CW01433389

A CONSTITUTIONAL ORDER OF STATES?

This collection celebrates the career of Professor Alan Dashwood, a leading member of the generation of British academics who organised, explained and analysed what we now call European Union law for the benefit of lawyers trained in the common law tradition. It takes as its starting point Professor Dashwood's vivid description of the European Union as a 'constitutional order of states'. He intended that phrase to capture the unique character of the Union. On the one hand, it is a supranational order characterised by its own distinctive institutional dynamics and an unprecedented level of cohesion among, and penetration into, the national legal systems. On the other hand, it remains an organisation of derived powers, the Member States retaining their character as sovereign entities under international law. This theme permeates both the constitutional and the substantive law of the Union. Contributors to the collection include members of the judiciary and distinguished practitioners, officials and academics. They consider the foundations, strengths, implications and shortcomings of this conceptual framework in various fields of EU law and policy. The collection is an essential purchase for anyone interested in the constitutional framework of the contemporary European Union.

A Constitutional Order of States?

Essays in EU Law in Honour of Alan Dashwood

Edited by

Anthony Arnull
Catherine Barnard
Michael Dougan
Eleanor Spaventa

·HART·
PUBLISHING

OXFORD AND PORTLAND, OREGON
2011

Published in the United Kingdom by Hart Publishing Ltd
16C Worcester Place, Oxford, OX1 2JW
Telephone: +44 (0)1865 517530
Fax: +44 (0)1865 510710
E-mail: mail@hartpub.co.uk
Website: http://www.hartpub.co.uk

Published in North America (US and Canada) by
Hart Publishing
c/o International Specialized Book Services
920 NE 58th Avenue, Suite 300
Portland, OR 97213-3786
USA
Tel: +1 503 287 3093 or toll-free: (1) 800 944 6190
Fax: +1 503 280 8832
E-mail: orders@isbs.com
Website: http://www.isbs.com

© The editors and contributors severally 2011

The editors and contributors have asserted their right under the Copyright,
Designs and Patents Act 1988, to be identified as the authors of this work.

All rights reserved. No part of this publication may be reproduced, stored
in a retrieval system, or transmitted, in any form or by any means,
without the prior permission of Hart Publishing, or as expressly permitted
by law or under the terms agreed with the appropriate reprographic
rights organisation. Enquiries concerning reproduction which may not be
covered by the above should be addressed to Hart Publishing Ltd at the
address above.

British Library Cataloguing in Publication Data
Data Available

ISBN: 978-1-84946-046-0

Typeset by Forewords Ltd, Oxford
Printed and bound in Great Britain by
TJ International Ltd, Padstow, Cornwall

Preface

This collection of essays celebrates the work and career of Professor Alan Dashwood CBE QC, who was a leading member of the generation of British academics who took an interest in European Union law before the accession of the UK in 1973. Having taught themselves the subject, Alan and his leading contemporaries then set about organising, explaining and analysing, for the benefit of lawyers trained in the common law tradition, a legal order heavily influenced by the civil law tradition of continental Europe.

Born in South Africa during the Second World War, Alan began his academic career in 1966 at the University of Glasgow and his earliest publications were on criminal law. In 1970, he began teaching European Union law and has specialised in that subject since he served as Legal Secretary from 1978 to 1980 to J-P Warner, the first British Advocate General at the European Court of Justice. Alan was the founding editor of the *European Law Review*, launched in 1975 and now one of the leading scholarly journals covering the law relating to European integration. Five years later, he published (with Derrick Wyatt) *The Substantive Law of the EEC*, a pioneering work which for the first time identified, for a common law readership, the salient features of the EU's substantive law (as opposed to the law relating to its institutions and decision-making processes). Now entitled *Wyatt & Dashwood's European Union Law*, the fifth edition by a team of authors (including three of us) was published in 2006.

The first edition of Wyatt & Dashwood was completed while Alan was at the European Court of Justice, but in the year of its publication he took up a chair in law at the University of Leicester, where he served as Head of Department from 1984 to 1987. While at Leicester, the close relationship Alan has always maintained with his students was underlined on a visit to the European institutions. During a long coach ride, the students organised a contest to see who could imitate most convincingly Alan's characteristic style of delivery. Ever competitive, Alan entered the contest himself and was crestfallen when he managed to come only third.

In 1987, Alan left Leicester to become one of four Directors in the Legal Service of the Council of the European Union. There he led an international team of lawyers responsible for giving oral and written advice to ministers, the Committee of Permanent Representatives and Council Working Groups, and for representing the Council in proceedings before the Union Courts. His portfolio initially comprised institutional questions; the Union budget and financial resources; social policy; cooperation with the African, Caribbean and Pacific countries; and staff matters. He advised the Presidency in the annual budget negotiations with the European Parliament and helped to devise and implement the new system of septenniel financing, which was initiated with the 'Delors package' in 1988. In the negotiations on 'Political Union', which culminated in the Maastricht Treaty, he advised on institutional matters. For nearly three years he was in charge of the legal aspect of agriculture and fisheries, and then moved on to external relations, where he was involved in the final stage of the Uruguay Round of multilateral trade negotiations and preparing the implementation of the WTO Agreement. He was responsible for the legal aspect of the common foreign and security policy when it was established post-Maastricht, and was the first legal advisor to the Political Committee. He was also put in charge of the drafting of the 1994 treaty on the accession to the EU of Austria, Finland and Sweden.

In 1995, Alan left the Council to become the first Professor of European Law at Cambridge and Fellow of Sidney Sussex College. He immediately assumed the Directorship of the Centre for European Legal Studies at Cambridge, a post he held until 2000. It was during that time that he founded the *Cambridge Yearbook of European Legal Studies*. He also inaugurated the annual Mackenzie-Stuart Lecture and a series of occasional papers. The conferences he organised, often reflecting interests he had developed while at the Council, became highlights of the academic calendar and led to a series of major publications: *Reviewing Maastricht: Issues for the 1996 IGC* (1996); *The Principle of Equal Treatment in EC Law* (edited with S O'Leary) (1997); *The General Law of EC External Relations* (edited with C Hillion) (2000); *The Future of the Judicial System of the European Union* (edited with A Johnston) (2001). From 1995 to 2008, Alan was also one of the joint editors of the *Common Market Law Review*.

All this might seem more than enough to fill a professional career. However, having been called to the Bar in 1969, in 1997 Alan became a tenant at 2 Harcourt Buildings (now Henderson Chambers) in the Temple and started to build a busy practice. He acted for the UK in several leading cases before the Union Courts, including *Pfeiffer*, *Advocaten voor de Wereld* and *Kadi and Yusuf*. He was made a Bencher of the Inner Temple in 2002. In the same year, at the invitation and with the support of the Foreign Office, Alan produced, with the help of a group of colleagues at Cambridge, a Draft Constitutional Treaty of the European Union, as a contribution to the work of the Convention on the Future of Europe. The draft was submitted to the Convention by Peter Hain MP, then the Minister for Europe, in 2003. It was subsequently published in the *European Law Review*.

Alan is frequently invited to give oral or written evidence to Parliamentary Committees on issues of EU law and to advise Government Departments on EU law matters. He also advises governments and parliaments of other Member States, as well as EU institutions. He was appointed CBE in 2004. Alan retired from his chair at Cambridge at the end of the 2008–09 academic session. However, he still plays an active part in the affairs of the Law Faculty and Sidney Sussex College and continues with his practice at the Bar, being made a QC in 2010.

One of Alan's most insightful contributions to the intellectual understanding of the distinctiveness of the European Union is his vivid description of it as a 'constitutional order of states', a phrase he coined in the first of his four magisterial position papers in *Reviewing Maastricht*. He intended that phrase to capture the unique character of the EU as a supranational order characterised by its own distinctive institutional dynamics, and by an unprecedented level of penetration into the national legal systems, yet which remained an organisation of only derived and limited powers, the Member States retaining their character as sovereign entities under international law. Although not uncontroversial, the phrase provides an invaluable conceptual tool for understanding the process of European integration. This collection takes the idea of 'a constitutional order of states' as its starting point, exploring its strengths and shortcomings in various fields of EU law and policy organised around the following broad themes: the EU's constitutional and judicial fabric, European substantive law and Europe's role in the wider world. These themes reflect some of the most important points of tension and development in the constitutional framework of the contemporary European Union as well as Alan's longstanding interests.

The editors were greatly assisted in the preparation of this collection for publication by Michelle Houston, who went through each contribution to check for inconsistencies of style that we ourselves had missed, and to all at Hart Publishing, who displayed their usual enthusiasm, forbearance and attention to detail. We are grateful to them all for their help. But our primary debt of gratitude goes to our contributors. Drawn from a range of professional backgrounds, all have close connections with Alan: he offered some their first job; some had their first article published by him; for some he supervised their PhD. Several of them battled through snow and ice to deliver drafts of their chapters at a lively seminar organised by the Centre for European Legal Studies at the University of Cambridge in December 2009. Our overriding memory of that seminar is the praise heaped on Alan by those who attended, not only for his intellectual contribution to the discipline, but also for his wit, warmth, stylish sense of dress and taste in exquisite whiskies.

AA
CSB
MD
ES
October 2010

Farewell and Thanks to Alan

It is appropriate in a collection such as this to say something about Alan Dashwood's contribution to European Union legal studies in his capacity as member of the Editorial Board of the *Common Market Law Review*.

We have to go back 16 years in time, to an announcement published in the December 1994 issue of the *Review*: 'The Editors and publishers are pleased to announce that Professor Alan Dashwood and Professor Jacqueline Dutheil de la Rochère have joined the Editorial Board'. The following issue suddenly ran to 383 pages—about double what was usual in those days. Now this is really a paradox—as this is the man whose succinctness is exemplary. My favourite e-mail from Alan ran to all of two words: 'Who he?' This was closely followed in brevity by: 'It's fine. Love Alan.'

In order to look at Alan's achievements in this area, we need to ask ourselves what a member of the Editorial Board does. He or she helps determine general policy, suggests authors and topics, assesses material received, and occasionally writes pieces, signed (if they are case notes and articles) and unsigned (if they are editorials)

These activities can be grouped naturally under three headings: Institutional balance; The Cambridge School; Passion.

INSTITUTIONAL BALANCE

In order to understand what lies behind the term institutional balance, one needs to know that, for many years, the *Common Market Law Review* had a special relationship with the Commission and its legal service. Specifically: three consecutive Deputy Directors-General of the Legal Service of the European Commission were on the Editorial Board. It was of course not Alan's intention to break up this happy marriage—but somehow to transform it into a *ménage à trois*. His thorough understanding of the nature of the European Community (though now we must get used to saying Union), where Commission and Council both play such important parts, led us to upgrade the input of the Council, directly and indirectly. Authors, points of view, even a member of the Editorial Board were sought from that august institution and given the attention they deserve. Linking this to the discussions on 'institutional rebalancing' as a result of the Lisbon Treaty, we can ask: does an increase in the influence of one Institution automatically lead to a decrease in influence of another? Did more influence from the Council mean less for the Commission?—it is open question! But in terms of input for the *Review* it was certainly added value.

THE CAMBRIDGE SCHOOL

This goes without saying! After Alan joined the Board, the *Review* soon published contributions by Michael Dougan and Christophe Hillion (they also joined the Editorial Board), and by Eleanor Spaventa, Oke Odudu, Angus Johnson, Catherine Barnard, Albertina Albors Llorens—all of whom were or are at Cambridge. Coincidence? No way! Alan inspired them all, and inspired them in particular to write for the *Review*.

PASSION—WITH STYLE

Certain of Alan's email reactions to articles and case notes indicate that legal issues could arouse strong feelings—though he might express this with delicacy.

- Oh dear! You know that the word 'governance' makes me reach for my revolver.
- This article is full and clear. A sound piece on an important topic (though one that leaves me somewhat cold). Eminently publishable.

But I should also mention the long telephone calls . . . Hours could pass discussing articles or judgments. While Alan can be as objective as any lawyer may need to be, he cared deeply about certain developments, certain judicial decisions—particularly of the Court of Justice. These were not just 'interesting', but could arouse fury. I can mention the example of *Mangold*—a case we have still not heard the last of!—where Alan was scathing about the Court's unwillingness to accept that where directives are invoked in horizontal situations, national courts will simply have to apply domestic provisions even if they are incompatible with EU law.

Alan's own publications in the *Review* are quite sparse, in terms of signed articles—since he had to spread his writing over the *European Law Review*, the *Cambridge Yearbook*, countless books, and so on. He gave us some brilliant editorial comments—in the last years, particularly in connection with the whole Treaty reform process, on which he was not afraid to hold clear opinions.

In February 2004, an editorial comment he drafted already revealed unconditional support for the Treaty reform process, and a clear rejection of suggestions to muddle through with the Treaties in their Nice versions. He identified early on the essential elements which needed to be retained in any new agreement replacing the Constitutional Treaty: a full-time president, a foreign minister, the extension of qualified majority voting in the Council, and absorption of what was left of the third pillar by the Community (whatever its name). He struggled with the problems which so-called depillarisation might bring—should the principle of primacy also apply within the former second pillar? Could infringement proceedings be started against Member States for failure to fulfil their obligations in the area of the common foreign and security policy?

Certainly, Alan could not be accused of failing to fulfil his obligations as a member of the *CMLRev* Editorial Board.

Alison McDonnell

Contents

PART III: EUROPEAN SUBSTANTIVE LAW

List of Contributors

ALBERTINA ALBORS-LLORENS is a University Senior Lecturer and Fellow, Girton College, University of Cambridge.

ANTHONY ARNULL is Barber Professor of Jurisprudence, University of Birmingham.

CATHERINE BARNARD is Professor of European Union Law and Employment Law and Fellow, Trinity College, University of Cambridge.

JOXERRAMON BENGOETXEA is Professor of the Philosophy of Law at the University of the Basque Country.

MARISE CREMONA is Head of the Law Department, Co-Director of the Academy of European Law and Professor of European Law at the European University Institute.

GEERT DE BAERE is Professor of EU Law at the University of Leuven Law Faculty and the Leuven Centre for Global Governance Studies.

MICHAEL DOUGAN is Dean of the Liverpool Law School and Professor of European Law at the University of Liverpool.

JACQUELINE DUTHEIL DE LA ROCHERE is Professor at the Université Panthéon-Assas (Paris II).

DAVID EDWARD was Judge of the European Court of Justice 1992-2004. He is now Professor Emeritus of the University of Edinburgh.

JONATHAN FAULL is Director General at the European Commission (DG Justice Freedom and Security).

BRUNO GENCARELLI is a member of the Legal Service of the European Commission.

LAURENCE GORMLEY is Professor of European Law and Jean Monnet Professor at the University of Groningen.

ROSA GREAVES is Professor at the Universities of Glasgow and Oslo.

JOSÉ A GUTIÉRREZ-FONS is Legal Assistant at the European Court of Justice.

JONI HELISKOSKI is an official at the Ministry for Foreign Affairs, Helsinki.

CHRISTOPHE HILLION is Professor of European Law, Universities of Leiden and Stockholm and the Swedish Institute for European Policy Studies.

MARGOT HORSPOOL is Professor of Law at Queen Mary, University of London. She is also a Professorial Fellow in European Law at the British Institute of International and Comparative Law.

FRANCIS JACOBS QC is Professor of Law at King's College London. He was previously Advocate General at the European Court of Justice (1988-2006).

ANGUS JOHNSTON is CUF lecturer at the University of Oxford and a fellow at University College Oxford.

PANOS KOUTRAKOS is Professor of European Law, University of Bristol.

KOEN LENAERTS is Judge and President of Chamber at the European Court of Justice and Professor of European Union Law at KU Leuven.

MARC MARESCEAU is Professor of European Law, European Institute, Ghent University, Faculty of Laws, Jean Monnet Centre of Excellence.

ALISON MCDONNELL is Associate Editor, Common Market Law Review.

INGOLF PERNICE is Professor and Director of the Walter Hallstein Institute for European Constitutional Law (WHI) at the Humboldt-Universität zu Berlin.

JEAN-CLAUDE PIRIS is the Legal Counsel of the European Council and of the Council of the European Union, Director General of the Legal Service of the Council.

RICHARD PLENDER is a Judge at the High Court of England and Wales.

MALCOLM ROSS is Professor of European Law, University of Sussex.

DAVID SCANNELL is a Barrister at Brick Court Chambers, London.

ROBERT SCHÜTZE is Reader in European Union Law, University of Durham.

ELEANOR SHARPSTON is Advocate General at the Court of Justice of the European Union.

PIET JAN SLOT is Professor of European Law, University of Leiden.

ELEANOR SPAVENTA is a Reader at the University of Durham and Director of the Durham European Law Institute.

JOHN R SPENCER is Professor of Law at the University of Cambridge, Fellow at Selwyn College and Co-Director of the Centre for European Legal Studies.

CHRISTIAAN TIMMERMANS is Pieter Sanders Professor of Law, University of Rotterdam, and a former Judge at the European Court of Justice.

ANTONIO TIZZANO is Judge at the European Court of Justice.

ROBIN WHITE is Professor of Law at the University of Leicester. He also holds a part-time judicial appointment as a Judge of the Upper Tribunal.

DERRICK WYATT is a QC, an Emeritus Professor of Law in the University of Oxford, and an Emeritus Fellow of St Edmund Hall, Oxford. He is currently a Visiting Professor of Law in the University of Oxford.

Table of Cases

EFTA COURT

EUROPEAN COURT OF HUMAN RIGHTS

EUROPEAN UNION

Commission

Court of Justice

Cases

Opinions

General Court/Court of First Instance

ICJ

NATIONAL

Czech Republic

Constitutional Court

Germany

Constitutional Court

Ireland

United Kingdom

United States

Table of Legislation

BILATERAL AND SIMILAR INSTRUMENTS

European Union

Other

EFTA

EUROPEAN ECONOMIC AREA

EUROPEAN UNION

Treaties and related Acts

Secondary legislation

Bilateral and similar instruments

See Bilateral and similar instruments, European Union

Other

INTERNATIONAL

NATIONAL

Czechoslovakia

Finland

France

Germany

Part I

Constitutional Fabric

Is the European Union an Organisation of Limited Powers?

DERRICK WYATT

I THE HYPOTHESIS

THE OBVIOUS ANSWER to the question posed by the title is in the affirmative. But to be satisfied with that simple answer would be misleading. It would gloss over the fact that the evolution and activities of the European Union have given far greater prominence to the existence and exercise of its powers than to limitations upon those powers.

The EU is an organisation of defined, attributed powers. It is this characteristic which Alan Dashwood ranked first among what he described as the 'conservatory principles' which he regarded as distinctive features of the 'constitutional order of states' which comprises the European Union. He identifies the principle of subsidiarity as a further conservatory principle.[1] My own perspective is that neither the principle of attributed powers nor the principle of subsidiarity has acted as effective constraints on the scope of Union competence.

The list of powers which are enumerated from time to time has never been regarded as a closed list, and that list has steadily expanded over the years. The scope of the lawmaking powers entrusted to the EU from time to time has been interpreted broadly by the lawmaking institutions. The Court of Justice has not been enthusiastic to enforce the limits of lawmaking competence, except in cases of clear breach of general principles of Community law, including fundamental rights. The Court of Justice has also contributed to the expansion of EU competence by an expansive reading of Treaty provisions, such as those which establish the internal market, and that expansive reading in turn has had an expansive effect on lawmaking competence.

The introduction of subsidiarity into the founding Treaties, and attempts to reinforce that principle in the Amsterdam Protocol, were a recognition

---

[1] See, eg A Arnull, A Dashwood, M Ross and D Wyatt, *Wyatt and Dashwood's European Union Law*, 4th edn (London, Sweet & Maxwell, 2000) ch 7.

that such mechanisms for competence control as existed were not working, and needed reinforcement through a system of structured self-restraint on the exercise of EU lawmaking powers. No such system of structured self-restraint has materialised. Responsibility for this is fairly evenly spread between the Member States, the lawmaking institutions and the Court of Justice. It remains to be seen whether the national parliaments can resuscitate subsidiarity under the arrangements introduced by the Lisbon Treaty.

My hypothesis is that the EU is an organisation of limited powers, but it has never fully reconciled itself to the fact, and has political ambitions which necessitate regular increases in its attributed competences, which encourage its institutions to act to the very limits of their powers, and which have stifled attempts to introduce a culture of self-restraint, to strike an appropriate balance between action at the centre and action at national, regional and local levels.

II   THE PROOF

A   The Expansion of Attributed Powers

It would be tedious to attempt an exhaustive chronological list of the series of Treaty amendments which have incrementally increased EU competence to the stage it has reached today, but instructive to refer to some of the major developments during the last 30 years or so. In 1987 the Single European Act (SEA) came into force, introducing a number of amendments to the EEC Treaty. Those who say that this remains the most significant step in the evolution of the European project have a seriously arguable case. The SEA introduced qualified majority voting (QMV) for certain existing lawmaking powers. The most significant change concerned QMV for measures designed to complete the 'internal market,' a term introduced essentially to rebrand the 'Common Market'. Significantly for the present discussion, it introduced sections on social policy and the environment. The third change brought about by the SEA was also significant. It signalled the end of the political arrangement whereby the numerous provisions for QMV voting contained in the original EEC Treaty, were actually used, rather than being ignored in favour of consensus.

The Maastricht Amendments of 1993 once more increased lawmaking powers, tempered by several distinct restraints on those powers. The Maastricht Treaty created Citizenship of the Union, made provision for a single currency, and extended European lawmaking powers in a number of ways. There were more possibilities for social legislation by QMV, but for some social issues (social security, unfair dismissal) unanimity was required. These developments prompted the UK's opt-outs, from the so-called Social chapter, and from the single currency. There was QMV for certain environmental measures, for development co-operation, for certain public health measures (though harmonisation in this context was excluded) and for economic sanctions resulting from common foreign and security policy decisions. And for the first time, a Treaty amendment offered a principle which claimed to restrict rather than expand Community competence. That principle was subsidiarity. A principle with neither detail to explain it, nor mechanism to enforce it, in the Maastricht Treaty; it acquired something of both in the Amsterdam Treaty.

The Amsterdam amendments (1999) authorised the Council to take unanimous action to combat discrimination based on sex, racial or ethnic origin, religion or belief, disability, age or sexual orientation. Amsterdam also transferred from intergovernmental co-operation to Community method, and to Court of Justice jurisdiction, various visa, asylum and immigration issues. It also devoted an entire protocol to defining Subsidiarity, and to identifying requirements and procedures for making the principle work more effectively in the legislative process. Controlling the exercise of Community competence still ranked highly on the agenda of the Member States, though in practice few Member States exercised self-restraint where Community action pursued policies in tune with national political priorities.

The Nice Treaty (2001) could not be described as an occasion for extending Community competence, though some competences were transferred from unanimity to QMV (eg implementation of citizenship rights of movement and residence). It was designed to pave the wave for enlargement, and it contained rules for QMV which defined the number of votes needed to carry proposals and the number of votes the present members and the newly acceding Member States would be entitled to cast in the process. The Declaration on the Future of the Union, annexed to the Nice Treaty, foreshadowed the process which would lead to the Constitution for Europe. First of all, the issue to be addressed in that process was 'how to establish and monitor a more precise delimitation of powers between the European Union and the Member States, reflecting the principle of subsidiarity'. That objective was to be achieved in part in the Draft Constitution. National Parliaments were to be made watchdogs of the principle of subsidiarity, and the Court of Justice was to be given increased jurisdiction in ensuring compliance with that principle by the Institutions of the Union. The Constitution for Europe was a step too far, but most of its provisions emerged in the Lisbon Treaty amending the Treaty on European Union and the Treaty establishing the European Community, which came into force on 1 December 2009.

The cumulative effect of the above series of amending Treaties on the scope of EU lawmaking competence has been substantial. It was for many years a truism that the EU lacked competence to harmonise criminal law.

When the Court of Justice ruled — in my view correctly — that in some cases it was essential that harmonised European rules be enforced by criminal sanctions and that making provision for this fell within Community competence, it did so against the opposition of 10 Member States.[2] The Court's judgment provoked a considerable academic literature.[3]

Under the rubric of judicial co-operation in civil and criminal matters, the Lisbon Treaty confers significant lawmaking power on the EU lawmaking institutions in the fields of criminal law and family law. As regards criminal law, following on from previous arrangements in Article 31 TEU, it authorises

> minimum rules concerning the definition of criminal offences and sanctions in the areas of particularly serious crime with a cross-border dimension resulting from the nature or impact of such offences or from a special need to combat them on a common basis.[4]

Specific areas with a cross-border dimension are identified, and the Council 'may adopt a decision identifying other areas of crime that meet the criteria specified'.[5] Furthermore, the TFEU provides express authorisation for the harmonisation of minimum rules for criminal offences and sanctions where this is essential to ensure the effective implementation of a Union policy in an area which has been subject to harmonisation measures, but there is the safeguard of consensus for a Member State considering that a draft directive would affect 'fundamental aspects of its criminal justice system', as well as provision for enhanced co-operation on the part of nine or more Member States in the event that consensus cannot be achieved.[6]

As regards judicial co-operation in civil matters, lawmaking competence is no longer confined to measures necessary for the functioning of the internal market. The scope of EU competence to harmonise family law is limited to subject matter with cross-border implications, and may be limited further by the aim of developing judicial co-operation in civil matters having cross-border implications. On the other hand, the scheme and scope of the provisions on judicial co-operation in criminal matters indicates that harmonisation of criminal law matters having cross-border implications may in itself be treated as providing a basis for judicial co-operation, and applying this proposition by analogy would suggest that

---

[2] Case C-176/03 *Commission v Council* [2005] ECR I-7879.

[3] Eg S White, 'Harmonisation of Criminal Law under the First Pillar' (2006) 31 *European Law Review* 2006 81–92; D Ruiz-Jarabo Colomer, 'L'incidence du droit communautaire sur le droit pénal en matière de protection de l'environnement' in La crisi dell'Unione Europea 2006, pp 125–44; C Philip,' Quelle compétence pénale pour l'Union européenne? (2006) *Gazette du Palais*, no 102–03 (II Doct) 9–13.

[4] Art 83(1) TFEU.

[5] Art 83(1), sub-para 3.

[6] Art 83(2) and (3).

harmonisation of elements of family law having cross-border implications can in itself provide the basis for judicial co-operation.

The Lisbon Treaty undoubtedly expands EU competence, and it reduces areas where unanimity is required for decision making. On the other hand, it does provide some safeguards for Member States, as has been demonstrated as regards harmonisation of criminal law. The residual lawmaking power contained in Article 308 EC is retained in Article 352 TFEU (and is still subject to unanimity), and appears to have been expanded, since it is no longer constrained by the requirement that action should prove necessary in the course of operation of the Common Market; now it is enough that action should prove necessary 'within the framework of the policies defined in the Treaties'. On the other hand, there are safeguards designed to curb abuse of this provision. In the first place, using the procedure for monitoring the subsidiarity principle referred to in Article 5(3) of the Treaty on European Union, the Commission shall draw national parliaments' attention to proposals based on this article. Secondly, measures based on this article shall not entail harmonisation of Member States' laws or regulations in cases where the Treaties exclude such harmonisation (such as harmonisation of public health measures). And thirdly, the provision cannot serve as a basis for attaining objectives pertaining to the common foreign and security policy.

B   Lawmaking Powers Have Been Interpreted Broadly by the Community Institutions

Even before any reference to legislative competence in the field of the environment appeared in the EEC Treaty, the Community institutions had adopted ambitious legislation for the protection of the environment on the basis of Article 100 EEC (subsequently Article 94 EC), in conjunction with Article 235 EEC (subsequently Article 308 EC and now Article 352 TFEU).[7] The preamble of Directive 76/160/EEC on the quality of bathing water, adopted on the basis of the latter articles, stated that, '. . . there exist in this area certain laws, regulations or administrative provisions in Member States which directly affect the functioning of the Common Market . . .'

No indication is given of how such laws might affect the functioning of the Common Market, nor how harmonisation might remedy such effects. The first reasoned recital of the preamble states that '. . . in order to protect the environment and public health, it is necessary to reduce the pollution of bathing water and to protect such water against further

---

[7] See, notably, Dir 76/160, on the quality of bathing water [1976] OJ L31/1 (Arts 100 and 235); Dir 80/778 on the quality of drinking water [1980] OJ L229/11(Arts 100 and 235).

deterioration . . .'. We are thus left in no doubt as to the real aim of the Directive. In truth, the Directive is adopted on the basis of an assumption that laws in Member States regulating (or not regulating) the quality of bathing water not only affect but directly affect the functioning of the Common Market. It might be objected that the Community legislature did not rely solely upon Article 100 EEC, but also upon Article 235 EEC. The latter article had two essential preconditions to its application: one that action by the Community should prove necessary to attain one of the objectives of the Community and the other that this necessity arose in the course of operation of the Common Market.[8] The preamble of Directive 76/160/EEC justifies reliance on Article 235 EEC as follows:

> . . . surveillance of bathing water is necessary in order to attain, within the framework of the operation of the Common Market, the Community's objectives as regards the improvement of living conditions, the harmonious development of economic activities throughout the Community and continuous and balanced expansion . . .

The objectives are indeed objectives of the Community, set out in the text of Article 2 of the EEC Treaty as it stood at the time. But the statement that the surveillance of bathing waters is necessary to attain the objectives referred to 'within the framework of the operation of the Common Market' is not explained, and it is not easy to see how it might be explained, except on the basis of the 'abstract risk' of obstacles to freedom of movement or of distortion of competition.[9]

The fact that decision making was at the time by unanimity (either because the Treaty so provided or by virtue of the practice subsequent to the Luxembourg accords) no doubt contributed to the tendency of the Member States to acquiesce in a broad reading of Treaty provisions conferring Community competence, and in particular Articles 100 and 235 EEC, which provided an opportunity to legislate in areas for which at the time no specific Treaty base existed. I accept that most legislation adopted under Article 100 EEC could be justified on the ground that it removed obstacles to the free movement of goods or persons and made a contribution to the Common Market, but the fact remains that the practice of the Community institutions, prior to the adoption of the Single European Act, was to treat competence to legislate for the Common Market on the basis of Articles 100 EEC and Article 235 EEC as a very wide compe-

---

[8] 'If action by the Community should prove necessary to attain, in the course of the operation of the Common Market, one of the objectives of the Community and the Treaty has not provided the necessary powers, the Council shall, acting unanimously on a proposal from the Commission and after consulting the European Parliament, take the appropriate measures.'

[9] Weatherill is right to observe that the reference in Art 308 to the 'course of the operation of the Common Market' has 'exerted little if any restriction on legislative resort to Art 308 . . .' See S Weatherill, 'Competence Creep and Competence Control' (2004) 23 *Yearbook of European Law* 1, 28.

tence indeed,[10] which required no detailed justification as regards effects on the functioning of the Common Market.

This generous conception of Community competence to regulate the Common Market survived the entry into force of the Single European Act, and was applied to the regulation of the internal market under the new Article 100a, later renumbered Article 95 of the EC Treaty and now Article 114 TFEU, and referred to hereafter as such. The Unfair Contract Terms Directive is an example.[11] The purpose of the Directive is to harmonise the laws of the Member States relating to unfair contracts concluded between a seller or supplier and a consumer.[12] The Directive is based on Article 114 TFEU. The preamble records that:

> Whereas the laws of Member States relating to the terms of contracts between the seller or supplier of services, on the one hand, and the consumer of them, on the other hand, show many disparities, with the result that the national markets for the sale of goods and services to consumers differ from each other and that distortions of competition may arise amongst the sellers and suppliers, notably when they sell and supply in other Member States . . .

This recital appears to be based simply upon the assumption that disparities between national laws can be equated with differences in the national markets, and that the resulting risk of distortions of competition justifies European wide legislation based on Article 114 TFEU. But the preamble adds a further consideration:

> Whereas, generally speaking, consumers do not know the rules of law which, in Member States other than their own, govern contracts for the sale of goods or services; whereas this lack of awareness may deter them from direct transactions for the purchase of goods or services in another Member State . . .

Reducing uncertainty for consumers contemplating cross-border purchases is presented as a basis for harmonisation. This recital has been described as foreshadowing the 'confidence-building' rationale for harmonisation of consumer law articulated in the preamble of Directive 99/44 on certain aspects of the sale of consumer goods and associated guarantees.[13] Cross-

---

[10] For reference to the debate in the House of Lords on 4 July 1978 on the 22nd and 35th Reports of the House of Lords Select Committee on the European Communities, in which criticism was levelled at over extensive use of Arts 100 and 235 EC in the environmental and consumer protection fields, and for a defence of the Community's harmonisation policy in this regard, see G Close, 'Harmonisation of Laws: Use or Abuse of the Powers under the EEC Treaty' (1978) 3 *European Law Review* 461. See also the reference to controversy over the issue at this time in John Usher's discussion of Case C-376/98 *Germany v Parliament and Council* [2000] ECR I-8419 in (2001) 38 *Common Market Law Review* 1519, 1527.

[11] Dir 93/13/EEC of 5 April 1993 on unfair terms in consumer contracts [1993] OJ L95/29.

[12] Ibid, Art 1.

[13] Dir 99/44/EC of the European Parliament and of the Council of 25 May 1999 on certain aspects of the sale of consumer goods and associated guarantees [1999] OJ L171/12. See S Weatherill, 'Constitutional Issues—How Much is Best Left Unsaid?' in S Vogenauer

border purchase of goods and services amount in principle to transactions covered by Article 28 EC or Article 49 EC (now Article 34 TFEU and Article 56 TFEU).[14] The above recital would support the proposition that internal market rules might properly be adopted at European level under, for example, Article 114 TFEU, whenever natural or legal persons might be deterred, by uncertainty created by disparities between national rules, from cross-border transactions which would—if carried out—amount to the exercise of a fundamental freedom. As indicated above, however, the legal uncertainty rationale did not stand alone in the preamble to the Unfair Contract Terms Directive, but supplemented a reference to disparities between national laws leading to distortions of competition.

Analogous considerations relating to legal uncertainty resulting from disparate national laws have been invoked to justify Community measures adopted to make it possible to facilitate cross-border co-operation and establish legal persons pursuant to Article 308 EC, and to justify the adoption of directives harmonising national provisions of company law under Article 50(2)(g) TFEU. The proposition that recourse to internal market measures might be justified by the need to eliminate legal uncertainty might also be seen as an aspect of a broader proposition, to the effect that internal market measures might generally be justified by the need to facilitate the exercise of fundamental freedoms, by, for example, providing appropriate language teaching for the children of migrants.[15] One potential difficulty with treating the need to eliminate legal uncertainty as a ground for harmonisation, from the point of view of seeking limits to Union powers, is that it would seem to provide a basis for harmonising virtually all national rules applicable to natural or legal persons engaged in cross-border activities.

C   The Reluctance of the Court of Justice to Enforce the Limits of Lawmaking Competence

I suggested at the outset that the Court of Justice has been reluctant to enforce the limits of lawmaking competence, except in cases of clear breach of general principles of Community law, including fundamental rights. One of the great judgments of the Court of Justice is that in the *Mulder* case,

---

and S Weatherill (eds), *The Harmonisation of European Contract Law: Implications for European Private Laws, Business and Legal Practice* (Oxford, Hart Publishing, 2006) 101. It is to be noted that the third recital of Dir 99/44/EC also refers to disparities of laws leading to distortion of competition between sellers.

[14] See, eg Case C-362/88 *GB-INNO-BM v Confédération du commerce luxembourgeois* [1990] ECR I-667 (cross-border shopping by Belgian residents in Luxembourg falls within the scope of Art 28 EC).

[15] Dir 77/486/EEC on the education of children of migrant workers.

in which it annuls Community rules on milk quotas for excluding dairy farmers rendered ineligible for quotas because they had taken advantage of Community schemes for accepting non-marketing premiums for the crucial base periods upon which quotas were calculated. That case was a reminder that a democratic political process is not always enough, and that the Commission and the Member States have to be reminded of the existence of the rule of law.[16] Another great judgment of the Court is that in *Kadi*, in which the Court refuses to abdicate its responsibility for the protection of fundamental rights in the legal order of the European Union.[17] But such cases do not touch the reach of EU competence—the scope of the subject matter which the EU lawmaking institutions may regulate, and which accordingly national lawmaking authorities may only regulate as long as the EU does not. The Court of Justice has almost invariably taken as expansive a view of EU competence as have the institutions themselves. It might be said that this latter proposition ignores the judgment in the *Tobacco Advertising* case, and certainly that case is of prime importance in the present context.

D   The Court Denies that the Community Institutions have a General Power to Regulate the Internal Market in the *Tobacco Advertising* Case

In the *Tobacco Advertising* case the Court of Justice denied that Article 95 EC bestowed on the Community legislature 'a general power to regulate the internal market', and insisted that the measures referred to in that article 'are intended to improve the conditions for the establishment and functioning of the internal market'.[18] The Court added that if

> a mere finding of disparities between national rules and of the abstract risk of obstacles to the exercise of fundamental freedoms or distortions of competition liable to result therefrom were sufficient to justify the choice of Article [114 TFEU] as a legal basis, judicial review of compliance with the proper legal basis might be rendered nugatory.[19]

It has already been noted that, prior to the *Tobacco Advertising* case, the practice of the Community institutions had been to treat Treaty

---

[16] Case 120/86 [1988] ECR 2321.

[17] Joined Cases C-402/05P and C-415/05P [2008] ECR I-6351.

[18] Case C-376/98 *Germany v Parliament and Council* [2000] ECR I-8419, paras 83 and 84. In this case Germany challenged the validity of Dir 98/43/EC of the European Parliament and of the Council on the approximation of the laws, regulations and administrative provisions of the Member States relating to the advertising and sponsorship of tobacco products [1998] OJ L213/9. See also Case C-74/99 *The Queen v Secretary of State for Health ex-parte Imperial Tobacco Ltd and others* [2000] ECR I-8599, a reference from the English High Court on the validity of the same directive. The two cases were joined for the oral hearing and the Opinion of AG Fennelly deals with both cases.

[19] Ibid, para 84.

competences to regulate the Common Market/internal market as if they were indeed a 'general power to regulate' that market, and the mere 'abstract risk' of obstacles to the exercise of fundamental freedoms or distortions of competition had been treated as a sufficient basis for recourse to, in particular, Article 94 or 95, and/or Article 308 EC. In what respects did the judgment of the Court of Justice in the *Tobacco Advertising* case suggest that the position thereafter would be any different?

The contested directive was based inter alia on Article 114 TFEU. It prohibited all forms of advertising and sponsorship of tobacco products and prohibited any free distribution having the purpose or the effect of promoting such products.[20] The directive prohibited (with certain exceptions) the use of the same names for tobacco products and for other products and services, and provided (with certain exceptions) that tobacco products must not bear the brand name, trademark, emblem or other distinctive feature of any other product or service.[21] The rationale of prohibiting such 'diversification products' was to prevent tobacco product manufacturers advertising their products indirectly by marketing and advertising products, such as clothing bearing the same trade mark as a tobacco product.

The Court annulled the directive because it could not be regarded as being justified by the need to regulate the internal market. The directive claimed to remove obstacles to cross-border provision of advertising services, and free movement of advertising media products. Yet in a number of cases (including that of diversification products), the directive removed obstacles to trade by banning the trade itself. It is clear that the Court regarded this approach as incompatible with Article 114 TFEU since it failed to achieve any genuine improvement in the operation of the internal market. The directive also claimed to remove the distortions of competition which resulted from diversity in the national rules regulating the advertising tobacco products. The Court rejected the proposition that such diversity per se could be regarded as sufficient distortion of competition to justify recourse to Article 114 TFEU, and held that only appreciable distortions of competition would suffice.

The Court's judgment in *Tobacco Advertising* contains both elements which are restrictive of Community competence to regulate the internal market and elements which are supportive of such competence. Two elements fall squarely in the former category—the requirement that Community measures regulating the internal market make a positive contribution to the internal market and the requirement that measures which make such a contribution through eliminating distortions of competition do so only in respect of distortions of competition which are appreciable. The Court's ruling in this latter regard is of potential significance. There

---

[20] Art 3(1) and (4).
[21] Art 3(2) and 3(3)(a).

mere existence of disparities between national rules cannot be regarded in itself as leading to the conclusion that distortions of competition exist which justify harmonisation. The weakness of the test is the lack of any objective criteria for its application.

Other elements of the Court's judgment are, however, strongly supportive of Community competence to regulate the internal market. In this category falls the Court's conclusion that a measure of harmonisation may be based on Article 114 TFEU if it makes some contribution to the internal market, even if the main objective is not to improve the internal market at all, but to achieve an objective such as public health, harmonisation of which is in principle denied to the Community institutions.

E   The Approach of the Court of Justice in Subsequent Cases has Largely Reversed the Competence-Restricting Effects of the *Tobacco Advertising* Case

Yet even the competence restricting effects of the *Tobacco Advertising* case have been largely reversed in the Court's subsequent case law. In *Swedish Match*,[22] the Court upheld a ban on oral tobacco, despite its earlier reasoning that removing obstacles to trade in advertising services and advertising media products by banning the trade itself could not be regarded as a genuine contribution to the internal market.

Again, in the *British American Tobacco* case,[23] the Court upheld labelling requirements concerning health warnings which could make no practical contribution to the free movement of packaged tobacco products, on the sole ground that a recital to the relevant directive refers to the existence of different national laws with respect to the presentation of such warnings.

In order to understand the significance of the Court's ruling in this case, it is necessary to refer briefly to relevant legislation and case law by way of context.[24] In the *Schwarzkopf* case,[25] the Court of Justice acknowledges that the rationale of common labelling rules at the European level is the possibility of multilingual labelling, which enables a product to be placed on the market on a number of Member States, and indicates that a directive laying down common labelling rules which does not facilitate

[22] Case C-210/03 *The Queen, on the application of: Swedish Match AB and Swedish Match UK Ltd v Secretary of State for Health* [2004] ECR I-11893; see also Case C-434/02 *Arnold André GmbH & Co KG v Landrat des Kreises Herford* [2004] ECR I-11825.
[23] Case C-491/01 *The Queen v Secretary of State for Health ex-parte British American Tobacco (Investments) Ltd and Imperial Tobacco Ltd* [2002] ECR I-11453.
[24] The following issues are discussed in A Arnull, A Dashwood, M Dougan, M Ross, E Spaventa and D Wyatt, *Wyatt and Dashwood's European Union Law*, 5th edn (London, Sweet & Maxwell, 2006) paras 21-026 to 21-029.
[25] Case C-169/99 *Hans Schwarzkopf GmbH & Co KG* [2001] ECR I-5901.

multilingual labelling would be invalid for inconsistency with Article 34 TFEU. The Court indicates that common labelling rules must not make it 'excessively difficult for . . . products having the same get-up to be marketed in several Member States'. 'Several' means more than two, and it seems that in the *Schwarzkopf* case it was, according to Advocate General Mischo, 'possible to print the warning, in three languages, on the tube and corresponding packaging'.[26]

The provisions on labelling of tobacco products were amended by Article 5(2) of Directive 2001/37/EC on the manufacture, presentation and sale of tobacco products.[27] Each unit packet of tobacco products must carry a general warning, on the most visible surface of the unit packet, and an additional warning, on the other most visible surface. The general warning

> shall cover not less than 30% of the external area of the corresponding surface of the unit packet . . . on which it is printed. That proportion shall be increased to 32% for Member States with two official languages and 35% for Member States with three official languages.

The additional warning

> shall cover not less than 40% of the external area of the corresponding surface of the unit packet of tobacco on which it is printed. That proportion shall be increased to 45% for Member States with two official languages and 50% for Member States with three official languages.[28]

Member States are furthermore entitled to stipulate that the warnings referred to are to be accompanied by a reference, outside the box for warnings, to the issuing authority.[29]

A challenge to the validity of the Directive by various tobacco companies in the English High Court led to a reference to the Court of Justice.[30] The applicants argued that Article 5 of the Directive was invalid because, contrary to the requirements of the *Schwarzkopf* case, that provision made it at the very least excessively difficult for tobacco products complying with the labelling rules in question to be marketed in several Member States, to the extent that parallel imports would in practice be excluded, and tobacco products would continue to be labelled exclusively for the Member State in which they are to be marketed.[31] The Court simply does not address these points.

The Court upholds the labelling requirements but does not even attempt

[26] Para 96 of the Advocate General's Opinion.
[27] [2001] OJ L194/26.
[28] Art 5(5) of Dir 2001/37/EC.
[29] Art 5(8) of Dir 2001/37/EC.
[30] *The Queen on the Application of (British American Tobacco (Investments) Limited, Imperial Tobacco Limited v The Secretary of State for Health, HM Attorney General* [2001] WL 1676838.
[31] Report for the Hearing, paras 73–75.

to demonstrate that the terms of Article 5 of the Directive remove obstacles to trade. The Court's reference to disparities between national laws, and the assertion that the Directive genuinely has as its aim the improvement of the conditions for the functioning of the internal market, are entirely formalistic. The only conclusion which can be drawn is that the fact that harmonisation of labelling rules in principle may contribute to the free movement of goods provides a justification for labelling rules which in fact make no such contribution. That would seem to amount to judicial endorsement of the very general power to regulate the internal market so emphatically denied by the Court of Justice in the *Tobacco Advertising* case.

F An Expansive Reading of Internal Market Freedoms Expands the Scope of Internal Market Competence

As well as tolerating an expansive reading of internal market competences on the part of the lawmaking institutions, the Court of Justice has increased the scope of those competences by its broad reading of internal market freedoms. I refer by way of example to judicial developments in the fields of health care and medical services, and collective action by trade unions.

There were initially some grounds for considering that health care and medical services provided within the framework of national social security schemes might not amount in all cases to services normally provided for remuneration within the meaning of Articles 49 et seq EC (now Article 56 TFEU).[32] In a number of cases,[33] the Court of Justice has found that medical services (including hospital care) fall within the internal market provisions on free provision of services. In one of the first of these cases the Court rejected the argument that hospital services cannot constitute an economic activity within the meaning of Article 50 of the Treaty, particularly when they are provided in kind and free of charge under the relevant sickness insurance scheme. The Court stated:

> It is settled case law that medical activities fall within the scope of the Treaty, there being no need to distinguish in that regard between care provided in a hospital environment and care provided outside such an environment . . .
>
> It is also settled case law that the special nature of certain services does not remove them from the ambit of the fundamental principle of freedom of movement . . ., so that the fact that the national rules at issue in the main

---

[32] See Case 263/86 *Humbel* [1988] ECR 5365, paras 17–19. The remarks of the Court were in connection with education, but seemed applicable by analogy to the provision of health care.

[33] See in particular Case C-157/99 *BSM Geraets-Smits v Stichting Ziekenfonds VGZ; HTM Peerbooms v Stichting CZ Groep Zorgverzekeringen* [2001] ECR I-5473, and Case C-385/99 *VG Müller-Fauré v Onderlinge Waarborgmaatschappij OZ Zorgverzekeringen UA* [2003] ECR I-4509.

proceedings are social security rules cannot exclude application of Articles [now 56 and 57] of the Treaty . . .[34]

This has implications for individual patients, who may in certain cases insist that their national health care systems pay for their health care in other Member States.[35] It also has another important implication. It brings the medical services in question within the scope of internal market regulation by the lawmaking institutions of the European Union.

I turn next to the example of collective action by trade unions. In the *Viking* case[36] the Court held that a private undertaking could rely on Article 43 EC (now Article 49 TFEU) against trade unions, where they took collective action which restricted the right of establishment of the undertaking concerned. The Court also held that trade unions could justify such collective action on grounds of overriding reasons of public interest, in particular the protection of workers, providing that the jobs or conditions of employment at issue were jeopardised or under serious threat, and providing that the collective action in issue was suitable for achievement of the objective pursued and did not go beyond what was necessary to attain that objective. This ruling would seem to have implications for the scope of Community regulatory competence, and it is instructive to refer to an argument rejected by the Court in *Viking*. The argument was to the effect that, since Article 137(5) EC (now Article 153(5) TFEU) excluded from the scope of Article 137 EC 'pay, the right of association, the right to strike or the right to impose lock-outs', such matters were also excluded from the scope of Articles 43 EC and 49 EC. The Court rejected this argument on the basis that the fact that such matters remained in principle within national competence did not release Member States from the obligation to exercise that competence consistently with Community law.[37] The argument that Article 137(5) EC militated against the application of Articles 43 and 49 EC to collective action perhaps received less attention than it deserved. The effect of holding that collective action including strike action falls within the scope of Articles 43 EC and 49 EC would seem to have the consequence that such action also falls within the regulatory competence of the Community institutions pursuant to Article 47(2) EC (applicable to services by virtue of Article 55 EC).[38] It is a somewhat curious position that strike action is excluded entirely from the scope of Article 137 and that, pur-

---

[34] *Geraets-Smits*, ibid, paras 53, 54.

[35] Case C-372/04 *Yvonne Watts v Bedford Primary Care Trust* [2006] ECR I-4325.

[36] Case C-438/05 *International Transport Workers Federation, Finnish Seamen s Union v Viking Line ABP, OÜ Viking Line Eesti* [2007] ECR I-10779.

[37] *Viking*, ibid, para 40. The argument was advanced by Denmark in *Viking*.

[38] It seems that strike action and the collective defence of workers' interests concerns 'the pursuit of activities as self-employed persons' within the meaning of Art 47(2) EC, since the Court in *Viking* holds that such action and collective defence of workers' interests is capable of restricting the right of establishment.

suant to that Article, Community measures concerning 'collective defence of the interests of workers . . .' are subject to unanimity in Council, and to mere consultation with the European Parliament,[39] while Community legislation based on Article 47(2) EC can apparently harmonise national rules covering both the collective defence of the interests of workers, and strike action, under the Article 251 procedure.[40] An argument to the effect that Article 137(5) EC implies that strike action does not fall within the scope of Articles 43 EC and 49 EC because if it did it would also fall within the regulatory competence of the Community under Articles 47(2) EC and 55 EC, and thereby deprive Article 137(5) EC of much of its practical effect, is at the very least a plausible argument, and it is not really addressed by the Court. Perhaps the argument was not put to the Court in those terms. However, the link between the scope of fundamental freedoms and the scope of Community competence to regulate the internal market is a significant link. Extension of the horizontal scope of Treaty provisions in principle brings with it increased competence at the Community level to regulate private conduct, and that in turn narrows the area within which national authorities are free to regulate without the risk of being over-ruled at Community level.

G   Subsidiarity Has So Far Failed to Instil a Culture of Self Restraint on the Part of the Member States and the Lawmaking Institutions

It is true that Member States have expressed support for subsidiarity and challenged Community legislation before the Court of Justice on the grounds of incompatibility with the principle of subsidiarity.

There is no doubt that at one level Member States have taken subsidiarity seriously and regarded it as a justiciable concept which could provide the basis for challenging the validity of Community acts adopted in breach of its requirements. Challenges to legislation on the basis of subsidiarity have been initiated by the Netherlands, Germany and the UK. But Member States have not necessarily been either consistent or rigorous in their capacity as Members of the Council, as regards voting on proposals for legislation.

---

[39] Art 137(2) EC.
[40] Voting in Council would be by qualified majority.

H   The Commission and Parliament Have Been Unenthusiastic about the Application of Subsidiarity in Practice

The Commission has never been sympathetic to the principle of subsidiarity, and has tried to minimise its application in practice. Subsidiarity has no application to areas which fall within the exclusive competence of the Community. From the outset the Commission argued for an interpretation of exclusive competence which included measures designed to remove obstacles to the free movement of goods, persons and services in the internal market. Since some of the most important and controversial of Community measures fall within this category, it is difficult to read this standpoint of the Commission as anything but a desire to minimise the practical effects of subsidiarity. The Commission maintained its position in this regard until the Court of Justice indicated that the principle of subsidiarity did indeed apply to such measures.[41] The European Parliament adopted the same approach as the European Commission, and indeed clung to its narrow view of the scope of subsidiarity even after its implicit rejection by the Court of Justice, precipitating an explicit rejection of this argument by the Court of Justice in a later case.[42]

Passages dealing with subsidiarity which appear in explanatory memoranda of the Commission are often perfunctory, in many cases simply stating that the requirements of subsidiarity are complied with. The qualitative and quantitative assessments referred to in points 4 and 5 of the 1997 Protocol (which were originally adopted as guidelines by the Edinburgh Council in 1992) were simply not undertaken, or not undertaken in any adequate way. Compliance with subsidiarity is commonly demonstrated by the claim that the legislation will lay down common standards, and/or that individuals expect to find common standards in the various Member States.

One example of perfunctory reasoning is to be found in the explanatory report to the Commission's proposal for revision of the Directive on drinking water quality (which became Directive 98/83/EC). The explanatory memorandum to the proposal addresses subsidiarity. It concludes that the subject matter has a Community dimension because 'All Member States are concerned by this action'. In addressing the question 'Which solution is most efficient comparing the means of the Community and of the Member States', the Commission states:

> the existing directive has been effective in improving the quality of drinking water throughout the Community;

[41] Case C-377/98 *Netherlands v European Parliament and Council* [2001] ECR I-7079, paras 30–34.
[42] Case C-491/01 *The Queen v Secretary of State for Health ex-parte British American Tobacco (Investments) Ltd and Imperial Tobacco Ltd* [2002] ECR I-11453, paras 175 and 179.

it has provided Member States and the water supply industry with a stable basis for their planning and investment;

consumers have become familiar with the directive and expect to receive water which they know will be safe to drink . . .

Another example of perfunctory reasoning concerns proposals for directives prohibiting discrimination on racial and ethnic origin, disability, religion, sexual orientation, etc, in various contexts (which became Directives 2000/43 and 2000/78). A Commission communication explains the subsidiarity justification as follows:

Most Member States have included in their constitutional and/or legal order provisions which assert the right not to be discriminated against. However, the scope and the enforceability of such provisions—and the ease of access to redress—vary greatly from one Member State to another.

The draft directives would lay down a set of principles on equal treatment covering key issues, including protection against harassment, the possibility for positive action, appropriate remedies and enforcement measures. These principles would be applied in all Member States, thus providing certainty for individuals about the common level of protection from discrimination they can expect. Common standards at Community level can only be achieved through co-ordinated action.[43]

If the requirements of subsidiarity can be be satisfied by measures which will ensure for individuals common standards wherever they go in Europe, then it is difficult to see how proposals for European legislation will ever 'fail the test'. Commission justifications for subsidiarity are in effect a statement of the rationale of the legislation itself; they are not a genuine criterion for deciding whether or not to advance the proposal in question.

I   The Court of Justice Has Been Unenthusiastic about the Application of Subsidiarity in Practice

The Court of Justice could have breathed constitutional life into subsidiarity had it so chosen. It has minimised the duty of the institutions to incorporate subsidiarity reasoning into the preambles of Community acts. And in the case of internal market measures, while accepting that subsidiarity applies to the measures in question, the Court has in effect held that if there is competence to adopt the measure, then that in itself resolves the question of compliance with subsidiarity. This is rather like the Commission's approach to subsidiarity and lawmaking generally— if there is competence to adopt common standards, the adoption of

---

[43] Communication from the Commission to the Council, the European Parliament, the Economic and Social Committee and the Committee of the Regions on certain Community measures to combat discrimination, [1999] OJ C369/3, heading 6.

common standards justifies the exercise of the competence. The Court could have adopted a much stricter approach to scrutiny of the procedural requirements of subsidiarity by insisting upon more detailed reasoning in legislative acts and by examining whether the lawmaking institutions had addressed those matters which they were obliged to address in the course of the lawmaking process, for example, whether or not the institutions had taken account of the guidelines in the Amsterdam Protocol and undertaken quantitative rather than purely qualitative assessments in substantiating the reasons for concluding that a Community objective could better be achieved at Union level than national level, as paragraph 4 of the Amsterdam Protocol requires. One response to criticisms such as this is that subsidiarity has large discretionary and political elements, and the Court of Justice is not as well placed as the lawmaking institutions to make the relevant assessment. This is of course true, but somewhat beside the point. The Court of Justice could clearly not be expected to review the substantive issue of whether or not the exercise of a particular competence in a particular case was consistent with subsidiarity. The Court could have been expected to examine whether the lawmaking institutions had addressed those matters which they were obliged to address, and included sufficiently detailed reasoning in legislative acts to make it possible for a reader to understand how the institutions went about the processes described in the Amsterdam Protocol.

III   CONCLUDING REMARKS

What is the explanation for institutional resistance to giving practical effect to the principle of subsidiarity? It is difficult to avoid the conclusion that the Commission, Parliament and Court have been reluctant to give full practical effect to subsidiarity because they consider that it runs against the grain of Community integration. In the case of the Commission and Parliament, application of the principle of subsidiarity leads to accepting restraints on the exercise of competences which in principle authorise Community action. Respect for subsidiarity may be outweighed by the universal institutional tendency to increase the scale of their activities rather than reduce them. Doing less, but doing it better, may give way in the collective institutional mind to doing the same, or more, and of course doing it to the best of our abilities.

So far, the contradiction between subsidiarity, and its exhortation to do less, on the one hand, and the established historic tendency of the institutions to stretch their competences to the outermost limits and to seek to bring home the reality of European integration through the mechanisms of European regulation, on the other, has been resolved in favour of the latter. There is little if any evidence that the principle of subsidiarity has modified the behaviour of the institutions in any significant way. It is possible that it has had some effect on the content of legislation (eg the reduction of the number of parameters in the water quality legislation referred to above), but such an example may involve as much the presentation of a decision taken on policy grounds as the reason underlying the decision itself.

The Council is made up of Member States, and to some extent might be thought of as a counterweight to the centralising tendencies of the Commission and Parliament. In terms of taking decisions as closely as possible to the citizen, it is championing democracy in so doing. But the Council is effective only up to a point in this respect. The Council is a political institution. When Member States vote on issues their first priority is whether they agree with the measure or not. If they do agree with a measure, there may be major advantages in supporting it, and in effect seeing government policy being pursued by the Community institutions. One advantage can be that a particular government policy may be unpopular but, if it is incorporated into the requirements of an EC directive, then the national authorities can 'blame Brussels'. Another advantage is that implementation of EC directives may expose governments to less parliamentary accountability than the implementation of purely national legislative measures (there is no doubt that in the UK implementation of Community obligations through the normal procedure of secondary legislation is much less costly in terms of parliamentary time than primary legislation). Quite apart from such considerations, Member States may simply not appreciate the 'precedent value' of adopting legislation on a particular subject matter on one Treaty basis rather than another, or of including certain subject matter in legislation proposed under a particular Treaty base. Most of the argument about the legislative process is about the merits in terms of policy of the legislation in question. Furthermore, the presidency system has to date given Member States in turn the incentive to be seen to be constructive in securing progress on agreement on pending Commission proposals. Securing agreement on the passage of Community legislation may be presented as evidence of the success of a Member State's presidency. The result of these various factors is that the actual effectiveness of the Council as a guardian of 'states' rights', acting as a counterweight to the Commission and Parliament, whose tendency is (no doubt in good faith and with every good intention) ever to increase their competence to act effectively at the European level, is questionable. The centralising tendencies of the Commission and Parliament exceed the ability and inclination of the Council to police the constitutional boundaries of Community action. In any event, it must be said that some Member States lack enthusiasm for the principle of subsidiarity. Belgium, like the European Parliament, continued to argue against application of the principle of subsidiarity to internal market measures even after the Court of Justice gave a strong indication that the principle did indeed apply in that context.[44] Subsidiarity has never been unequivocally embraced by the Community institutions, and some Member States at least have questioned its compatibility with the process of European integration.

Yet perhaps the Lisbon Treaty, with its role for national parliaments in scrutiny of proposed Union acts for compliance with subsidiarity, will give this so far neglected principle a new lease of life? It is certainly possible that the competences and responsibilities allotted to national parliaments and the lawmaking institutions under the Lisbon Protocol might be held to affect the course of any subsequent legal proceedings in which the compliance of a legislative act with the principle of subsidiarity were raised.

In the first place, a plea before the Court of Justice that the principle of subsidiarity had been infringed by a European legislative act, where national parliaments had not 'raised a yellow card', might be regarded by the Court of Justice as prima facie unfounded—even manifestly unfounded.

Where, by way of contrast, national parliaments had raised a yellow card to a Commission draft but the Commission had maintained its draft, with reasons, and the draft had been subsequently adopted, one possibility (which the present writer would advocate) would be that the Court of Justice would regard it as a procedural requirement essential to the validity of the act in question that the reasons of the Commission demonstrate that the national parliaments had made a manifest error of appraisal in objecting to the draft act on subsidiarity grounds. That is to say, the focus of the legal challenge would be on the question whether the national parliaments had acted rationally, in the sense of having properly directed themselves in fact and law and, having taken into account all relevant considerations, in objecting to the proposed act on subsidiarity grounds. To review compliance of a legislative act with the principle of subsidiarity via scrutiny of the defensibility of the objections raised by national parliaments would be preferable to purporting to review in its entirety the conduct of the lawmaking institutions in the lawmaking process. It would certainly be more practical.

It is difficult to be overly optimistic about the prospects for making subsidiarity a reality in the lawmaking process, but it is right to be concerned about the overcentralisation of decision making in the European Union. Subsidiarity honestly articulates the reason for that concern, by advancing the proposition that decisions should be taken as closely as possible to the citizen. In so many cases that will mean that decisions

---

[44] Case C-491/01 *The Queen v Secretary of State for Health ex-parte British American Tobacco (Investments) Ltd and Imperial Tobacco Ltd* [2002] ECR I-11453, paras 175 and 179.

should be taken at the local level, the regional level or the national level, rather than at the European level. Europe should confine itself to those activities which can only be undertaken effectively at the European level. That would keep it busy enough for the foreseeable future.

2

The Status and Rights of Sub-state Entities in the Constitutional Order of the European Union

DAVID EDWARD and
JOXERRAMON BENGOETXEA

Hugh Trevor Roper: *'If I must die in the ditch, it will be for the civilisation of old Europe, with its sophistication, its contradictions, its complexities, its hierarchies, its rich and varied cuisine, its wines.'*[1]

Back label on a bottle of 'Anarkos' wine from Apulia: *'The Academy says No to the sacrifice of millions of vines planted ad alberello; capitalist colonisation in the third millennium of the lands of Apulia; exploitation of their vineyards and their wines; enforced transfer of the right of replanting to other regions in the north; the complicity and factiousness of EU agricultural legislation; cultural oppression in the pattern of wine consumption; destruction of typicity; [and] domination of the market. Anarkos is an opposition wine!'*[2]

'Mir wëlle bleiwe wat mir sinn.' ('We want to remain what we are.')

W E HOPE IT is appropriate to begin an essay in honour of our friend Alan Dashwood, former Vice-Master of Sidney Sussex, oenophile and outstanding scholar and practitioner of EU law, with quotations from a former Master of Peterhouse, the back label on

---

[1] Hugh Trevor-Roper, letter to Valerie Paul, 29 August 1968, quoted in A Sisman, *Hugh Trevor-Roper—The Biography* (London, Weidenfeld & Nicolson, 2010).

[2] L'Accademia dei Racemi Sinfarosa Zinfandel Primitivo di Maduria was founded in 1998 to maintain the heritage of Apulian wines. Plantation of vines *ad alberello* dates from Roman times. The vines are trained on chestnut stakes in the pattern of a quincunx, which makes it impossible to tend them by machinery. The original text reads: 'Il sacrificio di milioni di viti piantate ad alberello, la colonizzazione capitalistica del terzo millennio nelle Terre di Puglia, lo sfruttamento dei suoi vigneti e dei suoi vini, l'emigrazione forzata dei diritti di reimpianto pugliesi negli altri regioni del nord, la complicità e la faziosità delle Leggi Comunitarie in Agricoltura, l'oppressione culturale nei modelli di consumo del vino, l'annientamento della tipicità, il dominio del mercato, L'Accademia dice No! Anarkos è un vino contro!'

a bottle of Apulian wine and the inscription on a building in the old Fishmarket of Luxembourg. Each of them illustrates, in its own way, a problem that continues to defy the ingenuity (or perhaps the will) of those who seek to build a 'Constitution for Europe': how are constitutional clothes to be put on the contradictions and complexities, not only of 'old Europe' but of the new Europe that has emerged since 1989? The rather vacuous motto 'united in diversity' recognises the problem but does little to solve it.

We come from two countries—Scotland and the Basque Country—whose constitutional arrangements illustrate the contradictions and complexities. Each is part of a single Member State, one of which has a written constitution while the other does not. Scotland enjoys substantial legislative autonomy, notably in the fields of civil and criminal law and procedure, but extremely limited fiscal autonomy. The Basque Country, by contrast, enjoys substantial fiscal autonomy but limited legislative autonomy, not including civil and criminal law and procedure. Each has some constitutional characteristics that are not shared even by other 'sub-state entities' in the same Member State, far less in others. Those who like tidy symmetrical constitutions will not look here for inspiration.

Up to now, EU law has largely been able to ignore the contradictions and complexities upon the view that, as Alan Dashwood has put it, the Union is 'a constitutional order of states'. It is states that have undertaken the legal obligations under the Treaties, and it is to them that the Union must look to ensure compliance with those obligations by sub-state entities. The Union cannot accept refusal, delay or obstruction on the part of such entities as a justification for non-compliance by the state.[3] The corollary is that—in theory—the Union does not prescribe, or interfere in, the internal constitutional order of the Member States.

But that is essentially the point of view of public international law. At an early stage, Advocate General Lagrange emphasised the constitutional nature of the ECSC Treaty and its internal consequences:

> [O]ur Court is not an international court but the Court of a Community created by six States on a model which is more closely related to a federal than to an international organisation, and although the Treaty which the Court has the task of applying was concluded in the form of an international treaty and although it unquestionably is one, it is nevertheless, from a material point of view, the charter of the Community, since the rules of law which derive from it constitute the internal law of that Community.[4]

---

[3] See the Opinion of Advocate General Sharpston in Case C-212/06 *Government of Communauté française and Gouvernement wallon v Gouvernement flamand* [2008] ECR I-1683, para 101 and following, and cases there cited.

[4] Case 8/55 *Fédération Charbonnière de Belgique v High Authority* [1954–56] ECR 245, 277.

Similarly, the extensive interaction between the internal circumstances of the Member States and the political process of implementing the EEC Treaty was stressed by Advocate General Roemer:

> There is a basic difference between the ECSC Treaty which brings about partial integration, and the EEC Treaty. As the objective of the latter is full integration of the whole of the economic life of the Member States, it must inevitably take into account the requirements of regional policy which are a component of the economic policy of each Member State. With regard to the Coal and Steel Community it was possible to disregard that aspect because it was feasible for the States to pursue a regional policy in the sector of the economy which was not integrated.[5]

Nevertheless, the Treaties have, from the beginning, recognised the asymmetrical character and interests of the Member States—for example, in the special provisions for overseas departments, countries and territories,[6] 'regional unions' such as those between Belgium, Luxembourg and the Netherlands[7] and (initially) for the special relationship between the Federal Republic of Germany and what were tactfully referred to as 'German territories to which the Basic Law does not apply'.[8]

In a variety of contexts, the ECJ has stressed the obligations of national courts to look below the formalities of state organisation, and to set aside or override internal rules of national law (including constitutional principles)—consider, for example (amongst many others), *Simmenthal*[9] (the obligation to set aside incompatible rules of national law), *Factortame (No 2)*[10] (the obligation to set aside the rule of English constitutional law that the courts may not grant an injunction against the Crown), *Marshall (No 1)*,[11] *Johnston*[12] and *Foster*[13] (direct effect of directives vis-à-vis 'emanations of the state'[14]) and, perhaps most controversially, *Köbler*[15] and *Traghetti del Mediterraneo*[16] (state responsibility for the conduct of supreme courts).

---

[5] Joined Cases 27–29/58 *Hauts Fourneaux de Givors v High Authority* [1960] ECR 241, 276.

[6] Now Art 355 and Part Four of the Treaty on the Functioning of the European Union (TFEU).

[7] Now Art 350 TFEU.

[8] Protocol to the EEC Treaty on German internal trade and connected problems.

[9] Case 106/77 *Amministrazione delle finanze dello Stato v Simmenthal SpA* [1978] ECR 629.

[10] Case C-213/89 *The Queen v Secretary of State for Transport, ex-parte Factortame Ltd and others* [1990] ECR I-2433; and the follow-up in the House of Lords [1991] 1 AC 603.

[11] Case 152/84 *Marshall v Southampton and South West Hampshire Area Health Authority (No.1)* [1986] ECR 723.

[12] Case 222/84 *Johnston v Chief Constable of the RUC* [1986] ECR 1651.

[13] Case C-188/89 *Foster v British Gas* [1990] ECR I-3313.

[14] The expression 'emanation of the state' seems to have been used for the first time in the order of the Court of Appeal referring *Marshall (No 1)*

[15] Case C-224/01 *Gerhard Köbler v Republik Österreich* [2003]ECR I-10239.

[16] Case C-173/03 *Traghetti del Mediterraneo SpA v Repubblica italiana* [2006] ECR I-5177.

Subject to the overriding requirement to give full force and effect to EU law, the institutions have been careful to stand aside from constitutional disputes within the Member States and likewise (as Marc Maresceau has described[17]) from the dispute within the Council of Europe as to the internal constitutional order of Liechtenstein, a Member State of the EEA.

The legal position that states are the actors in EU affairs, and that the Union does not prescribe or interfere in their internal constitutional order, has in some ways provided a comfort zone for EU lawyers, enabling them to work on the construction of the Union's legal order without becoming too much embroiled in national disputes and differences. The peace of the comfort zone is now disturbed for a variety of reasons. These include:

- The resurgence of 'nationalism' in various forms;
- The accession to the Union of a growing number of smaller states and the prospect of more, particularly following the dissolution of the former Soviet bloc;
- Measures taken by the larger states of western Europe to allay separatist sentiment by the adoption of various forms of devolved government, including the creation of 'regional' parliaments;
- The provisions of the Lisbon Treaty—notably the new definition of subsidiarity in Article 5, the assertion of democratic principles in Articles 9 and 10 of the Treaty on European Union (TEU), and Protocols (No 1) on the role of National Parliaments and (No 2) on the application of the principles of subsidiarity and proportionality; and
- The judgment of the German Constitutional Court (Bundesverfassungsgericht) of 30 June 2009.[18]

Before we go further, we should make it clear that we are not here arguing a 'nationalist' case. In our respective countries, one of us might be described as a moderate unionist, the other as a moderate nationalist. Our aim is, rather, to revisit some of the issues that were urged (largely unsuccessfully) on the Constitutional Convention by another friend and colleague, Neil MacCormick.[19] Some of his ideas did, directly or indirectly, find expression in the Constitutional Treaty, and now in the Lisbon Treaty. The question for us is whether the Treaties have really faced up to the issues he raised, or whether they conceal the seeds of continued dissatisfaction and dissent.

Nationalism has been seen as the scourge of Europe, the principal cause of successive conflicts and therefore, almost by definition, incompatible

---

[17] Chapter 26 below.

[18] BVerfG, 2BvE 2/08 vom 30.6.2009, Absatz-Nr (1–421).

[19] See his contributions to the Convention: 'Subsidiarity, Common Sense, and Local Knowledge', Conv 275/02, Contrib 94, 18 September 2002; 'Democracy at Many Levels: European Constitutional Reform', Conv 298/02, Contrib 101, 24 September 2002; and 'Stateless Nations and the Convention's Debate on Regions' Conv 525/03, Contrib 220, 31 January 2003.

with the ideal of European integration. But it is idle to pretend that there are not lively and serious nationalist (or separatist) feelings within the EU and on its outer margins, or that these can safely be ignored as being irrelevant to its nature and future structure.

There is a warning in two of the eleven lessons drawn by Robert McNamara, the former US Secretary of Defense, from the Vietnam War:

3. We underestimated the power of nationalism to motivate a people to fight and die for their beliefs and values.
4. Our judgements of friend and foe, alike, reflected our profound ignorance of the history, culture, and politics of the people in the area, and the personalities and habits of their leaders.

Whether in south-east Asia or in Europe or elsewhere, 'we want to remain what we are' is a sentiment that strikes a chord with most of humanity. It is true that virulent forms of nationalism have led to internecine disputes and, all too often, to the persecution of minorities and massacre. But the reality surely is that the complexities and contradictions of 'old Europe', of which nationalist sentiment is one, cannot be ironed out or reasoned away. The problem for the European constitution-builder is how best to accommodate them.

In the countries of the former Soviet bloc, the solution has been to accept the dissolution of larger states into smaller states, each having all the prerogatives of statehood. Most notably, the former Yugoslavia, which many people thought would be the first Iron Curtain country to join the (then) European Community, has now broken into seven separate states (Slovenia, Croatia, Serbia, Bosnia, Montenegro, Kosovo and FYROM), one of which is already an EU Member State while the others are candidate countries at various stages of acceptance. The growing number of small states acceding to the Union raises the issue of 'over-federalisation' criticised by the German Constitutional Court in its judgment of 30 June 2009, which we discuss below.

In parallel, several of the countries of western Europe have, since accession to the Union, adopted different forms of federal or quasi-federal arrangements as a way of solving, or at least defusing, their internal tensions. At the beginning, only one of the original six (Germany) was a federal state. (The constitution of the Netherlands, initially a confederal republic, provides for a high degree of administrative and regulatory, but not legislative, decentralisation.) Of the nine states that acceded between 1973 and the enlargement of 2004, only Austria was a federal state at the time of accession. Since accession, Belgium has become a federation, while Italy, Spain and the UK have each adopted some form of federal, quasi-federal or devolved constitutional arrangement.

It is interesting, in this context, to compare what are thought to be essential competences of the state (the central state). In Spain the administration of justice and substantive criminal law and procedure are national competences; in Germany they are shared competences; while in Scotland they are all devolved to the Scottish Parliament, subject to the overriding legislative competence of the national parliament. Taxation competences show comparable variations. This is unlikely to be the end of an evolving process of differentiation.

Against this developing patchwork of internal constitutional arrangements, we turn to consider the provisions of the Lisbon Treaty and the judgment of the German Constitutional Court.

The Treaty of Lisbon now formally affirms respect for 'the equality of Member States before the Treaties as well as their national identities, inherent in their fundamental structures, political and constitutional, inclusive of regional and local self-government',[20] and goes on to define the three basic principles of conferral, subsidiarity and proportionality.[21]

The principle of subsidiarity has been a mantra of the treaty-makers since Maastricht[22] and its formulation has been embroidered by successive Treaty amendments. However, as Derrick Wyatt observes,[23] 'Subsidiarity has so far failed to instil a culture of self-restraint on the part of the Member States and the law-making institutions'.

Immediately before Lisbon, the second paragraph of Article 5 of the EC Treaty read:

> In areas which do not fall within its exclusive competence, the Community shall take action, in accordance with the principle of subsidiarity, only if and insofar as the objectives of the proposed action cannot be sufficiently achieved *by the Member States* and can therefore, by reason of the scale or effects of the proposed action, be better achieved by the Community.

The Lisbon Treaty, as well as giving subsidiarity a more significant status in the Treaty on European Union, has introduced a small but significant amendment:

> Under the principle of subsidiarity, in areas which do not fall within its exclusive competence, the Union shall act only if and insofar as the objectives of the proposed action cannot be sufficiently achieved by the Member States, *either at central level or at regional and local level*, but can rather, by reason of the scale or effects of the proposed action, be better achieved at Union level.[24]

Thus, the Treaty now enjoins the Union legislator to consider the potential efficacy of action at regional or local level. This injunction is repeated,

---

[20] Treaty on European Union (TEU), Art 4(2), taken from Art I-5(1) of the Treaty establishing a Constitution for Europe (Constitutional Treaty), Art I-5(1).

[21] TEU, Art 5, following in essentials the Constitutional Treaty, Art I-11.

[22] EC Treaty as established at Maastricht, article 3b.

[23] Chapter 1 above.

[24] Treaty on European Union (TEU), as amended by the Treaty of Lisbon, Art 5(3), emphasis added.

for example, in Protocol (No 26) on Services of General Interest, which refers to 'the essential role and wide discretion of *national, regional and local authorities* in providing, commissioning and organising services of general economic interest as closely as possible to the needs of users'.

Again, following the Constitutional Treaty, the Lisbon Treaty asserts a number of democratic principles, including the following:

- In all its activities, the Union shall observe the equality of its citizens . . .[25]
- The functioning of the Union shall be founded on representative democracy.[26]
- Every citizen shall have the right to participate in the democratic life of the Union. Decisions shall be taken as openly and as closely as possible to the citizen.[27]

Next, the Lisbon Treaty includes a number of new provisions for the participation of national parliaments which are enjoined to 'contribute actively to the good functioning of the Union', inter alia, 'by seeing to it that the principle of subsidiarity is respected in accordance with the procedures provided for in the Protocol on the application of the principles of subsidiarity and proportionality [Protocol No 2]'.[28] The Protocol provides that:

- Before proposing legislative acts, the Commission shall consult widely. Such consultations shall, where appropriate, take into account *the regional and local dimension* of the action envisaged.[29]
- Any national parliament *or any chamber of a national parliament* may . . .send . . . a reasoned opinion stating why it considers that [a draft legislative act] does not comply with the principle of subsidiarity. It will be for each national parliament or each chamber of a national parliament to consult, where appropriate, *regional parliaments with legislative powers*.[30]

The separate rights of intervention granted to the chambers of national parliaments are particularly important where, as in Germany and Austria, one chamber is composed of representatives of the 'regions' (the *Länder*[31]). Such a chamber may be expected often to find it 'appropriate' to consult the *Land* Parliaments as to whether the principle of subsidiarity has been respected. Time will tell whether this obligation will be taken seriously by

---

[25] TEU, Art 9.
[26] TEU, Art 10(1).
[27] TEU, Art 10(3)
[28] TEU, Art 12(b).
[29] Protocol (No 2), Art 2, emphasis added.
[30] Protocol (No 2), Art 6, emphasis added.
[31] In Germany, the members of the Bundesrat are delegated by the *Land* governments; in Austria they are elected by the *Land* legislatures.

other national parliaments where neither chamber represents the regions.

Lastly (for present purposes), the Lisbon Treaty grants direct access to the Court of Justice to the Committee of the Regions 'for the purpose of protecting [its] prerogatives'[32] and, under the Subsidiarity Protocol, to bring 'actions against legislative acts for the adoption of which the [TFEU] provides that it be consulted'.[33] The Subsidiarity Protocol also contains a curious provision enabling Member States to 'notify' actions on grounds of infringement of the principle of subsidiarity 'on behalf of their national parliament or a chamber thereof'. The 'notification' is to be made 'in accordance with their legal order'.[34] It therefore appears, though it is far from clear, that a situation may arise where a Member State is the nominal applicant in an action for annulment of a legislative act on behalf of its national parliament or a chamber thereof (perhaps reflecting the wish of its internal parliamentary assemblies), even if the government of that state has voted in Council in favour of that act and would wish to argue that it should not be annulled.

All in all, the Lisbon Treaty recognises, albeit in a rather hesitant and piecemeal way, what Neil MacCormick called 'the manifest truth that European Democracy must operate at many levels, and that a concern for subsidiarity cannot be exhausted by reflection merely on relations between member states and union institutions'. In so doing, it moves us out of the comfort zone where only the states are the relevant actors. At least to some extent, it can no longer be said that the Union is a 'constitutional order of states'.

In more pompous terms, one might say that the two classical dynamics of European institutional integration—intergovernmental and supranational[35]—are no longer sufficient to explain the new, more complex, Treaty structures. Now the inter-parliamentarian dimension needs to be added, reflecting both democratic representation and multi-level governance.

On the other hand, it can hardly be said of the Lisbon Treaty, as Neil would have wished, that 'its structure is readily intelligible to its citizens and empowers them to have their full and proper say at all levels'. It persists in what he criticised as 'the inappropriate use of the term "region" to refer to territorial entities within the Union, which their citizens regard as "nations"'.[36] (German-speakers normally refer in English to the *Länder* as 'states', not 'regions'.) And while the Treaty gives enhanced status to the Committee of the Regions, it does nothing to redress the extraordinary

---

[32] TFEU, Art 263, third paragraph.
[33] Protocol (no 2), Art 8, second paragraph.
[34] Protocol (No 2), Art 8, first paragraph.
[35] See JHH Weiler, *Il sistema comunitario europeo* (Bologna, Il Mulino, 1985.)
[36] 'Democracy at Many Levels', above n 19, 2.

situation to which Neil drew attention,[37] where Malta has ten members (full and alternate) and Catalonia three.

This is an aspect of what the German Constitutional Court called 'over-federalisation' (*Überföderalisierung*).[38]

The judgment of the Constitutional Court has attracted attention particularly because of its insistence on the principle of electoral equality (*Wahlgleichheit*),[39] the continuing pre-eminence of the Member States as 'masters of the Treaties' (*Herren der Verträge*)[40] and the consequential reassertion of the right of the Constitutional Court to verify 'whether legal acts of the European institutions and bodies remain within the limits of the sovereign powers conferred on them or if the Community courts interpret the Treaties expansively tantamount to an inadmissible autonomous treaty amendment'.[41]

For our part, we take leave to doubt whether absolute statistical equality of voting power in parliamentary elections is an indispensable condition of democracy. Nor do we find it easy to see how the EU can function if the judicial organs of 27 Member States (or perhaps only those that have a Constitutional Court?) are able to declare acts of the institutions inapplicable within their territorial jurisdiction. That said, we are more concerned here with what we might call hidden aspects of the argument.

In the official English translation on the Court's website,[42] paragraph 279 of the judgment reads: 'The democratic basic rule of equal opportunities of success ("one man one vote") only applies within a people'. The original German reads: *Die demokratische Grundregel del wahlrechtlichen Erfolgschancegleichheit . . . gilt nur innerhalb eines Volkes*. The word *Volk* (which carries negative connotations too) can certainly be translated 'people', but also—and we would suggest more accurately in this context—as 'nation'. On this view, true democracy, or at least democracy in its fullest sense, can exist only within the context of a people or nation.

The Court introduces the idea of 'over-federalisation' after mentioning the 'marked imbalance' of representation in the European Parliament where

> According to the draft decision, a Member of the European Parliament elected in France would represent approximately 857,000 citizens of the Union and thus as many as a Member elected in Germany, who represents approximately 857,000 as well. In contrast, a Member of the European Parliament elected in Luxembourg would, however, only represent approximately 83,000 Luxembourg citizens of the Union, ie a tenth of them, in the case of Malta, it would be

---

[37] 'Stateless Nations', above n 19, 3.
[38] §288,
[39] §279ff.
[40] §334.
[41] §338–39.
[42] Available at http://www.bundesverfassungsgericht.de/entscheidungen/es20090630_2bve000208en.html.

approximately 67,000, or only roughly a twelfth of them; as regards a medium-sized Member State such as Sweden, every elected Member of the European Parliament would represent approximately 455,000 citizens of the Union from that country in the European Parliament.[43]

The Court notes, rather acidly, one might think, that 'representation in the European Parliament is not linked to the equality of citizens of the Union (Article 9 Lisbon TEU) but to nationality, a criterion that is actually an absolutely prohibited distinction for the European Union' and concludes that 'this contradiction can only be explained by the character of the European Union as an association of sovereign states'.[44] The judgment continues:

> It is true that the democracy of the European Union is approximated to federalised state concepts; if measured against the principle of representative democracy, however, it would show an excessive degree of federalisation (*Überföderalisierung*). With the personal composition of the European Council, of the Council, the Commission and the Court of Justice of the European Union, the principle of the equality of states remains linked to national rights of determination, rights which are, in principle, equal. Even for a European Parliament elected having due account to equality, this structure would constitute a considerable obstacle for the expression of the representative will of the parliamentary majority with regard to persons or subject- areas. For example, after the entry into force of the Treaty of Lisbon, the Court of Justice must still be composed according to the principle 'one state, one judge' and under the determining influence of the Member States regardless of their number of inhabitants.

Elsewhere in the judgment the Court asserts and seeks to protect (impliedly rather than expressly) the democratic interests of the *Länder* and of local government, where it refers to the school and educational system, the media and the status of churches,[45] the administration of justice,[46] the delivery of health services and 'the essential role and wide discretion of national, regional and local Governments in providing, commissioning and organising non-economic services of general interest'.[47] National, regional and local choice in these matters must be protected from unauthorised intrusion by the EU and its institutions.

The thrust of these arguments is to support the view that the legitimacy of the EU and its institutions depends upon its being, and remaining, 'a constitutional order of states'. The Member States are the source of legitimate authority and must be the ultimate judges of its limits. The discussion of democracy is concerned primarily with equality of voting

[43] §285.
[44] §287.
[45] §260.
[46] §352ff.
[47] §397.

power, while the references to regional and local choice or discretion seem to be designed to convey the message 'thus far and no further' or even 'keep your tanks off our lawn'.

In our opinion, this approach does not do justice to the complex problem with which the EU is faced. When it is said that the purpose of subsidiarity is to allow decisions to be taken as closely as possible to the citizen, the corollary must be that the decision makers, including legislative decision makers, who are closest to the citizen may legitimately make different choices in like circumstances. If the principle of equal treatment (or, put negatively, non-discrimination) means that all citizens must always be treated in the same way in the same circumstances, the range of choice that will be open to regional and local authorities is reduced to a level of banality. Anything in the nature of a 'postcode lottery' must be avoided, and uniformity of result must be imposed.

Thus, in our view, there is an underlying tension between the Treaty principles that, on the one hand, 'in all its activities, the Union shall observe the equality of its citizens' and, on the other, 'the functioning of the Union shall be founded on representative democracy' and 'every citizen shall have the right to participate in the democratic life of the Union'. This tension has been illustrated in recent cases before the Court of Justice: the Azores and Basque Country tax cases,[48] the Flemish/Walloon social security case,[49] and *Horvath*.[50] Each of these cases raised, in one form or another, the question whether differential arrangements adopted by 'regional' authorities within a single Member State were compatible with EU law.

In the Azores and Basque Country tax cases, the question at issue concerned the legitimacy of tax differentials as between, on the one hand, the Azores and the historic communities of the Basque Country and, on the other hand, other parts of Portugal and Spain respectively. The Court applied the threefold test of legitimate regional tax autonomy proposed by the Advocate General: institutional autonomy, procedural autonomy and economic autonomy.[51] In the Azores case, the criterion of economic autonomy was held not to be satisfied in relation to the particular provision at issue, while in the Basque cases all three criteria were held to be satisfied.

In the Flemish/Walloon social security case, there was no question that

---

[48] Case C-88/03 *Portuguese Republic v Commission* [2006] ECR I-7115; Joined Cases C-428/06 to C-434/06 *Unión General de Trabajadores de La Rioja (UGT-Rioja) and Others v Juntas Generales del Territorio Histórico de Vizcaya and Others* [2008] ECR I-6747.

[49] Case 212/06 *Government of Communauté française and Gouvernement wallon v Gouvernement flamand* [2008] ECR I-1683.

[50] Case 428/07 *The Queen, on the application of Mark Horvath v Secretary of State for Environment, Food and Rural Affairs* [2009] ECR I-6355.

[51] See the Opinion of Advocate General Geelhoed at para 54, and the judgment of the Court at para 67.

Flemish government was autonomous as regards the adoption of social security schemes. The question was whether the differential treatment resulting from the measures adopted was a 'purely internal situation' escaping the reach of EU law. It was held, for reasons explained by the Advocate General, that the situation was not purely internal. The Court did not, on the other hand, take up her invitation 'to reflect on the nature and rationale behind its doctrine in respect of purely internal situations'.[52]

Horvath concerned a difference in implementation, as between England on the one hand and Scotland, Wales and Northern Ireland on the other, of a regulation concerning direct support schemes for farmers under the Common Agricultural Policy. The complaint of Mr Horvath was that, as a farmer in England, he was made subject to an onerous obligation in respect of the maintenance of public footpaths to which he would not have been subject had he been a farmer in Scotland, Wales or Northern Ireland. This was because the measures taken by the UK government to implement the relevant Council regulation in England imposed such an obligation, while the measures taken by the devolved administrations of Scotland, Wales and Northern Ireland did not.

The Court held that 'divergences between the measures provided for by the various administrations cannot, alone, constitute discrimination', provided that they are compatible with the obligations on the Member State.[53] This conclusion has caused some perplexity amongst commentators. In the mid-1990s, albeit under different regulations, the Court had found it unacceptable that 'the competent authorities in the UK [had] tolerated differences in the application of the Milk Marketing Schemes' and found that the UK had failed in its obligations 'by allowing the Milk Marketing Boards to pursue divergent policies'.[54] *Horvath* has been seen as striking out a new line, more tolerant of differential implementation.

For our part, we do not see *Horvath* as an earth-shattering departure from previous jurisprudence. If anything, we regard it as facing up to the reality that, if the devolution of legislative and regulatory power is to be meaningful, some degree of difference must be tolerated.

That does not, however, address the underlying issue whether sub-state entities with a democratic mandate and accountability must have a right to participate in the formulation of legislative and administrative measures for whose implementation they will have constitutional responsibility. It is through them, in this respect, that the citizen will, in the words of the Treaty, 'participate in the democratic life of the Union'.

In her Opinion in the Flemish social security case, the Advocate General recognised the force of the argument:

[52] Opinion, para 121.
[53] *Horvath*, above n 49, para 57.
[54] Case 40/92 *Commission v United Kingdom* [1994] ECR I-989, paras 28–30.

105. Belgium is not the only Member State to have chosen a federal or otherwise decentralised structure. Community law has not made it impossible for other federal Member States, and/or their decentralised authorities, to exercise their competences as defined by national law. However, a Member State cannot use its decentralised structure as a cloak in order to justify a failure to comply with its obligations under Community law.

106. It might be said that, if so, decentralised authorities of Member States need some mechanism by which to participate in the elaboration of EU law, especially when the Member State itself is not competent. (I add in passing that analogous arguments arise in respect of locus standi in direct actions before the Court under Article 230 EC.)

107. That is a fair point. Appropriate institutional arrangements can, however, be set up to ensure such participation in the Community legislative process. This can be achieved, for example, through the first paragraph of Article 203 EC, which implicitly allows regional ministers to represent their Member State in the Council. I note that such arrangements have, indeed, been made within the Belgian constitutional structure.

In the event, the Lisbon Treaty does not open a direct right of action before the Court to sub-state entities, except through the channel of their national parliament or one of its chambers, or through the Committee of the Regions. Otherwise 'regional parliaments with legislative powers' may be consulted 'where appropriate'. This formulation does not appear to create an enforceable obligation to consult.

It is true that, as the Advocate General says, appropriate institutional arrangements can be set up to ensure participation in the legislative process through Article 203 EC, but this depends on the willingness of the government of the Member State concerned to accord this possibility. This is less likely to occur where, as often happens, the devolved administration is of a different political hue from the national administration.

What, then, is the solution? There appear to us to be two possible solutions, but there may be more.

The first solution would be further institutional reform, including a rethink of the role and composition of the Committee of the Regions. That is for the Greek kalends, even if it were realistic to think that the Member States would agree on a sensible structure.

The alternative is what might be called a 'Community solution', in the sense of developing a practice of organised consultation which can later become crystallised in law. After all, the European Council was in operation for some years before it was recognised as one of the EU institutions.

Neil MacCormick suggested[55] that parliaments of self-governing entities

---

[55] 'Democracy at Many Levels', above n 19, 5.

in Member States should be able to participate in COSAC.[56] It is open to question whether the representatives of the parliaments of Member States who constitute COSAC would accept the extensive widening of its membership that this would involve. More promising as potential interlocutors are REGLEG and CALRE. REGLEG is the Conference of European Regions with Legislative Powers, representing the governments of 73 regions from eight Member States. CALRE is the Conference of Regional Legislative Assemblies, representing the Presidents (Speakers) of 74 assemblies from the same eight Member States.[57]

The fact that there are two such bodies fits the new inter-parliamentary (or trans-parliamentary) dynamic that has begun to complement the inter-governmental and institutional structures of the EU, producing an increasingly complex constitutional structure of variable geometry. Within that structure there must surely be scope for the voice to be heard at Union level of those who are democratically accountable for giving *legislative* effect to Union action at a level closer to the citizen than national governments and parliaments.

A preparedness to give them a voice would be a pragmatic first step. But that requires the recognition, first, that there is a problem to be solved and, second, that symmetrical solutions do not always work for asymmetrical realities. We are not there yet.

---

[56] *Conférence des Organes Spécialisés dans les Affaires Communautaires.* Available at http://www.cosac.eu.

[57] See http://www.regleg.eu and http://www.calrenet.eu. The numerical difference is due to the composition of the Italian and Spanish delegations.

3

Ireland and the Lisbon Treaty: All's Well That Ends Well?

ANTHONY ARNULL[*]

I BACKGROUND

AFTER IRELAND'S ACCESSION in 1973 to what is now the European Union, the establishment of a position at the heart of Europe became a conscious objective of Irish policy.[1] Although particular EU initiatives and institutions sometimes attracted criticism, 'pro-Europeanism has become the default policy position of mainstream Irish politics'.[2] Indeed, the two largest parties, Fianna Fáil and Fine Gael, had been supportive of the integration process since the early 1960s. The leadership of the third party, the Labour Party, had moved to a similar position by the time of the 1987 referendum on the Single European Act.[3]

The enthusiasm of the political establishment for Europe was not wholly shared by Irish voters. The public's broadly favourable attitude towards the EU merely seemed to reflect a utilitarian desire to ensure that Ireland continued to enjoy the economic benefits of membership. The outcome of Irish referendums on the EU was consequently unpredictable.[4] It may therefore seem curious that, alone among the EU's Member States, Ireland risked holding a referendum on the Lisbon Treaty. The negative outcome of the one held on 12 June 2008 sparked a crisis in Ireland's relations with the EU. Although later reversed, it threatened to cause long-term damage to the country's standing in Europe. Could all this not have been avoided had the Treaty simply been ratified through the Oireachtas, the Irish Parliament?

---

[*] The comments of Robert Cryer and Colin Warbrick on some of the issues discussed in this chapter are gratefully acknowledged. The usual disclaimer applies.

[1] See Houses of the Oireachtas, Sub-Committee on Ireland's Future in the European Union, 'Ireland's Future in the European Union: Challenges, Issues and Options' (November 2008) 19.

[2] J FitzGibbon, 'Ireland's No to Lisbon: Learning the Lessons from the Failure of the Yes and the Success of the No Side', Sussex European Institute Working Paper No 110/European Parties Elections and Referendums Network Working Paper No 21, 6.

[3] Ibid, 5–6.

[4] Ibid, 8.

The explanation for Ireland's decision to hold a referendum lies in the decision of the Irish Supreme Court in *Crotty v An Taoiseach*[5] on the scope of Article 29.4.3 of the Irish Constitution, which was introduced to permit Irish accession to the European Community. The Supreme Court held in that case that Article 29.4.3 authorised the state 'not only to join the Communities as they stood in 1973, but also to join in amendments of the Treaties *so long as such amendments do not alter the essential scope or objectives of the Communities*'.[6] Amendments falling outside the scope of Article 29.4.3 would therefore require a further amendment of the Constitution. All such amendments require the approval of the Irish people in a referendum.[7]

At issue in the *Crotty* case was Irish ratification of the Single European Act. The Supreme Court held that the alterations to the Treaties made by that Act did not require further constitutional amendment. However, it found that Title III of the Single European Act, on European co-operation in the sphere of foreign policy, amounted to a separate treaty in its own right[8] and fell outside the scope of Article 29.4.3.[9] Because its effect would be to limit the freedom of action conferred by the Constitution on the government in matters of foreign policy, Title III could not be ratified without a further amendment of the Constitution.

The immediate effect of the *Crotty* decision was that a referendum was held on the Single European Act. The necessary constitutional amendment was approved comfortably, but in the longer term it proved difficult to ascertain whether or not a new European treaty contained provisions which altered 'the essential scope or objectives of the Communities'. The result was that all subsequent European treaties (other than accession treaties) were the subject of referendums in Ireland, even though a referendum might not always have been strictly necessary. An expectation was therefore created among the Irish electorate that a referendum would be held on any European treaty unless it merely provided for the accession of new Member States. This added a strong political imperative to the legal case for holding one on the Lisbon Treaty.[10]

An alternative strategy might have been the adoption by the Oireachtas of a Bill ratifying the Lisbon Treaty with a view to its submission to the Supreme Court by the President, under Article 26 of the Constitution, for

---

[5] [1987] IR 713. See N Fennelly, 'The Effect of European Community Law on Irish Law and the Irish Constitution' in A Arnull, P Eeckhout and T Tridimas (eds), *Continuity and Change in EU Law* (Oxford, Oxford University Press, 2008) ch 26, 450–51.

[6] Ibid, 767 *per* Finlay CJ (emphasis added).

[7] See Art 46 of the Irish Constitution.

[8] [1987] IR 713, 775 *per* Walsh J.

[9] Ibid, 783 *per* Henchy J.

[10] See G Barrett, B Laffan, R Thom, D Thomas and B Tonra, 'Ireland's Future in Europe: Scenarios and Implications' (UCD Dublin European Institute, 12 November 2008) 21–23.

a ruling on its constitutionality.[11] This would have had the advantage of giving the Supreme Court an opportunity to clarify the *Crotty* test and to specify which provisions of the Treaty, if any, required a constitutional amendment. Any subsequent referendum could then have been limited to the provisions singled out by the Supreme Court. Given previous practice, however, it would have had the political disadvantage that voters might have thought that the government was trying to avoid public scrutiny of the Treaty. The alternative of simply adopting an act and leaving it to an individual to challenge its constitutionality before the courts was equally unappealing. A defeat might have caused the government immense political damage without necessarily identifying all the provisions requiring an amendment to the Constitution. Either factor could have made it difficult to rectify the position by a later referendum.

II THE 2008 REFERENDUM CAMPAIGN

After much prevarication by the government, the date of the 2008 referendum was announced on 25 April 2008. The climate was not propitious for supporters of the Lisbon Treaty. Public confidence in politicians and the political process had been undermined by the Mahon Tribunal, whose enquiries into allegations of corruption[12] led Bertie Ahern, the so-called 'Teflon Taoiseach', to announce on 2 April 2008 that he would resign on 6 May.[13]

The 'yes' campaign was led by the Irish Alliance for Europe, a broad coalition which 'appeared to have operated almost exclusively at the elite level'.[14] It did not launch its campaign until the beginning of May 2008, by which time the 'no' campaign was already well under way.[15] It got off to a bad start when Charlie McCreevy, the then Irish Member of the European Commission, admitted that he had not read the Treaty.[16] Moreover, Fine Gael and Labour, the main opposition parties, were unable to resist the opportunity presented by the campaign to promote their candidates in the local and European elections due to be held in 2009. At the same time, Fianna Fáil linked the authority of the new Taoiseach, Brian Cowen, to the success of the 'yes' campaign. The result was to distract the attention of voters from the Treaty itself. FitzGibbon observed[17] that

---

[11] See L Pech, 'Le référendum en Irlande pour ratifier les traités Européens: obligatoire ou coutumier?' (Fondation Robert Schuman, October 2008) 8; Barrett et al, ibid, 23.

[12] Available at http://www.planningtribunal.ie/.

[13] See FitzGibbon, above n 2, 10.

[14] Ibid, 18.

[15] Ibid, 19–20.

[16] See 'Lisbon Treaty not an Easy Sell, Admits Irish EU Commissioner', *EUobserver*, 22 May 2008.

[17] Above n 2, 28.

'government and opposition party pro-European referendum campaigns can succeed but only when their pro-EU policy positions come first, and domestic policy differences are cast aside'.

On the no side, Sinn Féin and the Socialist Party were joined by various civil society groups independent of each other and of the main political parties. Many of the leading figures in these groups had built up considerable experience of campaigning against EU Treaties prior to previous referendums and had been involved in the successful campaign against the Nice Treaty in 2001. Prominent examples of such groups were Cóir (Justice) on the religious right and the People's Movement on the left. These groups offered an outlet for eurosceptic sentiment in the Catholic Church and the Irish Congress of Trade Unions, neither of which felt able to oppose the Treaty openly for fear of exclusion by the Government from the formulation of economic policy.[18] To these groups must be added Libertas, which attracted much media attention.[19] Established by a wealthy businessman, Declan Ganley, Libertas focused its somewhat contradictory campaign on making the EU more democratic, on national sovereignty and on corporate tax rates. It attracted support from disgruntled Fianna Fáil and Fine Gael voters who opposed the Treaty but did not wish to align themselves with the extreme left, fundamentalist Catholics or supporters of the IRA.[20]

III   THE RESULT AND THE DOMESTIC RESPONSE

Of those who took part in the June 2008 referendum, 46.6 per cent voted 'yes' while 53.4 per cent voted 'no'. The Nice Treaty had been rejected by almost exactly the same margin in June 2001. However, the turnout then (35 per cent) was significantly lower than in June 2008 (53 per cent). Indeed, the turnout in June 2008 was higher than that in October 2002 (49.5 per cent), when the Nice Treaty was approved. This suggested that there was unlikely to be a silent majority of 'yes' voters who could be relied on should the Lisbon Treaty be the subject of a second referendum. In addition, the range of issues that had been raised during the referendum campaign was diverse, making it difficult to establish what exactly it was that the majority had rejected.

In an attempt to address the latter difficulty, the Irish Department of Foreign Affairs commissioned research from marketing consultants Mill-

---

[18] Ibid, 18.
[19] Ibid, 13ff.
[20] Ibid, 20.

ward Brown IMS. Their report was published in September 2008.[21] Among its key findings were the following.[22]

- Sixty per cent of Irish voters believed that Ireland's interests were best pursued by remaining fully involved in the EU. Despite the referendum outcome, the attitude of people in Ireland towards the EU was among the most positive of all the Member States.
- Among those opposed to the Treaty, the key demographic groups were 25–34 year olds, the C2DE socio-economic group and women.
- Among those who supported the Treaty, the key demographic groups were those aged over 64, the AB socio-economic group and men.
- Among those who did not vote, 63 per cent were so-called voluntary abstainers, that is, people who were in a position to vote but decided not to do so.[23] Of this group, by far the most common reason given for not voting was 'lack of understanding/lack of information/too complicated'. People in the C2DE socio-economic group were much more likely to have abstained voluntarily than people in the ABC1 group.[24]
- The main reason given for voting no was 'lack of knowledge/information/understanding'. Booklets distributed by the government and the independent Referendum Commission were perceived as unduly complex and of little value.[25] Lack of knowledge of the EU, its institutions and decision-making processes was particularly widespread among 'no' voters.
- Yes campaign posters were disliked by both 'yes' and 'no' voters, many of whom felt that they were concerned more with self-promotion than with elucidating the benefits of the Treaty. Posters produced by the 'no' campaign, although disliked by some, were widely recalled and struck a chord with voters.[26]
- 26 per cent of 'no' voters mentioned Treaty-specific elements that were of concern to them, 20 per cent cited general issues around the referendum, while 16 per cent mentioned issues to do with loss of power/independence.
- The main areas of concern to all voters were: (i) retaining military neutrality; (ii) preventing excessive EU regulation; (iii) the loss of a

[21] 'Post-Lisbon Treaty Referendum Research Findings', available at http://www.imsl.ie/news/Millward_Brown_IMS_Lisbon_Research_Report.pdf.

[22] Ibid, i–iii.

[23] Thirty-four per cent were so-called circumstantial abstainers, who were unable to vote for a variety of practical reasons, such as being away from home on the day of the referendum or illness.

[24] An earlier survey conducted by Gallup for the EU Representation in Ireland (Flash Eurobarometer 245, 18 June 2008) found that younger people were much less likely to have voted than older people.

[25] Millward Brown report, above n 21, 9–10.

[26] Ibid, 10. The Flash Eurobarometer survey (above n 24) had found that 68% of voters—and 57% of 'yes' voters—had found the 'no' campaign to be more convincing than the 'yes' campaign.

permanent Irish Commissioner;[27] (iv) retaining control over the law on abortion; (v) workers' rights;[28] (vi) retaining control over public services; and (vii) corporate taxation. More 'no' voters than 'yes' voters considered these issues very important.

- No voters were far more likely than 'yes' voters to believe that the Treaty would lead to conscription to a European army.
- Yes voters were much more likely than 'no' voters to say that Ireland's economic prospects and influence in the EU had weakened as a result of the 'no' vote.
- Just over 22 per cent of 'no' voters believed that Ireland's position had been strengthened by the 'no' vote, possibly because they thought that the Treaty could now be renegotiated.

The picture that emerged from the Millward Brown report must have been received by the Irish Government with some satisfaction. It identified the need to provide voters with clearer information about the Treaty were there to be a second referendum and revealed several specific areas of concern that might be addressed. It specified the key demographic groups at which any new 'yes' campaign would need to be aimed, offered lessons about how such a campaign should be conducted and suggested that it was realistic to seek to persuade significant numbers of 'no' voters to vote 'yes'.

The second limb of the official response to the outcome of the 2008 referendum was the establishment by the Oireachtas of a Sub-Committee of the Joint Committee on European Affairs to consider Ireland's future in the EU. The Sub-Committee asked University College Dublin to produce a report on the options available to the government.[29] That report (hereafter the Barrett report) and the report of the Sub-Committee itself were published in November 2008. They were detailed and wide-ranging.

The Sub-Committee observed that, if a renewed attempt were to be made to ratify the Treaty, one possibility would be to put it to a second referendum after 'variations'[30] had been agreed with the other Member States. These might be achieved through the adoption of declarations, legally binding decisions (such as that adopted in 1992 after the failure

---

[27] This was ironic. Ireland risked losing the right to nominate a Commissioner in 2009 in any event under the Treaty of Nice, which was approved by Irish voters by referendum in 2003: see Art 213(1) EC, as amended. The Lisbon Treaty would have postponed the reduction in size of the Commission until 2014: see Art 17(5) TEU (as amended).

[28] On this issue, the debate had been affected by Case C-438/05 *The International Transport Workers' Federation and The Finnish Seamen's Union* [2007] ECR I-10779; Case C-341/05 *Laval un Partneri* [2007] ECR I-11767; Case C-346/06 *Rüffert* [2008] ECR I-1989; Case C-319/06 *Commission v Luxembourg* [2008] ECR I-4323. These cases had nothing to do with the Lisbon Treaty, which promised to strengthen the rights of workers by making the Charter of Fundamental Rights legally binding. See further S Kingston, 'Ireland's Options after the Lisbon Referendum: Strategies, Implications and Competing Visions of Europe' (2009) 34 *European Law Review* 455, 469–72.

[29] See above n 10.

[30] Above n 1, 45.

of the first Danish referendum on the Maastricht Treaty)[31] or protocols (though the need to avoid asking other Member States to re-ratify
the Treaty or jeopardising the elaborate compromises it enshrined was
acknowledged). Ireland, like a number of Member States, was already
the subject of a number of special provisions,[32] which might be extended
into new areas. However, the Barrett report warned that 'this may be
problematic, as Ireland would lose the capacity to shape or block further
policy developments in those areas from which it withdraws'.[33] As the
Sub-Committee put it, 'Opt outs are not cost free'.[34]

An alternative considered by the Sub-Committee was that the Treaty
might be ratified by the Oireachtas. However, it remained unclear whether
this was legally possible and 'an attempt to ratify the Treaty by parliament
alone could be interpreted as circumventing the democratic decision of
the people'.[35] A third possibility was a referendum on the Lisbon Treaty
with a commitment that, in the event of a second 'no' vote, the government would negotiate Ireland's withdrawal from the EU.[36] The Barrett
report had canvassed the possibility that Ireland might withdraw and join
the EEA or negotiate bilateral agreements with the EU along the lines
of Switzerland. However, it concluded that '[e]ven if Ireland retained the
euro while shifting to the EEA, the economic costs of losing EU membership are potentially very significant'.[37] It noted that 'EEA members do
not have access to the Common Agricultural Policy or Cohesion Funds',[38]
both of which had been of considerable benefit to Ireland. Switzerland
was significantly less dependent than Ireland on foreign investment. That
analysis of the position was endorsed by the Sub-Committee.

If it were concluded that there was no realistic chance of securing ratification of the Treaty, it was theoretically possible that the status quo might
continue. However, several Member States had made it clear that further
enlargement could not take place without the Treaty. If Ireland were seen
as the cause of the blockage, its standing both inside and outside the EU
would be severely damaged. It was unlikely that the other Member States
would be willing to abandon the Treaty for any significant period. The
Treaty could in principle be renegotiated, but there was no indication that
any other Member State would be willing to countenance such a step.
A final possibility was that an attempt would be made to find ways of

[31] See [1992] OJ C348/1.
[32] For details, see above n 10, 11–12.
[33] Ibid, 14.
[34] Above n 1, 5. See Kingston, above n 28, 464–67. *Cf* Case C-77/05 *United Kingdom
v Council* [2007] ECR I-11459; Case C-137/05 *United Kingdom v Council* [2007] ECR
I-11593.
[35] Ibid, 47.
[36] See Kingston, above n 28, 458.
[37] Ibid, 15.
[38] Ibid.

establishing a new treaty framework for co-operation between states who wished to participate. This could involve denouncing the existing Treaties or establishing a two-tier EU. 'If Ireland were to be part of the second tier of a "two-tier" Europe,' the Sub-Committee warned, 'the economic consequences would be serious.'[39]

The report of the Sub-Committee provided powerful evidence of how closely EU membership had become bound up with the identity of modern Ireland in the minds of the political establishment. It was not only a question of the economic benefits. Membership was seen as having brought independence from the UK[40] and a new set of secular values, such as human rights and equality, independent of the increasingly discredited Roman Catholic Church, along with an enhanced role on the world stage.[41] Running through the report of the Sub-Committee was the cold chill of fear that all this might be at risk if the Lisbon Treaty were not ratified.

IV   THE EUROPEAN RESPONSE

The result of the 2008 referendum in Ireland was greeted with dismay by Europe's political elite. In statements made the following day, the presidents of the European Commission and the European Parliament made essentially three points: that the outcome should be respected but that Member States which had not yet ratified the Treaty should continue with the process and that the Irish government should bring forward proposals for resolving the situation. Other statements were less restrained. The Prime Minister of Luxembourg declared that his government 'profoundly deplored' the result of the Irish referendum and that the Irish electorate had committed a fundamental error. The choice they had made was not good for Ireland or for Europe. The German Foreign Minister even said consideration would have to be given to how the EU might move forward without Ireland, though he quickly retracted that remark.[42]

The forum in which a way out of the impasse was found was the European Council, which considered the position on four occasions. Little emerged from its meeting in June 2008. At its meeting the following October, the European Council received an analysis by the Taoiseach of the results of the referendum. The elements of a solution began to emerge at its meeting in December 2008. The Presidency Conclusions

---

[39] Ibid, 51.
[40] When Ireland joined the EEC, 54% of its exports went to the UK. By the end of 2007, that figure had fallen to 18%. See the report of the Oireachtas Sub-Committee, above n 1, 19.
[41] Ibid, 1.
[42] See D Hierlemann, 'Lessons from the Treaty Fatigue' (Bertelsmann Stiftung, Spotlight Europe No 2008/13, December 2008) 4.

recalled that, under the Treaties as they then stood, the number of Commissioners would fall in 2009. However, it was agreed that, provided the Lisbon Treaty entered into force, a decision would be taken ensuring that the Commission would continue to comprise one national from each Member State. This is permitted by Article 17(5) of the revised TEU,[43] which would in any event postpone until 2014 any reduction in the size of the institution. Although Commissioners are formally independent,[44] the Member States' retreat from plans to cut their number may reinforce the trend for them to be seen as representatives of the Member States of which they are nationals.[45]

The European Council also agreed that, provided the Irish government sought to ratify the Treaty by the end of the term of the current Commission,[46] the concerns of the Irish people identified by the Taoiseach would 'be addressed to the mutual satisfaction of Ireland and the other Member States'.[47] Those concerns were set out in an annex to the Conclusions. They included neutrality; the right to life, education and the family; and taxation. Legal guarantees would be given that these matters were not affected by the Treaty. The high importance attached to other matters identified in the annex, including workers' rights, would be reaffirmed.[48]

The final shape of the European Council's response to the crisis emerged at its meeting in June 2009.[49] The main element was a 'Decision of the Heads of State or Government of the 27 Member States of the EU, meeting within the European Council, on the concerns of the Irish people on the Treaty of Lisbon' (the Decision). In addition, a 'Solemn Declaration on Workers' Rights, Social Policy and Other Issues'[50] was agreed. The European Council also took 'cognisance of the unilateral declaration of Ireland' dealing with defence and neutrality. That declaration was to be 'associated with the Irish instrument of ratification of the Treaty of Lisbon'. This followed the precedent set by Denmark in 1992. Although

---

[43] The EC Treaty contained no equivalent provision: see Art 213(1) EC, as amended by the Protocol on the enlargement of the European Union annexed at Nice to the TEU and the Treaties establishing the European Communities.

[44] See Art 17(3) TEU (ex-213(2) EC).

[45] See the report of the Oireachtas sub-committee, above n 1, 5; Kingston, above n 28, 458–59; 'Irish Commissioner Critical of Sarkozy', *EUobserver*, 20 December 2009. The willingness of the European Council to discard the notion of a smaller Commission occasioned some surprise: see D Dinan, 'Institutions and Governance: Saving the Lisbon Treaty—An Irish Solution to a European Problem' (2009) 47 *JCMS Annual Review* 113, 124–25.

[46] The Commission's term was due to end on 31 October 2009.

[47] Presidency Conclusions, para 3.

[48] In addition, the European Council adopted declarations on a range of institutional questions. These were necessary because of the continuing uncertainty about when reforms contained in the Lisbon Treaty would enter into force. See Dinan, above n 45, 120–25.

[49] At that meeting, the European Council also agreed to nominate José Manuel Barroso as President of the European Commission for 2009–14 and transitional measures concerning the composition of the European Parliament.

[50] The use of the word 'solemn' here seems devoid of legal significance.

described in the Presidency Conclusions as 'unilateral', the declaration itself is headed 'National Declaration by Ireland'. Its acceptance by the European Council would have the effect in international law of making it relevant to the interpretation of the Treaty as part of the context.[51]

The Presidency Conclusions[52] recorded the declaration of the Heads of State or Government that the Decision offered a 'legal guarantee that certain matters of concern to the Irish people will be unaffected by the entry into force of the Treaty of Lisbon'. The content of the Decision was said to be 'fully compatible' with that Treaty and not to necessitate 'any re-ratification' of it. The Decision was 'legally binding' and would take effect on the entry into force of the Lisbon Treaty. When the next accession Treaty (likely to be with Croatia) was concluded, the provisions of the Decision would be included in a protocol to be attached to the TEU and the TFEU. That protocol would not alter the relationship between the EU and its Member States. Its only purpose would be 'to give full Treaty status to the clarifications set out in the Decision'. It would 'clarify but not change either the content or the application of the Treaty of Lisbon'.

The Decision itself, which was annexed to the Presidency Conclusions, took the same form as that adopted by the European Council at its meeting in Edinburgh in December 1992 to meet Danish concerns about the Maastricht Treaty.[53] It comprised a short preamble followed by four lettered sections headed respectively 'Right to Life, Family and Education'; 'Taxation'; 'Security and Defence'; and 'Final Provisions'. The Decision had no basis in the EU Treaties and none was cited in its preamble. However, under the Vienna Convention[54] it seems to be binding in public international law as a treaty in its own right.[55] Like its predecessor concerning Denmark, the Decision was to be registered with the UN Secretariat in New York when it entered into force. This would confirm the intention

---

[51] See Art 31(2)(b) of the Vienna Convention on the Law of Treaties. On the status of the Vienna Convention in the EU legal order, see Case C-162/96 *Racke v Hauptzollamt Mainz* [1998] ECR I-3655; Case C-386/08 *Brita v Hauptzollamt Hamburg-Hafen*, judgment of 25 February 2010.

[52] Para 5.

[53] See above n 31.

[54] See Arts 2(1)(a), 7(2)(a) and 11.

[55] Alternatively, it may constitute an agreement made in connection with the conclusion of the Lisbon Treaty to be taken into account for the purposes of its interpretation as part of the context. See Art 31(2)(a), Vienna Convention; Institute of International and European Affairs, 'Lisbon—The Irish Guarantees Explained' (Dublin, June 2009); Editorial Comments, 'An Ever Mighty European Council—Some Recent Institutional Developments' (2009) 46 *Common Market Law Review* 1383, 1386–87. For discussion of the legal status of the corresponding decision concerning Denmark, see D Curtin and R van Ooik, 'Denmark and the Edinburgh Summit: Maastricht without Tears' in D O'Keeffe and P Twomey (eds), *Legal Issues of the Maastricht Treaty* (London, Wiley, 1994) ch 23, 353–58; Kingston, above n 28, 461–62.

of the parties to adopt an international treaty and enable the Decision to be invoked before the International Court of Justice.[56]

However, that Court only hears disputes between states. Any Member State which submitted to it a dispute concerning the effect of the Decision would infringe Article 344 TFEU (ex 292 EC) because the issue at stake would concern the interpretation or application of the EU Treaties.[57] Perhaps more likely is an attempt to invoke the Decision before the European Court of Justice (ECJ). This might occur in the context of an action for the annulment of a step taken by the EU under a provision affected by the Decision or proceedings in a national court in which the interpretation or effect of such a provision were contested. It is possible that the ECJ would treat the Decision as relevant to the interpretation of the EU Treaties. However, it might regard it as an attempt to circumvent, for a limited but indeterminate period, the procedure laid down in Article 48 TEU,[58] which is the only means by which the Treaties can be modified.[59] In that event, it might not accord the Decision any effect at all. Either way, the ECJ would clearly not give the Decision precedence over the Treaties.

The difficulty of invoking the Decision before the International Court of Justice and doubts about the status it would be given in its present form by the ECJ perhaps explain the Member States' promise to include it in a protocol when the next accession treaty is concluded. This again follows the precedent set by Denmark, elements of the comparable decision adopted in the case of that Member State having been included in the Protocol on the Position of Denmark annexed to the TEU and the EC Treaty at Amsterdam. This effectively rendered the decision itself redundant.[60] The ECJ was never asked to consider its status.

V THE 2009 REFERENDUM

In the immediate aftermath of the 'no' vote in June 2008, the Irish government was very guarded about how exactly the crisis might be resolved.[61] However, speculation about a second referendum began almost as soon as the outcome of the first became known. A poll taken in

---

[56] See Art 102(2), UN Charter.
[57] Cf Case C-459/03 *Commission v Ireland* [2006] ECR I-4635.
[58] But cf Editorial Comments, above n 55, 1387.
[59] See Case 43/75 *Defrenne v SABENA* [1976] ECR 455, para 58. In that case, the Court rejected an argument that a deadline laid down in the EEC Treaty had been altered by a so-called resolution of the Member States.
[60] See the Barrett report, above n 10, 20.
[61] See, eg the address to the Committee on Constitutional Affairs of the European Parliament on 6 October 2008 by the Irish Minister for Foreign Affairs, Micheál Martin.

July 2008 showed strong public opposition to a fresh vote,[62] but a poll published the following November[63] suggested for the first time that a majority would support the Treaty if there were a second referendum. By the time of the December meeting of the European Council it had become clear that, once the necessary guarantees were in place, the Irish government would make a renewed attempt to ratify the Treaty. On 8 July 2009, the Taoiseach duly announced that a second referendum would take place on 2 October 2009.[64]

Ireland was by then in the throes of a deep financial crisis.[65] Plummeting levels of confidence in the government led it to appeal to voters to treat the ratification issue as one of national importance beyond party politics.[66] The main opposition parties distanced themselves from the government by organising their own 'yes' campaigns, but did not seek to make political capital out of the government's travails.[67] The agricultural and business communities as well as the trade union movement gave unequivocal backing to the 'yes' campaign.[68] An important new development was the establishment of a number of pro-Lisbon civil society groups, some supported by the Irish Business Employers Confederation. One of them, 'Generation Yes', used new media such as social networking sites to target younger voters, most of whom had voted against the Treaty in 2008.[69] The European Commission also intervened, though it attracted controversy for doing so.

The 'no' campaign objected on principle to the notion of a second referendum on what it considered the same question. Cóir again played a prominent role. The leader of the UK Independence Party also campaigned against the Treaty, attracting considerable media attention.[70] The Irish editions of some British newspapers sought to counter the generally pro-Treaty attitude adopted by indigenous newspapers.[71] Following its poor performance in the June European elections, the leader of Libertas, Declan Ganley, had vowed not to participate in the campaign preceding the second referendum. However, in September he re-entered the fray, albeit on a reduced scale.[72]

---

[62] See Open Europe press release, 'New Poll Finds Irish Voters Are Strongly Against a Second Referendum' (27 July 2008), available at www.openeurope.org.uk.

[63] See 'Voters May Approve New Lisbon Treaty, Poll Reveals', *Irish Times*, 17 November 2008.

[64] See 'Ireland Announces Lisbon Referendum Date' *EUobserver*, 8 July 2009, available at http://www.rte.ie/news/2009/0708/eulisbon.html.

[65] See B Tonra, 'The 2009 Irish Referendum on the Lisbon Treaty' (2009) 5 *Journal of Contemporary European Research* 472, 473. The ramifications of the crisis, which remains unresolved, for Ireland's relations with the EU are as yet unclear.

[66] See FitzGibbon, above n 2, 29.

[67] Tonra, above n 65, 474; FitzGibbon, above n 2, 29.

[68] Tonra, ibid.

[69] FitzGibbon, above n 2, 29–30; Tonra, ibid, 473.

[70] Tonra, ibid, 475.

[71] Tonra, ibid, 476.

[72] 'Libertas Leader Rejoins Battle Against EU Treaty', *EUobserver*, 14 September 2009.

By then, the polls were running strongly in favour of the 'yes' campaign, but its margin of victory came as a surprise. On a turnout of 58 per cent, 67.1 per cent voted 'yes', while 32.9 per cent voted 'no'. Forty-one of the 43 electoral constituencies voted 'yes'. In some of them, the 'yes' vote exceeded 80 per cent.[73] At the request of the European Commission Representation in Ireland, a survey of voters was conducted between 3 and 7 October 2009.[74] The main findings of the survey included the following.[75]

- There was a marked increase in the number of those who believed that voting 'yes' would 'help the Irish economy'.
- In each broad segment of Irish society, 'no' voters were outnumbered by 'yes' voters. There was a marked increase in the number of women who voted 'yes', although men remained more likely to do so. Elderly people, the better educated, the self-employed and those living in urban areas were more likely to vote 'yes' than others.[76]
- The most widely cited reasons for voting 'no' were 'to protect Irish sovereignty' and 'lack of trust in politicians'. A significant number of respondents also said they had voted 'no' because of the outcome of the 2008 referendum and/or because they disagreed with the second referendum on principle.[77]
- Only 4 per cent of respondents said that they had been influenced in voting 'no' by a lack of information. This had been the main reason given for voting 'no' in 2008.
- No voters were again concentrated among the young, students, manual workers and those living in rural areas.
- The biggest swings by comparison with 2008 were from 'no' to 'yes' and 'no' to abstention. Of the considerable proportion of respondents who had voted 'no' or abstained in 2008 and voted 'yes' in 2009, important reasons for doing so were feeling better informed and more involved in the public debate. For those who had voted 'no' in 2008, a belief that voting 'yes' would help the Irish economy was also important.
- There was a dramatic increase in the number of people who thought the 'yes' campaign was convincing and an almost equally dramatic fall in the number of people who thought the 'no' campaign was convincing.[78]

[73] See Tonra, above n 65, 477.
[74] Flash Eurobarometer 284, 'Lisbon Treaty Post Referendum Survey Ireland 2009' (October 2009).
[75] Ibid, 5–6.
[76] Ibid, 8.
[77] Ibid, 12.
[78] The 'yes' campaign may have been assisted by guidelines issued by the Broadcasting Commission of Ireland in August 2009 stipulating that broadcasters were not required to continue the practice followed ahead of the 2008 referendum of allocating equal airtime to both sides. See F Mendez and M Mendez, 'Referendums and European Integration: Beyond the Lisbon Vote' [2010] *Public Law* 223, 227.

- A majority (sometimes substantial) of respondents thought the 'yes' vote would enable the EU institutions to work better, strengthen Ireland's position in the EU and help its economy while leaving unaffected Ireland's neutrality and tax system and its laws on abortion, gay marriage and euthanasia.

Following the enactment by the Oireachtas in mid-October of the Twenty-eighth Amendment of the Constitution (Treaty of Lisbon) Act 2009, the Irish instruments of ratification were deposited with the Italian government in accordance with Article 6(1) of the Lisbon Treaty on 23 October 2009.[79]

VI   ALL'S WELL THAT ENDS WELL?

If the EU is a constitutional order of states,[80] it is one in which some states are more equal than others.[81] Ireland's attempts to ratify the Lisbon Treaty show that this is not only true when the inequality is evident on the face of the Treaties. The view of opponents of the Treaty was that 'no' would simply mean 'no' and that, unless the Treaty were renegotiated, things would carry on much as before. That view was never shared by the political establishment, which openly contemplated extreme reactions by the other Member States to circumvent the requirement of unanimous support for Treaty changes laid down in Article 48 TEU. The fear was that the outcome might be to force Ireland to leave the EU or confine it to the 'slow lane'[82] of the integration process, with devastating economic and political consequences. Some of the witnesses who appeared before the Oireachtas Sub-Committee in 2008 claimed that Ireland's influence in the EU had already been damaged by the first referendum.[83] The apparent failure of any Irish candidate to be seriously considered as a potential President of the European Council in November 2009 may be seen as evidence of continuing damage to Ireland's standing.[84]

Despite the EU's oft-proclaimed commitment to 'solidarity among

---

[79] See J-C Piris, *The Lisbon Treaty: A Legal and Political Analysis* (Cambridge, Cambridge University Press, 2010) 60.

[80] See A Dashwood (ed), *Reviewing Maastricht: Issues for the 1996 IGC* (London, Sweet & Maxwell, 1996) 6–7.

[81] *Cf* Art 4(2) TEU.

[82] See the report of the Oireachtas sub-committee, above n 1, 51.

[83] See, eg the comment of Catherine Day, the Irish Secretary General of the European Commission, quoted in the Sub-Committee's report, above n 1, 23.

[84] John Bruton, former Taoiseach and Ambassador and Head of the European Commission Delegation in the United States, was reported to have indicated his interest in the post: 'Overworked Foreign Minister Likely to Rely on EU President, Says Candidate', *EUobserver*, 18 November 2009. Former Irish President Mary Robinson was also mooted. Bertie Ahern's chances of securing the post were probably dealt a terminal blow by the circumstances surrounding his resignation as Taoiseach: see Dinan, above n 45, 115.

Member States',[85] these fears seem to have been deliberately stoked by some of Europe's politicians. Although most of them spoke of 'respecting the Irish vote' in the 2008 referendum, some behaved as if they thought it would be 'easier . . . for the government to dissolve the people and elect another'.[86] In his statement issued a day after the vote, the Prime Minister of Luxembourg, who called it 'cet échec démocratique', compared it with the French and Dutch votes on the Constitutional Treaty in 2005. However, in circumstances such as these, the position of two founder Member States, one of them a large one, is immeasurably stronger than that of a small latecomer such as Ireland or Denmark, which experienced the same sense of isolation after its 1992 referendum on the Maastricht Treaty.[87] There was even criticism of Ireland for deciding to submit the Lisbon Treaty to a referendum,[88] although, as we have seen, the legal and political case for doing so was compelling. Such criticism seemed to reflect tacit agreement with the outspoken Charlie McCreevy's observation that the Treaty would have been rejected by most Member States if put to a referendum.[89] It is not helpful for politicians speaking on behalf of an organisation widely seen as suffering from a democratic deficit to criticise individual Member States for a democratic surplus.

Any revising Treaty is likely to be the subject of a referendum somewhere in the EU.[90] One could in theory envisage simultaneous referendums in all the Member States,[91] but that would not necessarily make a positive outcome more likely. It is not in any event provided for by the Lisbon Treaty. Suggested treaty amendments therefore have to be susceptible to explanation to a general public less willing than it used to be to accept assurances from politicians on trust. From this perspective, both the Constitutional Treaty and the Lisbon Treaty were disastrous, their bulk and complexity making them hard to sell on the basis that they would make

---

[85] Art 3(3) TEU. See also the Laeken Declaration of December 2001; 'Reforming Europe for the 21st Century', COM(2007) 412 final, 7.

[86] B Brecht, 'The Solution' (1953), English translation from J Willett and R Manheim (eds), *Bertolt Brecht, Poems 1913–1956* (Methuen, 1976) 440.

[87] See Hierlemann, above n 42, 4; Curtin and van Ooik, above n 55, 349.

[88] See, eg A Lamassoure, 'The European Union after the Irish "No"', European Interview No 26 (Fondation Robert Schuman, 23 June 2008).

[89] See 'EU Leaders' Attitude to No Vote Realistic, Says McCreevy', *Irish Times*, 27 June 2009.

[90] See generally Mendez and Mendez, above n 78. For a survey of referendum processes in the Member States, see Houses of the Oireachtas, Joint Committee on the Constitution, Second Report, 'Articles 46 and 47: Amendment of the Constitution and the Referendum-First Interim Report' (April 2009), available at http://www.oireachtas.ie/documents/Committees30thDail/J-Constitution/Report_2008/Report20090402.pdf (Appendix). The coalition government formed in the United Kingdom in May 2010 immediately announced its intention to amend the European Communities Act 1972 so that any future transfer of powers to the EU would require approval in a referendum.

[91] See Lamassoure, above n 88. *Cf* N MacCormick, 'A Union of its Own Kind? Reflections on the European Convention and the proposed Constitution of the European Union' (N MacCormick, 2004) 12.

the EU more democratic and transparent. The latter was particularly difficult to promote to ordinary voters, its form rendering it unreadable and vulnerable to charges that it was in reality the Constitutional Treaty in disguise. The EU's capacity to continue functioning following the demise of the latter Treaty[92] and speculation about what might be done to achieve some of its objectives under the existing Treaties[93] cast doubt on the need for the new Treaty.

A further problem confronting 'yes' campaigners was that of persuading voters whose knowledge of the EU was rudimentary to reject outlandish claims about the Treaty made by its opponents[94] and support a set of complex institutional reforms. Many of those who voted 'no' in 2008 believed that the loss of a permanent Irish Commissioner would mean that Ireland would have no voice at all in EU decision making.[95] This led the Oireachtas Sub-Committee to suggest the approval by the Member States each time a new Treaty is signed of an explanatory document 'setting out in clear and comprehensible terms the intentions of the governments framing the treaty and the effect of each of the treaty provisions'.[96] Although there would doubtless be some value in such documents, it may not be realistic to expect the general public to master abstract technical reforms to the EU decision-making process. As Donnelly observes, 'The sympathies of the European electorate are more likely to be engaged by proposals which are more demonstrably necessary to make specific policy areas work better'.[97]

The ECJ was singled out for criticism by some opponents of the Treaty, including the Socialist Party, Cóir and the People's Movement, who disapproved of particular decisions.[98] There is, however, a broader sense in which the Court's approach can be problematic in circumstances such as those of the Irish referendums. However much we may admire its case law, it has departed from the language used in provisions so often that it is sometimes hard to say where the *telos* will take it.[99] This can make it difficult to assuage the fears of those who argue that new provisions may lead the EU in unexpected and unwanted directions. Yet there is perhaps

---

[92] See Dinan, above n 45, 125–26; A Moravcsik, 'What Can We Learn from the Collapse of the European Constitutional Project?' (2006) 47 *Politische Vierteljahresschrift* 219.

[93] See, eg B Donnelly, 'After the Irish Referendum', Federal Trust Policy Commentary (June 2008); C Grant, 'Three Scenarios for the Lisbon Treaty' (August/September 2008) *Centre for European Reform Bulletin* issue 61.

[94] See Dinan, above n 45, 119; Editorial Comments, 'Protocology' (2009) 46 *Common Market Law Review* 1785, 1788; '"Lisbon Will Steal Your Children" Advert Denounced by MEPs', *EUobserver*, 9 September 2009.

[95] See the Millward Brown report, above n 21, ii and 17.

[96] See above n 1, 6.

[97] Donnelly, above n 93.

[98] See FitzGibbon, above n 2, 13.

[99] See further A Arnull, 'Me and My Shadow: The European Court of Justice and The Disintegration of European Union Law' (2008) 31 *Fordham International Law Journal* 1174.

a way in which the ECJ might play a positive role in resolving doubts about the effect of new treaties.

The understandable unwillingness of Member States to reopen treaties once they have been signed has made it difficult for binding guarantees to be offered where difficulties are encountered during the ratification process. The device of the 'decision of the heads of state or government meeting within the European Council' has worked on the two occasions it has been used, but it has about it the whiff of sophistry.[100] Such 'decisions' are legally binding only in a technical and limited sense. For practical purposes the most they can do is offer guidance on interpretation. One day they may cease to work their magic.

The Treaty amendment procedure was the subject of major changes at Lisbon. The revised Article 48 TEU lays down an ordinary revision procedure[101] and two simplified revision procedures. The scope *ratione materiae* of the simplified procedures, set out in Article 48(6) and (7) TEU, is limited. In both cases, the proposed changes will be contained in a unanimous decision of the European Council. At the national level, the second of the simplified procedures only requires no national parliament to have made known its opposition to the decision within six months of its adoption. The first of the simplified revision procedures and the ordinary revision procedure require the approval of all the Member States in accordance with their respective constitutional requirements. They are therefore vulnerable to a recurrence of the problem Ireland encountered with the Lisbon Treaty.

Under the first simplified procedure, the European Council would be able to review its decision in the event of difficulty in securing national approval. Because of the limited scope of the procedure, such a decision is perhaps less likely than an amending treaty to embody the complex compromises that might unravel if reopened. In the case of the ordinary procedure, the problem is potentially more serious. Article 48(5) TEU recognises the problem but offers no solution. It merely provides that if, two years after the signature of an amending treaty, 'four fifths of the Member States have ratified it and one or more Member States have encountered difficulties in proceeding with ratification, the matter shall be referred to the European Council'.

The ordinary procedure needs to provide a legal basis for the provision of an authoritative interpretation of new treaty provisions before they

---

[100] *Cf* Editorial Comments, above n 94, 1788.

[101] That procedure was used in June 2010 to agree an increase in the number of MEPs following the delay in the entry into force of the Lisbon Treaty, which would have effected such an increase, until after the June 2009 European elections. In view of the limited scope of the proposed amendments, the European Council decided, with the consent of the European Parliament, not to convene a Convention (see Art 48(3) TEU). To take effect, the changes agreed must be ratified by all the Member States in accordance with their own constitutional requirements. The number of Irish MEPs is not affected.

have entered into force. Such an interpretation cannot be provided by the European Council or the heads of state and government without appearing to undermine national constitutional requirements. It has to be given by the only institution that really matters in this context, the ECJ. Consideration should therefore be given to altering Article 48(5) TEU to allow the European Council to ask the ECJ to rule, within a short deadline,[102] on the effect of provisions contained in amending treaties where a small minority of Member States is holding up ratification. The request should seek to link the concerns of the state or states in question with specific provisions of the new treaty, on whose interpretation the ECJ could then rule. A mechanism such as this would not be without precedent. Article 218(11) TFEU (ex 300(6) EC) enables the ECJ to rule on whether an international agreement envisaged by the EU is compatible with the Treaties before it enters into force. There is also an analogy with the now-defunct Article 68(3) EC, which allowed the Council, the Commission or a Member State to ask the ECJ to give a ruling on the interpretation of Title IV of Part Three of the EC Treaty and of acts based on that Title.[103]

A procedure of the type proposed here would be a more transparent and legally effective way of 'clarifying' controversial new treaty provisions before they enter into force. It would therefore represent a distinct improvement on the current position, though it would not provide a perfect solution. Convinced opponents of a new treaty might point out that the ECJ is not bound by its own decisions and could in future change its mind. Conversely, proponents might worry that any ruling of the ECJ could limit its future freedom to adapt the meaning of the disputed provisions in the light of the vagaries of litigation. In practice, however, the ECJ rarely departs from its previous case law. Moreover, it is well aware of the potential for any of its judgments to constrain its future room for manoeuvre and adept at limiting their scope where it does not wish to make unduly broad statements of principle.[104]

Finally, the social and demographic profiles of 'yes' and 'no' voters in Ireland should be noted. Particularly striking is the difficulty the 'yes' campaign experienced in convincing voters aged between 18 and 24 of the merits of the Lisbon Treaty. The Laeken Declaration drew attention to the challenge of bringing the young 'closer to the European design'. If the Irish experience were to be repeated across the EU, the outlook would be bleak.

The 2009 Flash Eurobarometer[105] showed that the youngest respondents

---

[102] *cf* Art 269 TFEU (one month).

[103] *cf* also Art 47 ECHR and Chapter IV of the Statute of the International Court of Justice (both concerning advisory opinions).

[104] See L Coutron, 'Style des arrêts de la Cour de justice et normativité de la jurisprudence communautaire' (2009) 45 *Revue Trimestrielle de Droit Européen* 643, 670–72.

[105] Above n 74, 22.

and those still in education turned to the internet more often than other groups for information about the Treaty. Cóir had an extensive website[106] and 'Generation Yes' used Facebook[107] to reach younger voters during the 2009 campaign.[108] The EU should follow the example of national politicians and exploit the Internet imaginatively to connect with Europe's citizens, especially young people, and offer them an active role in policy-making.[109] Europe's leaders may thereby discover whether the opposition to the Treaty in Ireland among the young is replicated in other Member States. If so, technology may help them find an appropriate response. Although democracy remains a game played mainly at national level,[110] it is not enough for the EU to be a constitutional order merely of States. They derive their legitimacy from the people. The EU must also tap that source if it is to prosper.[111]

---

[106] Available at http://www.coircampaign.org/.

[107] Available at http://www.facebook.com/GenerationYes.

[108] See FitzGibbon, above n 2, 30.

[109] *Cf* the citizens' initiative provided for by Art 11(4) TEU; Editorial Comments, 'Direct Democracy and the European Union . . . Is that a Threat or a Promise?' (2008) 45 *Common Market Law Review* 929.

[110] See Dashwood, above n 80, 75. This situation is likely to persist: see the Lisbon judgment of the Bundesverfassungsgericht of 30 June 2009, paras 251 and 280–81; Art 12 TEU.

[111] See 'Project Europe 2030: Challenges and Opportunities', Report to the European Council by the Reflection Group on the Future of the EU 2030 (May 2010), 43; K Nicolaïdis, 'We, The Peoples of Europe . . .' (2004) 83(6) *Foreign Affairs* 97; U Everling, 'The European Union as a Federal Association of States and Citizens' in A von Bogdandy and J Bast (eds), *Principles of European Constitutional Law*, 2nd edn (Hart/Beck/Nomos, 2010) ch 19. *Cf* S Wernicke, 'Au nom de qui? The European Court of Justice between Member States, Civil Society and Union Citizens' (2007) 13 *European Law Journal* 380.

4

Where Will the Lisbon
Treaty Lead Us?

JEAN-CLAUDE PIRIS*

I
N ORDER TO try and answer that question, knowing the roots and
the history of the negotiations of the Treaty of Lisbon is of course
useful. It is also necessary to know what were the political aims of
the negotiators when drafting its provisions. It is obviously indispensable
to have a clear interpretation of what could be the actual legal effect of
those provisions. But the story of a treaty only begins with its implementation.[1] For the Lisbon Treaty, this story is difficult to foresee.

This is more the case for the Lisbon Treaty than for any preceding
European Treaty. First, some of its provisions deliberately leave room
for flexibility. This is, for example, the case for defining how the 'external action service' will be organised, or for establishing new rules on
comitology or the conditions under which the 'citizens' initiatives' might
be launched. Secondly, this is also the case for the large but vague role
given to the High Representative for Foreign Affairs and Security Policy
and, due to disagreements, for the largely undefined role conferred on the
President of the European Council. Thirdly, this is again the case for the
imprecision of the scope of some provisions, for instance on the Common
Agricultural Policy (Article 43(2) of the Treaty on the Functioning of the
European Union (TFEU)) or on the Common Commercial Policy (Article
207(4) TFEU); other examples could be quoted.

---

* The author is the Legal Counsel of the European Council and of the Council of the
European Union, Director General of the Legal Service of the Council. This contribution
is based by the author on the concluding chapter of his book *The Lisbon Treaty: a Legal
and Political Analysis* published in June 2010 (448 pp, Cambridge University Press) and on
a speech given in Victoria (British Columbia, Canada) on 30 April 2010, on the occasion
of the 8th Biennial Conference of the European Community Studies Association. The views
expressed in this contribution are purely personal. They do not represent the views of the
Council of the European Union nor of its Legal Service. This contribution is of course dedicated to Alan Dashwood, a very successful director in the Legal Service of the EU Council
for a number of years. His colleagues were lucky to have in Alan a colleague of high call-
bre, able to master any complex legal issue (which are amazingly numerous in the EU!), as
well as a good manager and a marvellous friend.

[1] See how many people criticised the Single European Act when it was adopted in 1986,
and found later that it was positive when implemented.

59

In any case, the fate of the Lisbon Treaty will not only depend on its text. A Treaty is a living document. Some of the provisions of the Lisbon Treaty can be implemented or not, the tools it provides can be used or not. It will depend on the persons and on the institutions having to interpret it and develop its potentialities, and on how they will act and react to each other. It will depend as well, as for all general treaties of this kind, on the economic and political context in which the Treaty will be applied. This is why, currently, the picture is still blurred, while some institutions are trying to assert their position better by drawing arguments on the provisions of the new Treaty. Stabilisation will come progressively. It may take two or three years for the Treaty of Lisbon to be really operational and for its effects to be appreciated.

This said, and in order to clarify the point of departure of this future story, one may try and answer some preliminary questions:

- Does the Lisbon Treaty take over the reforms envisaged in the failed 2004 Treaty, the aim of which was to establish a 'Constitution for Europe'?
- If the answer to that question is positive, does this mean that the Lisbon Treaty is a mere re-packaging of the so-called 'Constitution'?
- Does the Lisbon Treaty mark a leap towards the eventual establishment of a federal entity?
- Does this Treaty put an end to the imbalances which affect the EU in some areas?

I DOES THE LISBON TREATY TAKE OVER THE REFORMS ENVISAGED IN THE 'CONSTITUTION FOR EUROPE?

The Lisbon Treaty has taken on board the significant reforms to the Treaties which were foreseen in the failed Constitutional Treaty. The most important of these reforms, which aim at strengthening the Union, its effectiveness and its legitimacy, but which do not provide for any substantive extension of powers, are:

- The 'communitarisation' of the ex-'third pillar'. The improvements made to the Freedom, Security and Justice (FSJ) provisions by the Lisbon Treaty lie mainly in the 'communitarisation' of the former 'third pillar' through its incorporation into one title covering the whole FSJ area. This brings a more consistent and simple architecture. It will also allow a full parliamentary control (European and national) of measures which may affect every citizen, thus helping to guarantee a better protection of the rights of individuals. This means, in concrete terms, a more efficient decision-making procedure. There will be more qualified majority voting (QMV) in the Council and more co-decision with the European Parliament for the adoption of legal acts (except in specific cases such as family law, some forms of operational police co-operation or the establishment of a European Public Prosecutor's Office). This should help enhance the level of security within a border-free EU, while respecting individual rights. This also means full control by the Commission, the Court of Justice and national Courts over the implementation of these legal acts by the Member States, which should lead to a better level of implementation. However, the serious complications resulting from the 'variable geometry', with the specific positions of Denmark, Ireland and the UK, as well as the fact that a few other Member States do not (yet) participate in the Schengen area, will remain. The scope of the opt-outs of Denmark and of the UK and Ireland has even been extended. These complications will be increased when the 'brake–accelerator' mechanism is used. This mechanism might lead to enhanced co-operation[2] among groups of Member States, the composition of which might be different from one legislative act to another. All these flexibility measures were necessary for agreement to be reached between Member States during the Intergovernmental Conference (IGC), but they might lead to a patchwork of legislation and additional complexity.

- A significant increase in the powers of the European Parliament in the legislative and international areas. The trend to find a solution to the so-called 'democratic deficit' by extending the powers of the European Parliament has continued, despite the fact that the turnout to the European elections has declined steadily. At the same time, the national parliaments of the Member States, for the first time, have been given a possibility to intervene directly in the EU legislative process, and the Treaty provides citizens with the possibility to suggest new legislation, while some provisions aim at improving the possibility for 'civil society' to be better informed so as to allow it to play a role.

- The establishment of two new functions. The first new function is a full-time President of the European Council, a function to which Herman Van Rompuy was elected for a mandate of two and a half years, renewable once. The second one is a full-time High Representative for Foreign Affairs and Security Policy, a function to which Catherine Ashton was appointed for five years; this function makes her, at the same time, President of the Foreign Affairs Council and a Vice-President of the Commission. If effective and well coordinated with the Commission, these two new figures will considerably strengthen 'the centre' of the EU. They might, together with the other institutions and

---

[2] The normal provisions on 'enhanced co-operation' have, up to now, been used only once, in July 2010, in the case of divorce (Council Decision [CITE]authorising enhanced co-operation in the area of the law applicable to divorce and legal separation).

bodies which have 'federal' characteristics, become decisive actors in the development and progress of European policies. This should, in principle, result in better visibility for the EU on the international scene. However, nobody knows how this will work in the future. In particular, as several figures emerge as 'would-be rivals', they could fight each other and decrease the influence of the institutions.

- The Treaty contains a new definition and method of calculation of QMV in the Council (which will be fully applicable only in 2017) and an extension of its scope of application. This will allow for going in the direction of an enhanced democratic legitimacy for the decisions taken by the Council, either alone or in co-decision with the European Parliament.
- The Lisbon Treaty puts at the forefront the values on which the EU is based (Article 2 of the Treaty on European Union (TEU)).[3] It also takes the highly symbolic steps both of giving the Charter of Fundamental Rights the same legal value as the Treaties (Article 6(1) TEU) and of laying down an obligation for the EU to accede to the European Convention for the Protection of Human Rights and Fundamental Freedoms (ECHR) (Article 6(2) TEU).
- The Treaty also offers facilitated possibilities for enhanced co-operation between some Member States, especially in the area of security and defence ('permanent structured cooperation': Articles 42(6) and 46 TEU).
- Finally, after the entry into force of the Lisbon Treaty, the EU is still governed by two main Treaties which have equal legal value. However, the division of substance between the two new Treaties, the TEU and the TFEU, brings more clarity than that which existed between the former TEU and the Treaty establishing the European Community (TEC). The current TEU contains the general provisions applying to the EU, its values and objectives, its basic principles, the definition of its powers, the procedure for revising the Treaties and the main characteristics of its institutions, and a description of their powers. The TFEU contains the legal bases which enable the EU and its institutions to act, while setting limits to their powers. It is true that the result of the Lisbon IGC is difficult to read and that there are inconsistencies (the main one being the location of the provisions on Common Foreign and Security Policy (CFSP) in the TEU and not in the TFEU).[4] On the

---

[3] Art 2 TEU on the Union's values is not only a political and symbolic statement. It has concrete legal effects. First, it is a condition which a European State has to respect in order to be allowed to apply for membership: 'Any European State which respects the values referred to in Art 2 and is committed to promoting them may apply to become a member of the Union' (Art 49 TEU). Secondly, serious breaches of these values by a Member State may lead to the suspension of some of its rights resulting from Union membership (Art 7 TEU).

[4] This stresses the fact that CFSP remains a separate 'pillar' in the EU, governed by rules different from those applicable in the other areas of action of the EU.

whole, it does represent progress. Thus a reading of the 'consolidated' TEU on its own might be enough for the 'man in the street' to understand what the EU is about and how it functions, and all that in a reasonably short text (55 Articles in 30 pages).

The answer to be given to the first question is thus positive. By taking on the reforms envisaged in the failed 'Constitution for Europe', the Lisbon Treaty contains potential improvements for the effectiveness and legitimacy of the Union. It allows the EU to adopt common policies and actions more easily and more democratically in certain areas. Although the EU does not gain substantive new competences, it obtains better tools, in particular for it to be more active and visible on the international scene. The future will show whether and how these tools will be used.

II IS THE LISBON TREATY A MERE REPACKAGING OF THE FAILED 'CONSTITUTION FOR EUROPE'?

Despite the fact that it takes over the reforms envisaged by the so-called 'Constitution', it remains the case that, on a number of issues, the Lisbon Treaty is different from the Constitutional Treaty. These differences are far from being insignificant. The most important are political. All of them take the opposite direction to the federalist one:

- Not only has the term 'Constitution' been abandoned, but the Lisbon IGC also abandoned the constitutional approach . The Lisbon Treaty, contrary to what the Constitutional Treaty would have done, does not repeal all existing Treaties to replace them by a single text.
- Abandoning the constitutional concept was accompanied by the disappearance of all terms which might have been seen as steps towards the establishment of a state. This is the case for the terms 'Minister for Foreign Affairs', 'law' and 'framework law', as well as for the reference to the EU anthem, the EU flag, the EU motto and the 'European Day'. The text of the Charter on Fundamental Rights[5] and the formal enshrining of the primacy of EU law have also been removed from the Treaty.

The Lisbon Treaty also contains a number of legal differences from the Constitutional Treaty (Cst), which equally go in a direction opposite to a federalist one:

- For the first time, powers are given to national parliaments to intervene in the EU legislative procedure. The provisions contained in the

[5] However, the Lisbon Treaty gives the Charter Treaty legal value (Art 6(1) TEU).

Constitutional Treaty on this issue have been significantly strengthened by the Lisbon Treaty.

- A number of provisions, strengthened by the Lisbon Treaty, emphasise the fact that the EU is and remains an international organisation, whose masters are and remain the Member States:
- It is not the Treaty itself which establishes the EU, but its High Contracting Parties (Article 1 TEU; compare with Article I-1(1) Cst).
- The Union shall act 'only' within the limits of the competences conferred upon it by the Member States (Article 5(2) TEU; compare with Article I-11(2) Cst).

It follows that the answer to the second question is clear: the Lisbon Treaty is a different political animal,[6] as compared with the Constitutional Treaty. While the Constitutional Treaty represented a step in a federalist direction, this ambition has been abandoned with the Lisbon Treaty. To quote Angela Merkel, Federal Chancellor of Germany, in her 'Humboldt Speech on Europe' in May 2009: 'The European Union is not a State, and it is not meant to become one'.

III   DOES THE LISBON TREATY CHANGE THE NATURE OF THE EUROPEAN UNION OR MARK A LEAP TOWARDS THE EVENTUAL ESTABLISHMENT OF A EUROPEAN FEDERAL ENTITY?

The answer to this question is negative: the Lisbon Treaty does not go in the direction of an eventual establishment of a European federal state. All the elements of the Constitutional Treaty which had been obtained by the more 'eurosceptic' governments have been retained (and sometimes strengthened) in the Lisbon Treaty:

- For the first time, the EU Treaties oblige the EU to respect the 'essential functions' of the Member States (Article 4(1) and (2) TEU):
  '1.   In accordance with Article 5 [TEU], competences not conferred upon the Union in the Treaties remain with the Member States.
  2.   The Union shall respect the equality of Member States before the Treaties as well as their national identities, inherent in their fundamental structures, political and constitutional, inclusive of regional and local self-government. It shall respect their essential State functions.'

This article limits the competences of the EU in a stricter way than before, especially as there is no legal definition of exactly what the 'essential functions' of a state are.

---

[6] 'A sheep in sheep's clothing', as the Treaty of Lisbon was described by Alan Dashwood at a conference held in Dublin on 11 May 2009 in the Irish Centre for European Law.

- Other provisions go in the same direction. This is the case of the so-called 'flexibility clause' contained in Article 352 TFEU, which procedural requirements are stricter than in its former versions in Article 308 TEC (ex 235). This is also the case of Articles 2–6 TFEU on the classification of the EU's competences. It is again the case of the mechanisms contained in Protocol Nos 1 and 2, which give the national parliaments the power to control the EU institutions in their duty to respect the principle of subsidiarity (Article 5(3) TEU), and which have been significantly enhanced by the Treaty of Lisbon as compared to the Constitutional Treaty. The irruption of the national parliaments into the EU legislative process is especially important, at a time when the European Parliament has failed once again, in the June 2009 elections, to attract more voters and, therefore, more legitimacy.
- In the same vein, new limitations are imposed on the powers of the EU institutions. Thus, some provisions give to external entities powers which, before the Lisbon Treaty, were a monopoly of the EU institutions. This is the case of the citizens' initiative which enables citizens to request from the Commission the launching of a legislative proposal. This is also the case of the role given to national parliaments, for instance regarding control over Europol and Eurojust. The very aim of the EU Charter for Fundamental Rights is also to impose limits on the exercise of the powers of the EU institutions. Moreover, in the future, when the EU will become a party to the ECHR, the European Court of Strasbourg will control compliance with the provisions of the ECHR by the EU institutions. One could also mention the more precise limits of the EU's competences in certain areas, such as the freedom, security and justice area or public health.

Moreover, the limits of the EU's competences are, interestingly enough, highlighted several times in the Treaty or in its Protocols:

- That is the case in the new Protocol No 25 on the exercise of shared competences.
- It is also the case in the new Protocol No 26 on services of general interest.

In addition, despite the fact that they have no legal value, a number of Declarations approved by the 27 Member State representatives and attached to the Final Act of the IGC which adopted the Lisbon Treaty go in the same direction, stressing the limits or the absence of EU powers in one field or another. This is in particular the case of:

- Declaration No 1, which stresses that the Charter of Fundamental Rights does not extend or modify the powers and tasks of the Union;
- Declaration Nos 13 and 14, which both underline that CFSP will not

affect the responsibilities of the Member States to conduct their foreign policy;

- Declaration No 18, which recalls that '. . . competences not conferred
upon the Union in the Treaties remain with the Member States' (a repetition of the last sentence of Article 5(2) TEU);
- Declaration No 24, which confirms that the explicit conferral of legal
personality on the European Union 'will not in any way authorise the
Union to legislate or to act beyond the competences conferred upon it
by the Member States in the Treaties'; and
- Declaration No 31 on social policy, which stresses that this policy
'. . . [falls] essentially within the competence of the Member States'.

Most, if not all, of these Declarations are redundant; they are legally
inoperative. Nevertheless, politically, it is significant that they all go in the
same direction. They aim at stressing solemnly, and even to do so twice
if need be, the limits of the powers of the Union and of its institutions.
This is important politically, as it expresses a reduced trust, if not a lack
of trust of the Member States.

The Lisbon Treaty did not change the nature of the Union, which
remains 'a constitutional order of states'[7] according to Prof Alan Dashwood, or a 'partially federal entity'[8] according to others. This means that
the EU is neither a classic international intergovernmental organisation
nor a state. It does acts with federal powers in some fields (external trade
and competition policy, for instance), though, and remains similar to a
classic international organisation in other fields (notably foreign policy).
There is no realistic prospect in the foreseeable future that the EU, with
27 Member States or more, will become a federal state. In this regard,
one may stress the possibility offered by Article 50 TEU for a Member
State to decide to withdraw from the EU. Such a right normally exists in
confederations of states, but not in federal states. Therefore, the adoption
of this provision is politically significant, as it clarifies a basic issue—that
the Union is actually a voluntary association between states which remain
sovereign as to the question of whether or not they remain in that association. This does not mean that the EU cannot pursue political aims,
or that it cannot improve its political dimension; nor does it mean that
it cannot deepen the integration of its Member States in order to better
protect their interests and those of their citizens.

The challenge for the EU in the future is to continue to find the right
balance between, on the one hand, respect for the national identities of
its Member States, their cultures, traditions and diversities and, on the

---

[7] Alan Dashwood used this expression for the first time in 1996, in A Dashwood, *Reviewing Maastricht, Issues for the 1996 IGC* (London, Sweet & Maxwell, 1996) p 7.

[8] See J-C Piris 'The EU: Towards a New Form of Federalism?' in J Fedtke and B Markes-
inis (eds), *Patterns of Regionalism, The Clifford Chance Lectures*, vol 8 (Oxford, Hart
Publishing, 2006).

other hand, the necessity to develop an efficient, democratic, transparent central system of decision making and to ensure the uniform application of EU laws. This is what is needed in order to respond effectively to the economic, social, environmental and security challenges of this century, challenges which none of the Member States, whatever their size and importance, are able to answer on their own. Member States will keep their external identity in the world, and their participation in decision making and implementation will continue to be much more preponderant than in any existing federal state.

Consequently, the answer to the third question is that the Treaty of Lisbon does not change the nature of the Union. It preserves its unique characteristics, being neither a classic international organisation nor a federal state, and having a finally tuned and balanced system of decision-making powers, shared among the institutions according to the issues concerned. Moreover, the Treaty also marks a halt to the ambitions of the federalists. It might even be seen as a 'containment' of the powers of the European Union.

IV DOES THE LISBON TREATY PUT AN END TO THE 'IMBALANCES' WHICH AFFECT THE EU IN SOME AREAS?

In order to judge whether or not the Lisbon Treaty represents a great leap forward, the essential issue is to ascertain whether or not it has put an end to some of the major imbalances which seriously affect the strength and effectiveness of the Union. These imbalances, some of which are due to the fact that the EU remains a classic international organisation in some areas but works in a federal way in other areas, are at the very heart of the European project. They create uncertainty and may be a cause of instability. They may even be seen as making it difficult for the EU to continue to work efficiently in a durable way.

- The most well-known of these imbalances concerns Economic and Monetary Union (EMU). It affects the relationship between the two parts of this Union: economic and monetary. The euro is the single currency of 16 Member States (17 with Estonia on 1 January 2011), and it will probably become the currency of more of them in the future. There is an obvious link between the economic and the monetary parts, if one wants to be sure that the currency will remain stable while allowing reasonable economic growth. In the present EU, on one side, the euro is managed in a 'federal' way by the European Central Bank. On the other side, the fiscal, budgetary and economic policies remain

almost completely in the hands of the Member States.[9] For this economic part, the powers of the centre are, de jure or de facto, currently
limited to recommendations which are not effectively binding. This is
for good reasons, as Angela Merkel, Federal Chancellor of Germany,
stressed in her (already quoted) 'Humboldt Speech on Europe' in May
2009: 'The powers regarding budget, tax and social policy are held by
the Member States for good reasons'. It is certainly an inescapable fact
that there is a necessity for a direct link between these powers and an
effective political legitimacy (ie the link between the voters and those
who decide). Solving this asymmetry while keeping the present political
features of the EU represents an almost impossible task. However, a
monetary union which is based on loose rules on budget/tax/economic
governance will remain incomplete and, therefore, will not guarantee
stability, as the continuing 2009–10 financial crisis is proving. Many
coordinated efforts are currently being made, by the European Council under the presidency of Herman Van Rompuy, by the Commission
under the presidency of Jose Manuel Barroso, by the European Central Bank under the presidency of Jean-Claude Trichet, by the Council
of Ministers of Economic and Financial Affairs under the successive
six-monthly presidencies and by the Euro-Group under the presidency
of Jean-Claude Juncker. It remains to be seen if these efforts will lead
to measures which will be actually adopted, implemented and prove
to be sufficient.

- Another imbalance concerns the internal market: the aim of the internal market is to open the borders between the Member States to a
free flow of goods, services, capital and persons in a market of half
a billion persons. In principle, this aim has been largely achieved, but
it is not complete.[10] What has been done was accompanied by the
corollary condition that there should be no distortions of competition
between the Member States. A number of directives and regulations
have consequently been adopted with the aim of avoiding such distortions. This has not been the case for differences in tax and social
legislation and regulation, which are not considered in the Treaty as
being distortions of competition. The Treaty enables the EU to adopt
common rules on direct taxation and minimum rules on social policy,
but without making them necessary conditions for the internal market.

[9] This imbalance is all the more striking since, as the EU budget represents only around
1% of the total GNI of the EU, as compared with approximately 45% of the budget of
the public authorities of its 27 Member States (and, as far as the USA are concerned, with
20% of the GNI for the US federal budgets), the EU does not have the budgetary means
at its disposal which could help to deal with an economic and financial crisis.

[10] In particular in the area of services. See M Monti, 'A New Strategy for the Single Market
at the Service of Europe's Economy and Society', Report to the President of the European
Commission, 9 May 2010, 37: 'The Single Market is Europe's original idea and unfinished
business', available at http://ec.europa.eu/bepa/pdf/monti_report_final_10_05_2010_en.pdf.

Therefore, these common rules are almost always subject to unanimity in the Council and they are minimal. As a result, Member States keep almost complete freedom in those fields—hence the tensions over what is characterised by some as 'social dumping' or 'tax dumping', and the reactions to certain judgments of the EU Court of Justice (such as *Viking* or *Laval*).[11] Again, this asymmetry—which is not recognised by all, as some regard this situation as a normal area of competition between the Member States—is not easy to correct, as any solution would touch on the core sovereignty of the Member States and would necessitate strong democratic legitimacy on the part of the political decision makers.

- As concerns the free movement of persons, the asymmetry is between the external and the internal movement of persons. On the one hand, the EU, especially in its Schengen area, allows the free movement of persons inside its borders, and the rules and instruments regulating this freedom are governed in a 'federal' way. On the other hand, Member States fully keep their power to grant their nationality to non-EU citizens, or to allow them to immigrate for long-term stays, thus offering these new citizens or immigrants complete freedom to move to other EU states. The asymmetry between these two sides is clear. Again, it is difficult to correct, because changing the rules on national citizenship would touch upon the core sovereignty of the Member States.

- Another imbalance concerns the participation in military operations of the EU: the way it works is that those Member States which decide to participate with troops also have to pay for their expenses.[12] They thus pay twice (men and money), whereas those Member States which do not participate with troops in the operations do not contribute to their financing either, even though the military operations are carried out on behalf of the EU.

- Last, but not least, the most important of the EU's imbalances concerns its democratic legitimacy: the more competences to adopt legislation have been transferred by the Member States to the EU, the more this has reduced the powers of their national parliaments to adopt such legislation. Voters have the feeling that they have less control over the decisions which govern their life. It is true that, in parallel, more powers have been given to the European Parliament. Despite that, its members are elected by fewer and fewer voters (a turnout of only 43 per cent in the June 2009 elections, showing a constant decline since the first European elections in 1979, when the turnout was 63 per cent). A number of new measures were included in the Lisbon Treaty with

---

[11] See Case C-438/05 *Viking* [2007] ECR I-10806, judgment of 11 December 2007 and Case C-341/05 *Laval* [2007] ECR I-11845, judgment of 18 December 2007.
[12] A principle which comes from NATO, where it is expressed by the formula 'Costs lie where they fall'.

the aim of enhancing the democratic legitimacy of the Union. Among these provisions, the more important aim to increase the powers of the European Parliament, to give a concrete role to national parliaments and to provide the citizens with a possibility to request a legislative initiative from the Commission. However, the truth remains that there is no political game at the European level. The political game continues to be played out almost exclusively at the national level, in each of the 27 Member States.[13] Given the present opposition of most Member States to the establishment of something which would look like a federal entity, there are no 'simple' options which could be envisaged. It is difficult to assess a priori what will be the actual effects of the changes made to the provisions of the Treaties, especially on such an issue. Overall, one may hope that these changes will be a step towards a greater legitimacy in the functioning of the EU institutions.

It is a fact that the EU's decision-making process was already, even before the entry into force of the Lisbon Treaty, subject to many checks and balances. It is probably more open than most of the 27 national ones, as it is submitted to scrutiny both by the European Parliament and by the national parliaments, and also allows for an active input by 'civil society' and lobbies. Despite all this, one may wonder if citizens do think they have enough control over the way the EU's decisions and laws are made. The challenge is to find a way to convince them of the contrary. The Lisbon Treaty has begun moves in that direction, but further efforts are required.

In that framework, the fact that there is no political game at the European level has important and unavoidable consequences. One of these is the probability that any improvement in the situation should include an increase in the powers of the national parliaments. This would help to complement (not replace) the role of the European Parliament. This might be done according to different procedures and methods in each of the Member States, without necessarily amending the Treaties. Each Member State can organise itself in accordance with democratic principles, through its own constitutional practices. The manner in which each national parliament organises and implements scrutiny of the participation of its government in the EU decision-making process may result from different sources, such as:

- a provision of the national constitution;
- a law adopted at the time of ratification of a new EU Treaty;
- a judgment of the constitutional court;
- a formal agreement between the parliament and the government; and

---

[13] As the German Constitutional Court stressed in its 30 June 2009 judgment: '. . . it cannot be overlooked, however, that the public perception of factual issues and of political leaders remains connected to a considerable extent to patterns of identification which are related to the Nation State, language, history and culture' (para 251).

- practices accepted explicitly or implicitly by the government.

This is already happening in all Member States, to varying degrees, more or less effectively, thus providing for a certain degree of control by national parliaments over the participation of the representatives of their government in important decisions taken by the EU institutions. This control is more or less tight, depending on the Member State concerned: actually, the EU's 'democratic deficit' is also due to the fact that this control at the national level sometimes is not sufficient. Perhaps a declaration of the European Council could help to push the Member States concerned to act more, better and more quickly in this direction.

One of the problems which blur the picture is the usual mistake on the 'standards' to be taken into account as a benchmark.[14] Most people tend to judge the EU's institutional architecture through the prism of the political organisation of states. This is wrong. The separation of three distinct powers according to Montesquieu, the accountability of the executive power to the legislative one, etc are not adapted to the EU's uniqueness. With the Lisbon Treaty, the 'executive power' in the EU continues to be divided and shared between the European Council, the Council and the Commission, to which one should now add the President of the European Council and the High Representative for Foreign Affairs and Security Policy. As regards the 'legislative power', it is essentially shared between the European Parliament and the Council, but one should also note that the Commission's monopoly on legislative initiative has been strengthened, that the national parliaments have been given the means to play a role and that this is also the case for citizens, who will be able to submit 'citizen's initiatives'. Moreover, on a number of points, the European Parliament cannot be compared to a national parliament, where there is a majority supporting a government and which can be dissolved by the government.

One should also stress that there remains a large part of EU competences where the decision-making procedures provide for unanimity in the Council (tax, foreign policy, some areas of social policy, of environment policy, of economic and monetary policy, of justice and home affairs, the flexibility clause in Article 352 TFEU, etc), or even for the common accord of the Member States[15] (revision of the Treaties, appointment of judges, decisions on the seat of the institutions and on the language regime, etc). In those areas, the democratic control belongs to each national parliament, through a control of its national government. The consequence is that the EU system cannot be copied from the usual state democratic systems. If there was no solution to ensure democratic legitimacy in the EU other

---

[14] See G Majone, 'A Question of Standards' in *Dilemmas of European Integration—The Ambiguities and Pitfalls of Integration by Stealth* (Oxford, Oxford University Press, 2009).
[15] Unanimity in the Council allows for abstentions (Art 238(4) TFEU), whereas the common accord of the Member States requires a positive agreement by each of them.

than a system identical to a state one, that would mean there will be no future for the EU as it is conceived now. The EU should either become a federal state or be transformed into a classic international organisation. In its judgment of 30 June 2009, the German Constitutional Court considered that the Member States have shown that they are unable to establish a real democracy at the level of the EU. According to the Court, such real democracy cannot be established through something other than the election of a parliament on the basis of the democratic principle of 'one man, one vote', a parliament which should then be the basis for a European government.[16] Discussions should start on the basis of this opinion and could address the following questions:

- Is this solution (ie that the EU should be governed by a political system similar to those which govern democratic states) the only conceivable one? Would it be possible to conceive another system?
- Would it be the *sine qua non* option in order to be able to develop European integration further and to allow the EU to continue to enlarge its activities?
- Are there other options available?
- If there are none, would that mean that the EU is condemned to the status quo?
- Has it reached the limits of possible integration?

It is permissible to think that this is not necessarily the case. Europeans could continue to try and invent ways and means to pursue the European project in an innovative way. They should try to imagine new mechanisms and procedures for giving more political legitimacy to actions taken at the European level, in particular through better control by each national parliament over the participation of their government in the decisions taken at EU level.

This appears to be not only desirable, but also virtually unavoidable. If things do not change, it would become very difficult, if not impossible, to obtain the necessary acceptance by citizens to amend the EU Treaties to correct their imbalances, if there was such a need in the future. According to some, the only event which could change the mood of the citizens vis-à-vis the EU should be for the EU 'to deliver'. Of course, it would be helpful if the EU could show its capacity 'to deliver' concrete projects which would satisfy the needs and wishes of the citizens. However, one should not place too much hope on such a simple idea. Taking into account the current limits of the EU's powers, it does not look realistic. This is because most of the issues which directly concern the citizens in their daily life are currently outside the EU's scope of powers. This

---

[16] This does not mean that the German Constitutional Court is in favour of such a solution.

is the case for employment, taxation, industry, social security, pensions, most social policy, public health, education, culture, national security and public order, etc.[17]

With time, the imbalances described above have become more difficult to resolve, because the successive enlargements of the EU have led to a much greater heterogeneity—geographical, historical, cultural and economical—between its Member States. It remains the case that these imbalances have to be corrected, because the EU's present construction will hardly be able to remain stable in the future. This is so because these imbalances may not only prevent the EU from developing further, but may also prevent it from functioning in a satisfactory and sustainable way. If economic and financial tornadoes continue and escalate, they might push the EU towards a modification of the European architecture in order to correct these imbalances.

The very fact that the Lisbon Treaty has finally entered into force is a relief for the supporters of European integration. Moreover, the Treaty, by retaining the substantive reforms envisaged in the failed Constitutional Treaty, provides useful tools to deepen and strengthen the European project, should the political will be there. That said, it does not change the fact that this Treaty does not represent a great leap forward, or that it even marks a halt to the hopes of the 'federalists'.

As more European integration is and will remain necessary in order to preserve peace, freedom and prosperity in Europe and meet the challenges of the future, there is no other way forward than to have the support of the European citizens. The ways and means must be found to give them the power to exercise real democratic control over the EU's decisions, and to make them actually use this power. This should be done without transforming the EU into a federal state, which is unrealistic with 27 (more in the near future) Member States of such heterogeneity. This issue will not be resolved without strong political will, as it implies a change in political culture. In the absence of political will, one may expect, at best, a stagnation of the EU.

Such a stagnation would play against the interests of the Europeans, as none of the 27 EU Member States are able to deal on their own with the challenges of today. Whatever those challenges, the contribution of the European Union is needed to help tackle them, be it:

- protecting the environment and combating climate change;
- acting for better regulation of competition in the world and playing a role in world trade negotiations;
- fighting against international crime, traffic in human beings and the illegal drugs trade;

[17] See A Moravcsik 'The European Constitutional Settlement' (2008) 31(1) *World Economy* 158.

- acting to prevent war in the world;
- combating poverty and promoting democracy, human rights and equality between women and men in the world;
- protecting minorities in Europe, thus avoiding tensions which could, as often in the past, give birth to violence and armed conflicts;
- coordinating in order to act effectively in the case of international economic and financial crisis; and
- acting in favour of the poorest regions of Europe through solidarity on the part of the richest.

As Peter Sutherland said: 'the European project is the most noble political ideal in European history in a thousand years.'[18] Its primary and essential aim is reconciliation and peace among the European peoples, who have fought each other for centuries. Beyond this, common policies in some fields and co-operation in other fields are a necessity today for European states in order to preserve and improve the way of life and the needs and interests of their citizens. In order to achieve these aims, the ways followed in the past—intergovernmental co-operation or classic international organisations—have proved to be less efficient and less democratic than the (imperfect) EU. The priority now is to enhance the EU's democratic legitimacy and improve its visibility. The Lisbon Treaty is only one step in that direction, probably not the final one.

It will be fascinating to observe in the future how the Member States and the EU institutions will develop the potentialities of the Treaty of Lisbon, and if this will be enough to stabilise the EU, given the fact that the EU is, more than ever, indispensable for Europe to help face the challenges confronting its Member States and citizens.

---

[18] Peter Sutherland, interview by Harry Ayres, *Financial Times*, 3/4 January 2009.

5

Does Europe Need a Constitution? Achievements and Challenges After Lisbon

INGOLF PERNICE*

I INTRODUCTION

THE ATTEMPT TO give the European Union a 'constitution' has failed. It was as ambivalent as ambitious, since it is possible to argue that the Union already had a constitution even long before the 'post-Nice process' was started and long before the heads of state and government of the Member States used the word 'constitution' for the first time in 2001, in the Declaration of Laeken.[1] The historic work of the Convention was not useless, however. It first resulted in the 'Treaty Establishing a Constitution for Europe', which took the form of a Treaty and enhanced the constitutional character of European primary law substantially. Contrary to the name and the constitutional language used, however, it did not look at all like a constitution.[2] With the Lisbon

---

* The author expresses deep gratitude to Patricia Sarah Stöbener, LLM (King's College London) and Sebastian Leuschner for important assistance in finalising this contribution.

[1] Declaration on the Future of the European Union (Laeken Declaration), Annex I to the Presidency Conclusions of the Laeken European Council of 14 and 15 December 2001, II forth chapter, titled: 'Towards a Constitution for European Citizens', available at http://www.consilium.europa.eu/ueDocs/cms_Data/docs/pressData/en/ec/68827.pdf.

[2] See the criticism of JHH Weiler and A Moravcsik to name the Treaty, though it contained merely modest reforms, 'Constitution', JHH Weiler, 'The Constitution of Europe: Resquiescat in Pacem' in L Silva Morais, P de Pitta e Cunha (eds), *A Europa E Os Desafios do Seculo XXI: conferência internacional* (Coimbra, Almedina, 2008) 179, 182f; idem, JHH Weiler, 'Editorial: Marking the Anniversary of the Universal Declaration; The Irish No and the Lisbon Treaty' (2008) 19 *European Journal of International Law* 647, 652: 'Treaty which masqueraded as a Constitution . . .'; A Moravcsik, 'Europe without Illusions: A Category Error' (2005) 112 *Prospect*, available at http://www.prospectmagazine.co.uk/2005/07/europewithoutillusions.

Treaty, the name and the constitutional symbolism have been dropped, but the constitutional substance of the reform has been salvaged.

Alan Dashwood, with other experts, submitted a Draft Constitutional Treaty of the European Union in October 2002[3] that had great impact on the later outcome not only of the Convention's work but finally also of the Lisbon Treaty.[4] It has also contributed to a constitutional understanding of the primary law of the European Union—beyond Lisbon.

Yet, in order to salvage the substantive content of the Constitution for Europe after the negative votes in France and in the Netherlands, the European Council is said to have distanced itself expressly from the constitutional concept with the 'Brussels mandate' for the IGC 2007: 'The constitutional concept, which consisted in repealing all existing Treaties and replacing them by a single text called, "Constitution", is abandoned.'[5]

Careful reading, however, allows this statement to be interpreted as meaning that only a very specific constitutional concept is abandoned: to replace the Treaties by a Constitution. It leaves open the general question of a constitutional character of the primary law in substance. Its aim was to avoid further discussion on whether or not the reform establishes a European state, and to exclude any basis for arguing that another referendum is needed in certain Member States.

The original approach of the Convention thus created considerable 'constitutional confusion',[6] while its work has the merit of introducing substantial improvements in the primary law of the Union in terms of transparency, democracy and efficiency, underlining and enhancing its constitutional character in many important respects.[7]

Is there any purpose, then, in continuing to deal with the question: does Europe need a Constitution?

Joseph HH Weiler negated the need for a constitution as early as 1995, long before the reform process started. In the light of supremacy, direct effect and other 'constitutional elements', Europe in his view is

---

[3] A Dashwood, M Dougan, C Hillion, A Johnston and E Spaventa, 'Draft Constitutional Treaty of the European Union and Related Documents' (2003) 28 *European Law Review* 3, published among other drafts also at the ECLN website at http://www.ecln.net/index.php?option=com_content&task=view&idem=18&Itemid=36.

[4] For an overview on seventeen drafts submitted in this period see P Häberle, *Europäische Verfassungslehre*, 6th edn (Baden-Baden, Nomos, 2009) 600–31.

[5] ICG Mandate, Presidency Conclusions of the Brussels European Council of 21 and 22 June 2007, Annex 1, para. 1.1, available at http://www.consilium.europa.eu/ueDocs/cms_Data/docs/pressData/en/ec/94932.pdf, 16. For comments see I Pernice, 'Salvaging the Constitution for Europe—A Reform Treaty for the EU', lecture given at the University of Melbourne (2007), available at http://www.whi-berlin.de/documents/whi-paper0407.pdf.

[6] I Pernice, 'The Treaty of Lisbon. Multilevel Constitutionalism in Action' (2009) 15 *Columbia Journal of European Law* 349, 368, also available at http://www.whi-berlin.de/documents/whi-paper0209.pdf.

[7] Ibid 349, 368ff, 385–407; see below.

still part of a constitutional legal order. According to him, the European Union does not need a constitution but an ethos and *telos* to justify the existing constitutionalism.[8] Grimm's reply to the question of whether the European Union needs a constitution was negative, at least insofar as 'constitution' is understood as a 'constitution in its full sense of the term'. This would end up 'turning the European Union into a state'.[9] In his reply to Grimm, while sharing the analysis, Jürgen Habermas came to the opposite political conclusions.[10] History, as we have seen, has found its own way.

At least the entry into force of the Lisbon Treaty apparently did not put an end to the debate: in October 2009, the Union of European Federalists convened a conference and gave me the honour to talk about Europe's chances to adopt a constitution after the German Federal Constitutional Court's ruling on the Lisbon Treaty. My answer was clear: there is little chance for the European Union to give itself— or to be given—a constitution if this is meant to constitute a European federal state. A European federal state is neither needed nor desirable. The most original and promising feature of European integration is not to copy, on a larger level, the state model, but to question sovereign statehood and to reinforce effective sovereignty of the people by integrating states into a supranational constitutional compound that provides their people with an additional, complementary device of political authority to implement policies of common concern which individual states are unable or not efficient enough to implement. This approach would lose its sense if it were to lead to the same kind of statehood it searches to overcome.[11] Consequently, there is also no need to have a constitution in this sense. However, a constitution in another sense could be necessary.

This depends of how we judge upon three preliminary questions: First, what is a constitution? Second, what is or what should be the European Union? And third, what would be the added value of a constitution compared to the existing situation?

---

[8] JHH Weiler, 'Does Europe Need a Constitution? Demos, Telos and the German Maastricht Decision' (1995) 1 *European Law Journal* 219ff.

[9] D Grimm, 'Does Europe Need a Constitution?' (1995) 1 *European Law Journal* 282, 298ff.

[10] J Habermas, 'Remarks on Dieter Grimm's "Does Europe Need a Constitution?"' (1995) 1 *European Law Journal* 303. For more recent contributions. J Puente-Egido, ‚Braucht Europa eine Verfassung' in P Häberle, M Morlok and V Skouris (eds), *Festschrift für Dimitris Tsatsos* (Baden-Baden, Nomos, 2003) 530.

[11] For more detail see I Pernice, Zur Finalität Europas, in G Folke Schuppert, I Pernice and U Haltern (eds), *Europawissenschaft* (Baden-Baden, Nomos, 2005), 743, 763.

II   WHAT IS A CONSTITUTION?

The term 'constitution' is very complex and controversial.[12] Does it mean
a written document? Then the UK has no constitution. Does it mean the
fundamental legal order of a state? Then the European Union does not
have a constitution because it remains a supranational organisation. And
calling the basic statutes of certain international organisations, such as the
FAO, the UNESCO or the ILO, 'constitutions' would be mistaken.[13] Does
a constitution presuppose an existing people or nation, which has fought
for it in a revolution driven by the enthusiasm of freedom and equal
rights—as in France in 1789?[14] Then neither the US nor Germany would
have a constitution. The same is true if we believe that the people must
have adopted it by referendum. Even where no more than the adoption
by representative bodies expressing the sovereign will of the people is
required, the German Grundgesetz and the constitutions of Australia and
other countries of the British Commonwealth would not be constitutions.
Contrary to what seems to be implied in the recent judgment of the
German Federal Constitutional Court on the Lisbon Treaty,[15] no sovereign
people existed then in Germany to bring the Grundgesetz into effect.

What, then, are the essential criteria for defining a constitution?

For the present purpose, it might be sufficient to recall some ideas and
theories before explaining my understanding of the term 'constitution'.[16]

---

[12] See only from recent years, P Bastid, *L'idée de constitution*, Collection classiques (Paris, Economica, 1985); M Loughlin, 'In Defence of Staatslehre' (2009) 48 *Der Staat* 1, available at http://www.atypon-link.com/DH/doi/abs/10.3790/staa.48.1.1; UK Preuß (ed), *Zum Begriff der Verfassung: Die Ordnung des Politischen*, Philosophie der Gegenwart no 12246 (Frankfurt/Main, Fischer, 1994); J Raz, 'On the Authority and Interpretation of Constitutions: Some Preliminaries' in L Alexander (ed), *Constitutionalism: Philosophical foundations*, Cambridge Studies in Philosophy and Law (Cambridge, Cambridge University Press, 1998) 152ff. Concerning the European Union in particular see only P Craig, 'Constitutions, Constitutionalism, and the European Union' (2001) 7 *European Law Journal* 125; I Pernice, 'Europäisches und nationales Verfassungsrecht' (2001) 60 *Veröffentlichungen der Vereinigung der Deutschen Staatsrechtslehrer* 148, also available at http://www.whi-berlin.de/documents/whi-paper1301.pdf; N Walker, 'Taking Constitutionalism Beyond the State' (2008) 56 *Political Studies* 519.

[13] On this issue see A Dashwood, 'The EU Constitution—What Will Really Change?' (2004–05) 7 *Cambridge Yearbook of European Legal Studies* 33, 34. A Peters, 'The Constitutionalisation of the European Union—Without the Constitutional Treaty' in S Puntscher Riekmann and W Wessels (ed), *The Making of a European Constitution* (Wiesbaden, Verlag für Sozialwissenschaften, 2006) 35, 37.

[14] This is implied by H Hofmann, 'Von der Staatssoziologie zu einer Soziologie der Verfassung' (1999) 54 *Juristenzeitung* 1065, 1070; *cf* also U Haltern, *Europarecht und das Politische*, Jus publicum no 136 (Tübingen, Mohr Siebeck, 2005).

[15] German Federal Constitutional Court, judgment of 30 June 2009, Case 2 BvE 2/08, BVerfGE 123, 267, available at http://www.bverfg.de/entscheidungen/es20090630_2bve000208en.html, in particular paras 217, 228, 233 and 248.

[16] Pernice, above n 12, 148ff, and iden, 'Multilevel Constitutionalism in the European Union' (2002) 27 *European Law Review* 511, II.1.a, also available at http://www.whi-berlin.de/pernice-constitutionalism.htm, 4ff; both articles with further literature; I Pernice, FC Mayer, S Wernicke, 'Renewing the European Social Contract: The Challenge of institutional

A   Basic Elements: the 'Thin' and the 'Thick' Constitution

A number of minimum basic features are generally accepted as characterising a constitution. A constitution in this 'thin',[17] more functional sense is an arrangement that establishes and regulates the main organs of government in a legal order, their structure, powers and decision-making procedures, and the legal rules on the enactment and enforcement of law.

However, these features are not sufficient to describe the concept of a constitution. There is a wide discussion about what further criteria should be met. Joseph Raz enumerates seven features to define a constitution in a 'thick' sense, and a recent study by Jeffrey Dunoff and Joel Trachtman completes this list: beyond the establishment of the main organs and their powers and the allocation of governance authority in a vertical context, a constitution is meant to be stable, usually written, superior to ordinary law and justiciable. There are special requirements for the amendment of the constitution, and the term includes principles such as democracy, federalism and human rights that are 'generally held to express the common beliefs of the population about the way their society should be governed', a common ideology and also constraints and means of control of public power.[18]

However, this is a description of the general features of a western type of constitution rather than a normative theory. Not all constitutions contain all these features. Above all, this definition does not explain what a constitution must contain and, above all, what gives a constitution real authority.

B   The Authority of a Constitution

According to Dunhoff and Trachtman, this authority 'rests upon facts external to the constitution': the 'settlement regarding the fundamental structure of society' precedes and determines the structuring of legal constitutions. Therefore, legal constitutions are defined as 'efforts to effectuate or instantiate the chosen fundamental social structures'.[19]

---

reform and enlargement in the light of multilevel constitutionalism' (2001) 12 *King's Col lege Law Journal* 61, 68, also available at www.whi-berlin.de/documents/whi-paper1101.pdf.

[17] Raz, above n 12, 152, 153; see also: W Waluchow, 'Constitutionalism' in *Stanford Encyclopedia of Philosophy* (Stanford, CA, The Metaphysics Research Laboratory, Stanford University, 2007), available at http://plato.stanford.edu/entries/constitutionalism; P Cane and J Conaghan (eds), *The New Oxford Companion to Law* (Oxford, Oxford University Press, 2008) 210.

[18] Raz, above n 12, 153–154.; JL Dunoff and JP Trachtman, 'A Functional Approach to International Constitutionalization' in idem, *Ruling the World? Constitutionalism, International Law and Global Governance* (Cambridge University Press, 2009), 18–21.

[19] Ibid, 18.

Carl Schmitt distinguished between the fundamental settlement, which he named 'constitution', and its concrete instantiation by the constitution-making power, which he called 'constitutional law'.[20] This positivist concept does not include normative criteria but just acknowledges what decision has been produced by whoever holds effective power in the society. There is no explanation of what the will of constitution-making power is. It becomes visible and clear only through the constitution.[21] With this, the distinction between constitution and constitutional law becomes meaningless and the definition circular.

Loughlin distinguishes between the formal documents (the constitution of government) and the substantive constitution which forms a political unity and which is based on a political pact (the constitution of the state). The formal constitution is not self-authorising but valid only by virtue of an existing political will, the material constitution.[22] This political pact and hence the people are regarded as the ultimate source of sovereign authority.[23]

C   The Political Pact: a Contractualist Concept of Self-authorisation

In locating the source of authority of the constitution in a political pact, Loughlin makes it clear that the constitution is founded upon an act taken by or at least attributed to the people themselves, in which the people attributes political capacity to itself.[24]

It is true that, from empirical terms, many constitutions are not based upon the express approval of the people,[25] but where parliaments and governments are acting for the people, the citizens remain the legitimating subject. Representation is a basic democratic principle and there is no reason to qualify the actual consent given by a people's referendum as the single possible source of legitimacy.[26]

Where the authority of the constitution is based upon the will of the people, we find that contractualism and, with it, the concept of the *contrat*

---

[20] C Schmitt, *Constitutional Theory* (1928), translated and edited by Jeffrey Seitzer (Durham, Duke University Press, 2008), 75ff (*Verfassungsgesetz* as opposed to *Verfassung*).

[21] *cf* P Häberle, *Verfassungslehre als Kulturwissenschaft*, Schriften zum öffentlichen Recht no 436, 2nd edn (Berlin, Duncker & Humblot, 1998) 620; Hofmann (n 14); K Sobota, *Das Prinzip Rechtsstaat* (Tübingen, Mohr Siebeck, 1997) 30ff.

[22] Loughlin, above n 12, 1, 9f.

[23] Ibid, 4f, 20.

[24] *cf* Grimm, above n 9, 282, 290, 299.

[25] See only G Frankenberg, 'The Return of the Contract: Problems and Pitfalls of the European Constitutionalism' (2000) 6 *European Law Journal*, 257, 258f.

[26] *cf* Craig, above n 12, 125, 137f.

social as the origin and continuing basis for the validity of a constitution[27] is an appropriate theory for legitimising the constitution and government, at least in democratic societies. Though nobody would argue that people did—and would at any time—negotiate and agree upon a constitution in real terms, the institutions, procedures and allocation of powers laid down in constitutions, the reciprocal rights and duties of authorities and individuals can be constructed as the result of a political process in a given territory, involving people, social powers, and sometimes also advice or pressures from the outside.[28] They are terms which are finally agreed upon and recognised as the relevant and binding rules of the political process. In this sense, a constitution is the expression of a general agreement of the people concerned, a 'political contract',[29] a basic consensus (*Grundkonsens*) in the society reflected in the active participation and support of the citizens. Or, as Neil Walker describes it: the meta-democratic claim to self-authorisation, the idea of the people as author and owner of the constitution and the society as dedicated and integrated object of the constitution.[30] This concept of constitution is not limited to the adoption of a given legal settlement but rather is an open public process,[31] a concretisation, adaptation and recreation by the construction and interpretation in the day-to-day application, the continuous and repetitive confirmation of the basic agreement: as Rénan said: a *plébicite de tous les jours*.[32] 'Constitution' therefore means this steadily renewable agreement—or social contract—of the 'people', citizens of the given polity, providing ultimately for the legitimacy of all public authority, which it establishes, organises and limits.

---

[27] JJ Rousseau, *Du contrat social ou principe du droit politique* (1762); and reinstated by J Rawls, *Theory of Justice* (Cambridge, MA, Belknap Press of Harvard University Press, 1971) viii, 3, 11.

[28] Eg the German Grundgesetz and the Japanese Constitution, both made after World War II under the supervision of the Allies. For more recent cases see P Dann and Z Al-Ali, 'The Internationalized *Pouvoir Constituant*—Constitution-Making Under External Influence in Iraq, Sudan and East Timor' in A von Bogdandy and R Wolfrum (eds), *Max Planck Yearbook of United Nation Law*, Vol 10 (Leiden, Nijhoff, 2006) 423.

[29] This is the expression used by MP Maduro, 'From Constitutions to Constitutionalism: A Constitutional Approach for Global Governance' in D Lewis (ed), *Global Governance and the Quest for Justice, Vol 1. International and Regional Organisations* (Oxford, Hart Publishing, 2006) 227, 239ff.

[30] N Walker, 'Not the European Constitution' (2008) 15 *Maastricht Journal of European and Comparative Law* 135, 137, names it the popular and social register of constitutionalism. In N Walker, 'Reframing EU Constitutionalism' in J Dunoff and J Trachtman (eds), *Ruling the World? Constitutionalism, International Law and Global Governance* (Cambridge, Cambridge University Press, 2009) 149, he differentiates even between five frames: the legal order in juridical terms, a set of organs of government in political terms, self-authorisation, a integrated community in social terms and finally a common ideology in discursive terms.

[31] P Häberle, *Verfassung als öffentlicher Prozess*, Schriften zum öffentlichen Recht, no 353, 3rd edn (Berlin, Duncker &Humblot, 1998) especially at 121ff, 265ff.

[32] E Rénan, *Qu'est-ce qu'une nation? Conférence faite en Sorbonne le 11 mars 1882* (Paris, Calmann-Lévy, 1882) 26ff.

This consensus may consist in conventions, as in the UK,[33] or be laid down in written documents, as in most other countries. As soon as legislative powers come into play, constitutional criteria will have to apply. Thus, if the term 'constitution' has any particular meaning at all, it is this legitimising effect based, in a self-referential manner, upon the will and acceptance of the individuals who are affected and concerned by the acts of the public authority they have established.

D   Constitution for the State

The traditional polity having institutions vested with such powers is the state. A new setting is the EU. Hence the question arises whether the concept of constitution can be transferred to this supranational organisation or whether it is restricted to the state.

Carl Schmitt has even identified state and constitution.[34] In recent years Dieter Grimm has elaborated the origin of the concept of constitution as historically evolved in the frame of the state as the comprehensive political body that encompassed all public power over a territory and its people. The exclusivity of the state power to rule over a territory and the supremacy of the constitution are in his view essential elements of constitutionalism.[35] Also, Loughlin criticises a 'free-standing constitutionalism' as abandoning state theory and questioning the concept of constitutionalism as such.[36] The political pact and hence the people is regarded as the ultimate source of sovereign authority. Sovereignty shall thus be the absolute legal authority to rule and be both indivisible and inalienable. Only governmental powers, not sovereignty, can be divided or transferred.[37] With regard to the European Union, the legal nature of the primary law as international treaties implies that the public power emanates not from the people but from the Member States. Consequently, according to Grimm, the European integration shall not be a constitutionalisation but a mere 'juridification'.[38]

---

[33] *Cf* Dashwood, above n 13, 33f.

[34] Schmitt, above n 20 59ff.: 'The state does not *have* a constitution, which forms itself and functions "according" to a state will. The state *is* constitution.'

[35] D Grimm, 'The Constitution in the Process of Denationalization' (2005) 12 *Constellations*, 447. On the development of the term constitution see H Mohnhaupt and D Grimm, *Verfassung. Zur Geschichte des Begriffs von der Antike bis zur Gegenwart. Zwei Studien*, Schriften zur Verfassungsgeschichte no 47, 2nd edn (Berlin, Duncker & Humblot, 2002). More advocates of a restriction of the term constitution on the state: Pernice, above n 12, 148.

[36] Loughlin, above n 12, 1f, 26.

[37] Ibid, 1, 4f, 20.

[38] Grimm, above n 35, 447.

E The Changing Meaning of Constitution in a Changing World

Does this restriction of the concept of constitution to the state reflect what the essence of constitution is? If it is about a direct legal relationship between, on the one side, individuals defining themselves as citizens of a political community and, on the other side, the public authority so established on their behalf to exercise the powers conferred to it for implementing certain policies, then there is no reason to limit it to the traditional type of political community, which is the state. The changes caused by the process of globalisation need to be reflected in changes of minds and terms. States are increasingly unable to serve effectively the needs of their cititzens regarding peace, security, welfare etc. Supra- and international structures serve as complementary instruments to fill this growing lacuna. The historical development of the constitution as a means to limit state power cannot make the state a precondition of the constitution nor its exclusive object. Public functions are no longer bundled into one entity but dispersed in different political institutions.[39] Supranational legislation, the establishment of individual rights and the degree of integration at the European level are of a nature and impact on the individual life of the citizens which cannot be explained by terms of public international law or the idea of mere juridification.

The understanding of constitution and constitutionalism needed under such conditions is rather functional and pragmatic; it should not to be confused with statehood, but abstract from the form of political unity or system it establishes and organises.[40] According to a 'postnational'[41] concept of constitution, the definition of constitution includes all instru- ments—national, subnational and supranational—for the establishment, organisation and limitation of public authority by the people concerned. The distinctive feature of the constitution as compared to any other law is thus its fundamental characteristic of establishing an original and basic

---

[39] *Cf* Peters, above n 12, 35, 43ff.

[40] Pernice, above n 12, 148, and idem (above n 16) 511, 11.1.a. See also Dashwood, above n 13, 33, 34; A Peters, *Elemente einer Theorie der Verfassung Europas* (Berlin, Duncker & Humblot, 2001) 93ff; D Curtin, 'Civil Society and the European Union' (1996) 7 *Collected courses of the Academy of European Law* 185; J Habermas, 'Die postnationale Konstellation' in idem (ed), *Die postnationale Konstellation: Politische Essays* (Frankfurt/ Main, Suhrkamp, 1998) 91. C Möllers, 'Pouvoir Constituant—Constitution—Constitution- alization' in A von Bogdandy and J Bast (eds), *Principles of European Constitutional Law*, Modern Studies in European law no 8 (Oxford, Hart Publishing, 2006) 183, 195 even states: 'In European constitutional history any identification of nation-state and constitu- tion is unconvincing.' KH Ladeur, 'We, the European People . . .' (2008) 14 *European Law Journal* 147, 167, oversees this when criticising that 'protagonists of a European Constitu- tion . . . re-evaluate its (sc the nation state's) revival at a larger scale'.

[41] Pernice, above n 12, 148, 155; borrowing from J Shaw, 'Postnational Constitutionalims in the European Union' (1999) 6 *Journal of European Public Policy* 579; with important further thought M A Wilkinson, 'Civil Society and the Re-imagination of European Consi- tutionalism (2003) 9 *European Law Journal*, 451, 455, 468, 471.

legal relationship between the established institutions and the citizens. The citizens are considered as both the authors and the addressees of the authorities so established. A constitution is essentially self-referential, the statute by which people organise their political condition and the life of their polity. Contrary to legislative acts, it requires highest authority, and is in principle irrevocable and amendable only under particularly restrictive conditions. As Dashwood describes it in short: a constitution is a set of ground rules organising some form of collective human activity[42]—and this can be applied to the European Union.

III UNDERSTANDING THE EUROPEAN UNION

In order to assess whether or not the European Union needs a constitution, it is essential to know what the European Union is. This is also highly controversial. Some argue that it is—or should become—a state.[43] Establishing a federal state of Europe was the clear goal of the German Christian democrats for many years.[44] Likewise, Joschka Fischer, the former German foreign minister, called in his Humboldt Speech of 2000 for a United States of Europe.[45] However, in its Lisbon judgment the German Federal Constitutional Court has clearly stated that the German Constitution would not allow this step to be taken.[46] Rather, it considers the European Union as an association of sovereign national states.[47] Armin von Bogdandy proposed to describe it as 'supranational federation';[48] Christoph Schönberger, Olivier Beaud and Jean F Cohen

[42] Dashwood, above n 13, 33f.

[43] J Sack, ' Die Staatswerdung Europas—kaum eine Spur von Stern und Stunde' (2005) 44 *Der Staat* 67; in favour of the latter see also F Mancini, 'Europe: The Case for Statehood' (1998) 4 *European Law Journal* 29.

[44] H Kohl, former Chancellor of the Federal Republic of Germany, in his State of the Nation Adress from 1990, in *Verhandlungen des Deutschen Bundestages, 11. Wahlperiode, Stenographische Berichte, Plenarprotokolle 11/219—11/236*, available at http://www.kas.de/wf/de/71.4613/. See also J Rüttgers, Prime Minister of Nordrhein-Westfalen on 18 September 2009, postulating the United States of Europe, available at http://www.faz.net/s/Rub99C3EECA60D84C08AD6B3E60C4EA807F/Doc~E05BEA75D6C1146438C85BFB8E5582773~ATpl~Ecommon~Scontent.html.

[45] Speech of 12 May 2000, available at http://www.jeanmonnetprogram.org/papers/00/joschka_fischer_en.rtf.

[46] German Federal Constitutional Court, above n 15, para 228.

[47] German Federal Constitutional Court, Case 2 BvR 2134/92 and 2 BvR 2159/92, BVerfGE 89, 155, 190.

[48] A von Bogdandy, *Supranationaler Föderalismus als Wirklichkeit und Idee einer neuen Herrschaftsform. Zur Gestalt der Europäischen Union nach Amsterdam*, Forum Rechtswissenschaft no 28 (Baden-Baden, Nomos, 1999) 67.

propose 'federation';[49] and Stefan Oeter prefers the term 'federal union'.[50] The most common expression, however, is the organisation *sui generis*. This means that, with our traditional terminologies and categories of the state and the international organisation, based mainly upon the theory of Georg Jellinek,[51] we are unable to qualify and explain what the European Union really is, as distinguished from federal states, confederations or international organisations.

A The Features of the European Union

To describe the EU in the absence of a commonly agreed term, it is necessary, first, to summarise its basic features: it is a separate legal entity with its own legal personality, its own aims and powers conferred to its institutions representing the EU both, with regard to the Member States and their citizens, and towards third countries and international organisations. The Union is a body established by law, acting through law and bound to the rule of law—what Walter Hallstein coined a Community of law (*Rechtsgemeinschaft*).[52]

Indeed, the Union was established and developed by international treaties. However, these treaties are special: so procedurally, for ratification of the treaties and for ratifying amendments, most of the Member States have to apply special integration clauses of their constitutions providing for the powers and laying down particular procedural requirements and conditions for conferring sovereign powers to the Union. And substantively, the primary law contains many provisions and has many features which differ fundamentally from any other international treaty.

The European Treaties lay down common values, objectives and democratic principles of the Union and the Member States and establish the citizenship of the Union as the fundamental status of the citizens of the Member States.[53] The Treaties determine the specific rights and duties

[49] O Beaud, *Théorie de la fédération* (Paris, Presse Universitaires de France, 2007); C Schönberger, 'Die Europäische Union als Bund. Zugleich ein Beitrag zur Verabschiedung des Staatenbund-Bundesstaat-Schemas' (2004) 129 *Archiv des öffentlichen Rechts* 81; JL Cohen, 'A Global State of Emergency or the Further Constitutionalization of International Law: A Pluralist Approach' (2008) 15 *Constellations* 456, 465, 470ff.

[50] S Oeter, 'Federalism and Democracy' in A von Bogdandy and J Bast (eds), *Principles of European Constitutional Law*, Modern Studies in European law no 8 (Oxford, Hart Publishing, 2006) 53, 85ff.

[51] See especially G Jellinek, *Die Lehre von den Staatenverbindungen* (1882) newly edited by W Pauly, Bibliothek des öffentlichen Rechts no 3 (Goldbach, Keip Verlag, 1996), 16ff, 34, 172ff, who refers to the sovereign state with unlimited power on all fields, in contrast to the confederation which is established by sovereign states.

[52] See W Hallstein, *Die Europäische Gemeinschaft*, 1st edn (Düsseldorf, Econ-Verlag,1973) 31ff; cf ECJ Case 294/83 *Les Verts* [1986] ECR I-1339, para 23, 'The European Economic Community is a Community based on the rule of law'.

[53] ECJ Case 184/99 *Rudy Grzelczyk* [2001] ECR I-6293, para 30.

which are common and equally applicable to all citizens of the Member States, and which include democratic political rights and procedural participatory rights, fundamental rights and market freedoms. These rights are binding upon the European institutions, have direct effect in the national legal systems and have primacy over national law.[54] The European institutions are controlled by the European Court of Justice (ECJ) in the exercise of their powers, with the Lisbon Treaty in nearly all subject matters.

Contrary to intergovernmental decision-making processes, most European legislation is adopted both by the European parliament and—on the basis of qualified majority voting—by the Council in the co-decision procedure. Only certain sensitive areas, like foreign and security policies, economic policies and employment, are matters of intergovernmental co-operation and co-ordination. The Union has very limited or no powers in areas like taxation, social security systems, culture and education. However, in sum, it can regulate and co-ordinate matters which affect the internal sphere of the Member States and the daily life of the citizens considerably.

This is why not only fundamental rights (Article 6 TEU) but also safeguards of national identity and autonomy have been strengthened by the Lisbon Treaty. Article 4(2) TEU not only requires the Union to respect the national identity of the Member States, 'inherent in their fundamental structures, political and constitutional, inclusive of regional and local self-government', but more precisely states that 'it shall respect their essential State functions, including ensuring the territorial integrity of the State, maintaining law and order and safeguarding national security. In particular, national security remains the sole responsibility of each Member State.'

This provision reflects the fears of the governments to lose their power even in these areas and thus shows that the Union is exercising real powers that are far-reaching enough to threaten some key areas of traditional national sovereignty. Consequently, it requires the respect for the political structures and diversity of the states and cultures forming the Union as a specific system composed of at least two levels of action. To this end, Article 5 TEU lays down the limits for the use of the powers conferred to the Union and Protocol No 2, the 'early warning system' for the control of subsidiarity by the national parliaments. This mechanism ensures that those who would suffer most from an excessive use of the

---

[54] See *Van Gend, Costa ENEL, Simmenthal, Factortame* and other judgments of the ECJ, accepted by national constitutional courts in principle, though with reservations. For recent comments *cf* MP Maduro, L Azoulai (eds), *The Past and Future of EU Law: The Classics of EU Law Revisited on the 50th Anniversary of the Rome Treaty* (Oxford, Hart Publishing, 2010), in particular FC Mayer, 'Van Gend en Loos, The Foundation of a Community of Law', ibid, 16; I Pernice, '*Costa v ENEL and Simmenthal*. Primacy of European Law', ibid 47.

powers conferred to the Union can effectively intervene by political and also judicial instruments.

Such provisions for the allocation and use of public authority between two levels of action in a political system are constitutional by their nature. Also, the provisions for fundamental rights and on democratic principles of the Union are typically constitutional provisions. They can hardly be regarded as common elements of the statutes for international organisations or confederations. The principles of representative democracy in the Union with a directly elected parliament composed of representatives of the citizens of the Union and holding legislative powers together with the Council. These features demonstrate that this Union is designed to exercise public authority, as is traditionally known for states only, though in a balanced and limited manner, complementary to that of the Member States. They also indicate that the legitimacy of the Union and the European policies is rooted in the citizens having multiple identities, eg as citizens of their local communities, their respective Member States and citizens of the Union.

Special regard should be given to the functions and powers of national institutions in the political system of the Union, such as the new powers of the national parliaments—powers conferred upon them by the European Treaties, whereas most of the national constitutions remain silent about these new powers of their parliaments. Likewise, national ministers meeting in the Council exercise legislative authority at the European level. The administrative authorities and, in particular, judges of the Member States are empowered and bound to display European legislation, and to disapply national legislation in all cases of conflict with European law. This is special to the multilevel constitutional system of the European Union.

The Member States are essential part of the Union and vice versa. The system is based on pooled sovereignty and close interdependence between the European and national levels of action. It could not work without democratically elected and controlled national governments, nor could its legislation or policies—and even its judicial system—be effective without functioning national authorities implementing, applying and also scrutinising its action. On the other hand, Member States could not possibly be as effective as they are in acting for the interests of their citizens without this new device created for acting, where necessary, beyond national reach and influence. As the European Constitution is evolving, the national constitutions are progressively 'Europeanised'.[55]

Consequently, the Union cannot be seen in isolation but must be defined as an important part of the multilevel system based upon the Member States' constitutions. It is complementary to them and binds them together

---

[55] MP Maduro, 'Intergouvernementalismus contra Konstitutionalismus: Braucht das transformierte Europa eine Verfassung?' (2007) *Der Staat*, 319, 328.

with common values, common institutions, common law and for common purposes, with citizens having a common and equal status and equal rights under European law.

The relationship of European and national law, though, is not based on hierarchy between the European and the national levels but rather is pluralistic and co-operative. European law prevails in the case of a conflict with national law in order to be effective and to ensure equality between individuals from different Member States. On the other hand, supranational law is limited to certain purposes and policies, and is complementary to national law; it is not meant to jeopardise the validity of the law of the Member States or, in particular, the fundamental principles of the diverse national constitutions. Mutual consideration and co-operation as well as regard for the functioning of the European system, and for the basics of national constitutional law, are therefore required.[56] Thus, any definition of the Union without regard to the Member States as their very fundament and condition of life would be incomplete, as much as denying that the Union, with its powers and opportunites, changes the nature and functioning of its Member States and their institutions would be a mistake.

B   The Constitutional Character of the European Union

What does all this mean for determining whether or not the European Union needs a Constitution?

A theory of the European Union must be based upon these features and must aim at giving the system as a whole a comprehensive and meaningful name. The provisions of the Treaties mentioned have constitutional character. The Treaties establish a new legal entity, create institutions, confer powers to them, define the legal status, rights and duties of the citizens as well as the powers and duties of the Member States and their institutions in the system, lay down the form and legal value of action, the procedures of decision making and judicial control, etc. The primary law is superior to the secondary law made by the European institutions and has primacy over national law. Even if Member States or national constitutional courts still insist in being the 'masters of the Treaties', the Member States and

---

[56] N Walker, 'The Idea of Constitutional Pluralism' (2002) 65 *Modern Law Review* 317, 339–40. More detailed on multilevel constitutionalism and pluralism are Pernice, above n 6, 349, 383f; I Pernice, *Das Verhältnis europäischer zu nationalen Gerichten im europäischen Verfassungsverbund* (Berlin, Walter Hallstein Institut, 2006) 49ff, also available at http://www.whi-berlin.de/documents/whi-paper0507.pdf. *Cf* also MP Maduro, 'Contrapunctual Law: Europe's Constitutional Pluralism in Action' in N Walker (ed), *Sovereignty in Transition* (Oxford, Hart Publishing, 2003) 501, 542ff; M Kumm, 'The Jurisprudence of Constitutional Conflict: Constitutional Supremacy in Europe before and after the Constitutional Treaty' (2005) 11 *European Law Journal* 281; *cf* also U Preuss, 'The Constitution of a European Democracy and the Role of the Nation State' (1999) 12 *Ratio Juris* 417, 420, who cites the notion of an 'osmotic relationship'.

their governments are also subjects of the law, including European law. The Treaties are amendable only according to special procedures, and thus form a stable legal framework of the European Union. With the Lisbon Treaty, important parts of the doctrine of the ECJ have become part of the Treaties, so there can be no doubt that this constitution is also written. In short, the Treaties fulfil the elaborate features of a constitution in the 'thick' sense, as developed by Raz.[57]

Hence, even though the founding instruments of the European Union take the form of treaties governed by international law, the Union has evolved and is governed under rules of constitutional law. The ECJ has repeatedly underlined the specific character of the EEC Treaty, which, 'albeit concluded in the form of an international agreement, nonetheless constitutes the constitutional charter of a Community based on the rule of law'.[58] The German Federal Constitutional Court recognised this special character as long ago as 1967,[59] and also in its recent judgment on the Lisbon Treaty.[60] The national governments also accepted this development long time ago, and intended to codify in the Treaty Establishing a Constitution for Europe what had been constitutional reality for several decades. In a broad sense, at least, the European Union thus has a constitution.[61]

C   Discussing Constitutionalism for Europe

This understanding, however, is not undisputed. Loughlin concedes that the European Union has a 'constitution of government', but he rejects the thesis that it has original and autonomous authority. First, sovereignty

---

[57] See also Craig, above n 12, 125, 128ff.

[58] ECJ Opinion 1/91—European Economic Area, 1991 ECR I-06079, summary, para 1.

[59] German Federal Constitutional Court, Case 1 BvR 248/63 and 216/67, BVerfGE 22, 293, para 11, stating that the EEC Treaty represents something like the Constitution of this Community.

[60] German Federal Constitutional Court, above n 15, para 231, 'In a functional sense, the source of Community authority, and of the European constitution that constitutes it, are the peoples of Europe with their democratic constitutions in their states.'

[61] See also A Dashwood, 'The Constitution of the European Union after Nice: Law-making Procedures' (2001), 26 *European Law Review*, 215; A Dashwood, 'The Elements of a Constitutional Settlement for the European Union' (2001) 4 *The Cambridge Yearbook of European Legal Studies* 1. A few of many other authors are JHH Weiler, *The Constitution of Europe: Do the New Clothes Have an Emperor? and Other Essays on European Integration* (Cambridge, Cambridge University Press, 1999) 221ff; E Stein, 'Lawyers, Judges and the Making of a Transnational constitution'(1981) 75 *American Journal of International Law* 1; Peters, above n 40; Craig, above n 12, 125, 128ff; A Moravcsik, 'What Can We Learn from the Collapse of the European Constitutional Project?' (2006) 47 *Politische Vierteljahreszeitschrift* 219, 220, available at http://www.princeton.edu/%7Eamoravcs/library/PVS04.pdf, speaking of a 'de facto constitution'. See also Pernice, above n 16, 511, IIIII.A; idem, above n 12, 148, with further literature.

itself is in his view indivisible and inalienable[62]. Secondly, he cannot imagine a European social contract. In his eyes, my assumption that the European Union is based on the common decision of the peoples of the Member States is an exercise of pure representation.[63]

Loughlin is right insofar as the European Union has no sovereign power like a state, ia it is a Community of law and not based on force. However, in his statement he oversees that, from its basic function, the Union is merely complementing the national legal orders enabling the Member States to make effective policy in the era of globalisation. Moreover, Loughlin's understanding of state and sovereignty does not explain the system of a federal state, since the states that are part of a federal state have their own, original constitutional authority.[64] Multilevel systems of governance can hardly be explained with this theory of sovereignty.

Furthermore, if he rejects the idea of a European social contract as being based on the pure idea of representation, then the same would be true for the German Constitution and many other constitutions adopted by procedures other than referendum. Even if the European law rests formally upon international treaties, does this exclude that European public authority is understood as deriving from the will of the people who have constituted this Union under procedures laid down in their respective constitutions in common with the people of the other Member States? Is it possible, in democratic systems, to call the states 'masters of the Treaties'? Who are the people, if not the citizens of each state? Governments negotiate treaties on behalf of their citizens; the treaties are ratified by the parliaments representing the citizens, if the authorisation is not given directly by a popular vote. Thus, the constitution-making power ultimately rests with the citizens—and so too for the European Union, acting through their respective representatives.[65] In this regard, the Union can be understood as having original authority,[66] based on a social contract between the Member States in their identity as citizens of the European Union.[67]

---

[62] A view that corresponds to the classical notion of sovereignty but has become more and more questionable, as the Czech Constitutional Court recently pointed out in its second Lisbon judgment, Case ÚS 29/09 *Lisbon II* [2009], para 147ff, English translation available at http://www.concourt.cz/file/2506.

[63] Loughlin, above n 12, 1, 19.

[64] German Constitutional Court, Case 1 BvR 201/51, BVerfGE 1, 13, 34; Case 2 BvH 1, 2/82, 2 BvR 233/82 BVerfGE 60, 175, 207; B Grzeszick, in Maunz/Dürig, *Kommentar zum Grundgesetz* (München, CH Beck, 2006) Art 20.IV, para 15–16.

[65] More detailed is Pernice, above n 19, II.2.b; Pernice et al, above n 19, 61, 68.

[66] Dashwood, above n 13, 33, 48; P Badura, 'Bewahrung und Veränderung demokratischer und rechtsstaatlicher Verfassungsstruktur in den internationalen Gemeinschaften' (1964) 34 *Veröffentlichungen der deutschen Staatsrechtslehrer*, 34, 57; HP Ipsen, *Europäisches Gemeinschaftsrecht* (Tübingen, Mohr, 1972) 58ff; A von Bogdandy and M Nettesheim, in E Grabitz and M Hilf (eds), *Kommentar zur Europäischen Union: Vertrag über die Europäische Union, Vertrag zur Gründung der Europäischen Gemeinschaft*, Article 1 EGV (München, Beck, 1994), para 9.

[67] *Cf* also Weiler, above n 61, 346, with a specific concept of 'multiple demoi'.

This constitutionalism not only distiguishes the European Union from other transnational systems; it is the basis of the functioning of the European Union. As Weiler described it in 1999: 'Constitutionalism is the DOS or Windows', the operating system of the European Union, which is the condition of effective governance in all specific policies, from the internal market to criminal law.[68] This constitutionalism was even strengthened by the Lisbon Treaty giving the Charter of Fundamental Rights the same legal value as primary law, abolishing the pillar structure and extending the direct effect of European legislation as well as judicial review to measures regarding criminal law, providing for democratic principles, a citizens' initiative, strengthening the European Parliaments and giving the national parliaments an institutional role and responsibility in the legislative process.[69]

IV A CONSTITUTION FOR THE EUROPEAN UNION?

Given that, for all these reasons, the European Union must be understood as already having a constitution, what could the adoption of a 'real' constitution, written and structured in the traditional way and using the constitutional language we are familiar with from our national constitutions, reasonably add?

A Some Questions and Opinions

During the Convention's discussion on the Constitution for Europe, this was highly controversial, even among those who advocated that the European Treaties already have a constitutional character. It could be argued that, in substance, an express constitution is simply redundant. It could be questioned whether it is possible at all to reduce the existing primary law into a single self-contained documentary constitution, which respects the organic development and complex richness of the European aquis.[70] One of the aims of making a 'real' constitution could certainly be to further simplify and clarify the constitutional law of the Union and to integrate the doctrine of the ECJ.[71] This would include clarifying what the European Union really is. Rather than representing a simple reform, a constitution would be a statement of identity, of ideals, of the type of

---

[68] Ibid 221.
[69] *Cf* also Pernice, above n 6, 349.
[70] Walker, above n 29, 149, 150.
[71] Craig, above n 12, 125, 135; R Bellamy, 'The European Constitution is dead, long live European Constitutionalism' (2006) 13 *Constellations* 181, 181. *Cf* also Dashwood, above n 13, 33, 45.

society and polity it establishes and organises.[72]

On the other hand, Weiler doubted back in 2003 that it was possible to embed the acquis in a formal constitution respecting the acquis and not converting the Union into a federal state.[73] He also rejected the idea of a new constitution. Even if legally it is still correct to speak of a constitution, after the failed attempt, the vocabulary and concept of the constitution has been deeply damaged politically. A new attempt would have to go much beyond a mere reform treaty to be accepted as a real constitution if it were not to confirm the policy of deception.[74]

Others doubt whether a new constitutional debate would reopen the dispute on how far European integration should go. As was shown in the case of the Constitution for Europe, for some, the further integration does not go far enough, whereas for others it goes too far because they think that it already takes too much power away from the Member States and threatens their identities.[75]

For Andrew Moravcsik, a new constitutional debate would not only be difficult, it would be counterproductive. He has conceded that the—failed—constitutional reform has little legal and substantive justification because the changes are minor, and not worthy of the name 'constitution'.[76] Therefore, the failure of the Constitutional Treaty was, in Moravcsik's view, not coincidental and and is irreversible. It was not so much the substance of the constitution's modest institutional reforms that attracted opposition as its style and symbolism.[77] In Moravcsik's eyes, a relaunch of the project, as proposed, for example, by Michael Zürn,[78] is doomed to failure. Rather, he proposes to depoliticise the European constitutional evolution and return to the 'Europe of results' of which Commission President Barroso has spoken.[79] But do results legitimise action if those who are concerned do not understand the system producing these results or feel themselves to be adequately participating and represented in the policies led on their behalf? Every result benefits some and leaves others behind. To find general acceptance, the rules of the game providing equal participation and equal opportunities to all must be generally accepted. This is what a constitutional settlement is about.

---

[72] Weiler, above n 2, 179, 182.

[73] JHH Weiler, 'In defence of the status quo: Europe's constitutional *Sonderweg*' in JHH Weiler and M Wind, *European Constitutionalism Beyond the State* (Cambridge, Cambridge University Press, 2003) 7ff.

[74] Weiler, above n 2, 179, 183f.

[75] Bellamy, above n 71, 181.

[76] Moravcsik, above n 61, 219, 238.

[77] Moravcsik, above n 2.

[78] M Zürn, 'Zur Politisierung der Europäischen Union' (2006) 47 *Politische Vierteljahresschrift* 242, 245–47.

[79] Moravcsik, above n 61, 219ff, 237f with reference to J M Barroso, Press Release IP 06/595, 10 May 2006, available at http://europa.eu/rapid/pressReleasesAction.do?reference=IP/06/595&format=HTML&aged=0&language=en.

Therefore, a European Constitution which takes into consideration the popular and social registers of constitutionalism, as Walker describes it,[80] is still necessary in order to fill the legitimacy and efficacy gaps. In the longer term, at the latest with the next Treaty reform, it is inevitable that some version of a thicker constitutionalism for Europe will be resurrected and the constitutional concept will be 'unabandoned'. Even if constitutionalism was originally a state-shaped and state-fitting discourse, the mere criticism on the reference to constitutionalism for the EU does not compensate the absence of any adequate conceptual alternative. Constitutionalism defines how to do politics; that means determining what is in public interest. This can be applied to the policymaking in the EU.[81] Furthermore, the 'constituency' of the European Union has changed. With the increase in European competences and implication of the citizens, the meta-democratic presumption that the European nation states alone represent the peoples in the EU is challenged and the European constituency can also be represented as a compound people alongside the discrete peoples. The consequence would be that sooner or later Europe will need a 'real' constitution.

B The Added Value of a Constitution: the Perspective of the Citizen

In order to assess the added value of a constitution, it is necessary to take the perspective of those by whom and for whom the European Union is ultimately made: the citizens. For democratic countries, as the Member States are, the establishment, development and action of the Union is and must ultimately remain based upon the will of its citizens. Expressly giving the European Union a constitution would give the primary law the name that it deserves, in conformity with the constitutional reality of the Union. It would emphasise that the citizens are at the origin of its authority, whatever may have been the way in which their will has originally been formed for establishing or joining the Union. The form of a treaty, democratically ratified by states according to their respective constitutional procedures, is not an uncommon way to make a constitution.[82]

Furthermore, the European citizens are not in general against a constitution. Polls taken in the initial years of the reform process have shown that up to 79 per cent of the citizens of the EU 25 were in favour of a Constitution for the European Union; even in Britain there was a slight

---

[80] Walker, above n 30, 137.
[81] Ibid.
[82] For the example of the United States of America see M Tushnet, *The Constitution of the United States of America: A contextual Analysis* (Oxford, Hart Publishing, 2009) 9ff. For the German constitution see K Hailbronner and M Kau, 'Constitutional Law' in M Reimann and J Zekoll (eds), *Introduction to German Law*, 2nd edn (München, Beck, 2006) 53ff.

majority.[83] However, nobody expected a text of 400 pages, a constitution clothed in an international treaty with protocols and declarations, etc. Submitting such texts to national referendums is a provocation. Eleven per cent of the citizens surveyed complained about the complexity of the draft, 20 per cent about the lack of information.[84] It was a huge surprise, therefore, that the 2004 Treaty Establishing a Constitution for Europe found such great support from the voting peoples as it did. The citizens, thus, would be in favour of a constitution.

Would it then be undemocratic to start a new initiative?[85] Would it reverse democratic principles? Even if the French and Dutch referendums could be understood as votes against the idea of a Constitution for Europe—which does not seem to be the case[86]—democracy is an open process of forming and reforming political will in a public discourse with no limits except those laid down in the constitution. This means that any issue, even if one attempt to find a solution has failed, may be brought back to the table. It is for the people to decide whether or not they are ready to think about.[87] Therefore, continuing the debate on a Constitution for Europe is not undemocratic but, rather, the opposite: living democracy.

C   What Kind of Constitution?

However, as Weiler said, giving the European Union a 'real' constitution only makes sense if it makes a difference to the existing situation. Three questions seem to be among the most important to be answered:

- Would a new constitution realise and guarantee the equal participation of all citizens?
- What are the conditions and limits set by the national constitutions concerning a European people?
- Is it possible to use the term 'constitution' without making the European Union a state?

---

[83] EOS Gallup Europe, 'The Future of the European Constitution', Flash Eurobarometer 159 (Wavre, European Commission 2004), 21ff, available at http://ec.europa.eu/public_opinion/flash/fl159_fut_const.pdf; 159/2, 29ff, available at http://ec.europa.eu/public_opinion/flash/fl159_2en.pdf.

[84] EOS Gallup Europe, 'The Future Constitutional Treaty. First Results', Special Eurobarometer 214 (2005) 15, available at http://ec.europa.eu/public_opinion/archives/ebs/ebs214_en_first.pdf. Cf Dashwood, above n 13, 33, 45.

[85] Walker, above n 30, 135f; Weiler, above n 2, 179, 183f.

[86] See only Dashwood, above n 13; Zürn, above n 78, 245–47.

[87] With regard to the Lisbon Treaty, Pernice, above n 6, 349, 359–64.

(i) The Principle of Equal Participation

John Rawls, in defining the 'justice of the constitution', requires the constitution to be a 'just procedure satisfying the requirements of equal liberty':

> The precept of one elector one vote implies, when strictly adhered to, that each vote has approximately the same weight in determining the outcome of elections. And this in turn requires, assuming single member territorial constituencies, that members of the legislature (with one vote each) represent the same number of electors.[88]

The principle of degressive proportionality governing the composition of the European Parliament is clearly contrary to the idea of equal liberty. It is also the reason why the German Federal Constitutional Court, in its judgment on the Treaty of Lisbon, does not recognise the European Parliament as an institution able to provide sufficient democratic legitimacy to European legislation and policies and accepts it only as an additional or complementary source of democratic legitimisation.[89]

However, as made clear in Article 10(2) TEU, legitimacy of EU policies is rooted not only in the directly elected European Parliament, but also in the Member States as functioning democratic states with their respective — just — constitutions. Their national governments act in the Council and are accountable to their respective national parliaments. Losses in equal participation in the European Parliament are compensated by the additional weight of the citizen's will represented at the Council. This complex, intervowen structure of the Union thusdoes not follow the constitutional logic of nation-states, but finds its own ways of fair representation. Apart from direct comparison of figures, evidence for a lack of equal liberty in the practice of the European constitution has yet to be produced. This does not prevent, however, looking for more adequate devices to achieve in a future constitution what Rawls develops as conditions for a constitution to be just.

(ii) Constitutional Limits for Creating a European People

Achieving equal liberty and participation for all citizens of the European Union at this level might create a European *demos* and thus lead to formation of a federal state. According to the German Federal Constitutional Court, however, this would substitute the subject of constitutional legitimacy and not be covered by the German Grundgesetz. Due to the irrevocable transfer of sovereignty and the loss of the right to self-determination, it

---

[88] Rawls, above n 27, 221ff.
[89] German Federal Constitutional Court, above n 15, para 271, 274.

would require the directly declared will of the German people—in other words, a new constitution.[90]

Though this argument has little foundation in the Grundgesetz, the question comes to what is the ultimate source of legitimacy of the Union and its policies. The Constitutional Court's construction is basically that it is the collective will of the respective national peoples, or, more clearly, of the Member States, which remain the masters of the Treaties. With a European people, however, legitimacy of the Union policies would have its own source, and the Member States and their peoples would slip into a secondary role.

But this conclusion is valid only on the basis of a dichotomy between the Union being either an international organisation or a state—*tertium non datur*. As explained above, the constitutional reality of the European Union is different—or *sui generis*. Citizens may have two or more political identities: with regard to European areas of competence, they are Union citizens; with regard to national politics, they are citizens of their respective Member States; and in federal states they may be Bavarian or Berlin citizens in such areas of competences that remain at the sub-state level. Thus, as the former British Foreign Secretary, Jack Straw, correctly pointed out: 'Europe simply provides a further layer of identity'.[91] Acknowledging the European identity as co-existent with the citizen's local, regional, national and European political identities, and ensuring the principle of equal liberty at each level, by no means establishes a hierarchy of legitimacy in the Union.

(iii)   Implications of Constitutional Language and Terminology

The most difficult question is the third one, which concerns language and terminology. We have no other linguistic instruments for describing the institutions, their function and powers, the decision-making processes, the interdependence between national and European levels, and the principles governing the European Union than those available from the toolbox developed for state constitutions. Yet, the use of any of these terms—democracy, legislation, fundamental rights etc, even the word constitution itself—immediately implies a reference to the state. This is what we are used to. A considerable effort of abstraction is needed to dissociate this terminology from the state and to make clear that the context in which it is used is different and that the system to which it

---

[90] Ibid, para 228.
[91] J Straw, 'A Europe for its Citizens', lecture at the Royal Institute of International Affairs, Chatham House, 27 July 2001; see also C Carter and A Scott, 'Legitimacy and Governance Beyond the European Nation State: Conceptualising Governance in the European Union'(1998) 4 *European Law Journal* 429, 442–44; in more detail, see Pernice, above n 12, 148 and idem, above n 16) 511, II.1.a.

is applied is not a state but a supranational Union with its own logic and implications.[92]

D   Guiding Principles for Drafting a Constitution for Europe

To fulfil its purposes, a Constitution for Europe deserving its name would have to be short and clear in terms and concepts in order to make it accessible for the citizens, allowing them to take ownership of what they may otherwise continue to consider being just the subjects of. Like the Treaty on the European Union—except for its provisions on foreign and security policies—it should contain open and general provisions only, all details being dealt with in organic laws separated from the constitution.[93] It should underline the complementary character and subsidiary nature of the European Union and the Member States, but m also ake clear that both levels of action, including their constitutions, are part of one intervowen system, a composed political community. It must substantiate that the citizens, not the states, are the origin and the Masters of the Union (and its constitution), and that, with regard to the formation of will and the legitimacy of European policies, the Member States, their parliaments and governments are instruments to express the collective will of their citizens at the European level, while the will of the citizens—with their European identity as citizens of the Union— finds direct expression through their representatives in the European Parliament.

Pooling sovereignty this way can thus be explained as a substantial gain in political influence and effectiveness compared to national governments only, internally as well as at the global level.

V   CONCLUSIONS

The Laeken Declaration did not intend to say that the reform process initiated in Nice should lead to a constitution for the European citizens

---

[92] This is the problem of 'translation' as described by Weiler, above n 61, 270. *Cf* also E de Wet, 'The International constitutional Order' (2006) 55 *International Comparative Law Quaterly* 51, 51, 52; A von Bogdandy, 'Zur Übertragbarkeit staatsrechtlicher Figuren auf die Europäische Union—Vom Nutzen der Gestaltidee des supranationalen Föderalismus anhand des Demokratieprinzips' in M Brenner, *Der Staat des Grundgesetzes—Kontinuität und Wandel: Festschrift für Peter Badura zum siebzigsten Geburtstag* (Tübingen, Mohr Siebeck, 2004), 1033.

[93] For proposals in this sense regarding the competencies see I Pernice, 'Eine neue Kompetenzordnung für die Europäische Union' in P Häberle, M Morlok and V Skouris (eds), *Festschrift für Dimitris Tsatsos* (Baden-Baden, Nomos, 2003) 477, 502ff. *Cf* also Zürn, above n 78, and the complete draft of F Cromme, 'Die Zukunft des Lissabon-Vertrages—Ein kurzgefasster und dynamischer Verfassungsvertrag' (Baden-Baden, Nomos, 2010).

as a first step, but it asked whether it might 'lead in the long run to the adoption of a constitutional text in the Union'.[94] The 'long run' is not finished yet. The work of the Convention and the Lisbon Treaty resulting from it was a first important achievement. Further steps need to be taken. The Constitution for the European Union is an ongoing process.

The next step would be to initiate a broad and thorough Europe-wide debate about a Constitution for the European Union of the kind described. When the debate is concluded and the public opinion is ready for a new attempt, a draft should be prepared by a constitutional convention in an open and transparent process, which should be revised and adopted by the European Council and ratified by all the Member States. It should be submitted to a Europe-wide referendum to bring it into effect. Such a Constitution for the European Union could make a real difference.

After such a process, including the preparation of the referendum, people would be more familiar with the European Union, its aims and its structures, and might be able to participate more conciously and critically in the political life of the Union, as active citizens taking ownership of their Union.

[94] See above n 1.

6

Over the Rainbow: Languages and Law in the European Union

MARGOT HORSPOOL

I INTRODUCTION

THE EUROPEAN COMMUNITY and later the European Union as a 'constitutional order of states' did not, initially, concern itself to any great extent with problems which might be caused by language difficulties of any kind. The Member States in the fifties and sixties were still confident of a principal language such as French being sufficiently generally spoken and understood in the whole of the Community, not least by those actively involved in matters concerning the Community and its institutions, to feel the need (even if the political will had been present) to designate one or more 'official' languages. In any event, the need for the presence of several languages was accepted as natural in such an entity which did not aspire to become a unitary state with the need for just one official language. The European Coal and Steel Community (ECSC) Treaty, the first Community treaty in 1952, does not contain a provision concerning languages to be used in the Community. With growing membership, and a growing number of national languages in the membership, widening of the Union took place, perhaps at the expense of its deepening. The *Staatenverbund* referred to in the Maastricht and Lisbon judgments of the German Federal Constitutional Court (FCC) has no exact translation in English, and a 'constitutional order of states' may well come closer to the entity the FCC intends to describe than other versions such as 'confederation'. Other contributions deal with this question in detail. The multitude of views as regards the exact legal and political nature of the European Union is rarely concerned with the contribution of the 'language problem' created by the initial choice of more than one or two languages and the assumption that all languages were to be treated equally for all official purposes. This linguistic regime, together with the exponential growth in numbers of languages since (to 23 currently), has shaped the development of the nature of the European

Union to an extent perhaps not apparent from official published sources. This chapter attempts to shed some light on the difficulties and merits of the choices made by institutions and Member States as regards the use of languages in the European Union.

Among the many problems that have grown over the years in the European Union, the linguistic regime is increasingly referred to. In the past, and until major enlargement of the Union occurred in 2004 and 2007, language did not play a major role in the public perception of the functioning of the European Union. It was not seen as a significant problem in the interpretation of Community law contained in the European Court of Justice rulings. In fact, the Court of Justice has, over time, developed methods of interpretation which so far have succeeded in coping successfully with multilingual texts, ranging from the development of 'Community meanings' of words and expressions commonly used in the Member States (eg the term 'workers') to the frequent use of purposive or teleological interpretation of Community legislation, moving beyond the wording of the legislation to examine its objectives. Even when the common law countries (the UK and Ireland) joined the Union in 1973 these methods used by the Court of Justice, which contrast with the favoured literal interpretation approach in the common law, continued to be used. As a result, the use of these methods has increasingly filtered through into the statutory interpretation used by national common law courts.

However, with the enlargement of the European Union by another 12 members since 2004, there has been the addition of another set of languages (from 11 pre-2004 to 23 in 2010). There is a growing awareness of the multilingual aspects of the Union and of the problems this may be causing. At the same time, as the Treaty of Lisbon evidences, there is a need to emphasise the advantages of linguistic diversity, as expressed, for example, in the third paragraph of Article 3(3) TEU, which states that the Union 'shall respect its rich cultural and linguistic diversity'. However, the need to repeat this did not seem to arise in Title X Article 167 TFEU, which does not mention languages or linguistic diversity, only diversity of cultures. The Charter of Fundamental Rights, which has become binding under the Lisbon Treaty, states (in Article 22): 'The Union shall respect cultural, religious and linguistic diversity'. Perhaps the order of the words here is significant in terms of the desire to 'play down' the linguistic element.

In January 2007, a separate portfolio that included multilingualism was developed in order to 'reflect its political dimension in the EU given its importance for initial education, lifelong learning, economic competitiveness, employment, justice, liberty and security'.[1] This contribution sets out

---

[1] Europa Memo/07/80 press release. The Commissioner for Multilingualism was for a short time the Romanian, Leonard Orban. He was succeeded in January 2010 by the Cypriot Commissioner for Education, Culture, Multilingualism and Youth, Androulla Vassiliou.

firstly to explore the origins of the multilingual regime in the European Union, the efforts to come to grips with it and the attempts (none of which were wholly successful) to restrict the growing number of languages claiming official status with increasing membership. The multilingualism of EU Institutions is in stark contrast to the problem in the European Court of Justice, where the prevailing language is French, in particular in the deliberations of the Court. Although my original remit was to confine this contribution to the European Court of Justice, I feel it is necessary to contrast developments in practical and ideological terms within the various Institutions of the Union and, more widely, within the Member States, ultimately concentrating on the European Court of Justice. Looking to the future, I ask how it is possible to continue with the present regime at both ends of the spectrum. Finally, straying further from my original remit, I include a section on the new Directive on the Rights to Interpretation and Translation in Criminal Proceedings, adopted by the European Parliament on 16 June 2010 and awaiting adoption by the Council. This appears to be a major step in the recognition of the importance on language in legal proceedings in national courts in the European Union.

A   Multilingualism in the European Union

The story is often told how the language regime in the European Communities was dictated by the interests of the original Member States. It is said that, although the original intention was to confine the languages to one (French) or at the most two (French and German), it was in fact the interests of Belgium, as much as those of the Netherlands, that made it necessary to have three, and then four, languages.[2] Belgium has three official languages, French, Dutch (Flemish) and German. German is spoken by a small minority in the east of the country, but Dutch is now spoken by a majority of Belgians and even at the time of the establishment of the first Community, the European Coal and Steel Community, Dutch was one of the two major languages of Belgium. At that time, the Flemish part of the country was the less-developed and poorer part, with few people in the top echelons of politics and business, compared to the French-speaking Walloon part of the country. This has led to a long period of conflict based on language between political parties and generally in society. The rise of the Flemish part of the country has now brought the two groups to a position of parity, with arguably a predominance of the Flemish part.

Incidentally, at the time of writing, Belgium, in spite of just having held the Presidency of the EU for six months, is threatening to split up yet again, into its component parts. The split is along language lines, and the

---

[2] French, German, Italian and Dutch, respectively.

language problem is one of the main contributors to the crisis.[3] When, therefore, the European Communities were created, it was thought that it was the Belgians who insisted on having Dutch as one of the languages. This inevitably meant that Italian had to be added as well. The first indication of the linguistic regime is after the establishment of the European Economic Community, when the Treaty of Rome entered into force in 1958.[4] The first regulation adopted in pursuance to this Treaty sets out the 'official languages and the working languages' of the EEC: Dutch, French, German and Italian.[5] However, this was not the first treaty setting up the European Communities. The Treaty of Paris establishing the ECSC in 1952 did not contain a provision regarding the official languages. Nevertheless, it had been clear from the start that the languages would be French, German, Italian and Dutch. During the arduous negotiations leading up to the eventual conclusion of the Treaty of Paris in 1952, the linguistic regime had been one of the thornier problems to resolve. In fact, it turned out to be easier to agree on the persons who were to become the members of the High Authority, with Jean Monnet as its President, than on the language regime to be adopted. Robert Schuman, the French Foreign Minister, somewhat predictably, proposed that French should be the only official language. This was opposed in particular by Konrad Adenauer, the German Chancellor. Apparently a 'Benelux Minister' proposed English as the only language. We can only speculate how different developments would have been if that eminently practical (if counterintuitive) proposal had been followed. It would have made an initial saving on the budget and would now make a considerable difference in the expenditure of the Union and hence in the individual contributions by Member States. It would speed up the procedures and publications within the Union, and accelerate the rendering of judgments by the European courts. It would have done away with the problems attached to translation, comprehension and interpretation of so many languages. On the other hand, it would perhaps have made the entire enterprise even less democratic than it is accused of being already, as active participation would have been made dependent on knowledge of a second language, then, and even more now, the preserve of a certain elite.

The discussion then returned to a level more along the lines of national interest. The pressure for Dutch came from the Dutch, supported by the Belgians (at least as regards the Flemish Dutch-speaking part, which at

---

[3] The 'Belgian problem' is too complex to comment upon further here, and is beyond the remit of this article.

[4] Art 217 of the EEC Treaty (now Art 342 TFEU) provided as follows: 'The rules governing the languages of the Institutions of the Community shall, without prejudice to the provisions contained in the rules of procedure of the Court of Justice, be determined by the Council, acting unanimously by means of regulations'.

[5] Reg 1/58 determining the languages to be used by the European Economic Community, OJ B 017, 6 October 1958, 0385–86.

the time was still the weaker partner in the country). Eventually agreement was achieved concerning the four official languages: Dutch, French, German and Italian.[6] The negotiators were all versed in more than one language and it is interesting to note that, contrary to what one might expect, the negotiations between Adenauer, de Gasperi, Monnet, Schuman, Stikker, van Zeeland and Bech took place for the major part in German, which was their common language. Far from French being the obvious choice, therefore, if the selection had been based on a language spoken by most of the Member States, it would probably have been German. Of course, this would have been a clear political impossibility at that time. It should be pointed out that until enlargement in May 2004 German was still the native language of most citizens of the Union, taking into account that Germany, Austria and Belgium have German speakers, as well as parts of Italy. It will be interesting to see how the situation will now develop, bearing in mind that in most of the accession countries German, rather than French, appears to be the second most spoken foreign language after English. Therefore, after enlargement, the predominance of French as a second foreign language in the Union may continue to lose ground. Recent information indicates that 72 per cent of EU documents are published in English, 12 per cent in French and just 3 per cent in German.[7]

Until the establishment of the two European Communities in 1957, the language question was not regarded as important enough to be enshrined in official texts, and the four languages were all used equally in meetings, although with the determination of the official seat of the ECSC in Luxembourg it became inevitable that French began to dominate. A particular influence in this respect was exercised by the situation in the European Court of Justice, where from the beginning it had been determined (albeit not in any public document) that the prevailing language would be French.[8] What happened next is well known. First, in 1973, the UK, Ireland and Denmark were the first countries to accede to the Communities, adding English and Danish to the equation. At that stage it was no longer possible to avoid the addition of Danish, although in different circumstances, if Dutch and Italian had not already been there, it would have been unlikely that Denmark would have insisted on having Danish. In 1981 Greece joined, bringing in Greek, in 1986 Spain and Portugal followed, with Spanish and Portuguese respectively, and then in 1994 Austria, Sweden and Finland joined, bringing in Swedish and Finnish. Until May 2004, therefore, the European Union operated with 11 languages. The twelfth, Gaelic, was contributed by Ireland, but this language is not a working language and is practically never used, except

---

[6] D Spierenburg and R Poidevin, *Histoire de la Haute Autorité de la Communauté Européenne du Charbon et de l'Acier* (Brussels, Bruylant, 1993) 50.
[7] Published on EurActiv, http://www.euractiv.com, 29 June 29 2010.
[8] See below, Section B.

on ceremonial occasions when Ireland has the Presidency of the Union. The Treaty texts, too, were drawn up in 12 languages. Since 1 January 2007 the texts of the Treaties have been available in all 23 languages, with each being 'equally authentic'.[9]

The concept of official languages and working languages was introduced in Article 1 of Regulation 1/1958.[10] The Council, in determining the language regime—an indication of an awareness of the importance of the issue—based the Regulation on Article 217 of the EEC Treaty, which provides for unanimous voting. It refers to 'official' and 'working' languages only in its first article. The rest of the Regulation only refers to official languages. Article 4 states that regulations 'and other documents of general application' shall be drafted in the official languages. Thus, this applies to a vast amount of Community documentation, including regulations, directives and decisions, as well as many types of non-binding documents 'of general application'. Article 6 leaves it up to the various Institutions of the Community to decide in their rules of procedure which of the languages are to be used in specific cases. To take the example of the European Court of Justice, its rules of procedure stipulate the use of any of the official languages in cases before the Court; witnesses may be authorised to use a language other than one of the official languages.[11]

On 1 May 2004, nine further languages were added to the range: Czech, Estonian, Hungarian, Latvian, Lithuanian, Maltese, Polish, Slovakian and Slovenian. On 1 January 2007 there followed the accession of Bulgaria and Romania, adding their own languages to the list. The only country's language missing in this list is that of Cyprus. Although frantic efforts were made to bring about reunification of the island, only the Greek part of Cyprus has so far been included in the expansion, so this does not add another language to the EU range. At one time, it seemed possible that reunification would occur before the date for enlargement. Referenda were called for April 2004 in both the Greek and Turkish parts of the island, but only the Turkish referendum passed and reunification did not occur.[12] In spite of accession talks with Turkey having been opened in December 2004, those talks are still ongoing and it is not looking very likely at the time of writing that Turkish accession is imminent or even possible, in view of the continuing opposition of several Member States,

[9] See Art 55 TEU.
[10] Art 1: The official languages *and the working languages* (my emphasis) of the Institutions of the Community shall be Dutch, French, German and Italian.
[11] Art 29(4) of the ECJ Rules of Procedure [1991] OJ L176/7.
[12] The plan had been a quadrilateral meeting on 23 March 2004 to take forward the talks on reunification with a view to imminent accession to the European Union on 1 May 2004. The success of these talks put forward a referendum on both the Greek and Cypriot parts of the island. This had been planned so as to enable Cyprus to enter the European Union as a unified island on 1 May 2004. However, the referendum, although resulting in a positive vote by Turkish Cyprus, resulted in a negative vote by the Greek part.

in particular France and Germany. However, other Member States are much closer to accession, such as Croatia, Macedonia and Iceland, and possibly Serbia and Montenegro, and this would add another set of languages to the total.

Although the concept of the difference between 'working language' and 'official language' has been developed further (not necessarily enshrined in any legal texts, but purely in procedural working rules), there will still be many instances where all the languages of the Union will have to be used. To begin with, high-level official documents must be translated into all the languages. This includes any texts with legal force. Apart from the text of the Treaties, the primary source of all Union law, all secondary legislation, in particular regulations and directives, will have to undergo this process. Indeed, this has already started. The same applies in matters of interpretation. To take the example of the European Parliament, the most transparent of the Union institutions, which holds all its plenary sessions and most of its committee meetings in public, the plenary sessions will always have full interpretation from and into all the official languages. All official documents are also published in all the official languages, with a different colour for each language. The rainbow has long since run out of colours to provide these.

A distinction has been drawn between 'active' and 'passive' languages. Thus, passive languages are those which may be spoken or written, but where there will be no interpretation or translation into those, as it will be assumed that the speakers of those languages will have a sufficient understanding of one of the active languages. Active languages will be those which may be both written and spoken and into which other languages will be translated. It is usually assumed to be easier to read something in a foreign language than to write in the same language. It is generally also thought easier to understand a foreign language than to speak it. In both cases (the written and the spoken word), even this may sometimes be arguable. It is certainly easier to speak, say, standard English or German to a certain level, than necessarily to understand a Scottish, Irish, Cockney or Nigerian accent, or, for that matter, the upper-class mumble or estuary English for those who were not brought up in those circles or regions. An Austrian or Bavarian accent may well cause the same difficulty for German speakers.

Various solutions have been looked at in the past and are constantly being considered. Many working documents are now routinely produced in the 'working languages'. In 1994, the French Minister of Foreign Affairs, Alain Lamassoure, citing the example of the European Trade Mark Office, which works in five languages—English, French, German, Italian and Spanish—proposed the same practice should be followed in the internal workings of the European Institutions.[13] The European Parliament, however, reacted to this by referring to Article 6 of the EC Treaty (now Article 18 TFEU), which prohibits any discrimination on grounds of nationality, and to Article 128 of the Treaty (now Article 167 TFEU), which refers to Union's duty to 'contribute to the flowering of cultures of the Member States' and, in particular to the Union's duty to 'take cultural aspects into account in its action, in particular in order to respect and to promote the diversity of its cultures'.[14]

In practice, however, many working meetings of working groups and committees in the Commission or the Council, political groups in the European Parliament and cases heard by Chambers in the European Court of Justice will use a reduced number of languages, depending on the circumstances and practical requirements. This more or less informal practice is set to grow. In respect of the spoken word, there are additional physical difficulties. Any meeting which has an 'official' character, such as Council of Ministers' sessions, and plenary sessions of the European Parliament and of the European Court of Justice of the European Union and its Grand Chamber currently employ the full panoply of languages, using simultaneous interpretation. This means that 23 interpretation booths have to be used, with considerable dimensions. This rules out many conference venues, leaving purpose-built ones in the usual venues of these meetings. One solution would be obvious here. It is often mistakenly thought that all the languages are interpreted directly from one into another, for example Greek into Danish. In fact, those who can interpret (or translate) one into the other are very few and far between. The usual practice, which has existed since the very beginning of the Communities, is that of 'relay'. A 'minor' language, such as Dutch or Danish, will be understood by a minimum of two interpreters translating into one of the 'major' languages, such as French, English or German, which is the working language of a majority of interpreters and translators. All will master at least one, and often more, of these. Interpretation, say from Danish into English, will then be picked up by all the others and translated into their respective Greek, Czech and so on. There are two dangers inherent in this system. First, it means that, say, a Greek delegate will not only receive an interpretation with a greater delay than a French delegate, but also that his or her interpreter has to rely on a colleague, rather than on the original speaker, for what is being said. The danger of 'glitches' is readily apparent and there are myriad stories of misunderstandings that have arisen through this method. In the European Parliament, where speaking time is often restricted to seconds rather than minutes, a delegate will usually beware of saying anything remotely colloquial or ambiguous, not to

---

[13] Agence Europe, 22 December 1994.
[14] Art 167(4) TFEU.

mention anecdotes, in making his or her point. An idealistic but inexperienced British MEP, speaking about the European Community 'shooting the rapids of European integration' found himself confronted by puzzled Germans and others demanding what the shooting of *Kaninchen* (rabbits) could possibly have to do with the debate. And what of the German chairman, trying desperately to get a discussion going, whose question was rendered by the slightly bored interpreter as: 'Gentlemen, who will open the bowling?', only to be faced by the sudden response from the British delegate: 'Mr Chairman, it is the football season'? It is, in fact, surprising how few these incidents are, much of which, in my view, is undoubtedly largely attributable to the great conscientiousness and professionalism of the interpreters.

It has more and more become the practice to restrict the use of active languages in the Institutions, so that many meetings will use a greater number of passive than active languages. For example six or seven, up to 11, languages will be allowed to be spoken by delegates, but will only be interpreted into four or five, typically English, French, German, Spanish and Italian. Nevertheless, by law, all plenary sessions of the European Parliament, meetings of Councils of Ministers and many others still have to use the full array of official languages. The same applies, mutatis mutandis, to the translation of documents. Article 24 TFEU provides that 'every citizen of the Union may write to any of the institutions, bodies, offices or agencies referred to in this article or in Article 13 TEU' in one of the languages of the Member States. Documents are now often translated at one remove, for example from Greek into English and from there into Danish or Hungarian. Most documents will always exist in the major 'working languages'. However, what is now occurring is that if a piece of legislation has been drafted in French and English, some of the translations will take the English text as its base (probably mostly those into the languages of the more recent Member States) and others will use the French as a base (certainly Italy and Spain, and possibly Romania). At the present time, many people are being trained as translators and interpreters in the 'new' languages. However, there are fears that the EU will face a serious shortage of interpreters within five or so years' time. Various efforts are now being made to counter this threat. EU institutions are running joint awareness campaigns to encourage young people to consider language careers in Brussels. In November 2009, a 'European Education Salon' was held in Paris to promote interest in EU language careers. Apparently, a shortage of such linguists exists in the Czech Republic and in Latvia in particular, whereas the situation in respect of English is particularly grave. The knowledge of a foreign language by native English speakers has taken a rapid dive in the last decade. One of the causes was undoubtedly the decision by the British government to abolish the compulsory teaching of a foreign language at schools after the age of fourteen. The so-called 'Paris Declaration' adopted at the International Annual Meeting on Language Arrangements, Documentation and Publications (IAMLADP) at the OECD in June 2010 warns that a 'global shortage of qualified linguists' means that without a new generation of trained language professionals 'international organisations will be unable to perform their vital tasks'.[15] One cannot help but fear that there will be great difficulties in the future unless the many already existing informal arrangements could be agreed officially and, ideally, at least the number of active languages could be reduced to a minimum. Allowing all Union languages to be used as passive languages where necessary could preserve the democratic element. However, an official arrangement regarding this would undoubtedly require unanimous agreement by all the Member States, probably by way of Treaty amendment. This does not seem likely at the present time.

A number of Union Agencies and other bodies have adopted different language regimes. An example is the language regime of the Trade Mark Office, which has not been without its problems. This is illustrated in the case of Christina Kik, a Dutch trademark agent in the Netherlands.[16] When the Office for Harmonisation in the Internal Market (Trade Marks and Designs) was set up, provision was made for it to operate in just five languages: English, French, German, Italian and Spanish. These languages were given official status, but other EU languages could be used in an application.[17] However, in such a case the applicant was required to indicate a 'second language' on their application that would be the language of any proceedings, and this 'second language' had to be one of the 'official' languages. Ms Kik made her application to register the trademark KIK in Dutch and indicated Dutch also as the 'second language'. This application was dismissed as it was 'vitiated by a procedural irregularity'. The Court of First Instance and the ECJ considered whether there was a Community law principle of non-discrimination as between the official languages of the European Community as alleged by the applicant, based on the wording of Regulation 1/58. The applicant argued that, therefore, the entire language regime established by Article 115(2)–(6) of Regulation 40/94 was unlawful. This was rejected by both courts as Regulation 1/58, being a secondary instrument of Community law, could not be held to have laid down such a general principle. The ECJ stated:

> 84. Moreover, Article 217 of the Treaty [now Article 342 TFEU] authorises the Council to determine the rules governing the languages of the institutions of the Community, acting unanimously. It was in application of that provision

---

[15] Available at http://www.npld.eu/News/Events/Pages/JuneCommissioner Vassiliou backs international declaration supporting multilingualism.

[16] Case T-120/99 *Kik v Office for Harmonisation in the Internal Market* [2001] ECR II-2235.

[17] Art 115 of Reg 40/94, [1994] OJ L11/1 provides for the language regime of the Office.

that it adopted Regulation No 1, Article 1 of which lays down the official languages and working languages of the Community institutions. Those official languages are not, it will be observed, exactly the same as those identified in Articles 8d and 248 of the Treaty.

85. Further, Regulation No 1, in particular Article 4, requires that regulations and other documents of general application be drafted in the eleven official languages of the Union. It follows from that provision, and from Article 191 of the EC Treaty [now Article 294 TFEU] requiring publication in the Official Journal of the European Union of regulations, directives, and decisions adopted in accordance with the procedure referred to in Article 189b of the EC Treaty [now, after amendment, Article 294 TFEU], read in conjunction with Article 5 of Regulation No 1, which provides for the publication of the Official Journal in the official languages, that an individual decision need not necessarily be drawn up in all the official languages, even though it may affect the rights of a citizen of the Union other than the person to whom it is addressed, for example a competing economic operator.

B The Special Linguistic Status of the Court of Justice of the European Union

The linguistic issues with regard to the Court are somewhat different from those of the other institutions. First, there is the issue of the language of the proceedings before the Court. The Rules of Procedure provide here that it is even possible to use a language which is not one of the official languages of the European Union in the oral proceedings in the examination of witnesses or experts if the Court's permission is granted.[18] To take an example: some of the Baltic states (eg Latvia) have a substantial minority population that speaks Russian. Although Latvian is the only official language, Russian can be used in court proceedings there. It is thereforewholly conceivable that an Article 267 reference from a Latvian court to the Court of Justice would require the proceedings to be conducted partially in Russian. Secondly, although not specifically stated in the Court's Statute or Rules of Procedure (which do not refer to the language used in the judges' deliberations, whilst providing for everything else in respect of the use of language—even those which are not Community languages), it is known and accepted that officially the only language used in the Court's deliberations is French. When the Court was created in 1953 the reasons for this seemed self-evident. French was still regarded as the language spoken by the elite in the Member States,

---

[18] Art 29(4) of the Rules of Procedure of the Court of Justice of the European Communities of 19 June 1991, ([1991] OJ L176/7.

it was the language most used in international discussions and debates between European jurists, and it was the language in which most legal texts and articles intended for an international audience were written. Comparative law, as understood and studied at the time in Continental Europe, concerned principally the comparison between different civil law systems, particularly those of France and Germany. The International Court of Justice (ICJ) in The Hague and the European Court of Human Rights (ECtHR) in Strasbourg both use only French and English in their deliberations. It is quite likely, therefore, that the same practice would have been followed by the Court of Justice if the UK had been one of the founder members of the Community. As it was, the Court ended up with one language only in respect of its deliberations. This led quite naturally to French being used as the general working language of the Court as the procedural rules and the grounds for judicial review in the Treaties were closely aligned on the rules in French administrative law. This was perfectly acceptable with the six founder members, where jurists generally had a mastery of French. When Denmark, Ireland and the UK joined in 1973, this became less obviously the case. However, by then the practice was entrenched and, on the whole, care was taken to appoint judges and advocates general to the Court who had a mastery of French. This was becoming more difficult, however, with the first accessions, and with the advent of Greece, Spain and Portugal the problem was somewhat aggravated though still manageable. The addition of the two Nordic countries and Austria compounded the problem. Now, however, with 12 new members, 10 of whom are Central or Eastern European, where French is not widely spoken and English is the more prevalent language, the difficulties have become more serious. The judges rarely deliberate in a plenary composition as a full Court, and chambers consisting of three or five judges hear most cases. They sit as a grand chamber of 13 judges when this is requested by an institution or a Member State which is party to the proceedings.[19] It would seem that, at least in the case of the normal hearings in chambers, there could be a choice of either an additional language (possibly English in most cases) for the deliberations or another language as the single language for the Chamber, in order to avoid having to have interpretation. It is possible that in practice the latter is already be happening to some extent.

It is interesting to speculate how influential the French filtering effect has been in practice, both in the selection of judges and advocates general and that of other Court officials, such as registrars and, in particular, judges' clerks. As the choice of the language of deliberation is in law a matter for the Court to decide, in theory a change could be made in the near future. This, however, would require unanimous agreement by the

---

[19] Art 16 of the Protocol on the Statute of the ECJ added by the Treaty of Nice.

members of the Court, just as the judgments do. This may prove difficult, not least as the retention of French as the sole language of deliberation for so long may be attributed to some extent to judicial conservatism or, very likely, to a combination of French cultural hubris and others' cultural cringe. It should be pointed out, however, that neither the ICJ nor the ECtHR seem to experience any great difficulty from the fact that their deliberations are in both French and in English, with simultaneous interpretation. Even in the Vatican, admittedly not a court but surely one of the most conservative establishments in existence, Latin, while retaining its official status, has long since been abandoned as the sole language of debate, for example in meetings of the College of Cardinals.

Thirdly, there has been abundant case law dealing with the problems of interpretation of Union law in different languages when the language versions were not entirely equal or open to misinterpretation. It is inevitable that such instances will multiply with the advent of a large number of new languages. Conversely, it is true that the Court has become extremely adept at coping with the difficulties inherent in multilingualism, and has in a number of cases set out its view of how any discrepancies between statutory texts should be dealt with. In the well-known case of *CILFIT*,[20] which instructs national courts in the concept of 'Acte Clair', the Court stated that a matter does not have to be referred to the ECJ for a preliminary ruling in the following circumstance:

> The correct application of Community law may be so obvious as to leave no scope for any reasonable doubt as to the matter in which the questions raised is to be resolved'. However, before coming to this conclusion the national court must be convinced that the matter is equally obvious to the courts of the other member states and to the ECJ.

The ECJ adds more caveats:

> This possibility must be assessed on the basis of the characteristic features of Community law, as Community legislation is 'drafted in several languages' (only seven in 1982), all equally authentic and that, even if the different language versions are 'completely in accord with one another'. Community law first of all uses terminology which is peculiar to it, secondly legal concepts do not necessarily have the same meaning in Community law and in national law,[21] and thirdly 'every provision of Community law must be placed in its context and interpreted in the light of the provisions of Community law as a whole, regard being had to the objectives thereof and to its state of evolution at the date on which the provision in question is to be applied.[22]

---

[20] Case 283/81 *CILFIT et al v Ministry of Health* [1982] ECR 3415.
[21] For example in Case 53/81 *Levin v Staatssceretaris van Justitie* [1982] ECR 1035 the ECJ defined the concept of 'worker' as a Community concept, different from that in Member States; Art 17 of the EC Treaty introduces 'Citizenship of the Union' which 'shall complement and not replace national citizenship'.
[22] *CILFIT* Para 20 of the judgment.

In the early case of *Stauder v City of Ulm*,[23] when the Community only had four languages, the Court had to deal with a decision regulating the sale of 'Christmas butter' to poor pensioners. It stipulated that Member States had to take all necessary measures to ensure that the butter reached the right recipients, and to this end the German version stated that beneficiaries had to produce a coupon bearing their name, whereas in the other (French and Italian) versions the coupon simply had to 'refer to the person concerned', thus leaving other possibilities open. Mr Stauder felt his human rights had been infringed by the divulging of his name to retailers. The Court pointed out that, for the sake of uniform interpretation of Community law, in such a case one could not look at one version in isolation but the real intention of the draftsman could only be gleaned from looking at all four language versions. In the view of the Court, not surprisingly, the most liberal interpretation had to prevail, provided that it achieved sufficiently the objective pursued by the decision. It could not be accepted that the authors' intention was to impose a stricter obligation on one Member State than on another. Case C-72/95 *Kraaijeveld v Gedeputeerde Staten van Zuid-Holland*[24] concerned the Dutch interpretation of the text of a directive which provided for environmental protection consisting of 'canalization and flood relief works'. The Dutch government, which maintained that the Dutch version for its purposes was the only authentic one, contended that its implementation of the Directive excluding dykes below a certain size from this category (5 km in length) should be accepted. This would mean no environmental impact assessment would be necessary for such a dyke. Flood relief and canalisation work is carried out to regulate water flow or for the benefit of river navigation. This changes the character of the watercourse itself and the flora and fauna in and around the river. Dyke reinforcement work does not have any such effect. The Court answered these arguments by pointing out that, as it had said in *CILFIT*,[25] interpretation of a provision of Community law involved a comparison of the language versions. In case of divergence between these, the provision should be interpreted by reference to 'the purpose and the general scheme of the rules of which it forms part'.[26] There then follows an examination of all the language versions in the annex to the directive concerned. The English and Finnish are similar ('canalization and flood relief works'), whereas the German, Greek, Spanish, French, Italian, Dutch and Portuguese versions refer to canalisation and regulation of watercourses. The Danish and Swedish versions contain one single expression reflecting the idea of regulating watercourses. The Court then wisely points out that the purpose and

---

[23] Case 29/69 *Stauder v City of Ulm* [1969] ECR 419.
[24] [1996] ECR I-5403.
[25] See n 12.
[26] Para 28 of the judgment.

general scheme of the directive indicate that it has a broad objective and that, therefore, the annex must be interpreted to encompass all works for retaining water and preventing floods, and therefore dykeworks, 'even if not all the linguistic versions are so precise'.[27]

The Court's method of interpreting Union law according to the 'purpose and the general scheme' of the provisions in question is one it uses very generally, whether there is a linguistic diversion or not, as we can see in one of the earliest, and probably the best known, of its cases, Case 26/62 *van Gend & Loos v Nederlandsche Administratie der Belastingen*,[28] where it interprets a Treaty article 'in the light of the spirit and the general scheme of the Treaty' in order to define the doctrine of direct effect of Community law, entitling individuals to rely on Community law before their national courts. A further method used by the Court for overcoming the difficulty of different meanings of the same word is to give a 'Community definition' (now, presumably, to be referred to as a 'Union' definition) of such a word, as it did, for example, in Case 53/81 *Levin v Staatssecretaris van Justitie*[29] to forge a Community meaning for the word 'worker'. Over the years, the ECJ has developed not just its own style, but undoubtedly a unique way of looking at and interpreting Union law. Although many of the features and workings of the Court have grown to resemble common law methods, and much of the Court's reasoning, not to mention its straying beyond the confines of interpretation into the realms of lawmaking and setting precedent, is often regarded by civil lawyers as resembling that of the common law judge, the principal method of statutory interpretation in the common law, to look at the literal meaning, cannot be generally used by the Court. I have mentioned only some examples of the difficulties such interpretation would cause. Nor is the interpretation necessarily that of a civil law court, which would use 'travaux préparatoires' and teleological or contextual interpretation. It borrows from all these methods, but mostly prefers its own approach, accentuating the need to balance the interests of institutions against those of Member States and/or individuals, and interpreting Union law accordingly both in respect of the place of provisions in the Treaties, their 'spirit and general scheme', weighing them with a view to balancing those interests, and giving the maximum possible effect to those legal provisions in terms of Union interests.

In the interests of legal certainty, as the Court emphasised in *CILFIT*,[30] it is concerned particularly with the uniform interpretation of Union law.

---

[27] Para 31 of the *Kraaijeveld* judgment.
[28] Case 26/62 *van Gend & Loos v Nederlandsche Administratie der Belastingen* [1963] ECR 1.
[29] [1982] ECR 1035.
[30] See above n 20.

This was apparent in Joined Cases C-261/08 and C-348/08 *Zurita García and Choque Cabrera* (judgment of 22 October 2009), referred to the Court of Justice by the Spanish Tribunal Superior de Justicia de Murcia. These cases concerned the issue whether the Convention implementing the Schengen Agreement (the CISA) and the Schengen Borders Code require the competent authorities in the Member States to adopt a decision to expel any third-country national who has been determined to be unlawfully present on the territory of a Member State. Two expulsion orders were adopted against two Bolivian nationals, Mrs Garcia and Mr Cabrera, because they were unlawfully present on Spanish territory. Article 6b of the CISA, which has now been replaced with the same wording by Article 11(3) of Regulation 562/2006, provides:

> 1. If the travel document of a third-country national does not bear an entry stamp, the competent national authorities may presume that the holder does not fulfill, or no longer fulfils, the conditions of duration of stay applicable within the Member State concerned.

> 2. This presumption may be rebutted where the third-country national provides, by any means, credible evidence such as transport tickets or proof of his or her presence outside the territory of the Member States, which shows that he or she has respected the conditions relating to the duration of a short stay.

> 3. Should the presumption referred to in paragraph 1 not be rebutted, the third-country national may be expelled by the competent authorities from the territory of the Member States concerned.

Article 23 of the CISA states:

> 1. Aliens who do not fulfill or who no longer fulfill the short-stay conditions applicable within the territory of a Contracting Party shall normally be required to leave the territories of the Contracting Parties immediately.

> 3. Where such aliens have not left voluntarily or where it may be assumed that they will not do so or where their immediate departure is required for reasons of national security or public policy, they must be expelled from the territory of the Contracting Party in which they were apprehended, in accordance with the national law of that Contracting Party. If under that law expulsion is not authorized, the Contracting Party concerned may allow the persons concerned to remain within its territory.

According to Spanish law and the interpretation thereof, the penalty imposed in such an instance is to be restricted to a fine, except where there is an additional factor which would justify replacing the fine with expulsion. The Court stated that it was clear from the interpretation of the provision by the Spanish Supreme Court (Tribunal Supremo) that any decision must be specifically reasoned and must comply with the principle of proportionality.[31] Spanish law provides for a fine to be paid unless there are additional factors which would justify expulsion. The third-country national may, however, provide credible evidence to rebut the presumption of unlawful stay and show to have compliance with the conditions relating to the duration of a short stay. Pursuant to Article 6b(3) of the CISA (now Article 11(3) of Regulation No 562/2006[32]), should the presumption not be rebutted, the third-country national *may* (my italics) be expelled by the competent authorities from the territory of the Member States concerned. It was correct, as the Commission pointed out, that there is a discrepancy between the wording of the Spanish-language version of Article 11(3) of Regulation No 562/2006 and that of the other language versions. The Spanish language stated that the competent authorities 'shall expel' the third-country national if the presumption is not rebutted, whereas in all the other language versions expulsion is an option, not an obligation for those authorities.[33]

According to its settled case law, the Court emphasised the need for uniform application and interpretation of Community law,[34] which therefore made it impossible to consider one version of the text in isolation, but requires that 'it be interpreted on the basis of both the real intention of its author and the aim he seeks to achieve, in the light, in particular, of the versions in all languages'.[35]

Thus it came to the logical conclusion that wording used in one language version of a Community provision could not serve as the sole basis for the interpretation of that provision, or be made to override the other language versions in that regard. The discretionary nature of the power of expulsion was also confirmed by the Advocate General as appearing in the Spanish language version of the Article 6b of the CISA. The Court stated that:

> In the present cases, as the Spanish-language version of Article 11(3) of Regulation No 562/2006 is the only one which diverges from the wording of the other language versions, it must be concluded that the real intention of the legislature was not to impose an obligation on the Member States concerned to expel, from their territory, third-country nationals in the event that they have not succeeded in rebutting the presumption referred to in Article 11(1), but to grant those Member States the option of so doing.[36]

It was up to the national law to lay down the basic rules, but it was clear

[31] Para 22 of the judgment.
[32] [2006] OJ L105/11.
[33] Paras 52 and 53 of the judgment.
[34] Eg in Case 29/69 *Stauder* [1969] ECR 419, para 3; Case 55/87 *Moksel Import und Export* [1988] ECR 3845, para 15; Case C 268/99 *Jany and Others* [2001] ECR I8615, para 47; and Case C 188/03 *Junk* [2005] ECR I885, para 33).
[35] Para 55 of the judgment.
[36] Para 56 of the judgment.

from the information provided to the Court in the course of the written procedure that, under national law, a decision imposing a fine was not a permit for a third-country national unlawfully present in Spain to remain legally on Spanish territory. It was also apparent that in case of failure to comply with any decision to leave, irrespective of whether the fine had been paid, a third-country national may be prosecuted under Article 53(a) of the Law on Aliens and risks being expelled with immediate effect.

The Court therefore concluded that:

> Consequently, the reply to the question referred is that Articles 6b and 23 of the CISA and Article 11 of Regulation No 562/2006 must be interpreted as meaning that, where a third-country national is unlawfully present on the territory of a Member State because he or she does not fulfil, or no longer fulfils, the conditions of duration of stay applicable there, that Member State is not obliged to adopt a decision to expel that person.[37]

This is a striking example of the difficulty which may arise with a difference in translation which is considerably more than a nuance. In this case, there was, perhaps, an advantage in having many language versions. If there is only one version that is different from all the others, this may constitute a stronger argument in favour of coming down on the side of all those other language versions. This is true, in particular, when the Court wishes to give the widest possible interpretation favouring the individual to the language in EU legislation. However, what if a number of the other language versions also contained an obligation rather than an option?[38]

Examples of such language problems are still relatively rare, but are bound to increase with the rise in the number of languages in the Union. There are many other factors which will play a role in this respect. It is not just the number of languages which will contribute, there is also an increasing danger connected with educational factors. The teaching of languages in the Union has been steadily deteriorating, and not just in the UK, although it is being felt acutely there.

C The Draft Directive on Interpretation and Translation in Criminal Proceedings

The growing awareness of linguistic problems is shown in the proposed adoption of a directive concerned with interpretation and translation in criminal proceedings. On 30 November 2009, the Justice Council adopted a roadmap for strengthening the procedural rights of suspected or accused persons in criminal proceedings. The roadmap called for the adoption of

---

[37] Para 66 of the judgment.
[38] COM(2004) 328, 28.4.2004, [2009] OJ C295/1.

five measures covering some important procedural rights, based on a 'step-by-step' approach and invited the Commission to present the necessary proposals to this end. The first measure envisaged in the roadmap, which is now being implemented, concerns the right to interpretation and translation in criminal proceedings. A draft directive was approved by the European Parliament in June 2010 and is set to be adopted by the Council under the ordinary legislative procedure. The Stockholm Programme,[39] adopted by the European Council of 10–11 December 2009, refers to the roadmap and reaffirms the importance of the rights of the individual in criminal proceedings as a fundamental value of the Union and an essential component of mutual trust between Member States and of public confidence in the EU.

The explanatory memorandum to the Directive refers to rights to translation and interpretation under the ECHR and the EU Charter. Article 5 ECHR, the right to liberty and security, states, '(2) Everyone who is arrested shall be informed promptly, in a language which he understands, of the reasons for his arrest and of any charge against him . . .'

Article 6 ECHR, the right to a fair trial, states:

> (3) Everyone charged with a criminal offence has the following minimum rights:
> (a) to be informed promptly, in a language which he understands and in detail, of the nature and cause of the accusation against him;
> . . .
> (e) to have the free assistance of an interpreter if he cannot understand or speak the language used in court.

These rights are also enshrined in the Charter of Fundamental Rights of the European Union its Articles 6 and 47–50. In particular, Article 47 guarantees the right to a fair trial, including the right to legal advice and representation; Article 48 guarantees respect for the presumption of innocence and the rights of the defence. There are a few cases concerning the use of interpretation in the ECtHR, based on Article 6. In *Luedicke, Belkacem and Koç v Germany*,[40] the ECtHR stated that the accused has the right to interpretation free of charge, even in the event of his conviction. Interpretation should be of a high enough standard to enable the defendant to have knowledge of the case against him and to defend himself.[41] The right applies to documentary material and the pre-trial proceedings. In *Brozicek v Italy*[42] the ECtHR held that the standard of interpretation must

---

[39] European Council Conclusions, 10–11 December 2009.
[40] 28 November 1978, Series A No 29. 46. The Court thus finds that the ordinary meaning of the term 'free' in Art 6 para 3(e) is confirmed by the object and purpose of Art 6. The Court concludes that the right protected by Art 6 para 3(e) entails, for anyone who cannot speak or understand the language used in court, the right to receive the free assistance of an interpreter, without subsequently having claimed back from him payment of the costs thereby incurred.
[41] *Kamasinski v Austria*, 19 December 1989, A Series No 168.
[42] *Brozicek v Italy*, App No 10964/84, judgment of 19 December 1989, [1989] ECHR 23.

be 'adequate' and that details of the charge must be given to the person in a language that he understands. It is for the judicial authorities to prove that the defendant speaks the language of the court adequately and not for the defendant to prove he does not.[43] *Cuscani v UK*[44] is a case from the UK, where the trial judge at Newcastle Crown Court, confronted with an Italian-speaking defendant who had asked for an interpreter and whose command of English was clearly totally inadequate, asked whether anyone in court who knew the applicant was fluent in both English and Italian and could act as an interpreter for the applicant. The applicant's counsel, without consulting his client, pointed out that the applicant's brother was present, and the court agreed to make use of him, if need be. The applicant's brother was never requested to translate any statement during the course of the proceedings. It subsequently transpired that the brother had a lesser command of the English language than the defendant. The interpreter must be competent and the judge must safeguard the fairness of the proceedings.

The proposed Directive[45] provides for rights to interpretation and translation in criminal proceedings in EU countries. It specifically refers to cases brought under the European Arrest Warrant, which has shown the need for such a measure. The legal basis for the directive is Article 82(2) TFEU, which now provides for the ordinary legislative procedure to be used. The Article calls for minimum rules to be drawn up, of which this Directive is the first. Its provisions cover such matters as offering training to judges, lawyers and prosecutors, police and other relevant court staff,[46] and allows for a higher level of protection as these are only minimum rules. On the face of it, this measure provides for something which should be greatly welcomed, as some of the cases referred to above show. It builds on some initiatives taken by the Commission, such as a report with recommendations on the quality of interpretation and translation published in 2008 which include a curriculum in legal interpreting and a system of accreditation, certification and registration for legal interpreters, as well as the launch of an initiative for a master's degree in translation (EMT), using a network of existing programmes in legal translation at master's level throughout the EU.[47] The Recital of the draft[48] contains two alter-

---

[43] '41 . . . the Italian judicial authorities should have taken steps to comply with it so as to ensure observance of the requirements of Article 6 § 3 (a) (art 6–3-a), unless they were in a position to establish that the applicant in fact had sufficient knowledge of Italian to understand from the notification the purport of the letter notifying him of the charges brought against him. No such evidence appears from the documents in the file or the statements of the witnesses heard on 23 April 1989. On this point there has therefore been a violation of Article 6 § 3 (a) (art 6–3-a)'.

[44] *Cuscani v UK*, App No 3277/96, judgment of 24 September 2002.

[45] COM(2010)82/3 2010/0050 (COD).

[46] Art 5(2) and point 17 of the Recital.

[47] See points 17 and 18 of the Explanatory Memorandum.

[48] At 22.

native statements which provide for either an 'opt-in' or a maintenance of the 'opt-out' contained in Protocol 4 on the position of the UK and Ireland in respect of the area of freedom, security and justice annexed to the TFEU and a further statement that Denmark, under its Protocol annexed to the TFEU, is not taking part in the adoption of the Directive. It would seem unfortunate if the UK and/or Ireland would choose not to take part and it is to be regretted that Denmark will not take part either. This is a measure which appears to provide purely for the exercise of an individual's basic linguistic rights in criminal proceedings. A decision by the UK not to take part in this may well be taken on grounds of cost,[49] although the justification might well be that the system in place in the UK at present exceeds the requirements of the Directive. Such a decision could considerably diminish the effectiveness of the measure.

D   What of the Future?

Can a sensible solution be found for the problems described above? There is a need to strike a balance between democratic and cultural needs for multilingualism and practical and realistic considerations of language in a world which is increasingly 'globalised' and where the general language of communication is often inevitably English, in the use of computers, email and much else. This would call for concessions on the part of Member States which may be politically difficult to make, but should not be impossible if a realistic attitude prevails over outdated procedures and if, in particular, economic considerations are sensibly balanced against the basic human rights of individuals.

With the continuing expansion of the European Union, who knows how many languages will be 'official' languages in, say, 20 or 30 years' time? A number of 30, or even 35, languages would not appear to be fanciful. It is true to say that in the nearly 60 years which have elapsed since the first Community (ECSC) was established, when just four languages were used, the steady growth in numbers has been accommodated in various ways and by various methods without causing quite the enormous problems which one could have imagined. At first, the distinct impression was for a long time that the issue was simply being ignored, or at least dismissed as not important. Regulation 1/1958 only appeared after the establishment of the EEC, albeit as the first regulation. More recently, with the promotion of 'linguistic diversity' and the inclusion of language as part of a Commissioner's portfolio, the emphasis has been more on the

---

[49] Art 4 provides that Member States shall cover the costs of interpretation and translation irrespective of the outcome of the proceedings.

protection of minority languages in the European Union than on facing the issue of the official languages.

However, much of the practical side of the problem has been tackled by internal arrangements within the institutions without any binding rules ever being drawn up. It should not be forgotten that the EU has only ever been able to function as well as it has through the mutual co-operation and consensus between the Member States and institutions. Much of the legislation of the EU has been, and still is, passed by consent of all the Member States, something which is not always immediately realised by students studying the law of the European Union. It is not in the interest of institutions or Member States to propose, or try to pass, laws which Member States will simply try to avoid implementing, or even applying when they are implemented. It is, perhaps, a manifestation of the existence of a spirit of consensus in a constitutional order of states which transcends the character of a loose conglomerate of countries or even just a customs union concluded with purely national economic interests in mind, even if their interests still tend to converge based on national considerations. The Union's reactions to shocks such as the credit crisis in 2009 and the sudden realisation of the immigration issues arising from additional membership of what may be like-minded countries, but not countries with sometimes even approximately the same level of economic development, tend to show up the fault lines in the existing order. Even there, however, it would seem that a consensus often tends to emerge, perhaps not necessarily in every detailed action, but in a broader spectrum. The same kind of consensus may be able to persist as to the use of languages, determining numbers as and when convenient and according to the varying needs of institutions and agencies. Nevertheless, such informal arrangements must reach their limits somewhere. The number of translators and interpreters inside the EU institutions rises exponentially with each addition of a new language. Buildings to contain ever larger numbers of translators (or can it all be done online eventually?) and, even more ludicrously, ever larger numbers of interpreters in ever larger interpreters' booths would add an intolerable burden to the Union's building budget.

It would appear that the dilemma will have to be faced sooner rather than later.

Part II
Judicial Fabric

7

The Court of Justice as a Constitutional Adjudicator

ELEANOR SHARPSTON and GEERT DE BAERE*

I INTRODUCTION

T HIS CHAPTER EXAMINES the role of the Court of Justice of the European Union (the Court of Justice, or the Court) as an adjudicator in a specific category of cases raising constitutional issues. What are we to understand by the Court of Justice acting as a 'constitutional adjudicator'? This chapter does not endeavour to settle the debate if and to what extent the Court of Justice can be described as a constitutional court. That debate presupposes the settlement of a logically prior question, namely what a constitutional court is and, more specifically, what sort of disputes need to fall within a court's jurisdiction for it to merit the epithet 'constitutional'. A cursory look at the courts in the Member States bearing that title will reveal the usual unity in diversity, with quite a large helping of the latter, and such is even more the case if third countries are also examined.[1] This chapter therefore contents itself with the position that, at least in a number of respects, the Court of Justice can be so described.[2]

* The first author is Advocate General at the Court of Justice of the European Union. No views expressed in this study can be ascribed to the institution in which she serves. The second author is assistant professor of international law and EU law at the Faculty of Law and the Leuven Centre for Global Governance Studies, Katholieke Universiteit Leuven. Many thanks to Dr Tim Corthaut, Dr Kathleen Gutman and Dr Alicia Hinarejos for their comments and suggestions, to Dr Alexander Kornezov for valuable discussions on the topic, and to Ms Cath Hardle for proofreading. The usual disclaimer applies.
    [1] See, eg the list of links to constitutional courts and equivalent bodies on the website of the 'European Commission for Democracy through Law', better known as the 'Venice Commission' (ie the Council of Europe's advisory body on constitutional matters): available at http://www.venice.coe.int/site/dynamics/N_court_links_ef.asp?L=E.
    [2] In that sense, see, eg FG Jacobs, 'Is the Court of Justice of the European Communities a Constitutional Court?' in DM Curtin and D O'Keeffe (eds), *Constitutional Adjudication in European Community and National Law: Essays for the Hon. Mr. Justice O'Higgins* (Dublin, Butterworth, 1992) 25–32; A Dashwood and A Johnston, 'Synthesis of the Debate' in A Dashwood and A Johnston (eds), *The Future of the Judicial System of the European Union* (Oxford, Hart Publishing, 2001) 55–83; A Hinarejos, *Judicial Control in the European Union* (Oxford, Oxford University Press, 2009) 1–13.

It is over 20 years since the Court of Justice first held that the former EC Treaty, albeit concluded in the form of an international agreement, nonetheless constitutes the constitutional charter of a Community based on the rule of law.[3] It seems clear that that qualification can now be extended to both the EU Treaty and the FEU Treaty. Following the changes brought about by the Lisbon Treaty, both are not only of the same legal value,[4] but are also in principle subject to the jurisdiction of the Court.[5] Strictly speaking, therefore, the Court of Justice acts as a constitutional adjudicator every time it ensures that in the interpretation and application of the Treaties the law is observed.[6] This chapter focuses on one of the clearest examples of the Court performing a constitutional function,[7] namely the Court's role in adjudicating on the horizontal and vertical division of competences, viz that between the various institutions of the Union, and between the Member States and the Union, respectively. The Court itself has confirmed its constitutional role in that respect by holding that the choice of the appropriate legal basis has constitutional significance, since, having only conferred powers, the Community (now Union) must tie

---

[3] Case 294/83 *Parti écologiste 'Les Verts' v European Parliament* [1986] ECR 1339, para 23. See, later, Opinion 1/91 *Draft agreement between the Community, on the one hand, and the countries of the European Free Trade Association, on the other, relating to the creation of the European Economic Area* [1991] ECR I-6079, para 21 and, most recently, Joined Cases C-402/05 P and C-415/05 P *Kadi and Al Barakaat International Foundation v Council and Commission* [2008] ECR I-6351, para 81. See further K Lenaerts, 'The Basic Constitutional Charter of a Community Based on the Rule of Law' in M Poiares Maduro and L Azoulai (eds), *The Past and Future of EU Law* (Oxford, Hart Publishing, 2010) 295–315. But see Case 101/78 *Granaria* [1979] ECR 623, para 5, where the Court held that 'respect for the principle of the rule of law within the Community context entails for persons amenable to Community law the right to challenge the validity of regulations by legal action'.

[4] See the third para of Art 1 TEU and Art 1(2) TFEU. Unless otherwise indicated, references to the EU Treaty are to its post-Lisbon incarnation. A reference to an article of the old EU Treaty will be preceded by 'ex-'. What before Lisbon was known as the 'Community method' and 'Community external relations' will, in their post-Lisbon forms, be referred to as the 'ordinary Union method' and the 'the ordinary external relations of the Union', respectively. See also G De Baere, 'The Framework of EU External Competences for Developing the External Dimensions of EU Asylum And Migration Policy' in M-C Foblets, J Wouters, D Vanheule, Ph Debruycker, N Smith and M Maes (eds), *The External Dimension(s) of EU Asylum and Migration Policy* (Brussels, Bruylant, forthcoming 2010).

[5] With the notable exception (apart from monitoring compliance with Art 40 TEU and reviewing the legality of decisions providing for restrictive measures against natural or legal persons) of the common foreign and security policy (CFSP): see the second paragraph of Art 24(1) TEU and Art 275 TFEU.

[6] As per Art 19(1) TEU. Advocate General Poiares Maduro emphasises the connection between the Community as an autonomous legal order and the Court's role as a constitutional court: 'The EC Treaty, by contrast [with the European Convention on Human Rights], has founded an autonomous legal order, within which States as well as individuals have immediate rights and obligations. The duty of the Court of Justice is to act as the constitutional court of the municipal legal order that is the Community': Opinions in *Kadi and Al Barakaat*, above n 3, point 37.

[7] See, eg Jacobs, above n 2, 25–32; K Lenaerts, 'The Rule of Law and the Coherence of the Judicial System of the European Union' (2007) 44 *Common Market Law Review* 1651–1652.

each measure to a Treaty provision which empowers it to approve such a measure.[8] The choice of legal basis and its constitutional significance was also the subject of Professor Dashwood's famous inaugural lecture upon accepting the chair of European Law at the University of Cambridge.[9] It therefore seems a fitting topic for the present contribution.

This chapter will analyse a number of recent cases in which Professor Dashwood has acted as counsel for the UK, all of which show the Court in its constitutional role adjudicating on the vertical and/or horizontal division of competences within the Union.[10] First, however, we briefly examine the principle of conferral, which underlies any discussion of the vertical and horizontal division of competences.

II THE PRINCIPLE OF CONFERRAL

The principle of conferral[11] is one of the cornerstones of the EU legal order.[12] Pursuant to Article 5 TEU, under the principle of conferral,

> the Union shall act only within the limits of the competences conferred upon it by the Member States in the Treaties to attain the objectives set out therein. Competences not conferred upon the Union in the Treaties remain with the Member States.

---

[8] See Case C-370/07 *Commission v Council (CITES)* [2009] ECR I-8917, para 47 and, to that effect, Opinion 1/08 *Competence of the European Community to conclude with certain members of the WTO agreements modifying the Schedules of Specific Commitments of the Community and its Member States under the GATS (GATS Schedules)* [2009] ECR I, para 110 and Opinion 2/00 *Cartagena Protocol on Biosafety (Cartagena Protocol)* [2001] ECR I-9713, para 5.

[9] A Dashwood, 'The Limits of European Community Powers' (1996) 21 *European Law Review* 113.

[10] Opinion 1/03 *Competence of the Community to conclude the new Lugano Convention on jurisdiction and the recognition and enforcement of judgments in civil and commercial matters (New Lugano Convention)* [2006] ECR I-1145; *GATS Schedules*, above n 8; Case C-178/03 *Commission v Parliament and Council (Rotterdam Convention II)* [2006] ECR I-107; Case C-91/05 *Commission v Council (Small Arms and Light Weapons)* [2008] ECR I-3651; *Kadi and Al Barakaat*, above n 3; and Case C-411/06 *Commission v Parliament and Council (Basel Convention)* [2009] ECR I-7585. For a lively account of the role of counsel before the Court of Justice, see D Vaughan and M Gray, 'Litigating in Luxembourg and the Role of the Advocate at the Court of Justice' in A Arnull, P Eeckhout and T Tridimas (eds), *Continuity and Change in EU Law. Essays in Honour of Sir Francis Jacobs* (Oxford, Oxford University Press, 2008) 48–69.

[11] As used in Art 5(1) and (2) TEU. Various synonyms have been used in the Treaties, by the Court or in the literature, eg 'principle of conferral of powers' (Art 7 TFEU), the 'principle of conferred powers' (Opinion 2/94 *Accession by the Communities to the Convention for the Protection of Human Rights and Fundamental Freedoms (ECHR Accession)* [1996] ECR I-1759, para 24) or 'the attribution principle' (Dashwood, above n 9, 116).

[12] As well as, indeed, of the law of international organisations: CF Amerasinghe, *Principles of the Institutional Law of International Organizations*, 2nd edn (Cambridge, Cambridge University Press, 2005) 161 *et passim*; D Sarooshi, *International Organizations and Their Exercise of Sovereign Powers* (Oxford, Oxford University Press, 2005).

Specifically as regards the Court of Justice, that principle implies that it exercises only the jurisdiction conferred on it by the Treaties. Other cases involving Union law fall within the jurisdiction of the courts of the Member States, which function both as the 'juges de droit commun' in the Union legal order[13] and as the 'powerhouse' of European Union law.[14] More generally, the principle of conferral implies that the EU is incapable of extending its own competences, and that it does not have general lawmaking capacity. All Union measures[15] therefore require a legal basis in the Treaties. According to settled case law, the choice of that legal basis must be based on objective factors that are amenable to judicial review.[16] Moreover, the obligation to indicate the legal basis of a measure is related to the duty to state reasons under Article 296 TFEU: a measure subject to the latter duty is equally subject to the former obligation.[17]

Does every Union measure require a single legal basis? Not necessarily. If examination of a Union measure reveals that it pursues a twofold purpose or that it has a twofold component, and if one of those is identifiable as the main or predominant purpose or component whereas the other is merely incidental, the act must be based on a single legal basis, namely that required by the main or predominant purpose or component. Exceptionally, if it is established that an act simultaneously pursues a number of objectives or has several components that are indissociably linked, without one being secondary and indirect in relation to the other, such an act will have to be founded on the various corresponding legal

[13] Lenaerts, above n 7, 1625, 1645 and 1659. For an account of pluralist constitutional adjudication as an interaction between the Court of Justice and Member State constitutional courts see E Cloots, 'Germs of Pluralist Judicial Adjudication: *Advocaten voor de Wereld* and other References from the Belgian Constitutional Court' (2010) 47 *Common Market Law Review* 645. See, eg the Order of the German Bundesverfassungsgericht of 6 July 2010 (2 BvR 2661/06), in which, referring to its *Lisbon* judgment of 30 June 2009 (2 BvE 2/08, 2 BvE 5/08, 2 BvR 1010/08, 2 BvR 1022/08, 2 BvR 1259/08 and 2 BvR 182/09), it held that ultra vires review of EU acts could only be considered if a breach of competence on the part of the EU and its institutions were to be sufficiently qualified, and that the ECJ had not violated its competences by virtue of the outcome found in the *Mangold* judgment (Case C-144/04 *Mangold* [2005] ECR I-9981) in a sufficiently qualified manner.
[14] See D Edward, 'National Courts—the Powerhouse of Community Law' (2002–03) 5 *Cambridge Yearbook of European Legal Studies* 1. See also the second subparagraph of Art 19(1) TEU: 'Member States shall provide remedies sufficient to ensure effective legal protection in the fields covered by Union law'. On the possible implications of this provision for judicial protection see T Corthaut, 'Plus ça change, plus c'est la meme chose? A Comparison with the Constitutional Treaty' (2008) 15 *Maastricht Journal of European and Comparative Law* 29.
[15] See, nonetheless, Art 352 TFEU (ex-Art 308 TEC): 'If action by the Union should prove necessary, within the framework of the policies defined in the Treaties, to attain one of the objectives set out in the Treaties, *and the Treaties have not provided the necessary powers*, the Council, acting unanimously on a proposal from the Commission and after obtaining the consent of the European Parliament, shall adopt the appropriate measures' (emphasis added).
[16] See *GATS Schedules*, above n 8, para 172 and the cased-law cited there.
[17] *CITES*, above n 8, paras 38–40.

bases. [18] However, in accordance with the *Titanium dioxide* line of case law, recourse to a dual legal basis is not possible where the procedures laid down for each legal basis are incompatible with each other or where the use of two legal bases is liable to undermine the rights of the European Parliament.[19] We examine the application of these principles further in the section on the horizontal division of competences.

The principle of conferral applies as much to external action as to internal action of the Union,[20] and determines both the vertical and horizontal division of competences.[21] In other words, it determines whether the Union has competence to act and, if so, which institution can act in accordance with which procedure. The institutional aspect of the principle of conferral is explicitly confirmed in Article 13(2) TEU, according to which each institution is to 'act within the limits of the powers conferred on it in the Treaties, and in conformity with the procedures, conditions and objectives set out in them'.[22] Indeed, the institutional aspect of conferral has a longer pedigree in the EC Treaty than the general principle of conferral. The second subparagraph of the original Article 4(1) of the EEC Treaty already set out the principle in similar words to those that can now be found in Article 13(2) TEU, while Article 5 TEC, which introduced the general principle of conferral into the EC Treaty, was only added at Maastricht.

Both the EU as an organisation and the different institutions within the EU therefore only have those competences explicitly or impliedly conferred on them by the Treaties. Hence, the precise delineation of the vertical and horizontal division of competences is of the utmost constitutional importance. The Court took pains to explain the difference between vertical and horizontal division of competences in its judgment in the *Personal Data*

---

[18] *Basel Convention*, above n 10, paras 46–47 and the case law cited there.

[19] See Case C-300/89 *Commission v Council* (*Titanium dioxide*) [1991] ECR I-2867, paras 17–21; *Rotterdam Convention II*, above n 10, para 57; and Case C-155/07 *Parliament v Council* [2008] ECR I-8103, para 37 and the case law cited there.

[20] *ECHR Accession*, above n 11, para 24. See *Cartagena Protocol*, above n 8, para 5: 'The choice of the appropriate legal basis has constitutional significance. Since the Community has conferred powers only, it must tie the [international agreement in question] to a Treaty provision which empowers it to approve such a measure. To proceed on an incorrect legal basis is therefore liable to invalidate the act concluding the agreement and so vitiate the Community's consent to be bound by the agreement it has signed.' See further G De Baere, *Constitutional Principles of EU External Relations* (Oxford, Oxford University Press, 2008) 9–11.

[21] See, to that effect, *CITES*, above n 8, paras 46–48.

[22] This is followed by a stipulation that the institutions are to 'practice mutual sincere co-operation', which the Court of Justice had already made clear in Case 204/86 *Greece v Council* [1988] ECR 5323, para 16, and confirmed in Case C-65/93 *European Parliament v Council* [1995] ECR I-643, para 23. See also the Opinion of Advocate General Léger in Joined Cases C-317/04 and C-318/04 *European Parliament v Council and Commission* [2006] ECR I-4721, point 272.

Protection case.[23] There, the Court held that that the question of the 'areas of competence' of the European Union presents itself differently, depending on whether the competence in issue has already been accorded to the European Union in the broad sense or has not yet been accorded to it.

> In the first hypothesis, it is a question of ruling on the division of areas of competence within the Union and, more particularly, on whether it is appropriate to proceed [in the circumstances of the case] by way of a directive based on the EC Treaty or by way of a framework decision based on the EU Treaty. By contrast, in the second hypothesis, it is a question of ruling on the division of areas of competence between the Union and the Member States and, more particularly, on whether the Union has encroached on the latter's areas of competence.[24]

We believe, however, that it is more logical to examine these two hypotheses in reverse order. First, can the Union act at all? Secondly (if it can), under which precise competence may it do so and through which institutions? That said, the distinction between whether the Union can act and, if so, on what legal basis is useful mostly for analytical purposes. In practical terms, the two questions will often be dealt with simultaneously. We base our analysis on cases in which Professor Dashwood has acted as counsel and has thereby contributed to the exercise by the Court of its role as a constitutional adjudicator, viz the *New Lugano Convention* and *GATS Schedules* Opinions, and the *Rotterdam Convention*, *Small Arms and Light Weapons*, *Kadi and Al Barakaat* and *Basel Convention* cases.[25] Broadly speaking, all those cases raise issues as regards both the vertical and the horizontal division of competences. However, depending on the section in which they feature, they are here discussed only in relation to one or other aspect. Finally, it is no coincidence that most, if not all, of these cases concern the external relations of the EU. That is because battles concerning the vertical and horizontal division of competence are waged with particular antagonism when it comes to establishing who is allowed to act on the international scene and to what extent. It is therefore often in those areas that the Court is asked to act as a constitutional adjudicator or, in the words of a famous US constitutionalist, to 'umpire the federal system'.[26] Another good reason for choosing examples from external relations law is that it is one of the 'chasses préférées' of Professor Dashwood, as is evident not only from the fact that he was chosen to

---

[23] Case C-301/06 *Ireland v Parliament and Council (Personal Data Protection)* [2009] ECR-593.
[24] Ibid, para 56.
[25] Above n 10.
[26] PA Freund, 'Umpiring the Federal System' (1954) 54 *Columbia Law Review* 561.

act as counsel in each of the cases analysed, but also from his numerous scholarly writings on the matter.[27]

III VERTICAL DIVISION OF COMPETENCES

As a constitutional principle, the principle of conferral incorporates the idea, fundamental not only in the law of international organisations but also in the constitutional law of many federal states, that the Union only has those competences that the Member States have explicitly or impliedly conferred on it in the Treaties. Indeed, the second sentence of Article 5(2) TEU now explicitly confirms that residuary competences therefore belong to the Member States. That does not, however, mean that the principle of conferral is only there to safeguard the Member States' competences. The obverse of that coin is that competences once conferred on the Union cannot be repatriated to the Member States without amending the Treaties. That said, the principle tends to be viewed in terms of protecting the competences of the Member States against encroachment by the Union.[28] That was indeed the prism through which Professor Dashwood looked at the issue in his inaugural lecture at Cambridge. Famously describing the then Community as 'a constitutional order of states', he argued that it was of the essence of such an order that the powers exercisable at the centre be clearly demarcated, and that it should only be possible to extend those powers further with the explicit consent of the Member States, reached in accordance with each one's constitutional requirements.[29]

Has the Court managed to live up to those standards? To answer that question, we turn to examine its two most recent Opinions delivered on the basis of what is now Article 218(11) TFEU (ex-Article 300(6) TEC): the *New Lugano Convention* and *GATS Schedules* Opinions.

---

[27] Examples include 'External Relations Provisions of the Amsterdam Treaty' (1998) 35 *Common Market Law Review* 1019; 'The Attribution of External Relations Competence' in A Dashwood and C Hillion (eds), *The General Law of EC External Relations* (London, Sweet & Maxwell, 2000) 115–38; 'Opinion 2/00, Cartagena Protocol on Biosafety' (2002) 39 *Common Market Law Review* 353; 'Art 47 TEU and the relationship between first and second pillar competences' in A Dashwood and M Maresceau (eds), *Law and Practice of EU External Relations. Salient Features of a Changing Landscape* (Cambridge, Cambridge University Press, 2008) 70–103; 'Mixity in the Era of the Treaty of Lisbon' in C Hillion and P Koutrakos (eds), *Mixed Agreements Revisited* (Oxford, Hart Publishing, 2010) 351–66.
[28] See K Gutman, 'The Constitutionality of European Contract Law. Comparative Reflections with the United States', PhD dissertation, University of Leuven (2010) 303. We acknowledge, of course, that federalism as the division of competences between the Union and the Member States (or, more generally, the federal level and the federal entities) cannot be reduced to the principle of conferral alone: see K Lenaerts, 'Federalism and the Rule of Law: Perspectives from the European Court of Justice' (2010) 33 *Fordham International Law Journal* 1339.
[29] Dashwood, above n 9, 114.

A   The *New Lugano Convention* Opinion

The request for an Opinion concerned the exclusive or shared Community competence to conclude the new convention on jurisdiction and the recognition and enforcement of judgments in civil and commercial matters intended to replace the existing Lugano Convention.[30] In the course of the procedure leading up to the *New Lugano Convention* Opinion, the UK invited the Court to reconsider its decision in *Commission v Denmark*[31] that the scope of Community common rules may be affected or distorted by a Member State's international commitments where these commitments fall within an area which is already largely covered by such rules. In the latter case, Member States may not enter into international commitments outside the framework of the Community institutions even if there is no contradiction between those commitments and the common rules.[32] The UK argued that this test is neither clear nor precise, 'which gives rise to uncertainty and is unacceptable when it comes to limiting the competences of the Member States, whereas according to the first paragraph of Article 5 EC the Community enjoys conferred powers only'.[33] Abandoning that test, the UK concluded, 'would give greater precision in defining an *ERTA* effect whilst ensuring that the Member States fulfil their duty of loyal

[30] The following account of the *New Lugano Convention* Opinion draws on De Baere, above n 20, 47–51.

[31] Case C-467/98 *Commission v Denmark* [2002] ECR I-9519, para 82. This is one of the so-called *Open Skies* cases concerning infringement proceedings brought by the Commission against several Member States with respect to various breaches of Community law arising from the conclusion by those Member States of bilateral air transport agreements with the US: Case C-466/98 *Commission v United Kingdom* [2002] ECR I-9427; Case C-468/98 *Commission v Sweden* [2002] ECR I-9575; Case C-469/98 *Commission v Finland* [2002] ECR I-9627; Case C-471/98 *Commission v Belgium* [2002] ECR I-9681; Case C-472/98 *Commission v Luxembourg* [2002] ECR I-9741; Case C-475/98 *Commission v Austria* [2002] ECR I-9797; Case C-476/98 *Commission v Germany* [2002] ECR I-9855. See further R Holdgaard, 'The European Community's Implied External Competence after the Open Skies Cases' (2003) 8 *European Foreign Affairs Review* 365. The Court confirmed its approach in the 2002 *Open Skies* judgments in Case C-523/04 *Commission v Netherlands* [2007] ECR I-3267.

[32] *New Lugano Convention*, above n 10, para 46. This is a rendering of the so-called ERTA principle, which follows the logic of the principle of primacy: the Member States are not allowed to act internationally in a way that would affect existing EU law, because the situation cannot be remedied by merely disapplying the infringing national rule. The Member States' competence is thus excluded, which necessitates the existence of European Union competences to compensate for the Member States' inability to act (Case 22/70 *Commission v Council (ERTA)* [1971] ECR 263, para 17). That principle is now codified in Art 216(1) TFEU: 'The Union may conclude an agreement with one or more third countries or international organisations . . . where the conclusion of an agreement . . . is likely to affect common rules or alter their scope' and in Art 3(2) TFEU, which provides that the Union is to have exclusive competence for the conclusion of an international agreement 'insofar as its conclusion may affect common rules or alter their scope'. See De Baere, above n 4.

[33] *New Lugano Convention*, above n 10, para 47. Most of the Member State governments that submitted observations to the Court sought clarification of the case law arising from the *ERTA* judgment and supported the position taken by the UK (para 48).

co-operation when acting in the international sphere'.[34]

The Court, however, was not persuaded. It pointed out that what seemed to be general principles in *Commission v Denmark* were in fact 'only examples, formulated in the light of the particular contexts with which the Court was concerned'.[35] The Court then ruled 'in more general terms' that it had

> found there to be exclusive Community competence in particular where the conclusion of an agreement by the Member States is incompatible with the unity of the Common Market and the uniform application of Community law . . ., or where, given the nature of the existing Community provisions, such as legislative measures containing clauses relating to the treatment of nationals of non-member countries or to the complete harmonisation of a particular issue, any agreement in that area would necessarily affect the Community rules within the meaning of the ERTA judgment.[36]

The Court did, however, emphasise the importance of the principle of conferral; and pointed out that any competence, especially if it is exclusive or implied,

> must have its basis in conclusions drawn from a specific analysis of the relationship between the agreement envisaged and the Community law in force and from which it is clear that the conclusion of such an agreement is capable of affecting the Community rules.[37]

The Court also introduced the idea that there can be an *ERTA* effect where common rules constitute a system the integrity of which is liable to be compromised if Member States exercise their competences autonomously with respect to the agreement in question. It emphasised that it is essential to ensure a uniform and consistent application of the Community rules and the proper functioning of the system they establish in order to preserve the full effectiveness of Community law.[38] A comprehensive and detailed analysis must be carried out to determine the existence and nature of the Community's competence to conclude an international agreement. In doing so, account must be taken not only of the 'area' covered by the Community rules and by the provisions of the agreement envisaged, but also of the nature and content of those rules and those provisions, 'to ensure that the agreement is not capable of undermining the uniform and consistent application of the Community rules and the proper functioning of the system which they establish'.[39] The Court concluded that the Community rules on the recognition and enforcement of judgments are

---

[34] Ibid, para 48.
[35] Ibid, para 121.
[36] Ibid, para 122.
[37] Ibid, para 124.
[38] Ibid, para 128.
[39] Ibid, para 133.

indissociable from those on the jurisdiction of courts, with which they form a unified and coherent system; and that the new Lugano Convention would affect the uniform and consistent application of the Community rules as regards both the jurisdiction of courts and the recognition and enforcement of judgments and the proper functioning of the unified system established by those rules. It followed that the Community had exclusive competence to conclude the new Lugano Convention.[40]

In the *New Lugano Convention* Opinion, the Court may potentially have extended the scope of the Community's exclusive external competences.[41] It is now clear that common rules could be affected or distorted 'in any event within an area which is already largely covered by [common] rules' and that this gives rise to exclusive Community competence. It remains far less clear, however, from what moment an area is deemed to be 'largely covered' by common rules. It is unfortunate that the Court did not clarify its case law in that respect.

The problem lies not only in determining when an area is 'largely covered', but in the concept of 'area' itself. The EC Treaty did not, and the FEU Treaty does not, draw any clear lines between 'areas'.[42] Is 'area' an abstract concept that refers to different socio-economic categories such as banking, audiovisual services, medical services and the like? If so, the precise distinction between categories may be crucial to determining how completely the 'area' has been regulated. Or might the Court be referring to the specific subject matter of a given agreement or part of an agreement, and asking whether that subject matter is covered entirely or largely by common rules? The latter would make the concept of 'area' clearer and more manageable. If one takes the specific subject matter of the intended international agreement as being the 'area', it is much easier to determine whether this has been covered by Community legislation than attempting to find out whether a policy area *in abstracto* is covered by common rules.

It is, however, unclear what the Court's conception of 'area' encompasses, and the Court did not lift the veil in the *New Lugano Convention*

---

[40] Ibid, paras 172–73. See Council Decision 2009/430/EC of 27 November 2008 concerning the conclusion of the Convention on jurisdiction and the recognition and enforcement of judgments in civil and commercial matters [2009] OJ L147/1.

[41] Thereby arguably affirming its approach in Opinion 2/91 *Convention No 170 of the International Labour Organization concerning safety in the use of chemicals at work* [1993] ECR I-1061. Nonetheless, M Cremona, 'Community Report' in XL Xenopoulos (ed), *External Relations of the EU and the Member States: Competence, Mixed Agreements, International Responsibility, and Effects of International Law* (2006) 323–24 argues that *New Lugano Convention*, above n 10, should not be regarded as heralding a new wider reading of the scope of exclusivity, but as a signal that the analysis should focus on the overall nature and effect of an agreement on the Community legal order.

[42] See Protocol No 25 on the exercise of shared competence, which provides as regards Art 2(2) TFEU that 'when the Union has taken action in a certain area, the scope of this exercise of competence only covers those elements governed by the Union act in question and therefore does not cover the whole area'. Given what was said about the concept of 'area', the clarification provided by this Protocol is rather limited.

Opinion. Moreover, the entire analysis of whether or not an area is 'largely covered' by common rules seems redundant if one approaches the question from the perspective of a straightforward application of the *ERTA* doctrine. Surely the *ERTA* principle would apply if the agreement relates to matters that are covered by a particular piece of Community legislation, even if the 'area' within which that legislation belongs remains largely unregulated?

The *New Lugano Convention* Opinion shows the Court using the classical incremental and rather sibylline approach that has characterised its case law ever since the *ERTA* case. The Court's circumspect approach to EU external relations is manifest not only in its usually cautious technique of interpretation, but also in its apparent unwillingness to draw clear lines, especially with regard to the existence and nature of implied external competences. This undoubtedly has positive aspects, given the need for flexibility in external relations and the development of EU law. At the same time, the lack of precision in the Court's reasoning regarding the existence and nature of implied external competences is regrettable. It leads to a lack of legal certainty and predictability, and can have an unfortunate influence on future Treaty amendments, given that intergovernmental conferences have often relied on the Court's case law when (re)drafting Treaty provisions,[43] as is evident, for example, in the Treaty of Lisbon.[44]

B   The *GATS Schedules* Opinion

The Commission had requested the opinion of the Court on the conclusion of agreements under the GATS[45] concerning the modification and withdrawal of certain commitments and the provision of certain compensation which had become necessary as a result of the enlargement of the European Union. The Court was consulted on whether the conclusion of those agreements with the World Trade Organization (WTO) members who were affected thereby, pursuant to Article XXI of the GATS, fell within the sphere of exclusive competence of the Community or within the sphere of shared competence of the Community and the Member States. The Court's guidance was also sought as to whether Article 133(1) and (5) TEC (Common Commercial Policy), in conjunction with Article 300(2) TEC (procedure for concluding Community international agreements),

---

[43] cf Holdgaard, above n 31, 388–393.
[44] See A Dashwood, 'Mixity in the Era of the Treaty of Lisbon' in C Hillion and P Koutrakos (eds), *Mixed Agreements Revisited* (Oxford, Hart Publishing, 2010) 360–63 and 365; De Baere, above n 20, 67–71.
[45] General Agreement on Trade in Services, 15 April 1994, 1869 UNTS 183, 33 ILM 1167 (1994).

constituted the appropriate legal basis for the act concluding those agreements.

In its submissions, the Commission essentially relied once more on a familiar line of reasoning, which it had unsuccessfully advanced in the *GATS and TRIPS* Opinion. It argued that the agreements at issue fell within the Common Commercial Policy and, therefore, within a sphere of Community competence which is by definition exclusive. That policy, the Commission continued, is 'open and dynamic' and requires constant adjustment to take account of any changes of outlook in international relations, and requires a non-restrictive interpretation so as not to become nugatory in the course of time. That is what would happen if that policy were confined to the traditional aspects of trade without encompassing agreements designed, as in the present case, to modify the terms and conditions under which the Community commits itself to opening access to its market to the services and suppliers of services of other countries which are WTO members.[46]

What about the fact that the Court had clearly held in the *GATS and TRIPS* Opinion that only services provided under 'mode 1'[47] fell within exclusive Community competence in commercial matters—an outcome described by Professor Dashwood as 'All's well that ends well'?[48] In a rather adventurous interpretation of Article 133 TEC in its post-Nice form, the Commission argued the Court's dicta in the *GATS and TRIPS* Opinion had been superseded by the changes made by the Treaty of Nice. In its post-Nice version, Article 133(5) TEC provided that 'trade in services' fell, in general terms, within the Common Commercial Policy, subject only to the provisions of Article 133(6) TEC. According to the Commission, the aim of those changes was to simplify the situation and to reinforce the role of the Community in the negotiations to be undertaken within the WTO, by ensuring the consistency, effectiveness and credibility of the Community's action and by enabling it to perform its obligations swiftly and in good faith. Inasmuch as Article 133(6) TEC provided for an exception to the principle set out in Article 133(5) TEC, it had to be interpreted narrowly and did not therefore cover the agreements at issue.[49]

In its Opinion, the Court first pointed out that the exclusive or non-exclusive nature of the Community competence to conclude the agreements

---

[46] *GATS Schedules*, above n 8, para 45.

[47] That is to say: supply of a service from the territory of one Member into the territory of any other Member under Art I:(2)(a) of the GATS.

[48] Dashwood, above n 9, 119, also describing the Commission's claims of exclusivity in Opinion 1/94 *Competence of the Community to conclude international agreements concerning services and the protection of intellectual property (GATS and TRIPS)* [1994] ECR I-5267 as 'extravagant'.

[49] *GATS Schedules*, above n 8, paras 44–48. On whether Art 133(5) TEC excluded the operation of the ERTA doctrine and effectively established a parallel competence for the Community and the Member States: De Baere, above n 20, 63–64.

and the appropriate legal basis are two questions which are closely linked. Whether the Community alone has competence to conclude an agreement or whether such competence is shared with the Member States depends inter alia on the scope of the provisions of Community law which are capable of empowering the Community institutions to participate in the agreement. The Court therefore considered together (i) the question of which legal bases underpin the Community's competence to conclude the agreements at issue; and (ii) the question whether such Community competence is exclusive or whether, on the contrary, the Member States retain a share in competence to conclude those agreements.[50]

The scope of this chapter is too limited to provide a detailed analysis of what the Court decided. It suffices for present purposes that the Court did not accept the Commission's arguments. The Court held that the conclusion of the agreements fell within the sphere of shared competence of the European Community and the Member States, and that the Community act concluding those agreements had to be based on Article 133(1), (5) and (6), second subparagraph, TEC and on Articles 71 TEC and 80(2) TEC, in conjunction with Article 300(2) and (3), first subparagraph, TEC.

The Court pointed out that all international agreements relating to the fields mentioned in Article 133(6) TEC (ie culture, education, and social and human health services) fell within the shared competence of the Community and its Member States. The conclusion of such agreements therefore required the joint participation of the Community and the Member States, including in cases where these agreements did not concern the sectors in question exclusively or predominantly. The Court explicitly affirmed that it was necessary to preserve for the Member States an effective external competence in these particularly sensitive areas, in accordance with the specific provisions of Article 133(6) TEC.[51]

The Court further specified that commercial agreements in the field of transport implied the use of specific provisions relating to transport policy, included under Title V of the EC Treaty, as a legal basis. According to the Court, this results directly from the letter of Article 133(6) TEC, which provided that the negotiation and conclusion of international agreements in the field of transport are to continue to be governed by the provisions of Title V and Article 300 TEC. It is perhaps difficult to see how the Court could have reached a different conclusion.[52]

The *GATS Schedules* Opinion therefore features the Court in a role akin to the one it played in the *GATS and TRIPS* Opinion[53] and, indeed,

---

[50] *GATS Schedules*, above n 8, paras 111–13.

[51] *GATS Schedules*, above n 8, paras 139.

[52] The situation remains the same after Lisbon, as Art 207(5) TFEU makes clear: 'The negotiation and conclusion of international agreements in the field of transport shall be subject to Title VI of Part Three and to Art 218.'

[53] Above n 48.

in the first *Tobacco Advertising* judgment,[54] ie that of a court willing to adjudicate on the vertical division of competences *sine ira et studio*.[55] Both the *GATS and TRIPS* Opinion and the *GATS Schedules* Opinion show that, even if one might argue (as indeed the Commission did) that a unified approach towards the *WTO*[56] and *GATS*[57] agreements is so important for European integration that matters involving those agreements ought to come within the exclusive competence of the Community in their entirety,[58] the Court will recognise the limits that the Treaty places on claims to such competence.[59]

IV   HORIZONTAL DIVISION OF COMPETENCES AND INSTITUTIONAL BALANCE

As Advocate General Poiares Maduro has noted, the Court attaches so much importance to the choice of legal basis because it affects the institutional balance: it determines the applicable decision-making procedure and may ultimately have ramifications for the determination of

---

[54] Case C-376/98 *Germany v Parliament and Council* (*Tobacco Advertising I*) [2000] ECR I-8419; see also Case C-380/03 *Germany v Parliament and Council* (*Tobacco Advertising II*) [2006] ECR I-11573; see further Case C-491/01 *British American Tobacco (Investments) and Imperial Tobacco* [2002] ECR I-11453; Case C-434/02 *Arnold André* [2004] ECR I-11825 and Case C-210/03 *Swedish Match* [2004] ECR I-11893. See, however, D Wyatt, Chapter 1 above, for an argument that the Court's subsequent case law has effectively reversed the 'competence restricting effects' of the *Tobacco Advertising* case. The most recent example of the line of case law on the limits of Art 114 TFEU (ex-Art 95 TEC) is Case C-58/08 *Vodafone* [2010] ECR I-0000, in which the Court upheld the use of ex-Art 95 TEC as the proper legal basis for Reg (EC) No 717/2007 of the European Parliament and of the Council of 27 June 2007 on roaming on public mobile telephone networks within the Community and amending Directive 2002/21/EC [2007] OJ L171/32.

[55] 'Without anger and zeal': see Tacitus, *Annals*, I, 1, where the author uses this expression to explain that he will recount history in an impartial manner.

[56] Agreement Establishing the World Trade Organization, 1867 UNTS 154, 33 ILM 1144 (1994).

[57] Above n 45.

[58] Art 207 TFEU has extended the scope of the Common Commercial Policy, arguably to cover, in principle, all matters coming within the ambit of the WTO: see P-C Müller-Graff, 'The Common Commercial Policy enhanced by the Reform Treaty of Lisbon?' in A Dashwood and M Maresceau (eds), *Law and Practice of EU External Relations. Salient Features of a Changing Landscape* (Cambridge, Cambridge University Press, 2008) 188–201; regarding the Treaty establishing a Constitution for Europe *cf* P Eeckhout, *External Relations of the European Union: Legal and Constitutional Foundations* (Oxford, Oxford University Press, 2004) 54–55.

[59] The Court has shown a similar restraint in its case law on the interactions between trade and foreign policy in general and on dual-use goods and economic sanctions in particular: P Koutrakos, *Trade, Foreign Policy and Defence in EU Constitutional Law* (Oxford, Hart Publishing, 2001) 222–23. For a fuller account of Opinion 1/08, including as regards the issue of horizontal division of competences and the choice of legal basis, see M Cremona, 'Balancing Union and Member State Interests: Opinion 1/2008, Choice of Legal Base and the Common commercial Policy under the Treaty of Lisbon' (2010) 35 *European Law Review* 378.

the content of an act.[60] That neatly captures the pre-eminent importance of the choice of legal basis for the horizontal division of competences. The point may be illustrated by examining the *Rotterdam Convention, Kadi and Al Barakaat* and *Basel Convention* cases (all of which involved the combination of legal bases in the EC Treaty) and the *Small Arms and Light Weapons* case (which concerned the choice between a Community or a Common Foreign and Security Policy (CFSP) legal basis and the potential combination of those two). Here, we only examine the consequences of the choice of multiple legal bases for the decision-making procedures and for the institutional balance. A substantive analysis of how the Court performed its analysis of the legal instruments in question and its resulting choice of legal basis is beyond the scope of this contribution.

A The Horizontal Division of Competences within the Ordinary External Relations of the Union: the *Rotterdam Convention, Kadi* and *Al Barakaat,* and *Basel Convention* Cases

(i) The Rotterdam Convention Case

In the *Rotterdam Convention* case,[61] the Court annulled a regulation implementing the Rotterdam Convention on the prior informed consent procedure for certain hazardous chemicals and pesticides in international trade[62] on the grounds that it ought to have been adopted on the dual legal basis of Articles 133 and 175 TEC and not on Article 175 TEC alone.[63] Article 133 TEC, which concerned Community action in the field of the Common Commercial Policy, provided for qualified majority voting (QMV) in the Council with (at most) optional consultation of the European Parliament.[64] Article 175 TEC concerned Community action in the field of environmental protection, required QMV in the Council and provided for the European Parliament to be fully involved by way of the co-decision procedure.

Advocate General Kokott concluded that the two legal bases were mutually incompatible and could not therefore constitute a joint legal basis. She held it to be

---

[60] Opinion of Advocate General Poiares Maduro in Case C-133/06 *Parliament v Council* [2008] ECR I-3189, point 32.

[61] *Rotterdam Convention II*, above n 10, and see the similar C-94/03 *Commission v Council* (*Rotterdam Convention I*) [2006] ECR I-1. See further P Koutrakos, 'Annotation on Case C-94/03 *Commission v Council* and Case C-178/03 *Commission v Parliament and Council*' (2007) 44 *Common Market Law Review* 171.

[62] Signed by the European Community on 11 September 1998 and approved on the latter's behalf by Council Decision 2003/106/EC of 19 December 2002 [2003] OJ L63/27.

[63] Reg (EC) No 304/2003 of the European Parliament and of the Council of 28 January 2003 concerning the export and import of dangerous chemicals [2003] OJ L63/1.

[64] Art 133(7) TEC.

self-evident, on the one hand, that the Parliament's co-decision in the field of Article 175 EC cannot be dispensed with; since the Maastricht Treaty the co-decision procedure is one of the Parliament's most important rights of participation, and it makes an important contribution to the democratic legitimacy of Community legislation. Nor, on the other hand, could the procedure under Article 133(4) EC be abruptly supplemented by a co-decision right of the Parliament which is not provided for there.

That would appear to be a correct and sensible assessment. As the Advocate General argued,

> in either case there would be a danger that the decision-making process laid down in the relevant legal basis, and hence also the institutional balance laid down in the Treaty, could be distorted: a change to the legislative procedure can always also have an effect on the content of the act enacted.[65]

The Court nevertheless found that the two legal bases could be made mutually compatible by letting the Council decide by QMV (which was provided for in both articles anyway) and allowing the Parliament to be involved by way of the co-decision procedure (which was provided for only in Article 175 TEC). In other words, the Court appears to take the view that, when faced with seemingly incompatible decision-making procedures, the dilemma is solved by 'levelling up' to whichever procedure maximises the involvement of the European Parliament.[66]

However, as Advocate General Poiares Maduro argued in *Basel Convention*, levelling up in favour of the European Parliament has no basis in the Treaty. Referring to the double democratic legitimacy of the European Union, he argued that, while the level of direct democratic representativeness through the European Parliament is undeniably a relevant gauge of European democracy, it is not the only measure of legitimacy. European democracy also entails

> achieving a delicate balance between the national and European dimensions of democracy, without either one necessarily prevailing over the other. This is why the European Parliament does not have the same power as national parliaments in the legislative process and, although an argument could be made for stronger powers for the European Parliament, it is for the peoples of Europe to make that decision through treaty amendment . . . To accept a general principle of preference for a legal basis which maximises the participation of the European Parliament in the decision-making process would be tantamount to altering the institutional and democratic balance laid down by the Treaty.

The Advocate General concludes that

---

[65] Opinion of Advocate General Kokott in *Rotterdam Convention II*, above n 10, point 60.

[66] See the Opinion of Advocate General Poiares Maduro in *Basel Convention*, above n 10, point 6.

this analysis leads to a prohibition in practice on cumulative legal bases: either both provisions provide for the same decision-making procedure and an error as to legal basis would be of merely formal significance and therefore of no import,[67] subject to a possible incidence on the distribution of competence between the Community and the Member States; or they provide for different legislative procedures, which are therefore necessarily incompatible for the reasons I have just discussed, and they may not be combined.[68]

That is a cogent line of argument, though it plays down the significance of the choice of legal basis for the vertical division of competences.[69] If a measure were to be adopted on a dual legal basis akin to the one at issue in the *Rotterdam Convention* case (which would amount, post-Lisbon, to Article 192(1) TFEU (environment) and Article 207 TFEU (Common Commercial Policy)), both would fall under the ordinary legislative procedure and would thus be procedurally compatible (leaving aside, for present purposes, the need to consult the Economic and Social Committee and the Committee of the Regions under Article 192 TFEU). Yet, from the perspective of the vertical division of competence, the difference between a measure falling solely under Article 192 TFEU (and therefore, pursuant to Article 4(2)(e) TFEU, under shared competences) or solely under Article 207 TFEU (and therefore, pursuant to Article 3(1)(e) TFEU, under one of the few exclusive Union competences), or possibly partially under either, is significant.

(ii) The Kadi and Al Barakaat Cases

The Court's judgment in the *Kadi* and *Al Barakaat* cases endorsed a potentially even trickier combination of procedures by approving the combined legal bases of Articles 60, 301 and 308 TEC, even though the first and second provide for QMV in the Council and no involvement of the European Parliament, whilst the third provides for unanimity in the Council and consultation of the Parliament. However, the Court, like the General Court, omitted to address the issue of potential procedural incompatibility.

An indication as to how the Court might have reconciled the procedures laid down by those provisions may perhaps be gleaned from its decision

---

[67] The original French reads 'un vice purement formel, donc inopérant'. The English translation is somewhat unfortunate, in that 'without practical effect' would probably be a better translation of 'inopérant' than 'of no import' in this context.

[68] Opinion of Advocate General Poiares Maduro in *Basel Convention*, above n 10, point 6, fn 5. Is this perhaps Advocate General Poiares Maduro's equivalent of the famous 'footnote 4' written by Justice Stone of the US Supreme Court in *United States v Caroline Products Co*, 304 US 144, 152–53 (1938) (on which see W Mendelson, 'A Note on a Famous Legal Footnote' (1963) 25 *The Journal of Politics* 373–76).

[69] Not to mention the importance of the choice of legal basis for informing the contracting partners of the EU about the horizontal and vertical division of competences within the Union. See *Rotterdam Convention I*, above n 61, para 55.

in the *International Fund for Ireland* case.[70] There, the issue was the legal basis of a regulation concerning the Community's financial contributions to the International Fund for Ireland, adopted on the basis of Article 308 TEC.[71] The European Parliament argued that the regulation ought to have been adopted under the third paragraph of Article 159 TEC on economic and social cohesion, which required QMV in the Council and the co-decision procedure, while Article 308 TEC required unanimous voting in the Council and consultation of the European Parliament. Advocate General Bot concluded that the regulation should have been based solely on Article 159 TEC. The Community had, under the third paragraph of Article 159 TEC, the necessary competences to adopt the measures in the contested regulation, which therefore had to be annulled insofar as it was adopted on the basis of Article 308 TEC.

However, the Court held that Article 159 TEC could not in itself constitute a sufficient legal basis, ruling that the Community legislature ought to have had recourse to both the third paragraph of Article 159 TEC and Article 308 TEC, 'while complying with the legislative procedures laid down therein, that is to say, both the "co-decision" procedure referred to in Article 251 EC and the requirement that the Council should act unanimously'.[72] The Court thereby endorsed the rule of levelling up in favour of the Parliament that it had laid down in the *Rotterdam Convention* case. The rule as regards the Council is more difficult to deduce. Are conflicting legal bases resolved by favouring the 'more rigorous' decision-making procedure in the Council (here, the provision which allows for more input by each Member State by requiring unanimity)?[73]

Prima facie, the solution endorsed by the *International Fund for Ireland* judgment seems to be at odds with how the institutional balance and the system of double democratic legitimacy is normally organised. As a rule, that system implies that, where the 'centre of gravity' of the decision-making procedure in the Council lies at the level of the Union (as is the case with QMV), the democratic legitimacy of the decision is

---

[70] Case C-166/07 *Parliament v Council (International Fund for Ireland)* [2009] ECR I-7135. Here we refer briefly to a case in which Professor Dashwood was not involved, but only to illuminate cases in which he was.

[71] Council Reg (EC) No 1968/2006 of 21 December 2006 concerning Community Financial contributions to the International Fund for Ireland (2007–2010) [2006] OJ L409/86.

[72] *International Fund for Ireland*, above n 70, para 69. As to whether that conclusion departs from the *Titanium dioxide* case, above n 19, see Gutman, above n 28, 307–08.

[73] See, to that effect, the Opinion of Advocate General Tesauro in *Titanium dioxide*, above n 19, point 11. Commenting on the Court's ruling in Case 165/87 *Commission v Council* [1988] ECR 5547, para 11, that 'where an institution's power is based on two provisions of the Treaty, it is bound to adopt the relevant measures on the basis of the two relevant provisions', Advocate General Tesauro noted that 'that case concerned the relationship between two provisions, Articles 28 and 113, which could be applied together, merely by adopting the more rigorous voting system, the unanimity required by Article 28 (before the Single Act) rather than the easier procedure, the qualified majority provided for in Article 113.'

ensured predominantly through the involvement of the European Parliament, preferably through the co-decision procedure (now the 'ordinary legislative procedure').[74] However, when the centre of gravity of the decision-making procedure in the Council lies not at Union level but at the level of the Member States (as is the case with unanimity), democratic legitimacy needs to be guaranteed at the level of the Member States as well, ie through the democratic control of the ministers who vote in the Council by their respective national parliaments.[75] Normally, therefore, QMV in the Council is combined with the ordinary legislative procedure, while unanimity in the Council is combined with a procedure that involves the European Parliament to a lesser degree.[76] Nonetheless, under the pre-Lisbon framework, there were a number of examples of the combination of unanimity in the Council and co-decision with the Parliament.[77] Such is no longer the case in the post-Lisbon Treaties. However, in *International Fund for Ireland*, the Court did not explicitly rely in its reasoning on the presence of such possibilities in the EC Treaty. It is therefore not clear that it would feel constrained by the absence of that possibility in the current Treaties.[78]

It could be argued that a rule requiring levelling up towards more empowerment of both strata of the system of double democratic legitimacy (Council and European Parliament) is justified when combining two legal bases so as to allow the Union to take action which, at first glance, might seem to fall outside its explicitly attributed competences. However, the application of those rules is liable sometimes to lead to results that run counter to the *ratio legis* of one of the Treaty articles combined in the legal basis of the measure at issue.

That can be illustrated by looking at what the effect would be of applying those tentative rules to the legal basis in the *Kadi* and *Al Barakaat* cases. As will be recalled, the Court there sanctioned the adoption of the contested measure on the combined legal basis of Articles 60, 301 and 308 TEC. Articles 60 and 301 TEC provide for the Council to take measures by QMV on a proposal from the Commission (with no involvement from the European Parliament), while Article 308 TEC provides for the Council to act unanimously on a proposal from the Commission and after consulting the European Parliament. Applying the rules tentatively deduced from *International Fund for Ireland*, it would seem that

[74] Art 294 TFEU (ex-Art 251 TEC).

[75] See in that regard Protocol No 1 on the Role of National Parliaments in the European Union [2010] OJ C83/203 and Protocol No 2 on the Application of the principles of Subsidiarity and Proportionality [2010] OJ C83/206.

[76] See K Lenaerts and P Van Nuffel, *European Union Law*, 3rd edn (London, Sweet & Maxwell, forthcoming 2011), para 20-013.

[77] Arts 42, 47(2), and 151(5) TEC.

[78] As regards the possible combination of Arts 114 and 352 TFEU, see Gutman, above n 28, 389–90.

the measure would have to be adopted with unanimity in the Council after consultation of the Parliament. Such a procedure makes sense from the viewpoint of democratic legitimacy, as Union action at the limits of its attributed competences would in that way be endorsed by both levels of the system of double democratic legitimacy. However, that solution appears to jeopardise what must surely be the *ratio legis* for the decision-making procedure provided for in Articles 60 and 301 TEC (QMV and no involvement of Parliament): the need for speed.[79] When a decision has been taken under the CFSP that economic and/or financial sanctions are necessary, the Council needs to be able to act quickly and decisively. After all, the basic decision was taken by unanimity and therefore has the agreement of all the Member States. There might therefore be thought to be no need for lengthy reconsideration by Parliament and Council at the moment of taking an implementation measure.[80] The lack of involvement of the Parliament is problematic from a democratic point of view,[81] though it may (perhaps) be justified by the urgent nature of the sanctions in question. Parliamentary involvement would in principle be more essential at the stage of establishing a framework for imposing sanctions[82] than at the implementation stage of taking the actual sanctions. Regrettably, however, it is not provided for within the CFSP. From the perspective of the rule of law, there is at least the possibility for the Court of Justice to

[79] *Cf* A Dashwood, 'Dual-use Goods: (Mis)Understanding *Werner* and *Leifer*' in A Arnull, P Eeckhout and T Tridimas (eds), *Continuity and Change in EU Law. Essays in Honour of Sir Francis Jacobs* (Oxford, Oxford University Press, 2008) 359, pointing out that the choice of the then Art 113 TEC (which became Art 133 TEC after Amsterdam and Art 207 TFEU after Lisbon) as the legal basis for sanctions before the introduction of Arts 60 and 301 TEC was partly dictated by the simplicity of the procedure (QMV on a proposal by the Commission), because there would normally be a need for urgency.

[80] That is also why, as an exception to the unanimity rule in the Council for CFSP measures, Art 31(2) TEU provides for the Council to act by QMV when adopting a decision defining a Union action or position on the basis of a decision of the European Council relating to the Union's strategic interests and objectives, as referred to in Art 22(1) TEU and when adopting any decision implementing a decision defining a Union action or position. In both cases, the basic decision will have been adopted by unanimity.

[81] De Baere, above n 20, 275. See, however, the Opinion of Advocate General Poiares Maduro in *Basel Convention*, above n 10, point 6, fn 5.

[82] Art 75 TFEU (ex-Art 60 TEC) provides that the European Parliament and the Council, acting by means of regulations in accordance with the ordinary legislative procedure, are to 'define a framework for administrative measures with regard to capital movements and payments, such as the freezing of funds, financial assets or economic gains belonging to, or owned or held by, natural or legal persons, groups or non-State entities'. See, however, Case C-130/10 *European Parliament v Council*, pending. There, the Parliament is claiming that Council Reg (EU) No 1286/2009 of 22 December 2009 amending Reg (EC) No 881/2002 imposing certain specific restrictive measures directed against certain persons and entities associated with Usama bin Laden, the Al-Qaida network and the Taliban [2009] OJ L346/42, adopted on the basis of Art 215 TFEU, is invalid for the following reasons: (i) having regard to its aim and content, the correct legal basis for the Regulation is Art 75 TFEU; and (ii) in the alternative, the conditions for recourse to Art 215 TFEU were not fulfilled, because no proposal had been validly presented and the Council had not previously adopted a decision in accordance with Chapter 2 of Title V of the EU Treaty.

review the sanctions—and the scope of that possibility has rightly been enlarged with the entry into force of the Treaty of Lisbon.[83]

(iii)   The Basel Convention Case

The *GATS Schedules* Opinion shows that the Court takes a nuanced approach to the vertical division of competences. Although that approach may be criticised, it nevertheless shows the Court performing a genuine legal analysis in its role as a constitutional adjudicator. The *Basel Convention* case shows that the same can be said about the horizontal division of competences.[84] There, the Commission asked the Court to annul Regulation (EC) No 1013/2006[85] on shipments of waste insofar as it was based solely on Article 175(1) TEC and not on Articles 175(1) and 133 TEC. Rather, as it later argued in the *GATS Schedules* Opinion, the Commission relied essentially on settled case law, according to which the scope of application of the Common Commercial Policy is to be given a wide interpretation and a measure regulating trade with third countries does not cease to be a commercial policy measure merely because it also serves objectives in fields other than trade, such as protection of the environment.[86]

After a careful analysis of the objective and components of the contested regulation, the Court concluded that those relating to the protection of the environment were the main or predominant objective and component. The Court also held that a broad interpretation of the concept of Common Commercial Policy was not such as to call into question the finding that the contested regulation was an instrument falling principally under environmental protection policy, recalling that a Community act may fall within that area even when the measures provided for by that act are also liable to affect trade. A Community act falls within exclusive Community competence in the field of the Common Commercial Policy as provided for in Article 133 TEC only if it relates specifically to international trade in that it is essentially intended to promote, facilitate or govern trade and has direct and immediate effects on trade in the products concerned. The Court concluded that that was clearly not the case as regards the contested regulation.[87] The Commission had also relied on

---

[83] See Art 275 TFEU, pursuant to which the Court is to have jurisdiction to rule on proceedings, brought in accordance with the conditions laid down in the fourth paragraph of Art 263 TFEU, reviewing the legality of decisions providing for restrictive measures against natural or legal persons adopted by the Council on the basis of its CFSP competences in Chapter 2 of Title V of the EU Treaty.

[84] *Basel Convention*, above n 10.

[85] Reg (EC) No 1013/2006 of the European Parliament and of the Council of 14 June 2006 on shipments of waste [2006] OJ L190/1.

[86] *Basel Convention*, above n 10, para 31.

[87] Ibid, paras 70–72.

the *Rotterdam Convention* case to demonstrate the existence of a practice of adopting acts on the dual legal basis of Articles 133 EC and 175(1) TEC. The Court firmly rejected that line of argument, both on a substantive analysis of the contested measure and on the principle that the legal basis for an act must be determined having regard to its own aim and content and not to the legal basis used for the adoption of other Community acts which might, in certain cases, display similar characteristics.[88] The double legal basis sought by the Commission was therefore not endorsed by the Court.

B   The Horizontal Division of Competences between the Ordinary External Relations of the Union and the CFSP: the *Small Arms and Light Weapons* Case

The Commission brought an action seeking the annulment, for lack of competence, of Council Decision 2004/833/CFSP of 2 December 2004 implementing Joint Action 2002/589/CFSP with a view to a European Union contribution to the Economic Community of West African States (ECOWAS) in the framework of the Moratorium on Small Arms and Light Weapons.[89] In addition, the Commission raised a plea of illegality, pursuant to Article 241 TEC (now Article 277 TFEU), against Council Joint Action 2002/589/CFSP,[90] on which the disputed Decision was based. Both pleas were based on the same grounds. The Commission's quarrel was with the fact that the Council had adopted the disputed Decision under the then Title V of the EU Treaty, whereas the spread of small arms and light weapons is covered by Article 11 of the Cotonou Agreement.[91] The case is of great significance for the relationship between first and second pillar external relations in the pre-Lisbon constitutional framework, but we focus here only on the potential combination of legal bases from the first and second pillars.

The Court explicitly held that a combination of legal bases is impossible with regard to a measure that pursues a number of objectives or which has several components falling, respectively, within Community development co-operation policy and within the CFSP, and where neither

---

[88] Ibid, para 77.

[89] [2004] OJ L359/65. The following account of the *Small Arms and Light Weapons* case draws on De Baere, above n 20, 283–98.

[90] Council Joint Action 2002/589/CFSP of 12 July 2002 on the European Union's contribution to combating the destabilising accumulation and spread of small arms and light weapons and repealing Joint Action 1999/34/CFSP [2002] OJ L191/1.

[91] Partnership Agreement between the members of the African, Caribbean and Pacific Group of States of the one part, and the European Community and its Member States, of the other part, signed in Cotonou on 23 June 2000 [2000] OJ L317/3.

one of those components is incidental to the other.[92] The Court did not, however, base this conclusion on what would seem to us to be legally the most convincing argument. The *Titanium dioxide* line of case law, according to which 'recourse to a dual legal basis is not possible where the procedures laid down for each legal basis are incompatible with each other or where the use of two legal bases is liable to undermine the rights of the Parliament',[93] creates insuperable difficulties for cross-pillar internal measures involving the first and second pillars. As Advocate General Mengozzi noted, in a case concerning the distribution of competences between the second and first pillars, the use of two legal bases would appear to be impossible in view of the different procedural requirements laid down in the frameworks of Title V of the EU Treaty and of Title XX of the EC Treaty. Whereas a CFSP joint action was, in principle, to be adopted solely by the Council acting unanimously (subject to the application of ex-Article 23(2) TEU), Article 179(1) TEC provided, in respect of development co-operation, that 'the measures necessary to further the objectives referred to in Article 177 [TEC]' were to be adopted by the Council acting in accordance with the co-decision procedure in ex-Article 251 TEC.[94] Under the *Titanium dioxide* line of case law, these procedures would indeed seem incompatible and the rights of the European Parliament would therefore be likely to be undermined.

Nonetheless, such difficulties appeared to be surmountable with regard to international agreements based on both Article 300 TEC and ex-Article 24 TEU (for example by negotiating different parts of an agreement under different procedures, and concluding it by way of two separate decisions).[95] By basing its reasoning not on the procedural argument but on the position of principle that the Union could not have recourse to a legal basis falling within the CFSP in order to adopt provisions which also fell within a Community competence, did the Court shut the door not only to internal cross-pillar measures with a legal basis in both the first and second pillars, but also to cross-pillar international agreements? Such an approach would not have been conducive to the overall consistency and effectiveness of EU external relations in general and development co-operation policy in particular.[96]

---

[92] *Small Arms and Light Weapons*, above n 10, para 76.
[93] *Rotterdam Convention II*, above n 10, para 57. See also, to that effect, *Titanium dioxide*, above n 19, paras 17–21; Joined Cases C-164/97 and C-165/97 *Parliament v Council* [1999] ECR I-1139, para 14; Case C-338/01 *Commission v Council* [2004] ECR I-4829, para 57.
[94] Opinion in *Small Arms and Light Weapons*, above n 10, fn 76, adding that it was also doubtful whether the procedures for adopting decisions granting financial and/or technical support and based on acts of a general nature in one or the other pillar could be reconciled, because in the context of Title V of the pre-Lisbon EU Treaty competence for adopting such decisions fell to the Council, whereas in the context of development co-operation it was for the Commission to adopt measures of financial and/or technical support.
[95] As suggested by Eeckhout, above n 58, 184.
[96] De Baere, above n 20, 296–97.

The picture has become quite different since the entry into force of the Treaty of Lisbon (which, as Professor Dashwood has remarked, has probably ended the rather brief spell of significance of the *Small Arms and Light Weapons* judgment).[97] While ex-Article 47 TEU prohibited the CFSP from treading on Community territory, Article 40 TEU now prohibits any mutual invasion of territory between the 'Union competences referred to in Articles 3 to 6 of the Treaty on the Functioning of the European Union' (viz the former first pillar competences) and the CFSP.

Consequently, under the Treaty of Lisbon, the Court has to watch both sides of the border it finds itself patrolling. This will enable the Court to review cases in which instruments or procedures of ordinary external relations of the Union are used to the detriment of CFSP instruments and procedures. However, the CFSP under the Treaty of Lisbon loses its most important distinctive feature: its specifically conferred objectives. This would make the objectives-based analysis by the Court in the *Small Arms and Light Weapons* case difficult, if not impossible to undertake. For example, the distinction suggested by Advocate General Mengozzi between 'preserving peace and/or strengthening international security' (CFSP) and 'social and economic development' (development co-operation) would not resolve any border conflict between ordinary external relations of the Union and the CFSP. Both would fall under the general objectives of the Union's external action, under Articles 21(2)(c) and 21(2)(d) TEU, respectively. Ironically, while the Treaty of Lisbon has given the Court jurisdiction to arbitrate on 'encroachment' by the 'first pillar' on CFSP territory, the absence of specific CFSP objectives makes it more difficult to defend that territory against such encroachment.[98]

But what does the equality of the EU and FEU Treaties as per the third paragraph of Article 1 TEU and Article 1(2) TFEU imply for the possibility of legal instruments based on a combined legal basis in the EU Treaty as regards the CFSP and within the FEU Treaty as regards the ordinary external relations of the Union? We have noted the Court's willingness to combine seemingly incompatible legal bases and to 'level up' procedures in favour of maximum empowerment of both levels of the Union's system of double democratic legitimacy (Council and European Parliament). Is it conceivable that the Court would now be willing to endorse a decision integrating aspects of both development co-operation and security based

---

[97] A Dashwood, 'Article 47 TEU and the Relationship between First and Second Pillar Competences' in A Dashwood and M Maresceau (eds), *Law and Practice of EU External Relations. Salient Features of a Changing Landscape* (Cambridge, Cambridge University Press, 2008) 99.

[98] Similarly regarding the Constitution: MG Garbagnati Ketvel, 'The Jurisdiction of the European Court of Justice in Respect of the Common Foreign and Security Policy' (2006) 55 *The International and Comparative Law Quarterly* 104. See De Baere, above n 20, 299.

on a combination of Article 208 TFEU and Article 28 TEU? At first glance, that would indeed seem possible, given that the Court's objection to combining Community and CFSP legal bases appears now to have been met by granting the FEU and TEU Treaties equal status, and by the new wording of Article 40 TEU.[99] Another element pointing in that direction would seem to be that, whilst under the pre-Lisbon EU Treaty the CFSP operated through a separate set of legal instruments, the new EU Treaty provides for only one legal instrument for the CFSP (a decision) which is the same familiar legal instrument provided for by the ordinary Union framework in Article 288 TFEU.

Would the Court apply its 'levelling up' solution to such a combination of legal bases? If so, the result here would be (like in *International Fund for Ireland*) unanimity in the Council (pursuant to Articles 24(1) and 31(1) TEU) in combination with the ordinary legislative procedure (pursuant to Article 209(1) TFEU). However, it would seem that Articles 24(1) and 31(1) TEU (which exclude the adoption of legislative acts within the CFSP) would prevent any levelling up that resulted in applying a legislative procedure to a CFSP action. It is therefore unlikely that the Court would be willing to endorse such a result. Unless the Court distinguishes *International Fund for Ireland* and finds another way of combining legal bases from the ordinary external relations of the Union and the CFSP, it would seem that the Court may have to maintain its objection to such a combination of legal bases, albeit on different grounds from those advanced in *Small Arms and Light Weapons*.

V CONCLUSION

How should we evaluate the role played by the Court as an adjudicator in the 'constitutional order of states' that is the European Union? Does the Court manage to demarcate the Union's competences both vertically and horizontally so as to make their limits 'discernible with a tolerable degree of certainty'?[100] Clearly, that does not always seem to be the case. Indeed, it has been argued that the Court's standard phrase—that the choice of legal basis has to rest on 'objective factors'—is only partly accurate: the case law has produced no specific and easily identifiable criteria to predict the precise choice of legal basis.[101] The same could be said more generally about the limits of the Union's competence, particularly as regards the external relations of the Union. The *New Lugano Convention* Opinion

[99] See also Dashwood, above n 9, 101.
[100] Dashwood, above n 9, 114.
[101] P Koutrakos, 'Legal Basis and Delimitation of Competence in EU External Relations' in M Cremona and B de Witte (eds), *EU Foreign Relations Law. Constitutional Fundamentals* (Oxford, Hart Publishing, 2008) 184.

and the long line of case law since the *ERTA* judgment show that the Court finds it difficult to draw clear lines. While it is true that complete clarity and predictability in sensitive areas such as external relations are simply not possible,[102] it is unfortunate that the same lack of clarity has now found its way into the Treaties.[103]

The *Rotterdam Convention* and *Kadi and Al Barakaat* cases show the Court struggling to reconcile the vertical with the horizontal division of competences. It appears to be prepared to interpret the latter 'creatively' so as to allow the Union to act. The result is a gradual modification of the *Titanium dioxide* case law. The Court appears to be moving away from the idea that legal bases that are procedurally incompatible cannot be combined, in favour of an approach that allows for joint legal bases of seemingly incompatible Treaty articles by making them compatible. However, combining legal bases that are prima facie incompatible and 'levelling up' in order to make them compatible can lead to surprising results that, as *Kadi* and *Al Barakaat* show, can run contrary to the *ratio legis* of the decision-making procedure chosen by the Treaty draftsman for each of the individual legal bases that are being combined. It can, moreover, distort the institutional balance as enshrined in the Treaties.

What is the solution to these knotty problems? In a chapter based on a limited sample of the case law, we do not seek to propose a universal panacea. Sometimes, the answer may be to adopt two separate measures, each in accordance with the procedure required by the appropriate legal basis. There is no reason why that approach should lead to lack of co-ordination and loss of effectiveness. Precisely such an approach has been used for years for sanctions.[104] Alternatively, if it is considered vital to have a single integrated measure promulgated on a joint legal basis, a more flexible approach, taking account of the specific circumstances of the case and balancing the *rationes legis* of the procedures provided for in the relevant legal bases, seems preferable, from the perspective of the institutional balance, to giving automatic preference to the legal basis that maximises the involvement of the European Parliament, or to always requiring levelling up towards more empowerment of both strata of the system of double democratic legitimacy (Council and European Parliament).

It seems to us that, despite the problems we have identified, in broad terms the Court still acts as a competent constitutional adjudicator guided by principles of law rather than being 'skewed by doctrinal or idiosyncratic policy considerations' (in the words of a description of the Court explicitly negated by Professor Dashwood in his inaugu-

---

[102] Ibid, 197.
[103] See above n 44.
[104] As explained, these are adopted by way of a measure adopted under the ordinary Union method implementing a CFSP measure containing the basic decision.

ral lecture).[105] A missionary Court intent on turning the Union into a federal state would surely have grasped the opportunity offered in the *GATS and TRIPS* Opinion to assimilate the entire field of external economic relations into the Common Commercial Policy, where competence belongs exclusively to the Union.[106] The Court likewise declined to yield to temptation in the *GATS Schedules* Opinion.[107] The cases examined, albeit representing a necessarily limited sample, illustrate that the picture is nuanced. When faced with an ever-evolving scope of Union activities, which in turn is reactive towards the ever-evolving challenges on the external and internal front, the Court attempts to fit the square peg of allowing the Union to adapt to such evolutions into the round hole of compliance with the principle of conferral and with the institutional balance. The Court thus performs a delicate balancing act between principle and pragmatism. This is particularly clear in its case law on external relations,[108] but—as we see it—is also present throughout the case law on the horizontal and vertical division of competences.

As Paul Freund put it, the role of courts

> in maintaining a working federalism is precisely this task of mediation between large principles and particular problems, the task of interposing intermediate principles more tentative, experimental and pragmatic. The courts are the substations which transform the high-tension charge of the philosophers into the reduced voltage of a serviceable current.[109]

Substituting Member States and institutions for philosophers, it seems that this description admirably fits the Court of Justice's position within the EU legal order. The Court may not always get the balancing act quite right. Equally clearly, however, by feeling its way through intractable

---

[105] Dashwood, above n 9, 128.

[106] Ibid.

[107] The Court recalled that 'concerns relating to the need for unity and rapidity of external action and to the difficulties which might arise were the Community and the Member States to participate jointly in conclusion of the agreements at issue cannot change the answer to the question of competence. Replying to similar arguments advanced by the Commission in the procedure concerning the request for Opinion 1/94 relating to conclusion of the agreements annexed to the WTO agreement, the Court held that the resolution of the issue of the allocation of competence could not depend on problems which might possibly arise in administration of the agreements concerned' (above n 8, para 127).

[108] See T Tridimas and P Eeckhout, 'The External Competences of the Community and the Case-law of the Court of Justice: Principle versus Pragmatism' (1994) 14 *Yearbook of European Law* 143; cf P Koutrakos, *EU International Relations Law* (Oxford, Hart Publishing, 2006) 134, who argues that the Court's pragmatism confirms its place as the ultimate arbiter of any dispute arising in Community external relations.

[109] Freund, above n 26, 578.

competence issues and coming up with 'tentative, experimental and pragmatic' solutions, the Court performs the role of adjudicator or umpire which is necessary if a constitutional order of states such as the Union is to work at all.[110]

---

[110] See similarly, Hinarejos, above n 2, 193. The need for judicial review by constitutional courts is of course the subject of a lively debate. See, eg J Waldron, 'The Core of the Case against Judicial Review' (2006) *Yale Law Journal* 1346; R Fallon, 'The Core of an Uneasy Case For Judicial Review' (2008) *Harvard Law Review* 1693; M Tushnet, 'How Different are Waldron's and Fallon's Core Cases For and Against Judicial Review?' (2010) 30 *Oxford Journal of Legal Studies* 49.

8

The Relationship between the European Court of Justice and the European Court of Human Rights

CHRISTIAAN TIMMERMANS

I INTRODUCTORY REMARKS

I DO NOT remember exactly when Alan Dashwood and I first met. It might have been my first London–Leiden meeting in 1967 in London or a few years later in 1973 in a stuffy room at Old College, South Bridge, where at the time Alan was the assistant of Professor John Mitchell and I had come to give a lecture as a stand-in for Claus-Dieter Ehlermann.

I am grateful for the friendship and co-operation we established over many years, a co-operation culminating in our family relationship as cousins of the respective legal services of Council and European Commission (from time to time we had, I would say, not a conflictual but a good debate on topics of external relations law), subsequently in the Editorial Board of the *Common Market Law Review* and finally, over the last 10 years, as far as I am concerned, as a careful and most of the time grateful listener on the bench of the ECJ to the thorough and well thought out pleadings of AA Dashwood QC.

II THE RELATIONSHIP BETWEEN THE ECJ AND THE STRASBOURG COURT

EU external relations law is a subject on which Alan and I have occasionally crossed swords and one might be inclined to say that the relationship between the ECJ and the Strasbourg Court falls under that rubric. However, I do not think this would be correct. Over time, the relationship between the two courts has become so internalised into the EU legal system that in my view it can no longer be considered an external policy matter.

The process of internalising the Strasbourg Convention and the case law of the Strasbourg Court into the EU legal system has now culminated in the Charter, as from 1 December 2009, formally stating (Article 52, paragraph 3) that those fundamental rights recognised by the Charter which correspond to rights guaranteed by the European Convention have the same meaning and scope as the latter—though of course with the possibility for the EU to go further. Moreover, the preamble of the Charter explicitly refers in a receptive manner to the case law of the Strasbourg Court. So, before acceding to the Strasbourg Convention, the EU, by virtue of its own Treaty law, is already largely bound to respect that Convention, and I would think the case law of the Strasbourg Court.

The relationship between international courts is a topical subject these days, a favourite topic for international conferences and one that is extensively covered in academic writing, not only on a European but almost on a global level.[1] Similarly, the relationship between the ECJ and the Strasbourg Court is not a neglected subject.[2] Not only is the co-operation between the two courts through their case law followed closely by academics and court watchers, it is also regularly discussed in publications of individual members of both courts. That the ECJ follows and applies ever more closely the case law of the Strasbourg Court and that the Strasbourg Court has over the last 10 years developed a positive attitude—I would say a form of judicial comity vis-à-vis the ECJ as to the level of protection of fundamental rights granted by the latter—is well known. Indeed, in its *Bosphorus* judgment, the Strasbourg Court accepted the protection granted by the ECJ as being in principle equivalent to the protection ensured under the Convention as interpreted by the Strasbourg Court, justifying what I would say is only a remote or subsidiary control by that Court as to the respect of fundamental rights by the European Union.[3] The *Bosphorus* decision of 30 June 2005 has since been repeatedly confirmed by the Strasbourg Court.[4] This co-operation through the case law

---

[1] See the various contributions to the Symposium: 'Globalization and the Judiciary: Key Issues of Economic Law, Business Law, and Human Rights Law' (2004) 39 *Texas International Law Journal* 347; A-M Slaughter, 'A Global Community of Courts' (2003) 44 *Harvard International Law Journal* 191.

[2] See, eg L Scheeck, 'The Relationship between the European Courts and Integration through Human Rights' (2005) *Zeitschrift für ausländisches öffentliches Recht und Völkerrecht* 837; S Douglas-Scott, 'A Tale of Two Courts: Luxembourg, Strasbourg and the Growing European Human Rights *Acquis* (2006) 43 *Common Market Law Review* 629; J Callewaert, 'The European Convention on Human Rights and European Union Law: a Long Way to Harmony' (2009) *European Human Rights Law Review* 768; G Harpaz, 'The European Court of Justice and its Relation with the European Court of Human Rights: The Quest for Enhanced Reliance, Coherence and Legitimacy' (2009) 46 *Common Market Law Review* 105.

[3] *Bosphorus Airways v Ireland*, App No 45036/98, judgment of 30 June 2005, Reports of Judgments and Decisions 2005-VI.

[4] *Cooperatieve Producentenorganisatie van de Nederlandse Kokkelvisserij v the Netherlands*, App No 13645/05, decision of 20 January 2009; *Bernard Connolly v 15 EU Member*

is matched by an informal co-operation through regular informal meetings organised normally once a year, alternately in Strasboug and Luxemburg, in which delegations of both courts discuss recent developments of mutual interest in their respective case laws. Apart from those bilateral meetings, the presidents and other representatives of both courts meet in the various networks set up over the years to structure judicial co-operation in the EU. Indeed, the dialogue through the case law is prepared and fostered by the ever more intensive informal contacts.

All that being well canvassed, what should I add? Let me make three comments.

A Cooperation through the Case Law with a Real Impact and of Mutually Beneficial Effect

Real co-operation works both ways. That also holds true for the ECJ and the Strasbourg Court. The influence the one exerts on the other is mutual and real. References to each other's case law are not just a matter of judicial comity or of judicial diplomacy. These references demonstrate a real impact on the case law of each court. Not only do they influence the development of the case law, but, generally considered, this mutual influence is also in the interest of both courts. Both courts, by invoking each other's case law, may possibly increase their legitimacy and improve the acceptance of their own case law.

In the *Kadi* case, the ECJ, in claiming jurisdiction over Community instruments implementing Security Council resolutions on the blacklisting of presumed terrorists, made quite extensive reference to the case law on fundamental rights of the Strasbourg Court[5]. It may be considered that, in so doing, the ECJ was able to strengthen the motivation of its judgment by benefiting from the authority of the Strasbourg Court.

The Strasbourg Court, in turn, has occasionally referred to an evolution in the case law of the Luxembourg Court as an argument to further develop its own interpretation of the Convention. One such example is the recent decision of the Strasbourg Court in the case of *Scoppolla v Italy*,[6] accepting the retroactive application of the more lenient penalty as resulting from the principle of legality enshrined in Article 7 of the Convention, referring to that effect also to the Berlusconi judgment of the

---

States, App No 73274/01, decision of 9 December 2008; *Etablissements Biret et Cie SA and Société Biret International v 15 EU Member States*, App No 13762/04, decision of the same date.

[5] Case C-402/05 P *Kadi and Al Barakaat International Foundation v Council and Commission* [2008] ECR I-6351.

[6] App No 10249/03, judgment of 17 September 2009.

ECJ.[7] In this context, it will be highly interesting to see what approach the Strasbourg Court will follow in the case of *Youssef Nada v Switzerland*.[8] This involves a complaint against Switzerland relating to a decision of the Swiss Federal Court (Bundesgericht),[9] which decided a case somewhat similar to *Kadi*, on the justiciability of a national measure implementing a Security Council resolution on blacklisting, along the lines followed by the Court of First Instance (now the General Court) in the *Kadi* case (*ius cogens*).[10] More examples of such an influence of the Luxembourg case law might follow now that the Charter of Fundamental Rights of the European Union has become a binding instrument. I say that because the Charter can be considered to be a more up to date and detailed codification of fundamental rights, which may prompt the ECJ to further increase the level of protection of those rights. Incidentally, the Strasbourg Court has already occasionally referred to the Charter—and in fact did so even before the ECJ itself.[11]

Similarly, the ECJ has on occasion further developed its case law on fundamental rights, finding inspiration to do so in new developments in the case law of the Strasbourg Court: a right of privacy for companies, invoked in order to challenge the access to their premises by inspectors in competition law cases, in application of Article 8 of the Convention, was rejected in the *Hoechst* case of 1989.[12] However, in its *Roquette Frères* judgment of 2002,[13] the ECJ accepted such a right with explicit reference to the development in that regard of the case law of the Strasbourg Court.[14] Another example is the prohibition of discrimination based on sexual orientation with regard to benefits under a pension scheme accepted by the ECJ under Article 141 EC in the *KB* case of 2004,[15] invoking to that effect the decision of the Strasbourg Court in the *Goodwin* case of 2002.[16]

There is more to be said about this mutually beneficial effect of the co-operation between the two courts through their case law. This co-operation is not only beneficial to both courts insofar as it might strengthen their legitimacy; it might even have a much more direct beneficial effect

---

[7] Joined Cases C-387/02, C-391/02 and C-403/02 *Berlusconi and others* [2005] ECR I-3624.

[8] *Youssef Nada v Switzerland*, App No 10593/08.

[9] Case 1A.45/2007 *Youssef Nada*, judgment of 14 November 2007.

[10] ase T-315/01 *Kadi* [2005] ECR II-3649.

[11] *Goodwin v United Kingdom*, App No 28957/95, judgment of 11 July 2002, Reports of Judgments and Decisions 2002-VI.

[12] Joined Cases 46/87 and 227/88 *Hoechst* [1989] ECR 2859.

[13] Case 94/00 *Roquette Frères* [2002] ECR I-9011.

[14] *Niemietz v Germany*, App No 13710/88, judgment of 16 December 1992 and *Colas Est v France*, App No 37971/97, judgment of 16 April 2002, Reports of Judgments and Decisions 2002-III.

[15] Case C-117/01 *KB* [2004] ECR I-541

[16] See above n 11.

insofar as it might contribute to the solidity of each legal system by improving respect for that system. Indeed, both courts have been instrumental in strengthening each other's legal system.

In the *Hornsby* case of 1997, the Strasbourg Court indirectly condemned the non-execution of an ECJ judgment as being contrary to Article 6 of the Convention.[17] It has also ruled that a refusal by a national court to use the preliminary reference procedure might, if such refusal appears to be arbitrary, violate the right to a fair trial under Article 6 of the Convention.[18]

In the same vein, the position of the Convention in the EU and its Member States will be strengthened in a situation where Convention rights are accepted as fundamental Union rights and, when it comes to the enforcement of these rights within the Member States, benefit from the safeguards of the Union's legal system (direct effect, supremacy). So, in Germany, respect for fundamental rights by authorities of that Member State might be more effectively enforced through the Union's legal system than on the mere basis of the authority of the decisions of the Strasbourg Court as accepted by the Bundesverfassungsgericht.[19]

One could say, therefore, that the co-operation between the ECJ and the Strasbourg Court as it has developed over the years is beneficial to each court and more generally to the level of human rights protection. This co-operation can therefore be considered as a matter of well-understood self-interest. At the same time, this gives an important impetus for both courts to use their best efforts to avoid conflicts between their respective case laws.

B Will the Lisbon Treaty Change the Nature of this Cooperation?

My second remark relates to the Lisbon Treaty. What will be the consequences of the coming into force of that Treaty? Will it affect, or even fundamentally modify, the relationship between the two courts? Accession of the Union to the European Convention on Human Rights—which will admittedly take some time—will, at least formally, bring a fundamental change: the Union will become subject to the jurisdiction

---

[17] *Hornsby v Greece*, App No 18357/91, judgment of 19 March 1997, Reports of Judgments and Decisions 1997-II.

[18] See, eg *John v Germany*, App No 15073/03, decision of 13 February 2007 and *Herma v Germany*, App No 54193/07, decision of 8 December 2009.

[19] See the decision of that Court in the case of *Görgülü*, 14 October 2004, 2BvR 1481/04. According to the Bundesverfassungsgericht German Courts are not *de iure* bound to respect a judgment of the Strasbourg Court. They should however duly consider or take into account such a judgment. See more generally G Ress, 'The Effect of Decisions and Judgments of the European Court of Human Rights in the Domestic Legal Order' (2005) *Texas International Law Journal* 359.

of the Strasbourg Court. That would normally imply that the ECJ will be subordinated to that jurisdiction. At least, that is to be expected in view of the case law of the ECJ on the relationship between EU law and international law. The ECJ in principle accepted that the EU legal order can be made subject to the jurisdiction of an international court in the EEA Opinion.[20] The hurdle erected by Opinion 2/94 on the Human Rights Convention has now been removed by the Lisbon Treaty.[21] In that regard, I hope and expect that the ECJ will not follow the example of the Bundesverfassungsgericht as to the status of decisions of the Strasbourg Court in the EU legal system.[22]

Now, if the ECJ becomes subject to the jurisdiction of the Strasbourg Court, does that necessarily imply that the co-operation between the two courts as it has developed until now will change? To be more precise, would that mean the end of the *Bosphorus* case law?

It might, but it need not necessarily do so. It would seem rather paradoxical if the presumption of good behaviour accepted before accession would have to be abandoned because of accession. Also, the drafters of the Lisbon Treaty might have had a different view in that regard. Indeed, according to Protocol No 8 and Declaration No 2 on the arrangements for the accession of the EU to the Convention, emphasis is placed on the preservation of the specific characteristics of the Union and Union law. The Declaration refers in that respect to the existing regular dialogue between the ECJ and the Strasbourg Court, adding that this dialogue could be reinforced. So the idea seems to be continuing co-operation, rather than subordination. Maintaining the *Bosphorus* case law would be fully in line with that. Of course, the Strasbourg Court will have the final say in that regard, unless the Treaty of Accession of the Union to the Convention itself provides for some kind of mechanism to deal with this question. Personally, I would think it would be in the interest of both courts, and more generally of the Union and the Convention regime, if the existing co-operation between the two courts continued and possibly developed further, even after the Union's accession to the Convention.

In any event, accession as such raises a number of complex issues, one of which directly concerns the Court of Justice with regard to its basic function to ensure observance of the law in the interpretation and application of the Treaties.

The system of human rights protection provided for by the Strasbourg Convention is a subsidiary one. It can only be triggered after the available national legal remedies have been exhausted. A state can only be held liable for its acts before the Strasbourg Court after the person affected has allowed the state to correct the situation by going through the legal pro-

---

[20] Opinion 1/91 [1991] ECR I-6079, paras 39 and 40.
[21] Opinion 2/94 [1996] ECR I-1759.
[22] See above n 19.

cedures available in the national legal system. Transposed to the European Union, this would mean that, when a complaint concerns an EU act, in principle the Union Courts must first be addressed before the complaint can be held admissible in the Strasbourg Court.

It is precisely in this respect that the specific characteristics of the EU, to quote Protocol No 8, cause a problem because of the imbrication of the Union's legal system with those of the Member States. As a rule, a Union action affects a citizen not directly but only through national measures implementing or applying the Union act. So, where a person considers his rights affected, he has to bring a case before a national court against the national measure or its application, even if the fundamental rights problem, if there is one, has been caused by the Union act. He must then pursue the procedures available before the national courts before he can lodge a complaint against the Member State before the Strasbourg Court. And even when the Union act in question, for instance a regulation, directly affects that person, the scenario will normally be the same because he will only exceptionally have access to the Union's General Court to bring an action for annulment of that regulation.

The problem which arises here is that the Strasbourg Court could find itself pronouncing on the conformity of the Union act with the Convention without the ECJ having had the possibility to examine the issue. It seems difficult to accept, and at the same time hardly compatible with the *ratio* of the exhaustion of legal remedies principle, that the Strasbourg Court should be asked to rule directly or indirectly on the conformity of a Union act with the Convention without the court which, within the legal system from which the act emanates, has jurisdiction to ensure respect of fundamental rights, having had the possibility to examine the issue.

But what about the preliminary ruling procedure? That procedure is indeed the only possible way to involve the ECJ before the case is brought to the Strasbourg Court. However, that procedure is not in the hands of the parties; it is a prerogative of the national court. A last instance court is, of course, in principle obliged to refer, but only if that court detects a question of interpretation or validity of Union law which must be answered to solve the case and without prejudice to the exceptions of 'acte clair' and 'acte éclairé'. Where the validity of a Union act is questioned because of a possible violation of a fundamental right, there will not be an absolute obligation for the last instance court to refer that question to the ECJ. Indeed, as the ECJ has ruled in the *IATA* case, the fact that the validity of a Union act is contested before a national court is not in itself sufficient to warrant referral of a question for a preliminary ruling.[23] Consequently, it cannot at all be excluded that a case brought before the Strasbourg Court appears at that stage to raise serious ques-

---

[23] Case C-344/04 *IATA and ELFAA* [2006] ECR I-403, para 28.

tions about the conformity of a Union act with the Convention without the ECJ having been involved and even without the national court of last instance having necessarily infringed its obligation to refer.

It is already possible to envisage such a scenario, but the *Bosphorus* case law could reduce the consequences. Whether the *Bosphorus* approach will be continued after accession remains to be seen. In any event, it seems to me that, once the Union is a party to the Convention, the principle of exhaustion of legal remedies must be applied in such a way that, even when an action of the Union can only be challenged indirectly through the national courts, in principle where questions of validity of a Union act are involved, the Union Courts must be able to examine that question. It would seem to me difficult to accept, to give an example, that questions of respect of fundamental rights of such importance as those raised in such cases as *Bosphorus*,[24] *Kadi*[25] and *Ordre des Barreaux*[26] should be decided by the Strasbourg Court without the competent courts of the Union's legal system having had the opportunity to address these questions.

In my view, the problem is real and sufficiently serious to require a solution before the EU actually accedes to the European Convention. This is now also the official position of the Court of Justice as expressed in a memorandum of 5 May 2010.

What could the solution be?

1. Should the Strasbourg Court declare a complaint raising a question of conventionality of a Union action inadmissible if it has not first been made subject to a preliminary ruling procedure? That solution would be too indiscriminate by barring access to the Strasbourg Court to individual complainants who cannot determine the use of the preliminary procedure. It could also risk triggering a flow of questions to the Luxembourg Court, possibly overburdening it. But might a more discriminate use of that possibility not be the answer? Indeed, the Strasbourg Court has already ruled that an omission to refer preliminary questions by a national court may violate Article 6 of the Convention.[27] However, such a violation might possibly be established in exceptional cases only. Moreover, it would not seem very attractive for the exercise of the preliminary reference powers of the national courts—and, more particularly, the scope of the obligation to refer—to be more closely policed by the Strasbourg Court.

2. Another solution that has already been suggested would be to empower the Strasbourg Court to submit preliminary questions to the Luxembourg Court when the conventionality of Union law is put into

[24] Case C-84/95 *Bosphorus* [1996] ECR I-3953.
[25] See above n 5.
[26] Case C-305/5 *Ordre des Barreaux* [2007] ECR I-5305.
[27] See above n 18.

question. One of the disadvantages of that solution is that it could easily set both courts on a collision course. If the Luxembourg Court did not detect any problem but the Strasbourg Court, continuing the procedure after having received the answer of the Luxembourg Court, nevertheless established a violation, a direct conflict between the two courts would arise.

3. Still another solution, also under discussion, would be to introduce a procedural mechanism allowing the European Commission, in cases pending before the Strasbourg Court which appear to raise serious questions of conventionality of Union law, to bring those questions before the Luxembourg Court, the procedure before the Strasbourg Court then being suspended pending the answer of the Luxembourg Court. Of course, the decision or opinion of the Luxembourg Court would not bind the Strasbourg Court, which would have the final say. Access to the procedural mechanism need not be reserved to the European Commission only; it could also be granted to the European Parliament, the Council and Member States. The advantage of such a mechanism could be that a referral to the Luxembourg Court would not be automatic but would be reserved more particularly to cases where a serious question of conventionality arises, that issue to be assessed by the European Commission or the other parties to whom standing was granted.

Whatever solution is finally chosen, it should be so conceived as not to require an amendment of the existing Treaties; rather, it should be included in the Accession Treaty. Since we are dealing with a solution to a problem caused precisely by that accession and which is necessary to respect the characteristics of the EU, to quote Protocol No 8 once again, that Protocol itself already suggests that the issue can and should be regulated in the Accession Treaty.

C More General Consequences of the Lisbon Treaty as to Human Rights' Protection

My third and final point is this. Now that the Charter has become binding, it may be expected the ECJ will be confronted with even more fundamental rights issues and become more and more a fundamental rights court. This is the more to be expected because of the rapidly increasing Union legislation in the fields of immigration, asylum, family law, penal law, etc (implementation of the The Hague programme and now the Stockholm programme). Legislation in these fields regularly raises human rights issues. Important in this respect will also be the suppression of the former Article 68 EC, which limited the competence to refer preliminary questions in these areas to courts of last instance. Consequently, all national courts are now granted that competence under the Lisbon Treaty. It is true, as far as penal law is concerned, that there is still a five years transitional period, but those five years will quickly be over.[28] I may add that, looking at ECJ case law over the last 10 years, it is apparent that fundamental rights issues have become more and more frequent.

At first sight, Article 6 of the Union Treaty might leave the impression of an inflation of fundamental rights protection. Indeed, the Article establishes three layers or sources of fundamental rights: the Charter, the Strasbourg Convention to which the EU shall accede, and the only binding source before Lisbon—the general principles of what is now Union law relating to fundamental rights. One might expect that the Charter will become the primary source and absorb and largely replace the unwritten general principles covering fundamental rights. If so, the situation of the Union as to fundamental rights protection will become similar to that of those Member States having a Bill of Rights—a constitutional catalogue of fundamental rights—on the one hand, and the European Convention rights on the other.

However, one may wonder in this regard what the consequences of the already famous (or, for some, infamous) Protocol No 30 on the application of the Charter to Poland, the UK and, if ratified later on, the Czech Republic will be? According to the Protocol, the Charter shall not extend the ability of either the ECJ or the national courts in the Member States concerned to find national rules or practices of these states inconsistent with the rights confirmed by the Charter. This looks like a standstill clause. If so, it means that, as to fundamental rights protection, the Charter does not add new obligations to those already existing before the entry into force of the Lisbon Treaty. If that reading is correct, the general principles as a separate source will remain relevant at least for those Member States that are covered by Protocol No 30. However, it is difficult to imagine that, where a fundamental right, invoked as a general principle of Union law, is at the same time codified by the Charter, the ECJ will interpret the one differently from the other. Indeed, one might expect that both sources—that is, the Charter and the general principles—will in such cases function as communicating vessels. If so, the impact of the Protocol could remain largely optical. On the other hand, the Protocol clearly delivers a certain message, and the Court should take that message seriously. It would be too easy to say, as some have done, that the Protocol could simply be ignored.

III POST SCRIPTUM

My final word is addressed to Alan Dashwood, a 'brother in law', that is, a brother in European law: I wish him well.

---

[28] Protocol No 36 on Transitional Provisions, Art 10.

9

Reforming Some Aspects of the Role of Advocates General

ROSA GREAVES

I INTRODUCTION

A CONSTITUTIONAL ORDER of EU states operates within a distinct legal order which ensures that the rule of law is observed and interpreted uniformly by all the states and their citizens. The Court of Justice (ECJ) is the EU institution charged with the interpretation and review of the legality of EU measures. The Advocate General is a member of the Court but is not involved in the deliberation of the judgments. This chapter will consider some aspects of the role of the Advocate General and discuss how that role may be improved in order to continue to assist the Court in its task of developing a distinct EU legal order and strengthening its coherence. It will also propose some changes to the criteria and mechanism for the appointment of Advocates General. The rest of the chapter is divided into two sections. The first section will provide a general appraisal of the role and contribution of the Opinions of the Advocates General to the decision-making process of the Court based on research which has already been undertaken and published. It will then identify various positive and negative aspects of the role of the Advocate General within the EU judicature. In the second section, two proposals will be set out as to how the role and the working relationship between the judges and the Advocates General may be improved in order to increase the usefulness of the Opinions. This will be followed by proposals for a change in the appointment mechanism of the Advocates General in order to meet the principles of transparency and openness. Finally, the criteria for appointment will be considered and additional requirements will be proposed which are aimed at enhancing the quality and influence of the Opinions on the Court or, at the very least, ensure that the positive aspects of the role that have been identified are more secure for the future.

II THE PAST

A   Research and Conclusions on the Role and Function of the Advocate General

Given the popularity of the Opinions of the Advocates General within the academic community, it is surprising how little research has been undertaken on the role of this member of the Court of Justice.[1] One author has commented that perhaps the 'Advocate General is chronically understudied' because there is no equivalent position in any legal system of the EU Member States.[2] On the other hand, the fact that national legal orders have no direct equivalent of the position in their supreme or constitutional courts should have engaged the curiosity of the academic community to undertake such research. The reason for such scarcity of research in this area is not immediately obvious.

A review of the research that has been undertaken on the role and function of the Advocate General and on the contribution of the Opinions to the development of EU law supports the conclusion that it is possible to identify significant contributions by individual Advocates General. For example, the research undertaken by the author and Professor Noreen

---

[1] Only one book and a few articles have been written on the Advocate General: N Burrows and R Greaves, *The Advocate General and EC Law* (Oxford, Oxford University Press, 2007); A Barav, 'Le commissaire du gouvernement pres le Conseil D'Etat Francais et l'avocat general pres la Cour De Justice des Communautes Europeennes' (1974) *Revue Internationale de Droit Compare* 809; P Gori, 'L'Avocat General a la Cour De Justice Des Communautes Europeennes' (1976) *Cahiers de Droit Europeen* 375; A Dashwood, 'The Advocate General in the Court of Justice of the European Communities' (1982) 2 *Legal Studies* 202; K Borgsmidt, 'The Advocate General at the European Court of Justice: a Comparative Study' (1988) *European Law Review* 106; M Darmon, 'The Role of the Advocate General at the European Court of Justice' in S Shetreet (ed), *The Role of Courts in Society* (Dordrecht, Martinus Nijhoff 1988); N Fennelly, 'Reflections of an Irish Advocate General' (1996) *Irish Journal of European Law* 5; M Vranken, 'Role of the Advocate General in the Law-making Process of the European Community' (1996) 25 *Anglo-American Law Review* 39; T Tridimas, 'The Role of the Advocate General in the Development of Community Law: Some Reflections' (1997) *Common Market Law Review* 1349; JR Colomer, 'L'institution de l'Avocat General a la Cour de Justice des Communautes Europeennes' in GCR Iglesias, O Due, E Schintgen and C Elsen (eds), *Melanges en homage a Fernand Schockweiler* (Baden-Baden, Nomosa Velagsgesellschaft, 1999) 523; F Jacobs, 'Advocates General and Judges in the European Court of Justice; Some Personal Reflections' in D O'Keefe and M Adenas (eds), *LiberAmicorum for Lord.Slynn: Judicial Review in European Law* (Amsterdam, Kluwer, 2000); K Mortelmans, 'The Court under the Influence of its Advocates General: An Analysis of the Case Law on the Functioning of the Internal Market' (2005) *Yearbook of European Law* 127; A Pavlopoulos, *The Advocate General's Office and its Contribution to the Development of the Law and the Judicial Machinery of the European Communities* (Athens, Komotini, 1986); C Ritter, 'The Role and Impact of the Advocate General' (2006) 12 *Columbia Journal of European Law* 3, 751; I Solanke, 'Diversity and Independence in the ECJ' (2009) 15 *Columbia Journal of European Law* 1, 89; Advocates General are also briefly mentioned in other articles such as V Perju, 'Reason and Authority in the European Court of Justice' (2009) 49 *Virginia Journal of International Law* 307.
[2] I Solanke, 'Stop the ECJ: An Empirical Analysis of Activism at the Court' *European Law Journal*.

Burrows[3] concluded that the Advocates General included in the study assisted the Court mainly in fours ways: first, by arguing for innovation based on a teleological approach;[4] secondly, by arguing for consolidation based on existing case law or legislation; [5] thirdly, by arguing against past case law;[6] and fourthly, by arguing for a strict interpretation.[7]

Thus the authors concluded that Advocates General helped to establish methods of interpretation of EU law and extracted common principles of national legal systems which contributed to the development of a new legal order. The research also identified where the Advocates General may have failed in assisting the Court, mainly where lengthy Opinions are delivered (lack of time to read and language obstacles) or where Opinions are complex and written more like extended academic essays, which are not likely to be helpful to a Court that has to find a solution and take a decision that may have legal consequences for the parties.

It was also concluded that a dialogic relationship[8] exists between the Advocates General and the Court which is an important aspect of the role and should be protected. This is a kind of ongoing conversation on the interpretation of EU law both within the Court and with academics and practitioners outside the Court. Thus the Advocates General have a general role as facilitators of debate on EU law which was not envisaged when the decision to include Advocates General as members of the ECJ was taken. The authors also concluded that Opinions which address the question and propose a solution supported by analysis of case law and

---

[3] Above n 1.

[4] Burrows and Greaves, above n 1, ch 4 on Maurice Lagrange. Lagrange's teleological approach to the interpretation of the EC Treaties and the comparative approach he adopted in his Opinions were very helpful to the Court in the development of a separate EU legal order. However, it may be that the significance of the contribution of the Opinions needs more careful assessment in respect of some important later developments. For example, there is evidence that the contribution of the Advocate General was not prominent in the establishment of the principle of state liability (ch 9) but, on the other hand, it was important in the context of developing the concept of EU citizenship (ch 10).

[5] Ibid, Jacobs' contribution to the development of a coherent EU trade mark law as demonstrated in his Opinions in Case C-427/93 *Bristol-Myers Squibb v Paranova A/S* [1976] ECR I-3457 (ch 6); Leger's contribution on the principle of direct effect and on the duty of consistent interpretation illustrated in his Opinion in Case C-287/98 *Luxembourg v Linster* [2000] ECR I-6917 (ch 8).

[6] Jacobs's Opinion in Case C-10/89 *HAG II* [1990] FCR I-3711, where the Court followed his Opinion and reversed prior case law. However, it should also be noted that the strong Opinions of Advocates General Van Gerven, Jacobs and Lenz on reversing the Court's consistent case law of not granting horizontal direct effect of directives failed to persuade the Court. Nevertheless, such strong advocacy no doubt was influential in the Court's robust insistence on imposing on national judges a duty of consistent interpretation of national law with EU law and the adoption of the doctrine of State liability.

[7] Jacobs' Opinion in Case C-292/00 *Davidoff & Cie SA and Zino Davidoff SA v Gofkid Ltd* [2003] ECR I-389; Warner's Opinion in Case 792/79R *Camera Care Ltd v Commission* [1980] ECR 119.

[8] This description is mentioned by D Kostakopoulou in 'Ideas, Norms and European Citizenship: Explaining Institutional Change' (2005) 68 *Modern Law Review* 233.

legislation are the most useful. Furthermore, not surprisingly, there is also evidence to suggest that, in difficult cases, clear and succinct arguments appear to benefit the Court more than abstruse and convoluted (academic) interpretations of EU law. The evidence also indicates that it is rather immaterial whether the Opinion is 'followed' in a particular case.[9]

A more empirical type of research has been undertaken by other academics. For example, Dr Iyola Solanke interviewed approximately 20 Advocates General and legal secretaries.[10] This research is particularly helpful in providing a view of the role of the Advocate General from an inside-the-court perspective. The study also demonstrates the individualism of the role and the influence and importance of the legal secretaries who not only debate the legal issues that arise in the cases with the Advocate General but, in a large number of cases, write the first draft of the Opinion. The degree of influence that legal secretaries have over the approach that an Advocate General may take remains a mystery, given the secrecy that surrounds the internal operation of Advocates General's chambers and the lack of a uniform practice. Both the appointment of the legal secretaries and the working methods of Advocates General's chambers are matters for each individual Advocate General to determine.[11]

Other authors have also commented on the function and role of the Advocate General and tried to describe it in a variety of ways. The function of the Advocate General within the decision-making process of the ECJ has been compared to the French Commissaire du Gouvernement in the Conseil d'Etat, though significant differences are evident. [12] The Opinion itself has been viewed as akin to a judgment of a court of first instance,[13] a judgment of first instance which is 'subject to instant and invariable appeal',[14] a second opinion which is in fact delivered first[15] or a dissenting judgment when the ECJ reaches a different conclusion.[16] A wider function has been recognised as shedding light 'in the meaning of

---

[9] See also former member of the ECJ Sir David Edward's interview with Don Smith at the University of Denver, Sturm College of Law, available at http://law.du.edu/index.php/judge-david-edward-oral-history.

[10] I Solanke, 'Diversity and Independence in the European Court of Justice' (2008–09) *Columbia Journal of European Law* 89.

[11] The appointment, role and function of the Legal Secretaries is also understudied. However, such an exercise is well beyond the scope of this chapter.

[12] Darmon and Borgsmidt, above n 1 and G Bebr, *Judicial Control of the European Communities* (1962) 24. TC Hartley, *The Foundations of European Community Law*, 5th edn (Oxford, Oxford University Press, 2003) 57.

[13] JP Warner, 'Some Aspects of the European Court of Justice' (1976) *Society of Public Teachers of Law* 15, 18; AA Dashwood, 'The Advocate General in the Court of Justice of the EC' (1982) *Legal Studies* 215.

[14] Hartley, above, n 12.

[15] Ibid.

[16] Darmon, above n 1.

an obscure judgment'[17] or adding value by being more accessible in their reasoning to 'practising lawyers, academics or simply members of the general public'.[18] More recently, authors have written of the task of the Advocate General as being to discern the public interest in any case,[19] although the ECJ has stated that the Advocates General 'are not entrusted with the defence of any particular interest'.[20]

Significant doctrinal research has been undertaken to try to evaluate the contribution that Advocates General have made to the development of EU case law. As already commented above, this is not an easy task and the conclusions reached are by their very nature tentative. Tridimas and Arnull have written on the role from a general perspective and Mortelmans has focused on the Opinions delivered in cases concerning the internal market. Tridimas concluded that the Opinions of the Advocate General should be seen as an invisible influence on the Court and that the most important aspect of the Opinion is its explanatory value.[21] Arnull also concluded that it is difficult to measure empirically the influence of the Opinions on the development of EU law, given that ECJ deliberations are held in closed session, there is a single committee style judgment and no dissenting views are expressed.[22] Nevertheless, he acknowledged the value of the Opinions for those who are concerned with the activities of the ECJ. Mortelmans, on the other hand, undertook a comprehensive analysis of the contribution of Advocates General to the functioning of the internal market,[23] and concluded that 'the Advocate General has a supporting task; a task which is aimed at shaping the law'.[24] He found that, in practice, the Advocates General have been innovative in important cases concerning the internal market and constructive commentators of the ECJ judgments by their analysis of legal writing and careful interpretation of the earlier case law, consequently contributing to the refinement of the course taken by the ECJ.

Thus the research undertaken so far has found evidence that the Opinions have significantly contributed to the development of EU law by assisting the Court to reach its decisions and also by reaching a wider

---

[17] P Craig and G de Burca, *The Evolution of EU Law* (Oxford, Oxford University Press, 1999) 94.

[18] A Arnull, *The European Union and its Court of Justice* (Oxford, Oxford University Press, 1999) 9.

[19] D Chalmers, C Hadjiemmamuil, G Monti and A Tomkins, *European Union Law: Text & Materials* (Cambridge, Cambridge University Press, 2006) 123.

[20] Case C-17/98 *Emesa Sugar (Free Zone) NV v Aruba* [2000] ECR I-665.

[21] T Tridimas, 'The Role of the Advocate General in the Development of Community Law' (1997) 34 *Common Market Law Review* 1349.

[22] Above n 18.

[23] K Motelmans, 'The Court under the Influence of its Advocates General; An Analysis of the Case Law on the Functioning of the Internal Market' (2005) *Yearbook of European Law* 127.

[24] Ibid, 167.

audience. The latter has been achieved because most of the Opinions have provided detailed analysis of relevant ECJ judgments and clarity of reasoning often absent from the committee-style ECJ judgment. The limited in-depth case studies that have been undertaken also seek to identify the degree of influence that the Opinions have had on the ECJ judgments. This is a much more difficult task, as researchers have had to rely mostly on circumstantial evidence, given that the judges' deliberations, including the written notes that are exchanged between them in preparation for the deliberation, remain secret.

B   The Strengths and Weaknesses of the Role of the Advocate General

Another approach to examining the role of the Advocate General, and, in particular, where the aim is to identify how the role might usefully be changed without damaging positive elements of the role, is to carry out, in the abstract, a SWOT analysis.[25]

The analysis identifies the main strengths of the role of the Advocate General as: impartial assessment which helps the Court by the delivery of an objective opinion without compromises; a coherent text which is an effective dissemination of the Court's judgments where the same conclusion is reached by both the Advocate General and the Court; a complete overview of the case, exploring arguments and answers not proposed in the submissions and shedding light on certain aspects of the case; the membership of the Court, which enables them to participate in case flow management;[26] and stable periods of appointments, which assist consistency and continuity of argument and a stable development of a new legal order. A more controversial though still perceived strength of the Advocate General is the pursuit of extrajudicial activities.

The current role of the Advocates General does have some weaknesses. First, Advocates General do not deliver judgments as such but a single learned individual's view of the case. Secondly, they do not participate in the deliberation of the Court and the Court has no obligation to engage actively with the Opinion when delivering a decision. Thirdly, the Opinions are not always of the highest quality or clarity. Fourthly, there has not been much diversity amongst the Advocates General.

The SWOT analysis also identifies opportunities to make the role of Advocates General more effective. It would be useful for Advocates General to project the consequences of the legal choices that they explore in their Opinions and particularly to warn the Court of the risks of taking

---

[25] SWOT stands for strengths, weaknesses, opportunities and threats.

[26] Case flow management assists the Court to take decisions as fast as possible by moving cases in a timely fashion from filing to conclusion. Effective case flow management minimises delays and makes optimum use of resources.

a particular interpretation of EU law. Some degree of specialisation by some Advocates General might also increase the potential for Opinions to influence the Court as these would then be the views of experts. An opportunity may also exist for a closer relationship between the Advocate General and the reporting judge as to which issues of EU law concern the Court in any particular case. However, care would need to be taken if this idea were pursued, given that the impartiality and independence of the Advocates General must not be prejudiced.

The threats facing the Advocate General mainly concern Article 6 of the ECHR. As they have been discussed in depth elsewhere,[27] they will not be considered in this chapter save to comment that this threat could be mitigated by wider publication of the ability of the parties to seek reopening of the oral procedure. However, the threat of case overload leading to unacceptable delays in concluding cases before the ECJ is a matter of concern which needs to be addressed.

Thus the research undertaken so far underlines the importance of the ongoing dialogic relationship between the Advocates General and the Court as well as the importance of high quality, authoritative and well reasoned Opinions. There are also some issues as to the appointment mechanism and criteria for appointment which will be addressed in the second part of the paper.

III   THE FUTURE

Although there have been regular debates on the European judicial architecture, often during the periods leading to intergovernmental conferences (IGCs) to amend the European Treaties, no amendments to the role of the Advocate General were achieved until the Nice IGC, where the overwhelming increase in the Court's workload had to be addressed. The Member States agreed to increase the number of judges by empowering the EU Council to establish a Civil Service Tribunal to deal with staff cases and to reduce the workload of the Advocates General by providing that the delivery of an Opinion was no longer required in every case before the ECJ.[28] The Court may decide that, after hearing the Advocate General, the case does not raise a new point of law and therefore an Opinion is not required. However, this reform has not eliminated the Advocates General's workload problem, which is likely to increase as litigation in the new areas

---

[27] Burrows and Greaves, above n 1, ch 3. See also the decision of the ECtHR in *Cooperatieve Producentenorganisatie van de Nederlandse Kokkelvisserij UA v The Netherlands*, App No 13645/05, judgment of 20 January 2010, where a challenge to the compatibility of the Advocate General's role in the proceedings before the ECJ with Art 6 ECHR was rejected as manifestly ill-founded.

[28] For a descriptive narrative of these events, see Burrows and Greaves, above n 1, 20–22.

of competences filter through to the ECJ from the national courts. An increase in the number of Advocates General is not likely (at least in this author's view),[29] given the cost, the lack of evidence that the Opinions of Advocates General are essential to the workings of the Court and the lack of political will. It is submitted that other solutions should be explored that can safeguard the strengths of the role of Advocate General which are well recognised and eliminate some of the weaknesses that have been identified above. It will be an additional bonus if the proposed reforms accrue benefits from the opportunities the system provides and/or if some of the threats are marginalised.

The major changes that are proposed in this chapter for wider debate are the following: a reconsideration of some aspects of the working relationship between the Advocates General and the judges; a fundamental change in the manner in which Advocates General are appointed; and the identification of specific requirements that are essential and/or desirable for appointment to the position of Advocate General.

However, in order for such a proposal to be given a fair hearing amongst the academic, judicial and political communities, it is important that we recognise that Advocates General are not judges and their influence on the judgments of the Court is not measurable with certainty. It is true that in every other way Advocates General are treated as members of the Court, but the fact remains that they do not decide cases. It is worth emphasising that the Opinions have no legal effect on the parties, their main function and objective being to provide the Court with an informed, impartial and reasoned view of the legal issues on which the Court will have to reach a decision. If the function of the Opinion and the auxiliary role of the Advocates General in the EU judicial architecture are emphasised more in the literature and in the debates in which academics, practitioners and policy makers engage at international conferences, then perhaps the governments of the Members States will find it politically more acceptable to have a more open and transparent mechanism for the appointment of Advocates General.[30]

A   The Working and Dialogic Relationship with the Judges

It is difficult to evaluate how well the relationship between the Advocates General and the Court has worked because hard evidence is unavailable.

---

[29] Art 252 TFEU does provide specifically that '[s]hould the Court of Justice so request, the Council, acting unanimously, may increase the number of Advocates-General'. Declaration 38 on Artile 252 TFEU regarding the number of Advocates General in the ECJ [2008] OJ C115/350 provides for an increase from 8 to 11 on a request by the ECJ.

[30] Although the criteria and the appointment mechanism for the ECJ judges are outside the scope of this essay, it also needs addressing. For a discussion on the appointment of judges see Solanke's article on Diversity and Independence, above n 10.

The practice of the Court not to engage openly with the Opinions of the Advocates General when delivering judgments or preliminary rulings makes it impossible to be confident, when reaching conclusions, as to the degree of influence that Opinions have on the Court. It is difficult to undertake research, since no hard evidence is available.[31] Furthermore, there appears to be very little dialogue between the reporting judge and Advocate General assigned for each case. Evidence of contact between the chambers via legal secretaries is for the most part concerned with the chambers of the judges sitting in the same case rather than between the chambers of the Advocate General and the reporting judge. Furthermore, it would probably be inappropriate for such closeness to occur, given the requirement of independence that is stipulated in the Treaty. However, it is submitted that the term 'independence' in Articles 252 and 253 the Treaty on the Functioning of the European Union (TFEU) relates to independence from the Member States that nominate them and the parties arguing before the Court rather than independence from the internal workings of the Court.[32]

Nevertheless there is sufficient evidence to support the conclusion that the dialogic relationship between the Advocate General and the Court and the ongoing conversation on the interpretation of EU law within the Court with academics and practitioners outside the Court have been important elements in building a coherent EU legal order.[33] One of the weaknesses identified in the role of the Advocate General is not so much that the deliberation takes place without the presence of the Advocate General but that there is no evidence that the judges, in taking their decision, engage in any form with the Opinion of the Advocate General. Comments from individual judges that their deliberations start with the Opinion may be correct, but it begs the question as to why the reporting judge prepares the Court's draft judgment whilst the Opinion is being drafted. It would be more logical, though it would lengthen proceedings, for the reporting judge to wait for the Opinion to be delivered and then start the draft.

Thus the first proposed reform on the working relationship between the Advocate General and the Court is that a duty be imposed on the Court to be more transparent in how much it relies on the reasoning of the Advocate General. Judgments of the Court should expressly refer to any reasoning in the Opinion which the Court has followed. Similarly, the

---

[31] Former judge, Sir David Edward has commented that the Opinion of the Advocate General is the 'starting point' for the Court's deliberation in 'How the Court of Justice Works' (1995) *European Law Review* 539, 555.

[32] For an excellent discussion on the meaning of 'independence' as perceived by Advocates General that were interviewed by Solanke see above n 10, 98–101.

[33] eg See Part III of Burrows and Greaves, above n 1 which traces the influence of Advocates General in developing some fundamental concepts of EU Law, namely, direct effect, state liability and citizenship.

Court should also be more specific as to which aspects of the reasoning set out in the Opinion it has not followed.

Another suggestion for a pragmatic reform that may enhance the dialogic relationship between the Advocates General and the Court concerns the specialism of some Advocates General. The EU has now acquired competences in very sensitive areas of law, such as family law, where decisions taken by the Court will not only have direct legal effect on EU citizens but may also impact on areas of national law which have evolved in each Member State, reflecting different national traditions and culture. These differences are then embedded in the national laws and procedures of the Member States.

According to Article 252 TFEU, the Court shall be 'assisted' by eight Advocates General. As already stated above, research has indeed shown that the Advocates General have assisted the Court in various manners. One such manner has been the way in which certain technical or complex areas of EU law have benefited from having a number of Opinions delivered by the same Advocate General. The most striking example is Advocate General Jacobs, who delivered over 20 opinions on the interpretation of provisions of the Trade Mark Directive[34] over a short period of 10 years.[35] Another example is Advocate General van Gerven, who may be considered to have acquired a specialism, given that he delivered Opinions in 15 cases involving aspects of gender discrimination in the short period of six years.[36]

The studies on Jacobs and van Gerven also suggest that cases are not allocated to Advocates General on a rotation basis, as sometimes stated by members of the Court and the academic literature,[37] though there is certainly no evidence that expertise and specialism play any role in the method by which Member States choose their nominees.

Thus the second proposed reform is to appoint some Advocates General on the basis of their expertise in sensitive or complex fields of law where the EU has acquired new competences. It is submitted that the Court would benefit and be 'assisted' by a specialist Opinion from an independent and impartial Advocate General,[38] and that the time is right to experiment, given the EU's new competence in criminal and family matters.

---

[34] Council Dir 89/104 of 21 December 1988 to approximate the laws of the Member States relating to trade marks [1989] OJ L40/1.

[35] For a full evaluation of his contribution to the development of EU trade mark law see Burrows and Greaves, above n 1, ch 6.

[36] Burrows and Greaves, ibid, ch 5.

[37] L Neville Brown and F Jacobs, *The Court of Justice of the EC* (by L Neville Brown and T Kennedy), 5th edn (London, Sweet & Maxwell, 2000) 71.

[38] Burrows and Greaves, above n 1, ch 11, 298.

B The Appointment of Advocates General

In accordance with Article 253 TFEU, Advocates General and judges of both EU courts are appointed 'by common accord of the governments of the Member States for a term of six years, after consultation of the panel provided for in Article 255'. The panel comprises seven persons and gives an opinion on the suitability of the candidates nominated by the Member States to perform the duties.[39] There is no provision for a uniform mechanism to be agreed as to how the national candidate is chosen.[40]

The appointment or renewal of appointment of an Advocate General will now be subject to an opinion from the Selection Panel.[41] However, given that the number of Advocates General is limited to eight, the system of nominations for Advocates General is not exactly identical to that for the appointment of judges. A political agreement has resulted in France, Germany, Italy, Spain and the UK having the right to nominate an Advocate General each,[42] whilst the other 22 Member States have to take their turn in nominating the remaining three Advocates General.[43] Thus, five Advocates General are permanently appointed, as long as the Member States concerned nominate them every six years,[44] while the nomination of the other Advocates General rotates amongst the rest of the 22 EU Member States.

A number of commentators, including Sally J Kenney, have expressed surprise that there is 'little public scrutiny of appointments to the ECJ within the Member State and there is none within Community institutions'.[45] The recent changes that have been introduced for the appointment of members of the ECJ, including its Advocates General, are an improvement, but are still far short of what is required. The current (improved) method of selection of the members of the EU courts remains intergovernmental in nature, discriminatory on the grounds of nationality and

---

[39] The panel was introduced by the TFEU. For further details see Council Decisions 2010/124 and 2010/125 of 25 February 2010 relating to the operating rules of the panel and to the appointment of the members of the panel provided for in Art 255 TFEU [2010] OJ L50/18 and L50/20. This change in the appointment mechanism is too recent for any valuable comment to be made on its success.

[40] In the UK, for example, the vacancy is advertised and there is an open competitive process. For the processes used in other countries see Solanke above n 10.

[41] For an examination of this new appointment process see Burrows, 'The Lisbon Treaty and the Revised Appointments Process for the Advocate General', work in progress paper presented at UACES, Bruges 2010.

[42] Declaration 38, above n 29.

[43] Not surprisingly Poland made a fuss that if the number of Advocates General is increased they want a permanent nomination and they got it!

[44] Eg Francis Jacobs was nominated by the UK for three mandates from 1988 to 2006.

[45] S Kenney, 'The Members of the Court of Justice of the European Communities' (1998) 5 *Columbia Journal of European Law* 101, 102.

outdated given what has already been achieved, namely the establishment and development of a distinct legal order.

The dilemma, therefore, is to find an appropriate mechanism for the appointment of Advocates General which respects to some extent the fundamental EU principle of no discrimination on the grounds of nationality but also accommodates the political reality that the EU is a 'a constitutional order of states'. At the very least, there is a need to ensure geographical spread and that no two Advocates General are nationals of the same Member State. The appointment mechanism should also ensure that there is a fair representation of female and male appointees.[46]

Thus, the first proposed reform is the abolition of the right of the large five Member States to have a permanent Advocate General each. It is difficult to find objective justifications for this arrangement whereby five Member States are so privileged.

Even if it is conceded that having permanent Advocates General from France, Germany and Italy, and then from the UK, was initially justifiable to assist the Court to take decisions that were compatible with the national legal systems of the larger Member States, the argument is no longer sustainable, given the ease of accessibility to information and the general legal expertise on national legal systems that exists at the Court. The research and library resources available at the ECJ, the electronic accessibility of national laws and the expertise of national lawyers pleading before the ECJ should ensure that differences in national legal systems are taken fully into account when proposing solutions to legal problems facing the ECJ. What possible non-political justification could be envisaged for having a permanent Advocate General from France, Germany, Italy, Spain and the UK?

The second proposed reform is more radical. It is advocated in this chapter that a different mechanism from the one applied for the ECJ judges should be introduced for the appointment of Advocates General. An appointment mechanism more similar to the one that has been designed for the appointment of judges to the EU Civil Service Tribunal[47] seems more suitable. The main features of the Civil Service Tribunal appointment mechanism are that there is an open call for applications, an opinion and long short-list from the Selection Committee and a Council decision on appointment. This open approach should be encouraged, with vacancies for the position of Advocates General being advertised throughout the EU, both in the Official Journal and in appropriate leading national

---

[46] A similar appointment process has been adopted for the International Criminal Court. See T Ingadottir, 'The International Criminal Court—Nomination and Election of Judges' (June 2002), available at http://www.ru.is/publications/CV/Thordis-Ingadottir_2008.pdf.

[47] See H Cameron, 'Establishment of the European Union Civil Service Tribunal' in *The Law and Practice of International Courts and Tribunals* (The Netherlands, Koninklijke Brill NV, 2006) 273–83.

journals and newspapers. This radical reform will not be popular with various interested parties, including the Member States. It is clear that, in accepting this very different method of selection for appointment to the EU Civil Service Tribunal, the Member States were anxious to make sure that it was not taken as a precedent for other appointments[48] and, therefore, will undoubtedly strongly resist the proposed reform for the appointment of Advocates General.

Even if the first proposed reform is not acceptable to the five Member States and they continue to have permanent Advocates General, some reforms should be adopted. All five Member States should have to adopt a uniform, transparent and open method of appointment, and apply the same uniform criteria for appointment as outlined below. Furthermore, the EU Council should only appoint the nominees if a favourable opinion is received from the Selection Panel.

Nevertheless, these two proposed changes in the appointment mechanism would strengthen the independence and impartiality of Advocates General that is enshrined in Article 253 TFEU. It would liberate them totally from the governments that currently nominate them. A more open system of recruitment may also address the weakness of lack of diversity[49] and provide an opportunity for a wider range of suitably qualified EU citizens to consider applying for the position. There is very much a feeling of lack of transparency in the manner in which Member States select the individuals they nominate as Advocates General. This is not felt so much in the UK, where these positions are now advertised.

C The Criteria for Appointment

Article 252 TFEU provides for the appointment of eight Advocates General, with the possibility of the EU Council, acting on a request from the ECJ and acting unanimously, to increase that number. The TFEU does not set out any nationality requirements for appointment, the only essential requirement being that they 'shall be chosen from persons whose independence is beyond doubt and who possess the qualifications required for appointment to the highest judicial offices in their respective countries or who are juriconsults of recognised competence'.[50] Thus the TFEU does

---

[48] At the time of the introduction of this new mechanism for the appointment of members of the EU Civil Service Tribunal it was specifically stated that this appointment mechanism was not a precedent for other judicial appointments (statement entered in the Council's minutes at the time of the adoption of Council Decision 2004/752 [2004] OJ L333/7). However, circumstances do change and it would not be the first time that political statements have been ignored as long as political will exists to take a different direction.

[49] I Solanke, 'Diversity and Independence in the European Court of Justice' (2009) 15 *Columbia Journal of European Law* 89, 91–93.

[50] Art 253 TFEU.

neither require that members of the Court be EU citizens or that they have competence in EU law!

It is argued in this chapter that it is not sufficient that nominees are suitably qualified for appointment to 'the highest judicial offices in their respective countries'. Nominees may be highly qualified to hold these national judicial offices but be totally ignorant of EU law and procedures. The presumption that if nominees are qualified for a national judicial office they are also qualified for an appointment to the European courts is not sustainable. This seems particularly pertinent in the context of the Advocate General, whose function is not to judge a case on the basis of the arguments that have been presented both in written submissions and in the oral proceedings but to deliver 'reasoned submissions on cases which, in accordance with the Statute of the Court of justice of the European Union, require his involvement'.[51] The cases before the ECJ require either interpretation or declaration of invalidity of EU law,[52] or require disputes to be decided between various parties.[53] It is to state the obvious that knowledge of the legal system on which the Advocate General is required to submit an Opinion should be an essential requirement for an appointment to that position.[54]

The requirement that the nominee should be qualified for the highest judicial office in their home country may have been sensible in the 1950s, when the EU legal system had yet to be created. That creation was to be based on the European Treaties and on the principles common to the national legal systems of the six original Member States. Sixty years later, such a requirement for appointment seems outdated and irrelevant.

Thus, the first proposed essential requirement for appointment is that nominees or applicants for the positions of Advocates General should be not only qualified for appointment to the highest judicial offices in their respective countries but also have demonstrable knowledge of substantive and procedural EU law.[55] There has been so much integration of EU law in the national legal systems of the Member States, as well as the introduction of EU remedies in national courts, that demonstrable knowledge of EU law should not be a difficult requirement to meet for those intending to seek an appointment as an Advocate General. Knowledge of EU law may be obtained by academic qualifications or by experience as a practitioner, a government lawyer or an in-house lawyer.

---

[51] Art 252 TFEU.

[52] These are primarily cases which reach the ECJ as preliminary references from national courts (Art 267 TFEU) or direct judicial review actions brought by privileged parties (eg Art 263 TFEU).

[53] A large number of disputes before the ECJ are between the Member States and the Commission.

[54] For a wider ranging discussion on appropriate criteria see Solanke, above n 10, 105–11.

[55] Knowledge of EU law also ranks high with the Advocates General interviewed by Solanke, above n 10, 105.

A requirement of knowledge of EU law may also address perceived weaknesses, namely that the quality of Advocates General's Opinions can be variable, and address the threat that the quality of the Opinions may deteriorate to such an extent that they lose their usefulness or are totally ignored.

The second proposed essential requirement for appointment is that the selected applicant should have a degree of fluency in French and English before taking up the appointment. The counter argument to make language ability an essential requirement for appointment is that Advocates General write in their own language; therefore language skills may be an advantage but are not an essential requirement. Nevertheless, given the fact that Advocates General are now so heavily involved in case flow management,[56] perhaps a language requirement is more important than in the past as it can help the management of the workload of the Court.

A third proposed reform is to make provision that some of the candidates for appointment are recognised specialists in areas of law which are either particularly technical, such as intellectual property law and competition law, or in areas where the EU has acquired new competences. Thus, in listing the requirements for appointment as an Advocate General, it may be that some consideration should also be given to appointing some Advocates General on the basis of the specialisation of the applicant.

Two of the strengths that have been identified in Advocates General's Opinions are consistency and continuity, which have assisted the ECJ in developing EU law in areas where new competences have been transferred from the Member States to the EU.[57] There may also be an opportunity here for specialist Advocates General to influence the judges by writing with authority as specialists in the field. The ECJ should be invited to identify areas of EU competences in which the Court would benefit in having a specialist Opinion. Some of the areas that immediately come to mind are: intellectual property, competition law, criminal law, family law and tax law.

Given the acknowledged contribution of the Advocates General to the case flow management of the ECJ, it should be a desirable requirement for those seeking a position as Advocates General to have demonstrable experience of management of work flows. As far as case flow management is concerned, the Advocates General play an important role which is fully recognised by the judges. Advocates General are very much involved in the decisions taken by the Court as to which Court Chamber to refer a case, and in judging the importance of the issues raised in the case and how the case should proceed. The decision not to have an Opinion in a

---

[56] This is the expression used for the coordination of court processes and resources to ensure efficiency and speed from the filing of a case to its conclusion.

[57] An example is the creation of a EU trademark law. See Burrows and Greaves, above n 1, ch 11.

case that raises no new point of EU law is taken by the Court after consultation with the Advocate General appointed for that particular case. The allocation of cases amongst the Advocates General is done by the First Advocate General, who is appointed on a yearly basis.

D Concluding Observations

There is much that can be discussed as to how the role of Advocates General may be improved, how Advocates General should be appointed and what criteria candidates should have to meet in order to be considered for such a position. This chapter does not seek to provide all the answers but merely to address a few issues and promote ideas for further debate.

None of the proposed reforms discussed in this chapter impair the continuance of the extrajudicial activities that members of the Court, and in particular Advocates General, undertake, such as publishing articles, contributing chapters to edited books, attending conferences and engaging generally with the national judiciary, practitioners and academics. This manner of dissemination of EU law and ECJ practice has been identified as one of the strengths of the role of the Advocate General and should be encouraged. Similarly, the proposed reforms do not resolve the perceived threat to the Opinion in respect of Article 6 ECHR. This difficult issue will have to be resolved one day and should be directly addressed when negotiations start for the EU to accede to the ECHR.[58]

It is submitted that the reforms that have been proposed above are likely to strengthen the role of the Advocate General. The dialogic relationship between the Advocate General and the Court, which has been identified as an important feature of the role of the Advocate General, would be strengthened by a requirement that the Court engages with the Advocate General's reasoning, particularly when it reaches the same conclusion but follows a different route. Thus the Court should identify in its judgment which aspects of the reasoning in the Opinion it has rejected. The Advocates General in their Opinions sometimes explore arguments and answers not proposed in the submissions of the parties or the interveners, and the Court should be required to comment expressly on them in the judgment. An Opinion delivered by a specialist, particularly in areas which are complex or where the EU has obtained new competences, would also encourage this important aspect of the role of the Advocate General.

The proposed reforms as to the appointment of Advocates General would ensure that the requirement of independence is fully met. There is no doubt that the mechanism devised for the appointment of judges

---

[58] Although the ECtHR has not found the role of the Advocate General in the proceedings of the ECJ as incompatible with Art 6 ECHR, above n 27, it is submitted that this is too important an issue not to be settled by expressed terms in the negotiated agreement.

to the Civil Service Tribunal is more transparent and more appropriate for a constitutional order of states than a selection panel mechanism which remains intergovernmental as long as the system of nominees is maintained. The current nationality discrimination that is embedded in permanently having Advocates General from five Member States should be removed. Any EU citizen who meets the criteria for appointment should be free to apply for the position of Advocate General.

It has also been demonstrated that Opinions which focus on the legal issues and propose solutions that are supported by analysis of existing case law and legislation are the most useful to the Court. Thus the proposed essential requirement of knowledge or experience of EU law and practice seems fundamental in ensuring that the quality of the Opinions is maintained. The desirable requirement that some Advocates General are appointed for their specialist knowledge also seems to be a further step in enhancing the quality of the Opinion delivered to the Court, particularly in the areas identified above. Language and management skills may seem luxuries, but in the context of a very busy Court whose working language is French and is continuously facing an increasing case load, such skills should be regarded at the very least as desirable.

10

The Role of General Principles of EU Law

KOEN LENAERTS and JOSÉ A GUTIÉRREZ-FONS*

T
HE FUNCTION OF general principles in the EU legal order appears to be threefold.[1] First, they enable the European Court of Justice (ECJ) to fill normative gaps left either by the authors of the Treaty or by the EU legislator, to ensure the autonomy and coherence of the EU legal system. Secondly, they serve as an aid to interpretation, since both EU law and national law falling within the scope of EU law must be interpreted in light of the general principles. Finally, they may be relied upon as grounds for judicial review. EU legislation in breach of a general principle is to be held void and national law falling within the scope of EU law that contravenes a general principle must be set aside.[2]

In addition to these three functions, general principles may also be said to contribute to the creation and development of a common constitutional space or, as Groussot puts it, a 'ius commune europaeum'.[3] Since general principles are inspired by the constitutional traditions of the Member States,[4] national constitutional law and jurisprudence influence the way in which the ECJ incorporates general principles into the EU legal order. Thus, national constitutions and national constitutional courts play an important role in the formation of general principles, giving rise to a 'bottom-up' effect. Once a general principle is recognised, however, the autonomy of the Union legal order requires the ECJ to take into account

* All opinions expressed herein are personal to the authors.
[1] See generally U Bernitz and J Nergelius (eds), *General Principles of European Community Law*, European Monograph 25 (The Hague, Kluwer, 2000); T Tridimas, *The General Principles of EU Law*, 2nd edn (Oxford, Oxford University Press, 2006); X Groussot, *General Principles of Community Law* (Groningen, European Law Publishing, 2006); U Bernitz, J Nergelius, and C Cardner (eds), *General Principles of EC Law in a Process of Development*, European Monograph 62 (The Hague, Kluwer, 2008).
[2] These last two functions are grounded in the 'constitutional status' of general principles in the hierarchy of norms. See Case C-101/08 *Audiolux* [2009] ECR I-9823, para 63 and Case C-174/08 *NCC Construction Danmark* [2009] ECR I-10567, para 42.
[3] Groussot, above n 1, 421.
[4] See Joined Cases C-387/02, C-391/02 and C-403/02 *Berlusconi and Others* [2005] ECR I-3565, paras 67 and 68 (qualifying as such the retroactive application of the more lenient criminal sanction).

the special features and objectives laid down by the founding Treaties. In other words, while the recognition of general principles may be grounded in the constitutions of the Member States, when interpreting and applying them, the ECJ must break free of the moorings of the national legal systems in which they originated, sail unhindered through the uncharted waters of an autonomous legal order and attempt not to capsize when balancing the general interest against the claims of individuals. Accordingly, the outcome reached by the ECJ when applying general principles may be more, or less, beneficial to individuals than the solution that would have been reached under the law of a particular Member State. The answer adopted by the ECJ may, in certain cases, provide a plausible alternative to long-standing national legal traditions at odds with more recent developments. Thus, for instance, when the approach of the ECJ encourages the protection of certain individual rights, this may in turn put pressure on national legislators and courts to move in the same direction. Hence, general principles may also give rise to a 'top-down' effect and thus influence national constitutional traditions. This mutual cross-fertilisation creates a continuous flux of ideas and exchange of opinions between the ECJ and its national counterparts, giving rise to a common constitutional space defined by a dynamic dialogue.

The purpose of this chapter is to focus on this latter function of general principles. More specifically, we aim to examine how the creation and development of a common constitutional space affect the allocation of powers between the Union and its Member States, as well as between the EU legislator and the ECJ. This contribution unfolds as follows. In section I, we argue that the Charter of Fundamental Rights of the European Union (the Charter)[5] provides an adequate source of inspiration for the establishment of general principles, while enabling the ECJ to show respect for the political process. This section then proceeds to examine two recent cases where the ECJ drew explicitly the distinction between constitutionally protected situations that give rise to the establishment of general principles and other set of circumstances calling for legislative intervention. We welcome this development, which not only highlights the constitutional status of general principles but is also respectful of the prerogatives of the EU legislator or, where appropriate, the national legislator. Next, we argue that the establishment of specific constitutional expressions of a general principle does not upset the vertical and horizontal allocation of powers, provided that the scope of application of the general principle at issue is clearly defined. Section II posits that, not only with regard to the establishment of general principles but also in relation to their development, national constitutional traditions have made

---

[5] The Charter has been binding primary law of the Union since 1 December 2009. See Art 6(1) TEU and for the text of the Charter [2010] OJ C83/02.

and will continue to make an important contribution to the preservation of a common constitutional space. Drawing on a moderate discourse on constitutional pluralism, we favour the application of 'a margin of appreciation' in the development of general principles, insofar as the conferral of such a margin does not jeopardise the basic values of the EU. Finally, a brief conclusion supports the contention that the role played by the general principles of EU law is not incompatible with the idea that the Union is a 'constitutional order of states'.[6]

I THE ESTABLISHMENT OF GENERAL PRINCIPLES

A The Evaluative Approach, the Risk of Judicial Activism and the Charter

The interaction between general principles and national law can be described as a continuing two-way process. As Koopmans puts it, general principles 'are, in a certain sense, commuters'[7] who travel back and forth from the national legal systems to the EU. To preserve this two-way process when establishing and developing general principles, it is vital that the Court follows a methodology that satisfies the expectations of national courts. Otherwise, the latter may perceive general principles as illegitimate judicial lawmaking and decide to stop engaging with the ECJ.

In establishing and developing general principles, the laws of the Member States have proved to be very influential. In this regard, there is a strong correlation between the deference shown to national law by the ECJ and the degree of convergence existing among the different national legal systems. The more convergence there is among the legal orders of the Member States, the more the ECJ will tend to follow into their footsteps.[8] Where convergence is not total but a particular approach is common to a large majority of national legal systems, then the ECJ will normally follow that approach, adapting and developing it to fit within the EU context. A good example is provided by the ECJ's case law on the general principle of State liability in damages.[9] Although the introduction of that judge-made principle was justified on the ground that it 'is inherent in the system of the EC Treaty',[10] it has subsequently been refined and developed on the

---

[6] A Dashwood, 'The Limits of European Community powers' (1996) 21 *European Law Review* 113.

[7] T Koopmans, 'General Principles of Law in European and National Systems of Law: A Comparative View' in U Bernitz and J Nergelius (eds), *General Principles of European Community Law*, above n 1, 25.

[8] K Lenaerts, 'Interlocking Legal Orders in the European Union and Comparative Law' (2003) 52 *International & Comparative Law Quarterly* 873, 886.

[9] Ibid, 887.

[10] Joined Cases C-6/90 and C-9/90 *Francovich and Others* [1991] ECR I-5357, para 35.

basis of comparative law methodology. Thus, in *Brasserie du Pêcheur*,[11] drawing on the comparative law analysis carried out by AG Tesauro in his Opinion, the ECJ ruled that liability for loss or damage caused by a Member State could not be made conditional upon a finding of fault or negligence.[12] As for the obligations imposed on the injured party, relying again on the Opinion of AG Tesauro, the ECJ found that there was a duty to mitigate loss incumbent on the party claiming damages which was 'common to the legal systems of the Member States'.[13] Likewise, in *Köbler*, the ECJ drew on the rules applicable in national legal systems in order to dismiss the arguments based on the principle of res judicata and the principle of the independence of the judiciary, which were put forward by a number of Member States opposed to state liability for the conduct of national courts. Referring to the Opinion of AG Léger, the Court held that those arguments were indeed invoked by national legal systems to justify the imposition of limits on state liability for such conduct, but not in such a way as to create an insurmountable obstacle to such liability in all circumstances. On the contrary, the Court observed that, in spite of divergences on the content and scope of the principle of state liability for acts of the judiciary, there was a common trend at national level in favour of recognising that individuals could claim compensation for damages caused by national courts.[14]

By contrast, where there are important divergences among national legal systems, the ECJ will be careful before adopting an 'EU' solution. The ruling of the ECJ in *Grant* illustrates this point.[15] In this case, the Court was asked whether Article 141 EC (now Article 157 TFEU) precluded an employer from refusing to award a travel concession to the same-sex partner of an employee in a stable relationship. The ECJ took a close look at the solutions provided for by national legislatures, observing that Member States had taken quite different stands. Some of them had given same-sex registered partnerships the same status as marriages. Most of them treated these unions as stable heterosexual relationships outside marriage only with respect to a limited number of rights. Finally, only a few recognised no rights for same-sex partners. In light of these divergences, the ECJ ruled that

> in the present state of the law within the [Union], stable relationships between two persons of the same sex are not regarded as equivalent to marriages or stable relationships outside marriage between persons of opposite sex. Consequently, an employer is not required by [Union] law to treat the situation

---

[11] Joined Cases C-46/93 and C-48/93 *Brasserie du Pêcheur and Factortame* [1996] ECR I-1029.

[12] Ibid, para 80. See also Opinion of AG Tesauro in the same case, paras 85–90.

[13] Ibid, para 85.

[14] Case C-224/01 *Köbler* [2003] ECR I-10239, para 48.

[15] Case C-249/96 *Grant* [1998] ECR I-621.

of a person who has a stable relationship with a partner of the same sex as equivalent to that of a person who is married to or has a stable relationship outside marriage with a partner of the opposite sex.[16]

Moreover, in discovering general principles, it is well established that the ECJ does not seek to identify the lowest common denominator from national constitutional traditions. Instead, the ECJ follows 'an evaluative approach', according to which the Court incorporates the solution provided for by the national legal orders that fits better or is in line with the objectives and structure of the Treaty. As AG Lagrange eloquently expressed,

> the case law of the Court, insofar as it invokes national laws (as it does to a large extent) to define the rules of law relating to the application of the Treaty, is not content to draw on more or less arithmetical 'common denominators' between the different national solutions, but chooses from each of the Member States those solutions which, having regard to the objects of the Treaty, appear to it to be the best or, if one may use the expression, the most progressive. This is the spirit, moreover, which has guided the Court hitherto.[17]

Herdegen opines that the ECJ must be cautious when having recourse to this evaluative approach 'that harbours the potential for excessive judicial activism'.[18] To that effect, he echoes the critiques of AG Mazák in *Palacios de la Villa*[19] regarding the methodology employed by the ECJ in *Mangold*[20] when establishing the principle of non-discrimination on grounds of age. Herdegen and AG Mazák posit that neither national constitutional traditions nor international law provide an adequate source of inspiration for the Court's position. Only two national constitutions recognise the principle at issue,[21] whilst the various international instruments to which the Member States are signatories refer to the principle of equality in general but remain silent on the principle of non-discrimination on the specific grounds of age.[22] Additionally, Herdegen and AG Mazák criticise the Court for deducing the principle of non-discrimination on grounds of age from the principle of equality. Recalling *Grant*,[23] they argue that it falls to the EU legislator and, where appropriate, to the national

---

[16] Ibid, para 35.
[17] Opinion of AG Lagrange in Case 14/61 *Hoogovens v High Authority* [1962] ECR 253. See also Opinion of AG Roemer in Case 18/70 *Duraffour v Council* [1971] ECR 515.
[18] M Herdegen, 'General Principles of EU Law- The Methodological Challenge' in U Bernitz, J Nergelius, and C Cardner (eds), *General Principles of EC Law in a Process of Development*, above n 1, 343, 348.
[19] Opinion of AG Mazák in C-411/05 *Palacios de la Villa* [2007] ECR I-8531, paras 92–95.
[20] Case C-144/04 *Mangold* [2005] ECR I-9981.
[21] Only the Portuguese and Finnish constitutions recognise this principle.
[22] Herdegen, above n 18, 350–51. See also J Jans, 'The Effect in National Legal Systems of the Prohibition of Discrimination on Grounds of Age as a General Principle of Community Law' (2007) 34 *Legal Issues of Economic Integration* 53, 65.
[23] See Grant, above n 15.

legislature to identify the criteria on which the differentiation between individual situations cannot legitimately be based. Herdegen goes even further, suggesting that, since the ECJ encroached upon the competences reserved to the Member States, this invites German courts to read the ruling in *Mangold* as ultra vires[24] (German courts would thus refer this question to the German Constitutional Court,[25] which would then decide, in light of its *Maastricht* decision,[26] whether *Mangold* should be declared inapplicable in Germany[27]).

Nevertheless, these objections overlook the internal source of inspiration supporting the findings of the ECJ in *Mangold*, namely the Charter.[28] In effect, Article 21(1) of the Charter states that 'any discrimination based on . . . age . . . shall be prohibited'. If *Mangold* had been delivered after *Parliament v Council*,[29] perhaps the ECJ would have made an express reference to this instrument.[30] In the latter case, the Court held for the first time that, while the Charter was not legally binding at the time, it could operate as a source of inspiration for the establishment of general principles.[31] Since then, the Court has continued this trend, often citing articles of the Charter as a source of inspiration for general principles.[32] This is a positive development. Not only is the aim of the Charter to reaffirm the European *acquis* regarding fundamental rights, but the Charter also embodies contemporary European values and is designed to meet the challenges of social and technological change.[33] In fact, since 1 December 2009, when the Treaty of Lisbon entered into force, the Charter stands on an equal footing with the TEU and the TFEU. Accordingly, the Charter provides a sound legal basis for the establishment of general principles. By rendering rights visible and by merging and systematising in a single document the sources of inspiration scattered in various national and international legal instruments, the Charter brings clarity for both citizens

---

[24] Herdegen, above n 18, 348.

[25] In its decision on the Treaty of Lisbon of 30 June 2009, the German Constitutional Court claimed jurisdiction to decide whether EU law is ultra vires or whether it runs counter to the core content of the constitutional identity of the German Basic Law. See German Constitutional Court, BVerfG, 2 BvE 2/08 vom 30.6.2009, Absatz-Nr (1–421), 241. Available in English at http://www.bverfg.de/entscheidungen/es20090630_2bve000208en.html.

[26] See German Constitutional Court, BVerfGE 89, 155. For the English version, see *CMLR* [1994] 57ff.

[27] It is worth noting that the ruling of the ECJ in *Mangold* was examined by the German Constitutional Court. See German Constitutional Court, case *Honeywell*, decision of 6 July 2010, BVerfG, Constitutional Complaint, 2 BvR 2661/06.

[28] See above n 5.

[29] Case C-540/03 *Parliament v Council* [2006] ECR I-5769.

[30] Herdegen, above n 18, 351 (holding that the change in the ECJ's attitude towards the Charter was, in part, triggered by the severe criticism against *Mangold*).

[31] *Parliament v Council*, above n 29, para 38.

[32] See, eg Case C-432/05 *Unibet* [2007] ECR I-2271, para 37; Case C-12/08 *Mono Car Styling* [2009] ECR I-6653, para 47. After the entry into force of the Treaty of Lisbon, see especially Case C-555/07 *Kücükdeveci*, judgment of 19 January 2010, para 22.

[33] Tridimas, above n 1, 358.

and national courts as to how fundamental rights are protected at the EU level.[34] An express reliance on the Charter as a ground for incorporating a new general principle cannot awaken national sensitivities. On the contrary, since the Charter is the result of a pan-European consensus, drawing on its articles for inspiration is a sign of judicial deference to the political process. The Charter thus provides an adequate basis to cope with the objections raised by AG Mazák and Herdegen.[35]

B Distinguishing between Constitutionally Protected Situations and Other Sets of Circumstances Calling for Legislative Intervention

In addition, two recent decisions of the ECJ demonstrate that recognising the principle of equality as a general principle does not allow the ECJ to interfere with the prerogatives of the EU legislator. In *Audiolux*,[36] the ECJ was asked whether there was a principle of equal treatment of minority shareholders. This principle would seek to protect minority shareholders by obliging the dominant shareholder of a company, to offer to buy their shares under the same conditions as those agreed when the takeover of the company took place.[37] The ECJ began by denying that the alleged principle of equal treatment of minority shareholders could be found in secondary legislation.[38] Next, it examined whether such a principle could be inferred from the general principle of equality. The Court replied in the negative. It held that not only would such a principle require weighing the interests of the dominant shareholder against those of minority shareholders, it would also necessitate an evaluation of the legal consequences for corporate takeovers. Likewise, in light of the principle of legal certainty, this principle would require a precise expression,[39] ensuring that interested parties were able to act in complete awareness of their obligations and rights. In any event, even assuming that minority shareholders deserve special protection, the general principle of equality does not provide the right avenue for guaranteeing this protection.[40] The Court also observed that, while the general principle of equality has a constitutional status, the alleged principle of equal treatment of minority

---

[34] P Eeckhout, 'The EU Charter of Fundamental Rights and the Federal Question' (2002) 39 *Common Market Law Review* 945, 951–52.

[35] But see Herdegen, above n 18, 352 (opining that 'it remains to be seen whether the reference to the Charter . . . ensures methodological added value with respect to the scope of fundamental rights and the justification of interference by EU legislation or Member Sates' action').

[36] *Audiolux*, above n 2.

[37] Ibid, para 32.

[38] Ibid, para 52 (reaching the same conclusion, AG Trstenjak also examined Treaty provisions and international law. See her Opinion in *Audiolux*, above n 2, paras 75–80).

[39] Ibid, para 58.

[40] Ibid, para 59.

shareholders would require such a degree of specificity that its formulation inevitably involves legislative choices.[41] Therefore, the ECJ concluded that the alleged principle of equal treatment of minority shareholders could not be recognised as a general principle of EU law.

In *NCC Construction Danmark*,[42] the ECJ again stressed that, in the absence of legislative choices, the application of the general principle of equality is confined to constitutional questions. The facts of the case may be summarised as follows. Under Danish law, a construction business had to pay VAT on any construction carried out on its own account, while the subsequent sale of that real estate was an exempt transaction. This meant that if a construction business paid VAT for goods and services used for both the construction of a building on account of its customers and the sale of a building constructed on its own account, it could only deduct the VAT charged on those goods and services in relation to its taxable activities, ie the construction of a building on account of its customers. The applicant, a construction company, argued that the Sixth VAT Directive[43] had not been properly transposed into Danish law. It contended, among other grounds, that the right to deduction of VAT had been infringed by Denmark, since that Member State had legislated in a way that subjected the applicant to less advantageous treatment (partial deduction) than that to which building businesses were entitled under the Sixth VAT Directive (full deduction). The Court began by observing that the right to deduction is a fundamental principle underlying the common EU system of VAT. Indeed, it is the embodiment of the general principle of equality within that common system.[44] Next, basing its approach on *Audiolux*, the Court ruled that, in contrast to the general principle of equality, which has a constitutional status, the right to deduction is grounded in secondary EU law.[45] Since the Danish legislator had exercised its legislative discretion in compliance with the Sixth VAT Directive, Denmark was entitled to impose a limitation on the right to deduction for goods and services used for both taxable and exempt activities. Moreover, the ECJ pointed out that the general principle of equality read in the context of the common VAT system only required Denmark to treat comparable economic operators alike.[46] This was indeed the case, since the first sale of a building effected by both construction businesses and property developers was exempted from VAT.[47] As a result, the Court ruled that Danish law was compatible with the right to deduction provided for in the Sixth VAT Directive.

It follows from *Audiolux* and *NCC Construction Danmark* that it falls

---

[41] Ibid, para 63.
[42] *NCC Construction Danmark*, above n 2.
[43] [1977] OJ L145/1.
[44] *NCC Construction Danmark*, above n 2, para 41.
[45] Ibid, para 42.
[46] Ibid, para 44.
[47] Ibid, para 46.

to the EU legislator (or, where appropriate, to the national legislature) to identify the criteria on which differentiation between individual cases cannot legitimately be based. Yet, as *Mangold* demonstrates, the general principle of equality may be relied upon without further legislative intervention in relation to 'constitutionally protected categories' of people (eg nationality, sex, age). In summary, the distinction between constitutionally protected situations and other sets of circumstances calling for legislative intervention is a positive development. It shows that, beyond constitutionally protected categories, the general principle of equality cannot be relied upon to replace legislative choices. Otherwise, the ECJ would risk being dragged into policymaking based on its own conception of redistributive justice.[48] However, this does not mean that the general principle of equality is confined to protecting constitutional situations. As *NCC Construction Danmark* shows, it only implies that, when legislative discretion is involved, that principle intervenes at a later stage: as an *ex post* review of the internal consistency of the choices made by the legislator.

C The Establishment of Specific Constitutional Expressions of a General Principle and its Impact on the Vertical and Horizontal Allocation of Powers

The question is then whether, by establishing specific constitutional expressions of a general principle, the ECJ has encroached upon the powers of the EU legislator or of the national legislator. In concrete terms, has the establishment of the general principle of non-discrimination on grounds of age turned the vertical and horizontal allocation of powers on its head? We reckon that, insofar as the scope of application of general principles is clearly defined, the reply should be in the negative.

First, it should be pointed out that, from the fact that a general principle applies without further legislative intervention, it does not follow that a link with EU law is no longer necessary. Otherwise, the boundaries of the EU legal order would be continually extended to the detriment of national sovereignty. This point is illustrated by contrasting the facts in *Bartsch*[49] with those in *Mangold*. However, before examining these two cases, one should recall that the scope of application of general principles covers three different situations: (i) when Member States implement EU legislation[50] ('the agency situation'[51]); (ii) when the Court examines

---

[48] See Opinion of AG Trstenjak in *Audiolux*, above n 2, paras 107 to 109.
[49] Case C-427/06 *Bartsch* [2008] ECR I-7245, para 24.
[50] Case 5/88 *Wachauf* [1989] ECR 2609.
[51] Term borrowed from JHH Weiler and N Lockhart, '"Taking Rights Seriously" Seriously: The European Court and its Fundamental Rights Jurisprudence—Part I' (1995) 32 *Common Market Law Review* 51, 73.

the validity of national measures derogating from EU requirements[52] ('the derogation situation'); and (iii) where some specific substantive EU rule is applicable to the situation in question[53] ('measures falling within the purview of EU law').

In *Mangold*, the ECJ was asked whether German employment law that allowed successive fixed-term contracts for workers older than 52 years without requiring any justification was contrary to Directive 2000/78.[54] This directive establishes a general framework for equal treatment in the field of employment law. Thus, differences in treatment based on age are forbidden unless they pursue a legitimate objective in a proportionate fashion. In the event of German employment law not complying with Directive 2000/78, the national court also asked about the legal consequences for the contractual relationship between the employee and the employer, both being private parties. The ECJ found that the objective pursued by the national legislation in question was legitimate, insofar as it promoted employment for older workers. However, it failed to meet the proportionality test, since it took into account neither the personal situation of employees before they were 52 years old nor the structure of the labour market.[55] At this juncture, the Court observed that, at the time of the facts, the deadline for the transposition of Directive 2000/78 had not expired. Therefore, Directive 2000/78 could neither be invoked nor bring in the application of a general principle of EU law.[56] However, since the contested German legislation in fact implemented Directive 1999/70,[57] whose period for transposition had long expired, '[t]here was, therefore, a [Union] law framework of relevant rules . . . to which the general principle of equal treatment (including equal treatment irrespective of age) could be applied'.[58] By contrast, in *Bartsch*, the ECJ found no link with EU law. In that case, the deadline for the transposition of Directive 2000/78 had not expired at the relevant time. However, in contrast to *Mangold*, the conflicting national provisions—an occupational pension scheme which excluded a widow(er) from being entitled to a survivor's pension where her (or his) deceased husband (or wife) was a private-sector employee 15 years older than her (or him)—did not implement Union legislation. Nor was there any substantive rule of EU law applicable to the situation. Accordingly, the ECJ held that the general principle forbidding unequal treatment on grounds of age could not be relied upon by the applicant.

Furthermore, *Kücükdeveci* may be distinguished from *Mangold* and

[52] Case C-260/89 *ERT* [1991] ECR I-2925.
[53] See Opinion of AG Sharpston in *Bartsch*, above n 49, para 69. See also Tridimas, above n 1, 39–42.
[54] [2000] OJ L303/16.
[55] *Mangold*, above n 20, para 65.
[56] Opinion of AG Sharpston in *Bartsch*, above n 49, para 72.
[57] [1999] OJ L175/43; *Mangold*, above n 20, para 75.
[58] See Opinion of AG Sharpston in *Bartsch*, above n 49, para 70.

Bartsch in that the contested conduct took place after the deadline for the transposition of Directive 2000/78 had already expired. Thus directive 2000/78 provided a link with EU law given that the national legislation at issue—under which the calculation of the notice period for dismissal did not take into account the time an employee had worked before the age of 25 years—concerned rules on the conditions for employees' dismissal which is a matter covered by Article 3(1)(c) of that directive.[59]

Secondly, if a given constitutional expression of a general principle is codified by the EU legislator, should national courts evaluate the consistency of national law with EU law by reference to secondary EU legislation or by reference to the general principle enshrined therein? For instance, should national provisions of employment law that treat employees differently according to their age be examined in light of Directive 2000/78 or of the general principle of non-discrimination on grounds of age? Far from being trivial, the answer to this question is of paramount importance for the interaction between judge-made principles and secondary EU legislation. Indeed, finding the right answer, which should be in line with the principle of separation of powers, will become more pressing to the extent that, as opposed to directives,[60] general principles might produce horizontal direct effects.

In this regard, some Advocates General have argued that the horizontal application of general principles would operate to the detriment of the EU legislator. For instance, AG Ruiz-Jarabo Colomer argued in *Michaeler* that a horizontal application of general principles would 'convert . . . typical [Union] acts into merely decorative rules which may be easily replaced by the general principles'.[61] In a similar vein, AG Kokott opined in *Kofoed* that parties should not be able to rely on a general principle where the latter is given specific effect and expressed in a concrete manner in a directive. Since the content of general principles is 'much less clear and precise', the Advocate General considered that, for situations falling within the scope of a directive, 'there would [otherwise] be a danger . . . that the harmonisation objective of [the] Directive . . . would be undermined and the legal certainty . . . which it seeks to achieve would be jeopardised'.[62] Likewise, in the context of Directive 2000/78, AG Mazák observed in *Palacios de la Villa* that if general principles can be invoked independently of Union implementing legislation, not only would legal certainty be threatened, since an obligation not laid down in national law would be imposed on certain subjects of the law, but the vertical and horizontal allocation of powers laid down in Article 13 EC (now Article 19 TFEU)

---

[59] *Kücükdeveci*, above n 32, paras 24–26.
[60] Joined Cases C-397/01 to C-403/01 *Pfeiffer and Others* [2004] ECR I-8835.
[61] Opinion of AG Ruiz-Jarabo Colomer in Joined Cases C-55 and 56/07 *Michaeler & Others* [2008] ECR I-3135, paras 20–22.
[62] Opinion of AG Kokott in Case C-321/05 *Kofoed* [2007] ECR I-5795, para 67.

would also be disturbed.[63] The vertical allocation of powers would be disturbed because the unanimity requirement laid down in that provision protects the competences of the Member States. The horizontal allocation of powers—between the legislature and the judiciary—would be disturbed by the horizontal application of general principles as it would render meaningless the political choice which the Council can make to enact Union legislation lacking horizontal direct effect.[64]

However, these objections seem to overlook that general principles enjoy a 'constitutional status'. In light of the hierarchy of norms, this means that whether a general principle produces horizontal direct effects is a determination that takes place at the level of 'primary law'. Such a determination does not fall within the purview of the Union legislator. Nor is it a prerogative of the Member States. *Defrenne*[65] and *Angonese*[66] illustrate this point.

In the former case, the ECJ ruled that the general principle of equal pay for equal work—grounded in Article 119 EEC (now Article 157 TFEU)—may produce horizontal direct effects. After looking at the aim, the nature and the place of the principle of equal pay for equal work in the scheme of the Treaty, the ECJ held that this principle is 'mandatory in nature' and, accordingly, applies to public authorities and private individuals alike.[67] By contrast, not only was Directive 75/117,[68] which sought to improve the legal protection of workers suffering from unequal pay caused by sex discrimination, irrelevant to determine whether the principle of equal pay for equal work could produce horizontal direct effects, but the ECJ actually pointed out that in no way could Directive 75/117 reduce the effectiveness and the temporal scope of that principle.[69] Likewise, in *Angonese* the ECJ observed that Regulation No 1612/68,[70] which implemented the free movement of workers as laid down in Article 39 EC (now Article 45 TFEU), was not applicable to a competition for a post organised by a private bank. This circumstance, however, did not prevent the principle of free movement of workers—a specific application of the general principle of non-discrimination on grounds of nationality—from producing horizontal direct effects. The ECJ reasoned that its findings in *Defrenne* could, a fortiori, apply to the free movement of workers, since both principles

---

[63] Opinion of AG Mazák in *Palacios de la Villa*, above n 19, paras 133–138.

[64] Ibid, para 138 (Art 13 EC (now Art 19 TFEU) states that the Council 'may take appropriate action to combat discrimination'. Therefore, it is for the Council to decide whether such action requires the adoption of a regulation or a directive.)

[65] Case 43/75 *Defrenne* [1976] ECR 455.

[66] Case C-281/98 *Angonese* [2000] ECR I-4139.

[67] *Defrenne*, above n 65, para 39.

[68] [1975] OJ L 45/19.

[69] *Defrenne*, above n 65, para 60. See also Case 96/80 *Jenkins* [1981] ECR 911, para 22 (holding that Dir 75/117 could not alter the content or scope of that general principle); Case C-17/05 *Cadman* [2006] ECR I-9583, para 29.

[70] [1968] OJ Spec Ed Séries I-475.

are 'mandatory in nature' and seek to combat discrimination, albeit based on different grounds, on the labour market.[71] In the field of social law, could *Defrenne* support the horizontal application of other 'constitutional categories' of the principle of non-discrimination which are 'mandatory in nature' but are not laid down in a Treaty provision? In this regard, one could argue that, in order to preserve the vertical and horizontal allocation of powers, only those general principles which are enshrined in a Treaty provision may produce horizontal direct effects. Stated differently, in the absence of a Treaty provision, *Defrenne* may not be relied upon. Yet this argument does not seem convincing. A close reading of *Defrenne* reveals that the wording of Article 119 EEC did not play a major role in the rationale of the ECJ.[72] Indeed, the ECJ did not focus on whether this Treaty provision was sufficiently precise to produce direct effects, preferring, instead, to 'identify and isolate' the general principle of equal pay for equal work.[73] Most importantly, *Defrenne* shows that, in deciding the horizontal application of the principle of equal pay for equal work, the ECJ was respectful of the prerogatives of the Union legislator and of the Member States. To this effect, the ECJ drew a distinction between situations where a 'purely legal analysis' sufficed to detect the presence of sex discrimination and complex situations where such a presence could not be ascertained unless legislative measures were adopted.[74] While, in relation to the former type of situations, the ECJ is in a position to hold that the general principle of equal pay for equal work produces horizontal direct effects, in the latter type of situations the ECJ is not. Therefore, insofar as this distinction is complied with, the vertical and horizontal allocation of powers is not disturbed by the horizontal application of a general principle. This is so regardless of whether the general principle is grounded in a Treaty provision.

It is in this sense that the ECJ confirmed in *Kücükdeveci* that the general principle of non-discrimination on grounds of age, now enshrined in Article 21 of the Charter, is to be applied horizontally in an employment relationship covered by Directive 2000/78.[75]

---

[71] *Angonese*, above n 66, paras 34–35.

[72] Eg the ECJ observed that, while Art 119 EEC was formally addressed to the Member States, this circumstance did not exclude 'rights from being conferred on individuals' who seek to enforce the duties laid down therein. *Defrenne*, above n 65, para 31.

[73] P Craig and G De Búrca, *EU Law: Text, Cases and Materials*, 4th edn (Oxford, Oxford University Press, 2007) 276–77.

[74] *Defrenne*, above n 65, paras 19–22.

[75] *Kücükdeveci*, above n 32, paras 50–55.

II THE DEVELOPMENT OF GENERAL PRINCIPLES

With respect to the development of general principles, should the ECJ adopt a hierarchical approach, whereby national constitutional traditions would have no say as to the standard of protection to be adopted at EU level? Or, conversely, should the ECJ recognise that constitutional values may legitimately differ from one Member State to another ('value diversity')?

This latter option would fit well with the notion of 'constitutional pluralism', a legal theory that seeks to provide a non-hierarchical explanation of the interaction between Union and national law.[76] For general principles, a moderate discourse on 'constitutional pluralism' would posit that, beyond a core nucleus of shared values where the ECJ must ensure uniformity, the 'ius commune europaeum' resulting from the application of general principles cannot disregard the cultural, historical and social heritage that is part and parcel of national constitutional traditions.[77] To this effect, the ECJ cannot rely on general principles, particularly fundamental rights, as an unstoppable centripetal force that would ensure uniformity while destroying constitutional diversity.[78] When touching upon sensitive areas of national constitutional law which lie outside a core nucleus of shared values, respect for constitutional pluralism implies that the ECJ should exercise a degree of judicial deference. The decision of the ECJ in *Omega*[79] illustrates this approach. There, the Bonn police authority prohibited Omega from offering games involving the simulated killing of human beings on the ground that it infringed human dignity. Given that Omega had entered into a franchise contract with a British company, it argued that the ban was contrary to the freedom to provide services embodied in Article 49 EC (now Article 56 TFEU). Thus, the ECJ was called upon to strike a balance between Article 49 EC and human rights, as applied by a national authority. After noting that the ban constituted a restriction on the freedom to provide services which, nevertheless, pursued a legitimate objective—the protection of human dignity—the ECJ ruled that, for the purposes of applying the principle of proportionality,

> [i]t is not indispensable . . . for the restrictive measure issued by the authorities of a Member State to correspond to a conception shared by all Member States as regards the precise way in which the fundamental right or legitimate interest in question is to be protected.[80]

[76] For an account on the different views of constitutional pluralism, see M Avbelj and J Komárek (eds), 'Four Visions of Constitutional Pluralism' (2008) 21 EUI Law Working Papers, available at <http://cadmus.eui.eu/dspace/handle/1814/9372> .

[77] M Cartabia, 'Europe and Rights: Taking Dialogue Seriously' (2009) 5 *European Constitutional Law Review* 5.

[78] Ibid, 17.

[79] Case C-36/02 *Omega* [2004] ECR I-9609.

[80] Ibid, para 37.

Put simply, the fact that a Member State other than Germany has chosen a system of protection of human dignity less restrictive of the freedom to provide services does not render the German measure contrary to the EC Treaty. Given that the ban satisfied the level of protection guaranteed by the German constitution and did not go beyond what was necessary to that effect, the ECJ considered that it was a justified restriction. Thus, *Omega* demonstrates that the ECJ did not seek to impose a common conception of human dignity. Nor did it embrace the national conception, which was more protective of free movement. Instead, it endorsed a model based on 'value diversity', where national constitutional traditions are not in competition with the economic objectives of the Union but form an integral part of it.[81]

A moderate discourse on constitutional pluralism introduces a welcome element of balance into the development of general principles. However, the ECJ must still guarantee a core nucleus of shared values vital to the integrity of the EU legal order. In relation to those values, the ECJ has no choice but to follow a hierarchical approach. The question that then arises is how to define the outer limits of this nucleus. In this regard, Weiler argues that 'the [Union] should not impose its own standard on the Member State measure but allow a wide margin of appreciation, insisting only that the Member State does not violate the basic core encapsulated in the ECHR'.[82] Thus, by having recourse to a margin of appreciation, not only would the ECJ mediate between the 'European commonality' and 'national particularism', it would also reinforce its commitment to subsidiarity.[83]

However, the application of a margin of appreciation is a complex task, given that its operation depends, to a large extent, on the right whose exercise is being restricted, the factual context and the legitimate aims pursued by the restrictive measure.[84] This complexity is highlighted by contrasting *Schmidberger*[85] and *Omega* with *Viking*[86] and *Laval*.[87] In the two former cases, the ECJ held that the contested national measures fell within the margin of appreciation and thus were submitted to a soft proportionality test. By contrast, in *Viking* and *Laval*, even though the

---

[81] Tridimas, above n 1, 341.

[82] JHH Weiler, 'Fundamental Rights and Fundamental Boundaries' in JH.H Weiler, *The Constitution of Europe: 'Do the New Clothes Have an Emperor' and Other Essays on European Integration* (Cambridge, Cambridge University Press, 1999) 126.

[83] The terms 'European commonality' and 'national particularism' are borrowed from J Sweeney, 'A "Margin of Appreciation" in the Internal Market: Lessons from the European Court of Human Rights' (2007) 34 *Legal Issues of Economic Integration* 27.

[84] Ibid, 45.

[85] Case C-112/00 *Schmidberger* [2003] ECR I-5659.

[86] Case C-438/05 *ITF and FSU v Viking Line ABP and OÜ Viking Line Eest* [2007] ECR I-10779.

[87] Case C-341/05 *Laval un Partneri Ltd v Svenska Byggnadsarbetareförbundet* [2007] ECR I-11767.

ECJ recognised for the first time the right to take collective action 'as a fundamental right which forms an integral part of the general principles of [Union] law',[88] it submitted collective action restricting the Treaty provision on free movement of persons to stricter scrutiny.[89] Does this mean that it is impossible for the ECJ to adopt a margin of appreciation approach without giving rise to inconsistencies? A close reading of *Viking* and *Laval* may provide a negative answer to this question.

In *Laval*, Directive 96/71 (the Posted Workers Directive)[90] was decisive in determining the area of discretion enjoyed by the Member States. This Directive provides a list of mandatory rules of minimum protection in relation to the terms and conditions of employment of posted workers which the host Member State may impose on the posting undertaking.[91] Since the trade unions in *Laval* sought to force the posting undertaking to sign a collective agreement containing obligations not specifically referred to in the Directive, their action was a disproportionate obstacle to the freedom to provide services.[92] Furthermore, the Directive also lays down the regulatory means by which the host Member State can establish the list of mandatory rules for minimum protection, namely, by law, administrative provisions, or universally applicable collective agreements or arbitration awards. Neither Swedish legislation nor administrative regulations provided for a minimum wage. Nor was any collective agreement or arbitral award recognised as universally applicable. Therefore, the ECJ considered that, even though guaranteeing payment of a minimum wage to posted workers was an overriding reason of public interest, collective action forcing the posting undertaking to enter into negotiations on pay without any legal frame of reference would render it impossible or

---

[88] Ibid, paras 90 and 91. *Viking*, above n 86, paras 43 and 44 (quoting the Charter as a source of inspiration).

[89] It is worth noting that one of the main criticisms of these judgments lies in that the ECJ applied the fundamental freedoms to trade unions, despite the fact that trade unions, unlike public authorities, represent not the general interest but that of their members. In addition, it is also argued that, unlike non-governmental regulatory bodies to which the fundamental freedoms apply (Case 36/74 *Walrave and Koch* [1974] ECR 1405; Case C-415/93 *Bosman* [1995] ECR I-4921), trade unions do not enjoy exclusive control to regulate an area of the economy. See, eg A Davies, 'One Step Forward, Two Steps Back? The *Viking* and *Laval* Cases in the ECJ' (2008) 37 *Industrial Law Journal* 126, 136–37. However, as Professor Dashwood points out, where a Member State delegates the regulation of employment relations to both sides of the industry, 'recourse to collective action by trade unions form[s] an integral part of the process of regulating the provision of services in that [Member State]'. Insofar as trade unions enjoy legal autonomy which allows them 'to regulate working conditions in a Member State by way of collective agreements, underpinned by the threat or use of collective action', he posits that their ability to hinder free movement is analogous to that of non-governmental regulatory bodies. A Dashwood, '*Viking* and *Laval*: Issues of Horizontal Direct Effect' (2007–08) 10 *Cambridge Yearbook of European Legal Studies* 525, 535 and 539. See also Opinion of AG Mengozzi in *Laval*, above n 87, para 160.

[90] [1997] OJ L18/1.

[91] *Laval*, above n 87, para 80. Besides, Sweden had not made use of Art 3(10), which could grant further rights to posted workers. See para 84.

[92] Ibid, para 108.

excessively difficult for that undertaking to identify its legal obligations regarding minimum pay.[93] As a result, in *Laval*, the legislative framework adopted by the EU legislator conditioned the way in which the ECJ could apply the principle of proportionality.

Further, in contrast to the contested measures in *Schmidberger* and *Omega*, the collective action taken in *Viking* and *Laval* involved measures which potentially cloaked protectionist, albeit socially legitimate, claims. In *Schmidberger*, environmentalists interrupted the traffic on the Brenner motorway for a couple of hours in order to raise awareness about pollution. Their goal, however, was not to restrict imports from a particular source.[94] In *Omega*, activities involving 'playing at killing' were banned because they were incompatible with a basic value of the German constitution. Despite the effect on trade, the German authorities' attitude had nothing to do with the fact that the equipment was imported from the UK.[95] Hence, there was no intent to insulate the local market from external competition in either of the two cases. Conversely, in *Viking* and *Laval*, trade unions sought protectionist measures by struggling to keep jobs at home.[96] While it may be legitimate for trade unions to seek to protect workers from social dumping, it is equally true that trade unions are not entitled to shield local labour markets from competition coming from other Member States. For this reason, the ECJ may have felt that granting a margin of appreciation to trade unions in such a broad way, as if they were Member State authorities, was inappropriate.[97] The opposite decision might have tilted the balance in favour of a 'social Europe' that arguably excludes a large part of its new citizens.[98] Trade unions could easily engage in social protectionism, leading to retaliatory measures and eventually to the fragmentation of social groups across Europe.[99] In this

[93] Ibid, para 110.

[94] *Schmidberger*, above n 85, para 86.

[95] *Omega*, above n 79, para 29.

[96] *Viking*, above n 86, para 15 ('[i]n press statements FSU justified its position by the need to protect Finnish jobs').

[97] For an alternative explanation, see L Azoulai, 'The Court of Justice and the Social Market Economy: The Emergence of an Ideal and the Conditions for its Realization' (2008) 45 *Common Market Law Review*. 1335, 1350–53.

[98] A Rosas, 'Finis Europae Socialis?' in *Chemins d Europe, Mélanges en l'honneur de Jean Paul Jacqué* (Paris, Dalloz, 2010) 591, 606–07. For an overview of the submissions of the Eastern European Member States on the case, see B Bercusson, 'The Trade Union Movement and the European Union: Judgment Day' (2007) 13 *European Law Journal* 279.

[99] Whilst it is true that in *Viking*, the ITF engaged its members in a coordinated and internationally agreed action to counter the problems associated with the flag of convenience and social dumping, the transnational character of such an action does not rule out that it might give rise to social protectionism. To this effect, AG Poiares Maduro correctly observed that '[a] policy of coordinated collective action could easily be abused in a discriminatory manner if it operated on the basis of an obligation imposed on all national unions to support collective action by any of their fellow unions'. In his view, a compulsory coordinated industrial action would enhance the bargaining powers of some trade unions to the detriment of others, fragmenting the labour market and hindering free movement. In this regard, it is

regard, had the Scandinavian trade unions in *Laval* and *Viking* reacted to cheaper labour coming from the Baltic states with a transnational mindset, perhaps seeking to raise standards throughout the EU rather than seeking to exclude workers from other Member States, the ECJ might have been more sympathetic to their claims.[100] For example, fears of social protectionism might have been alleviated had the Scandinavian trade unions joined forces with their Baltic counterparts to provide a 'European solution' to relocations within the Union or to the remuneration of posted workers.[101]

It follows that the ECJ leaves to the Member States a margin of appreciation when defining the social objectives to be protected as well as when setting out the means to attain them, provided that no fundamental EU value, such as the prohibition of protectionism, is at stake.

III   CONCLUSION

In his well-known inaugural lecture entitled 'The limits of European Community powers',[102] Professor Dashwood argued in favour of understanding the European Union as a 'constitutional order of states'; he advocated a model of limited integration, below the level of a fully functioning federal structure. This model posits that 'the powers exercisable at the centre [should be] clearly demarcated; and that it should only be possible to extend those powers further with the explicit consent of the Member States, reached in accordance with each one's constitutional requirements'.[103] Is the role played by general principles of EU law compatible with this model? In our submission, the reply should be in the affirmative.

First, general principles do not only have a 'top-down' dimension that pre-empts national constitutional traditions to the benefit of a single EU standard. On the contrary, general principles canvas the very essence of EU constitutionalism insofar as they facilitate 'constitutional dialogue' in a system of multi-level governance.

Secondly, in *Kücükdeveci* the ECJ ruled that, unlike Directive 2000/78, which cannot of itself impose obligations on an individual, the general principle of non-discrimination on grounds of age may be relied upon—in civil proceedings—to set aside a national provision falling within the

---

worth recalling that a trade union member of the ITF which fails to comply with an ITF circular would expose itself to sanctions and even to the loss of membership. See Opinion of AG Poiares Maduro in *Viking*, above n 86, paras 7 and 71.

   [100] C Barnard, '*Viking* and *Laval*: An Introduction' (2007–08) 10 *Cambridge Yearbook of European Legal Studies* 463, 492.
   [101] Opinion of AG Poiares Maduro in *Viking*, above n 86, paras 70 and 71.
   [102] Dashwood, above n 6, 114.
   [103] Ibid, 114.

scope of EU law which is incompatible with that principle. In so doing, the ECJ has arguably taken an important step towards adopting a unitary understanding of the EU and national legal orders.[104] Yet this important development in the ECJ's case law does not seem contrary to the model of integration supported by Professor Dashwood. It is indeed not the normative force of general principles that might call 'the constitutional order of states' into question, but rather how the ECJ determines the existence of a substantive EU law link between national law and a general principle, as well as how the ECJ defines the interaction between judicial lawmaking and the Union legislature. In other words, a clear definition of the scope of application of general principles is of paramount importance for Dashwood's model. But as *Bartsch*, *Audiolux* and *NCC Construction Danmark* show, the credibility of the EU as a 'constitutional order of states' is not under threat, since the ECJ takes very seriously the vertical and horizontal limits to the application of general principles.

Last but not least, the theory of 'constitutional pluralism' provides useful guidance on how general principles must be developed. Beyond the bounds of a core nucleus of key shared values vital to the Union's integrity, the ECJ should have recourse to a 'margin of appreciation' analysis which would strike the right balance between 'European commonality' and 'national particularism'. Thus, the national identities are preserved as the Union continues to be based upon a model of 'value diversity'.

To conclude with the nautical metaphor mentioned at the beginning of this contribution, while general principles may force the ECJ to sail alone in unchartered waters of constitutional law, national legal systems provide an indispensable compass.

---

[104] M Dougan, 'When Worlds Collide! Competing Visions of the Relationship between Direct Effect and Supremacy' (2007) 44 *Common Market Law Review* 931.

I I

The Horizontal Application of Fundamental Rights as General Principles of Union Law

ELEANOR SPAVENTA

I INTRODUCTION

T HE PECULIARITY OF the constitutional order of states is fully reflected in the difficulties inherent in delimiting the exact scope of Union law. This is true both in relation to fleshing out the Treaty provisions (especially those declared to grant rights to individuals) and in relation to the effect of the general principles of Union law, and particularly fundamental rights, on the domestic constitutional systems. In this respect, the interaction between the ever expanding scope of the Treaty rights-granting provisions (mainly of the Union citizenship and the free movement provisions) and the general principles has created a complex web of intersecting jurisdictions where domestic, Union and European Convention rights concur, as well as sometimes compete, with one another. As a result, the determination of the 'proper' scope of application of Union fundamental rights is of paramount constitutional importance—the broader the scope of the former, the deeper the impact on both national regulatory sovereignty and national conceptions of fundamental rights.

Here, it should be noted that this is not a zero sum game, where gains and losses can be precisely determined so that a 'gain' at EU level exactly corresponds to a 'loss' at national level (or vice versa): first of all, a loss in national sovereignty might well be compensated by the gain in individual rights; secondly, fundamental rights, and especially the balance between competing interests, reflect cultural and social values and anxieties so that a loss in national sovereignty might also determine a loss in societal compromises, in the collective dimension, in favour of an individualistic (and possibly selfish) view of mutual rights and responsibilities; thirdly, an individual's gain might translate into another individual's loss, regardless of whether there has been a gain to the national or Union dimension; fourthly, a 'gain' in the Union's jurisdiction is also a gain for a certain vision of the European Union (more supranational, more constitutionally independent from its Member States). This chapter does not seek to explore all of these issues, although it touches upon them; rather, it focuses on exploring the extent to which fundamental rights as general principles of Union law can (or/and should) be invoked against other individuals. More generally, an investigation into those issues might help in answering one of the main questions Alan has been interested in: if the Union can correctly be described as a constitutional order of states, which 'constitutional' order is this?

I will first look at the scope of application of fundamental rights as general principles of Union law, then concentrate on those situations in which fundamental rights apply to acts of the Member States. I will then analyse the extent to which general principles, and fundamental rights in particular, are horizontally applicable and look at some reasons why these developments might not be altogether wise.

II THE SCOPE OF APPLICATION
OF FUNDAMENTAL RIGHTS

It is well known that, lacking any express reference to fundamental rights in the original Treaties, the European Court of Justice held that fundamental rights formed part of the general principles of (then) Community law which it would protect.[1] The political institutions, in turn, endorsed this case law first by means of a political declaration,[2] then through Treaty revisions[3] and most importantly through the declaration of the Charter of Fundamental Rights,[4] which, following the entry into force of the Treaty of Lisbon, has become 'officially' legally binding.[5] As for the sources of those rights, pre-Charter, the Court mainly referred to the

---

[1] Case 11/70 *Internationale Handelsgesellschaft* [1970] ECR 1125.

[2] Joint declaration of Council, Commission and Parliament concerning the Protection of Fundamental Rights and the European Convention for the Protection of Human Rights and Fundamental Freedoms [1977] OJ C103/1.

[3] Starting with the Maastricht Treaty (but already in a preamble to the SEA), every Treaty revision contained a fundamental rights element; see generally A Arnull, A Dashwood, M Dougan, M Ross, E Spaventa, D Wyatt, *Wyatt and Dashwood's EU Law*, 6th edn (London, Sweet & Maxwell, 2006) ch 7.

[4] Charter of Fundamental Rights of the European Union [2000] OJ C364/1 (Nice version); the original version has been then modified (amended version [2010] OJ C83/02). Hereinafter, all references to the Charter or the Charter of Fundamental Rights refer to the amended version now in force.

[5] Art 6 TEU. The Court, as well as its Advocates General (eg Case C-341/05 *Laval un Partneri* [2007] ECR I-11767), had already extensively referred to the Charter before its official entry into force; given that, in theory, the Charter is only codifying existing rights, such references are less problematic than it might be thought at first sight.

European Convention of Human Rights[6] and the common constitutional traditions,[7] as well as other international instruments of fundamental rights protection.[8]

Whilst the fact that the Union should be bound by fundamental rights is not generally contested, the extent to which such fundamental rights might also permeate in the domestic legal systems is more controversial. Thus, when discussing the scope of application of fundamental rights as general principles of Union law, we need to distinguish three possibilities: first of all, the applicability of fundamental rights in relation to acts of the EU institutions; secondly, those cases where fundamental rights as general principles of Union law apply to the acts of the Member States implementing Union law; and thirdly, those cases in which fundamental rights apply because the matter falls within the scope of application of Union law. I will briefly analyse the scope of application of fundamental rights in relation to acts of the EU institutions, then concentrate on those instances in which fundamental rights apply to the acts of the Member States, as a result of a connection with EU law. I shall then focus on the possibility that fundamental rights as general principles of Union law might have direct and/or indirect horizontal effects in litigation between private parties.

III FUNDAMENTAL RIGHTS AGAINST THE EU

As mentioned above, this is the least controversial of categories. When the EU acts as a regulator or as an administrative body, it is bound by the Charter as well as by the general principles.[9] Here fundamental

---

[6] eg Case 36/75 *Rutili v Minister for the Interior* [1975] ECR 1219. The EU is due to accede to the ECHR (Art 6(2) TEU); see also Protocol (no 8) Relating to Art 6(2) of the Treaty on European Union on the Accession of he Union to the European Convention on the Protection of Human Rights and Fundamental Freedoms ([2010] OJ C83/273). The negotiations for accessions have now started (see Press Release IP/10/906, 10 July 2010) and Justice and Home Affairs Council Press Release, 3–4 June 2010, 10630/1/10/REV 1. See also Draft Council Decision authorising the Commission to negotiate the Accession Agreement of the European Union to the European Convention for the Protection of Human Rights and Fundamental Freedoms, 'Involvement of the ECJ Regarding the Compatibility of Legal Acts of the Union with Fundamental Rights', Doc No 10568/10 (2 June 2010); and 'Co Respondent Mechanism', Doc No 10569 (2 June 2010). For reasons better known to the Council, the Draft Council Decision authorising the Commission to negotiate is classified (Doc No 9689/10—request for access denied). See also 'Discussion Document of the Court of Justice of the European Union on certain aspects of the accession of the European Union to the European Convention for the protection of Human Rights and Fundamental Freedoms', document of 5 May 2010 (unnumbered), available at http://curia.europa.eu/jcms/upload/docs/application/pdf/2010-05/convention_en_2010-05-21_12-10-16_272.pdf.

[7] Eg Case 11/70 *Internationale Handelsgesellschaft* [1970] ECR 1125; Case 4/73 *Nold v Commission* [1974] ECR 491.

[8] Generally eg Case 4/73 *Nold v Commission* [1974] ECR 491.

[9] Although in this context the distinction seems rather redundant and due to disappear.

rights are capable of having direct effect, ie of providing individuals with a cause of action against the EU institutions. Of course, not all rights listed in the Charter are capable of having such an effect, and the more programmatic or inspirational rights would have more limited application since the margin of discretion left to the legislature would presumably be broader.[10] Aside from traditional judicial review cases, where individuals rely on fundamental rights to challenge the acts of the institutions, it is difficult to imagine a situation in which fundamental rights might be invoked against another individual. In this respect, it is just conceivable that an employee of one of the EU institutions might attempt to rely on the Charter against another employee; yet, in these instances, their relationship should be governed either by EU rules (in which case there would not be any horizontal effect but rather either a vertical or an incidental effect) or by the relevant national law (according to where the institution is located).

In those cases in which fundamental rights are invoked against the EU institutions, the standard of fundamental rights protection is (or should be)[11] solely that decided by the Union judicature, with the proviso that the level of protection cannot fall below that set by the European Convention of Human Rights.[12] Of course, this might create tensions should the standard of protection afforded by the Union judicature fall considerably below that afforded at national level;[13] yet both Union and national judicatures seem to be well intentioned to avoid such conflicts.[14]

[10] See the rather unhelpful distinction between principles and rights, Art 52(5) Charter of Fundamental Rights.

[11] Although in the terrorist cases the General Court seems to have delegated, at least to a certain extent, the protection of the claimants' fundamental rights to the national courts; see E Spaventa, 'Annotation on the PMOI Cases' (2009) 46 *Common Market Law Review* 1239.

[12] See Art 52(3) Charter of Fundamental Rights of the EU.

[13] There was a danger of a conflict of this type in the German bananas saga in relation to Reg 404/93 on the common organization of the market in bananas [1993] OJ L47/11; here some German courts deemed the Regulation to be incompatible with the traders' right to property; the issue was eventually settled by the German Federal Constitutional Court, which restated the so-called Solange II case law, refusing to scrutinise the compatibility of the Regulation with fundamental rights as protected by the German Constitution (see Federal Constitutional Court, decision 7/6/00 [2000] Human Rights Law Journal 251). See generally, U Everling, 'Will Europe Slip on Bananas? The Bananas Judgement of the Court of Justice and National Courts' (1996) 33 *Common Market Law Review* 401; N Reich, 'Judge Made 'Europe à la carte': Some Remarks on Recent Conflicts between European and German Constitutional Law Provoked by the Banana Litigation' (1996) *European Journal of International Law* 103; C U Schmid, 'All Bark and No Bite: Notes on the Federal Constitutional Court's "Banana Decision"' (2001) *European Law Journal* 95.

[14] See the 'happy' ending to the bananas saga; and also the reactions to the legal challenges against the European Arrest Warrant; see eg German Constitutional Court's ruling declaring the German legislation implementing the European Arrest Warrant void but not engaging with the compatibility of the EAW with fundamental rights, decision of 18 July 2005, 2 BvR 2236/04 (press release in English available at http://www.bundesverfassungsgericht.de/en/press/bvg05-064en.html); see also H Satzger and T Pohl, 'The German Constitutional Court and the European Arrest Warrant: "Cryptic Signals" from Karlsruhe' (2006) 4 *Journal of International Criminal Justice* 686. See also Protocol (No 35) on Article 40.3.3. of

IV   FUNDAMENTAL RIGHTS AGAINST THE MEMBER STATES WHEN IMPLEMENTING UNION LAW AND WHEN ACTING WITHIN ITS SCOPE – VERTICAL SITUATIONS

More controversially, European Union fundamental rights can also be invoked against the Member States when they are either implementing EU law or acting within its scope.[15] I will briefly recall the extent of the Member States' duty in both situations.

A   Fundamental Rights when Implementing Union Law

When the Member State is exercising discretion in implementing EU law,[16] it has to respect the constitutional principles of the EU, including fundamental rights. The reason for this obligation is that the Member State in such cases is acting as an agent of the EU and therefore cannot overstep the constitutional limits that constrain the latter. However, the extent of this obligation was not altogether clear: the pre-Charter case law, starting from the *Wachauf* case,[17] seemed to limit the effect of fundamental rights to a duty of consistent interpretation so that the national act/rule implementing Union law would have to be interpreted insofar as possible in a way that was consistent with Union fundamental rights. In other words, the case law seemed not to impose a duty to disapply national rules implementing Union law when those conflicted with EU fundamental rights.[18] However, such a restrictive reading would have been inconsistent with the case law on the scope of fundamental rights when Member States act within the scope of Union Law (see below), where the national court's obligation is more far reaching and extends to a duty to disapply national law when inconsistent with Union fundamental rights.

In any event, the debate now seems to be obsolete, since the Charter does not contain such a limitation rather expressly binding the Member States when they implement EU law.[19] Therefore, post-Charter, there should not

---

the Constitution of Ireland [2010] OJ C83/321, which was a direct reaction to the challenge brought in Case C-159/90 *SPUC v Grogan* [1991] ECR I-4685 to the Irish rules on advertising of abortion services in other Member States.

[15] See, eg the rather confused (and of dubious legal usefulness) Protocol (No 30) on the application of the Charter of Fundamental Rights of the European Union to Poland and the United Kingdom [2010] OJ C83/313.

[16] If there were no discretion the potential fundamental rights breach would be ascribable to the EU, not to the Member State (eg Case C-84/95 *Bosphorus* [1996] ECR I-3953; and in front of the ECHR App No 45036/98).

[17] Case 5/88 *Wachauf* [1989] ECR 2609; C-20/00 and C-64/00 *Booker Aquaculture Ltd at al v Scottish Ministers* [2003] ECR I-7411.

[18] For this interpretation see T Hartley, *The Foundations of European Community Law*, 5th edn (Oxford, Oxford University Press, 2003), 146, footnote 60.

[19] Art 51(1) Charter of Fundamental Rights of the EU.

be any doubt that an individual may bring proceedings against a Member State when the latter, in implementing EU law, infringes European Union fundamental rights. Furthermore, in those cases, it is open to an individual to also rely on national fundamental rights since, if a discretion is conferred, Member States are under a dual obligation to respect both Union and national fundamental rights (and must in any event respect the European Convention of Human Rights). So when a Member State is implementing Union law, the applicable fundamental rights standard is the highest between the national and the EU one.

A different, and more complex question, to which I shall return later, is whether the Member State is bound by Union fundamental rights when it should have implemented Union law but it has not, ie in the absence of any legislative provision.

B   Fundamental Rights when Acting within the Scope of Union Law

Member States are also bound by Union fundamental rights when they act within the scope of Union law,[20] ie when they limit a right granted by Union law. Here, in *ERT* and *Familiapress*,[21] the Court made clear that, when the Member State is invoking a Treaty derogation or a mandatory requirement in order to justify limiting one of the Treaty free movement rights, it must respect fundamental rights as general principles of Union law. This interpretation is more contested as it has been seen as an undue interference with national sovereignty:[22] after all, the Member States have their own system of fundamental rights protection which can be relied upon in those situations; and, it is argued, the very fact that the Member State is derogating from a free movement right should place it outside the reach of Union law. However, in this author's opinion, this case law is entirely consistent with the Union's own constitutional premises: when a Member State is limiting, or derogating from, a Treaty provision it must respect the Treaty and its constitutional principles. Much in the same way as any limitation/derogation from these rights must be proportionate, it must also respect fundamental rights. That said, the continuing expansion of the scope of the free movement provisions, the fact that the link between barrier and rule contested might be extremely tenuous,[23] so that the free

---

[20] Fundamental rights are also relevant as an aid to interpretation, eg 222/84 *Johnston v Chief Constable of Royal Ulster* [1986] ECR 1651; C-13/94 *P v S Cornwall County Council* [1996] ECR I-2143.

[21] Case C-260/89 *ERT* [1991] ECR I-2995; Case C-368/95 *Familiapress* [1996] ECR I-3689; this was to be expected to an extent following the ruling in Case 36/75 *Rutili* [1975] ECR 1219.

[22] See, eg F Jacobs, 'Human Rights in the European Union: the Role of the Court of Justice' (2001) 26 *European Law Review* 331, which is, however, rather inconsistent with his more generous approach in his opinion in Case C-168/91 *Konstantinidis* [1993] ECR I-1191.

[23] Case C-60/00 *Carpenter* [2002] ECR I-6279.

movement provisions might become a simple vehicle for the enforcement of fundamental rights, is clearly constitutionally problematic.[24] The reason for this particular problem lies in the expansion of the scope of the Treaty rather than in the application of fundamental rights to limitations and derogations. Yet it is this fear of an undue expansion of the scope of Union law towards establishing some sort of free-standing Union fundamental rights that explains why the scope of the Charter is limited to the actions of the Member States when implementing, rather than also acting within the scope of, Union law.

Having briefly recalled the scope of application of fundamental rights against the acts of the Member States, it is now time to consider the extent to which fundamental rights as general principles of Union law might be relied upon in litigation against private parties (horizontal application) by virtue of the fact that the situation has a connection with Union law. Here I will start by analysing those cases in which private parties rely on the general principles to displace national law (incidental horizontal application), before turning to pure horizontal effect cases, ie where there is no provision in national law.

V INCIDENTAL HORIZONTAL APPLICATION OF FUNDAMENTAL RIGHTS AS GENERAL PRINCIPLES OF UNION LAW

Having dealt with vertical situations, it is now time to address the extent to which the general principles of Union law, and in particular fundamental rights, apply in horizontal situations. Here the answer is far from clear, both because of the paucity of case law and because of the very nature of the problem, which raises complex constitutional and policy issues.[25] In order to attempt disentangling the matter, I will first analyse those cases in which (i) national rules falling within the scope of the Treaty are incompatible with a general principle of EU law and are invoked in litigation between private parties; I shall then turn my attention to (ii) the same situation involving a directive rather than the Treaty (*Mangold*-type situation).

---

[24] On this point see also E Spaventa, 'Seeing the Woods Despite the Trees? On the Scope of Union Citizenship and its Constitutional Effects' (2008) 45 *Common Market Law Review* 13.

[25] See generally eg J Krzeminska-Vanvaka, 'Horizontal Effect of Fundamental Rights and Freedoms—Much Ado About Nothing? German, Polish and EU Theories Compared after *Viking Line*', Jean Monnet Working Paper 11/09; M Tushnet 'The Issue of State Action/ Horizontal Effect in Comparative Constitutional Law' (2003) 1 *International Journal of Constitutional Law* 79; M Safjan and P Miklaszewicz 'Horizontal Effect of the General Principles of EU Law in the Sphere of Private Law' (2010) *European Review of Private Law* 475.

A   Incidental Horizontal Application—Situations Falling within the Treaty

It has been mentioned before that when a national rule falls within the scope of the Treaty, either because the rule is giving effect to one of its provisions or because it is limiting it, the national rule must also comply with the general principles of Union law, including fundamental rights.

The same principle applies when the national rule is invoked in litigation between private parties (as was the case in *Familiapress*),[26] so that a rule falling within the scope of the Treaty, in order to be compatible with Union law, must also comply with the general principles; if it does not, the national court will be under the same obligation to disapply it as if the rule were incompatible with one of the Treaty provisions. The fact that such application of Union law might have effects on litigation between private parties is immaterial in the same way as it is immaterial when private parties rely on Article 34 TFEU, which is not horizontally applicable, against other private parties.

The only question in this respect is whether, in order to be able to invoke the general principles, the Treaty provision which brought the matter within the scope of Union law must be directly effective: here, the answer seems to be positive. If the Treaty provision invoked is not directly effective, there would be no cause of action and therefore Union law would not apply at all (unless, of course, there is a provision in secondary legislation that attracts the national rule within the orbit of Union law, of which more in the next section). The fact that the Treaty provision triggering the general principles needs to be directly effective is demonstrated by the rulings on age discrimination:[27] as is well known, Article 19 TFEU, which provides Union competence in the field of discrimination on grounds of age, is not directly effective. In those cases, in order to be able to trigger the general principles, the Court had recourse to secondary legislation rather than the Treaty.

The application of the Treaty might also trigger the general principles in another way: here, when the Treaty provisions apply horizontally (such as in the case of the free movement provisions and sex discrimination), private parties have been allowed to rely on the general principles to attempt to resist the application of the Treaty. This was particularly the case in *Viking* and *Laval*, and will be the subject of detailed analysis below.[28]

---

[26] Case C-368/95 *Familiapress* [1996] ECR I-3689.
[27] Eg Case C-144/04 *Mangold* [2005] ECR I-9981; Case C-555/07 *Kücükdeveci*, judgment of 19 January 2010.
[28] Case C-438/05 *International Transport Workers' Federation and Finnish Seamen's Union v Viking Line ABP and OÜ Viking Line Eesti* [2007] ECR I-10779; Case C-341/05 *Laval un Partneri* [2007] ECR I-11767

B Incidental Horizontal Application—Situations Falling within a Directive (*Mangold*-type)

If the application of the general principles in situations which fall within the scope of Union law by virtue of a directly effective Treaty provision is relatively straightforward, the situation in relation of matters falling within the scope of Union law by virtue of secondary legislation is more complex.[29] I will first briefly recall the case law, then assess whether it is constitutionally sound.

It is well known that in *Mangold* the Court applied a general principle to a horizontal situation.[30] It might be recalled than in that case the issue related to a dispute (possibly fictitious) between two private parties as to whether a German rule which allowed a derogation from the general limitations on the use of fixed-term contracts for workers above the age of 52 was compatible with (then) Community law. Directive 2000/78, establishing a general framework on equal treatment,[31] including equal treatment regardless of age, was of limited help to the claimant since the time limit for implementation had not yet expired. This notwithstanding, the Court held that (i) the principle of non-discrimination on grounds of age was a general principle of Community law; (ii) the matter at issue fell within the scope of (then) Community law by virtue of Directive 1999/70 on the framework agreement on fixed-term work;[32] and therefore (iii) the national court was under an obligation to provide the legal protection necessary to ensure that the principle of non-discrimination on grounds of age could be fully effective also by setting aside any incompatible national rule.

---

[29] And, more generally, the debate on the extent to which directives might have effects on individuals is still open; aside from Case C-194/94 *CIA Security International SA v Signalson SA* [1996] ECR I-2201 and Case C-443/98 *Unilever Italia Spa v Central Food Spa* [2000] ECR I-7535, which might be limited to a specific directive (83/189), see Case C-201/02 *Wells v Secretary of State for Transport, Local Government and the Regions* [2004] ECR I-723 (which in the writer's opinion was not very surprising as it was a judicial review/vertical situation); Joined Cases C-152/07 to C-154/07 *Arcor AG and Co KG, Communication Services TELE2 GmbH, Firma 01051 Telekom GmbH v Bundesrepublik Deutschland* [2008] ECR I-5959; on these cases see the interesting contribution by R Král,'Questioning the Limits of Invocability of EU Directives in Triangular Situations' (2010) 16 *European Public Law* 239. In Joined Cases C-37/06 and C-58/06 *Viamex and Agrar Handels GmbH v Hauptzollamt Hamburg-Jonas* [2008] ECR I-69, the Court upheld the validity of a regulation which provided that in order to qualify for an export refund for live animals the conditions provided for in Dir 91/628 would have to be respected. Critical of this approach is P Craig, 'The Legal Effect of Directives: Policy, Rules and Exceptions' (2009) 34 *European Law Review* 349, who interprets this case as a further relaxation of the no horizontal direct effect rule because, through the medium of a regulation, a directive is capable of producing legal effects vis-à-vis a private party.

[30] Case C-144/04 *Mangold* [2005] ECR I-9981.

[31] Dir 2000/78 establishing a general framework for equal treatment in employment and occupation [2000] OJ L303/1.

[32] Dir 1999/70 concerning the framework agreement on fixed-term work concluded by ETUC, UNICE and CEEP [1999] OJ L175/43.

The *Mangold* ruling gave rise to intense criticism from both Advocates General[33] and scholarship (not least by Alan Dashwood himself),[34] both because of its far-reaching implications and because of the ease with which the Court discovered a 'new' general principle.[35] Yet, despite the negative reactions, *Mangold* has been confirmed in subsequent case law. In particular, in *Kücükdeveci*[36] the Court again applied the general principle of non-discrimination on grounds of age in litigation between private parties. In that case, German rules provided that work completed before the age of 25 should not be taken into account in the calculation of the notice period required for lawful dismissal. As a result, Ms Kücükdeveci benefited from a shorter period of notice from her employer, a private company, than it would have otherwise been the case. This time, the period for implementation of Directive 2000/78 had expired; yet, since the litigation was between private parties, and since directives are not capable of being applied to horizontal situations, Directive 2000/78 was of little use to the claimant. The Court restated that the principle of non-discrimination on grounds of age is a general principle of Union law; it then found that the German legislation at issue was inconsistent with Directive 2000/78. After having reaffirmed the lack of horizontal direct effect of directives, and the limits of the duty of consistent interpretation, the Court instructed the national court of its duty to disapply, if need be, any provision of national law contrary to the general principle of non-discrimination on grounds of age.[37] At first sight, then, the *Mangold* case law seems to imply that the general principles, including fundamental rights, are applicable whenever the situation falls within the scope of Union law, regardless of whether

---

[33] Several Advocates General have criticised the Court's decision in *Mangold*; eg AG Mazák in Case C-411/05 *F Palacios de la Villa v Cortefiel Servicios SA* [2007] ECR I-8531; AG Ruiz-Jarabo Colomer in Joined Cases C-55 and 56/07 *Michaeler and Others* [2008] ECR I-3135; AG Kokott in Case C-73/07 *Tietosuojavaltuutettu v Satakunnan Markkinapörssi Oy and Satamedia Oy* [2008] ECR I-9831; more open is AG Sharpston in Case C-427/06 *B Bartsch v Bosch und Siemens Hausgeräte (BSH) Altersfürsorge GmbH* [2008] ECR I-7245, esp paras 79–85 (however, in that case, both the AG and the Court found that the matter fell outside the scope of (then) Community law so that the general principles did not apply).

[34] See Editorial Comment, 'Horizontal Direct Effect: A Law of Diminishing Coherence' (2006) 43 *Common Market Law Review* 1.

[35] Although, to be fair to the Court, given that the right not to be discriminated against on grounds of age had been included in the Charter and that the Charter was merely a codifying rather than an innovative document, it should have not been such a surprise.

[36] Case C-555/07 *Kücükdeveci*, judgment of 19 January 2010.

[37] The *Mangold* case law does not seem to be limited to age discrimination: in *Audiolux* (Case C-101/08 *Audiolux SA and Others v Groupe Bruxelles Lambert SA (GBL) and Others, Bertelsmann AG and Others* [2009] ECR I-9823) the Court examined whether Union law encompassed a general principle of protection of minority shareholders; again, the litigation giving rise to the reference was between private parties and the matter fell within the scope of Union law by virtue of the company law directives. Whilst it found that there is no such principle in Union law, the fact that it accepted to analyse whether such a principle existed might be taken as an indication of the breadth of the *Mangold* approach (see below).

the trigger is the Treaty or a directive, and regardless of whether the litigation is vertical or horizontal.

It has been argued[38] that *Mangold* does not support the view that general principles, and fundamental rights, are 'truly' horizontally applicable. In that case, it is argued, the Court merely instructed the national court not to apply the legislation breaching the general principle of Union law much in the same way as it would if a national rule breached Article 34 TFEU, which also does not have horizontal direct effect. Thus, for instance, rules imposing a non-justified product requirement cannot be invoked against a private party since they infringe EU law. Regardless of any spillover effect on the contractual relationship between private parties, such application of Union law does not amount to horizontal effect. In order to appreciate the difference, take the following example: an individual enters into a contract with a supermarket in another Member State for the sale of her locally produced wine; the Member State enacts legislation prohibiting the sale of foreign wine; the supermarket attempts to rely on said legislation to get out of its contractual obligations but is prevented from doing so since the national court must, as a matter of EU law, disregard the national rule which is inconsistent with the Treaty (vertical effect with incidental effects on individuals). On the other hand, take the case of an individual looking to sell wine produced in her own country: a small shop refuses to buy such wine since it specialises on products from another Member State; the individual would not be able to rely on Article 34 TFEU to force the shop to stock her wine (no horizontal effect).

The difference between the duty of national courts to disregard national rules inconsistent with the Treaty and horizontal effects might appear at times counterintuitive, yet it is important in that, in the first case, there is no free-standing cause of action, whilst when a piece of legislation applies horizontally it provides a free-standing cause of action against another individual. It is with this in mind that some authors have argued that the *Mangold* ruling is less dramatic than it might appear at first sight: thus, we would not be dealing with horizontal effect of general principles but, rather, with the normal application of the constitutional rules of the European Union, constitutional rules which are formed by the Treaty and the general principles of Union law. The only difference here would be that in some cases the situation falls within the scope of Union law by virtue of the Treaty, whilst in the *Mangold*-type situation it would be brought within the orbit of Union law by virtue of a directive. Seen in this way, *Mangold* would not signal any great change in the constitutional principles of the EU; rather, it is 'surprising' for the creative way in which the

---

[38] See M Dougan, Chapter 12 below.

Court found the existence of a previously unknown general principle of non-discrimination on grounds of age.[39]

From a constitutional perspective, the analogy might need further reflection (and there is no precedent for it—even in cases involving Treaty provisions a general principle was never applied to displace a national rule in cases concerning individuals). In cases relating to the Treaty, it is accepted that the Treaty provision (if directly effective) can be invoked to displace national rules regardless of whether it has a real horizontal effect: thus there is a correlation of effects between a trigger and the effects acquired by the general principles by virtue of the trigger.

However, in the case of directives, this is not the case: directives cannot be used to displace national rules in horizontal situations; indeed, as said above, the Court resisted calls for such 'exclusionary' effects in *Pfeiffer*.[40] So *Mangold* determines a rather curious constitutional effect whereby the directive triggers the application of general principles in a way that is broader than what could be achieved through the sole trigger. It is this dissonance between trigger and general principle that is both novel and problematic. Furthermore, if there is no longer a need for a similarity of scope between trigger and triggered principle, then there is no reason why such interpretation should not be of broader application so that it could be used to impose obligations on individuals beyond exclusionary effects. I shall now turn to this issue by analysing cases where there is no national rule that might be 'excluded' by the general principle.

VI   THE EFFECT OF GENERAL PRINCIPLES IN
THE ABSENCE OF CONFLICTING NATIONAL
RULES—PURE HORIZONTAL EFFECT?

A   Treaty Provisions

I have mentioned above that, in order to be compatible with the Treaty, a national rule limiting or giving effect to one of the Treaty provisions must also be compatible with the general principles of Union law (regardless of whether the situation is horizontal or vertical). In this regard, the general principles, including fundamental rights, apply exactly in the same way as the Treaty provision which brought the situation within the scope of Union law. However, the situation in respect of the effect of the general principles in the absence of national rules is more uncertain. Is it possible for a general principle to be capable of true horizontal direct effect, so that it can be invoked to impose obligations on private parties? If so,

---

[39] But see n 35.
[40] Joined Cases C-397/01 to 403/01 *Pfeiffer and others* [2004] ECR I-8835; see in particular AG Ruiz-Jarabo Colomer's Opinion.

does the answer depend on whether the Treaty provision which acts as a trigger is itself capable of true horizontal effect? In order to answer this question, I will first analyse the rulings in *Viking* and *Laval* to assess whether they provide authority either way.

It is well known that the rulings in *Viking* and *Laval* concerned litigation as to the compatibility of industrial action with the Treaty's free movement of persons provisions. Two companies complained that such industrial action interfered with their free movement rights: in *Viking*, the action was aimed at preventing the reflagging of a ship to another Member State;[41] in *Laval*, it was aimed at forcing the foreign company, which was posting its workers abroad, to enter into a local collective agreement.[42] In both cases, the companies were relying on the Treaty against the trade unions: a finding of incompatibility with Union law of the national rules regulating industrial action would in fact have been of little help to the claimants since the industrial action would not have been rendered unlawful. For this reason, the companies relied on Articles 43 and 49 TEC (now 49 and 56 TFEU), arguing that the industrial action, directed at preventing movement in one case and at imposing additional contractual obligations on foreign companies in the other, affected their right to move within the European Union. In order to resist the companies' claims, the trade unions relied, inter alia, on the right to strike as guaranteed by Union law. The Court accepted that the right to strike was a general principle of Union law and that it could be invoked to resist the companies' claims so as to justify the barrier to movement.[43] For this reason, it could be argued that *Viking* and *Laval* are authority to hold that, at least in those cases in which the Treaty is applied horizontally, the general principles are also horizontally applicable.

Yet it is not obvious that we can infer all of this from those two cases. The horizontal application of the general principles in *Viking* and *Laval* was a by-product of the horizontal application of the Treaty provisions: they were used to curtail the scope of application of the free movement of persons, to ensure (or at least to attempt to ensure) that, like almost any other right at national level, the economic free movement provisions would find some limit when clashing with other (non-economic) rights. In

---

[41] Case C-438/05 *International Transport Workers' Federation and Finnish Seamen's Union v Viking Line ABP and OÜ Viking Line Eesti* [2007] ECR I-10779.

[42] Case C-341/05 *Laval un Partneri* [2007] ECR I-11767.

[43] The Court therefore imposed its own vision of the appropriate ambit of the right to strike, see further E Spaventa, 'Federalization v Centralization: Tensions in Fundamental Rights Discourse in the European Union' in M Dougan, S Currie (eds), *50 Years of the European Treaties* (Oxford, Hart Publishing, 2008), 343; see also eg C Barnard, 'Social Dumping or Dumping Socialism?' (2008) 67 *Cambridge Law Journal* 262; R O'Donoghue and B Carr, 'Dealing with *Viking* and *Laval*: from Theory to Practice' (2008–09) 11 *Cambridge Yearbook of European Legal Studies* 179.

this respect, consider *Bosman*,[44] the precursor of horizontal application of
the Treaty free movement of persons provisions: there the football association argued, inter alia, that the Court should refrain from allowing Article
39 TEC (now 45 TFEU) from having horizontal effect since private parties
would not be able to invoke the Treaty derogations, which are linked to
'public' rather than 'private' interests and would therefore not apply to
private parties.[45] The Court rejected this argument, explicitly accepting
that private parties might be able to justify restrictions imposed on other
people's Treaty freedoms.[46] Now, it seems clear that if private parties can
objectively justify limitations imposed on other people's Treaty freedoms,
it follows that they can also attempt to justify imposing a limitation on
a Treaty freedom because the limitation is due to the (legitimate) exercise
of their own fundamental rights.[47]

For this reason, it is difficult to say whether *Viking* and *Laval* might
give any indication about whether general principles are capable of true
horizontal application if, for true horizontal application, we mean the
ability of a private party to rely on a general principle to impose obligations on another party, such as to impose obligations which little have
to do with the exercise of Treaty rights. Thus, for instance, would a
migrant worker be able to rely on the general principles of Union law to
enforce her fundamental right—say, her right to privacy or freedom of
expression—against her employer merely by virtue of falling within the
scope of the free movement of workers provisions? Would a tenuous link,
such as the one established in the *Carpenter* case,[48] be enough to trigger
fundamental Union rights against private parties? As far as this author
is concerned, it is to be hoped that an individual who has exercised her
right to move would not be able, for that sole reason, to invoke a fundamental right as a general principle of Union law against a private party.
I will come back to this issue in the last section.

[44] Case C-415/93 *Union Royale Belge des Sociétés de Football Association and others
v Bosman and others* [1995] ECR I-4921; in the writer's opinion *Bosman* is not strictly
speaking a horizontal effect case but rather a semi-horizontal one (confirming the approach
in Case 36/74 *Walrave v Union Cycliste Internationale* [1974] ECR 1405) since the rules
at issue collectively regulated footballers contracts.
[45] Case C-415/93 *Union Royale Belge des Sociétés de Football Association and others v
Bosman and others* [1995] ECR I-4921, para 85.
[46] See also Case C-291/98 *Angonese* [2000] ECR I-4139.
[47] In fact, I would argue that the legitimate exercise of a competing fundamental right
should not be qualified as a barrier at all, so as to escape from the centralising jurisdiction
of the ECJ, and instead be left to the assessment of the national courts (subject to the principles of equality and effectiveness). Of course this is very far from being the Court's view;
see also Case C-112/00 *Schmidberger* [2003] ECR I-5659. On the horizontal effect of the
Treaty provisions and its application to contractual relations see also D Wyatt, 'Horizontal
Effect of Fundamental Freedoms and the Right to Equality After *Viking* and *Mangold* and
the Implications for Community Competences' (2008) 4 *Croatian Yearbook of European
Law and Policy* 1.
[48] C-60/00 *Carpenter* [2002] ECR I-6279.

B Directives

There is no case law to enlighten us as to the scope of application of the general principles, including fundamental rights, in situations in which a matter falls within the scope of Union law by virtue of a directive, but where there is no national rule to be displaced. The issue arose in *Audiolux*,[49] where minority shareholders who had suffered a takeover bid from another company claimed that they should be protected by Union law, in particular by the alleged general principle of equal treatment of minority shareholders. In their view, the principle of equal treatment should have afforded them a right to sell their shares to the acquiring company under the same conditions as the majority shareholders. The national court referred the case to the European Court of Justice, asking it to address two separate (if obviously) related issues: first of all, whether such a general principle actually existed; secondly, whether general principles could be relied upon against private parties even in the absence of national rules. The Advocate General found that there was no general principle guaranteeing the equal treatment of minority shareholders. In the event that the Court's assessment differed, she then proceeded to refute the idea that such a general principle could be invoked against a private party. The Court found that the proposed principle was not a general principle of Union law,[50] and hence avoided the question as to the effects of general principles on the relationship between private parties.

There is therefore no authority to suggest that the application of fundamental rights as general principles in cases falling within the scope of Union law by virtue of a directive can be invoked against a private party beyond the 'exclusionary' effects endorsed by the Mangold case law. Yet, as we shall see in the next section, it is difficult to accept *Mangold* but then limit its scope.

VII SOME CONSTITUTIONAL OBJECTIONS AGAINST THE HORIZONTAL APPLICATION OF FUNDAMENTAL RIGHTS

The analysis carried out above can be summarised in the following way:

---

[49] Case C-101/08 *Audiolux SA and Others v Groupe Bruxelles Lambert SA (GBL) and Others, Bertelsmann AG and Others* [2009] ECR I-9823.

[50] *Audiolux*, para 63, 'The general principles of Community law have constitutional status while the principle proposed by Audiolux is characterised by a degree of detail requiring legislation to be drafted and enacted at Community level by a measure of secondary Community law. Therefore, the principle proposed by Audiolux cannot be regarded as an independent general principle of Community law.'

Treaty provisions

- For any national legislation which falls within the Treaty to be compatible with it, it must also be compatible with the general principles of Union law, regardless of whether the Treaty is invoked in litigation between private parties (*Familiapress*) or in vertical situations (*ERT, Carpenter*).
- Treaty provisions must also be interpreted so as to be compatible with fundamental rights as general principles of Union law (*Schmidberger*); this means that, when the Treaty is invoked by an individual against another individual, the scope of application of the Treaty provision (or the content of the Treaty right) finds its natural limit in the general principles (*Viking* and *Laval*).

Directives

- National legislation which falls within the scope of a directive must comply with the general principles of Union law, including fundamental rights (*Booker Aquaculture*). This is true even if a party is invoking the Union principle against another party in a way which would not be allowed under the directive (*Mangold*).
- If a matter falls within the scope of Union law by virtue of a directive, but there is no national rule which needs to be displaced by the general principle, then there is no authority to say that the general principle could be invoked against a private party.

Thus, the extent to which fundamental rights as general principles of Union law can be applied horizontally is not at all clear. In this respect, the *Mangold* case law poses very important hermeneutic questions. Thus, it has been noted above that one of the striking elements of that case law is the dissonance between the scope of application of the trigger (a directive) and the scope of application of the general principle. This dissonance is important as it makes it more difficult to confine the *Mangold* case law to those cases in which the general principles are merely used to 'displace' (or exclude) conflicting national rules. In other words, even were one to share the enthusiasm shown by some of the scholarship for a constitutional distinction between effects which only determine the 'exclusion' of national law and those which entail a (allegedly more problematic) 'substitution' of the Union norm for the national one,[51] there is no reason why *Mangold* should not apply also in 'substitution' cases. I am first going to look at this dissonance problem, then turn to the reasons

---

[51] See, eg K Lenaerts and T Corthaut, 'Of Birds and Edges: the Role of Primacy in Invoking Norms of EU Law' (2006) 31 *European Law Review* 287; AG Ruiz-Jarabo Colomer, Opinion, Joined Cases C-397 to C-403/01 *Pfeiffer and others* [2004] ECR I-8835.

why the current approach is not only constitutionally problematic but also practically untenable.

A   The Dissonance between Trigger and Triggered Principle

I have said above that, if one were to be consistent, the *Mangold* approach cannot be confined to those situations in which the general principle is used to displace conflicting national rules. Thus, once we accept that the mode of application of the general principle, and of fundamental rights, is independent from the scope of application of the Union law norm that determined its applicability in the first place, then we open the doors to a much broader effect of the Union law's general principles. In other words, if there is no longer any equivalence in application between the two (Union norm and general principle), then there is no way we can justify such a difference in application between cases. As a result, it is difficult to understand why, if a rule falls within the scope of a non-directly effective Treaty provision (eg Article 19 TFEU), it should not attract the application of the general principle but, if the rule falls within the scope of application of a non-(horizontally) directly effective directive, it should attract the general principle. Or why, if a directive cannot impose exclusionary effects, can such effects be imposed by virtue of a general principle which was triggered by that directive?

Thus, if the *Mangold* case law can be justified, then it is difficult to confine its application to those cases in which national law creates an obstacle to the full effectiveness of a general principle, whether or not such a principle has been enshrined in the directive which brought the matter within the scope of application of Union law. If we were to be hermeneutically consistent, by virtue of the *Mangold* case law, general principles and fundamental rights would become applicable in all cases falling for whatever reasons within the scope of Union law; they should arguably have both exclusionary and substitution effects; and they should be fully applicable against private parties. This would entail a rather major constitutional development, so that something which is not permissible in many national constitutional systems, such as the horizontal applica-tion of fundamental rights, might become possible through the medium of Union law. Furthermore, there seems to be no awareness of the fact that, in codifying Union fundamental rights in the Charter, the (consti-tutional) legislature clearly intended the Charter to apply only in vertical situations and, as a result, addressed it only to Union institutions and Member States. That such a dramatic constitutional development should happen through badly reasoned rulings is then all the more regrettable.

In any event, and even should the *Mangold* case law be limited to determining the lack of applicability of national law falling within the scope of a directive when the former conflicts with (some?) EU fundamental rights, one should consider whether such a development is desirable. Here, one could recall the well-rehearsed arguments against the distinction between exclusion and substitution in relation to the horizontal effect of directives.[52] Those arguments also apply, and perhaps even more so, to fundamental rights. Thus, such a distinction risks being arbitrary, since it is based on random elements upon which private parties have little control, such as whether there is a provision of national law and how that provision is phrased. The end result is both to increase different standards of protection within the EU (all the more problematical in matters relating to fundamental rights) and to increase legal uncertainty so that private parties who have acted lawfully and in good faith might find themselves liable for what is ultimately a failure of the national authorities. Moreover, the distinction between exclusion and substitution increases this uncertainty because it fails to establish one simple clear rule. So, if we accept the *Mangold* ruling (and the present writer does not), we should be prepared to accept that fundamental rights should be applicable horizontally also in the absence of national rules; otherwise, we should reject the constitutional soundness of the *Mangold* approach.

B   Fundamental Rights, Anyone? Transforming State Liability in Individual Responsibility

In both *Mangold* and *Kücükdeveci*, the Court might have been motivated by the dual desire of maximising the rights of individual claimants, a feature which has become common in post-citizenship case law,[53] and of maximising the effectiveness of Union law, so as to further reduce the scope for Member State's mis- or non-implementation of directives. Two issues need to be considered in this respect. First of all, and as mentioned in the introduction, in cases relating to litigation between private parties the gain in individual rights often translates into a loss for another individual. Mr Mangold's employer would be bound by a contract that he thought in good faith would be terminated after a given period of time;[54] Ms Kücükdeveci's employer would be liable to pay compensation

---

[52] See, eg AG Jacobs' Opinion in Case C-443/98 *Unilever Italia Spa v Central Food Spa* [2000] ECR I-7535; generally M Dougan, 'When Worlds Collide: Competing Visions of the Relationship between Direct Effect and Supremacy' (2007) 44 *Common Market Law Review* 931.

[53] See, eg E Spaventa, *Free Movement of Persons in the European Union: Barriers to Movement in their Constitutional Context* (Alphen aan den Rijn, Kluwer Law International, 2007), esp chs 5–7.

[54] Of course, and as mentioned above, the litigation in *Mangold* was probably fictitious; yet, since the national court and, as a consequence, the ECJ treated it as genuine, we must do the same; on the relationship between judicial prounouncements and the (re)writing of history see C Ginzburg, *Il giudice e lo storico* (Torino, Einaudi, 1991, reprinted 2006).

for having given a shorter notice than what was required by the Court. In both cases, the employers acted in compliance with the applicable national law.[55] In this respect, the fact that those effects might be confined to cases of 'exclusion' might, from a legal certainty viewpoint, be even worse since a party that acts following an unambiguous national rule might face disastrous economic consequences by virtue of the, sometimes random, application of Union law.

Secondly, this transfer of liability from Member State to individual might signal the fact that the Court no longer considers *Francovich* damages to be an adequate means to remedy the negative effects on individuals arising from a Member State's failure to comply with Union law.[56] Thus, traditionally, in horizontal situations covered by directives, individuals would need to seek redress from the state since only the state bore the responsibility for implementing directives. The *Francovich* damages represented a compromise between giving horizontal effects to directives and the reality of patchy implementation across the Union's territory. Whilst the conditions imposed by the Court might have made the recovery of damages difficult or costly at times, the solution was not without sense. It provided a financial incentive for correct implementation (which is more effective for the internal market and eliminates the distorting effect of non-compliance) and afforded some protection to individuals. However, the *Mangold* case law transfers that financial risk onto the individual, who, in many jurisdictions, would not even be able to recover the damage from the state through a *Francovich* action since the connection between mis-implementation and damage suffered by the (national) law-abiding citizen might be considered too remote.[57]

Thus, the horizontal application of general principles, and fundamental rights in particular, poses significant problems. From a hermeneutic viewpoint, the dissonance between trigger and triggered principle is either untenable or should be extended to cover all cases falling within the ambit of Union law. From the perspective of legal certainty, the *Mangold* approach makes it impossible for private parties to foresee their obligations yet transfers liability from the Member State onto them. From a constitutional perspective, this interpretation disregards those national constitutional traditions which have so far resisted (for good reasons) the horizontal application of fundamental rights; and, in doing so, it curtails the discretion of both the Union and the national legislature, limiting the effectiveness of political choices.

---

[55] This is a problem which is common to other areas of Union law, such as the horizontal application of Treaty rights, where the lack of proper implementation by the state translates in liability of a private party.

[56] Case C-479/03 *Francovich v Italy* [1995] ECR I-3843.

[57] The same can be said in relation to the *Laval* approach, where liability was transferred from the state, who had mis-implemented the Posted Workers' Directive, to the trade union, which acted in compliance with national law.

VIII   CONCLUDING REMARKS

The result of the *Mangold* approach is not to maximise individual rights, but rather to take from some (employers) to give to others (employees and indirectly the state); it is to reduce legal certainty so that mutual rights and obligations can no longer be easily ascertained but are the result of judicial developments which are difficult to conceptualise in a coherent manner; it is to confuse the scope of application of Union law to an extent to which it becomes difficult to predict when and to what extent fundamental rights as general principles of Union law apply. Furthermore, as noted by many Advocates General, this case law also affects the ability of the legislature to lay down detailed rules on the way a given right should be implemented. Finally, following the adoption of the Charter, and the generous approach to rights/principle codification followed therein, the explosive potential of this case law should not be underestimated. After all, all rights/principles contained in the Charter are general principles of Union law; and most of those are sufficiently clear to be capable of imposing obligations on individuals. Will all of these rights then have horizontal application? In the writer's opinion, an opinion probably shared by Professor Dashwood, given his scepticism about both *Mangold* and an excessive reliance on fundamental rights, the Court should abandon the horizontal application of the general principles and accept that it, by itself, cannot correct all evils of society, much less all of the constitutional accidents inherent in the Union project. At present, the Court risks transforming the constitutional 'order' of states in a constitutional chaos.

12

In Defence of *Mangold*?

MICHAEL DOUGAN*

I INTRODUCTION

THIS CHAPTER COULD never hope to provide a fitting tribute to a scholar who has exercised a profound influence on my own academic life. Alan Dashwood's passionate emotional commitment to the ideals of European integration, combined with a rigorous critical legal intellect and a healthy realism about some of the bolder ambitions of European union, will ever provide the standard to which I aspire in my own work. Indeed, I consider myself remarkably lucky that so much of that work has been conducted directly under Alan's tutelage—a tutelage that has been not only challenging and stimulating, but also truly generous of spirit, not to say sparkling with wit, and touching in warmth. But of course, papers are what a Festschrift seeks to offer by way of tribute to our dearest colleagues, and my chapter will honour Alan's contribution to EU legal scholarship by examining certain aspects of the ruling in *Mangold*—one of the most controversial judgments to be delivered by the Court of Justice (ECJ) in recent years,[1] attracting considerable academic criticism, including a number of important contributions by Alan himself.[2]

The essence of the *Mangold* judgment is by now so well known that it calls for only the briefest of summaries: the ECJ found the prohibition of discrimination on grounds of age to be a general principle of Union law, binding upon the Member States whenever they act within the scope of the Treaties; this was despite the fact that Directive 2000/78, specifically guaranteeing equal treatment on grounds of age in the field of employment,[3] lacked direct effect in the instant case because (first) the time limit for the Directive's implementation had not yet expired when the relevant

---

* I am very grateful to participants at the Cambridge conference in honour of Alan Dashwood, and also to those at a research seminar in the University of Paris II (Panthéon-Assas), for their comments and discussion. I am also indebted to Tony Arnull, Catherine Barnard and Eleanor Spaventa for their invaluable suggestions on earlier drafts.

[1] Case C-144/04 *Mangold* [2005] ECR I-9981.

[2] In particular: A Dashwood, 'From *van Duyn* to *Mangold* via *Marshall*: Reducing Direct Effect to Absurdity?' (2006–07) 9 *Cambridge Yearbook of European Legal Studies* 81.

[3] [2000] OJ L303/16.

dispute arose[4] and (secondly) the litigation involved two private parties, yet directives cannot of themselves impose obligations upon individuals.[5]

This contribution takes as its cue the generally frosty reception afforded to *Mangold*, and enquires just how far the ruling deserves various of the criticisms levelled against it.[6] As we shall see, it is in fact possible to defend certain apparently controversial elements of the *Mangold* ruling. But other aspects of the jurisprudence do indeed emerge as rather problematic in nature—not least the question of when a Member State acts within the scope of the Treaties, for the purposes of triggering its obligation to respect the general principles of Union law, particularly as that question has been addressed by the ECJ in its post-*Mangold* case law.[7] Moreover, it will be argued that such problems have potentially important implications for the concept of the Union as a 'constitutional order of states', insofar as they suggest that the Court is engaged in a process of gradually but steadily expanding the effective space of the 'European public law order', even into situations where it is far from obvious that the nature and content of the rule of law, through which we judge the legality of public action, should be defined by the Union rather than by the Member States themselves.

II RECOGNISING A GENERAL PRINCIPLE OF UNION LAW PROHIBITING DISCRIMINATION ON GROUNDS OF AGE

It is useful to begin with one of the most commonly aired causes for complaint about the reasoning in *Mangold*. To be recognised as a general principle of Union law, a given proposition must either represent a constitutional tradition common to the Member States or derive from an international agreement on which the Member States have collaborated or to which they are signatories.[8] Yet equal treatment on grounds of age

---

[4] Eg Case 148/78 *Ratti* [1979] ECR 1629; Case C-212/04 *Adeneler* [2006] ECR I-6057.

[5] Eg Case 152/84 *Marshall* [1986] ECR 723; Case C-91/92 *Faccini Dori* [1994] ECR I-3325.

[6] We will not engage with other important aspects of the *Mangold* ruling, eg interpretation of the 'non-regression' clause; or the Member State's obligations pre-transposition deadline. See further, eg Case C-212/04 *Adeneler* [2006] ECR I-6057; Cases C-378–380/07 *Angelidaki* [2009] ECR I-3071; Cases C-261/07 and C-299/07 *VTB-VAB* [2009] ECR I-2949; Case C-98/09 *Sorge*, judgment of 24 June 2010. Cp C Tobler, 'Putting *Mangold* in Perspective' (2007) 44 *Common Market Law Review* 1177; A Masson and C Micheau, 'The *Werner Mangold* Case: An Example of Legal Militancy' (2007) 13 *European Public Law* 587.

[7] In particular: Case C-427/06 *Bartsch* [2008] ECR I-7245; Case C-555/07 *Kücükdeveci*, judgment of 19 January 2010.

[8] Eg Case 4/73 *Nold* [1974] ECR 491; Case 44/79 *Hauer* [1979] ECR 3727; Case C-540/03 *Parliament v Council* [2006] ECR I-5769. The Treaties themselves may also provide the basis for a general principle of Union law: consider, eg Art 18 TFEU (ex-12 EC) or Art 340 TFEU (ex-288 EC).

could hardly have been said to reflect any such common constitutional tradition,[9] and was not clearly expressed in any international agreement to which the Member States were party,[10] creating the impression that the Court in *Mangold* was insufficiently observant of its own methodology for identifying the general principles of Union law[11]—in fact, appears simply to have made up 'new law' as it went along, with no proper legal basis for doing so.[12]

There have been several attempts to defend the ECJ's reasoning in that regard: for example, on the grounds that *Mangold* did not envisage a right to equal treatment specifically on the grounds of age, but merely manifested the much broader rule that comparable situations should be treated the same;[13] or that any given general principle of Union law need not command significant support amongst the national constitutional traditions, provided it resonates with the specific aims and values of the Union itself.[14] A rather different defence of the ECJ's ruling (even if not its reasoning) in *Mangold* would be to observe that equal treatment on grounds of age was expressly included in the Charter of Fundamental Rights proclaimed by the Union's political institutions in December 2000.[15] Since the Charter purported merely to codify those basic rights and principles which already existed under the Union legal order, the Court would therefore have been entitled to treat the Charter as an authoritative reference point for the elucidation of its own general principles of Union law. On that basis, the ECJ in *Mangold* could have saved itself much trouble simply by referring to the Charter as a sound basis for recognising that the pro-

[9] It appears to have been constitutionally recognised by only two of the (then) 25 Member States, ie Finland and Portugal: see AG Kokott in Case C-550/07 *Akzo Nobel Chemicals*, para 96 and note 78 of the Opinion of 29 April 2010, judgment pending. See also AG Mazák in Case C-411/05 *Palacios de la Villa* [2007] ECR I-8531; AG Bot in Case C-555/07 *Kücükdeveci*, Opinion of 7 July 2009.

[10] In particular: no specific provision of the ECHR prohibits discrimination on grounds of age.

[11] See further, eg Editorial, 'Horizontal Direct Effect—A Law of Diminishing Coherence?' (2006) 43 *Common Market Law Review* 1; E Muir, 'Enhancing the Effects of Community Law on National Employment Policies: The *Mangold* Case' (2006) 31 *European Law Review* 879; J Jans, 'The Effect in National Legal Systems of the Prohibition of Discrimination on Grounds of Age as a General Principle of Community Law' (2007) 34 *Legal Issues of Economic Integration* 53; J Raitio, 'The Principle of Legal Certainty as a General Principle of EU Law' in U Bernitz, J Nergelius and C Cardner (eds), *General Principles of EC Law in a Process of Development* (The Hague, Kluwer Law International, 2008).

[12] A criticism famously levelled by R Herzog and L Gerken, 'Stop the European Court of Justice' in *Frankfurter Allgemeine Zeitung* (8 September 2008). Cf Editorial, 'The Court of Justice in the Limelight—Again' (2008) 45 *Common Market Law Review* 1571.

[13] Eg AG Sharpston in Case C-227/04 *Lindorfer* [2007] ECR I-6767 and Case C-427/06 *Bartsch* [2008] ECR I-7245. For criticism, eg AG Mazák in Case C-411/05 *Palacios de la Villa* [2007] ECR I-8531.

[14] Eg AG Kokott in Case C-550/07 *Akzo Nobel Chemicals*, Opinion of 29 April 2010, judgment pending. Cp M Herdegen, 'General Principles of EU Law: The Methodological Challenge' in Bernitz et al, above n 11.

[15] In particular: Art 21(1) of the Charter [2000] OJ C364/1.

hibition on age discrimination constitutes a general principle of Union law.[16] The Court in fact began to employ the Charter in precisely such a manner only with its later *Family Reunification Directive* judgment—but exactly analogous reasoning could have extended, in hindsight, to the situation in *Mangold* itself.[17]

That explanation is more persuasive, but it also causes certain problems. There is a degree to which the proclamation of the Charter by the Union's political institutions and its subsequent emancipation by the Union courts constituted an act of self-levitation, and one which floated a little uncomfortably beside the fundamental principle that the Union is an organisation of attributed powers which enjoys only those competences conferred upon it by the Member States. However laudable its aims and content, the Charter was a mere declaration by the political institutions. Its judicial endorsement might have given the false impression that an expression of political will can be converted into legal doctrine via a process which operates altogether outside the ordinary framework for revision of the Treaties or the adoption of secondary legislation.[18] So, while reference to the relevant text of the Charter (even if the time did not seem ripe in the *Mangold* dispute itself, then at least with the benefit of hindsight after the *Family Reunification* case) could have absolved the ECJ from some of the criticism that it was making up 'new law' as it went along, it would nevertheless have come at the expense of a different accusation: that the Court was conferring constitutionally problematic legal effects upon the unincorporated Charter.

However, even insofar as one accepts that the latter critique possesses certain merit, it must be admitted that such problems are not unique to *Mangold*: similar misgivings could be expressed in respect of a range of other Charter provisions which appeared to go beyond a mere codification of the Union's pre-existing jurisprudence.[19] More importantly, this

---

[16] Cp D Schiek, 'The ECJ Decision in *Mangold*: A Further Twist on Effects of Directives and Constitutional Relevance of Community Equality Legislation' (2006) 35 *Industrial Law Journal* 329; M Herdegen, 'General Principles of EU Law: The Methodological Challenge' in Bernitz et al, above n 11.

[17] Case C-540/03 *Parliament v Council* [2006] ECR I-5769. Thereafter also in, eg Case C-432/05 *Unibet* [2007] ECR I-2271; Case C-303/05 *Advocaten voor der Wereld* [2007] ECR I-3633; Case C-438/05 *Viking Line* [2007] ECR I-10779; Case C-450/06 *Varec* [2008] ECR I-581. See further, eg E Drywood, 'Giving with One Hand, Taking with the Other: Fundamental Rights, Children and the Family Reunification Decision' (2007) 32 *European Law Review* 396.

[18] See further, eg M Dougan, 'Legal Developments' in U Sedelmeier and A Young (eds), *Journal of Common Market Studies: The European Union Annual Review 2006/2007* (Oxford, Blackwell Publishing, 2007).

[19] Consider, for example, the right to collective action referred to in Art 28 of the Charter but only recognised by the ECJ in its case law for the first time in Case C-438/05 *Viking Line* [2007] ECR I-10779. See further, eg L Besselink, 'The Member States, the National Constitutions and the Scope of the Charter' (2001) 8 *Maastricht Journal of European and Comparative Law* 68; K Lenaerts and E de Smijter, 'A 'Bill of Rights' for the European Union' (2001) 38 *Common Market Law Review* 273; P Carozza, 'The Member States' in S

entire critique of the *Mangold* ruling should now be considered of largely historical interest: since the entry into force of the Treaty of Lisbon, the Charter (albeit in its revised 2007 version) has acquired legally binding force, thus providing a more compelling constitutional underpinning to the guarantee of equal treatment on grounds of age as a matter of primary Union law.[20] That much was recognised by the ECJ itself in *Kücükdeveci*: having recalled that the existence of a general principle of Union law concerning age discrimination was first acknowledged in *Mangold*, the Court continued to note that the Charter now enjoys the same legal value as the Treaties, and includes a specific provision on equal treatment as regards age.[21]

The problem is that incorporation of the Charter could prove to be a double-edged sword in this context. On the one hand, it may well be true that the legally binding character of the Charter helps provide stronger doctrinal support for the Court's recognition of equal treatment on grounds of age as a general principle of Union law. On the other hand, such support begs the question: what does the Court now consider to be the proper legal basis for the prohibition on age discrimination as a matter of primary Union law? It might be that the relevant source will continue to be the Court's own general principles of Union law, with the Charter being referred to in *Kücükdeveci* only as a useful prop for the previously scant reasoning in *Mangold*; it might be that the newly incorporated provisions of the Charter will in the future entirely displace the general principles of Union law as the primary reference point for further developing the *Mangold* jurisprudence; or it might be that the case law develops through some more complex combination of the general principles and the Charter.[22] Such questions about the interplay between unwritten and written fundamental rights within the Union's revised legal order resonate far beyond the specific context of this chapter.[23] But, as we shall see, the potential for the Charter to play a substantive rather than merely cosmetic role here creates potential new complications in the future development of important aspects of the *Mangold* case law.[24]

For now, suffice to conclude: the ECJ's reasoning in *Mangold* may not

Peers and A Ward (eds), *The EU Charter of Fundamental Rights: Politics, Law and Policy* (Oxford, Hart Publishing, 2004).

[20] Art 6(1) TEU. Full text of the revised Charter published at [2010] OJ C83/389.

[21] Case C-555/07 *Kücükdeveci*, judgment of 19 January 2010.

[22] Cp the case of 'general principles' which are not also 'fundamental rights' within the meaning of the Charter, eg legal certainty or legitimate expectations.

[23] See further, eg M Dougan, 'The Treaty of Lisbon 2007: Winning Minds, Not Hearts' (2008) 45 *Common Market Law Review* 617. At the time of writing, the available case law provides only limited insights into this important question: besides *Kücükdeveci*, consider also, eg Case C-403/09 PPU *Detiček*, judgment of 23 December 2009; Case C-578/08 *Chakroun*, judgment of 4 March 2010; Case C-211/10 PPU *Povse*, judgment of 1 July 2010.

[24] See Sections V and VI (below).

have been very convincing, and such poor reasoning is not something to be excused or encouraged, but it is now beyond doubt that the general principle of Union law prohibiting age discrimination forms a legitimate part of the Union's (post-Lisbon) primary law.

III   EXTENDING THE APPLICATION OF THE GENERAL PRINCIPLES OF UNION LAW BEYOND THE PUBLIC INTO THE PURELY PRIVATE SPHERE?

The ruling in *Mangold* has also been considered controversial insofar as it suggests that the general principles of Union law are capable of going further than controlling the (public law) actions of the Union institutions and Member States when acting within the scope of the Treaties, so as also to serve as a direct source of legally binding (private law) obligations for individuals acting as such within their own sphere of autonomy. Thus, in *Mangold* itself, the general principle of Union law prohibiting discrimination on grounds of age provided the basis for the Court to meddle in the contractual freedom of two private parties (employer and employee).[25]

Closer inspection suggests that that interpretation of *Mangold* is not terribly persuasive. There is an easy, though unfortunate, confusion between the question of whether Union law which creates (public law) duties for the Member State can also be invoked collaterally during the course of horizontal proceedings between two private parties and the issue of whether Union law instead imposes (private law) obligations directly upon an individual which may be apt for enforcement in litigation before the national courts.[26] *Mangold* was clearly an example of the former type of situation: the general principle of Union law prohibiting age discrimination was treated by the Court as an 'administrative law' obligation for the Member State, albeit one that was (quite rightly) capable of having certain legal effects in relations between two private parties. After all, the disputed terms and conditions of the claimant's fixed term contract of employment were directly based upon legislation adopted by Germany pursuant to its own regulatory powers. The unlawful discrimination was therefore not derived from the exercise by two private parties of their contractual autonomy, but had a clear public law basis, the latter providing the necessary administrative wrongdoing against which the general principles of Union law were ultimately directed.

Mangold thus illustrates no more than the simple proposition that,

---

[25] See further, eg Editorial, above n 11.
[26] Cp A Hartkamp, 'The Effect of the EC Treaty in Private Law: On Direct and Indirect Horizontal Effects of Primary Community Law' (2010) 18 *European Review of Private Law* 527.

where the general principles of Union law are binding upon a Member State acting within the scope of the Treaties, public law acts which are tainted by illegality in accordance with the standards of administrative conduct laid down by the ECJ may be impugned, not only directly in an action for judicial review against the delinquent public authorities themselves, but also indirectly where such public law acts are challenged collaterally in a dispute between two private individuals.[27] That proposition is analogous to the well-established case law concerning primary Treaty provisions such as Article 34 TFEU (ex 28 EC):[28] the rules on the free movement of goods impose obligations only upon the Member State and other public bodies as defined by the Court, but those obligations can be invoked also in horizontal disputes involving two private parties, where the outcome hinges upon the compatibility of the relevant public measures with substantive Union law.[29] Nor would it have made much sense for the Court in *Mangold* to have extended, wholesale, the general principles of Union law so as to catch directly the purely private actions of individuals acting within their own sphere of autonomy. After all, why should private parties be held to the same standards of behaviour, as regards principles such as legal certainty and legitimate expectations, as those imposed upon public entities entrusted with the exercise of power in the general good?

Of course, one may leave open to debate the question of whether certain of the general principles of Union law might still evolve in the future so as to become horizontally applicable in the true sense of that term.[30] But that would imply a significant change in the constitutional function of the general principles of Union law, including the need to distinguish carefully between those general principles which would continue to perform their traditional function of furnishing the Union legal order with

---

[27] Cp AG Sharpston in Case C-427/06 *Bartsch* [2008] ECR I-7245, especially at paras 79–85 of the Opinion. Also, eg AG Trstenjak in Case C-80/06 *Carp* [2007] ECR I-4473 and in Case C-101/08 *Audiolux*, judgment of 15 October 2009. See further, eg Schiek, above n 16; Jans, above n 11.

[28] The same is not true, whether we like it or not, in the case of unimplemented directives, where the preclusion of horizontal direct effect generally applies regardless of whether the situation involves the Member State's substantive wrongdoing or that of a private individual. But note 'triangular' situations such as Case C-201/02 *Delena Wells* [2004] ECR I-723; and the much-debated question of whether the same is true of troublesome rulings such as Case C-194/94 *CIA Security International* [1996] ECR I-2201.

[29] Eg Case 74/76 *Iannelli & Volpi v Meroni* [1977] ECR 557; Case C-315/92 *Verband Sozialer Wettbewerb v Clinique Laboratories* [1994] ECR I-317; Case C-33/97 *Colim v Biggs* [1999] ECR I-3175; Case C-159/00 *Sapod Audic v Eco-Emballages* [2002] ECR I-5031; Case C-322/01 *Deutscher Apothekerverband* [2003] ECR I-14887.

[30] Consider, in particular, Case C-101/08 *Audiolux*, contrasting Opinion of 30 June 2009 with judgment of 15 October 2009. See further, eg X Groussot and HH Lidgard, 'Are There General Principles of Community Law Affecting Private Law?' in Bernitz et al, above n 11; M Safjan and P Miklaszewicz, 'Horizontal Effect of the General Principles of EU law in the Sphere of Private Law' (2010) 18 *European Review of Private Law* 475; and also the contribution by Eleanor Spaventa in this collection (Chapter 11).

its unwritten code of administrative law, as compared to those general principles which would also or instead serve as the basis for an entirely novel body of Union law aimed at regulating also the private legal sphere (albeit still only within the scope of application of the Treaties).[31] Whatever else *Mangold* has done, it has certainly not done that.

IV EXPANDING THE SITUATIONS IN WHICH THE RIGHT TO EQUAL TREATMENT ON GROUNDS OF AGE MAY HAVE DIRECT EFFECT WITHIN THE NATIONAL LEGAL SYSTEMS

Perhaps the most common criticism of the *Mangold* ruling concerns the allegation that the ECJ improperly relied upon the general principles of Union law so as to expand the situations in which the right to equal treatment on grounds of age could produce independent effects within the national legal systems.[32] In the first place, the Court effectively ignored the limits placed upon the legal effects of Article 19(1) TFEU (ex 13(1) EC), which had been consciously drafted by the Member States under the Treaty of Amsterdam so as to ensure that the various grounds of discrimination contained therein did not have direct effect, and would only produce legal effects (if at all) through the adoption of implementing measures by the Union legislature.[33] Secondly, for those very purposes, the Union legislature had indeed adopted Directive 2000/78 giving effect to the prohibition on age discrimination—yet the Court managed slyly to bypass both the principle that directives should not have direct effect before the deadline for their transposition has expired and the rule that directives are not capable in themselves of imposing obligations upon private parties.[34] In other words: the *Mangold* ruling had the effect of

---

[31] Consider, eg the right to equal pay in Case 43/75 *Defrenne v Sabena* [1976] ECR 455 or to equal treatment in Case C-281/98 *Angonese* [2000] ECR I-4131: even if one were to accept that their 'true' horizontal application was capable of deriving from their status as general principles of Union law, rather than as express Treaty provisions, such 'private law' effects would still best be distinguished from the 'public law' functions of those (and other) general principles of Union law in situations concerning Member Sate conduct (whether vertical or horizontal in dress). Cp Jans, above n 11.

[32] Eg AG Mazák in Case C-411/05 *Palacios de la Villa* [2007] ECR I-8531. Note also AG Sharpston in Case C-427/06 *Bartsch* [2008] ECR I-7245, especially at para 31 of the Opinion. See further, eg Dashwood, above n 2; A Arnull, 'Editorial: Out With the Old . . .' (2006) 31 *European Law Review* 1.

[33] Cp AG Geelhoed in Case C-13/05 *Chacón Navas* [2006] ECR I-6467. See further, eg L Waddington, 'Art 13 EC: Mere Rhetoric or a Harbinger of Change?' (1998) 1 *Cambridge Yearbook of European Legal Studies* 175; M Bell, 'The New Art 13 EC Treaty: A Sound Basis For European Anti-Discrimination Law?' (1999) 6 *Maastricht Journal of European and Comparative Law* 5; L Flynn, 'The Implications of Art 13 EC: After Amsterdam, Will Some Forms of Discrimination be More Equal Than Others?' (1999) 36 *Common Market Law Review* 1127.

[34] See Section I (above).

distorting both the balance between the roles of the Union legislature and its judiciary, and the division of competences between the Union and its Member States—an accusation which directly challenges the integrity of Dashwood's 'constitutional order of states'.

It is certainly true that, for those reasons, *Mangold* looks like an exercise in judicial mischief-making. Nevertheless, the Court's recourse to the general principles of Union law in *Mangold* was, in principle, entirely legally defensible.

The general principles of Union law are an autonomous body of constitutional doctrine within the Union legal order, distinct from both the primary provisions of the Treaties and any provisions of Union secondary legislation. As long as (first) the relevant situation falls within the scope of Treaties for the purposes of triggering the application of the general principles of Union law at all and (secondly) the relevant general principle fulfils the usual threshold criteria requiring its substantive content to be clear, precise and unconditional, then it should be capable of having direct effect and thus producing independent effects within the national legal orders. Such direct effect in respect of a general principle of Union law per se is unaffected by whatever limitations might apply to the direct effect of any legally distinct Treaty provision or implementing directive covering the same or similar subject matter. Indeed, it is worth recalling that, when it comes to sidestepping the inability of unimplemented directives to impose obligations upon private individuals, specifically by reference to a hierarchically superior norm of Union law, *Mangold* is not entirely without precedent: after all, the Court has previously held that the Equal Pay Directive merely elaborates upon the provisions of Article 157 TFEU (ex 141 EC) and, as such, can be relied upon even in horizontal disputes against national rules which do not fully comply with the requirements imposed by Union law.[35]

There is no doubt, of course, that the inter-relationships between the general principles of Union law, the provisions of the Treaties themselves and secondary legislation adopted by the Union institutions are constitutionally complex and potentially problematic. Consider, for example, how far the Member States, even in their capacity as 'masters of the Treaties', may be able to curb the full legal effects of a given right which enjoys the status of a general principle of Union law by having recourse to the expedient of express Treaty drafting that seeks to rule out any possibility of direct effect.[36] Or again, consider how far the substantive content

---

[35] Dir 75/117 [1975] OJ L45/19; eg Case 96/80 *Jenkins v Kingsgate* [1981] ECR 911; Case C-381/99 *Brunnhofer* [2001] ECR I-4961. See now Dir 2006/54 [2006] OJ L204/23. See further, eg Jans, above n 11.

[36] Consider, eg the possible legal effects of Protocol No 30 on the application of the Charter of Fundamental Rights of the European Union to Poland and to the United Kingdom [2010] OJ C83/313. See further, eg Dougan, above n 23.

of Union secondary legislation should affect the interpretation of Union primary law (whether a Treaty provision or a general principle of Union law), for example, by defining a particular balance of competing interests or imposing a specific limitation on the scope or strength of a given right.[37] But such difficult questions are hardly unique to *Mangold* (even if they are partly illustrated by it). They reflect a more general state of complexity and opaqueness in the relationship between the 'superior' legal sources within the Union's hierarchy of norms.[38] Nor do such problems detract from the veracity of the underlying point of principle: the potential direct effect of a given general principle of Union law remains legally distinct from that of a given Treaty provision or Union secondary instrument.

Accepting the potential direct effect of the general principles of Union law to be an autonomous issue, critical evaluation of *Mangold* should perhaps focus rather on the manner in which the Court actually addressed the capacity of the general principles of Union law to produce independent effects within the national legal orders. In particular: when precisely will a dispute fall within the scope of the Treaties, so as to trigger the possible application of the general principles of Union law at all (Section V)? And when exactly will a given general principle of Union law be considered sufficiently clear, precise and unconditional as to be capable of producing direct effect in practice (Section VI)? If we have hitherto been eager to defend the Court from the zeal of its academic critics, our approach to the *Mangold* case law is now about to take a rather more sceptical turn.

V   WHEN WILL A SITUATION FALL 'WITHIN THE SCOPE OF THE TREATIES' FOR THE PURPOSES OF APPLYING THE GENERAL PRINCIPLE OF UNION LAW PROHIBITING AGE DISCRIMINATION?

Consistently with the logic of the general principles of Union law, the latter should only apply to situations falling within the scope of the Treaties. The precise definition of what falls 'within the scope of the Treaties' for those purposes remains unclear,[39] but there is broad consensus on the proposition that it embraces three main situations: where the Union institutions are

[37] Consider, eg the relationship between Art 56 TFEU (ex-49 EC) and Dir 96/71 [1997] OJ L18/01 as interpreted in rulings such as Case C-341/05 *Laval un Partneri* [2007] ECR I-11767 and Case C-346/06 *Dirk Rüffert* [2008] ECR I-1989. See further, eg the essays collected together in (2007/2008) 10 *Cambridge Yearbook of European Legal Studies*; and the contribution by Catherine Barnard in this volume (Chapter 17).

[38] As opposed to the relationship between the inferior norms dealt with by the Treaty of Lisbon: see Arts 289–91 TFEU.

[39] See further, eg T Tridimas, *The General Principles of EU Law*, 2nd edn (Oxford, Oxford University Press, 2006); X Groussot, *General Principles of Community Law* (Groningen, Europa Law Publishing, 2006).

exercising powers conferred by or pursuant to the Treaties;[40] where the Member State is discharging its duty under the Treaties to implement Union law within its own legal system;[41] and where the Member State seeks rather to derogate from its binding obligations under Union law.[42] Where national measures fall outside the scope of the Treaties, there are no grounds for assessing their compatibility with the general principles of Union law.[43]

The inevitable consequence of such logic is that the scope of application of the general principle of Union law prohibiting age discrimination as recognised in *Mangold* will differ from, and should be considerably broader than, the scope of application of the right to equal treatment on grounds of age as entrusted to the Union's political institutions under Article 19 TFEU and given effect through implementing measures such as Directive 2000/78. Article 19 TFEU empowers the Union legislature to enact measures prohibiting age discrimination within the limits of the powers conferred by the Treaties upon the Union; the Union institutions have thus far exercised that competence only in respect of employment matters as defined by the relevant provisions of Directive 2000/78.[44] By contrast, the general principle of Union law prohibiting age discrimination will apply throughout the scope of application of the Treaties, including for matters other than (and independently of) those actually regulated under Article 19 TFEU/Directive 2000/78, provided only that the national legislation in question can be considered to implement or derogate from the Member State's obligations under Union law.

In *Mangold* itself, the latter requirement was satisfied because Germany's disputed legislation was in fact intended to transpose another Union measure, ie Directive 1999/70 giving effect to the Framework Agreement on Fixed Term Work.[45] The fact that the Member State was implementing Directive 1999/70 meant that the situation in *Mangold* fell within the

---

[40] Eg Case C-377/98 *Netherlands v Parliament and Council* [2001] ECR I-7079 (Union legislature); Case C-404/92P *X v Commission* [1994] ECR I-4737 (Union executive); Case C-185/95P *Baustahlgewebe v Commission* [1998] ECR I-8417 (Union judiciary).

[41] Eg Case 5/88 *Wachauf* [1989] ECR 2609; Cases C-31/91 to C-44/91 *Lageder* [1993] ECR I-1761; Case C-2/92 *Bostock* [1994] ECR I-955; Case C-292/97 *Karlsson* [2000] ECR I-2737; Cases C-20/00 and 64/00 *Booker Aquaculture* [2003] ECR I-7411; Case C-101/01 *Lindqvist* [2003] ECR I-12971. This includes the obligation to provide for the enforcement of Union law within the domestic legal system: consider, eg Case 222/84 *Johnston* [1986] ECR 1651; Case C-276/01 *Steffensen* [2003] ECR I-3735.

[42] Eg Case C-260/89 *ERT* [1991] ECR I-2925; Case C-368/95 *Familiapress* [1997] ECR I-3689; Case C-60/00 *Carpenter* [2002] ECR I-6279; Cases C-482 and 493/01 *Orfanopoulos* [2004] ECR I-5257. In this context, note also the 'balancing of rights' rulings, eg Case C-112/00 *Schmidberger* [2003] ECR I-5659; Cases C-570 and 571/07 *Blanco Pérez*, judgment of 1 June 2010.

[43] Eg Case 12/86 *Demirel* [1987] ECR 3719; Case C-159/90 *SPUC v Grogan* [1991] ECR I-4685; Case C-299/95 *Kremzow* [1997] ECR I-2629. Cp Arts 4(1) and 5(2) TEU.

[44] See Art 3 Dir 2000/78.

[45] [1999] OJ L175/43.

scope of the Treaties, thus providing the necessary legal context within which the general principles of Union law could be considered binding. In the absence of Directive 1999/70—or another such 'third measure' of Union secondary legislation—one might have assumed that the German rules on fixed term contracts would not have fallen within the scope of Union law at all, and the general principle of equal treatment on grounds of age would have been entirely inapplicable to the relevant dispute.

Left at that, one would have to admit that *Mangold* could not act as a substitute for Directive 2000/78 in every case, but only as regards those situations which, because they are already regulated at the supranational level, are capable of bringing the relevant national legislation within the scope of Union law so as to become subject to its general principles. That in turn would provide the basis for another critique of the ECJ's ruling: being dependent upon the happenchance existence of some 'third measure' capable of linking the dispute to Union law, even though that 'third measure' has no further relevance to or involvement in resolution of the legal problem at hand, *Mangold* implies that some citizens will be able to overcome all the usual limitations working upon the direct effect of Directive 2000/78, whilst others will just have to live with their unequal treatment. Such distinctions, even if constitutionally natural to the Union legal order, would nevertheless seem merely to bring another layer of arbitrariness to a field already characterised by an undesirable degree of inconsistency and confusion.[46]

The solution to this problem lies, if at all, in the question: can Directive 2000/78 itself provide the necessary link to Union law, such that implementation of Directive 2000/78 (even though that measure might lack any direct effect of its own) is nevertheless capable of triggering application of the general principle of Union law prohibiting age discrimination (which can then extend its direct effect in favour of the claimant)?[47] If so, that would help restore a more coherent system of judicial protection for individual citizens: the right to equal treatment on grounds of age could apply across the entire regulatory field occupied by Directive 2000/78, without having to demonstrate that the general principles of Union law have also been mediated through some additional but essentially random 'third measure'.

In its rulings in *Bartsch* and *Kücükdeveci*, the ECJ seemed to confirm that Directive 2000/78 can in itself provide the necessary link to the Treaties.[48] Further analysis of that proposition involves two subsidiary

---

[46] See further, eg M Dougan, 'Legal Developments' in U Sedelmeier and A Young (eds), *Journal of Common Market Studies: The European Union Annual Review 2005/2006* (Oxford, Blackwell Publishing, 2006).

[47] A question posed already by Dashwood, above n 2, 107–108.

[48] Case C-427/06 *Bartsch* [2008] ECR I-7245; Case C-555/07 *Kücükdeveci*, judgment of 19 January 2010.

questions: whether a non-directly provision of Union legislation should in principle be capable of providing the trigger for a directly effective general principle of Union law; and the precise circumstances under which implementation of Directive 2000/78 may in practice be classified as a situation where the Member State is acting within the scope of the Treaties. Taken together, those subsidiary questions illustrate how the benefits of *Bartsch* and *Kücükdeveci* in terms of creating a more coherent system of judicial protection for individual victims of age discrimination must nevertheless be balanced against the aggravation of certain broader constitutional difficulties for the Union as far as concerns its relationship to the national legal systems.

A   Can a Non-Directly Effective Legislative Instrument Trigger a Directly Effective General Principle?

In principle, there seems no objection to the proposition that a non-directly effective Union legislative instrument may legitimately provide the trigger for invoking a general principle of Union law—even if the latter might then be capable of having direct effect for itself.[49]

After all, it is the fact of the Member State's implementation of or derogation from its Treaty obligations that provides the relevant criterion for applying the general principles of Union law. The amenability of those obligations, or general principles, to independent application and enforcement before the domestic courts—in other words, their direct effect—simply does not appear to be a decisive factor in that regard. In particular, if there is a good constitutional justification for the Union to impose upon the Member States its own body of administrative law responsibilities—based on the fact that the national authorities are either acting as delegated agents for the executive enforcement of Union law or instead seeking to avoid their ordinary duties under the Treaties—then that justification loses none of its force simply because the relevant provisions of Union legislation are incapable of free-standing application before the national courts. Indeed, it would seem odd to decide that, just because a given provision of Union law lacks direct effect of its own, for example, because it is somehow insufficiently clear or unconditional, the Member State should thereby be absolved from its duty to observe the adminis-

---

[49] Eg case law on proportionality: Case C-186/98 *Nunes and de Matos* [1999] ECR I-4883; Case C-491/06 *Danske Svineproducenter* [2008] ECR I-3339. Eg case law on equal treatment: Case C-442/00 *Caballero* [2002] ECR I-11915; Case C-520/03 *Olaso Valero* [2004] ECR I-12065; cp Case C-177/05 *Guerrero Pecino* [2005] ECR I-10887; Case C-81/05 *Cordero Alonso* [2006] ECR I-7569. Eg case law on legal certainty: Case 80/86 *Kolpinghuis Nijmegen* [1987] ECR 3969; Case C-60/02 *Criminal Proceedings Against X* [2004] ECR I-651; Case C-387/02 *Berlusconi* [2005] ECR I-3565; Case C-105/03 *Pupino* [2005] ECR I-5285.

trative law requirements which would otherwise be imposed under the Treaties—not least because such a provision of Union law necessarily calls for the exercise of national legislative/executive discretion of precisely the sort which the general principles of Union law are intended to control.[50]

If the general point of principle seems clear, perhaps its specific manifestation in rulings such as *Bartsch* and *Kücükdeveci* feels less secure because of the peculiar coincidence of subject matter between the non-directly effective provisions of Directive 2000/78 and the directly effective general principle of Union law which they had triggered: there is something of a legal conjuring trick about the idea that the ECJ is prepared to substitute a general principle of Union law for an unimplemented directive, covering the same substantive obligations as regards the same material scope, without the intermediary of some entirely independent 'third measure' which can at least provide a more respectable constitutional link to the Treaties.

In that regard, it is arguable that the substantively identical nature of the unimplemented provisions of Directive 2000/78 (on the one hand) and the general principle of Union law guaranteeing equal treatment on grounds of age (on the other hand) should have been given greater weight by the ECJ in rulings such as *Bartsch* and *Kücükdeveci*. The point here is not to deny that non-directly effective Union instruments should be capable, in principle, of triggering directly effective general principles of Union law. The argument rests rather on a feeling that considerations of legal certainty, of the sort that have traditionally led the Court to deny that an unimplemented directive should be capable in itself of imposing obligations upon individuals, appear applicable also in a situation where reliance upon the general principles of Union law would actually lead to exactly the same outcome as if the Court had permitted full enforcement of that directive in a horizontal dispute between two private parties.[51]

We have grown increasingly accustomed in recent years to the idea that normal expectations concerning the direct effect and supremacy of Union law might have to be compromised by more fundamental considerations of legal certainty: for example, where the relevant Union law was not

[50] Similarly, if exercise of the Member State's discretion as regards implementation succeeds in rendering the non-directly effective Union obligation complete as a matter of national law, the general principles of Union law should still apply (even though there is still no direct effect as such for the relevant Union legislation).

[51] That would not have been the case in *Mangold*, given that Dir 1999/70 (rather than Dir 2000/78) provided the requisite link to Union law. But it has been argued that considerations of legal certainty should also have been a decisive factor weighing against any obligation to enforce the general principle of Union law prohibiting discrimination on grounds of age also in *Mangold* itself: see, eg AG Kokott in Case C-321/05 *Kofoed* [2007] ECR I-5795; AG Mazák in Case C-411/05 *Palacios de la Villa* [2007] ECR I-8531; AG Colomer in Cases C-55 and C-56/07 *Michaeler* [2008] ECR I-3135; AG Kokott in Case C-73/07 *Satakunnan Markkinapörssi and Satamedia* [2008] ECR I-9831. Cp P Craig, 'The Legal Effect of Directives: Policy, Rules and Exceptions' (2009) 34 *European Law Review* 349.

adequately published in a form accessible to the citizens;[52] or where a contrary national decision has already acquired the force of res judicata.[53] It is therefore arguable that, where the legislative instrument relied upon as a trigger for the general principles of Union law is an unimplemented directive, and recognising the direct effect of a given general principle of Union law would precisely replicate the substantive legal framework as it would result from simply granting horizontal direct effect to the directive itself, the Court should have permitted the principle of legal certainty to intervene and effectively short-circuit the system for enforcing Union law before the national courts. Such an approach would help preserve the legitimate interests of an individual otherwise faced with the imposition of novel obligations on account of Union law—particularly in a situation where the relationship between two private parties is on the point of being altered by a collateral challenge based upon the Member State's own 'administrative' wrongdoing. Yet the approach in cases such as *Bartsch* and *Kücükdeveci* shows that the Court did not believe such considerations to be sufficiently compelling: legal certainty will prevent an unimplemented directive of itself from imposing obligations upon an individual, but it will not prevent exactly the same directive from triggering the general principles of Union law so as to reshape that individual's obligations in exactly the same manner.

B Precisely When May Directive 2000/78 Act as a Trigger for the General Principles of Union Law?

Accepting that a (non-directly effective) secondary instrument can in principle act as a valid trigger for the application of a (directly effective) general principle of Union law, and that the ECJ will admit no exception to that approach in practice based upon concerns about legal certainty for private individuals, we can now move on to consider our second subsidiary question: when precisely, in the sense of under which circumstances, will Directive 2000/78 in itself prove capable of bringing a situation 'within the scope of the Treaties'?

The ECJ first addressed this question in the *Bartsch* case.[54] *Bartsch* (like *Mangold* itself) concerned facts occurring before the deadline for transposition of Directive 2000/78 had expired. But in *Bartsch* (unlike in *Mangold*), the relevant dispute arose in a field of employment law (qualification for an occupational survivor's pension) as regards which there

---

[52] Consider, eg Case C-108/01 *Asda Stores* [2003] ECR I-5121; Case C-161/06 *Skoma-Lux* [2007] ECR I-10841; Case C-345/06 *Heinrich*, judgment of 10 March 2009.

[53] Consider, eg Case C-453/00 *Kühne & Heitz* [2004] ECR I-837; Case C-234/04 *Kapferer* [2006] ECR I-2585; Cases C-392 & 422/04 *i-21 Germany* [2006] ECR I-8559.

[54] Case C-427/06 *Bartsch* [2008] ECR I-7245.

was no 'third measure' of Union secondary legislation. The question was thus posed directly: could the general principle of Union law guaranteeing equal treatment on grounds of age be triggered simply on the basis of Directive 2000/78 alone? The Court denied that the Directive was capable in itself of acting as the necessary link to Union law in this case: in particular, the disputed national rules were not a measure implementing Directive 2000/78; furthermore, the case had arisen before expiry of the deadline for the Directive's transposition into domestic law.[55]

Bartsch therefore seemed to suggest that, in order for the Member State's conduct to fall within the scope of the Treaties for the purposes of applying the general principles of Union law, based on Directive 2000/78 alone and without the intermediary of some 'third measure', the claimant must fulfil two (cumulative) requirements: first, that the disputed national rules constitute a specific implementation measure in respect of Directive 2000/78; and secondly, that the deadline for the latter's transposition had already expired at the time of the relevant facts. Conversely, it appeared from the ruling in *Bartsch* that, if the disputed measures were not intended to act as a specific implementation of Directive 2000/78, there could be no link to Union law, even if the deadline for transposition of Directive 2000/78 had indeed expired, and regardless of the fact that the disputed domestic rules did nevertheless fall within the Directive's material scope of application (in particular) because they regulated some relevant aspect of the employment relationship.[56]

On the one hand, to make expiry of the deadline for transposition of Directive 2000/78 a determinative factor in its ability to act as an autonomous trigger for the general principles of Union law might seem entirely consistent with the broader case law on the legal effects of unimplemented directives. Until the deadline for transposition has passed, the Member State is bound only by a negative obligation not to take steps that would seriously compromise achievement of the objectives of Union law;[57] it is not subject to any more far-reaching positive obligations (for example) to construe existing national law as far as possible in conformity with the relevant Union instrument.[58] It is therefore compatible with the constitutional principles underlying the particular nature of directives to hold that the deadline for transposition acts as a crucial threshold for quantifying the nature and extent of the Member State's obligations under Union law—including whether the situation should be treated as 'within

---

[55] See, in particular, para 17 of the ruling in *Bartsch*.
[56] Though consider AG Sharpston in Case C-427/06 *Bartsch* [2008] ECR I-7245, especially at paras 91–92 of the Opinion.
[57] Eg Case C-129/96 *Inter-Environnement Wallonie* [1997] ECR I-7411.
[58] Eg Case C-212/04 *Adeneler* [2006] ECR I-6057.

the scope of the Treaties' for the purposes of imposing the (positive) obligation to respect the general principles of Union law.[59]

On the other hand, certain problems do arise with the Court's suggestion in *Bartsch* that the specific implementing character of the disputed national measures acts as an additional determinative factor in the capacity of Directive 2000/78 to provide an autonomous trigger for the general principles of Union law. Of course, such a requirement would considerably reduce the range of situations that might benefit from *Mangold*: for example, it is doubtful whether a case like *Bartsch* would have been decided any differently even if the deadline for transposition had expired, since the disputed German rules on occupational pensions were not specifically intended to implement Directive 2000/78 (even if they clearly fell within its material scope of application). More importantly, perhaps, it would appear rather difficult in practice to maintain any clear distinction between those national measures which count as a 'specific implementation' and those which merely 'fall within the material scope' of any given instrument of Union secondary legislation. Particularly when one considers the flexibility with which Member States are entitled to implement directives into national law, including by reference to pre-existing legislation or to judicial interpretation, or by various combinations of old and new legislative and judicial measures, identifying a specific relationship of implementation between disputed national measures and Union secondary legislation might become an arbitrary or even impossible task.[60]

For those reasons, one might argue that, provided the deadline for transposition of Directive 2000/78 has passed and the disputed national measures fall within the material scope of application of Directive 2000/78, there should be no need to demonstrate (in addition) that those measures constitute a specific implementing measure, before the situation can be treated as falling within the scope of the Treaties for the purposes of enforcing the general principles of Union law. That position seems to have been confirmed by the ECJ itself in *Kücükdeveci*.[61] The case involved German rules concerning calculation of the notice period for dismissal from employment which were alleged to discriminate on grounds of age. As in *Bartsch*, such rules could not be considered as implementing some 'third measure' of Union legislation; they could only be considered to fall within the scope of the Treaties based on their relationship to Directive 2000/78 itself. In that regard, unlike in *Bartsch*, the employer's allegedly discriminatory conduct on the basis of the disputed German rules occurred

---

[59] However, note the peculiar situation underpinning the (otherwise apparently contradictory) rulings in Case C-81/05 *Cordero Alonso* [2006] ECR I-7569 and Case C-246/06 *Velasco Navarro* [2008] ECR I-105.

[60] Consider, eg Case C-81/05 *Cordero Alonso* [2006] ECR I-7569. See further, eg S Prechal, *Directives in EC Law*, 2nd edn (Oxford, Oxford University Press, 2005) ch 5.

[61] Case C-555/07 *Kücükdeveci*, judgment of 19 January 2010.

after the deadline for transposition of Directive 2000/78 into national law had already expired. According to the Court, upon that date, Directive 2000/78 had the effect of bringing within the scope of Union law the disputed German legislation as regards conditions of dismissal (which was a matter governed by the Directive). The ruling makes no reference to the additional requirement in *Bartsch* that the disputed national rules should constitute a measure implementing Directive 2000/78; indeed, just as in *Bartsch* itself, it would have been difficult to see how the German dismissal rules could possibly have fulfilled that criterion.

The ECJ thus seems to have shifted from expecting (in *Bartsch*) that the relevant national rules amount to a specific implementing measure in respect of Directive 2000/78, to accepting (in *Kücükdeveci*) that the disputed domestic legislation need merely fall within the general scope of application of Directive 2000/78.[62] That shift could make even an ardent defender of *Mangold* wonder whether there are any meaningful constitutional limits to the Court's creativity: the unwritten right to equal treatment can be enforced against incompatible provisions of national law, also within the context of a horizontal dispute between two private parties, even where there is no 'third measure' to bring the situation within the scope of the Treaties, based on the fact that the relevant national law falls within the material scope of Directive 2000/78 and provided only that the transposition deadline has already passed, despite the fact that the general principle of Union law and the unimplemented directive which acted as its trigger are, for all intents and purposes, identical in terms of their substantive content. Even if most of those propositions can be justified individually as a matter of Union constitutional law, perhaps their cumulative effects do in the end begin to resemble the pulling of a startled bunny out of a magical legal hat—creating the impression that *Mangold* and its subsequent jurisprudence together add up to something more radical than the sum of their largely orthodox parts.

More importantly, perhaps, for the ECJ in *Kücükdeveci* to imply that the Member States act 'within the scope of the Treaties', and are thus bound by the general principles of Union law, whenever the exercise of their own regulatory competences happens to touch upon a matter also subject to some form of legislative intervention by the Union itself, has the potential greatly to expand the scope of application, not only of *Mangold* and its right to equal treatment on grounds of age, but also of

---

[62] Note that *Kücükdeveci* goes further in this regard than Case C-81/05 *Cordero Alonso* [2006] ECR I-7569 and Case C-246/06 *Velasco Navarro* [2008] ECR I-105 (where the disputed national legislation had already been adopted in implementation of an existing Union directive, and was capable of transposing the amendments now required by another Union directive, even though that national legislation could not be described as a specific implementation measure in respect of that subsequent directive).

the entire system of Union administrative law which the general principles represent.[63]

It was mentioned above that the understanding of when a situation falls 'within the scope of the Treaties' is not entirely clear,[64] and it is true that some commentators have indeed argued in favour of recognising a 'default' category of situation in which Member State action—even though not implementing or derogating from the Treaties as such—should nevertheless be capable of triggering the general principles of Union law, ie where the Member State's conduct simply falls within the same scope of application as some substantive measure of Union law.[65] Further support for that approach was added by Advocate General Sharpston in *Bartsch*, where she observed that Member State action could trigger the general principles of Union law 'because some specific substantive rule of [EU] law is applicable to the situation'.[66]

However, the legal authorities capable of supporting the latter proposition have traditionally appeared to be both quantitatively and qualitatively weaker than those available in respect of the more accepted categories of situation falling 'within the scope of the Treaties'.[67] If anything, the weight of available case law directly contradicts (rather than supports) the approach in *Kücükdeveci*.[68] Consider, for example, the well-established principle that more stringent national regulatory standards adopted within the field of application of a Union measure providing for only minimum (rather than exhaustive) harmonisation nevertheless fall outside the scope of the Treaties for the purposes of triggering the general principles of Union law[69] unless such national rules give rise to an independent infringement of Union law (for example) by creating a prime facie breach of

---

[63] Particularly in the case of 'horizontal' measures such as Dir 2000/78, which impose specific obligations (the right to equal treatment) as regards significant fields of national policy (employment law), important aspects of which are not otherwise regulated by specific measures of Union law (eg wages and dismissal).

[64] See the introduction to Section V above.

[65] Consider, eg H Schermers and D Waelbroeck, *Judicial Protection in the European Union*, 6th edn (The Hague, Kluwer Law International, 2001) 35–37.

[66] Case C-427/06 *Bartsch* [2008] ECR I-7245, para 69 of the Opinion.

[67] The main authority cited is usually Cases C-286/94, C-340/95, C-401/95 and C-47/96 *Garage Molenheide* [1997] ECR I-7281; but this ruling could more naturally be understood as a manifestation of the right to effective judicial protection for the enforcement of the relevant substantive Union law rights: see M Dougan, *National Remedies Before the Court of Justice* (Oxford, Hart Publishing, 2004) ch 5.

[68] Consider, eg Case C-144/95 *Maurin* [1996] ECR I-2909; Case C-309/96 *Annibaldi* [1997] ECR I-7493; Case C-36/99 *Idéal Tourisme* [2000] ECR I-6049. See further, eg P Eeckhout, 'The EU Charter of Fundamental Rights and the Federal Question' (2002) 39 *Common Market Law Review* 945; A Knook, 'The Court, the Charter and the Vertical Division of Powers in the European Union' (2005) 42 *Common Market Law Review* 367.

[69] Consider, eg Case C-2/97 *Borsana* [1998] ECR I-8597; Case C-6/03 *Deponiezweckverband Eiterköpfe* [2005] ECR I-2753; Case C-82/09 *Dimos Agiou Nikolaou Kritis*, judgment of 22 April 2010.

the Treaty rules on the free movement of goods or services.[70] The only authority which appears inconsistent with that principle—and points in the same direction as *Kücükdeveci*—is the judgment in *Karner*.[71] But academic opinion has been divided over the significance of *Karner*—whether it marks a new departure from the established case law or was merely decided *per incuriam*—such that it hardly provides a solid jurisprudential foundation for the approach since adopted by the Court in *Kücükdeveci*.[72]

The Court's approach to defining the scope of the Treaties in *Kücükdeveci* also sits uneasily with its earlier invocation of the Charter of Fundamental Rights, so as to bolster the legal basis upon which Union law recognises the general principle prohibiting discrimination on grounds of age: after all, Article 51(1) states that the provisions of the Charter are addressed to the Member States 'only when they are implementing Union law'—a formulation closer to the Court's approach in *Bartsch* than to that in *Kücükdeveci*. Insofar as the true source, under Union primary law, for the right to equal treatment on grounds of age remains the general principles of Union law, *Kücükdeveci* shifts the latter's scope of application even further away from that of the Charter—exacerbating the already difficult problems created by Lisbon in defining the proper relationship between the case law on fundamental rights and the revised Article 6 TEU.[73] Conversely, if the true source, under Union primary law, for the right to equal treatment on grounds of age is now to become the Charter of Fundamental Rights, *Kücükdeveci* suggests that the Court will adopt a very liberal interpretation of the concept of 'implementation' under Article 51(1)—effectively ignoring the drafters' clear desire to limit the potential impact of the Charter upon national competences in favour of a sweeping approach which equates 'implementation' with a mere coincidence of subject matter between Union and national law.[74]

Furthermore, is not entirely clear on what constitutional basis the Court in *Kücükdeveci* intended to rationalise (let alone legitimise) extending the concept of when a Member State acts within the scope of the Treaties, beyond the accepted situations of implementing Union law, or derogat-

---

[70] Consider, eg Case C-410/96 *André Ambry* [1998] ECR I-7875; Case C-322/01 *Deutscher Apothekerverband* [2003] ECR I-14887; Case C-441/04 *A-Punkt Schmuckhandels* [2006] ECR I-2093.

[71] Case C-71/02 *Karner* [2004] ECR I-3025.

[72] See further, eg F de Cecco, 'Room to Move? Minimum Harmonisation and Fundamental Rights' (2006) 43 *Common Market Law Review* 9; M Dougan, 'Minimum Harmonisation after *Tobacco Advertising* and *Laval Un Partneri*' in M Bulterman, L Hancher, A McDonnell and H Sevenster (eds), *Views of European Law from the Mountain: Liber Amicorum Piet Jan Slot* (The Hague, Kluwer Law International, 2009); J Kühling, 'Fundamental Rights' in A von Bogdandy and J Bast (eds), *Principles of European Constitutional Law*, 2nd edn (Oxford, Hart Publishing, 2010).

[73] See further, eg Dougan, above n 23.

[74] See further, eg G de Búrca, 'The Drafting of the European Union Charter of Fundamental Rights' (2001) 26 *European Law Review* 126; Besselink, above n 19; Eeckhout, above n 68; Knook, above n 68.

ing from the Treaties, so as now also to embrace simply an overlap in subject matter between national and Union action. Why should existing national rights and obligations be replaced with an entirely new corpus of Union law, not because the Member State is acting as a direct delegatee of Union law by enforcing, or as a conscious detractor from Union law by seeking to avoid, its Treaty obligations, but merely because there is a coincidence of subject matter between some measure of Union secondary law and the exercise of national regulatory competence?[75] To be sure, such a coincidence of subject matter can justify scrutiny to determine whether the Member State is in strict compliance with its obligations under the Treaties and Union secondary legislation (within the limits to which the latter may produce independent effects in the national legal systems). But why should a Member State, in such circumstances, be expected also to demonstrate its allegiance to the entire Union system of administrative law? Such a prospect could dramatically expand the reach of the 'European public law order': the Union would effectively assume a far-reaching authority to define and enforce the rule of law, even for situations where the relationship between the assertion of Union and the exercise of Member State competences is relatively tenuous. If that really is what the Court intended in *Kücükdeveci*, it would surely constitute a very significant legal development, with important implications for the prevailing balance of power within our 'constitutional order of states', yet one urgently lacking any persuasive normative justification.[76]

VI   ESTABLISHING THE DIRECT EFFECT OF THE GENERAL PRINCIPLES OF UNION LAW

So much for the problem of when a dispute falls within the scope of the Treaties, so as to trigger the potential application of the general principles of Union law. The other main limb of the *Mangold* equation concerns the question: once triggered in principle, when exactly will a given general principle of Union law be considered sufficiently clear, precise and unconditional as to be capable of producing its own direct effect in practice? There are in fact two aspects to this question: the direct effect

[75] On justifications for scrutiny of national action under the general principles of Union law, consider E Spaventa, 'Federalisation v Centralisation: Tensions in Fundamental Rights Discourse in the EU' in M Dougan and S Currie (eds), *50 Years of the European Treaties: Looking Back and Thinking Forward* (Oxford, Hart Publishing, 2009). Note that EU fundamental rights scrutiny even as regards Member State derogations still remains controversial: see further, eg P Huber, 'The Unitary Effect of the Community's Fundamental Rights: The *ERT* Doctrine Needs to be Reviewed' (2008) 14 *European Public Law* 323; N Nic Shuibhne, 'Margins of Appreciation: National Values, Fundamental Rights and EC Free Movement Law' (2009) 34 *European Law Review* 230.
[76] Apparently of the same view, eg Kühling, above n 72; G Thüsing and S Horler, Annotation of *Kücükdeveci* (2010) 47 *Common Market Law Review* 1161.

of the general principle per se; and its relationship to any corresponding Union secondary legislation.

A   When Will a General Principle of Union Law Produce Its Own Direct Effect?

In *Mangold* itself, the legal content of the general principle of Union law prohibiting age discrimination could readily be considered legally complete and capable of being ascertained without reference either to the Treaties or any implementing measure of Union secondary legislation. After all, every equal treatment dispute follows the same essential pattern of legal analysis: whether it is possible to establish comparability, whether the disparity in treatment constitutes discrimination and of what nature, whether such discrimination can be justified in principle by reference to a legitimate objective, and whether the disputed measures comply with the principle of proportionality.[77] Other cases have already established the free-standing justiciability of such questions within the context of the general principles of Union law, so there is little objectionable in the Court's finding in *Mangold* that the right to equal treatment on grounds of age is similarly capable of its own independent application before the national courts.[78]

Moving beyond the prohibition on age discrimination, the ECJ in *Mangold* seemed to anticipate that its ruling should apply also to the other forms of equal treatment referred to in Directive 2000/78 (religion or belief, disability and sexual orientation);[79] one assumes that the same would be true for the prohibition on race discrimination as regulated by Directive 2000/43.[80] In fact, although the Court passed over the opportunity to recognise the prohibition of discrimination on grounds of sexual orientation as a general principle of Union law in *Maruko*,[81] Advocate General Jääskinen in the *Römer* dispute has since urged the ECJ to do precisely that.[82] In any event, there is surely a strong case for arguing that the principle of equal treatment on grounds of sex should be recognised as a general principle of Union law capable of giving rise to enforceable rights, within the scope of the Treaties, *à la Mangold*, even in horizon-

---

[77] Cp AG Tizzano in Case C-144/04 *Mangold* [2005] ECR I-9981, especially at paras 83–85 of the Opinion.
[78] Eg Case C-442/00 *Caballero* [2002] ECR I-11915; Case C-520/03 *Olaso Valero* [2004] ECR I-12065; Case C-300/04 *Eman and Sevinger* [2006] ECR I-8055. For a more sceptical view, see Craig, above n 51.
[79] See paras 74 and 76 of the ruling in *Mangold*; cp AG Mazák in Case C-411/05 *Palacios de la Villa* [2007] ECR I-8531.
[80] [2000] OJ L180/22.
[81] Case C-267/06 *Maruko* [2008] ECR I-1757; though note AG Colomer at para 78 (fn 82) of the Opinion.
[82] Case C-147/08 *Römer*, Opinion of 15 July 2010, judgment pending.

tal disputes where the Equal Treatment Directive has not been correctly implemented into national law.[83] Familiar disputes about whether the employer is an emanation of the state for the purposes of enforcing the unimplemented directive, or whether the duty of consistent interpretation can cure the apparent incompatibility of national law, would thus become a thing of the past.[84] By contrast, one can readily imagine various propositions which—even if they were to be treated as general principles of Union law—would surely not be considered sufficiently clear, precise and unconditional as to be capable of producing their own direct effect within the national legal systems.[85] Consider, for example, a principle such as consumer protection: it is surely too nebulous to be capable of creating justiciable individual rights and obligations, independently of the various instruments of secondary legislation adopted by the Union institutions to deal with specific categories of consumer disputes, and thus seems destined to perform a primarily interpretative role within the Union legal order.[86]

Once again, however, this issue is perhaps complicated by the entry into force of the Treaty of Lisbon and the conferral of binding status upon the Charter of Fundamental Rights. In particular, we have already noted that the ECJ—particularly after *Kücükdeveci*—may have to decide whether the proper basis under Union primary law for any given putative fundamental right is either to remain the general principles of Union law or instead to become the written provisions of the Charter itself. In the latter event, the reference point for addressing the direct effect question would necessarily change: the Court would have to clarify which of the Charter's substantive provisions are capable of fulfilling the criteria for producing independent legal effects, as opposed to those which require further implementation and/or should act merely as interpretative guides.[87] For those purposes, the Court would be obliged to take into account the general provisions governing the interpretation and application of the Charter, as contained in Title VII (2007 version)—including the awkward distinction between (fully justiciable) rights and (partially justiciable) principles as set out in Article 52(5)[88]—though the final outcome of such assessments would, in

[83] Equal treatment on grounds of sex has long been recognised as a general principle of Union law by the ECJ, eg Case 149/77 *Defrenne v Sabena* [1978] ECR 1365, paras 26–27; more recently, eg Case C-25/02 *Rinke* [2003] ECR I-8349. There is as yet no post-*Mangold* authority, though note the rather reticent approach of AG Kokott in Case C 104/09 *Roca Álvarez*, Opinion of 6 May 2010, especially at paras 55–56.
[84] Cp Case 152/84 *Marshall* [1986] ECR 723; Case C-185/97 *Coote v Granada Hospitality* [1998] ECR I-5199.
[85] Cp Case C-101/08 *Audiolux*, judgment of 15 October 2009.
[86] Consider, eg Case C-233/94 *Germany v Parliament and Council* [1997] ECR I-2405. See further, eg Editorial, above n 11; Muir, above n 11.
[87] Cp AG Bot in Case C-555/07 *Kücükdeveci*, Opinion of 7 July 2009, especially at para 90.
[88] See further, eg M Dougan, 'The Convention's Draft Constitutional Treaty: a "Tidying-Up Exercise" That Needs Some Tidying-Up of Its Own . . .' Federal Trust Constitutional Online Essay 27/03, available at www.fedtrust.co.uk/eu_constitution.htm.

most situations, seem likely to remain the same as when dealing with the unwritten general principles of Union law.[89]

B   When Will Union Legislation Merely Embody or Rather Go Beyond the General Principles?

Assuming any given general principle of Union law to be capable of producing its own direct effect, a final question concerns how far any relevant but unimplemented directive might merely embody that general principle of Union law without adding anything extra to its substantive content, or instead go appreciably beyond the scope of the relevant general principle of Union law so that the claimant should remain unable to benefit from some specific type or level of protection.[90]

To illustrate that problem, consider the situation in *Mangold* itself. The ECJ's ruling expressly adverted to the distinction between the general principle of Union law prohibiting discrimination on grounds of age (on the one hand) and the specific provisions of Directive 2000/78 dealing with various 'supplementary' issues (on the other hand)—issues such as the provision of legal remedies, the burden of proof, protection against victimisation, engagement in social dialogue and the possibility of affirmative action.[91] Was the Court suggesting that that distinction could act as an appropriate division of labour between the directly effective substance of the general principle of equal treatment on grounds of age (on the one hand) and the still non-directly effective supplementary provisions of Directive 2000/78 (on the other hand)? If so, the picture may actually prove more complex than the Court suggests. It is true that the right to effective judicial protection, although undeniably a general principle of Union law,[92] does not necessarily have direct effect in every case involving the choice of remedies for victims of discrimination: the Member State still enjoys a margin of discretion about the precise form of relief to be provided under national law for vindication of the right to equal treat-

---

[89] As with Art 38 of the Charter on consumer protection. Consider also, eg Art 22 (cultural, religious and linguistic diversity); Art 25 (rights of the elderly); Art 37 (environmental protection).

[90] We will not investigate further the important question of when the ECJ will rely on either the general principles of Union law or Dir 2000/78 where it has an equal choice between the two. Consider cases where the ECJ relied entirely on Dir 2000/78 (eg Case C-388/07 *Age Concern England* [2009] ECR I-1569; Case C-88/08 *Hütter* [2009] ECR I-5325; Case C-229/08 *Wolf*, judgment of 12 January 2010; Case C-341/08 *Petersen*, judgment of 12 January 2010) and the possible explanation offered by AG Kokott in Case C-499/08 *Andersen*, Opinion of 6 May 2010, judgment pending; though cf AG Trstenjak in Case C-45/09 *Rosenbladt*, Opinion of 28 April 2010, judgment pending.

[91] See para 76 of the ruling in *Mangold*.

[92] Eg Case C-432/05 *Unibet* [2007] ECR I-2271; Case C-268/06 *Impact* [2008] ECR I-2483.

ment.[93] Similarly, the right to protection against retaliation for victims of discrimination has been held in previous cases to derive from Union secondary legislation, and should therefore be incapable, in itself and without adequate national transposition measures, of imposing obligations upon individual employers.[94] By contrast, however, the allocation of the burden of proof in discrimination cases has long been held to be an aspect of the substantive right to equal treatment and as such regulated directly by Union law.[95] The mere fact that the Court's approach has since been effectively codified in Union secondary legislation should not detract from the fact that precise standards for allocation of the burden of proof could well form an integral part of the substantive right to equal treatment under the general principles of Union law.[96]

Mangold thus invites—indeed, requires—detailed further analysis so as to identify those aspects of an unimplemented directive which can justly be described as merely derivative from the general principles of Union law, as opposed to those elements of Union secondary legislation which are genuinely additional to the level of protection offered under Union primary law. Again, however, that task has become potentially even more complicated since the conferral of legally binding force upon the Charter of Fundamental Rights. Article 52(2) states that Charter rights for which provision is made in the Treaties shall be exercised under the conditions and within the limits defined by those Treaties.[97] On the assumption that the Court will in the future prefer to adjudicate disputes about fundamental rights on the basis of the written text of the Charter rather than under its own general principles of Union law, yet more difficult questions may arise about whether Article 52(2) has the effect of limiting not just the direct effect, but even the substantive content, of a given individual right, ie by tying the latter's scope and/or content to the conditions provided for under the primary Treaty provisions and/or any implementing legislation adopted by the Union institutions.[98] One begins to wonder

[93] Eg Case 14/83 *von Colson* [1984] ECR 1891; Case C-271/91 *Marshall II* [1993] ECR I-4367; Case C-460/06 *Paquay* [2007] ECR I-8511; Case C-63/08 *Pontin*, judgment of 29 October 2009.

[94] Eg Case C-185/97 *Coote v Granada Hospitality* [1998] ECR I-5199.

[95] Eg Case 170/84 *Bilka-Kaufhaus* [1986] ECR 1607; Case 109/88 *Danfoss* [1989] ECR 3199; Case C-381/99 *Brunnhofer* [2001] ECR I-4961; Case C-17/05 *Cadman* [2006] ECR I-9583.

[96] Previously Dir 97/80 [1998] OJ L14/6. Now Dir 2006/54 [2006] OJ L204/23. Cp Case C-8/08 *T-Mobile Netherlands* [2009] ECR I-4529 concerning the burden of proof in competition cases.

[97] See further, eg Lenaerts and de Smijter, above n 19. For a different view, see M Bell, 'The Right to Equality and Non-Discrimination' in T Hervey and J Kenner (eds), *Economic and Social Rights under the EU Charter of Fundamental Rights: A Legal Perspective* (Oxford, Hart Publishing, 2003).

[98] Consider, eg the various 'citizens' rights' contained in Title V of the Charter, most of which derive from the Treaties and are regulated in detail by Union secondary legislation. Note also Art 52(6), according to which full account shall be taken of national laws and

whether the conferral of binding legal status upon the Charter was, after all, really such a victory for the transparency and effectiveness of fundamental rights within the Union's constitutional order . . .

VII   CONCLUSIONS

Is the *Mangold* ruling as poorly reasoned and constitutionally objectionable as has been portrayed in many of the scholarly analyses? On the whole, our reflections suggest that much of the criticism of *Mangold* is either misplaced or exaggerated: the proclamation and subsequent incorporation of the Charter provide a legitimate basis for recognising the existence of a general principle of Union law prohibiting discrimination on grounds of age; that general principle was directed merely against Member State action falling within the scope of the Treaties, not against the exercise of their contractual autonomy by purely private parties; and the system governing the potential direct effect of the general principles quite rightly operates parallel to that of the Treaties themselves, or of any secondary measures adopted by the Union legislature (such as Directive 2000/78).

That is not to deny that *Mangold* raises certain difficult doctrinal issues. It has been argued that the Court's understanding of when a dispute will fall within the scope of the Treaties, for the purposes of triggering the general principles of Union law, has been stretched to (or even beyond) its tolerable constitutional limits by rulings such as *Kücükdeveci*. Questions also remain concerning the precise range and content of those general principles of Union law which might be considered sufficiently clear, precise and unconditional so as to be capable of producing independent legal effects within the domestic legal systems. Overshadowing many such issues is the potential impact of the Charter of Fundamental Rights: how far it will replace the general principles as the primary legal reference point for resolving cases involving fundamental rights; and if so, what approach the Court might adopt towards the problematic 'horizontal' provisions contained in Title VII. But those difficult doctrinal issues either existed before *Mangold* or would have arisen regardless of *Mangold*. At worst, that ruling has simply made finding useful answers more urgent—and also, one must admit, more interesting. Given such a combination of constitutional importance and intellectual complexity, one can well understand why the *Mangold* ruling fired Alan's scholarly imagination so strongly and fruitfully.

---

practices as specified in the Charter: that provision could again have a significant limiting effect on how the ECJ evaluates the direct effect and/or defines the substantive content of various Charter rights (particularly the 'solidarity rights' contained in Title IV).

13

Edging Towards Closer Scrutiny? The Court of Justice and Its Review of the Compatibility of General Measures With the Protection of Economic Rights and Freedoms

ALBERTINA ALBORS-LLORENS*

I INTRODUCTION

IT IS UNDENIABLE both that the protection of fundamental human rights in the European Union has come a long way since the inception of the European Communities and that the Court of Justice has played a crucial role in this process. The Court was indeed solely responsible for the initial incorporation of this principle within the Community legal order and its elevation to the rank of a primary norm of EU law against which the compatibility of the acts of EU Institutions and of the Member States, acting in the sphere of Community law, could be tested. The last decade has seen important developments, such as the solemn proclamation of the Charter of Fundamental Rights at Nice and the entry into force of the Treaty of Lisbon, which has finally given legally binding force to this Bill of Rights, thus enhancing the visibility of fundamental rights as part of the Union legal order. However, these developments would possibly never have seen the light of day without the groundbreaking work of the Court, whose case law gave initial recognition to many of the now catalogued rights and developed their content and scope by draw-

* University Senior Lecturer and Fellow, Girton College, University of Cambridge. I am extremely grateful to Anthony Arnull, Catherine Barnard and Angus Johnston, for their very helpful comments on an earlier draft.

ing inspiration from the national legal systems and international treaties for the protection of human rights.[1]

Despite the unquestionable value of the Court's endorsement of human rights and freedoms as primary sources of what we must refer to now as EU law, questions still remain as to the intensity with which the Court applies this general principle of law in the judicial scrutiny of EU measures. In particular, the limited success which applicants have experienced when challenging the legality of EU measures on grounds of breach of fundamental rights and general principles of law has long been highlighted by academic commentators.[2] This outcome is particularly obvious in cases concerning the challenge of measures of a general nature such as regulations and directives, where the Court has been strongly deferential to the discretion enjoyed by the political institutions and hence has been reluctant to annul these measures unless there has been a manifest error of law or fact attributable to the enacting institutions.[3] The Court has frequently emphasised that restrictions to some of these rights can be justified by overriding considerations in the public interest and, while it is necessary to strike a balance between safeguarding fundamental rights and the protection of the general interest, questions still remain as to how scrupulous the Court has been in its examination of these competing claims.

It is evident that the Court might want to avoid continuous challenges to legislative measures, but it is also clear that the consequences of the annulment of such measures are very serious because they are applicable in all the Member States. However, it is debatable whether these practical considerations should overshadow the protection of fundamental rights and freedoms and determine a lower level of protection at the Union level than that offered, for example, by the national legal systems. This has certainly been a bone of contention between the Court of Justice and some national courts.[4]

The purpose of this chapter is to consider the evolution of this area of law, and in particular of the cases where fundamental economic rights and freedoms have come into conflict with EU measures. Under the Common Union Policies, such as the Common Agricultural and Transport Policies, the EU institutions have always enjoyed broad discretion to adopt measures such as the imposition of levies, the application of quotas and the

---

[1] See below, Section II.

[2] See A Clapham, 'A Human Rights Policy for the European Community' (1990) 10 *Yearbook of European Law* 309, 331; S Douglas-Scott, 'A Tale of Two Courts: Luxembourg, Strasbourg and the Growing European Human Rights Acquis' (2006) 43 *Common Market Law Review* 629, 633; B de Witte, 'The Past and Future Role of the European Court of Justice in the Protection of Rights' in Alston (ed), *The EU and Human Rights* (Oxford, Oxford University Press, 1999) 859, 882–883.

[3] See below, Section II.

[4] See, eg the reaction of the national referring court following the preliminary ruling of the Court in Case 11/70 *Internationale Handelsgesellschaft* [1970] ECTR 1125, discussed below in Section II.

introduction of prohibitions on the use of certain substances or of marketing restrictions. These measures were bound to collide with individual economic rights, such as the right to property and the freedom to pursue a trade or profession. Consequently, these areas offer fertile ground for the examination by the Court of this conflict of interests.

The tension with economic rights has also arisen in other cases, such as those where the Community has implemented UN sanctions. Some of those rulings will be examined below, as will the impact of the raft of recent terrorist asset freezing cases. In some of these, the Court found the Council regulation that gave effect to a UN Security Council resolution to be, inter alia, in breach of the right to property. A pivotal issue in these cases was the competence of the Union's judicature to review the compatibility of this regulation with the principle of protection of fundamental human rights guaranteed in the Union's legal order. Predictably, this attracted a great deal of interest from European and international lawyers alike, as it referred directly to the relationship between international and EU law.[5] However, another very important aspect of these judgments is whether they heralded a different or more intrusive level of judicial scrutiny for discretionary Community measures or whether they simply sat comfortably with the established case law.

II THE SUBSTANTIVE CHALLENGE OF EU REGULATIONS AND DIRECTIVES: A BRIEF OVERVIEW OF THE CASE LAW

One of the aims of this chapter is to examine whether there has been an evolution in the level of substantive review applied by the Union judicature when examining the compatibility of legislative measures adopted by the Union institutions with the protection of fundamental economic rights. In this context, the term 'fundamental economic rights' will refer to the rights to property and freedom to pursue a trade or profession, which rapidly established themselves as natural contenders for conflict with the principles of the Common Union Policies—in particular, the Common

---

[5] There has been a wealth of literature covering this issue. See, among others, B Kunoy and A Dawes, 'Plate Tectonics in Luxembourg: The *Ménage à Trois* Between EC Law, International Law and the European Convention on Human Rights following the UN Sanction Cases' (2009) 46 *Common Market Law Review* 73; C Tomuschat, 'Annotation on Case T-306/01 *Yusuf and Al Barakaat v Council and Commission* and Case T-315/01 *Kadi v Council and Commission*' (2006) 43 *Common Market Law Review* 537; A Garde, 'Is it Really for the European Community to Implement Anti-terrorism UN Security Council Resolutions?' (2006) 65 *Cambridge Law Journal* 281; P Eeckhout, 'Community Terrorism Listings, Fundamental Rights and UN Security Council Resolutions: in Search of the Right Fit' (2007) 3 *European Constitutional Law Review* 183; M Payandeh and H Sauker, 'European Union: UN Sanctions and EU Fundamental Rights' (2009) 7 *International Journal of Constitutional Law* 306.

Agricultural Policy. This section will consider some of the cases where the Court of Justice considered the legality of regulations and directives which encroached on the exercise of these rights and will reveal a profoundly deferential approach towards the exercise of discretion by the Union institutions. Furthermore, it will show that the guarded approach taken by the Court has extended to other aspects of the judicial control of regulations and directives, and not only to the substantive examination of their legality.

A   Regulations

The quartet of seminal cases—*Stauder*,[6] *Internationale Handelsgesellschaft*,[7] *Nold*[8] and *Hauer*[9]—where the Court first gave meaning to the principle of protection of fundamental human rights in EU Law concerned preliminary references on either the interpretation or validity of Community measures.[10] The last three also involved ownership and economic rights. Following the initial recognition of the status of the protection of fundamental human rights as a general principle of EU law in *Stauder*,[11] where the Court interpreted a Commission decision, the first opportunity to consider claims referring to a possible violation of fundamental human rights by a Community regulation arose in the *Internationale Handelsgesellschaft* case.[12] There, a Community regulation on the common organisation of the market for cereals required, as a condition for the grant of export licences, the lodging of a deposit, which would be forfeited in its entirety if exportation did not take place during the period of validity of the licence. The national court made a reference to the Court of Justice on the validity of the relevant provision in the regulation, questioning the compatibility of the system of deposits with national standards of protection of human rights and in particular with the principles of freedom of action and disposition and of economic liberty and proportionality, as protected by the German Constitution. The Court vigorously asserted the autonomy

---

[6] Case 26/69 *Stauder v City of Ulm* [1969] ECR 419.

[7] Case 11/70 *Internationale Handelsgesellschaft* [1970] ECR 1125.

[8] Case 4/73 *Nold* [1974] ECR 491.

[9] Case 44/79 *Liselotte Hauer v Land Rheinland-Pfalz* [1979] ECR 3727.

[10] Challenges to the action of Member States when these derogate from EU law began in 1975 with *Rutili* (Case 36/75 *Rutili* [1975] ECR 1219), where a national authority relied on one of the express derogations available under Art 45(3) TFEU (ex-Art 39(3) EC) to the provisions on free movement of workers. In the context of challenges to the action of the Member States when these implement Community measures, an early example was provided by Case 5/88 *Wachauf* [1989] ECR 2609. It thus became clear that the respect for fundamental human rights bound not only the Union Institutions but also the Member States when acting in the sphere of EU law (See Case 260/89 *ERT* [1991] ECR 2925).

[11] Case 26/69 *Stauder v Ulm* [1969] ECR 419.

[12] Case 11/70, above n 4.

of EU law by stating that national standards of protection could not be simply transposed to test the legality of Community acts. However, it went on to say that it would draw inspiration from the constitutional traditions of the Member States when giving meaning to the protection afforded to human rights at Community level, which it would then adapt to the structure and objectives of the Community.[13]

Thereafter, the Court's analysis was divided into two parts. First, it concluded that the system of deposits itself was legal, given that there were no other mechanisms that could be as efficient in the fulfilment of the aims of the regulation—namely, to place the institutions in a position to follow constantly trade movements so that they could implement the principles of the Common Agricultural Policy.[14] There was, however, little consideration of whether the institutions would be able to use the information acquired to execute the objectives of that policy—which was presumably the ultimate reason why the restrictions imposed by the deposits could be justified.[15] Secondly, it examined whether the system imposed an excessive burden on traders to the extent of breaching their fundamental human rights. Despite the strong claim made by the Court only a few paragraphs earlier, the judgment did not contain at this stage any evidence of the Court drawing inspiration from the national legal systems on limitations to economic rights and freedoms but merely a rather brief examination of some of the peripheral aspects of the scheme. For example, the Court considered the proportionality of the costs and charges involved in lodging a deposit rather than that of the actual forfeiture of the entire deposit—in respect of which the Court felt that traders were adequately protected by the provisions in the Regulation for cases of *force majeure*.[16] The conclusion of the Court was that the system did not violate any fundamental right. As a result, a very strong statement of principle was followed by a relatively shallow level of scrutiny.[17] Although the Court appeared to strike a balance between the protection of the objectives pursued by the

---

[13] Ibid, paras 3–4 of the judgment. Tridimas rightly describes this part of the judgment as a 'testament to the Court's creative jurisprudence' in *The General Principles of EU Law*, 2nd edn (Oxford, Oxford University Press, 2007) 301.

[14] The Court considered that a system of declaration of exports would be unreliable while a system of fines a posteriori would be difficult to implement, particularly when transnational transactions were involved.

[15] In fact, the applicants had argued that the Commission was not technically in a position to exploit the information, an argument that was swiftly dismissed by the Court (see para 19 of the judgment).

[16] The traders in the main proceedings before the national court had also contested the construction of the notion of *force majeure* adopted by the Regulation as excessively narrow and this constituted the basis of the second question raised by the national court.

[17] Unsurprisingly, the reaction from the national referring court was robust. The German Administrative Court found that the system of deposits contravened the fundamental principles set out in the German constitution and made a reference to the German Constitutional Court, which led to the well-known *Solange I* judgment (reported at 2 *CMLR* [1974] 540), widely construed as a direct threat to the supremacy of EU law.

Regulation and of the rights of the applicants, a structured pattern of analysis failed to emerge from this decision.

Although it was not until nine years later that the Court again considered the potential breach of property rights by a Community regulation in *Hauer*,[18] the *Nold*[19] case, decided in 1974 and concerning a reference on the validity of a Commission decision enacted in the field of the ECSC Treaty, was of twofold significance. Not only did the Court recognise international treaties for the protection of fundamental human rights as a second source of inspiration,[20] it also introduced the important idea, borrowed from both the national systems and international Treaties, that property rights are not absolute but may be subject to limitations in order to protect the public interest.[21] While the necessity of such a balancing act was evident, the assessment of the proportionality of the imposed limitations was to become a crucial aspect of subsequent cases.

The judgment in *Hauer* provided a fuller analysis than in *International Handelsgesellschaft*. In Hauer, the key issue was the compatibility of the Community Regulation on the common organisation of the market on wine, which prohibited the planting of vines for a period of three years, with the right to property and the freedom to pursue a trade or profession—two economic rights that soon became closely associated in the challenge of Community regulations in subsequent cases. This time, the Court took as a starting point that restrictions to the right of property on grounds of protection of the public interest were lawful both under the ECHR[22] and under the constitutions of the Member States.[23] Having established that restrictions could, prima facie, be justified the next step was to elucidate whether the restrictions were in fact excessive to achieve the required benefits to the common interest. The Court held:

> [I]t is still necessary to examine whether the restrictions introduced by the provisions in dispute in fact correspond to objectives in the general interest pursued by the Community or whether, with regard to the aim pursued, they *constitute a disproportionate and intolerable interference with the rights of the owner, impinging on the very substance of the right to property.*[24]

The Court therefore chose a three-tiered formula which incarnated a very high threshold for a full review: only disproportionate and intolerable restrictions that affected the very essence of the right could be found incompatible with EU law. While the Court considered that the regulation did have the purpose of achieving objectives in the public interest only

---

[18] Case 44/79, above n 9.
[19] Case 4/73, above n 8.
[20] Ibid, para 13.
[21] Ibid, para 14.
[22] Art 1 of the First Protocol to the ECHR.
[23] The Court made reference to the German, Italian and Irish Constitutions.
[24] Para 23 of the judgment (emphasis added).

after careful consideration,[25] the conclusion that it did not impose a disproportionate and intolerable interference on the right to property that impinged on the very substance of the right was swiftly reached. The same conclusion followed, almost automatically, in relation to the possible breach of the freedom to pursue a trade or profession. Such a high bar suggested that the task of obtaining the annulment of a general measure on grounds of a breach of the right to property would prove to be a formidably difficult one.

The case set a trend that would be repeated in later cases where EU regulations were contested as incompatible with economic rights. For example, in *Schräder*,[26] the applicant was a processor of cereals who objected to paying a co-responsibility levy when producers alone were responsible for the actual surpluses of cereals. The Court held that the levy was in fact passed on by processors to producers and that, as a result, the former only bore an administrative and accounting charge in connection with the payment and transfer of the levy. Therefore, according to the Court, the interference with the rights to property was non-existent and minimal in the case of the freedom to exercise a trade or profession.

In the same case, the applicant had additionally argued an infringement of the principle of proportionality, a natural component of the balance of conflicting legal interests but also an independent general principle of EU law.[27] In relation to this argument, the Court took the view that, given the broad discretion of the Community legislator in matters of the Common Agricultural Policy, a breach of the principle would only be found if the measure was 'manifestly inappropriate' to fulfil the objectives that the institution intended to pursue. Such a cursory examination revealed not only an intensely deferential approach to the review of general measures, but also the conclusion that the invalidity or annulment of a general measure would only follow in extreme cases of breach of an economic right or a general principle of law. While it is clear that there are limits to judicial interpretation where political institutions make broad social or economic choices, it is also easy to understand that such standpoint could be controversial, particularly at a stage of development of EU law where claims of democratic deficit in the adoption of Community legislation were still prominent.[28]

---

[25] See paras 24–28 of the judgment.

[26] Case 265/87 [1989] ECR 2237.

[27] See, eg Case C-331/88 ex-*parte Fedesa* [1990] ECR I-4023.

[28] This case was decided before the signature of the Treaty on European Union and hence the legislative procedure of co-decision (which post Lisbon is known as the ordinary legislative procedure) had not even been introduced in the Union legal order. Regulations were thus adopted mainly on the basis of the consultation and co-operation procedure, both of which raised serious concerns in terms of the limited participation of the European Parliament in the adoption of legislation.

The first *Bananas* judgment[29] provides another example of the deep-seated reluctance of the Court to engage in the review of measures taken in the exercise of broad discretion by the Community legislature—with extreme consequences for holders of economic rights. In that case, a Council regulation on the common organisation of the market in bananas altered dramatically the importation arrangements that had been enjoyed by German traders, who suffered a large reduction in their quota of imports of third country bananas. The German government claimed this measure to be, inter alia,[30] in breach of the traders' rights to property and freedom to pursue a trade or profession and the principle of proportionality. Again, the Court found that the arrangements introduced by the regulation were justified by the general interest and the fact that the German traders had thus far enjoyed a particularly beneficial regime did not entitle them to expect that this state of affairs should continue. While this is true and acceptable as part of the normal commercial risk associated with a commercial activity, it remains a fact that the Court gave very little weight to the actual impact that the measure had on the traders, again dismissing arguments of lack of proportionality on the basis that the institution had broad discretion to act in the field of the Common Agricultural Policy. It is also noteworthy that the regulation in question had not even provided transitional arrangements for those traders that would be particularly affected by the new regime.[31] As one commentator pointed out at the time, this approach 'reduce[d] judicial control to a minimum'.[32]

A few years later, the ruling in *Bosphorus*[33] showed again the difficulties that arise in the challenge of regulations on grounds of breach of economic rights. There, a national court made a reference for a preliminary ruling on the interpretation of a Community regulation that gave effect to UN sanctions against the former Yugoslavia. In particular, a provision in the regulation provided, inter alia, that aircraft in which a majority or controlling interest was held by a person or undertaking operating from the former Yugoslavia should be impounded by competent authorities of the Member States. A Turkish airline specialising in charter flights and organised travel leased an aircraft owned by the Yugoslav national airline

[29] Case C-280/93 *Germany v Council* [1994] ECR I-4973.
[30] There were also claims that the regulation discriminated against traders of third country bananas and in favour of importers of Community and traditional ACP bananas.
[31] But see the later decision in Case C-68/95 *T. Port* [1996] ECR I-6065, where the Court held that the Commission should take transitional measures to protect the situation of traders whose economic rights were significantly affected by the drastic quota reductions introduced by the Bananas Regulation.
[32] U Everling, 'Will Europe Slip on Bananas? The Banana Judgment of the Court of Justice and National Courts' (1996) 33 *Common Market Law Review* 401, at 419, see also p 415. See also De Witte, above n 2 at 880–81 and Case C-306/93 *Winzersekt v Land Rheinland-Pfalz* [1994] ECR I-5555.
[33] Case C-84/95 [1996] ECR I-3953.

for a period of four years. As the aircraft was preparing to take off at Dublin airport, it was impounded by the Irish authorities on the basis of the Community regulation. One of the arguments of the Turkish airline in the national proceedings was that they were not undertakings based in the former Yugoslavia but simply carried out the day-to-day operation and control of the leased aircraft and that the confiscation of the aircraft was contrary to their right to the peaceful enjoyment of property and freedom to pursue a trade or profession, as well as to the principle of proportionality. They argued that the owners of the aircraft had already been sanctioned because the rent paid for the aircraft was held in blocked accounts and that impounding the aircraft resulted in an additional and unjustified penalty imposed on an innocent party that had no connexion with the former Yugoslavia.

The reasoning of the Court was terse. In a handful of paragraphs, it stressed that the measure pursued objectives of general interest of such fundamental importance for the international community that the restrictions of economic rights that it imposed could not be regarded as inappropriate or disproportionate.[34] While the importance of the objectives pursued was beyond question, the Court again did not really consider whether the impounding of the aircraft was disproportionate, particularly when it was being operated by a non-Yugoslav undertaking which would suffer considerable damage to its economic activity. Noticeably, there was no allusion to any procedural safeguards that should have been upheld in connection with the restrictions of economic rights, such as the right to be heard or the right to effective judicial protection. In this respect, and as will be seen below, the recent cases on the freezing of terrorist assets present a very useful basis for comparison, given that they seem to show a fuller level of judicial scrutiny by the Court in the review of general measures that pursue imperative considerations in the public interest.[35]

In *Pfizer v Council*,[36] a private applicant brought an action for annulment under Article 263 TFEU (ex-Article 230 EC) to challenge the legality of a regulation that amended a directive containing rules concerning the authorisation and withdrawal of authorisation of antibiotics used as additives in feedstuffs. As a result of this amendment, the authorisation for the use of virginiamycin, an antibiotic used as a growth promoter, was withdrawn. The ruling is one of several that have considered the application of

---

[34] A few years later, the European Court of Human Rights confirmed that there had been no breach of fundamental rights given that the general interest pursued by the contested regulation was of considerable weight and hence capable of justifying restrictions of economic rights, within the meaning of Art 1 of Protocol No 1 of the European Convention. See *Bosphorus Hava v Ireland*, App 45036/98 (2006) 42 EHRR1.

[35] See below Section IV.

[36] Case T-13/99 [2002] ECR II-3305.

the precautionary principle[37] by the Community institutions.[38] The applicant, who was the only producer of virginiamycin in the world, argued,
inter alia, the infringement of the principle of proportionality and of the
right to property. The usual line of reasoning was taken in dismissing these
claims. First, and given the breadth of the discretion of the institutions
in matters of Common Agricultural Policy, a breach of proportionality
would only be established if the measure adopted was 'manifestly inappropriate'. Secondly, and as the objective of protecting public health was an
important one, it could justify restrictions on economic rights. Although it
was clear that the regulation would entail serious economic consequences
for the applicant, the Court held that alternative methods of husbandry
were available—even if they were more expensive– and that a transitional
period of six months had been put in place during which the substance
could still be marketed and used. These guarantees, which arguably did
little to remedy the negative consequences that befell the applicant, were
deemed to be sufficient to conclude that there was no disproportionate
or intolerable interference with the right to property. Again, the review
by the Court touched only the surface of the action of the Community
legislator in terms of the possible infringement of the applicant's rights.[39]

B   Directives

A quick overview of the cases involving the challenge of directives shows
a similar degree of deference to the broad discretionary powers of the
institutions. For example, in *Spain and Finland v European Parliament and
Council*,[40] the applicants sought the annulment of a Community directive
on the organisation of the working time of persons performing mobile
road transport activities, whose purpose was to improve the health and

[37] This principle implies that where there is uncertainty as to the existence or extent of
risks to health, the institutions may take precautionary measures without having to wait
until the reality and seriousness of those risks become fully apparent (Case C-180/96 *United
Kingdom v Commission* [1998] ECR I-2265, para 99, and Case T-199/96 *Bergaderm and
Goupil v Commission* [1998] ECR II-2805, para 66). The principle was incorporated in
the EC Treaty at the time of the Maastricht Treaty in old Art 174(2) EC (now 191 TFEU)
within the title concerning environmental provisions.

[38] See Case C-331/88 *FEDESA* [1990] ECR I-4023; Case T-74/00 *Artegodan v Commission* [2002] ECR II-4945; Case T-344/00 *Ceva Santé Animale v Commission* [2003]
ECR II-229; Case C-236/01 *Monsanto* [2003] ECR I-8105. See further Heyvaert, 'Facing
the Consequences of the Precautionary Principle in European Community Law' (2006) 31
European Law Review 185.

[39] However, it is also noticeable that in this case several other grounds of challenge had
been put forward, such a breach of legitimate expectations, lack of reasoning and manifest
error, and, although the Court formally adopted a traditionally deferential formula to the
review of the measure, the ruling contained a much more exhaustive analysis of these considerations than that present in previous cases.

[40] Case C-184/02 [2004] ECR I-7789.

safety of drivers and road safety, and to align conditions of competition. This directive included, amongst others, provisions concerning maximum weekly working time, breaks, rest periods for apprentices and trainees, patterns of work and night work. One of the arguments of the applicants was that the inclusion of self-employed drivers in the scope of the directive constituted an excessive interference with their freedom to pursue a trade or profession, and that the objective of road safety was already taken into account by an existing regulation that regulated driving time and rest periods. The Court applied the same two-limb test that it had used in actions concerning the challenge to regulations. While it recognised that economic rights were protected by the Community legal order, it held that these could be restricted so long as the restrictions corresponded to objectives in the general interest and did not constitute a disproportionate or intolerable interference 'impairing the very substance of the rights'.[41] The Court made reference to the fact that the directive just limited the economic activity of self-employed drivers but did not affect the very essence of their right. It is therefore hard to avoid the conclusion that only where a Community measure essentially led to the exclusion of an economic activity could a holder of an economic right be successful in proving the infringement of that right.[42] In relation to the proportionality of the interference, the Court referred to the broad discretion of the institutions in matters of the Common Transport Policy and again applied a very limited scrutiny, only examining whether the measures were manifestly inappropriate.[43] This analysis stood in contrast to the fuller reasoning followed by Advocate General Stix-Hackl, who applied a full-blown proportionality test.[44]

In *Booker Aquaculture*,[45] a national court made a preliminary reference to the Court on the validity of a Community directive that introduced measures for the control of certain diseases in fish. The applicants in the

[41] See above n 24 and accompanying text.

[42] See, in this respect, the Opinion of Advocate General Stix-Hackl, paras 115–16. See also Tridimas's observations in cases concerning a possible infringement of the right to property, where he concludes that the protection afforded to this right effectively has the purpose to 'prohibit expropriation' (above n 13, 317).

[43] Ibid, para 52 of the judgment. A similar approach was followed in Case C-154/04 *Alliance for Natural Health and Others v Secretary of Health* [2005] ECR I-6451. The case concerned a reference on the validity of a Community directive that prohibited the marketing of food supplements which did not comply with the directive. The examination of a possible breach of the freedom to pursue a trade or profession was peremptory and only focused on the fact that the measure in question was not manifestly inappropriate. For an earlier example, see also Case C-200/96 *Metronome Musik* [1998] ECR 1953.

[44] The Advocate General pointed out that, although a low level of scrutiny commonly applied to legislative measures, the question of the proportionality of the restrictions should be examined in depth. She considered whether the measure pursued an objective in the general interest, or was suitable, necessary and reasonable. Her conclusion was that the measure embodied a proportionate restriction of economic rights (see paras 120–41 of the Opinion).

[45] Case C-20/00 *Booker Aquacultur Ltd and Hydro Seafood GSP Ltd v The Scottish Ministers* [2003] ECR I-7411 (joined with Case C-64/00).

national proceedings argued that, unless they were compensated for the fish that had to be destroyed in pursuance of the directive, they would suffer an intolerable interference impairing the very substance of their right to property. Arguably, the effect of the measures taken by national authorities in implementation of this directive amounted to a real deprivation of the right to property and not merely to a simple restriction. The Court disagreed with these arguments, emphasising the importance of the general objectives pursued by the directive and pointing out that, although the Community legislature could, by exercising its broad discretion in the field, approve the award of compensation for farmers or owners whose animals had been destroyed, a general right to compensation could not be automatically inferred. Again, the way in which the Community institutions exercised their discretion was subject to no more than a light touch review.

The cases considered above therefore illustrate the considerable difficulties involved in obtaining the substantive review of a Community regulation or directive on the basis that they infringe economic rights.

III   OTHER ASPECTS OF THE JUDICIAL CONTROL OF REGULATIONS AND DIRECTIVES

The difficulties present at the level of the substantive examination in the judicial review of regulations and directives are also reflected in other aspects of the system of judicial protection of individual rights devised by the Treaties. A first example is furnished by the case law concerning the non-contractual liability of the Community institutions arising from legislative acts under Articles 268 and 340(2) TFEU (ex-235 and 288(2) EC), which vividly shows the deferential approach taken by the Court in relation to the discretion of the Community legislator in cases where serious economic loss of damage has followed for private parties as a result of a potentially illegally general act. In *Zuckerfabrik Schöppenstedt* the Court held that:

> where legislative action involving measures of economic policy is concerned, the Community does not incur non-contractual liability for damage suffered by individuals as a consequence of that action . . . unless a *sufficiently flagrant violation of a superior rule of law for the protection of the individual* has occurred.[46]

The severity of this formula and its interpretation by the Court meant

---

[46] Case 5/71 *Zuckerfabrik Schöppemstedt v Council* [1971] ECR 975, para 11 of the judgment (emphasis added).

that private applicants were rarely successful in actions for damages.[47] By contrast, mere illegality appeared sufficient to attract liability for individual/administrative acts. However, more recent case law, following the ruling in *Bergadem*,[48] has suggested that the general or individual nature of the act is no longer decisive but that the '*Schöppenstedt* formula' will apply whenever the institution has discretion on how to act. Despite the fact that this non-formalistic approach to the consideration of the claims in damages is to be welcomed, the presence of broad discretion on the part of the Community institution—and most general measures will involve the exercise of discretion—continues to be a key factor in determining the extent of the protection given to individual rights when a private applicant brings a claim in damages arising from a potentially illegal Community act.

A second example refers to the draconian conditions of standing that natural or legal persons must satisfy before they can bring an action for annulment under Article 263 TFEU (ex-Article 230 EC); these have been well documented in the academic literature.[49] Many actions brought against Community regulations in the field of the Common Agricultural Policy were dismissed as inadmissible without the applicants having even the chance to have their substantive claims examined—even though in some of those cases there were serious allegations of breach of fundamental rights and general principles of law.[50] Until the decision of the

---

[47] See, eg Cases 83 and 94/76, and 4, 15 and 40/77 *HNL v Council and Commission* [1978] ECR 1209 and Cases 116 and 124/77 *Amylum v Council and Commission* [1979] ECR 3497.

[48] Case C-353/98 P [2000] ECR I-5291. See also Case T-178/98 *Fresh Marine Co v Commission* [2000] ECR II-3331 and Case C-390/95P *Antillean Rice Mills* [1999] ECR I-769 at paras 43–44 of the judgment.

[49] See A Arnull, 'Private Applicants and the Action for Annulment under Art 173 EC' (1995) 32 *Common Market Law Review* 7 and P Craig, 'Standing, Rights and the Structure of Legal Argument' (2003) 9 *European Public Law* 493. See also the landmark Opinion of Advocate General Jacobs in Case C-50/00P *Unión de Pequeños Agricultores v Council* [2002] ECR I-6677 and the discussion of this case in A Albors-Llorens, 'Standing of Private Parties to Challenge Community Measures: Has the European Court of Justice Missed the Boat?' (2003) 62 *Cambridge Law Journal* 72.

[50] See, eg Case 191/87 *Covale v Commission* [1988] ECR 515, where the Court dismissed as inadmissible an action for the annulment of a Community regulation which, according to the applicants, breached the principle of proportionality or Case 55/86 *ARPOSOL* [1988] FCR 13, where the applicants were unable to challenge a Community regulation that effectively introduced a penalty without giving concerned parties the right to a hearing. The latter case pertained to a cluster of cases where Spanish fishermen who were accused of illegal fishing tried to challenge Community legislation which was arguably contrary to the principles of non-retroactivity, the right to a hearing, proportionality and non-discrimination. The Court had considered the merit of similar claims through some earlier preliminary rulings (see eg Joined Cases 138 and 139/81 *Directeur des Affaires Maritimes du Litoral du Sud-Ouest v Marticorena-Otazo and Parada* [1982] ECR 3819). However, even in these cases the lack of a robust analysis of the human rights claims was criticised by commentators. See N Foster and R Churchill, 'Double Standards in Human Rights? The Treatment of Spanish Fishermen by the European Community' (1987) 12 *European Law Review* 430.

European Court in *Codorníu* in 1994,[51] private parties had to overcome not only the already restrictive tests of direct and individual concern, but also, in many cases, the infamous 'abstract terminology' test, which meant the almost impossible proof that an act labelled as a regulation was a decision in substance.[52] Even though, following the Lisbon reforms, the new Article 263 TFEU has recognised the *Codorníu* finding that only direct and individual concern needs to be satisfied in order to prove standing to challenge general Community acts,[53] the traditional construction of the test of individual concern continues to be a major obstacle to a more liberal approach to *locus standi* and hence to the freedom of private parties to invoke substantive claims of breach of their economic rights.[54] The Court's argument that an indirect challenge via a preliminary ruling on validity provides a satisfactory alternative[55] does not always hold true, and a few cases have highlighted how the unavailability of this avenue has resulted in the absence of a right to effective judicial protection.[56] This means that a private party whose rights may have been infringed by a general Community measure may face considerable obstacles not only at the stage of substantive review but also in being able to mount a challenge in the first place.

---

[51] Case C-308/89 *Codorniu v Council* [1994] ECR I-1853.

[52] Cases 789 and 790/79 *Calpak* [1980] ECR 1949. The case law concerning directives presented similar problems until the decision in Case T-135/96 *Union européenne de l'artisanat et des petites et moyennes entreprises (UEAPME) v Council* [1997] ECR II-373, which made it clear that even a directive could be challenged by a private applicant if the applicant showed direct and individual concern (see paras 64–69 of the judgment).

[53] The new wording of Art 263 TFEU, however, allows the possibility that, if the act is capable of constituting a 'regulatory' act, only direct concern might need to be shown to prove standing where no implementing measures are required. The significance of this amendment may become clearer once the Court interprets the notion of a 'regulatory' act, which is currently not defined anywhere in the Treaty.

[54] See the Opinion of Advocate General Jacobs in *UPA*, above n 49, and also his Opinion in Case C-263/02 *Commission v Jégo Quéré* [2004] ECR I-3425, paras 43–47. See also Case C-258/02P *Bactria v Commission* [2003] ECR I-15105, where the applicants claimed that a Community regulation affected their property rights. The Court simply confirmed the findings of the (then) Court of First Instance that the applicants were not individually concerned and hence had no standing to challenge the measure (see paras 48–52 of the Order of the Court). Their action was therefore dismissed as inadmissible and therefore there was no opportunity to consider the substantive grounds for challenge put forward by the applicants.

[55] See, eg Case C-321/95P *Greenpeace v Commission* [1998] ECR I-1651 at para 33.

[56] For a very early example of the fallibility of this argument, see Case 40/64 *Sgarlata* [1965] ECR 203, 227, where the applicants argued that the inadmissibility of the action for annulment would deprive them for any judicial protection both at Union and national level. In Case C-50/00 *Unión de Pequeños Agricultores v Council*, above n 49, an action for the annulment of a Community regulation that discontinued aid for small producers of olive oil was held inadmissible even though it was clear that the applicants would not be able to institute national proceedings that could result in a reference for a preliminary ruling on the Regulation's validity to be made to the European Court. See also paras 36–49 of Advocate General Jacobs' Opinion where he showed conclusively that the system of preliminary references does not always provide and alternative and equally satisfactory avenue for private applicants.

IV THE TERRORIST ASSET-FREEZING CASES: A NEW LEVEL OF SUBSTANTIVE REVIEW?

Few judgments in the history of the European Union have generated as much academic commentary as the decisions of the General Court (then the Court of First Instance)[57] and the Court of Justice[58] in *Kadi* and *Yusuf*.[59]

These cases concerned challenges to a Council regulation that gave effect in the European Union to some UN Security Council resolutions introducing a package of measures intended to suppress international terrorism in the aftermath of the September 2001 attacks. The regulation in question provided for the freezing of funds of persons and organisations with suspected links with Osama bin Laden, Al-Qaeda and the Taliban. The applicants were persons listed in the annex of the contested regulation whose funds had been frozen, and they challenged the regulation on the basis that it breached their fundamental rights, in particular their right to property and the right to a fair hearing.

The General Court asserted the primacy of the UN Charter over EU law. It held that it was not competent to review the compatibility with fundamental human rights of a Union regulation that simply implemented UN Security Council resolutions and did not involve the exercise of any discretion on the part of the Union institutions. According to the Court, if it were to declare such a regulation illegal, this would implicitly amount to a declaration that the Security Council resolutions were themselves incom-

---

[57] Case T-315/01 *Kadi v Council and Commission* [2005] ECR II-3649 and Case T-306/01 *Yusuf and Al-Barakaat* [2005] ECR II-3533.

[58] Joined Cases C-402/05P and C-415/05P *Kadi and Al Barakaat International Foundation* [2008] ECR I-6351. See A Gattini, 'Joined Cases C-402/05P and 415/05P *Kadi and Al Barakaat International Foundation v Council and Commission*' (2009) 46 *Common Market Law Review* 213.

[59] The rulings of the General Court in these cases marked the beginning of a cascade of rulings concerning the compatibility of Community measures imposing economic sanctions with fundamental human rights. See Case T-228/02 *Organisation des Modjahedines du people d'Iran (OMPI I)* [2006] ECR II-4665; Case C-229/05 *PKK and KNK v Council* [2007] ECR- 439; Case C-354/04P *Gestoras Pro Amnistia v Council* [2007] ECR I-1579 and Case C-355/04 *Segli v Council*, [2007] ECR I-1657; Case T-47/03 *Sison v Council* [2007] ECR II-73 and Case T-327/03 *Stichting Al-Aqsa v Council* [2007] ECR II- 79; Case C-117/06 *Möllendorf* [2007] ECR I-8361; Case T-256/07 *People's Mojahedin Organisation of Iran v Council (OMPI II)* [2008] ECR II-3019; Case T-284/08 *People's Mojahedin Organisation of Iran v Council (OMPI III)* [2008] ECR II-3487; Case T-318/01 *Othman*, judgment of 11 June 2009; Cases C-399/06 and C-403/06P *Hassan v Council and Commission*, judgment of 3 December 2009. See the commentaries on some of these decisions by A Garde, 'Is it Really for the European Community to Implement Anti-terrorism UN Security Council Resolutions?' (2006) 65 *Cambridge Law Journal* 281 and by A Johnston, 'Thawing Out? The European Courts and the Freezing of Terrorist Assets' (2007) 66 *Cambridge Law Journal* 273; 'The European Union, the Ongoing Search for 'Terrorists' Assets and a Satisfactory Legal Framework: Getting Warmer or Colder?' (2007) 66 *Cambridge Law Journal* 523; 'Freezing Terrorist Assets again: Walking a Tightrope over Thin Ice?' (2008) 67 *Cambridge Law Journal* 31; and 'Frozen in Time? The ECJ Finally Rules on the *Kadi* Appeal' (2009) 68 *Cambridge Law Journal* 1.

patible with the protection of fundamental human rights. The only review that the Court could carry out was that of the compatibility of the regulation—and thus indirectly of the resolutions—with norms *ius cogens*.[60] As a result, the Court only examined the compliance of the regulation with peremptory norms of international law. In reference to arguments that the right to property of the applicants had been violated, the Court held that only an '*arbitrary deprivation* of that right might be regarded as contrary to *ius cogens*'.[61] Similarly, claims of breach of the right to be heard and the right to an effective judicial remedy were dismissed as no breach of *ius cogens* was deemed to have occurred.[62]

As seen in the previous section, the review of general Community measures has always been notably difficult for private parties, generally on the basis of the broad discretion inherent in the exercise of legislative power, which the Community judicature has always viewed with great deference. This led to the rather superficial scrutiny of the compatibility of these measures with the principle of protection of economic and other fundamental rights. The decisions of the General Court in *Kadi* and *Yusuf* appeared to raise the threshold for full review to an even higher level. For example, and in reference to the right to property, only the arbitrary dispossession of assets could guarantee the possibility of judicial review of Community acts implementing UN Security Council Resolutions.[63]

It is also worth noting two important differences between these cases and previous cases involving regulations and directives discussed in Section II. First, although the sanctions were imposed by regulation, namely through a general act, the substantive character of the measure was more that of an administrative/individual measure in relation to the applicants, given that it imposed penalties on specific and named individuals.[64] Traditionally, private parties have enjoyed a greater rate of success when challenging individual rather than general acts, given that broad choices of legislative power are not involved.[65] Secondly, the Council in these cases

---

[60] See further C Tomuschat, 'Case Note on Case T-306/01 *Yusuf* and Case T-315/01 *Kadi*' (2006) 43 *Common Market Law Review* 537.

[61] See *Yusuf*, above n 57, para 291 and *Kadi*, above n 57, para 242 (emphasis added). In the *Bosphorus* case, above n 33, where the Court of Justice had interpreted Community regulation also giving effect to a UN Security Council Resolution imposing economic sanctions, there was no reference to this higher threshold of review to be applied to these cases.

[62] See *Yusuf*, above n 57, paras 304–47 and *Kadi*, above n 57, paras 253–92.

[63] For a criticism to the Court's approach to the protection of fundamental human rights see P Eeckhout (above n 5, 195–206).

[64] In the one previous case concerning sanctions (see Case C-84/95 *Bosphorus*, above n 33) the Regulation provided for a general sanction to be applied by the national authorities to individual cases. As a result there was no identification of any private parties in the Regulation itself.

[65] See J Weiler and N Lockhart, '"Taking Rights Seriously": The European Court and its Fundamental Human Rights Jurisprudence—Part I' (1995) 32 *Common Market Law Review* 51, 85; see also P Craig and G de Búrca, *EU Law*, 4th edn (Oxford, Oxford University Press, 2008) 391–94.

effectively had no discretion and was simply giving effect to UN Security Council resolutions. This time, the deference shown by the General Court referred to the broad decision-making powers of the UN Security Council and not to those of the EU institutions.

The judgments of the Court of Justice, on appeal, adopted a radically different approach to the standard of protection of fundamental human rights.[66] Contrary to the findings of the General Court, the Court of Justice held that it was competent to review fully the lawfulness of the regulation in the light of principles of protection of fundamental human rights. In considering whether the regulation was incompatible with the right to property, the Court took the view that, although the measures were temporary, they were not intended to deprive the persons mentioned in the annex to the regulation of their right to property. However, they imposed important restrictions on that right, and hence it was necessary to examine whether the restrictions were justified. In doing so, the Court abandoned the ultra-restrictive approach followed by the General Court and took instead the well-trodden path of considering whether the freezing measures constituted a 'disproportionate and intolerable interference impairing the very substance of the right'.[67] After alluding to the broad margin of discretion of the legislature, the Court felt that a balance between protecting the imperative requirements in the public interest present in this case and the protection of property rights had been achieved. Hence, the restrictions of property rights were found to be justified at a general level. This reasoning, consistent with that followed in earlier cases involving the challenge to regulations, showed that even regulations designed to give effect to UN Security Council resolutions would be subject to a full review in terms of their conformity with fundamental human rights.

However, the judgment was groundbreaking when it considered whether the right to property had been respected in relation to the applicants. On this point, the Court followed the lead of its Advocate General[68] and concluded that Mr Kadi had not been able satisfactorily to put across his case before the competent authorities. Therefore, and because adequate

---

[66] See the very comprehensive commentary by T Tridimas and J Gutierrez-Fons, 'EU Law, International Law and Economic Sanctions against Terrorism: The Judiciary in Distress' (2009) 32 *Fordham International Law Journal* 901 and T Tridimas, 'Terrorism and the ECJ: Empowerment and Democracy in the EC Legal Order' (2009) 34 *European Law Review* 103.

[67] See Joined Cases C-402/05P and C-415/05P, above n 58, para 357.

[68] The decisions of the Court were preceded by a robust Opinion from Advocate General Poiares Maduro. In relation to an alleged infringement of the right to property, he had argued that the freezing of all financial interests of the applicants for several years without limit of time and without the possibility of challenging the accusations of wrongdoing constituted a far-reaching interference with the peaceful enjoyment of the right to property. While he accepted that restrictions to the right to property could be justified on the protection of imperative requirements in the public interest, procedural safeguards had to be respected in order to show that such restrictions were justified (see para 47 of the Opinion).

procedural safeguards had not been met, the measures constituted an unjustified restriction of his right to property.[69]

The recognition of the necessity to protect procedural safeguards where restrictions to the right of property are imposed to protect the public interest was a step of great significance because it introduced a more thorough review of the compatibility of Community measures with the protection of economic rights, even if this only referred to satisfactory standards of procedural rather than substantive fairness.

It would be easy to confine the findings of the Court to the narrow field of general Community measures imposing sanctions. As mentioned earlier, such measures (even where labelled as general) have a very strong individual element when applied to the specific individuals or organisation that are the subject of the sanctions and listed or named in the regulation. This distinguishes them from the regulations and directives enacted in the field of the common organisation of the market, which rarely identify any private parties and have an effect on categories of people entirely defined in an objective and abstract way. However, there are some indications that the path taken by the Court in *Kadi* might be just the beginning of a trend that could spill over into the substantive review of measures involving the exercise of broad discretion in other areas of Community law.

Among the various cases decided in the aftermath of the *Kadi* decision were the rulings of the General Court on the *People's Mojahedin Organisation of Iran v Council (OMPI/PMOI) II and III*, decided only a few months apart in 2008.[70] They involved decisions adopted by the Council updating the list of entities and individuals with terrorist links in the annex of another Council regulation freezing terrorist assets. In doing so, the Council deferred to the assessment of the national authorities in the identification of persons of entities to be kept on the list—an important difference from the facts at issue in *Kadi*, and one that intensified the legal complexity of these cases. In an earlier ruling,[71] the General Court had annulled a Council decision that had placed the applicants on the list on basis that their basic process rights had not been respected. Further challenges followed when the Council decided to maintain the applicants on the list—in the *OMPI/PMOI III* case this was done even after they had been removed from the national terrorist list following a

---

[69] Ibid, paras 367–70. The same finding was made in some more recent cases (see *Hassan*, above n 59, paras 92–93; *Othman*, above n 59, paras 91–92). In *Kadi*, the Court had found, earlier in the judgment, that the right to an effective judicial remedy and the right to a hearing had also been breached as the applicants had not been informed of the evidence used against them and therefore could not exercise the right to be heard (see paras 331–53 of the judgment).

[70] See Case T-256/07, above n 59 and Case T-284/08, above n 59. For an excellent critical commentary on these decisions, see E Spaventa, 'Case Note on Case T-256/07 and Case T-284/08' (2009) 46 *Common Market Law Review* 1239.

[71] Case T-228/02 *Organisation des Modjahedines du people d'Iran v Council (OMPI/PMOI I)* [2006] ECR II-4665.

decision from a national tribunal. These cases raised a panoply of issues which are beyond the scope of this chapter and were argued from the perspective of the breach of the rights of the defence, with no mention of a breach of any economic rights. Nevertheless, the approach of the Court to the review of the decisions was illuminating and potentially relevant to future challenges of measures involving the exercise of discretion and to the issues considered here.

In both cases, the General Court affirmed that the Council had broad discretion in the adoption of economic sanctions.[72] However, it then crucially pointed out that this did not mean that the Court could not review the interpretation made by the Council of the relevant facts. It held that:

> The Community judicature must not only establish whether the evidence relied on is factually accurate, reliable and consistent, but must also ascertain whether that evidence contains all the relevant information to be taken into account in order to assess the situation and whether it is capable of substantiating the conclusions drawn from it. However, when conducting such a review, it must not substitute its own assessment of what is appropriate for that of the Council.[73]

Although the Court was cautious to show a degree of deference in the last sentence of this statement, the first part of it shows a bold move towards more intense judicial scrutiny of measures involving a margin of discretion.

In the *OMPI/PMOI II and III* rulings, the Court then went on to emphasise that, in cases where an institution enjoys wide discretion, the observance of procedural guarantees is particularly important, a point that the *Kadi* decision and its progeny had already made abundantly clear. It therefore appears, as already remarked by Tridimas in relation to the *OMPI/PMOI II* case, that a new and more intrusive standard of review has emerged in the context of the challenge of sanctioning measures.[74] This is borne out, in particular, by the judgment of the General Court in the *OMPI/PMOI III* case. There, the Court felt it could not review the substantive legality of the contested decision due to the refusal of the Council and the national authorities to communicate the relevant evidence used to maintain the applicants' names in the terrorist list and the decision was annulled on the basis of the breach of the right to judicial protection.[75] However, the Court sent a clear signal that it would be

---

[72] See Case T-256/07, para 137 and Case T-284/08 para 55, although see Spaventa, above n 70, 1260–1261 on whether such broad discretion really existed.

[73] See Case T-256/07 para 138 and Case T-284/08 para 55.

[74] Tridimas, above n 70, 125. See also Spaventa, above n 70, 1252 in relation to the *OMPI/PMOI III* decision.

[75] For a consideration of the problems arising in these cases from the division of competences between national authorities and the Council in these cases, see Spaventa, above n 70, 1252–63.

willing to carry out a robust review of 'the lawfulness and merits' of the measures to freeze funds.[76]

V CONCLUDING REMARKS

The premise of this chapter was that the EU judicature has traditionally shown a great reluctance to scrutinise fully the legality of legislative measures such as regulations and directives, even where claims of breach of fundamental rights have been made. The broad discretion enjoyed by the institutions in the enactment of these measures seems to have been one of the reasons for the application of a very high threshold of substantive review. In particular, and as discussed in Section II, only where a measure adopted in the general interest entailed a disproportionate and intolerable restriction that affected the very essence of the right would a finding of illegality follow. Deference to institutional discretion was also patent when applicants argued the infringement of general principles such as proportionality, where only a 'manifestly inappropriate measure' would be found to be disproportionate.[77] In the specific context of restrictions of economic rights, these formulae have meant that it has proved practically impossible for a holder of these rights to be successful in challenging this type of measures.

However, recent developments in the terrorist assets freezing cases suggest that the Court may be prepared to undertake a more intense scrutiny not only of the procedural fairness but also of the substantive lawfulness of discretionary measures and, in particular, to assess the evidence used by the Council in the imposition of sanctions.

The ruling of the Court of Justice in *Commission v Tetra Laval*,[78] in the field of competition law, shows a similar result in the review of merger decisions, where the Commission also enjoys a wide margin of discretion, this time not in the imposition of sanctions but in the assessment of economic matters. That case concerned an appeal against a ruling of the General Court annulling a Commission decision declaring a merger incompatible with the Common Market. It is accepted that the Commission enjoys broad discretion in the assessment of economic matters, and this had generally translated in previous cases into a very cautious approach followed by the Union judicature at the level of the substantive review of decisions enacted in the exercise of this discretion.[79] However,

---

[76] Case T-284/08 at para 75.

[77] But see Weiler and Lockhart, above n 65, 90–91, who, providing some examples from the case law, showed that private applicants have been comparatively more successful in invoking the breach of the principle of non-discrimination.

[78] Case C-12/03 P *Commission v Tetra Laval* [2005] ECR I-987.

[79] See Joined Cases C-68/94 and C-30/95 *France and Others v Commission (Kali und Salz)* [1998] ECR I-1375 at paras 223 and 224 of the judgment.

in *Tetra Laval*, the Court of Justice held that this did not mean that the Union judicature could not review the Commission's interpretation of information of an economic nature. As a result, the Court of Justice had to assess whether 'the evidence relied on is factually accurate, reliable and consistent', and also whether it contained 'all the information that must be taken into account in order to assess a complex situation and is capable of substantiating the conclusions drawn from it'.[80] The judgment was a landmark one in that it showed the readiness of the Court to engage in a fuller substantive review than before. The Court of Justice dismissed the appeal and upheld the ruling of the General Court declaring the illegality of the Commission's decision.

The argument made here is that these developments may well have an impact in the field of restrictions on economic rights and other fundamental rights imposed by general measures such as regulations and directives by making a successful challenge more feasible than hitherto. As a result, a move towards wider and potentially deeper review by the Union judicature in these areas could become a reality, as it has become in the framework of the terrorist asset-freezing cases.

First, the Court of Justice's judgment in *Kadi* upheld the applicant's claim of a breach of the right to property because procedural safeguards had not been complied with by the relevant regulation. This in itself was a significant step forward because it highlighted that challenges to restrictions on the right to property could be made (and more importantly be successful) where process rights had not been respected. This is, for the moment, confined to measures imposing sanctions, but further case law may unveil its potential in other areas or its extension to challenges where, for example, the freedom to exercise a trade or profession (normally closely associated to the right to property) is argued to have been infringed.

Secondly, should the EU judicature show a willingness to extend a more thorough substantive review of measures involving the exercise of discretion to regulations and directives in the common organisation of the market, it may be prepared to assess more fully, for example, the evidence held by the enacting institution that justifies the proportionality of the restrictions imposed upon individual rights in order to achieve public interest objectives. This will prove a difficult and delicate task for the Court, which must also respect the limits of judicial intervention and not substitute its own assessment for that of the political institutions.

In cases like *UPA*, the Court dashed hopes for a broader access to judicial review and hence for greater protection of individual rights. In particular, the maintenance of the restrictive interpretation of the test of individual concern—itself the creation of the Court—meant that stand-

---

[80] See Case C-12/03P above n 78, para 39 of the judgment.

ing remains a forbidding barrier when directly challenging the legality of measures of a legislative nature. Thereafter, even if this barrier was overcome or if a reference for a preliminary ruling on validity was made, applicants also had to contend with a formidably high threshold for the substantive review of these measures. However, unless the new found willingness of the Court to consider the procedural aspects of making intrusions on fundamental rights becomes just a formalistic exercise and not the first sign of an evolution, the developments discussed above may indicate that the Court is willing to be more progressive in the assessment of the substance of the claims than in issues of admissibility. Although it is undeniable that the protection of the general interest justifies restrictions on individual rights—particularly economic rights—the manner in which the justification and proportionality of these restrictions is assessed might well begin to change.

14

Union Law and Final Decisions of National Courts in the Recent Case Law of the Court of Justice

ANTONIO TIZZANO and BRUNO GENCARELLI*

I INTRODUCTION

O VER THE PAST few years, the Court of Justice has on several occasions found itself passing judgment on the interaction between the principles of supremacy of Union law and res judicata. These opportunities presented themselves through challenges to a series of judicial and administrative national decisions that, whilst reached contrary to European law, had nonetheless become final and, as such, benefited from binding status.

It is no exaggeration to say that the Court's varying responses to this question provoked considerable unrest,[1] ranging from surprise to concern,

---

* The ideas and opinions expressed in this contribution belong exclusively to the authors and do not represent those of any of the institutions to which they are affiliated.

[1] The astonishment, criticisms and fears can instantly be seen in the choice of title of the many articles and commentaries written on this case law. Whilst this is particularly true in relation to Italian doctrine, 'country of origin' of some of the most controversial cases on the subject, these concerns are, however, far from limited to those south of the Alps. See, in particular: P Bříza, 'Lucchini SpA—Is There Anything Left of Res judicata Principle?' (2008) 27 *Civil Justice Quarterly* 40; C Consolo, 'Il primato del diritto comunitario può spingersi fino a intaccare la 'ferrea' forza del giudicato sostanziale?' (2007) 9 *Corriere Giuridico* 1189; F Lajolo, 'L'Europa abbatte un mito: il giudicato' (2007) *Diritto del Commercio Internazionale* 724; PA Negrelli, 'Il primato del diritto communitario e il giudicato nazionale: un confronto che si poteva evitare o risolvere altrimenti' (2008) 5 *Rivista italiana di diritto pubblico communitario* 1217; PJ Wattel, 'Köbler, Cilfit and Welthgrove: We Can't Go on Meeting Like This' (2004) 41 *Common Market Law Review* 177. More measured, or less 'alarmist', analyses can, however, be found. To this effect see R Caponi, 'Corti europee e giudicati nazionali', Relazione al XXVII Congresso nazionale dell'Associazione italiana fra gli studiosi del processo civile, Verona, 25 September 2009, available at http://www.personaedanno.it/cms/data/articoli/files/013606_resource1_orig.pdf; X Groussot and T Minssen, 'Res judicata in the Court of Justice Case-Law' (2007) 3 *European Constitutional Law Review*, 385; R Kovar, 'L'incidence du droit communautaire sur l'intangibilité des décisions nationales définitives' in *Chemins d'Europe—Mélanges en l'honneur de Jean Paul Jacqué* (Paris, Dalloz, 1999); F Spitaleri (ed), *L'incidenza del diritto communitario e della CEDU*

even a certain irritation, as is always the case when the Kirchberg judges are seen to be meddling with supposedly untouchable rules and principles, ones that are recognised as belonging to a sort of impenetrable core of national legal heritage.

It seems to us, however, that another reading—more faithful and less alarmist—can be found for this evolving case law. These developments fall primarily within the wider search for a balance (one that is certainly delicate, often even precarious) between two imperatives: upholding legal certainty and ensuring the effectiveness of Union law.

In any case, the fact that this body of law does not call into question respect for the principle of res judicata should not really surprise anyone. As is true with any legal order, the Union cannot allow itself to disregard a principle that is a cornerstone of all modern systems of justice, one that is crucial to the stability of the law, the authority of the judiciary and in fine civil order. 'The importance, both for the Community legal order and national legal systems, of the principle of res judicata', as underlined by the Court on a number of occasions,[2] is therefore to a certain extent self-evident and cannot in all seriousness be questioned.

II RES JUDICATA OF THE COURT'S OWN JUDGMENTS

The argument above is especially true in relation to the force of res judicata in decisions of the Union's own judges. In particular, bearing witness to this is the far-reaching significance accorded to this principle within the case law, extending not only to the operative part of judgments and orders, but also to the legal grounds upon which they are based,[3] as well as the substantive examination favoured by the Court in order to ascertain whether two or more actions have the same subject matter, concern the same parties and are founded upon the same legal grounds.

Of course, our aim here is not to provide a detailed examination of this case law. Rather, it is perhaps more interesting to focus upon some

---

sugli atti nazionali definitivi (Milan, Giuffrè, 2009). Some even seem to regret the fact that the Court did not go far enough or criticise its approach, which, according to them, is too 'timorous' with regard national jurisdictions. Cf, respectively, L Coutron, 'La revanche de Kühne? À propos de l'arrêt Kempter (CJCE, 12 février 2008, aff C-2/06)' (2007) 45 *Revue trimestrielle de droit européen* 69; and D-U Galetta, *L'autonomia procedurale degli Stati membri dell'Unione europea: Paradise Lost* (Turin, Giappichelli, 2009).

[2] Case C-224/01 *Köbler* [2003] ECR I-10239, para 38; Case C-234/04 *Kapferer* [2006] ECR I-2585, para 20; Case C-2/08 *Fallimento Olimpiclub*, judgment of 3 September 2009, para 22; Case C-40/08 *Asturcom Telecomunicaciones*, judgment of 6 October 2009, para 35; Case C-526/08 *Commission v Luxembourg*, judgment of 29 June 2010, para 26; also Case T-24/07 *ThyssenKrupp Stainless v Commission* [2009] ECR II-2309, para 112.
[3] Eg Joined Cases 97, 193, 99, 215/86 *Asteris e a. v Commission* [1986] ECR 2181; Case C-310/97 *Commission v Assi Domän Kraft Products e a.* [1999] I-5363, para 54.

recent examples that are symptomatic of an underlying tendency to accord a wide interpretation to res judicata originating in the Kirchberg plateau.

In particular, the ECJ tends to show a certain flexibility, to say the least, in relation to the condition of identity of subject matter. So, in the case of an appeal against a Commission decision replacing a previous one that has been the subject of an action for annulment, the fact that the disputed measure is technically different from the previously annulled decision is not in itself decisive. Instead, in order to establish whether the condition of identity of subject matter is fulfilled, the Court will carry out an overall substantive examination of the extent of the similarities between the content of the two decisions. Consequently, where, for example, the first decision has been annulled for a straightforward 'mere' procedural irregularity and—after this has been corrected—the decision is readopted in largely similar terms, the condition will be considered to be satisfied.[4]

From time to time, it seems that the Court is holding itself up as a yet more strict guardian of the authority of its own case law. For example, the *P&O European Ferries (Viscaya)*[5] case raised, amongst others, a question surrounding qualification as state aids of measures which aided the transport company P&O to exploit shipping routes between Spain and the UK. This issue had already been the subject of a judgment by the Court of First Instance, which annulled an initial Commission decision on the point and had acquired res judicata. The question was whether the issue could be newly contested within the framework of an appeal against a second Commission decision adopted after—and in order to comply with—the Court's first judgment.

As was noted in the conclusions presented in this case,[6] it is possible to argue that, besides the fact that the two judicial procedures did not concern the exact same parties[7] and addressed two technically distinct acts,

---

[4] See, in particular, the recent Court of First Instance cases: *ThyssenKrupp Stainless v Commission*, above n 2, paras 136–45; and Case T-66/01 *Imperial Chemical Industries v Commission*, judgment of 25 June 2010, paras 196–210. In the context of the latter case concerning an abuse of dominant position in the soda ash market, an initial decision of the Commission had been annulled because of a breach of a procedural requirement relating to its authentication then readopted using the correct procedure, once again becoming the object of an action for annulment. In response to an argument concerning the applicant's rights of defence and, specifically, right of access to the file (one which had been raised in the context of the original decision), the Court noted that, whilst the Commission had formally adopted two decisions, it had not carried out a new measure of instruction between the delivery of the judgment for annulment and adopting the new decision, that the content of the two decisions was identical (except for one party), and that the applicant was once again arguing that his right to access the file had been violated. As such, the Court was able to conclude that the two disputes concerned the same object and had the same purpose (paras 207 and 208).

[5] Joined Cases C-442/03 and 471/03, *P&O European Ferries (Vizcaya) e Diputación Foral de Vizcaya v Commission* [2006] ECR I-4845.

[6] See Opinion of AG Tizzano in *P&O European Ferries*, ibid, paras 60–79.

[7] Indeed, the Diputación Foral de Vizcaya, one of the parties in the second case, was not

their subject matters were, in part, different. This is because the Commission had carried out further investigations and put forward a new set of appraisals, as compared to those found in the first decision. Indeed, in light of the decision of the Court of First Instance, the Commission reopened its formal investigation procedure into the aids, as provided for in ex-Article 88 EC (now Article 108 TFEU), thus giving the parties the opportunity—which they duly took—to present further information and observations. These new elements were then taken into account by the Commission when adopting its second decision. Notwithstanding these factors, which tended to point to divergences between the two cases, the Court nonetheless held that, due to the substantially identical nature of the support measures in the two proceedings, their qualification as state aids could no longer be called into question. As such, by delivering a new judgment on this question, the judge at first instance had failed to respect the absolute authority of the principle of res judicata protecting the previous decision.[8]

From these cases, as well as others,[9] the extent to which res judicata is, for the Union judge, a principle to be protected and respected with a particular vigilance, perhaps even rigour, can clearly be seen.

III   REVIEW OF FINAL DECISIONS OF NATIONAL COURTS IN BREACH OF UNION LAW: THE RETURN TO DOMESTIC LAW

The same approach, as that outlined above, which could be said to clearly respect the binding nature of final decisions, also, and perhaps inevitably, characterises the Court's now settled case law on national administrative or judicial acts which have become final and are in breach of Union law. This level of inviolability constitutes a limit which is, in principle, an absolute limit to the application of Union law, even where the EU provisions infringed by the national decision have been qualified by the European judge himself as being a matter of public policy.

Indeed, this is the principal lesson of the well-known *Eco Swiss* case,[10] decided in 1999 following a preliminary reference ruling from the Dutch Court of Cassation. Here the question was whether Union law requires a national judge to set aside domestic procedural rules according to which an arbitration award which has become res judicata cannot be called into question by a subsequent arbitration award. Under the relevant national

---

involved in the appeal against the first Commission decision.

[8] See *P&O European Ferries*, above n 5, paras 48 252.

[9] For a more in-depth analysis of these questions, see, in particular L Querzola, 'Spunti sui limiti oggettivi del giudicato comunitario' [1998] *Rivista Trimestrale di Diritto Processuale Civile* 331.

[10] Case C-126/97 *Eco Swiss* [1999] ECR I-3055.

law, any such review was not permitted, even where it was necessary in the context of annulment proceedings concerning the subsequent award in order to establish if the contract that the initial arbitration had held to be valid may in fact be void, because of a conflict with ex-Article 85 of the EC Treaty (now Article 101 TFEU).

As we know, the Court answered this question in the negative. Its decision was founded on respect for the fundamental principle of legal certainty, notwithstanding the fact that—as the Luxembourg judge expressly underlined—the Treaty article in question constituted a matter of public policy.[11]

Even though there are some who may question the current status of a precedent such as this, particularly in light of subsequent developments in the case law, the recent *Asturcom* case would seem to dispel any such doubts.

This judgment is significant for more than one reason. First of all, its timing is significant: it was delivered on 6 October 2009, that is, subsequent to several cases which have over the past few years clarified the boundaries between Union law and final national decisions, particularly the controversial *Lucchini* judgment.[12] Secondly, the facts surrounding *Asturcom* shared some important similarities with those of *Eco Swiss*: this case also concerned an arbitration award which had become final, even though it had been adopted contrary to provisions of Union law considered by the Court to be 'of equal standing to national rules which rank, within the domestic legal system, as rules of public policy'.[13] More specifically, the referring court, hearing enforcement proceedings in relation to the award, asked whether Union law required it to annul the final award because it was based on an unfair arbitration clause according to Directive 93/13/EC,[14] even though national law would not allow such an examination for the very reason that the award had become final. Lastly, this case concerned an area in which the Court had always ruled in favour of the need to ensure effective application of Union law in relation to consumer protection, rather than upholding the procedural autonomy of its Member State. In relation to the latter point, this was notably by requiring the national judge to set aside any domestic procedural rules that limit the possibility of the unfair character (and therefore the nullity) of a contractual clause being raised by its own motion,[15] and not to apply those establishing a limitation period that

---

[11] *Eco Swiss*, ibid, paras 39–47.
[12] Case C-119/05 *Lucchini* [2007] ECR I-6199.
[13] *Asturcom Telecomunicaciones*, above n 2, para 52.
[14] Council Dir 93/13/EEC of 5 April 1993 on unfair terms in consumer contracts [1993] OJ L95/29.
[15] See Joined Cases C-240/98 to 244/98 *Océano Grupo Editorial et Salvat Editores* [2000] ECR I-4941; Case C-168/05 *Mostaza Claro* [2006] ECR I-10421; and C-243/08 *Pannon GSM*, judgment of 4 June 2009.

prevents a ruling on any such unfairness.[16] In the eyes of the Luxembourg judge, outcomes such as these are essentially based on the need for positive intervention by a third party to the contract, which is the relevant national jurisdiction, to redress the substantial imbalance between the consumer and the seller or supplier, as the former may in particular be unaware of his rights or unable to bring legal proceedings because of the associated costs.[17]

The *Asturcom* case does, however, show that any such protection is not absolute and is subject to limits, particularly when it comes into conflict with the principle of res judicata. In terms that could hardly have been clearer, and echoing those used 10 years earlier in the *Eco Swiss* judgment, the Court reaffirmed that:

> Community law does not require a national court to disapply domestic rules of procedure conferring finality on a decision, *even if to do so would make it possible to remedy an infringement of a provision of Union law*, regardless of its nature, on the part of the decision at issue.[18]

The protection for consumers against unfair terms intended by Directive 93/13/EC cannot, the Luxembourg judge continues, be interpreted as going so far as 'to make up fully for the total inertia on the part of the consumer',[19] the applicant in the *Asturcom* case having neither participated in the arbitration proceedings nor brought an action for annulment of the arbitration award, which therefore became final.

Contrary to certain appearances, this line of case law, which pays particular respect to the inviolability of the res judicata principle, is not at all in conflict with that which has emerged from another set of judgments in relation to the fate reserved for final national decisions, of an administrative or judicial nature, and whose infringement of Union law only became apparent a posteriori.

More specifically, in this series of cases, the question addressed was whether national authorities must set aside or revise a final decision which, in light of a subsequent intervention by the Court, contains an interpretation of Union law that has been shown to be incorrect. This arises where a preliminary reference ruling is made in relation to another case on a date following the expiration of the limitation period or after all avenues of appeal against a national decision have been exhausted. In other words, does respect for the principle of supremacy of Union law and the retroactive effect of preliminary rulings (to the extent that, in principle, they take effect from the date the relevant provisions enter into force) always

---

[16] See Case C-473/00 *Cofidis* [2002] ECR I-10875.

[17] See *Océano Grupo Editorial et Salvat Editores*, ibid, paras 26 and 27; *Cofidis*, above n 16, paras 32–34; and *Mostaza Claro*, ibid, paras 26–28.

[18] *Asturcom Telecomunicaciones*, above n 2, para 37. Emphasis added.

[19] Ibid, para 47.

and necessarily call into question the inviolability of decisions that have become final?

Although a lot of ink has been spilled over the responses provided to this question, the judgments are reflective of a certain 'conventionality' on the part of the Court. It was established in *Kühne & Heitz*,[20] *i-21 Germany*[21] and *Kempter*[22] that a review of the provisions under scrutiny (which could ultimately lead to their revocation) is only required if and when this is imposed by relevant national law. By virtue of the first of the conditions laid down in this line of case law, the national body in which proceedings for a review of the decision have been brought must, as a result of its own domestic law, have the power to reopen a decision that has become final for the purposes of taking account of subsequent case law.[23] Therefore, it is only through reference to national procedural rules applicable to the referring court that the Kirchberg judges have recognised the existence of this obligation.

They have, in addition, been even more cautious in recognising such an obligation where the final decision is of judicial nature. In the *Kapferer* case,[24] the court considered the possible application of the principles set out in the aforementioned *Kühne & Heitz* case law—which dealt with the revision of administrative acts—to a judicial decision which had acquired res judicata. It addressed this only as a somewhat moot point, however, and did not give a final ruling on the issue.[25] Even supposing it is possible to apply these principles to an act of this nature, the Court nonetheless went on to exclude the requirement to review the decision in light of the specifics of the case before it. This was because the relevant national law—here, that of Austria—did not allow for the possibility of reopening decisions that had become final in order to consider their compatibility with a legal provision of superior hierarchy and, as such, the condition outlined above was not fulfilled.[26]

In other words, in accordance with the well-known principles of equivalence and effectiveness,[27] Union law must be able to benefit from the same

---

[20] Case C-453/00 *Kühne & Heitz* [2004] ECR I-837.

[21] Joined Cases C-392/04 and 422/04 *i-21 Germany et Arcor* [2006] ECR I-8559.

[22] Case C-2/06 *Kempter* [2008] ECR I-1411.

[23] *Kühne & Heitz*, above n 20, para 28 and reasoning. In the sense of a 'codification' of this requirement, see the *Kempter* decision, ibid, which categorised as 'conditions' the 'circumstances' which would give rise to an obligation to review as outlined in the *Kühne & Heitz* case.

[24] Case C-234/04 *Kapferer* [2006] ECR I-2585.

[25] *Kapferer*, ibid, para 23, which begins with the following clarification: 'Even assuming that the principles laid down in that judgment [Kühne & Heitz] could be transposed into a context which, like that of the main proceedings, relates to a final judicial decision . . .'.

[26] Ibid.

[27] According to settled case law, the respect of these principles requires that procedural rules relating to appeals designed to ensure the protection of the rights which individuals acquire through provisions of Union law cannot, on the one hand, be less favourable than those governing similar domestic actions (principle of equivalence) and are not framed in

procedural rules as would apply to analogous domestic disputes when the principle of res judicata is at stake. This is, no less, but equally no more, than what is already found within the relevant national legal order. The inevitable consequence of this for the parties concerned is that the possibilities of obtaining a review or revocation of a decision that has become final contrary to European provisions can vary considerably according to the procedural rules that apply and the exceptions that they allow to the principle of res judicata—'the other side of the coin', so to speak, to any line of cases that respects national procedural autonomy.[28]

IV THE LUCCHINI CASE

Against this backdrop—one of, on the whole, peaceful coexistence between the requirements of Union law and the need for legal certainty—the *Lucchini* judgment was like a bolt from the blue. Here, the Court stated that 'Community law *precludes* the application of a provision of national law, such as Article 2909 of the Italian Civil Code, which seeks to lay down the principle of res judicata',[29] insofar as this would prevent the recovery of state aid granted in violation of the Treaty. This ruling, seemingly barely reconcilable with the direction of the case law outlined above, could hardly be met with indifference. In particular, contrary to the reasoning used by the Luxembourg judges in the cases above, this time the challenge to, and defeat of, the principle of res judicata was based upon Union law. Specifically, the decision was founded upon the principle of supremacy, as well as the rules governing the division of competences between the Union and its Members in relation to state aids, without the need to take a 'detour' via the any national legal system. That said, if one looks a little more closely, it seems that, rather than marking a complete overhaul of the case law, the decision was essentially, if not exclusively, guided by the nature, perhaps even the pathology, of the particular case before the Court.

such a way as to render impossible in practice the exercise of rights recognised by the European legal order (principle of effectiveness). See, inter alia, Case C-78/98 *Preston ea* [2000] ECR I-3201, para 31; Joined Cases C-222/05 and 225/05 *van der Weerd ea* [2007] ECR I-4223, para 28.

[28] An outcome criticised, in particular, by AG Ruiz-Jarabo Colomer who, in his opinion on *i-21 Germany and Arcor*, above n 21, para 67, observed that: 'reliance on national law, as advocated by the Court of Justice in such cases, raises serious problems, including, in particular, disparities in the protection of rights derived from the Community legal order'. On the same point see L Coutron, 'Cour de justice, 13 janvier 2004, Kühne & Heitz NV/ Productschap voor Pluimvee en Eieren' (2003–04) 3 *Revue des affaires européennes* 417; and A Bouveresse, 'La mise en conformité des mesures nationales contraires au droit communautaire: le retrait, une obligation à géométrie variable' in G Eckert, Y Guatier, R Kovar and D Ritling (eds), *Incidences du droit communautaire sur le droit public français* (Strasbourg, Presses universitaires de Strasbourg, 2007).

[29] *Lucchini*, above n 12, para 63 and reasoning. Emphasis added.

In fact, it was clear that the case presented a number of elements which made it anomalous for several reasons. The first of these concerned its object: a measure authorising the grant of state aid which was adopted by the Italian administrative authorities and subsequently confirmed by the Tribunal and the Court of Appeal in Rome, although it completely ignored the exclusive competence enjoyed by the Commission in relation to the compatibility of state aid with the Common Market. Furthermore, it disregarded the fact that, in this particular case, the Commission had exercised this competence through Decision 90/555/EEC, which concluded that the aid was incompatible with the Common Market.[30] Faced with such a serious 'encroachment' by the national authorities in an area in which they did not have competence, and such a flagrant infringement of the principle of supremacy and the direct effect of Union acts, it could be argued that, at least from the perspective of European law, the necessary elements for a res judicata claim were not present.[31] If this were to be the case, the 'radical' element of the solution adopted by the Court is easier to understand, as is the absence of any reference to the principle of res judicata in the reasons given by the Court for the decision in *Lucchini*.

The exceptional nature of this case also stems from the role played by the various parties in the context of the main proceedings. One could mention the number of manifest errors or the condemnable passivity, to say the least, of the Italian authorities, national administrations and civil jurisdictions;[32] and even, above all, the 'ingenuity' of the claimant who was the beneficiary of the illegal aid. She did not bring a claim for annulment to the Court of First Instance to contest Decision 90/555/ESCC, an option available to her. Instead, she preferred simply to let the delay for bringing the relevant action expire, before finally turning to the national judge to request payment of the aid, thus bypassing the one-month time limit provided for in Article 33(3) ESCC. The result was that the very foundations, not only of state aid control, but also the Union's wider system of legal remedies, were called into question, forcing the Luxembourg judge to take action.[33] After all, desperate times call for desperate

---

[30] [1990] OJ L314/17.

[31] An entirely different situation from that in *Kühne & Heitz* (above n 23), *i-21 Germany* (above n 21), *Kapferer* (above n 24) and *Kempter* (above n 22) in the context of which the conflict between national res judicata and Union law arose *ex post*, that is following an interpretation by the Court of Justice that intervened after the point at which the domestic decision at issue became final.

[32] For an eloquent discussion of the various shortcomings and failings of the Italian authorities, see the Opinion of AG Geelhoed in *Lucchini*, above n 12, paras 13 and 65–67.

[33] Indeed, as the Court recalled in para 55 of the *Lucchini* decision, the case law excludes, once the time limit laid down in the Treaty has expired, the beneficiary of state aid forming the subject matter of a Commission decision from contesting its legality both before a Union judge in a direct action and before the national courts through an appeal against the implementing measures. See, in particular, Case C-188/92 *TWD Textilwerke Deggendorf* [2004] ECR I-833, para 13; and Case C-241/01 *National Farmers' Union* [2002] ECR I-9079, para 34.

measures, a conclusion which seems to have been confirmed by the fact that subsequent case law, such as the *Asturcom* case (one which, as we noted previously, follows a more 'orthodox' approach to the issue), either does not mention the *Lucchini* case or refers to it only to immediately limit its scope. This can be seen in the *Fallimento Olimpiclub* case, examined below.

That said, and even if we adopt a reading which significantly limits the effects of the *Lucchini* decision, the case nonetheless remains an important precedent—one which, furthermore, was delivered by the Court's Grand Chamber—which is unlikely to remain an isolated decision with no future impact.

Other areas of Union law may, in the same way, be prone to similar conflicts between Union obligations and the national principle of res judicata. Let us imagine, for example, the *Lucchini* case 'the other way around' and in the context of merger control. Here, one might see a merger or acquisition which had been authorised by the Commission on the back of Regulation 139/2004 EC (which grants the Commission exclusive competence in this area)[34] being later prevented, or at least subjected to further conditions, by a Member State in order to protect its national economy, or for other 'strategic' reasons. It would be wrong to think that this is simply an academic question or a 'nightmare scenario', as the *Enel/Acciona/Endesa* saga in the area of electricity demonstrates. In fact, even if this particular case led to infringement proceedings against Spain, it arose from the exact situation where the acquisition of the energy supplier Endesa by the Enel and Acciona groups had been the object of several measures imposing certain restrictive conditions, even though this operation had already been authorised by a decision of the Brussels executive. [35]

---

[34] Council Reg (EC) No 139/2004 of 20 January 2004 on the control of concentrations between undertakings, [2004] OJ L24/21. As we know, this regulation grants the Commission exclusive competence to examine concentrations with a 'Community' dimension' (that is, those which reach a certain threshold of turnover for the undertakings concerned) and sets out, to this end, a system of control of their compatibility with the Common Market.

[35] See European Commission press release IP/08/746, 'Mergers: Commission Requests Spain to Lift Conditions Imposed on Acquisition of Endesa by Enel and Acciona' (15 May 2008). The incriminating provisions, considered by the Commission as contravening the regulation on the control of concentrations as well as the provisions of the Treaty on free movement, included the obligation, amongst others, to ensure the independence of Endesa, not to transfer its centre of operations out of the Spanish territory, to purchase a stated amount of national coal, and to maintain the assets of insular and non-continental electricity networks within the Endesa group. In this regard, it should be noted that the system for prior authorisation on the basis of which the National Energy Commission (NEC) had imposed these conditions on Enel and Acciona has since been ruled by the Court as contrary to the principles of free movement of capital and freedom of establishment (Case C-207/07 *Commission v Spain* [2008] ECR I-111). We might also consider B Gencarelli, 'Alcune riflessioni conclusive sui rapporti tra diritto comunitario e atti nazionali definitivi' in F Spitaleri (ed), *L'incidenza del diritto comunitario*, above n 1.

V   THE FALIMENTO OLIMPICLUB CASE

In any case, the Court soon had the opportunity to clarify the scope of the *Lucchini* decision as the issue was at the heart of a reference for a preliminary ruling from the Italian Court of Cassation in the *Fallimento Olimpiclub* case. The Luxembourg judge was asked about the circumstances in which the principle of res judicata could be set aside due to an infringement of Union law in a different area from that of state aids; here, in relation to VAT.

The Italian court considered itself bound by certain judgments which had acquired the force of res judicata and which related to VAT adjustment notices issued following the same tax investigation, in respect of the same taxable person, but relating to a different tax year. These previous and final judgments had all concluded that there was no fraud or abuse involved. It follows from the order for reference that, whilst these judgments related to different taxation periods, the observations made in them, and the decision that was reached, were binding upon the main proceedings. This conclusion was reached by virtue of a recent interpretation of the principle of res judicata in the Italian tax case law, according to which the outcome of a final decision in a dispute cannot be called into question in the context of a different case which addressed the same parties and which raised similar questions, even when the first judgment relates to a different taxation period from that at issue in the proceedings in which this judgment is invoked.[36] In the present case, the referring court raised the incompatibility of the concerned definitive decisions with the notion of abuse of rights in the area of VAT, as developed by the ECJ case law.

Following a fairly brief, but particularly clear and effective, line of reasoning, the European Court made the following statement on this approach to the principle of res judicata:

> [N]ot only does the interpretation in question prevent a judicial decision that has acquired the force of res judicata from being called into question, even if that decision entails a breach of Union law; it also prevents any finding on a fundamental issue common to other cases, contained in a judicial decision which has acquired the force of res judicata from being called into question in the context of judicial scrutiny of another decision taken by the relevant tax authority in respect of the same taxpayer or taxable person, but relating to a different tax year.[37]

Hence, if the principle of res judicata were to have the effect outlined above, there would be no opportunity to make the necessary corrections to a national judge's erroneous interpretation of EU law, thereby leading to

---

[36] In this area of Italian law, we talk about 'giudicato esterno' or of 'external' effects of res judicata, as opposed to the principle known as 'discreteness of judgments'.

[37] *Fallimento Olimpiclub*, above n 2, para 29.

an inescapable repetition of this mistake. From this, the Court concluded that 'such extensive obstacles to the effective application of the Community rules on VAT cannot reasonably be regarded as justified' by arguments relating to legal certainty, thus contravening the principle of effectiveness.[38]

Thus, this ruling would seem to mark a shift in the emphasis of the case law from arguments relating to the principle of equivalence—allowing only those derogations and adjustements to res judicata permitted by national law—to those emphasising the requirements of effective application of Union law—involving no such 'diversion' via the domestic legal order. One might conclude from this that *Fallimento Olimpiclub* has delivered a decisive, or even fatal, blow to the status of the principle of res judicata, already severely shaken by the preceding case law. On this point also, however, a more nuanced reading is needed.

On the one hand, in fact, the Union judge, perhaps aware of the reactions provoked by the *Lucchini* judgment, was at pains to highlight the 'highly specific' nature of the case and explicitly limited its scope to situations in which 'the division of powers' between the Member States and the Union was called into question.[39] Therefore, the *Lucchini* precedent was not binding in *Fallimento Olimpiclub*, given that the regulation of VAT and the levying of tax fall within the competence of the national authorities.

On the other hand, a reading of the reasoning in the *Fallimento Olimpiclub* decision suggests that the conclusion reached by the Court was, once again, motivated by the particular facts of the case and the characteristics of the disputed interpretation of res judicata that the Italian Court of Cassation had adopted. In fact, the Luxembourg judge did not, as such, censor the national court's requirement that the inviolability of a final judgment be respected (even where this is in conflict with a decision of the European Court). Instead, its disapproval was limited to the systematic extension of this inviolability—and with it the perpetuation of an incorrect interpretation of Union law—to a different and subsequent tax dispute which relates to a different tax year and, further, is still pending before the referring court, so that, by definition, this dispute cannot have already given rise to a final judgment. In other words, it is not the principle of res judicata that must give way to the needs of the Union's legal system, as much as some of its more specific and far-reaching consequences[40]—(ones that are, moreover, described by Italian law as being

---

[38] Ibid, para 31.
[39] Ibid, para 25.
[40] In this respect, Professor Simon even talks of the 'atypical' character of the Italian definition of res judicata. See D Simon, 'Autorité de chose jugée d'un arrêt national' (2009) 11 *Europe* 11.

'external' effects and arise from a far from settled national case law which is far from settled).[41]

VI   CONCLUSION

By focusing on the specific effects of this judicial interpretation, the *Fallimento Olimpiclub* decision, like the case law which preceded it, is firmly set within the search for a proper balance, based on the particular circumstances of each case, between, on the one hand, the need to guarantee the application of Union law and the protection of rights it confers on individuals[42] and, on the other, respect for the procedural autonomy of Member States. This is an exercise which is very familiar to the European judge and which has characterised entire chapters of Luxembourg case law. Notwithstanding the inevitable nuances and distinctions that result from an approach which is, by definition, undertaken on a case-by-case basis, certain dominant themes emerge from the cases examined in this contribution. This case law finds its unifying thread in, first, the importance that the Court attaches to the principle of res judicata and to its corollary, the inviolability of final decisions of national administrative authorities and judicial courts, even where they may prove to be contrary to common EU provisions. Thus, in principle, there are no obstacles, one might say, to the application of national rules relating to res judicata, in perfect accordance with the respect for the procedural autonomy of Member States. The constraints of Union law are only felt when national rules prevent the revocation or the review of a provision that has been subject to a final decision in a way that is contrary to the long-established principles of equivalence or effectiveness.

All in all, it seems to us that, notwithstanding the cries of outrage which have at times been heard, the case law that we have examined here does not entail an upheaval, or a reversal, of the principle of res judicata as recognised and protected by national laws.[43] Instead, these decisions limit

---

[41] In its referral order of 21 December 2007, the Italian Court of Cassation clarified that the principle known as 'discreteness of judgments' has been significantly altered by recent case law and, in this respect, referred in particular to the change in interpretation found in Judgment No 13916/06, given by the its united sections.

[42] In respect of the principle at issue here, let us note, however, that the non-application of domestic rules on res judicata does not necessarily benefit the party to the case and can lead to the denial of rights that previously been accrued. This was the case elsewhere in the *Lucchini* case, in respect of the company that illegally received a state aid, and in the *Fallimento Olimpiclub* decision for the party that was previously not subject to the payment of VAT on the basis of Italian law alone.

[43] Besides, we should note, in passing, that generally the principle of res judicata is not absolute and is subject to certain exceptions in every national legal system. See, in this respect, the arguments put forward by AG Geelhoed in his Opinion in the Lucchini case (above n 32, para 37). This is equally true of the EU legal order: Art 44 (1) of the Statute of the Court of Justice provides that '[a]n application for revision of a judgment may be

themselves to reaffirming and clarifying a method of interpretation which is consistent with the rules governing the relationship between national legal systems and the Union's own legal order. Here, this means that, as fundamental as it may be, the interpretation of the effect of a general principle such as res judicata is not only a question for national law, but rather one which must also take account of the requirements imposed by EU law.[44] In the end, we are only talking about the 'price' of, or rather an essential condition for, the harmonious functioning of our common legal order, as well as the effective protection of the rights which its subjects draw from it.

made to the Court of Justice only on discovery of a fact which is of such a nature as to be a decisive factor, and which, when the judgment [that has subsequently acquired the force of res judicata] was given, was unknown to the Court and to the party claiming the revision'.

[44] On these points, see R Adam and A Tizzano *Lineamenti di diritto dell'Unione europea* (Turin, Giappichelli, 2008) 365.

Part III

European Substantive Law

15

The Struggle for EU Citizenship: Why Solidarity Matters

MALCOLM ROSS*

I INTRODUCTION

C AN THE EUROPEAN Union be described as a Europe of citizens rather than an order of states? Or, perhaps more important than this routine question, why would a positive answer matter? Inevitably, any response is likely to come hedged with caveats depending on what kind of citizenship is envisaged and the character of the polity in which citizenship is housed. After all, the distinguishing features of citizenship (European or not) classically tend to revolve around status, entitlements and responsibility within a definable political community. The development of EU citizenship, at least in the rhetoric and reasoning of case law from the Court of Justice, has hitherto been driven by at least two motors. On the one hand, the language and methodology of the single market have provided a genetic imprint to the point where citizenship has been described as the fifth freedom[1] built on equal treatment and requiring obstacles to it to be justified against overriding public interests.[2] On the other, a thread of fundamental rights is also discernible,[3] suggesting a more personal character and the possibilities of a citizenship not necessarily tied to cross-border movement.[4] Indeed, a case can be made for saying that EU citizenship has reached sufficient maturity as a force for change that now it is shaping the single market rather than the other way round.

---

* I am very grateful to Yuri Borgmann-Prebil, Julie Dickson, Tony Arnull and, especially, Helen Compton for comments and suggestions. The usual disclaimer applies.

[1] 'Editorial' (2008) 45 *Common Market Law Review* 1.

[2] Y Borgmann-Prebil, 'The Rule of Reason in European Citizenship' (2008) 14 *European Law Journal* 328.

[3] Traceable even to pre-citizenship cases such as Case C-168/91 *Konstantinidis* [1993] ECR I-1191, per AG Jacobs. See also N Nic Shuibhne, 'The Outer Limits of EU Citizenship: Displacing Economic Free Movement Rights?' in C Barnard and O Odudu (eds), *The Outer Limits of European Law* (Oxford, Hart Publishing, 2009) ch 8.

[4] Especially visible in the cases about the registration of names: Case C-148/02 *Garcia Avello* [2003] ECR I-11613, Case C-353/06 *Grunkin and Paul* [2008] ECR I-7369.

The recent elevation in status of the EU Charter of Fundamental Rights to have the 'same legal value as the Treaties'[5] adds further ammunition to that particular argument. Nevertheless, this rights-led dynamic to EU citizenship trumpeted by lawyers still arguably lacks the heart or moral compass that might make a 'Europe of citizens' a plausible proposition for political scientists or sociologists. Indeed, more boldly, citizenship that is lacking in solidarity is hardly citizenship at all.

It is therefore the purpose of this chapter to assess the evidence in support of a more embedded EU citizenship struggling to emerge from the conceptual shadows of both the single market and fundamental rights. The key to weighing this evidence, it is submitted, is to be found in the presence (or otherwise) of solidarity as a concept with which to give spirit to the letter of citizenship. In short, without acknowledging and confronting solidarity, the development of EU citizenship will remain a thin and largely gutless project. Greater engagement with solidarity, as the case law only inconsistently does to date, may prove the catalyst that meaningful citizenship still requires. The analysis that follows compares the characteristics of citizenship and solidarity with a view to examining the relationship between the two ideas in recent case law and how the dynamics of that arrangement can impact upon the constitutional evolution of the post-Lisbon EU.

II   CITIZENSHIP AND SOLIDARITY COMPARED

There is no space here to depict the rich histories of citizenship and solidarity.[6] Both contested concepts, they occupy congruent terrain. In a political and sociological sense, the two ideas are deeply connected with questions of identity and belonging, and the extent to which these can evolve in deterritorialised, transnational or cosmopolitan settings. There is consequently an overarching 'them and us' dimension to both concepts: between citizens and non-citizens, and between members of a solidaristic group and non-members. Establishing and defending borders accordingly seems integral to the conceptualisation of citizenship and solidarity, although there might be many ways of doing this and hostility towards

---

[5] Art 6(1) TEU. Acknowledged, without further elaboration, by the Grand Chamber in Case C-555/07 *Kücükdeveci v Swedex GmbH & Co, KG*, judgment 19 January 2010, para 22.

[6] As a familiar idea in Greek city-states, citizenship has the longer pedigree. But solidarity can certainly be traced back two centuries and explicitly occurs in the 1804 Code Civil. On solidarity generally, see S Stjernø, *Solidarity in Europe: The History of an Idea* (Cambridge, Cambridge University Press, 2005). For a variety of disciplinary perspectives on solidarity see N Karagiannis (ed) *European Solidarity* (Liverpool, Liverpool University Press, 2007); M Ross and Y Borgmann-Prebil (eds), *Promoting Solidarity in the European Union* (Oxford, Oxford University Press, 2010). For contemporary citizenship studies, see J V Ciprut (ed), *The Future of Citizenship* (Cambridge MA, MIT Press, 2008).

the outsider does not necessarily follow.[7] Moreover, the barriers to entry do not have to be set high, and membership of more than one group simultaneously may well be possible. For the purposes of this particular chapter, the relevance of this delimiting aspect of the two concepts is in trying to pin down the important elements that establish the necessary foundational bonds and, on that basis, whether there is any overlap or causal connection between them. Put another way, does sustainable citizenship depend on solidarity from its members,[8] or does solidarity cement, strengthen or even supplant citizenship? Clearly, it is possible to envisage solidarities without citizenship (eg the rise of transnational political movements or inter-generational solidarities to confront threats such as climate change[9]), but is the reverse meaningful? The development of EU citizenship, as will be elaborated further below, seems to have proceeded without a cogent underpinning of solidarity, but its future direction may be dependent upon a change to this state of affairs.

A further crossover between citizenship and solidarity can be found in what might be described as the degree of mutuality demanded or experienced between members. In citizenship this is often expressed formally in terms of duties or responsibilities as well as rights, as seen in Article 20(2) TFEU. Nevertheless, as is famously the case in its EU manifestation, there may be a considerable imbalance between the rights and duties components of the citizenship package. Solidarity, at the very least, carries a concern for others and a willingness to make sacrifices for them.[10] Members of a group are, or at least they *feel*, obliged to promote the well-being of other members.[11] It is this presence of some degree of mutuality that distinguishes solidarity from charity, love or mere empathy. This mutuality does not have to be based on high moral ground or altruism. As Williams observes,[12] risk exposure may well dictate movements between or within solidaristic groups as, for example, states otherwise reluctant to engage with climate change realise the implications of migration challenges arising from displaced populations. In the current context of EU citizenship predominantly mediated by cases in the social welfare arena, it is exposure to the financial consequences of increased solidarity that seems to be inhibiting the development of citizenship. Indeed, it has been asked whether case law extending the benefits of EU law 'might not

[7] D Heyd, 'Justice and Solidarity: The Contractarian Case against Global Justice' (2007) 38 *Journal of Social Philosophy* 112.

[8] *cf* J Habermas' description of citizenship as 'an abstract, legally mediated solidarity between strangers' in 'Why Europe Needs a Constitution' (Sept–Oct 2001) 5 *New Left Review* 16.

[9] See A Williams, 'Solidarity, Justice and Climate Change Law' (2009) 10 *Melbourne Journal of International Law* 493.

[10] See further S Derpmann, 'Solidarity and Cosmopolitanism' (2009) 12 *Ethical Theory and Moral Practice* 303.

[11] Ibid, 304.

[12] Williams, above n 9, 498–502.

ultimately risk producing the opposite effect, ie of provoking a backlash among the host society against individuals who have not acquired membership of the solidaristic community according to the latter's traditional or accepted criteria'.[13]

This tension points to another key element of common ground between citizenship and solidarity, namely their political character. Again, the EU variant of citizenship is perhaps unusual since active political engagement remains embryonic, at least in relation to the exercise of civic rights.[14] Of course, this is not to deny the highly contentious politicisation of EU citizenship arising from the concomitant fears it generates about the security and future of national citizenship. The political aspirations and consequences of nascent EU citizenship are themselves reasons for local political opposition to its entrenchment.[15] This might explain why citizenship's development has focused instead upon welfare rights as these, at least, can be mediated through law and courts. In other words, some expansion of EU citizenship has been possible through the attempt to depoliticise it by the legal language of rights and equal treatment. In this sense, of course, the shaping of EU citizenship is consistent with the patterns of constitutionalisation demonstrated in the history of the single market and, more broadly still, the whole panoply of judicial protection principles developed by the Court of Justice for the purpose of allowing individuals to access EU law.

However, as will be argued further below, this rights-based approach is unhelpful insofar as it inhibits transparency in facing up to the real challenge of solidarity in such cases. Crucially, discourses of solidarity and citizenship can be seen to appeal to different audiences and constituencies. Solidarity is unabashedly political in the sense that it requires commitment to the 'others' on the basis of a threat to one being a threat to all—clearly visible, of course, in classical struggles of class and labour. Seen in this way, solidarity flows from a political, moral or emotional 'as if' stance, ie my reaction to seeing benefits or access denied to someone else is as if I had suffered the same detriment. Whilst it is possible to formalise this as equal treatment (in EU law as the proposition that a migrant should be treated as if he/she were a national of the host state), this distancing

[13] M Dougan, 'The Spatial Restructuring of National Welfare States within the European Union: The Contribution of Union Citizenship and the Relevance of the Treaty of Lisbon' in U Neergaard, R Nielsen and L Roseberry (eds), *Integrating Welfare Functions into EU Law—From Rome to Lisbon* (Copenhagen, DJØF Publishing, 2009) 147, 165.

[14] Art 22 TFEU set outs limited voting rights. For their contribution to polity-building, see J Shaw, *The Transformation of Citizenship in the European Union* (Cambridge, Cambridge University Press, 2007).

[15] According to Art 20(1) TFEU, 'Citizenship of the Union shall be additional to and not replace national citizenship'. This replaces the 'shall complement and not replace' formulation of Art 18 EC.

from solidarity as the rationale obscures the active, experienced dimension to citizenship that might be necessary to ensure its durability or appeal.

Citizenship and solidarity are thus closely intertwined, but with different voices and perhaps also a different centre of gravity. Citizenship necessarily directly connects the citizen to the polity, whether that is a state or some transnational governance arrangement. Solidarity connects members of the group themselves and is accordingly a more horizontally characterised social phenomenon. The extent to which these two relationships engage with, or are distinct from, each other forms the struggle for citizenship that is being played out in the EU. Put crudely, it is presumably in the interests of Member States to keep the lid on citizenship, as it were, without encouraging a solidarity dimension. However, the interesting question is whether Member States actually have the ability to maintain that position. An embedded solidarity between EU citizens, were it to develop, would be capable of bypassing Member States' ownership of EU citizenship. This is obviously not a political or social reality at the moment, but the possibility merits examination. After all, at a general level, there are plenty of precedents for Member States failing to keep areas of policy 'ring-fenced'. In relation to citizenship more specifically, analogies for putative EU citizenship might recall Marshall's historical analysis[16] in a national context where social rights are arguably more inextricably linked to identity than civil or political ones. The contestation, through EU law, of what might broadly be termed participation in a state's social environment (not just financial benefits under State welfare systems but even matters such as the recognition of names) accordingly forms a particularly apposite focus for analysis below. In particular, it is the examination of how that contestation is being conducted that may indicate the prospects for an EU citizenship to acquire the horizontal aspect that solidarity connotes.

In short, when discussing the question of the EU as a constitutional order of states, there is thus a real significance to be attached to whether its transnational citizenship remains firmly mediated through states or whether a solidarity model of citizenship—detached, or at least significantly disconnected from state control—is capable of emerging. The next section therefore addresses some of the case law complexities that have arisen, it is submitted, because of a failure to distinguish properly the relationship between citizenship and solidarity. This, in turn, has created further inconsistencies in delineating the place of both concepts in the evolving constitutional order of the EU.

---

[16] TH Marshall, *Citizenship and Social Class* (London, Pluto, 1992), originally written in 1950.

III   THE SOLIDARITY DISCOURSE
IN CITIZENSHIP CASE LAW

'Solidarity' is certainly a theme in the European citizenship case law, but has hitherto lacked a uniform meaning or context. Indeed, even in relation to basic questions the case law displays variations or ambiguity as to what kind or extent of solidarity is relevant and between whom it might exist. Some authors have discerned different axes of solidarity in free movement cases, eg between host state and EU migrant or between EU migrant and home state.[17] Expressions and concepts that sound like solidarity in describing these relationships—such as 'real link', 'genuine link' or 'effective link'—have attracted extensive scholarly inquiry. However, for many commentators that analysis consists of dismissing any notion of a putative European solidarity in the course of assessing whether the solidarity internal to national welfare systems might be under threat as a result of the EU mobility case law.[18] This propensity in the literature perhaps inevitably reflects the fact that even the Court of Justice and its Advocates General often tend to restrict engagement with explicit use of the term to the financial solidarity owed by a host state to a migrant gaining access to its system of welfare benefits. Solidarity, in the sense of bonding or emotional pull, appears instead in the Court's characterisation of nationality rather than European citizenship. As the Grand Chamber observed in *Rottmann* when dealing with the consequences of the withdrawal by a Member State of nationality from one its naturalised citizens, it is legitimate for a Member State to wish to protect the special relationship of solidarity and good faith between it and its nationals and also the reciprocity of rights and duties, which form the bedrock of the bond of nationality.[19]

Although the Court went on in that case to decide that Member States are still required to exercise their own rules about nationality in accordance with EU law, especially the principle of proportionality, the allusion to solidarity in only its national context is symptomatic of the nature of

---

[17] Notably M Dougan, 'Expanding the Frontiers of Union Citizenship by Dismantling the Territorial Boundaries of National Welfare States?' in C Barnard and O Odudu (eds), *The Outer Limits of European Law* (Oxford, Hart Publishing, 2009) ch 7. He distinguishes between 'solidaristic real links' and 'membership real links' in the context of objective justifications for national restrictions on the grant of benefits.

[18] See, particularly, C O'Brien, 'Real Links, Abstract Rights and False Alarms: The Relationship between the ECJ's "Real Link" Case Law and National Solidarity' (2008) 33 *European Law Review* 643; A Somek, 'Solidarity Decomposed: Being and Time in European Citizenship' (2007) 32 *European Law Review* 787; S Giubboni, 'A Certain Degree of Solidarity—Free Movement of Persons and Access to Social Protection in the Case Law of the European Court of Justice' in M Ross and Y Borgmann-Prebil, above n 6, ch 9.

[19] Case C-135/08 *Rottmann v Freistaat Bayern*, judgment of 2 March 2010, para 51; see T Konstadinides, 'La fraternité européene? The Extent of National Competence to Condition the Acquisition and Loss of Nationality from the Perspective of EU Citizenship' (2010) 35 *European Law Review* 401.

the challenges facing the development of European citizenship. Is the latter a clone of national citizenship or, if different, is it detachable from any solidarity base? Put more starkly, does a solidarity kept in the confines of nationhood serve to circumscribe transnational citizenship?

The relationship between citizenship and solidarity is complicated further by the gradations that operate within both concepts. As will be elaborated below, the current state of EU law creates a situation in which some citizens are more equal than others and some solidarities are stronger or more favoured than others. The reasons for these nuances are not hard to explain on a political level, since both ideas can easily be framed as threats to national sovereignty, financial stability, local identity or any combination thereof. However, the more interesting question is whether the contestation of citizenship and solidarity follows similar patterns and whether either concept is being enhanced or restricted because of, or at the expense of, the other. In particular, the discussion below considers whether the conversation (or, perhaps more accurately, argument) between the Court of Justice and the Member States over the development of citizenship could be productively deployed in the context of solidarity discourse.

Visions of EU citizenship remain as diverse as they were at the time of the concept's introduction in the 1990s. At one extreme, Advocate General Poiares Maduro has referred to the 'miracle' of EU citizenship as one not determined by nationality:

> It strengthens the ties between us and our States (insofar as we are European citizens precisely because we are nationals of our States) and, at the same time, it emancipates us from them (insofar as we are now citizens beyond our States). Access to European citizenship is gained through nationality of a Member State, which is regulated by national law, but, like any form of citizenship, it forms the basis of a new political area from which rights and duties emerge, which are laid down by Community law and do not depend on the State. This, in turn, legitimises the autonomy and authority of the Community legal order.[20]

In the same Opinion, the Advocate General refers to European citizenship as more than a body of rights; rather, it presupposes a political relationship that unites the peoples of Europe with a mutual commitment to open their respective bodies politic to other European citizens. Crucially, in his view, EU citizenship does not require the existence of a people, or belonging to a people, but is founded on the existence of a European political area.

This approach obviously chimes with the 'fundamental status' tag attached to citizenship by the Court of Justice in *Grzelczyk*.[21] However, there is no surprise that this bullish attitude contrasts with the less ambitious or enthusiastic moods of Member States. Their more sanguine

---

[20] Opinion in Case C-135/08 *Rottmann*, above n 19, para 23.
[21] Case C-184/99 *Grzelczyk* [2001] ECR I-6193; recently repeated by the Grand Chamber in Case C-135/08 *Rottmann*, above n 19.

approach, manifested most obviously in Directive 2004/38[22] and its gra-
dated forms of citizenship,[23] reflects both a wish not to undermine national
versions of citizenship and a resistance to financial exposure in terms of
access to welfare benefits. The extent to which this directive either puts the
brakes on, or even reverses, the jurisprudence of the Court of Justice or
previous secondary legislation has become an increasingly prevalent issue
in litigation. Again, this is an entirely predictable development, given the
constitutional significance of the personal and material scope of EU citizenship.[24] As discussed below, the initial deference of the Court towards
the Union legislature in *Förster*[25] has been followed by studied deafness
in *Vatsouras*[26] and much more robust judgments by the Grand Chamber
in *Ibrahim*[27] and *Teixeira*.[28] The result is a complex and incomplete picture, where the music of EU citizenship is played by different instruments,
and not always in harmony.

The tensions and inconsistencies in these recent judgments raise three
main concerns: the extent to which citizenship has failed to eradicate the
significance attached to 'worker' status, the relevance of personal circumstances and the intensity of proportionality as a measure of review of
national obstacles to enjoyment of EU citizenship. These debates, explored
in cases that significantly all involve access to a host state's financial benefits, bring into sharp relief the extent to which the Court has been willing
to find ways round the states' attempted use of the EU legislative process to curtail in express terms the judicial (over-?)exuberance that marked
earlier cases such as *Grzelczyk*[29] and *Bidar*.[30] In this sense, the iterative
process of contestation over citizenship reflects the more general dynamics
of constitutionalisation and provides a measure of how far the shaping of
the Union remains under the effective control of Member States.

The particular focus giving rise to the *Förster* and *Vatsouras* cases was
the impact of the remarkably two-faced Article 24 of Directive 2004/38,
which, it will be recalled, creates a presumption of equal treatment for
Union citizens residing in a host Member State in paragraph (1) subject

[22] Dir 2004/38 on the Right of Citizens of the Union and their Family Members to Move
and Reside within the Territory of the Member States [2004] OJ L158/77.
[23] In the sense of rights and protection varying according to time periods of three months,
up to five years and beyond five years of residence in another Member State.
[24] See E Spaventa, 'Seeing the Wood Despite the Trees? On the Scope of Union Citizenship and its Constitutional Effects' (2008) 45 *Common Market Law Review* 13; see also
Dougan, above n 17.
[25] Case C-158/07 *Förster* [2008] ECR I-8507.
[26] Joined Cases C-22/08 and C-23/08 *Vatsouras and Koupatantze*, judgment of 4 June
2009.
[27] Case C-310/08 *London Borough of Harrow v Ibrahim and Secretary of State for Home
Department*, judgment of 23 February 2010.
[28] Case C-480/08 *Teixeira v London Borough of Lambeth and Secretary of State for the
Home Department*, judgment of 23 February 2010.
[29] Above n 21.
[30] Case C-209/03 *Bidar* [2005] ECR I-2119.

to the specific derogations in paragraph (2). The latter provides that the host state

> shall not be obliged to confer social assistance during the first three months of residence . . . nor shall it be obliged, prior to acquisition of the right of permanent residence, to grant maintenance aid for studies . . . to persons other than workers, self-employed persons, persons who retain such status and members of their families.

The *Förster* case gave the Court the opportunity to review the scope and even the validity of this potentially far-reaching derogation. Advocate General Mazák was willing to use the ammunition of the pre-existing case law to limit the impact of Article 24(2), observing that the five-year rule for the maintenance grant in question should be seen as an outer limit and that the personal circumstances of the applicant should form the subject of analysis for any proportionality review. The Court, however, rolled over in puppy-dog fashion to endorse the advantages of a clear, known and foreseeable qualification rule, with no regard for the applicant's individual position. Further, in a bizarre pronouncement that any undergraduate law student with a modicum of knowledge about the single market case law would find preposterous,[31] the Court took such a blanket five-year residence requirement as proportionate in principle. Whilst it would be naive to claim that the Court could easily have confronted the Member States head-on in the first case to discuss a provision that was obviously designed to achieve a particular result, it nevertheless seems curious that the derogation was defended and justified with such gusto and without any reference to the proper relationship between an exception in secondary legislation and primary Treaty provisions (citizenship) and Union law principles (equal treatment). Moreover, this cursory attention to proportionality seems all the more flawed, given that the Court of Justice has taken to describing general principles of EU law as having 'constitutional status'.[32]

Although the retreat by the Grand Chamber in *Förster* might be unappealing to fans of its robustness and independence, the ruling could perhaps claim an old-fashioned merit of certainty. However, this could not be said to characterise the subsequent *Vatsouras* ruling by the Third Chamber of the Court. Turning a deaf ear to the intentions of the legislature, and sticking with the case law that the legislation had been designed to limit,[33] the Court decided that benefits under Book II of the German Code of Social Law were not 'social assistance' within the meaning of Arti-

---

[31] *Cf* the Advocate General's analysis in Case C-224/01 *Köbler* [2003] ECR I-10239.

[32] See, eg Case C-101/08 *Audiolux SA and Others v Groupe Bruxelles Lambert SA (GBL) and Others, Bertelsmann AG and Others*, judgment of 15 October 2009, para 63; Case C-174/08 *NCC Construction Danmark A/S v Skatteministeriet*, judgment of 29 October 2009, para 42.

[33] Particularly Case C-138/02 *Collins* [2004] ECR I-2703.

cle 24(2) and accordingly not part of the derogation available to Member States. As Fahey has noted, 'it is this fine line between social assistance *simpliciter* and work seeker assistance that the Court ultimately fails to distinguish with force, despite its importance to the interpretation of the Directive and especially to the solidarity provisions'.[34]

Vatsouras hardly inspires confidence in citizenship-building by the Court. There are, after all, limits to how far Article 24(2) can be ignored through interpretation, and the idea of declaring it incompatible with the Treaty is presumably a ship that has sailed already, given the number of decisions about the Directive that have not taken this route. Indeed, the Court in *Vatsouras* expressly stated[35] that the question referred disclosed no factor affecting the validity of Article 24(2), although this negative expression only flows from the fact that the Court had already deemed the exception not to apply in the first place to the type of national benefit at issue. Instead, the evolution of citizenship appears at risk of having stalled in face of determined Member State resistance and an affirmation of the sacred status of workers. It is perhaps no surprise that even the Advocate General in *Förster* argued for the claimant's worker status. Moreover, Advocate General Ruiz-Jarabo Colomer preferred to characterise Messrs Vatsouras and Koupatantze as more than 'ordinary jobseekers'. Even the Court seems to have sent a strong hint to contemplate the application of Article 39 EC (now Article 45 TFEU) for the latter. Indeed, in a curious line of reasoning, the Court stated that Article 24(2) of the Directive had to be interpreted in the light of Article 39(2).[36] This unfortunately begs the question of whether Article 24(2) should be interpreted in the light of the Treaty's citizenship provisions as well, although it is hard to see how this could not also be the case.

Yet if *Förster* and *Vatsouras* display a Court uncertain or disinclined to elaborate citizenship further, the subsequent cases of *Ibrahim* [37]and *Teixeira*[38] provide limited evidence of its more robust pre-Directive thinking being revived. These cases, decided on the same day by the Grand Chamber, were closely similar factually, involving access to the UK's housing assistance regime. In both cases the claimants had been spouses of EU citizens but were no longer living with them and had care responsibilities for the children of those relationships. Both Teixeira (herself an EU citizen) and Ibrahim (a Somali national) had made applications for housing assistance that had been turned down by local authorities. In a challenging approach, the UK government's argument in these cases before the

---

[34] E Fahey, 'Interpretive Legitimacy and the Distinction between "Social Assistance" and "Work Seekers Allowance"' (2009) 34 *European Law Review* 933.

[35] Cases C-22/08 and C-23/08 *Vatsouras and Koupatantze*, above n 26, para 46.

[36] Ibid, para 44.

[37] Case C-310/08 *Ibrahim*, above n 27.

[38] Case C-480/08 *Teixeira*, above n 28.

Court of Justice was built around the idea that Directive 2004/38 had swept away previous law and put in place an exhaustive regime in which the applicants would need to be self-sufficient.

The answers given by the Grand Chamber are interesting on two counts. First, and not altogether surprisingly, it pointedly refused to adopt the arguments of the UK that tried to paint the Directive as a new, restrictive approach. The Court underlined the fact that the Directive had not repealed Article 12 of Regulation 1612/68[39]—a provision which was not dependent on Article 10 of the same legislation (which had been repealed) for the right of residence of children of workers. Thus, maintaining its *Gaal*[40] and *Baumbast*[41] jurisprudence, Article 12 of Regulation 1612/68 is to be applied independently of the EU rules relating to rights of residence in another Member State. Moreover, the Court expressly referred to the *travaux préparatoires* to Directive 2004/38 and to recital 3 of that legislation for this purpose. Thus, a parent who is the primary carer of children of a national of a Member State who works or has worked in the host state can claim a right of residence on the sole basis of Article 12 without being required to satisfy the conditions of Directive 2004/38.[42] Invoking its familiar weapon of effectiveness[43] to interpret Article 12, the Court forcefully refused to turn the fact that the Baumbast family had been self-sufficient into a legal requirement for later cases.[44] Both Teixeira and Ibrahim therefore had a right of residence as primary carers.

This reasoning, although again arguably restricted to a numerically restricted class of potential claimants,[45] can be seen as a more robust defence of solidarity—in the sense of integrating children and families into the host state society—than the more textually evasive approach taken in *Vatsouras*. However, it is still noticeable that the Grand Chamber did not stray far from the general language of effectiveness and the economic objectives of Regulation 1612/68 (designed for workers and their families). In this sense, the Court seems to have preferred the more conservative line taken by Advocate General Mazák in *Ibrahim* rather than the express endorsement of solidarity adopted by Advocate General

[39] [1968] OJ L257/2.
[40] Case C-7/94 *Gaal* [1995] ECR I-1031.
[41] Case Case C-413/99 *Baumbast and R* [2002] ECR I-7091.
[42] *Ibrahim*, para 50; *Teixeira* para 61.
[43] More generally, see M Ross, 'Effectiveness in the European Legal Order(s): Beyond Supremacy to Constitutional Proportionality?' (2006) 31 *European Law Review* 474.
[44] The local authority in *Ibrahim* had tried to elevate self-sufficiency into an essential principle of EC law.
[45] Though the UK may have thought the numbers significant enough to be politically contentious, the Home Office voicing its 'disappointment' with the rulings and council officials saying 'we have a floodgates issue': see 'EU Court Ruling over Migrant UK Child Benefit Claims' reported at www.news.bbc.co.uk/1/hi/england/london/8535625.stm and 'Somali woman in London wins EU case to claim benefits' www.news.bbc.co.uk/1/hi/uk/8532868.stm.

Kokott in *Teixeira*. The latter had pointed to the justification for financial solidarity being owed by the host state as the 'relatively high level
of integration' of both Ms Teixeira, who had been continuously resident
in the UK for 18 years, and her daughter, who had been born in the UK
and had pursued her entire education there.

Nevertheless, and this provides the second point of interest about the
recent cases, the Court did pay attention to the personal circumstances
of the daughter in relation to the relevance of the fact that she had been
aged 15 when the application for housing assistance was made and had
reached the age of majority in UK law by the time the Court heard the
case. Responding directly to the Court of Appeal's question whether the
parent carer's rights ended on majority of the child, the Court replied
that to make the application of Article 12 subject to an age limit or to
the status of the dependent child would conflict with both the letter and
the spirit of that provision. Thus, although a child attaining majority
would be assumed in principle to be capable of meeting their own needs,
the right of residence of a parent 'may nevertheless extend beyond that
age, if the child continues to need the presence and care of that parent
in order to be able to pursue and complete his or her education'.[46] The
key point of more general significance here is that this is a tailored, per-
sonalised assessment of the type that had been prevalent in the *Grzelczyk*
and *Bidar* case law. It is not the general, certainty-oriented proportionality
test of *Förster*. Whilst it may be too early to treat *Förster* as some kind
of submissive aberration on the part of the Court of Justice, the stance in
Teixeira and *Ibrahim* at least potentially restores a person-centred effectiveness approach in the face of rendering politically unpopular results.

At this juncture, it might reasonably be asked whether there is sufficient
evidence in just a handful of post-Directive benefit cases to construct a convincing case for a narrative in which the Court stands up to the avowedly
restrictive political agenda of Member States on the basis of a citizenship
conceptualised around the principled use of solidarity. Or, to put it another
way, whether the case law has travelled in any substantial direction towards
the position canvassed by Advocate General Poiares Maduro, in which

> in principle, a Member State can no longer make an obligation of solidarity
> dependent on integration established by a condition requiring a connection with
> national territory. Citizenship of the Union must encourage Member States to
> no longer conceive of the legitimate link of integration only within the narrow
> bounds of the national community, but also within the wider context of the
> society of peoples of the Union.[47]

---

[46] *Teixeira*, para 86.
[47] Case C-499/06 *Nerkowska* [2008] ECR I-3993 at para 23 of his Opinion. See also
AG Trstenjak in Joined Cases C-396/05, C-419/05 and C-450/05 *Habelt and Others* [2007]
ECR I-11895, paras 82–84.

Since it is perhaps to be expected that the Court would be tentative in dealing with cases bubbling away in the politically hot cauldron of access to welfare benefits, it may be illuminating to consider briefly the evidence from the discussion of citizenship and solidarity in other contexts. Although the illustrations may present less controversy in terms of financial cost for Member States, they still involve issues that may be contentious and sensitive for other reasons closer to either core values or emotional ties.

In particular, it is submitted that the emergence of a jurisprudence addressing obstacles to the enjoyment of citizenship, in effect an analogy to established notions in free movement law,[48] is explicable in terms of weighing the expectations of EU citizens in relation to the solidarity owed them by host states. On one level, these cases could perhaps throw greater light on what it is that makes citizenship 'fundamental'. Cases involving the registration of children's names,[49] the conditions for exemptions from toll road payments to disabled drivers,[50] the withdrawal of naturalised citizenship[51] and restrictions placed upon the numbers of non-resident students having access to particular higher education courses[52] have all been discussed as potential violations of rights conferred by EU citizenship. The feature of these cases is that they subject spheres that are prima facie under Member States' policy control to review against EU citizenship requirements. The relevance of solidarity is in the extent to which it forms part of the proportionality assessment that decides whether a particular State's action is incompatible with those requirements. Whilst it may be argued that the subjecting of these rules to EU law in the first place inevitably follows from the Court's reasoning in *Grzelczyk*,[53] the incorporation of solidarity into the subsequent evaluation methodology is qualitatively a different and additional step. In this sense, whilst the Treaty rules on citizenship play a vital jurisdictional role (taking a set of circumstances beyond the 'purely internal'), it is solidarity that occupies the judgmental aspect for the purposes of deciding the compatibility of a state's act or system of rules with EU law. Thus, although the Court still refers to the obstacles to movement

---

[48] Ie the notions of indistinctly applicable restrictions in relation to goods and non-discriminatory obstacles to the free movement of persons, establishment and services.

[49] Case C 148/02 *Garcia Avello* and Case C-353/06 *Grunkin and Paul*, above n 4.

[50] Case C-103/08 *Gottwald v Bezirkshauptmannschaft Bregenz*, judgment of 1 October 2009.

[51] Case C-135/08 *Rottmann*, above n 19.

[52] Case C-73/08 *Bressol and Others, Chaverot and Others v Gouvernement de la Communauté française* judgment of 13 April 2010.

[53] Art 18(1) TFEU (ex-12 EC) prohibits non-discrimination on grounds of nationality only in situations 'within the scope of application of the Treaties'. Holding the status of an EU citizen in a host state triggers the application of the Treaties. Cf the presumption of equal treatment to be accorded to EU citizens moving to a host state under Art 24(1) of Dir 2004/38.

that might be created for a child in the future through confusion over having different names and documents in different states, the reality in such cases is that Member States are presumed to recognise the chosen personal identity of that child across the EU. Mutual recognition, itself arguably a market subset of the idea of solidarity insofar as it requires sacrifice of autonomy for a wider (economic) benefit, is the departure point here unless rebuttable for EU-compatible reasons. Likewise, in *Rottmann*, the subtext that is arguably at work is that no EU national should be left stateless within the EU political space without a very good justification. Thus a German decision to revoke a naturalised citizenship and, a notable inclusion in the Grand Chamber's judgment, given that it had not yet occurred, any future Austrian decision (not) to reinstate the individual's original nationality are not unfettered national decisions, even though the individual's own deception in obtaining German natu-ralised status might be admissible as a justification for, ultimately, the loss of any EU state nationality and thereby EU citizenship.

The measurement of proportionality was also the key question in *Bres-sol*[54] once it had been (predictably) established that the limitation of students' access to higher education on predominantly residence-based criteria constituted discrimination under the TFEU. The Grand Chamber's ruling is perhaps harder to read in solidarity terms than the other cases here, and not just because the concept is absent from the judgment.[55] On one reading, the Court's forceful rejection of economic justifications for discrimination might imply a more rigorous defence of the mutual soli-darity owed by Member States to each other's non-economic citizens (in this case, students). But, as explicitly articulated by the Advocate General, *Bressol* is a case about a restriction on direct access to education, not just the more indirect question of financial support for studies that has dogged the *Bidar* line of case law. In that sense, *Bressol* could be under-stood as a classic free movement case but with rights of citizenship put on the same footing as the older freedoms. Indeed, the Advocate Gen-eral expressly argued that the 'sufficient integration' tests could not be transposed to the *Bressol* context.[56] Nevertheless, the extremely robust approach taken towards the evidential burden to be satisfied by a Member State in relation to all the pleaded justifications (ie the claims about exces-sive financial burdens, risks to the homogeneity of the education system and threats to the maintenance of national health care levels posed by 'foreign' students not staying after qualification) might also have wider implications to the extent that attempts to circumscribe and limit solidar-

---

[54] Case C-73/08 *Bressol*, above n 52.

[55] AG Sharpston refers to solidarity in the final paragraph of her Opinion but only in the sense of the obligation upon Member States to work together in seeking solutions to common problems such as the effects of student mobility.

[56] Opinion, para 94.

ity obligations in any context might be that much harder to sustain. In short, *Bressol* illustrates the precise issue of discourse and conceptualisation that this chapter seeks to explore. Is it a case about the very essence of a student-citizen's right of mobility[57] or is it about the responsibilities of Member States to demonstrate solidarity towards non-economically active 'foreigners' unless defended against (very) strict evidential requirements? These are closely intertwined factors in *Bressol*, but the preference for the language of citizenship in the judgment may suggest an unwillingness to bite on the arguably more politically contentious delineation of the burdens of solidarity.

A final interesting example (even though decided ultimately in favour of the state) is provided by *Gottwald*, where a disabled German national driving on holiday in Austria sought to challenge a fine imposed for not paying the fees due for travelling on a toll road there. Discs conferring annual exemption from toll payments were available under Austrian law to disabled persons resident or ordinarily resident in Austria. Ordinary residence for this purpose could be established by showing a permanent or regular connection to the territory by, for example, pursuing an occupation, or by private activities of a regular kind in Austria. Having characterised Mr Gottwald as an EU citizen exercising his freedom to move in order to take holidays, the Court of Justice accordingly analysed the rules for toll discs against the Treaty prohibition on nationality discrimination. Noting that the rules did not require any minimum period of residence, the Court found that the indirect discrimination contained in the disc conditions were justified and did not offend proportionality. The national rules were intended to facilitate regular journeys in Austria by disabled persons with a view to their integration in national society and the place of residence was accordingly a suitable and, on the evidence of local application, a broadly interpreted criterion. The apparent weight given to the wide view taken by the Austrian authorities to 'ordinary residence' seems to have been crucial and provides a further example of the individualisation of circumstances being important when applying proportionality. But, of course, the finding that the Austrian position was justifiable and proportionate still suggests that the extent of solidarity actually owed may be relatively modest. This sits in contrast to the more generalised approach in *Bressol*, unless the latter is to be explained by the greater importance (and stricter analysis) attached to a blanket restriction on access to education.

Seen in terms of the constitutional discussion that runs through this volume, these recent cases reveal a difficult tension in the presentation of citizenship. Its fundamental status is hardly confirmed by being the weaker sibling of workers and jobseekers. Yet a stronger content—one

---

[57] See para 79 of the judgment.

that transparently declares obligations of solidarity—is an unpalatable prospect for Member States and one that the Court of Justice seems only to be flirting with at present.

IV   CONCLUSIONS

The complex coupling of citizenship and solidarity, it is submitted, works to the detriment of the latter's development as a *communautaire* concept at a time when the exact opposite might be expected, given the numerous references to solidarity in the amended Treaty on European Union. Whilst some of these might be more rhetorical than real, such as the contribution of the Union to solidarity and mutual respect among peoples in the wider world,[58] it can be expected that others will be subject to much closer and more rigorous judicial scrutiny. These, it is suggested, include the intergenerational solidarity that is demanded by Article 3(3) TEU and the listing of solidarity as one of the core values of the Union in Article 2.

The increasingly granular nature of both citizenship and solidarity, to date, means that these general concepts have been reduced to a degree of factual specificity that undermines their potential as principles of foundational constitutional significance. New cases seemingly have to be analysed according to the type of benefit or claim that is being pursued, yet still often leaving the applicant better off as a worker or jobseeker than as a 'bare' citizen. As the discussion of the case law demonstrates, a cynical interpretation is that citizenship and—especially—solidarity are fine so long as they do not involve too much cost to (usually) the host state. The idea that financial concerns (unreasonable burdens) form the acceptable justifications for limiting citizenship—itself a departure from the attitude adopted in relation to the rule of reason applied to obstacles to the single market—operates as the lifeline for Member States to keep the lid on EU citizenship for the time being. It remains to be seen whether the *Bressol* ruling constitutes a more robust and more generalised defence of citizenship and/or solidarity. It is perhaps too easily characterised as a case so transparently discriminatory and flimsily evidenced in its justifications to serve as a real benchmark of the Court's direction of travel.

Perhaps the key point to emerge from this discussion of recent case law is that the conduct of the discourse of citizenship is absolutely critical to the credibility to be attached to its tag as fundamental. A watershed point appears to have been reached as to just how 'fundamental' EU citizenship can meaningfully be, and the Court is seemingly uncertain as to how best to proceed or the concepts to prioritise. Reinforcing the need to classify individuals according to the legal hat they wear is hardly an

---

[58] Art 3(5) TEU.

upgrade for citizenship; indeed, it is quite possibly the reverse. But, at the same time, subjecting areas of presumptively national discretion to EU law review under the familiar banner of proportionality could prove highly significant, depending upon the intensity of that scrutiny and the criteria that are deployed in its exercise. Proportionality, it should be said, is more than just a procedural device for judicial review of public acts and can instead—depending on what values are used as the appropriate standard—be a substantive methodology for reorienting the balance or direction of citizenship's content.

Here, it is suggested, is the key to understanding solidarity's present significance and power. Rather than becoming fixated on an approach predicated upon elucidating certain fundamental rights of citizenship (hitherto identified as movement, residence and equal treatment—none of which are new in EU law), solidarity potentially scrutinises and limits the resistance of Member States to accommodate the personal situations of other States' nationals and extend social justice to them as part of an EU-wide political community. Yet the response of the Court has been to apply only a limited concept of solidarity that seems to be secondary in the sense of a role in justifying or negating limitations to specific rights within the institution of EU citizenship. Consequently, the preponderance of the case law seems to retain the language of a rights-based, thin, disembodied citizenship capable of being restricted for economic reasons in at least some situations. Indeed, it is notable in *Bressol* that Advocate General Sharpston states that the 'key underlying principle is that all citizens of the Union must be treated as individuals, without regard to their nationality'.[59] Whilst it may be politically more marketable to represent EU citizenship as a body of individual or fundamental rights rather than as obligations of solidarity on Member States (and, at least indirectly, host citizens), that discourse conceals and potentially throttles open engagement with the deeper issue of quite how much solidarity is owed to all EU citizens.

What seems to be up for grabs now is whether the benchmark against which to apply proportionality could engage with broader values than unreasonable financial burdens and, in particular, open up a transparent debate about solidarity even if not immediately endorsing more wide-ranging claims[60] that could argue for its broader constitutional status as an interpretive principle of EU law. Without EU-level solidarity funds in place, such claims will continue to appear highly tentative despite the increasing presence of allusions to solidarity in a wide range of politi-

---

[59] Opinion, para 142.
[60] See M Ross, 'Solidarity—A New Constitutional Paradigm for the EU?' in M Ross and Y Borgmann-Prebil, above n 6, ch 2.

cal developments[61] and EU policy documents.[62] Moreover, it should not be forgotten that solidarity is hardly likely to emerge as (or from) a top-down, imposed strategy. Instead, solidarity is perhaps more plausibly grown from confidence in shared values and transnational approaches to social justice via what is increasingly termed 'reflexive governance'.[63]

It should now be clear that, even if confined to the context of the tendencies of Member States to maintain obstacles against other EU states' nationals in areas of prima facie policy discretion, there is a battle going on over the extent and reasoning behind intervention by EU law. In the context of EU citizenship, that is precisely why solidarity matters. EU citizenship currently owes much of its shape to a rights-led approach that remains strongly susceptible to Member State influence through restrictive justifications that satisfy (often unevenly applied) tests of proportionality. To that extent, the description of the EU as a constitutional order of states holds good. Solidarity, an altogether more powerful or threatening concept, depending on political persuasion, has remained buried or at least camouflaged in the discourse of EU citizenship. The extent to which solidarity becomes an active and articulated element in citizenship and general principles of EU law or takes root in the practices of EU governance will be crucial tests of how far emerging transnational core values can drive constitutional development with less control or direction by Member States.

---

[61] Eg the handling of the recent Greek debt crisis.

[62] Notably in relation to healthcare. See European Commission, 'Solidarity in Health: Reducing Health Inequalities in the EU', COM(2009) 567. See also European Commission, 'Renewed Social Agenda: Opportunities, Access and Solidarity in 21st Century Europe' COM(2008) 412, which claims that 'Solidarity is part of how European society works and how Europe engages with the rest of the world'.

[63] See generally, O de Schutter and J Lenoble (eds), *Reflexive Governance, Redefining the Public Interest in a Pluralistic World* (Oxford, Hart Publishing, 2010).

16

Social Solidarity and
Social Security

ROBIN CA WHITE*

I INTRODUCTORY REMARKS

ALAN DASHWOOD FAMOUSLY described the European
Community as 'a constitutional order of states'.[1] The Treaty of
Maastricht added to that constitutional structure the concept of
citizenship of the Union.[2] This is a citizenship enjoyed and shared by
nationals of all the Member States. Initially ridiculed by some as a cosmetic attempt to bring Europe closer to its people,[3] the concept is being
increasingly used by the Court of Justice as a constitutional status with
real benefits. The current mantra of the Court is as follows:

> in accordance with settled case law, citizenship of the Union is destined to
> be the fundamental status of nationals of the Member States, enabling those
> who find themselves in the same situation to receive the same treatment in
> law irrespective of their nationality, subject to such exceptions as are expressly
> provided for . . .[4]

However, provisions of the Treaty on the Functioning of the European
Union[5] and secondary legislation[6] both include exclusionary words plac-

---

* All views expressed are purely personal.

[1] A Dashwood, 'The Limits of European Community Powers' (1996) 21 *European Law Review* 113, 114.

[2] Now Arts 18–25 TFEU

[3] J Weiler, 'Citizenship and Human Rights' in J Winter, D Curtin, A Kellermann and B de Witte (eds), *Reforming the Treaty on European Union* (The Hague, Kluwer, 1996) 57, especially 65–68.

[4] Case C-103/08 *Gottwald* [2009] ECR I-9117, para 23. See also, among many examples, Case C-209/03 *Bidar* [2005] ECR I-2119, para 31; Case C-403/03 *Schempp* [2005] ECR 6421, para 15; Joined Cases C-482/01 and C-493/01 *Orfanopoulos and Oliveri* [2004] ECR I-5257, para 65; Case C-148/02 *Garcia Avello* [2003] ECR 11613, para 22; and Case C-184/99 *Grzelcyk* [2001] ECR I-6193, para 31. These words are also used in Dir 2004/38/EC on the right of citizens of the Union and their family members to move and reside freely within the territory of the Member States (cited in this chapter as the Citizenship Directive), corrected version at [2004] OJ L229/35, further corrected at [2005] OJ L197/34, preamble, para 3, giving them legislative legitimacy.

[5] Arts 20 and 21 TFEU.

[6] Citizenship Directive, preamble, para 1.

ing limitations on the benefits which flow alone from enjoying the status of a citizen of the Union. The genetic code in the Treaty[7] is slowly but surely being unravelled to reveal a powerful constitutional status, and a corresponding narrowing of the limitations in its application.[8] The status is of real benefit to the 500 million citizens of the Union, particularly when they are in a Member State other than that of their own nationality. The current battleground is the extent to which the status itself entitles citizens to equal treatment with nationals when they are in a Member State other than that of their own nationality, and, in the period prior to the acquisition of permanent resident status,[9] need some form of assistance from the Member State of residence.

The enquiry in this chapter explores the extent to which the constitutional status of citizenship of the Union is reflected in national practice in the field of social security in the UK. In doing so, it touches on the distinction between social security and social assistance, and reflects on whether the case law of the Court of Justice of the European Union is generating a principle of social solidarity required of Member States when addressing the needs of citizens of the Union who are not their own nationals.

The context is the requirements in UK social security law that, to be entitled to housing assistance and certain means-tested benefits, the claimant must have a 'right to reside' in the UK, the Channel Islands, the Isle of Man or the Republic of Ireland.[10] The phrase 'right to reside' is not defined, but it is readily conceded that a person's right to reside may flow from European Union law just as much as national law.[11] What has proved highly contentious is when a person has a 'right to reside' under European Union law.

The question of who has a right to reside has proved troublesome for First-tier Tribunals, the Upper Tribunal[12] and the courts. There are two recent judgments on references from UK courts to the Court of Justice and at least a further three pending references touching on who has a right to reside, and when such a right arises.

---

[7] A phrase coined in F Mancini and D Keeling, 'Democracy and the European Court of Justice' (1994) 57 *Modern Law Review* 175, 186.

[8] See M Dougan, 'The Constitutional Dimension to the Case Law on Union Citizenship' (2006) 31 *European Law Review* 613.

[9] After five years of lawful residence: Art 16 of the Citizenship Directive.

[10] See generally A Berry, 'Social Rights under Directive 2004/38/EC' [2007] *Journal of Immigration Asylum and Nationality Law* 233.

[11] P Larkin, 'The Limits to European Social Citizenship in the United Kingdom' (2005) 68 *Modern Law Review* 435.

[12] The Social Entitlement Chamber of First-tier Tribunals hears first instance appeals in social security matters, with an appeal on a point of law, with permission, lying to the Administrative Appeals Chamber of the Upper Tribunal. Thereafter appeal lies to the Court of Appeal and House of Lords.

II THE CITIZENSHIP DIRECTIVE
AND SOCIAL ENTITLEMENTS

A Background

The Citizenship Directive provides that Member States need not grant social assistance in the first three months of residence, and must grant complete equality of treatment once permanent residence is acquired after five years of lawful residence.[13] Entitlement arising in the period from three months until permanent residence is attained would seem to turn on the degree of social integration of the citizen in the fabric of the host Member State.[14] Residence conditions for benefit entitlements might be appropriate provided that they pursue a legitimate public interest and are proportionate.[15]

Where a person has, or is able to retain, worker status, there is a further route to benefit entitlement in Article 7(2) of Regulation 1612/68,[16] which requires workers to be afforded the same social and tax advantages as nationals. This covers not just social security benefits and social assistance, but all manner of benefits flowing from worker status. In addition, Article 12 of Regulation 1612/68 provides:

> The children of a national of a Member State who is or has been employed in the territory of another Member State shall be admitted to that State's general educational, apprenticeship and vocational training courses under the same conditions as the nationals of that State, if such children are residing in its territory.
>
> Member States shall encourage all efforts to enable such children to attend these courses under the best possible conditions.

Additionally, there is the possibility that claims to equality of treatment with nationals, and so entitlement to all the benefits those nationals would receive in the same circumstances, may be grounded in the rights to be found in Article 21 TFEU where that article alone gives the claimant

---

[13] Art 24 of the Citizenship Directive. Art 16 requires a person to have 'resided legally for a continuous period of five years' in order to acquire permanent residence. What constitutes legal residence has proved contentious.

[14] See, by analogy, the ruling in Case C-209/03 *Bidar* [2005] ECR I-2119, which concerned entitlement to educational grants under the pre-existing Community provisions. This case established a number of principles but was not decided on the basis of the terms of the Citizenship Directive. See also C O'Brien, 'Real links, Abstract Rights and False Alarms: the Relationship between the ECJ's "Real Link" Case Law and National Solidarity' (2008) 33 *European Law Review* 643.

[15] See Case C-138/02 *Collins* [2004] ECR I-2703; see also commentaries by O Golynker, 'Jobseekers' Rights in the European Union: Challenges of Changing the Paradigm of Social Solidarity' (2005) 30 *European Law Review* 111; and J. Muelman and H de Waele, 'Funding the Life of Brian: Jobseekers, Welfare Shopping and the Frontiers of European Citizenship' (2004) 31 *Legal Issues of Economic Integration* 275.

[16] [1968] OJ L257. See, eg Case C-212/05 *Hartmann* [2007] ECR I-6303.

a right to reside in the host Member State. It will be recalled that the Court of Justice in *Baumbast and R*[17] ruled that there could be rights of residence flowing from what was then Article 18 EC in circumstances not contemplated by the provisions on the free movement of persons and the secondary legislation implementing those rights where the situation was sufficiently analogous to those for which specific provision had been made, and where the application of restrictions by the host Member State would not be proportionate.[18] The Court ruled:

> [A] citizen of the European Union who no longer enjoys a right of residence as a migrant worker in the host Member State can, as a citizen of the Union, enjoy there a right of residence by direct application of Article 18(1) EC. The exercise of that right is subject to the limitations and conditions referred to in that provision, but the competent authorities and, where necessary, the national courts must ensure that those limitations and conditions are applied in compliance with the general principles of Community law and, in particular, the principle of proportionality.[19]

B   Transposition of the Citizenship Directive in the UK

The earlier free movement directives have been transposed into national regulations by the Home Office as immigration regulations. That pattern was followed in relation to transposition of the Citizenship Directive, notwithstanding that it is more than an immigration measure. The current national regulations are The Immigration (European Economic Area) Regulations 2006, as amended in 2009.[20] Somewhat anomalously (given the restrictive view taken by the national institutions of the right to reside), those regulations go beyond the requirements of the Directive in one respect in regarding as a qualified person (and so having a right to reside) someone who is a jobseeker.[21]

The transposition of the Citizenship Directive has proved to be problematic in all the Member States. In its December 2008 report,[22] the Commission reported that no Member State had, in its view, fully imple-

---

[17] Case C-413/99 *Baumbast and R* [2002] ECR I-7091.
[18] Paras 76–96.
[19] Para 94.
[20] SI 1996/1003 as amended by SI 2009/1117.
[21] Reg 6(1)(a) of the Immigration (European Economic Area) Regulations 2006. Simply being a jobseeker appears to give the right of residence. But note that there is doubt about whether a person who has ceased to be self-employed can be a jobseeker: *Secretary of State for Work and Pensions v RK* [2009] UKUT 208 (AAC).
[22] 'Report from the Commission to the European Parliament and the Council on the Application of Directive 2004/38/EC on the Right of Citizens of the Union and their Family Members to Move and Reside Freely within the Territory of the Member States', COM(2008) 840/3. See also 'Communication for the Commission to the European Parliament and the Council on Guidance for Better Transposition and Application of Directive 2004/38/EC

mented the requirements of the Directive, and that no single provision of the Directive had been fully implemented in every Member State. Why should this be so?

Though the drafting of the Citizenship Directive leaves much to be desired and hardly disguises the political compromises it contains, the poor implementation of the Directive is not, in my view, wholly the fault of its drafters.

In relation to the UK, some of the difficulties of interpretation have arisen because the Department for Work and Pensions has elected in drafting national legislation to make entitlement to certain means-tested benefits conditional on the claimant having a right to reside. The concept is being used for purposes rather different from the determination of immigration status.

There is a second condition of entitlement to the benefits which require the claimant to have a right to reside; such claimants must also have their 'habitual residence' in the UK.[23] This was an earlier requirement which at the time stood alone. It was designed to narrow the group of new arrivals who would be eligible for means-tested benefits. After several years of litigation, both in tribunals and in the courts, the requirement of habitual residence has come to be regarded by decision makers in the Department for Work and Pensions as largely satisfied once someone has been here for three months, notwithstanding the more detailed requirements of the formal legal test.[24]

There have been further complications because of transitional arrangements operative for A8 and A2 nationals, but the specific problems of application of the requirement to show a right to reside for this group are not the subject of this chapter, since many cases which have come before tribunals and courts involve nationals of other Member States who are not in any transitional situation.

[2004] L229/35, on the Right of Citizens of the Union and their Family Members to Move and Reside Freely within the Territory of the Member States', COM(2009) 313/4.

[23] Introduced in 1994, and which led to a number of challenges in relation to its compatibility with European Union law. See generally, M Adler, 'The Habitual Residence Test: a Critical Analysis' (1995) 2 *Journal of Social Security Law* 179; S Cox, 'The Habitual Residence Test and EC Law' (1999) 21 *Journal of Social Welfare and Family Law* 416; P Rogerson, 'Habitual Residence: the New Domicile?' (2000) 49 *International & Comparative Law Quarterly* 86; and E Crawford, 'Payment Postponed: Exploring the Extent of Nacca's Authority' (2003) 10 *Journal of Social Security Law* 52.

[24] P Wood et al, *Social Security Legislation 2010/11. Volume II, Income Support, Jobseeker's Allowance, State Pension Credit and the Social Fund* (London, Sweet & Maxwell, 2010), para 2,175. The habitual residence test is not applicable to many EEA nationals. See generally Case C-90/97 *Swaddling* [1999] ECR I-1075.

III DECISION-MAKING IN UNITED
KINGDOM COURTS AND TRIBUNALS

A Taking a Narrow View of the Right to Reside in the National Legal Order

I do not know the overall number of social security appeals to First-tier Tribunals involving issues of the right to reside, but I do know that the number of appeals finding their way to the Upper Tribunal runs into the hundreds. Housing assistance cases go elsewhere and tend to become visible when an appeal against the local authority's decision wends its way through the county courts to the Court of Appeal, or when a decision is challenged through judicial review.

The approach of the Secretary of State for Work and Pensions, who will be the respondent in proceedings before the First-tier Tribunal in social security cases, has been to take a very narrow view of the right to reside.[25] The starting point for national authorities is, of course, the national regulations which implement the Citizenship Directive.

Let me give a very simple example from the one appeal I have determined as a Judge of the Upper Tribunal, since in some ways it typifies the national approach.[26] I can do so because the outcome is, I think, uncontentious (and my decision has not been appealed). It is immaterial that I was concerned with the predecessor to the 2006 regulations which implemented the pre-Citizenship Directive equivalents to the provision of the Citizenship Directive. The appeal concerned a Dutch national (of Somali origin) with two young children. She arrived in the UK in June 2004. She worked as a shop cleaner for nine months, from December 2004 to September 2005, when she was made redundant. In November 2005 she claimed income support for herself and her children. The decision maker ruled that she was not entitled to the benefit since she had no right to reside in the UK. The First-tier Tribunal found in her favour, accepting her evidence that she had spent time looking for other work before claiming. The Secretary of State appealed. The Secretary of State argued that she had severed her relationship with the labour market by leaving her work in September and not claiming benefit for two months. Furthermore, she had claimed income support rather than jobseeker's allowance—the tribunal had found that she claimed this benefit because she had been so advised by the Department for Work and

---

[25] There is the possibility of enforcement action against the UK over its approach to the right to reside. The Child Poverty Action Group has reported (P Fitzpatrick, 'UK's Application of EC Law Investigated' (October 2009) *Welfare Rights Bulletin* No 212, 4) that the Commission has responded to its expressions of concern about the application of the 'right to reside by communicating its intention to treat the CPAG representations as a formal complaint'.

[26] CIS/0519/2007 (unreported).

Pensions. The Department for Work and Pensions also argued that she had not had her involuntary unemployment registered in an employment office, though they also had to concede that the Department had no procedures for enabling this to be done.[27] I upheld the tribunal's decision that she remained a worker, and hence had a right to reside in European Union law. I also ruled that, although a long delay in claiming benefit could indicate that someone had severed their connections with the labour market, a short delay,[28] as in this case, did not have that result. Furthermore, there was nothing inconsistent in claiming income support and being available for work; the benefit can be awarded to those in part-time work not exceeding 16 hours a week. A person working, say, 15 hours a week would almost certainly have little difficulty in establishing that such work was genuine and effective work to the exclusion of work that is purely marginal or ancillary so that she would be a worker within what was then Article 39 EC. Though the tribunal had not spelled things out in quite the detail I was able to do at the appellate level, they had essentially come to the same conclusion for the same reasons. I therefore dismissed the Secretary of State's appeal.

What are some of the other issues which have become contentious? Do the *Baumbast* principles remain? In some cases, it has been argued that the Citizenship Directive is a complete code, which replaces not only the repealed legislation, but also certain principles established in pre-existing case law from the Court of Justice. What periods are taken into account in determining whether a person has obtained permanent residence? What impact does the holding of a residence permit under the previous regime with an unexpired period on it have on a person's right to reside? What does 'legally reside' mean in the Directive?

B   Guidance from the Court of Justice

(i)   Five References from UK Courts

There have been five references from UK courts relating to the interpretation of the Citizenship Directive and the meaning of the right to reside. Two rulings have been given; in a further case the Advocate General has delivered her Opinion, and the final two cases remain pending.[29]

The two cases where rulings have been made relate to the right to reside of a parent whose children are in education.[30] The Advocate General has

---

[27] Other than in connection perhaps with making a claim to jobseeker's allowance.

[28] The First-tier Tribunal had found as a fact that the claimant was looking for work during this period.

[29] As at 1 September 2010.

[30] See *London Borough of Harrow v Ibrahim and Secretary of State for the Home Department* [2008] EWCA Civ 386; *Teixeira v London Borough of Lambeth* [2008] EWCA Civ

308 Robin CA White

delivered her Opinion in a reference concerning the interpretation of the temporal aspects of the operation of Article 16 of the Citizenship Directive.[31] The two pending cases also concern the detail of the way in which a right of permanent residence can be acquired. The *McCarthy* case[32] concerns the concept of legal residence, while the *Dias* case[33] concerns the effect of a period of prior residence under a residence permit issued under the provisions replaced by the Citizenship Directive.

(ii)   The Right to Reside of Parents of Children in Education

Both *Ibrahim* and *Teixeira* concerned the right to reside of the parent of children who were in education in the context of claims for housing assistance. They raised questions concerning the interpretation of Article 12 of Regulation 1612/68 and of the principles established in the *Baumbast* case.[34] The cases might have been joined, but it appears that they were not, because *Ibrahim* concerned a claim by a third-country national married to a citizen of the Union, whereas *Teixeira* concerned a claim by a Portuguese national.

Ibrahim concerned a Somali woman with four children, who was married to a Danish national. Some of the children were in primary education throughout the relevant period. The husband had worked in the UK, but became unfit for work and received benefit. The couple became estranged and the husband left the country. There was a brief reconciliation some time later, but this did not work out. The couple remained married. The woman applied for housing assistance for herself and her children. She argued that she had a right to reside as the parent of children in education, relying on Article 12 of Regulation 1612/68 and the principles established in the *Baumbast* case. The local authority and the Home Secretary argued that the woman could only have a right to reside if she could bring herself within the terms of the Citizenship Directive, which, they argued, was a complete code which had replaced any earlier case law entitlement.

Teixeira was also a homelessness case. Advocate General Kokott neatly summarises the question raised by the Court of Appeal in this case:

1088; and now Case C-310/08 *Ibrahim* Judgment of 23 February 2010 and Case C-480/08 *Teixeira* Judgment of 23 February 2010. Both judgments are of the Grand Chamber.

[31] *Secretary of State for Work and Pensions v Lassal* [2009] EWCA Civ 157. Case C-162/09 *Lassal* [2009] OJ C153/29 (pending). Advocate General's Opinion of 11 May 2010.

[32] *McCarthy v Secretary of State for the Home Department* [2008] EWCA Civ 641. Case C-434/09 *McCarthy* [2010] OJ C11/18 (pending).

[33] *Secretary of State for Work and Pensions v Dias* [2009] EWCA Civ 807. Case C-325/09 *Dias* [2009] OJ C256/13 (pending).

[34] See text accompanying n 17 above.

Can a Union citizen who is not gainfully employed and who does not have sufficient resources of her own claim a right of residence as her daughter's carer in the Member State in which her daughter, as the child of a former migrant worker, is in education?

The UK government, supported in this argument by the Danish and Irish governments, argued that the Citizenship Directive provided the sole basis for the conditions governing the right of residence, with the result that no right of residence could, following the entry into force of the Citizenship Directive, be derived from Article 12 of Regulation 1612/68. This argument is roundly rejected by the Court of Justice. There was nothing to suggest that the Citizenship Directive was intended to be a complete code which limited the normative content of Article 12 of Regulation 1612/68 to a mere right of access to education.[35] Indeed, the objective of the Citizenship Directive was to simplify and strengthen the right of free movement and residence. The proper interpretation of Article 12 of Regulation 1612/68 is that children have, in connection with the right of access to education, an independent right of residence where they are residing in a Member State in which one of their parents is or has been employed.[36] The continuing application of the ruling in the *Baumbast* case is expressly confirmed to the effect that a parent (regardless of their nationality) who is the primary carer of a child exercising the rights in Article 12 of Regulation 1612/68 has a right of residence during the period of the child's education in order to make the right to education practical and effective.[37]

The second issue was whether the right to reside of the child and the parent is conditional on the family having sufficient resources and comprehensive sickness insurance cover. The Court observes that Regulation 1612/68 makes no reference to such conditions, and that there is nothing in the Citizenship Directive to bring those conditions into play.

The ruling in the *Teixeira* case is the same, but adds two further clarifications. It is not necessary for one of the parents to have been a migrant worker 'at the precise moment when the child started in education'.[38] However, the right to reside of a parent in the capacity of primary carer 'ends when the child reaches the age of majority, unless the child continue to need the presence and care of the parent in order to be able to pursue and complete his or her education'.[39]

The outcome of these cases is dramatic. The tendency of Member States to make the right to reside in all circumstances conditional on self-sufficiency is severely eroded. The conditions of self-sufficiency and of

[35] Para 45.
[36] Para 33.
[37] Paras 47 and 55.
[38] Para 72.
[39] Para 87.

having comprehensive medical cover apply only where these are expressly mentioned as conditions of residence. The rulings are, however, entirely consistent with a policy of encouraging integration of those exercising the right of free movement into the host Member State. In very many cases, the limitation that the right to reside of the parent as primary carer will end when the child reaches the age of majority will not be a major inhibition, since very many such parents will have acquired permanent residence under the Citizenship Directive by that time.

These rulings also make clear that the Citizenship Directive is just one part of the bundle of rights relating to the right of free movement of citizens of the Union. The rights in the Directive must be read in the context of both the provisions of the Treaty on citizenship, but also in the context of other provisions of the secondary legislation of the Union. In interpreting national legislation implementing the Citizenship Directive, it will be necessary to look beyond the Citizenship Directive alone and to consider the place of that measure in the larger bundle of rights which flow from the Treaty and the secondary legislation of the Union. There is a progressive continuity in the rights attaching to citizens of the Union.

(iii)   Acquiring Permanent Residence

The questions raised in the *Lassal* case[40] concerned the extent to which a person could claim the right of permanent residence on the basis of lawful residence prior to the date for implementation of the Citizenship Directive. Taous Lassal, a French national, had been a worker in the UK from September 1999 to February 2005. She then gave up work and returned to France to visit her mother. She returned to the UK in December 2005 and looked for work. She was paid unemployment benefits from January to November 2006. In November 2006, she claimed income support, a means-tested benefit, on the basis that she was pregnant, but her claim was refused.

In the *McCarthy* case[41] the House of Lords asked whether a person with dual Irish and British nationality who had lived all her life in the UK could claim to be a beneficiary of the provisions of the Citizenship Directive, and whether she had 'resided legally' within the host Member State for the purpose of Article 16 of the Directive in circumstances where she was unable to satisfy the requirements of Article 7 of the Citizenship Directive. In the *Dias* case[42] questions were raised relating to the computation of the period of five years of lawful residence required to qualify for permanent resident status. The circumstances of the claimant provide

---

[40] *Lassal*, above n 31. Advocate General's Opinion of 11 May 2010. See now judgment of 7 October 2010.
[41] *McCarthy*, above n 32. See now Advocate General's Opinion of 25 November 2010.
[42] *Dias*, above n 33.

a helpful illustration of the potential problems which arise in determining entitlement to permanent resident status. Maria Dias is a Portuguese single parent with the following pattern of residence in the UK:

- Arrived in January 1998 and in work until the summer of 2002;
- 13 May 2000: granted a residence permit valid until 13 May 2005;
- Summer 2002 to 17 April 2003: on maternity leave;
- 18 April 2003 to 25 April 2004: not working;
- 26 April 2004 to 23 March 2007: in work;
- 23 March 2007 onwards: not working;
- March 2007: claimed means-tested benefit.

It was argued that the significance of the residence permit was that it covered a period when Maria Dias was not working; she argued that she was residing legally during this period, notwithstanding that she was not economically active. This allowed her to join up the earlier periods of residence as a worker with economically active residence from 26 April 2004 until after the entry into force of the Citizenship Directive. Therefore she had a right of permanent residence and so was entitled to means-tested benefits on the same terms as applied to UK nationals.

Advocate General Trstenjak delivered her Opinion in the *Lassal* case on 11 May 2010. The questions posed by the national court raised a number of issues requiring advice from the Court of Justice.

First, could permanent residence, as a new right introduced by the Citizenship Directive, only be acquired on the basis of lawful residence after 1 May 2006? This would mean that no one could acquire permanent residence prior to May 2011. It was argued that recital (17) in the preamble to the Citizenship Directive containing reference to residence 'in the host Member State in accordance with the conditions laid down in this Directive' led to this outcome. The Advocate General recognises the complexity and ambiguity of the words of the recital, and expresses some sympathy with the view that a right of permanent residence only arises where 'the continuous period of five years' residence has been completed in accordance with the provisions of Community law'.[43] She comes to no clear conclusion on this issue, but is clear that 'a period of residence completed in accordance with the predecessor provisions of Directive 2003/38 is also a period of legal residence under Article 16(1)'.[44] That must surely be right, and it would be a shock if the Court of Justice did not take the same view.

Secondly, could permanent residence arise prior to 1 May 2006? It follows from the conclusions of the Advocate General in her Opinion that a right of permanent residence cannot arise until the implementation date of

---

[43] [2003] OJ L120/22; para 88 of the Opinion.
[44] Para 93 of the Opinion.

the Citizenship Directive. That would be determined by either the expiry of the implementation date in the Directive, namely 1 May 2006, or from an earlier date on which a Member State correctly transposed the requirements of the Directive. That too would seem to be a conclusion which is unlikely to be contradicted by the ruling of the Court of Justice.

Thirdly, could permanent residence arise by completion of a period of residence completed prior to the entry into force of the Directive? In the particular circumstances of the *Lassal* case, could Taous Lassal claim a right of permanent residence in November 2006 on the basis of having resided and worked in the UK from September 1999 to February 2005?

The Advocate General concludes that the terms of Article 16(4) are determinative here. This provides: 'Once acquired, the right of permanent residence shall be lost only through absence from the host Member State for a period exceeding two consecutive years'.

The Advocate General acknowledges (with rather obscure reasoning) that periods of residence in the distant past should not ground claims to permanent residence, but emphasises that the Directive:

> . . . proceeds from the assumption that the required level of integration is achieved where there has been a continuous period of five years' residence and that the required link with the host state no longer exists after a period of absence of two years.[45]

The result is that, provided there has not been a period of more than two years' absence on a date on or after 1 May 2006[46] from the date on which a person had completed at least five years' continuous residence, then that person has a right of permanent residence. In other words, in November 2006, Taous Lassal could ground a claim to permanent residence on her period as a worker between September 1999 and February 2005.

An interpretative approach to the Citizenship Directive which focuses on the achievement of a particular level of social integration is supported by this approach to the acquisition of permanent residence, but it will require national decision makers to abandon a narrow, perhaps pedantic, approach to the basis of residence at any given time.

Applying this reasoning to the circumstances in the *Dias* case would result in the conclusion that she had the status of permanent resident from 30 April 2006, since the residence prior to that date was all residence in accordance with either the Citizenship Directive or its predecessor measures. It would be exceedingly strange to rule that the period when she was not working but was the holder of a Community residence permit did not count as lawful residence under Community law.

---

[45] Para 96 of the Opinion.

[46] Or an earlier date if the national implementing measure so provides. In the UK the operative date is 30 April 2006. The Opinion is broadly followed in the judgment of the Court of 7 October 2010.

That leaves the questions referred in the *McCarthy* case. The response to the first question looks straightforward. Article 3 describes the beneficiaries of the Directive as those who 'move to or reside in a Member State other than that of which they are a national'. Shirley McCarthy resides in the UK while holding the nationality of both the UK and Ireland. The Court has always taken a broad view of nationality, and has been resistant to approaches within Member States which seek to deny the holding of a particular nationality.[47] The second question raised will require the Court of Justice to provide guidance on the nature of the exercise of rights of residence, and whether a sharp distinction should be drawn between rights arising under the Citizenship Directive, under Article 21 TFEU, and those arising under under national law. It is to be hoped that the social integration approach is followed, which would allow the appropriate level of social integration to be achieved whatever the basis of the lawful residence in the host Member State. It would be consistent with the approach adopted in the *Trojani* case[48] to define lawful residence as including residence lawful under national law. In the *Trojani* case the Court of Justice ruled that equal treatment under what was then Article 12 EC was required in relation to lawful residence for a certain time regardless of whether that residence arose under Community law, or under national law.

(iv) The Writing on the Wall

It would be surprising if the Court of Justice departed from an integrationist line in responding to these references. That line has been firmly established in the two rulings already issued, and is signalled—albeit with some mild reservations—in the Advocate General's Opinion in the *Lassal* case. If this prediction is correct and the outcome is that there are more wide-ranging rights of residence flowing from European Union law than the UK government had assumed in its social security legislation, then there will be a welcome entitlement to housing and other social assistance for a group of migrants who can either more readily establish permanent residence[49] or can argue that they are on the way to full social integration into the UK. The words of Advocate General Kokott in the *Teixeira* case

---

[47] Case C-369/90 *Micheletti* [1992] ECR I-4239, although this case concerned an attempt to give priority to the nationality of Argentina at the expense of that of Italy. The question of recognition did not involve the denial of the nationality of one Member State against another. But in Case C-200/02 *Zhu and Chen* [2004] ECR I-9925 Catherine Chen was able to rely on her Irish nationality in a claim against the UK, whose nationality she also held without having moved from Ireland to the UK.

[48] Case C-456/02 *Trojani* [2004] ECR I-7573.

[49] Indeed, in Case C-480/08 *Teixeira*, the Advocate General questions whether Teixeira (i) had not, in fact, acquired permanent residence at the date of her claim or (ii) could not establish an entitlement to equal treatment on the basis of the *Trojani* case, and invites the national authorities to consider these questions: paras 116–22 of the Opinion.

seem apposite in support of this approach:

> Moreover, a certain degree of financial solidarity by the host Member State with nationals of other Member States has, until now, already been inherent in all Community instruments relating to the rights of free movement and residence, not least in regard to persons not gainfully employed . . . This idea finds renewed expression in the preamble to Directive 2004/38 in that, even during a person's initial period of residence in the host Member State, recourse to the social assistance system is not categorically ruled out, although it should not become an unreasonable burden on the system . . . In addition, Article 14(3) of Directive 2004/38 provides that an expulsion measure is not to be the automatic consequence of a Union citizen's or his or her family member's recourse to the social assistance system.[50]

IV DISTINGUISHING SOCIAL SECURITY AND SOCIAL ASSISTANCE

European Union secondary legislation refers to social assistance but does not define it.[51] Nor has the Court of Justice provided a definitive definition of social assistance and its relationship with social security. The most comprehensive summary of a line of case law can be found in the Opinion of Advocate General Kokott in the *Skalka* case.[52]

The Court of Justice has said in a number of cases that a benefit is a social security benefit:

> insofar as it is granted, without any individual and discretionary assessment of personal needs, to recipients on the basis of a legally defined position and relates to one of the risks expressly listed in Article 4(1) of Regulation No 1408/71.[53]

However, the distinction between social security and social assistance is not always easy to draw. The *Hughes* case[54] concerned a claim to family credit, a UK cash-based means-tested non-contributory weekly benefit designed to top up the earnings of families in low-paid work. The UK argued that it was social assistance. The Court reiterated its earlier case law and, in doing so, addressed a specific objection of the UK government

---

[50] [2004] OJ L120/22; Case C-480/08 *Teixeira* judgment of 23 February 2010, para 82 of the Opinion (footnotes omitted).

[51] Social assistance is referred to as outside the scope of Reg 883/2004/EC on the coordination of social security systems, corrected version at [2004] OJ L200I, under Art 3(5) of that regulation; and in Art 24(2) of the Citizenship Directive.

[52] Case C-160–02 *Skalka* [2004] ECR I-1771. See paras 50–56 of the Opinion.

[53] Case C-215/99 *Jauch* [2001] ECR I-1901, para 25. The eight heads of benefit referred to in Art 4(1) of Reg 1408/71 are sickness and maternity benefits; invalidity benefits; old-age benefits; survivors' benefits; benefits for accidents at work and occupational diseases; death grants; unemployment benefits; and family benefits. Reg 883/2004 adds two further areas: paternity benefits and early retirement benefits.

[54] Case C-78/91 *Hughes* [1992] ECR I-4839

to the effect that the claimant was not in a legally defined position because the benefit was subject to a means test. The Court said that the need to satisfy an individual assessment of needs did not preclude the benefit from being social security, since the criteria applied were objective, legally defined criteria which, if met, conferred an entitlement to the benefit.[55] The Court went on to find that there was a sufficient link with the family for the benefit to constitute a family benefit falling within Article 4(1) (h) of Regulation 1408/71. Advocate General Kokott in *Skalka* questions whether the analysis in *Hughes* should be generalised:

> 53. . . . The definition of a social security benefit, as it is construed in that judgment, might, conversely, support the argument that a benefit constitutes social assistance only if it is granted on the basis of an assessment of the needs of the person concerned, which falls within the discretion of the competent authority, rather than on the basis of objective, legally defined criteria.

> 54. However, in many national legal orders, social assistance is granted on the basis of objective, legally defined criteria for assessing personal need simply so as to observe the principle of equal treatment. Furthermore, guaranteeing the minimum level of subsistence is no longer considered to be a charitable measure on the part of the State. On the contrary, in many modern welfare States, individuals have such a right as an expression of their human dignity.

> 55. It follows that a benefit can display social assistance features, which are the criteria necessary for its classification as a special benefit, even when it is granted according to personal need which can be determined on the basis of objective, legally defined criteria.

The trend over many years in the UK has been to make means-tested benefits a matter of legal entitlement when statutory conditions are met.[56] There is usually no link with insurance in the context of benefits which are income-related. This makes the dividing line between social security and social assistance much more difficult to place. This is especially true in the UK, where some benefits designed to meet the same social need exist in a contribution-based form and on an income-related basis.[57]

It is possible to discern a trend to reduce the scope of social assistance in the case law of the Court of Justice. In the *Vatsouras and Koupatantze* case,[58] the Court was considering a German means-tested benefit in favour of jobseekers. The Court ruled:

> Benefits of a financial nature which, independently of their status under national law, are intended to facilitate access to the labour market cannot be regarded as

---

56 See R Titmuss, 'Welfare "Rights", Law and Discretion' (1971) 42 *Political Quarterly* 113.
57 Current examples are employment and support allowance, and jobseeker's allowance.
58 Joined Cases C-22/08 and 23/08 *Vatsouras and Koupatantze*, judgment of 4 June 2009.

constituting 'social assistance' within the meaning of Article 24(2) of Directive 2004/38.[59]

V   SOCIAL SOLIDARITY AS A COMMUNITY PRINCIPLE

A CEPS Special Report notes:

> one of the most common sources of friction between citizens of the Union and host Member States arises around access to social benefits . . . Member States tend to apply a sufficient resources test to all citizens of the Union whether or not they are workers or self-employed . . .[60]

Writing in the CESIfo DICE Report 4/2006, which is devoted to a number of comments on the Citizenship Directive, Hailbronner refers to the Court of Justice's concept of social solidarity,[61] although he is critical of the deliberate ambiguities left in the Citizenship Directive by the legislature, as well as the fact that the 'Court has never even considered the potential economic impact of its social benefits legislation'.[62]

In his legal analysis of citizenship of the Union, Francis Jacobs comments:

> It seems worth keeping in mind—when discussing the balancing of citizenship rights and national welfare systems—that financial obligations might also arise for states as a consequence of merely respecting the right to residence on the basis of citizenship. Though a right to residence as such is a non-financial benefit, there is also a risk for the host state to face costs in case the citizen is not capable of covering his own expenses.[63]

That is exactly the position in which the UK finds itself, and its choice of requiring a right to reside as a condition of entitlement to benefits might spectacularly backfire in that what it has seen as a restrictive condition of entitlement may become an expansive condition of entitlement.

Mention has already been made of Advocate General Kokott's reference to a degree of financial solidarity in this area. I would argue that it is not surprising to find notions of national solidarity which underpin

[59] Para 45.
[60] S Carrera and A Faure Atger, 'Implementation of Directive 2004/38 in the Context of EU Enlargement. A Proliferation of Different Forms of Citizenship', CEPS Special Report/ April 2009, para 2.2.3; see also para 2.2.4.2.
[61] K Hailbronner, 'The EU Directive on Free Movement and Access to Social Benefits', CESIfo DICE Report 4/2006, 8, available at http://www.cesifo-group.de/ (accessed 4 December 2009). See also K Hailbronner, 'Union Citizenship and Access to Social Benefits' (2005) 42 *Common Market Law Review* 1245; and various contributions in U Neergaard, R Nielsen and L Roseberry (eds), *Integrating Welfare Functions into EU Law* (Copenhagen, DJØF 2009).
[62] Ibid, 13.
[63] F G Jacobs, 'Citizenship of the European Union—A Legal Analysis' (2007) 13 *European Law Journal* 591, 596.

national social security systems overflowing into the transnational arena as a result of the creation of citizenship of the Union. The concept of solidarity is, of course, very well known to European Union law, finding Treaty expression in Article 10 EC.[64]

Solidarity is a key aspect of national social security systems.[65] It is often embodied in the principle that a nation will act in solidarity with individuals who need support. But it is also a principle which is recognised at the European Union level. Advocate General Fennelly described social solidarity as envisaging 'the inherently uncommercial act of involuntary subsidisation of one social group to another'.[66] Nor has the concept gone unnoticed by academic commentators.[67]

Pieters speaks of circles of solidarity.[68] Traditionally the circle of solidarity has been drawn around the nationals of a state (and those assimilated with nationals). Citizenship of the Union challenges us to broaden the circle of solidarity, so that solidarity operates to protect not just the nationals of the Member State concerned, but also those with whom those nationals share a citizenship of the Union. There are signs of a widening of the circles of solidarity, but there are also signs of a tightening of

---

[64] Following entry into force of the Treaty of Lisbon, Art 10 is not re-enacted as part of the TFEU, but rather located in the Treaty on European Union as Art 4(3), which reads:

Pursuant to the principle of sincere co-operation, the Union and the Member States shall, in full mutual respect, assist each other in carrying out tasks which flow from the Treaties.

The Member States shall take any appropriate measure, general or particular, to ensure fulfilment of the obligations arising out of the Treaties or resulting from acts of the institutions of the Union.

The Member States shall facilitate the achievement of the Union's tasks and refrain from any measure which could jeopardise the attainment of the Union's objectives.

[65] D Pieters, *Social Security: An Introduction to the Basic Principles* (The Hague, Kluwer, 2008), esp ch 1. See also Commission on Scottish Devolution (the Calman Commission), 'Serving Scotland Better: Scotland and the United Kingdom in the 21st Century', final report (June 2009), para 2.24.

[66] Case C-70/95 *Sodemare* [1997] ECR I-3395, para 29; see also para 29 of the judgment.

[67] T Hervey, 'Social Solidarity: A Buttress against Internal Market Law?' in J Shaw (ed), *Social Law and Policy in an Evolving European Union* (Oxford, Hart Publishing, 2000), 31; K Ting and E Verbraak, 'Solidarity: An Indispensable Concept in Social Security' in J van Vugt and J Peet (eds), *Social Security and Solidarity in the European Union* (Nijmegen, Physica-Verlag, 2000), 254; S O'Leary, 'Solidarity and Citizenship Rights in the Charter of Fundamental Rights of the European Union' in G de Búrca (ed), *EU Law and the Welfare State. In Search of Solidarity* (Oxford, Oxford University Press, 2005), 39; C Barnard, 'EU Citizenship and the Principle of Solidarity' in E Spaventa and M Dougan (eds), *Social Welfare and EU Law* (Oxford, Hart Publishing, 2005), 157; M Dougan and E Spaventa, '"Wish You Weren't Here . . ." New Models of Social Solidarity in the European Union' in E Spaventa and M Dougan (eds), *Social Welfare and EU Law* (Oxford, Hart Publishing, 2005), 181; C Barnard, 'Solidarity and New Governance in Social Policy' in G de Búrca and J Scott (eds), *Law and New Governance in the EU and the US* (Oxford, Hart Publishing, 2006) 153; and M Dougan, 'The Spatial Restructuring of National Welfare States within the European Union: The Contribution of Union Citizenship and the Relevance of the Treaty of Lisbon' in U Neergaard, R Nielsen and L Roseberry (eds), *Integrating Welfare Functions into EU Law. From Rome to Lisbon* (Copenhagen, DJØF, 2009), 147.

[68] D Pieters, *Social Security: An Introduction to the Basic Principles* (The Hague, Kluwer, 2008), 21.

conditions of entitlement in order to keep the circle of solidarity no wider than is a matter of formal legal obligation.

If this principle of social solidarity acquired clearer identification as a general principle of European Union law, then it could be used as a further aid to the interpretation of such secondary legislation as the Citizenship Directive. There is, I would argue, not much wrong with the logic that sharing a citizenship with the nationals of 26 other Member States entitles us to a certain level of social protection when in a country other than that of our own nationality. That level of social protection should not put us at an advantage over nationals of the Member State, but should enable us to claim equal treatment with nationals of the host Member State. The Citizenship Directive does not go that far. It leaves a period beyond three months and before the attainment of permanent residence as a period in which our rights should increase as our level of social integration increases. Social integration arises from many bases of residence, not just a substantial period of economic activity. Over time, it may become much easier to sustain the argument that citizenship alone as a constitutional status entitles us to equality of treatment with nationals of any Member State in which we reside.[69]

VI CONCLUDING REMARKS

This chapter has explored the application of European Union law from the contrasting perspectives of a national legal order in the context of entitlement to social assistance and of the Union legal order as evidenced by rulings of the Court of Justice. The startling difference in approach is attributed to a failure in transposing the Citizenship Directive to appreciate that it goes far beyond an immigration measure. The Department for Work and Pensions, in seeking to use a measure, essentially drafted as an immigration measure, as a gatekeeper for entitlement to social assistance, may have seriously misinterpreted the scope of the Directive. It is certainly true that those involved in social security adjudication find it difficult to match up the words of national regulations implementing the Directive with the social construction of citizenship of the Union. An approach which recognised social solidarity as an interpretative principle, and could perceive the needy citizen of the Union who is not our national in the same light as the needy citizen who is our national, would avoid much of the

---

[69] Although in relation to entitlement to educational benefits, the Court of Justice has confirmed the legitimacy of the five year qualifying period in Art 24 of the Citizenship Directive: Case C-158/07 *Jacqueline Förster*, [2008] ECR I-8507. See also the note on this case by O Golynker, 'Case C-158/07, *Jacqueline Förster v Hoofddirectie van de Informatie Beheer Groep*, Judgment of the Court (Grand Chamber) of 18 November 2008' (2009) 46 *Common Market Law Review* 2021, especially the comments on the relationship of this ruling with that in Case C-209/03 *Bidar* [2005] ECR I-2119.

hardship which the delays inherent in judicial decision making invariably bring. Requiring an appropriate level of social integration matched to social entitlements is a means of accommodating Member State concerns— largely unfounded by empirical evidence—about benefit tourism.[70] Ultimately the problem has arisen because the national regulations are seen as restrictive in application, whereas the Court of Justice tells us that the rights granted by the Citizenship Directive, considered in the light of what are now Articles 18, 21 and 45 FTEU, must be viewed expansively.

But the criticism is not all for the national authorities. Notions promulgated in the Treaties and interpreted in the Court of Justice need to be capable of easy delivery in day-to-day decision making within national administrations. Concepts must filter down to the practicalities of such decision making if a constitutional order of states is to be a reality for the ordinary citizen. Only in this way will Europe be brought closer to the citizen. In this context, the troublesome distinction between social security and social assistance needs further elaboration. Under the Citizenship Directive, Article 24(2) would appear to require greater access to support from a host Member State the greater the level of integration achieved, which is arguably reinforced by the specific reference to a stricter five-year qualifying period for grant maintenance aid for studies in Article 24(2).[71] The underlying rationale of many the judgments of the Court of Justice clearly points in this direction, but such decisions are hard to apply within the decision-making machinery of national administrations. It is much easier to apply a rule which says there is no entitlement until permanent residence is achieved. That would not be a desirable development, but at present the exercise of tricky judgments based on levels of social integration is such that social solidarity as a European Union concept informing decision making is likely to remain part of an academic discourse rather than a mechanism for the delivery of assistance to needy citizens of the Union.

---

[70] See, eg T Coles, 'Telling Tales of Tourism: Mobility, Media and Citizenship in the 2004 Enlargement' in P Burns and M Novelli (eds), *Tourism and Mobilities. Local-Global Connections* (Oxford, CAB International, 2008), 65–80; D Blanchflower, J Saleheen and C Shadforth, *The Impact of Recent Migration from Eastern Europe on the UK Economy*, Bank of England External MPC Unit Discussion Paper No 17, 15; and N Doyle, G Hughes and E Wadensjö, 'Freedom of Movement for Workers from Central and Eastern Europe. Experiences in Ireland and Sweden', Swedish Institute for European Policy Studies Report No 5, 2006.

[71] See material cited at n 69 above.

17

Social Policy and the Shifting Sands of the Constitutional Order: The Case of Posted Workers

CATHERINE BARNARD*

I. INTRODUCTION

SOCIAL POLICY WAS never Alan Dashwood's favourite area of EU law. As always with these things, he showed prescience. When the EEC Treaty was drafted, social policy was really an add-on extra and the content of the Treaty's text scarcely merited the title 'Social Policy'. In the original constitutional order of states envisaged by the Treaty of Rome, social policy was a matter solely for the domestic realm. It was a manifestation of state sovereignty and so it was a national—and thus territorial—matter. The EU's task was to create an effective single market. This would have ancillary benefits for national social policy since greater prosperity would provide states with the resources to develop their social policy but that is as far as EU involvement should go.[1] It is a perspective that still prevails in many quarters to this day.

However, the winds of both positive and negative integration have prompted a reconsideration of this fundamental understanding. A now—fairly substantial—body of EU rules have been adopted in the 'social' (for which read employment) field.[2] Although something of a patchwork, the legislation has covered matters as diverse as equality rights, information and consultation for workers and health and safety. The rationale for adopting such legislation has been mixed, ranging from the political (the need to give the EU a 'social' face) to the economic (the need to avoid social dumping/the creation of a level playing field). This legislation com-

* I am grateful to Michael Dougan for his helpful comments.
[1] See S Giubboni, *Social Rights and Market Freedom in the European Constitution. A Labour Law Perspective* (Cambridge, Cambridge University Press, 2006), 29ff.
[2] See further, C Barnard, 'EU "Social" Policy from Employment Law to Labour Market Reform' in G De Búrca and P Craig, *Evolution of EU Law* (Oxford, Oxford University Press, 2011).

plements, supplements and, at times, replaces national employment law but, crucially, key pillars of employment law, in particular laws against unfair dismissal and laws on redundancy, the minimum wage, 'family friendly policies' and industrial action remain subject to domestic law only. In part this is due to the fact that the EU's competence to act in the areas of pay and collective action remains heavily circumscribed,[3] but it also reflects a lack of commitment on the part of the states to act at EU level in those areas where successive Treaty amendments have actually provided the EU with competence.

Yet it is the EU's rules on negative integration, as interpreted by the Court of Justice, which have posed the greatest challenge to attempts to seal domestic social policy off from EU law. In particular, the Court's increasing use of the 'market access' or 'restrictions' test, introduced by the Court in *Säger*[4] and more recently confirmed in *Commission v Italy (motor insurance)*,[5] as the driving interpretative principle of the four freedoms has threatened to undermine national employment laws. Thus, in the days when the non-discrimination approach applied, a national minimum wage whose rates were neither directly nor indirectly discriminatory on the grounds of nationality would be immune from challenge under, for example, Article 45 TFEU[6] because nationals and migrants were being treated alike. However, that same legislation could now be considered a restriction on, say, freedom of establishment of companies under Article 49 TFEU because the requirement to pay the minimum wage, while non-discriminatory, hinders the company's freedom to pay its employees what it chooses (ie wage rates below the minimum wage).[7] Of course, any such restriction can be justified but, depending on the mood of the Court, may not withstand a strict proportionality test.

This issue was brought into sharp focus by the controversial rulings of the Court of Justice in *Viking*[8] and *Laval*.[9] In *Viking*, a decision by

---

[3] See esp Art 153(5) TFEU.

[4] Case C-76/90 *Säger v Dennemeyer & Co Ltd* [1991] ECR I-4221. See also Case C-55/94 *Gebhard v Consiglio dell'Ordine degli Avvocati e Procuratori di Milano* [1995] ECR I-4165, para 37; Case C-19/92 *Kraus v Land Baden-Württemberg* [1993] ECR I-1663, para 32.

[5] Case C-518/06 *Commission v Italy (motor insurance)* [2009] ECR I-3491.

[6] See, eg Case 167/73 *Commission v France* [1974] ECR 354, para 45 considered below. See also the effect of the Rome I Regulation.

[7] For a discussion of the market access test *v* the non-discrimination test, see C Barnard, *The Substantive Law of the EU: The Four Freedoms* (Oxford, Oxford University Press, 2010; for criticism of the market access test, see E Spaventa, 'From *Gebhard* to *Carpenter*: Towards a (Non-) Economic European Constitution' (2004) 41 *Common Market Law Review* 743; J Snell, 'The Notion of Market Access: A Concept or a Slogan?' (2010) 47 *Common Market Law Review* 437; G Davies, 'Understanding Market Access: Exploring the Economic Rationality of Different Conceptions of Free Movement Law' (2010) *German Law Journal* http://www.germanlawjournal.com/index.php?pageID=11&artID=1264 (accessed on 2 September 2010).

[8] Case C-438/05 *Viking Line ABP v The International Transport Workers' Federation, the Finnish Seaman's Union* [2007] ECR I-10779.

[9] Case C-341/05 *Laval un Partneri Ltd v Svenska Byggnadsarbetareförbundet* [2007] ECR I-11767.

the Finnish seaman's union (FSU) to call its members out on strike, in accordance with Finnish law on industrial action, was found to constitute a restriction on freedom of establishment contrary to Article 49 TFEU, a restriction which could possibly be justified on the grounds of worker protection but was, almost certainly, not proportionate.

Laval (and the subsequent cases of *Rüffert* and *Commission v Luxembourg*[10]), concerned the issue of posted workers, that is workers temporarily sent by their companies to work in another Member State but who return after a certain period to their home state. The case of posted workers demonstrates in microcosm the shifting sands of the constitutional order of states in the social sphere: no longer is it simply the case that domestic, and now EU, labour laws apply in a state. The combined effect of the Rome I Regulation, the Posted Workers Directive and the Court's interpretation of Article 56 TFEU is that labour laws of other Member States may also apply in that state. In other words, the new constitutional order of states created by the EU involves the extra-territorial application of laws of other states.

The case of posted workers is the most overt example of extra-territorial application, but it is not the only one. As Harry Arthurs vividly puts it,[11] 'foreign' labour laws 'sneak' into Member States though a number of other mechanisms,[12] including human resources policies of transnational corporations and, in the EU context, the open method of coordination (OMC). He says:[13]

> [OMC] has contributed, or may contribute to several developments with quasi-extraterritorial implications: some approximation of national adherence to broad community policy (which in turn is significantly influenced by the leading states); the conscious imitation by some states of successful policy experiments originating in others ('flexicurity' is a case in point); and the explicit borrowing of labor law institutions or doctrines (especially by new Member States that adopted—with modifications—those of older members)

The mention of OMC and new governance makes Alan's blood boil ('You know how the word governance makes me want to reach for my revolver') and so will not be discussed further. But for our purposes it serves to underline the fact that the initial constitutional arrangement envisaged by the drafters of the EEC Treaty, premised on the traditional idea that labour law is a domestic matter, is breaking down in perhaps surprising and unexpected ways. Moreover, the original constitutional order is being

---

[10] Case C-346/06 *Rüffert* [2008] ECR I-1989. Case C-319/06 *Commission v Luxembourg* [2008] ECR I-4323.

[11] H Arthurs, 'Extraterritoriality by Other Means: How Labor Law Sneaks across Borders, Conquers Minds, and Controls Workplaces Abroad' (2010) 21 *Stanford Law and Policy Review* 101.

[12] For further details, see B Hepple *Labour Laws and Global Trade* (Oxford, Hart Publishing, 2005) ch 7.

[13] Ibid, 110.

reconfigured to accommodate the interests of old and new Member States. *Laval* is an interesting study on how the Court attempts to achieve this balance and so forms the focus of this chapter. However, in order to understand *Laval* and its progeny, some background needs to be provided.

II   WHICH LAW APPLIES?

A   Introduction

The issue of which law applies to migrant workers is a sensitive one. A number of Member States, notably the UK and Ireland, adopt a territorial approach to their laws. This means that, provided the individual falls within the personal scope of the relevant provision and has worked the relevant period of service (for example, they are an 'employee' with one year's service), domestic employment rights will apply, irrespective of the individual's nationality and the duration of his or her employment in the state. Various explanations for the territorial approach have been offered, but generally they turn on principles of equality, fairness and good industrial relations.

As the analysis below shows, the Rome Convention 1980 and now the Rome I Regulation[14] appear to endorse this position in respect of *migrant* workers, as does Article 45 TFEU[15] and Article 7(1) of Regulation 1612/68[16] (which expressly refers to the territorial principle[17]), but not in respect of posted workers. Articles 56 TFEU and the Posted Workers Directive (PWD) 96/71[18] also cast serious doubt on the territorial application of national labour law to posted workers. In respect of *posted* workers, the starting point of Article 56 TFEU, the PWD and the Rome I Regulation is that home state employment rules apply (ie country of origin principle). This is also the approach in the field of social security in respect of posted workers. Article 12(1) of Regulation 883/2004[19] provides:

> A person who pursues an activity as an employed person in a Member State on behalf of an employer which normally carries out its activities there and who is posted by that employer to another Member State to perform work on that employer's behalf shall continue to be subject to the legislation of the first

---

[14] Reg 593/2008 [2008] OJ L177/6, which applied from 17 December 2009.

[15] A lot of case law still decided under Art 45 TFEU is still governed by the discrimination approach but the Court has recognised that the restrictions/market access test also applies here too: Case C-464/02 *Commission v Denmark (Company Cars)* [2005] ECR I-7929.

[16] [1968] OJ SE L 257/2, p 475.

[17] 'A worker who is a national of a Member State may not, *in the territory of another Member State*, be treated differently from national workers by reason of his nationality in respect of any conditions of employment and work, in particular as regards remuneration, dismissal, and should he become unemployed, reinstatement or re-employment' (emphasis added). See also Art 7(4) of Reg 1612/68.

[18] [1997] OJ L18/1.

[19] [2004] OJ L166/1.

Member State, provided that the anticipated duration of such work does not exceed twenty-four months[20] and that he is not sent to replace another person.

The starting point of our analysis is, however, the Rome I Regulation on the choice of law which, to labour lawyers, is a somewhat neglected, though nevertheless important, piece of legislation.

B The Rome I Regulation

As far as individual employment contracts are concerned, the law which applies to individuals working in other Member States is governed by the Rome I Regulation, which applies without prejudice to the Posted Workers Directive. The Rome I Regulation envisages two situations:

1. where the parties have chosen the applicable law; and
2. where they have not.

We shall consider these two situations.[21]

(i) No Choice of Law Clause

Where the parties have not chosen the applicable law, Article 8(2) applies. This says:

> To the extent that the law applicable to the individual employment contract has not been chosen by the parties, the contract shall be governed by the law of the country in which or, failing that, from which the employee habitually carries out his work in performance of the contract. The country where the work is habitually carried out shall not be deemed to have changed if he is temporarily employed in another country.

So, in the case of a Polish worker who has come to the UK as a migrant worker under Article 45 TFEU but without a choice of law clause in his contract, the effect of the first part of Article 8(2) of the Rome I Regulation is that English law will be the objectively applicable law. Under this analysis, the UK would be able to apply all of its labour law rules to domestic and migrant workers alike.

However, in the case of a Polish worker temporarily[22] posted to the UK by a Polish company under Article 56 TFEU, the effect of the first part of

---

[20] In the original Reg 1408/71 this period was 12 months.

[21] Fuller details can be found in C Barnard 'The UK and Posted Workers: The Effect of *Commission v Luxembourg* on the Territorial Application of British Labour Law' (2009) 38 *Industrial Law Journal* 122.

[22] According to the 36th Recital of the Rome I Regulation, work is regarded as temporary 'if the employee is expected to resume working in the country of origin after carrying out his tasks abroad'. In an attempt to deal with evasion techniques, it continues 'The conclusion of a new contract of employment with the original employer or an employer belonging to the same group of companies as the original employer should not preclude the employee from being regarded as carrying out his work in another country temporarily'.

Article 8(2) and the second sentence of Article 8(2) is that the objectively applicable law will be Polish. Therefore, in principle the UK should not be able to apply all of its labour law rules to the Polish posted worker.

(ii)   Choice of Law Clause

Where, on the other hand, the parties have chosen the applicable law,[23] Article 8(1) of the Rome I Regulation says 'An individual employment contract shall be governed by the law chosen by the parties in accordance with Article 3'. Article 8(1) continues that 'Such a choice of law may not, however, have the result of depriving the employee of the protection afforded to him by provisions that cannot be derogated from by agreement under the law that, in the absence of choice, would have been applicable pursuant to [Article 8(2)] . . .'. So, if the parties have chosen English law to govern the employment contract and the English workers are posted temporarily to Poland, then English law is likely to be the objectively applicable law under Article 8(2) as well as the chosen law. Similarly, where the Polish employer, posting Polish workers to the UK, has chosen Polish law to govern the contract, the chosen law will be, and the objectively applicable law is likely to be, Polish.

(iii)   Summary

This analysis shows that when considering the position of the Polish worker temporarily posted to the UK, with or without Polish law being the choice of law, Polish law may well apply to the contract. Even if the parties have chosen a different law, such as English law, the contract will remain subject to mandatory provisions of Polish law which cannot be derogated from. English courts will be able to apply English law only if (i) the foreign law is considered contrary to UK public policy under Article 21 of the Rome Regulation (unlikely in the labour law context), or (ii) English law applies as an overriding mandatory rule of the forum under Article 9(2) of the Rome I Regulation.[24]

The chance of the UK being able to invoke Article 9(2) in the labour law context looks slim. 'Overriding mandatory provisions' are defined in Article 9(1) as

> provisions the respect for which is regarded as *crucial* by a country for safeguarding its public interests, such as its political, social or economic organisation, to such an extent that they are applicable to any situation falling

[23] Parties can choose the relevant law under Art 3 of the Rome I Regulation: 'A contract shall be governed by the law chosen by the parties'.
[24] This provides: 'Nothing in this Regulation shall restrict the application of the overriding mandatory provisions of the law of the forum.'

within their scope, irrespective of the law otherwise applicable to the contract under this Regulation.[25]

It is hard to argue that, for example, laws on unfair dismissal, however central to a system of employment protection, are 'crucial' to safeguarding a country's social organisation. It is therefore now difficult to maintain that Polish workers temporarily posted to the UK will be subject to key aspects of UK employment protection legislation which apply as overriding mandatory provisions of the forum. The UK's territorial approach in respect of posted workers therefore appears hard to sustain under the Rome I Regulation.

C The Application of the Treaty Provisions pre-*Laval* and the PWD

(i) *Rush Portuguesa*

At first, the UK's territorial approach to labour law did not appear sustainable under Article 56 TFEU following the decision in *Rush Portuguesa*.[26] Rush Portuguesa, a Portuguese company, entered into a subcontract with a French company to carry out rail construction work in France. It used its own third country national workforce,[27] contravening French rules which provided that only the French Office d'Immigration could recruit non-EU workers. The Court ruled that Articles 56 and 57 TFEU[28] precluded a Member State (France) from prohibiting a person providing services established in another Member State (Portugal) from moving freely on its territory with all his staff and precluded that Member State (France) from making the movement of staff in question subject to restrictions such as a condition as to engagement in situ or an obligation to obtain a work permit. However, the Court added that:[29]

> [Union] law does not preclude Member States from extending their legislation, or collective labour agreements entered into by both sides of industry, to any person who is employed, even temporarily, within their territory, no matter

---

[25] Emphasis added. As the Commission's explanatory memorandum says (COM(2005) 650, 7), this test explicitly draws on the Court of Justice's decision in Joined Cases C-369/96 and C-376/96 *Arblade* [1999] ECR I-8453, para 31.
[26] Case C-113/89 *Rush Portuguesa v Office national d'immigration* [1990] ECR I-1417.
[27] The workforce was actually Portuguese, but at the time the transitional arrangements for Portuguese accession to the EU were in place, which meant that the rules on freedom to provide services were in force but not those relating to the free movement of workers. Therefore, Portuguese workers did not enjoy the rights of free movement and so for our purposes the Portuguese workers constitute third country nationals (see para 4 of the judgment).
[28] Para 12, emphasis added.
[29] Para 18.

in which country the employer is established; nor does [Union] law prohibit Member States from enforcing those rules by appropriate means.[30]

Thus, by allowing the host state to extend its labour laws and conditions to the staff employed by service providers working in its territory, the Court, in one (unreasoned) paragraph, put a stop to a threat of 'social dumping' (from the perspective of the richer states). In so doing, the Court apparently rejected Advocate General Verloren van Themaat's view, in the earlier case of *Seco*,[31] that 'when providing services in another Member State any employer may in principle make use of the cost advantages existing in his country, including lower wage costs, under the conditions of undistorted competition which constitute another objective of the [Treaties]'. In other words, the Court in *Rush* denied states from countries with lower labour costs the possibility of exploiting their comparative advantage.

For the purposes of this chapter, the Court in *Rush* did not make a clear distinction between the *workers* provision of the Treaties and the *services* provisions. The Court appeared to consider that the host state was entitled to apply the principle of equal treatment and thus the full panoply of its laws to both migrant *and* posted workers. In other words, the host state could adopt a territorial approach, a view given some support by the preambular paragraph of the Workers' Regulation 1612/68:

> Whereas such right [the right of all workers in the Member States to pursue the activity of their choice within the [Union]] must be enjoyed without discrimination by permanent, seasonal and frontier workers and by those who pursue their activities for the *purpose of providing services*.[32]

The rationale for applying host state laws to all working in its territory was explained by the Court in the early workers' case of *Commission v France*:[33]

> The absolute nature of this prohibition [against discrimination], moreover, has the effect of not only allowing in each state equal access to employment to the nationals of other Member States, but also, in accordance with the aim of Article 177 of the Treaty [stet[34]], of guaranteeing to the state's own nationals that they shall not suffer the unfavourable consequences which could result

---

[30] Citing Joined Cases 62/81 and 63/81 *Seco SA and Another* [1982] ECR 223, para 14 where the Court said 'It is well-established that [Union] law does not preclude Member States from applying their legislation, or collective labour agreements entered into by both sides of industry relating to minimum wages, to any person who is employed, even temporarily, within their territory, no matter in which country the employer is established, just as [Union] law does not prohibit Member States from enforcing those rules by appropriate means'. See also Case C-43/93 *Van der Elst* [1994] ECR I-3803, para 23.

[31] Joined Cases 62/81 and 63/81 *Seco SA and Another* [1982] ECR 223.

[32] Emphasis added.

[33] Case 167/73 [1974] ECR 354m para 45.

[34] The French language version uses 'Art 117' EEC (now 151 TFEU), which is more likely to be correct in the context.

from the offer or acceptance by nationals of other Member States of conditions of employment or remuneration less advantageous than those obtaining under national law, since such acceptance is prohibited.

In other words, by applying the principle of equal treatment and thus the territorial approach, the terms and conditions of employment of nationals of the host state would be protected against undercutting by migrants. Nevertheless, subsequent case law cast significant doubt on this approach.

(ii) The Subsequent Case Law

(a) Terms of Employment
In subsequent cases the Court retreated from its bold, but unreasoned, approach in *Rush Portuguesa*, and brought its decisions squarely within the framework of its services jurisprudence. This break was made most explicit in *Finalarte*, where the Court firmly distinguished the situation of posted workers from that of migrant workers,[35] making it clear that the position of the posted workers would be considered 'solely in the light of Articles [56 and 57]'[36] and not under Article 45 TFEU. This paved the way for the Court to apply its *Säger*[37] restrictions jurisprudence. This involves considering four questions:

1. Do the requirements imposed by the host state on the service provider restrict the freedom to provide services?
2. Can the measure be justified on the grounds of, for example, worker protection,[38] especially the interests of the posted workers?[39]
3. Is the same interest already protected in the state of establishment?
4. Are the steps taken proportionate?[40]

The four-stage *Säger* approach can be seen in *Mazzoleni*.[41] ISA, a French company, provided security guards who worked on a part-time basis for brief periods at a shopping mall in Belgium. In the course of an inspection by the Belgian labour inspectorate, it was found that the monthly wage

---

[35] Joined Cases C-49, 50, 52, 54, 68 and 71/98 *Finalarte Sociedade de Construção Civil Lda* [2001] ECR I-7831, para 23.

[36] Ibid, para 26. *Cf* Case C-109/04 *Kranemann* [2005] ECR I-2421, where the Court said that Art 45 could apply to a German trainee lawyer temporarily working in the UK. H Vershcueren, 'Cross-Border Workers in the European Internal Market: Trojan Horses for Member States' Labour and Social Security Law?' (2008) 24 *International Journal of Comparative Labour Law and Industrial Relations* 167, 176.

[37] Case C-76/90 [1991] ECR I-4221, para 12, emphasis added.

[38] *Finalarte*, above n 35, paras 41–49, for a careful scrutiny of the worker protection justification and that the national measures did actually confer a genuine benefit on the posted workers. See also Case C-164/99 *Portugaia Construções Lda* [2002] ECR I-787, paras 28–9.

[39] *Finalarte*, ibid, para 41.

[40] See, eg Joined Cases C-369 and 376/96 *Arblade* [1999] ECR I-8453.

[41] Case C-165/98 *Criminal proceedings against André Mazzoleni and Inter Surveillance Assistance SARL* [2001] ECR I-2189.

of ISA workers was less than the minimum wage in Belgium, albeit that their remuneration package as a whole, including tax and social security contributions, was similar to, if not more favourable than, remuneration under Belgian law. The Court said that (i) while Belgian law in principle breached Article 56, because by subjecting service providers to all conditions required for establishment, it deprived the provisions on services of practical effectiveness, and (ii) the requirement to pay the host state's minimum wage could be justified on the grounds of worker protection. However, the Court suggested the application of the Belgian rules might be disproportionate.[42] It said that (iii) the Belgian objective of worker protection would be attained if all the workers concerned enjoyed an equivalent position overall in relation to remuneration, taxation and social security contributions in the host Member State and in the Member State of establishment.[43] It continued that (iv) the application of Belgian law on minimum wages to service providers established in a frontier region of a Member State could result, first, in an additional, disproportionate administrative burden, including, in certain cases, the calculation, hour-by-hour, of the appropriate remuneration for each employee according to whether he has, in the course of his work, crossed the frontier of another Member State and, secondly, in the payment of different levels of wages to employees who were all attached to the same operational base and carried out identical work. That last consequence might, in its turn, result in tension between employees and even threaten the cohesion of the collective labour agreements that are applicable in the Member State of establishment.[44]

Thus, *Mazzoleni* suggested that the host state was justified in requiring that, in appropriate circumstances, the service provider pay its workforce minimum wages laid down by the host state's law or, as in *Arblade*,[45] collective agreement, provided that the provisions of the collective agreement were sufficiently precise and accessible and they did not render it impossible or excessively difficult in practice for the employer to determine his obligations. In *Wolff*[46] the Court added the host state was also justified in extending to service providers measures intended to 'reinforce the procedural arrangements enabling a posted worker usefully to assert his right to a minimum rate of pay'. In a similar vein, the Court said in *Finalarte*[47] that the host state could require the service provider to give the posted workers the equivalent of 30 working days of paid leave per year, even

---

[42] Para 34.
[43] Para 35.
[44] Para 36.
[45] Joined Cases C-369/96 and C-376/96 [1999] ECR I-8453.
[46] Case C-60/03 *Wolff & Müller v Pereira Félix* [2004] ECR I-9553, paras 36 and 41.
[47] Joined Cases C-49/98, C-50/98, C-52/98 to C-54/98 and C-68/98 to C-71/98 *Finalarte Sociedade de Construção Civil Ld^a* [2001] ECR I-7831, para 58.

though this amount exceeded the four weeks' paid leave laid down by the Working Time Directive 2003/88,[48] provided this was proportionate.

The upshot of this line of case law is to endorse the country of origin principle, thereby preventing the host state (the UK in our example) from imposing its employment laws on the posted workers unless those laws are justified, proportionate and, crucially in the services context, take account of the employment protection already provided in the home state (Poland in our example). As Vershueren pithily puts it, 'the application to workers of labour law of the host Member State, which is the rule under the free movement of workers provisions, can be seen in principle as an obstacle to the free movement of services'.[49] The result of this case law is that the blanket, territorial application of labour law by host states such as the UK already looked suspect by the early 2000s.

(iii) Monitoring and Enforcement Rules

So far I have concentrated on the case law concerning terms of employment imposed by the host state. This became a particular issue in *Laval* (considered below). A number of other cases concerned other, largely administrative, obligations imposed on employers of posted workers. Generally the Court has found that rules of a more substantive kind are not compatible with Article 56 TFEU, while those of a more procedural nature might be compatible with Article 56 TFEU.

In respect of the more substantive rules, the Court has said that host state laws requiring the posted worker to have been employed by the service provider for at least six months in the case of Luxembourg[50] (a year in the case of Germany)[51] were not lawful. A requirement for the posted workers to have individual work permits which were only granted where the labour market situation so allowed was also not compatible with the EU law.[52] Similarly, a requirement for the service provider to provide, for the purposes of obtaining a work permit, a bank guarantee to cover costs in the event of repatriation of the worker at the end of his deployment was not permitted,[53] nor was a requirement that the work

---

[48] [2003] OJ L299/9.

[49] Above n 37, 177.

[50] Case C-445/03 *Commission v Luxembourg* [2004] ECR I-10191, paras 32–33. See also Case C-168/04 *Commission v Luxembourg* [2006] ECR I-9041, which found the 'EU Posting confirmation' which required the posted worker to have an employment contract of at least one year was contrary to Art 56 TFEU.

[51] Case C-244/04 *Commission v Germany* [2006] ECR I-885.

[52] Case C-445/03, above n 50, paras 42–43. See also the earlier case of Case C-43/93 *Vander Elst* [1994] ECR I-3803.

[53] Ibid, para 47.

be licensed,[54] or a requirement that the service provider designate an *ad hoc* agent resident in the territory of the host state.[55]

On the other hand, rules of a more procedural nature have been upheld by the Court provided they are clear and transparent and proportionate.[56] So, in *Commission v Germany*[57] the Court said that it was compatible with Article 56 TFEU for the host state to insist that the service provider furnish a 'simple prior declaration certifying that the situation of the workers concerned is lawful', particularly in the light of the requirements of residence, work visas and social security cover in the Member States where the provider employs them. In *Commission v Luxembourg*[58] the Court also said that the host state could require the service provider to report beforehand to the local authorities on the presence of one or more posted workers, the anticipated duration of their presence and the provision or provisions of services justifying the deployment.[59]

These sorts of administrative rules are particularly prevalent in Continental Europe. They are not found in the UK (which is one of the reasons why the UK has no statistics on how many posted workers there are actually working in the UK). The case law applying the Treaty to administrative rules is likely to remain good law even after *Laval*'s interpretation of the Posted Workers' Directive, since Article 5 of the Directive expressly envisages that Member States must take appropriate measures if the Directive's provisions are not complied with.[60] This line of case law therefore suggests that, while the Court may not countenance the application of many substantive host state labour law rules to posted workers, it will give considerable leeway to the host state authorities to supervise the activities of those service providers in its state—more than the unsuccessful Bolkestein draft of the Services Directive appeared to allow them.[61]

---

[54] Ibid, para 30.
[55] Case C-319/06 *Commission v Luxembourg* [2008] ECR I-4323, paras 93–94.
[56] Ibid, para 82. See also Case C-458/08 *Commission v Portugal* [2010] ECR I-0000.
[57] Case C-244/04, above n 51.
[58] Case C-445/03, above n 50.
[59] Para 31.
[60] On the problems of enforcement of the PWD, see the Commission's Communication COM(2006) 159.
[61] Art 24 of the Bolkestein draft of the Services Directive required the host state to check whether the service provider complied with the provisions of the PWD. However, the host state could not require, inter alia, the service provider 'to hold and keep employment documents in its territory or in accordance with the conditions applicable in its territory': COM(2004) 2. *Cf* the Commission's position in its guidance document COM(2006) 159, which predated Case C-490/04 *Commission v Germany* [2007] ECR I-6095: 'On the basis of the aforementioned case law, it must be concluded that, in order to be able to monitor compliance with the conditions of employment laid down in the Directive, the host Member State must be able to demand, in accordance with the principle of proportionality, that documents be kept in the workplace which are, by their nature, created there, such as time sheets or documents on conditions of health and safety in the workplace. The host Member State cannot demand a second set of documents if the documents required under the legislation of the Member State of establishment, taken as a whole, already provide.'

III THE POSTED WORKERS' DIRECTIVE

A The Provisions of the Directive

For the purposes of this chapter, the other key piece of legislation in this complex jigsaw is the Posted Workers' Directive 96/71, which had not come into force at the time when the facts of *Arblade*, *Mazzoleni* and *Finalarte* arose. This Directive is intended to promote the transnational provision of services and to ensure a 'climate of fair competition[62] and measures guaranteeing respect for the rights of workers'.[63] Despite the reference to worker protection, the Directive is primarily a measure to facilitate the free movement of services, as its legal basis—Articles 53(1) and 62 TFEU (ex-Articles 47(2) and 55 EC)[64]—makes clear, a view now confirmed by the Court.[65]

The Directive applies to undertakings established in a Member State[66] which, in the framework of the transnational provision of services, post workers to the territory of another Member State.[67] The posting of workers can take one of three forms,[68] the most important for our purposes being the situation where a worker[69] is posted under a contract concluded between the undertaking making the posting (which is established in a Member State other than that where the service is provided) and the party for whom the services are intended (the situation in *Rush Portuguesa* and in *Laval*).

According to Article 3(1) PWD, whatever the law applicable to the employment relationship, the undertakings identified above must guarantee posted workers the host state's terms and conditions of employment in respect of:

---

[62] See *Laval*, above n 9, para 75: This 'prevents a situation arising in which, by applying to their workers the terms and conditions of employment in force in the Member State of origin as regards those matters, undertakings established in other Member States would compete unfairly against undertakings of the host Member State in the framework of the transnational provision of services, if the level of social protection in the host Member State is higher'.

[63] Preambular, para 5 cited by the Court in Case C-60/03 *Wolff & Müller v Pereira Félix* [2004] ECR I-9553, para 42. For a full discussion of the background to the Directive, see S Evju 'Revisiting the Posted Workers Directive: Conflict of Laws and Laws in Contrast' (2009–10) 12 *Cambridge Yearbook of European Legal Studies* 151.

[64] For a full analysis of the Directive, see P Davies 'Posted Workers: Single Market or Protection of National Labour Law Systems?' (1997) 34 *Common Market Law Review* 571.

[65] *Rüffert*, above n 10, para 36.

[66] Art 1(1). Art 1(4) provides that undertakings established in non-Member States must not be given more favourable treatment than undertakings established in a Member State.

[67] Art 1(1).

[68] Art 1(3).

[69] A posted worker means a worker, as defined by the law of the host state, who for a limited period, carries out his work in the territory of a Member State other than the state in which he normally works: Art 2(1) and (2).

- maximum work periods and minimum rest periods;
- minimum paid holidays;
- minimum rates of pay,[70] as defined by the host state's law and/or practice, including overtime. This does not apply to supplementary occupational retirement pension schemes;
- the conditions of hiring out of workers, in particular the supply of workers by temp agencies;
- health, safety and hygiene at work;
- protective measures with regard to the terms and conditions of employment of pregnant women or women who have recently given birth, of children and young people; and
- equality of treatment between men and women and other provisions on non-discrimination.

These mandatory rules can be laid down by law, regulation or administrative provision.[71] In the case of building work, the terms and conditions can be laid down not only by law, regulation or administrative provision, but also by collective agreements. The specific details of this complex provision are considered below. Article 4 of the Directive imposes obligations of co-operation in respect of information sharing between national administrations, a system which, as both the Court[72] and the Commission[73] note, is not functioning effectively. Article 5 requires Member States to take appropriate measures in the event of failure to comply with the Directive.

B   Analysis

Unlike a number of social policy directives, the PWD is not a standard harmonisation measure. Instead, it aims to co-ordinate the legislation—and the rules laid down by collective agreements—of the Member States. It therefore does not harmonise the material content of rules on, say, the minimum wage.[74] This is a matter for the individual Member States.[75] Rather, the Directive attempts to accommodate the diverse national employment law within the framework of an EU Directive. In this process of co-ordination, the Directive adopts a conflicts of laws approach. Article 3(1) identifies the hard core of mandatory rules using the language of the Rome Convention (now called 'overriding mandatory provisions' in Article

---

[70] Allowances specific to the posting shall be considered to be part of the minimum wage, unless they are paid in reimbursement of expenditure actually incurred on account of the posting, such as expenditure on travel, board and lodging (Art 3(7), para 2).

[71] Art 3(1).

[72] *Arblade*, above n 40, para 61.

[73] COM(2006) 159, 9.

[74] *Laval*, above n 9, paras 60 and 68.

[75] Ibid.

9(2) of the Rome I Regulation), which must be respected by undertakings assigning their employees to work in the host state. In this way, the Directive goes further than *Rush Portuguesa*, which merely permitted (as opposed to requiring) Member States to extend certain rules to employees posted to their territory. However, the Directive is narrower than *Rush Portuguesa* because Article 3(1) limits the areas of national rules which can be extended by the host state; *Rush Portuguesa* envisaged that all host state rules could be applied to the posted worker.

Of the rules that the host state can apply, some areas overlap with existing EU legislation (eg working time, paid holidays, discrimination law); others do not (eg minimum rates of pay). Moreover, the list in Article 3(1) is exhaustive, a view confirmed by *Laval* (see below). So there are key areas of national employment law, such as unfair dismissal, redundancy and family friendly laws, which the host state cannot apply to the posted worker (and from which the domestic, but not the posted, workers can benefit) since those areas are not listed in Article 3(1). These matters will therefore be left to the home state unless the terms of Article 3(7) (the minimum standards clause) or Article 3(10) on public policy are satisfied (both these provisions are considered further below).

In conclusion, the effect of the PWD is that, in a posting situation, generally the laws of the posted workers' home state apply, except in the areas exhaustively listed in Article 3(1). In practical terms, and of relevance for the purpose of this chapter, is that posted workers carry with them the rules of their home state into the territory of the host state.

IV   THE EFFECT OF *LAVAL* AND ITS PROGENY

A   The Decision in *Laval*

As we have seen, the general thrust of the Rome I Regulation, the PWD and the Court's more recent case law under Article 56 TFEU is that generally home state employment laws apply to posted workers. *Laval* and its progeny confirm this in spades.

Laval concerned a Latvian company which won a contract to refurbish a school in Sweden using its own Latvian workers, who earned about 40 per cent less than comparable Swedish workers. The Swedish construction union wanted Laval to apply the Swedish collective agreement but Laval refused, in part because the collective agreement was unclear as to how much Laval would have to pay its workers, and in part because it imposed various supplementary obligations on Laval, such as paying a 'special building supplement' to an insurance company to finance group life insurance contracts. There followed a union picket at the school site, a blockade by construction workers and sympathy industrial action by the electricians unions. Although this industrial action was permissible under Swedish law, Laval brought proceedings in the Swedish labour court, claiming that this action was contrary to Union law, in particular Article 56 TFEU and the PWD.

The case raised a number of interesting legal issues which have been discussed extensively elsewhere.[76] For the purposes of this chapter, I want to focus on the Court's consideration of the PWD. The Court emphasised that Article 3(1) contained an exhaustive list of host state employment rules which could be applied to the posted worker and its terms had to be complied with to the letter. Sweden had failed to do this. For example, Article 3(1) does not cover matters such as the 'special building supplement' and the other insurance premiums employers were required to pay in Sweden under the relevant collective agreement. Although Sweden could, in principle, extend such an obligation to service providers if such a matter could be considered a 'public policy' provision under Article 3(10),[77] Member States must positively opt to rely on Article 3(10)—something Sweden had not done. Further, since trade unions were not a public body, they could not rely on Article 3(10), so the trade union could not force Laval to pay the various insurance premiums under Union law.[78]

In respect of the provisions on pay, the host state can insist on payment of its rates of pay but only if they are minimum and laid down in one of the ways prescribed by the Directive, ie by:

1. law, regulation, or administrative provision; and/or
2. in respect of activities referred to in the Annex (ie all building work relating to the construction, repair, upkeep, alteration or demolition of buildings), collective agreements or arbitration awards which have been declared universally applicable within the meaning of Article 3(8).

If they are not laid down in one of these ways, then they cannot be

---

[76] See, eg chs 17–22 of (2007–08) 10 *Cambridge Yearbook of European Legal Studies* as well as J Malmberg and T Sigeman 'Industrial Actions and EU Economic Freedoms: The Autonomous Collective Bargaining Model Curtailed by the European Court of Justice' (2008) 45 *Common Market Law Review* 1115; C Kilpatrick, '*Laval*'s Regulatory Conundrum: Collective Standard-setting and the Court's New Approach to Posted Workers' (2009) 34 *European Law Review* 844; P Syrpis and T Novitz, 'Economic and Social Rights in Conflict: Political and Judicial Approaches to Their Reconciliation' (2008) 33 *European Law Review*, 411.

[77] Art 3(10) allows Member States, on a basis of equality of treatment, to apply to national undertakings and to undertakings of other Member States terms and conditions of employment on matters other than those referred to in the bullet points above in the case of public policy provisions, and terms and conditions of employment laid down in collective agreements or arbitration awards concerning activities other than those relating to building. In Case C-319/06 *Commission v Luxembourg* [2008] ECR I-4323, paras 49 and 50 the Court gave such a restrictive reading to Art 3(10) that it is unlikely to be successfully invoked in the labour law context.

[78] Ibid, paras 83–84. See also Case C-319/06 *Commission v Luxembourg* [2008] ECR I-4323.

applied to the posted workers. The trade unions in *Laval*, and in the subsequent German case of *Rüffert*, learned this the hard way. Since there is no law on the minimum wage in Sweden (or Germany)[79] (ie limb (1) does not apply), both cases focused on Article 3(8) dealing with collective agreements (ie limb (2)).

Article 3(8) also has two paragraphs. The first deals with those systems which do have a doctrine of extension (also known as the *erga omnes* effect) of collective agreements. This says that collective agreements, or arbitration awards which have been declared universally applicable, are those which must be observed by all undertakings in the geographical area and in the profession or industry concerned. This paragraph was at issue in *Rüffert*. Germany has a system for declaring collective agreements universally applicable. However, in the particular situation at issue, the collective agreement setting pay in the building industry had not been declared universally applicable,[80] so the collectively agreed rules on pay rates could not be applied to the posted workers,[81] no matter that the German state law on the award of public contracts required contractors and their subcontractors to pay posted workers at least the remuneration prescribed by the collective agreement in force at the place where those services were performed.

The second paragraph of Article 3(8) deals with those systems which do not have a procedure for extending collective agreements to all workers (systems such as those in the UK and Sweden). In these situations,

> *Member States* may, *if they so decide*, base themselves on collective agreements or arbitration awards which are generally applicable to all similar undertakings in the geographical area and in the profession or industry concerned, and/or collective agreements which have been concluded by the most representative employers' and labour organisations at national level and which are applied throughout national territory. (emphasis added)

Once again, as with Article 3(10), the Court required Member States positively to opt for either of these possibilities.[82] Because Sweden had not taken advantage of the second paragraph of Article 3(8),[83] the trade unions could not impose on Laval enterprise-level collective bargaining.[84]

---

[79] *Laval*, above n 9, para 8; *Rüffert*, above n 10, para 24. All other terms and conditions laid down by Art 3(1) of the Posted Workers Directive have been implemented by Swedish law: *Laval*, para 63.

[80] *Rüffert*, above n 10, para 26.

[81] Ibid, para 31.

[82] *cf* AG Mengozzi in *Laval*, above n 9, especially paras 179–181ff. He concludes at para 187: 'It is therefore beyond doubt, in my view, that the right to take collective action granted by Swedish law to trade unions to enable them to impose the wage conditions laid down or governed by Swedish collective agreements provides a suitable means of attaining the aim of protecting posted workers laid down in Art 3 of Directive 96/71.'

[83] *Laval*, above n 9, para 67.

[84] Ibid, para 71.

The minimum standards clause in Article 3(7) of the PWD[85] did not help the Swedish trade unions either. Many, including Advocate General Bot in *Rüffert*,[86] had thought that Article 3(7) meant that, while the Directive provided the floor, the state—always assumed to be at least the host state—could go further and impose higher standards, subject to the ceiling of Article 56 TFEU. However, this was not the Court's understanding of Article 3(7). It said in *Laval*—and repeated in *Rüffert*—that Article 3(7) applied to the situation of out-of-state service providers voluntarily signing a collective agreement in the host state which offered superior terms and conditions to their employees. It also covered the situation where the home state laws or collective agreements were more favourable and these could be applied to the posted workers[87] (ie the situation where a German worker was posted by a German company to Portugal. The German worker would continue to enjoy superior German terms and conditions of employment while working in Portugal). It did not allow the host state to impose terms and conditions employment which went 'beyond the mandatory rules [in Article 3(1)] for minimum protection'.[88] The Court thus came close to making Article 3(1) not a floor but a ceiling. And, in reaching this conclusion, the Court prevented the Swedish trade unions from relying on Article 3(7) to impose higher (host state) standards on the Latvian employer.

B   Analysis

So what are the implications of this decision for the territorial application of labour law? As we have seen, the Court has adopted a restrictive reading of Article 3(1). In this respect, its view stands in sharp contrast to that of Advocate General Bot but coincides with the arguments advanced by the Commission. This means that host states can insist on applying their laws only in the situations envisaged in Article 3(1)/Article 3(8); all other employment matters must be left to the home state. Moreover, if a host state fails to comply with the strict terms of Article 3 PWD, the laws of the home state will apply to the posted workers in these areas as well.

The question, then, is why has the Court taken such a narrow view of Article 3(1)? One clue can perhaps be gained from Advocate General Mengozzi's Opinion: he said that Article 3(1) was a 'derogation'[89] from the principle of home state control laid down in Article 8(2) of the Rome I

---

[85] This provides: 'Paragraphs 1 to 6 shall not prevent application of terms and conditions of employment which are more favourable to workers.'
[86] *Rüffert*, above n 10, paras 82–83.
[87] *Laval*, above n 9, para 81.
[88] Ibid, para 80. See also *Rüffert*, above n 10, para 33.
[89] *Laval* Opinion, above n 9, para 132.

Regulation. According to traditional jurisprudence, derogations must be narrowly construed.[90]

Another clue can be gained from the Court's marriage of the PWD with Article 56 TFEU, which was clearly expressed in *Rüffert*. The Court said that its interpretation of Directive 96/71 is 'confirmed by reading it in the light of Article [56 TFEU], since that Directive seeks in particular to bring about the freedom to provide services, which is one of the fundamental freedoms guaranteed by the [Treaties]'.[91] The pre-*Laval* but post-*Rush* case law under Article 56 TFEU already provided a strong indication that the Court was suspicious of host states trying to apply the full panoply of their employment laws to posted workers (thereby depriving companies like Laval of their comparative advantage). *Laval* confirms this and may even require a reconsideration of some of the pre-*Laval* cases such as *Mazzoleni* and *Arblade*. It now seems unlikely that the host state can require posted workers to enjoy any more than the minimum remuneration which must be strictly laid down in one of the ways prescribed by Article 3(1).

V CONCLUSIONS

The full territorial application of labour law has reached the end of the road, at least as far as posted workers are concerned. The combined effect of Rome I, the PWD and Article 56 TFEU is to introduce a system of regime portability. This means that firms can choose the 'least regulative' labour law regime to which a given contract or transaction is related and then, relying on Article 56 TFEU, bid for—and probably win—contracts in states with more prescriptive (and thus more expensive) labour law regimes. These firms can then post their workers to fulfil these contracts. These posted workers can then, snail-like, take their home state regime with them when they go to work in another Member State. In limited circumstances (basically those set out in Article 3(1)), host state laws will apply (and from that perspective the judgments in *Laval* et al should come as a relief to trade union lawyers because at least some host state laws will apply to posted workers, provided that the host state complies precisely with the terms of the Directive).

However, the default position is that home state employment laws (if any) apply. In this way, there is little difference between posted workers and posted goods. In the latter situation, goods carry the imprint of their home state laws with them when being sent to another Member State under the principle of mutual recognition. The same is now being applied to posted workers. Also in this way, the Court is essentially giving

---

[90] If this reasoning is correct, then Arts 3(7) and (10), as derogations to derogations, must be particularly narrowly construed.

[91] Para 36.

employers from the new, Eastern European states a green light to exploit their comparative advantage, as Advocate General Verloren van Themaat had argued for in *Seco*, nearly 30 years ago. Inevitably, this raises the fears of social dumping—or undercutting—in the old Member States. For example, John Monks, General Secretary of the European Trade Union Confederation (ETUC), addressed the European Parliament in February 2008 on the implications of the *Viking* and *Laval* judgments. He said:

> So we are told that the right to strike is a fundamental right but not so fundamental as the EU's free movement provisions. This is a licence for social dumping and for unions being prevented from taking action to improve matters.[92]

However, the Court's approach in *Laval, Rüffert* and *Commission v Luxembourg* is the inevitable result of the parallel application of domestic labour law regimes and one which benefits the new Member States.

The original Treaty drafters might well be surprised by this result. While the first half of the original prescription found in the Treaty of Rome still holds good (that domestic labour law continues to be applied by states, albeit now supplemented by an ever larger body of EU legislation), the second half of the prescription (the creation of the single market) has produced the unexpected result that increasingly, domestic labour law of other Member States applies in host states too.

---

[92] Available at http://www.etuc.org/IMG/pdf_ETUC_Viking_Laval_-_resolution_070308.pdf, accessed 21 December 2010.

18

EU Criminal Law—the Present and the Future?

JOHN R SPENCER

I WAS VERY pleased to be invited to make a contribution to A Con-
stutitonal Order of States, a project in honour of Alan Dashwood.
To my pleasure was added an element of surprise, however, because
my involvement with EU law is rather a narrow one. I am primarily a
'pénaliste', whose involvement with EU law is a sideline that began by
accident when, some 15 years ago, I was co-opted to the group that
eventually produced the *Corpus Juris* project: the controversial proposal
which, as readers will presumably remember, suggested as a solution to the
problem of frauds on the Community budget a special code of criminal
offences, enforced by a European Public Prosecutor who could operate
in all the Member States.[1]

My contribution to this book of essays is a general essay about the EU
and criminal law. General as it is, I hope it will be useful, even in a book
of essays that is aimed at what might be called 'hard-core EU lawyers'.
At present, EU criminal law is a double mystery, because each of the two
groups of people who ought to be interested in it firmly believes that it
is exclusively a matter for the other. Criminal lawyers usually refuse to
look at EU criminal law because they see it as a topic for the EU lawyers, and mainstream EU lawyers avoid it because they see it as a topic
for the criminal lawyers. So a general essay of the type that follows has
its place, I believe, even in this more specialist type of book.[2]

---

[1] M Delmas-Marty (ed), Corpus Juris, *Introducing Penal Provisions for the Purpose of
the Financial Interests of the European Union* (Paris, Editions Economica, 1997). A revised
version of the project appeared in 2000, together with a three-volume supporting study, as
M Delmas-Marty and JAE Vervaele (eds) *The Implementation of the Corpus Juris in the
Member States* (Antwerp, Groningen and Oxford, Intersentia, 2000). See JR Spencer, 'The
Corpus Juris Project and the Fight against Budgetary Fraud' (1998) 1 *Cambridge Yearbook
of European Legal Studies* 77; JR Spencer, 'The Corpus Juris Project—Has it a Future?'
(1999) 2 *Cambridge Yearbook of European Legal Studies* 355; and the House of Lords
Select Committee on the European Communities, 9th Report, 1998–99 Session, 'Prosecuting
Fraud on the Communities' Finances—the Corpus Juris', HL Paper 62.

[2] The recent appearance of two excellent books on the subject written in English may help
to dispel the mystery: V Mitsilegas, *EU Criminal Law* (Oxford, Hart, 2009) and A Klip,
European Criminal Law (Antwerp, Oxford and Portland, Intersentia, 2009). For a succinct

I   EU CRIMINAL LAW: WHY?

The first question that arises is in this context is why there should be such a thing as EU criminal law at all. The purposes of the EEC (as it originally was) were economic: to promote peace, first by linking the economies of the European nation states together in such a way that war between them would in future be unthinkable, and secondly, by diverting the energies of their inhabitants from national rivalry to national and collective economic growth—along the lines of Dr Johnston's famous comment that 'There are few ways in which a man can be more innocently employed than in getting money'.[3] The cornerstone of this operation was the creation of a single economic area in which there would be free movement of workers, services, goods and capital. At first sight, it is not obvious to see where criminal law appears on this agenda—particularly as criminal justice is usually regarded as an area where national differences are particularly marked, national sovereignty is guarded with particular jealousy, and all talk of harmonisation is particularly unrealistic. To quote Harold Gutteridge, a famous comparatist and Cambridge professor of an earlier age, studying the criminal law of other countries is interesting, but 'the unification of criminal law is either impossible or, if possible, would be undesirable'.[4]

However, a reflection quickly shows that EU law must necessarily impinge on the criminal law of the Member States in a negative sense; and experience over recent years shows a growing practical need for it to do so positively as well.

EU law impinges negatively on national criminal law because it takes precedence over national law, including national criminal law, and therefore nullifies rules of national criminal law that conflict with it. Thus, for example, EU law provides for free movement of capital, which means that it is not open to national criminal law to penalise the removal of money from one Member State to another.[5] Less obviously, it also negatively impinges on national criminal justice systems because it prohibits them being used (or selectively not used) in ways that frustrate the purposes and policies of the Union—including, first and foremost, its central policy of free movement. It is one of the central Treaty obligations of the Member States that they shall 'take any appropriate measures, general or particular, to ensure fulfilment of the obligations arising out of the Treaties or

account of the recent history of EU criminal law see E Baker, 'The European Union's "Area of Freedom, Security and (Criminal) Justice" Ten Years On' (2010) *Criminal Law Review* 833.

[3] Boswell, *Life of Johnson* (LF Powell's revision of GB Hill's edition) (Oxford, Oxford University Press, 1964–71) vol II, 323.

[4] HC Gutteridge, *Comparative Law—an Introduction to the Comparative Method of Legal Study and Research* (Cambridge, Cambridge University Press, 1949) 30.

[5] Joined Cases C-358/93 and C-416/93 *Aldo Bordess and Others* [1995] ECR I-361.

resulting from the acts of the institutions of the Union'.[6] Situations some-times arise in which the only effective 'appropriate measure' is the use, by a Member State, of its criminal justice system: and a Member State that fails to bring its criminal justice system to bear in such a case will be in breach of this obligation. So it was that, some years ago, France was condemned when the French authorities failed to use the criminal law to stop rioting French farmers physically blocking the import of agricultural products from other Member States.[7]

EU law impinges on national criminal law positively when the EU con-sciously creates new rules at European level that force the criminal justice systems of the Member States to change their existing rules and practices and replace them by new ones: for example, by requiring them in future to co-operate with new bodies and organisations set up by 'Brussels', requiring their criminal courts to give automatic recognition to decisions of the criminal courts of other Member States, or requiring them to pass laws creating new criminal offences or to punish already-existing crimi-nal offences more severely. The last 15 years have seen a rapid growth of EU legislation of this type, the collective product of which is usually called 'EU criminal law'. In the following pages, we shall see a number of practical examples of all of these.

The main reason for this rapid growth of EU criminal law is a practi-cal one: the appearance of what might be called the 'fifth freedom'. In the wake of the free movement of workers, services, goods and capital has come a form of free movement that was both unintended and unde-sirable, namely that of criminals and crime. At the simplest and most obvious level, open borders and cheap transport between Member States combine to make it far easier than it used to be for a crime to be com-mitted in state A and the criminal to remove himself to state B, where the police and prosecutors of state A cannot catch him or her. In the face of this, the traditional process of extradition—by which the transfer of a wanted person across the Channel could be achieved, but it might take six years and cost the taxpayer £120,000[8]—obviously had to be replaced by a process that was quicker and cheaper; as it was, with effect from 31 December 2003, by the European Arrest Warrant,[9] of which more later. The 'fifth freedom' also means an increase in 'trans-border' crimes—for example, smuggling and carousel fraud—where part of the offence takes

---

[6] Treaty on European Union, Art 4(3); reproducing an obligation already existing by virtue of Art 10 of the EC Treaty.

[7] Case C-265-95 *Commission v French Republic* [1997] ECR I-6959. See E Baker, 'Crimi-nal Jurisdiction, the Public Dimension to "Effective Protection", and the Construction of Community–Citizen Relations' (2001) 4 *Cambridge Yearbook of European Legal Studies* 25.

[8] An example given to Parliament by the Minister of State, Mr John Denham, on the Second Reading of the Extradition Bill in the Commons: HC 396 col 396, 9 December 2002.

[9] Council Framework Decision of 13 June 2002 on the European Arrest Warrant and the Surrender Procedures Between Member States (2002/584/JHA), [2002] OJ L190/1.

place in one Member State and part of it in another, and these also create a need for various forms of EU criminal law. The effective prosecution of a 'trans-border' offence is likely to be dependent on the ability of one Member State to obtain evidence from another: whence pressure to replace the traditional process of 'mutual legal assistance', which is cumbersome and slow, with a new and swifter process, modelled on the European Arrest Warrant.[10]

Criminal offences committed across borders also give rise to practical issues of co-ordination. Suppose a people-smuggling operation is planned in London, using a route that brings the illegal immigrants into Europe via Belgium, whence they are distributed to France, Germany and Italy with the help of associates operating there. In this situation, which Member State or States should be responsible for the investigation and resulting prosecution? It was to deal with issues of this sort that Eurojust was created in 2002.[11] The fact that several different states have jurisdiction also raises the oppressive possibility of successive prosecutions, in different Member States, of the same people for the same offence. To deal with this concern, an article on 'double jeopardy', alias *ne bis in idem*, was included in the Schengen Agreement,[12] the interpretation of which has given rise to a series of cases before the ECJ;[13] and with the same aim in mind, a framework decision was adopted in 2009.[14]

Trans-border criminality also raises broader and more theoretical issues of co-ordination. To deal with certain types of it effectively, it is necessary, first and foremost, that all the Member States should treat the behaviour in question as a criminal offence, and secondly, that they all should visit it with penalties that are broadly similar. As Jean Pradel puts it, 'It is necessary to discourage "criminal tourism" which might encourage potential criminals to choose the country which is the least repressive'.[15] It is this concern that lies behind a number of framework decisions and other instruments which require Member States to criminalise certain forms of undesirable activity and to make them punishable with certain types of penalty—for example, the Framework Decision of 2002 on terrorism.[16]

---

[10] Hence the proposal for a 'European Investigation Order', discussed at p 353 below.

[11] Council Act of 29 May 2000 establishing in accordance with Art 34 of the Treaty on European Union the Convention on Mutual Assistance in Criminal Matters between the Member States of the European Union, [2000] OJ C197/01; Council Decision 2009/492/JHA of 16 December 2008 on strengthening Eurojust and amending decision 2002/187/JHA, [2009] OJ L138/14.

[12] Art 54 of the Convention Implementing the Schengen Agreement. See Klip, above n 2, 231ff; Mitsilegas, above n 2, 143ff.

[13] On this see Klip, above n 2, 231ff; Mitsilegas, above n 2, 143ff.

[14] Council Framework Decision 2009/948/JHA of 30 November 2009 on prevention and settlement of conflicts of exercise of jurisdiction in criminal proceedings, [2009] OJ L328/42.

[15] J Pradel, 'Les grandes tendances de l'européanisation des systèmes pénaux nationaux' (2009) 50 *Les Cahiers de Droit* 1015, 1032.

[16] Council Framework Decision of 13 June 2002 on combating terrorism (2002/475/JHA) [2002] OJ L164/3.

Terrorism, obviously, is behaviour that directly threatens the interests of each Member State. In some cases, however, behaviour must be punished because it poses a threat, not to the Member States themselves, but to the interests of the European Union as an institution. An obvious example, since the arrival of the 'single currency', is counterfeiting the euro.[17] Another example is fraud on the Community budget.[18]

As well as practical reasons for the growth of EU criminal law, there are ideological ones. In 1999, the Treaty of Amsterdam amended the Maastrict Treaty by proclaiming the objective of the European Union to be the creation of 'an area of freedom, security and justice'—a commitment now reiterated in Article 67(1) of the TFEU. Though capable of being used by authoritarians as a pretext for the creation of an area in which the authorities have *freedom* to bring those who threaten the *security* of the state to *justice*, the 'AFSJ' potentially conveys a message that is more positive: the idea of area in all parts of which citizens can be sure that the criminal justice system will treat those who come into contact with it with a certain minimal level of humanity, consideration and efficiency. It was in that spirit that, in 2001, a framework decision was adopted which guarantees certain minimum rights for victims in criminal proceedings.[19] It is also in reality the spirit that animates the current move towards a series of instruments designed to guarantee various minimum rights for suspects and defendants—though, as will be explained later in this chapter, these are officially justified on instrumental grounds, as being necessary to build 'mutual trust' between the criminal justice systems of the Member States, in the absence of which 'mutual recognition' measures, like the European Arrest Warrant, are unlikely to work smoothly.[20]

II EU CRIMINAL LAW—WHAT IS IT?

The phrase 'EU criminal law' suggests a European criminal code and a European criminal procedure code, with a European public prosecutor to enforce them. Such were indeed the elements of the system that was proposed 13 years ago in the Corpus Juris project. Of this, no part has so far been implemented—although the TFEU does now provide a treaty

---

[17] Council Framework Decision of 29 May 2000 on increasing protection by criminal penalties and other sanctions against counterfeiting in connection with the introduction of the euro (200/383/JHA), [2000] OJ L104/1; Council Reg (EC) No 1338/2001 of 28 June 2001 laying down measures necessary for the protection of the euro against counterfeiting, [2001] OJ L181/6.

[18] Hence the so-called 'PIF Convention'; see n 71 below.

[19] Council Framework Decision of 15 March 2001 on the standing of victims in criminal proceedings. This was the instrument that gave rise to the famous *Pupino* case, Case C-105/03 [2005] ECR I-5285; see n 76 below.

[20] See p 352 below.

basis for a European Public Prosecutor, should the Member States at some future point decide they want to have one.

At present, EU criminal law exists only in a looser sense, and in concrete terms comprises the following four elements: (i) a group of European organisations created to secure the better functioning of criminal justice; (ii) a group of European instruments enacted with the aim of enabling the criminal justice systems of the Member States to tackle trans-border cases more effectively; (iii) a group of European instruments prescribing uniform rules of substantive criminal law which the Member States are required to adopt; and (iv) a smaller group of European instruments which, in a similar way, prescribe rules of criminal procedure. In the next section of this chapter each of these four elements will be examined in turn.

A Organisations

(i) OLAF[21]

The oldest of these specialist organisations is the European Anti-Fraud Office, usually known as OLAF, the acronym for its French name, l'Office européen de lutte anti-fraude. This started life in 1988 as UCLAF (Unité de lutte anti-fraude), and when relaunched in 1999 as OLAF, it gained greater independence, a bigger staff, more extensive powers and a supervisory body. Its powers and duties are set out in the regulation adopted when it was reconstituted.[22] Its office, like that of the Commission to which it is formally attached, is situated in Brussels.

As prescribed in the OLAF Regulation, the task of OLAF is to:

> conduct administrative investigations for the purpose of fighting fraud, corruption and any other illegal activity affecting the financial interests of the European Community [and] investigating to that end serious matters relating to the discharge of professional duties such as to constitute a dereliction of the obligations of officials and other servants of the Communities . . .[23]

To this end, it was given wide inquisitorial powers. It is thus an example of the 'vertical' approach to the problems of crime within the European Union—as against the 'horizontal' approach, in which the role of the Union is limited to co-ordinating the efforts of national authorities. The investigations that OLAF carries out are of two types: 'external' ones, where suspected fraud is investigated in Member States, and 'internal' ones, which target suspected frauds within the central organs of the Union.

[21] Mitsilegas, above n 2, 210ff.
[22] Reg (EC) No 1073/1999 of the European Parliament and of the Council of 25 May 1999 concerning investigations conducted by the European Anti-Fraud Office (OLAF), [1999] OJ L136.
[23] Art 1(3).

Having carried out an investigation, and found what it believes to be criminal offences, OLAF has no power to prosecute. It forwards its reports to the competent authorities of the Member State whose courts have jurisdiction, who are then free to act on them. The tendency of national prosecutors to ignore reports which OLAF believes to be well founded is, of course, a source of deep frustration within OLAF—a matter which explains why OLAF and its officials are staunch supporters of the proposal to create a European Public Prosecutor.

If OLAF's internal critics are mainly concerned about its inability to ensure that action is taken against the frauds that its investigations bring to light, its external critics have highlighted other and different matters.[24] One of these is its awkward constitutional position, because OLAF is at once a part of the Commission and the organ responsible for investigating frauds and improper practices within it. Another is the occasional heavy-handedness with which it has exercised its powers—which has led to several well-publicised pieces of litigation.[25]

(ii) Europol[26]

The origin of Europol, the European Police Office, was a 'third pillar' convention concluded in 1995, which—after the usual delays for ratification which bedevil legislation by convention—eventually came into force in 1998. After the Convention had been repeatedly modified, in April 2009 Europol acquired a new constitutional document: the Europol Decision, a Council decision,[27] with effect from 1 January 2010. Under this document, as before, Europol comprises a Management Board with a representative from every Member State, a Director (with three Deputy Directors) and a Supervising Body. It has legal personality, and its seat is in The Hague.

By Article 3 of the Europol Decision, the objective of Europol is 'to support and strengthen action by the competent authorities of the Member States and their mutual cooperation in preventing and combating organised crime, terrorism and other forms of serious crime affecting two or more Member States.'

Though the idea of a 'European FBI' has had its vocal supporters,[28] Europol bears little resemblance to the Federal Bureau of Investigation in

---

[24] Mitsilegas, above n 2, 215–18; X Groussot and Z Popov, 'What's Wrong with OLAF? Accountability, Due Process and Criminal Justice in European Anti-fraud Policy' (2010) 47 *Common Market Law Review* 605. And see the House of Lords European Union Committee, 24th Report of Session 2003–04, 'Strengthening OLAF, the European Anti-Fraud Office', HL Paper 139.

[25] Notably the *Tillack* case: (Case T-193/04, *Tillack v Commission*, [2006] ECR II 3995) For this and other litigation see Mitsilegas, and Groussot and Popov, previous note.

[26] Mitsilegas, above n 2, 161ff; Klip, above n 2, 387ff.

[27] Council Decision of 6 April 2009 establishing the European Police Office (Europol) (2009/371/JHA), OJ L121/37, 15.5.2009.

[28] Including Helmut Kohl: see Mitsilegas, above n 2, 162.

the US. It is a 'horizontal' body, which has no operational powers, the basic task of which is the collection, storage, analysis and exchange of information about criminals and crimes. To this end, it runs the Europol Information System. Much of the Europol Decision is concerned with the management of this Information System, and the issues of data protection that arise from its existence.

However, Europol can become involved in operational policing to some limited extent. First, by Article 6 of the Decision, Europol staff may participate in 'joint investigation teams' set up groups of national police forces. Secondly, by Article 7, Europol has the power to make a formal request to a Member State to take action in respect of a particular case. A Member State that receives such a request is obliged to consider it, but is not required to act on it. If it decides not to act on it, however, it must give Europol its reasons, unless to do so would 'harm essential national security interests' or 'jeopardise the success of investigations under way or the safety of individuals'.

(iii)   Eurojust [29]

Eurojust is another manifestation of the 'horizontal' concept: an organisation designed to co-ordinate the activities of public prosecutors in the different Member States. As such, it actually represents the last in a line of three attempts to do so. The first, which began in 1996, was a scheme under which Member States lent one another 'magistrats de liaison'—prosecutors from one Member State who are seconded to another, in order to provide help and advice.[30] The second, which was launched two years later, was a more ambitious scheme for a 'European Judicial Network'—a network of public prosecutors who, as 'national contact points', are available to advise one another, and who meet all together at least once a year, usually in the Member State which currently holds the Presidency of the Council.[31] Perhaps surprisingly, both of these earlier schemes have continued after the creation of Eurojust, the EJN even acquiring a new constitutional document by a Council decision in 2008.[32]

Eurojust came into being by a Council decision in 2002,[33] its constitution being amended by a second Council decision seven years later,[34] and

---

[29] Mitsilegas, above n 2 187ff; Klip, above n 2, 401ff.
[30] Established by the Joint Action of 22 April 1996, [1996] OJ L105.
[31] Established by the Joint Action of 29 June 1998, [1998] OJ L191.
[32] Council Decision 2008/976/JHA of 16 December 2008 on the European Judicial Network, [2008] OJ L348/130.
[33] Council Act of 29 May 2000 establishing in accordance with Art 34 of the Treaty on European Union the Convention on Mutual Assistance in Criminal Matters between the Member States of the European Union, [2000] OJ C197/1.
[34] Council Decision 2009/492/JHA of 16 December 2008 on strengthening Eurojust and amending decision 2002/187/JHA, [2009] OJ L138/14.

its legal position then being further regulated by Articles 85 and 86 of the TFEU. The body that results from this jigsaw of legislation is bigger, heavier and much more formal than the two schemes for ensuring co-operation between prosecutors that preceded it, and in broad terms it does for public prosecutors what Europol has done for the police.

The structure of Eurojust is rather similar to that of Europol. Eurojust, like Europol, is a legal entity and, like Europol, it has its official seat in The Hague. Again, like Europol, it consists of representatives sent by Member States. At a formal level, it is composed of 'one national member seconded by each Member State in accordance with its legal system, being a prosecutor, judge or police officer of equivalent competence'.[35] The resulting 'college' elects a President and Vice-Presidents.[36] Eurojust has a permanent staff, headed by an Administrative Director. Like Europol, it also has an external Supervisory Body.

According to Article 85(1) of the TFEU,

> Eurojust's mission shall be to support and strengthen co-ordination and co-operation between national investigating and prosecuting authorities in relation to serious crime affecting two or more Member States or requiring a prosecution on common bases, on the basis of operations conducted and information supplied by the Member States' authorities and by Europol.

This set of objectives are elaborated in greater detail by the 2002 Council Decision.[37] In the pursuit of its objectives Eurojust, like Europol, has no power, as such, to require a Member State to investigate a case or institute a prosecution, much less does it have the power to do either of these things itself. By Article 6 of the Decision it has the power 'ask' a Member State to do either of these things and, indeed, a range of other things as well. Among these other things, Eurojust may ask a Member State to set up a joint investigation team together with another Member State and, in cases where two Member States are both engaged in investigating or prosecuting the same person, it may also invite one of them to 'keep off the grass' and leave it to the other. As when Europol issues an invitation of this sort, where Eurojust asks a Member State to take a course of action, that Member State is at liberty to refuse—though, as when a Member State refuses to accede to a request from Europol, it must give its reasons, unless to do so would 'harm essential national security interests or would jeopardise the safety of individuals'.[38]

If Eurojust's powers are limited, its practical significance is considerable. As one commentator puts it:

[35] Eurojust Decision, article 2(1) (as amended)
[36] At the time of writing the President is a Briton, Aled Jones.
[37] Eurojust Decision, Art 3.
[38] Under the 2002 Decision, Member States could also refuse to give reasons where to do so would 'jeopardise the success of investigations under way', but this phrase was dropped from the 2008 revision.

The improvement which the establishment of Eurojust has brought to international co-operation is twofold. First, it provides practical assistance at prosecutorial level for the transmission and execution of requests for international assistance. Second, it creates a forum in which decisions on the best place for the prosecution can be made. Eurojust does not have a formal competence to decide upon matters of plural jurisdiction. However, the very fact that prosecutors with expertise in the international co-operation of the relevant member States can take up consultations on a specific case is *de facto* of enormous importance. The permanent structure should be conducive to the prevention of jurisdictional conflicts, and to multiple prosecutions and to *ne bis in idem* problems.[39]

The politics that lay behind the creation of Eurojust are closely connected with public reaction to the Corpus Juris project, and in particular, to its central proposal for the creation of a European Public Prosecutor. Though this idea was strongly supported by the Commission and by UCLAF (later OLAF), this 'vertical solution' to the problems of trans-border crime, and to trans-border frauds on the Community budget in particular, was strongly opposed by many Member States, with the UK at the forefront. To solve the current problems, whose existence the opposing Member States did not deny, they came up with an alternative solution: a 'horizontal' solution the twin elements of which were 'mutual recognition'—of which more is said below—and improved co-ordination between the prosecution services of the different Member States, to which end Eurojust was rapidly created. But this solution was to some extent a compromise and, like many compromises, meant different things to different people. Whereas, for some, Eurojust was the end of the process, for others it was a beginning. Among those who supported the creation of Eurojust, there were some who hoped that, in time, it would grow from being a body that merely co-ordinates the efforts of the prosecutors of the different Member States to become a body that actually does the job itself: an independent European Public Prosecutor.[40]

When the Lisbon Treaty was drawn up, this point of view prevailed, to the extent of the inclusion in the Treaty of what is now Article 86 of the TFEU. This provides that, by a decision that is unanimous, the Council 'may establish a European Public Prosecutor's Office from Eurojust'; and it further provides that, where the Council is not unanimous, it is open to a group of at least nine Member States to 'go it alone'.

---

[39] Klip, above n 2, 404.
[40] See Mitsilegas, above n 2, 188ff.

B European Instruments on 'Mutual Recognition'

'Mutual recognition' is when the courts of two different legal systems recognise and enforce each other's rulings and decisions automatically, without any examination of the factual basis upon which they were made. It is the arrangement that has long existed between the criminal courts of the different parts of the UK, but until recently it was not at all the system that operated between the criminal courts of the EU Member States. In the European context, the basic principle was that the judges in criminal courts did not normally recognise each other's orders and decisions, although they might sometimes do so exceptionally, and as a special favour. In those exceptional cases where the criminal courts of one Member State might be able to invoke the help of those of another to enforce its order, the procedure would typically involve the making of a formal request, transmitted from court to court indirectly, via the two countries' governments. The executive of the requested state would usually screen incoming requests and, in some cases, might not allow them to proceed. Where the request did eventually reach the court system of the requested state, the court would usually grant it only where a number of conditions were met. Typically, these were two: first a 'double criminality' requirement, ie a requirement that the behaviour should be criminally punishable in the requested state as well as in the requesting state, and secondly a requirement that the requesting state produce enough evidence to show a 'prima facie case' justifying the measure asked for. In some situations, the executive of the requested state would then exercise a further control at what might be called the 'output stage'. This was so, in particular, with extradition in its traditional form, where the final removal of the requested person required the consent of the executive of the requested state—in the UK, the Home Secretary.[41] All this tended to make the prosecution of trans-border crimes where the wanted person, or the evidence, or some of it, was in another Member State slow, costly and uncertain. It was in reaction to this problem that the team that drafted the Corpus Juris project proposed, for offences of budgetary fraud, the 'vertical' solution of a European Public Prosecutor, armed with powers that could be exercised in any part of the territory of the European Union.

Not wishing to go down this route, the Member States, led by the UK,[42]

---

[41] As is still the case in the UK where extradition is sought by States that are not part of the EU.

[42] See the evidence of K Hoey, Under-Secretary of State at the Home Office, to the House of Lords Select Committee on the European Communities, 'Prosecuting Fraud', above n 1, Appendix 4, §297: 'The simplest way of putting it is that we support cooperation between jurisdictions rather than creating a single jurisdiction. Particularly as I come from Northern Ireland and Lord Hope is from Scotland, a very good model for this cooperation is what we already have here, working between the separate jurisdictions within the United Kingdom . . .'

proposed 'mutual recognition' as part of an alternative solution. First publicly floated, in outline only, at the Cardiff Council in June 1998,[43] it was then proclaimed with greater force at the Tampere Council in October 1999. In section IV of the Presidency Conclusions it was stated that:

> [35] . . . The European Council therefore endorses the principle of mutual recognition which, in its view, should become the cornerstone of judicial co-operation in both civil and criminal matters within the Union. The principle should apply to both judgments and to other decisions of judicial authorities . . .

The first concrete step in this direction was, of course, the European Arrest Warrant (EAW), created by a framework decision adopted in the summer of 2002.[44] This replaced traditional extradition within the EU by a system under which, if certain basic conditions are met, the transfer of the wanted person takes place automatically, without the intervention of the executive, and within a stated set of time limits. If the offence for which the person is wanted is one of the 32 listed in Article 2(2) of the Framework Decision, the traditional 'dual criminality' requirement is suppressed: the requested state must hand the wanted person over, provided the offence carries at least three years' imprisonment in the requesting state. If the offence is not on this 'framework decision list', the EAW is still available if the offence carries a maximum penalty of at least 12 months, or (in the case of a convicted person) a sentence of at least four months has been imposed; though here, the requested state may insist upon 'dual criminality'. The implementation date fixed by the framework decision was 31 December 2003: a date which many Member States complied with, though for various reasons some were late. The new measure eventually survived constitutional challenges in several Member

---

[43] Presidency Conclusions, Cardiff 15 and 16 June 1998, §39, 'The European Council underlines the importance of effective judicial cooperation in the fight against cross-border crime. It recognises the need to enhance the ability of national legal systems to work closely together and asks the Council to identify the scope for greater mutual recognition of decision of each others' courts.'

[44] Council Framework Decision of 13 June 2002 on the European Arrest Warrant and the Surrender Procedures Between Member States (2002/584/JHA), [2002] OJ L190/1. The literature on the EAW is now substantial. See, inter alia, S Allegre and M Leaf, *The European Arrest Warrant: a Solution Ahead of its Time?* (London, Justice, 2003); R Blekxtoon and W van Ballegolij, *Handbook on the European Arrest Warrant* (The Hague, TMC Asser Press, 2004); N Keizer and E van Sliedregt (eds), *The European Arrest Warrant in Practice* (The Hague, TMC Asser Press, 2009); JR Spencer, 'The European Arrest Warrant' (2003–04) 7 *Cambridge Yearbook of European Legal Studies* 201. For a review of the workings of the EAW in the UK, see the House of Lords European Union Committee, 30th Report of Session 2005–06, 'European Arrest Warrant—Recent Developments', HL Paper 156. For a critique of the UK implementing legislation, see JR Spencer 'Implementing the European Arrest Warrant: a Tale of How Not to Do It' (2009) 30 *Statute Law Review* 184.

States,[45] and a further challenge before the ECJ.[46]

Though widely criticised in the popular press (at least in the UK) as forcing our courts to send Britons to face unfair trials for offences of which they are innocent, the governments of the Member States (including ours) view the EAW as a big success. This has led to moves to create further 'mutual recognition' measures to replace the existing leisurely and uncertain 'mutual legal assistance' regime[47] that currently applies when the courts of one Member State wish to obtain evidence from another, or make other dispositions in the case ahead of trial. However, once the political pressure resulting from the attack on the World Trade Centre on 11 September 2001 had died down, progress was much slower. In 2003 a framework decision was adopted that sought to impose a 'mutual recognition' regime in respect of 'freezing orders'.[48] Eventually, after lengthy negotiations, in December 2008 a further framework decision was adopted providing for a so-called 'European Evidence Warrant', which Member States are required to implement by January 2011;[49] however, as the scope of this is limited, its new 'mutual recognition' regime being applicable to some types of evidence but not others, it is widely seen as half-measure of questionable utility. The restricted scope of this instrument, and the generally slow progress in producing others, arose from an underlying political difficulty: framework decisions required unanimity, which with 27 Member States had become hard to achieve. Once the Lisbon Treaty was in force, under which the EU can now legislate in the area of criminal law by means of directives, adopted by a qualified majority vote, there were moves to replace this framework decision with a new directive creating a 'European Investigation Order', the scope of which would be much wider. At the time of writing, a draft directive emanating from a group of Member States, led by Belgium, is under discussion; and the UK government—despite the protests of the eurosceptic press, which reported the proposal it is usual alarmist terms[50]—has decided to opt in.

Meanwhile there have been parallel moves to extend 'mutual recognition' to sentences—so that the sentence imposed by a criminal court in

[45] The literature is substantial. For a succinct discussion, see Mitsilegas, above n 2, 133–38; and see the special issue (2008) 6(1) *International Journal of Constitutional Law*.
[46] Case C-303/05 *Advocaten voor de Wereld VZW v Leden van de Ministerraad* ECR [2007] I-3633.
[47] Within Europe, this is based on the European Convention on Mutual Assistance in Criminal Matters of 20 April 1959, together with the EU Convention on Mutual Assistance in Criminal Matters (Council Act of 29 May 2000, [2000] OJ C197/1).
[48] Council Framework Decision 2003/577 JHA of 22 July 2003 on the execution in the European Union or orders freezing property or evidence, [2003] OJ L196/45.
[49] Council Framework Decision 2008/978/JHA of 18 December 2008 on the European evidence warrant for the purpose of obtaining objects, documents and data for use in proceedings in criminal matters, [2008] OJ L350/72.
[50] 'Britons to be Spied on by Foreign Police' was the headline in the *Daily Telegraph* when reporting, on 26 July 2010, that a UK opt-in was imminent. For a summary of the arguments for and against, see JR Spencer (2010) 6 *Archbold Review* 4.

one Member State will be automatically recognised by the others, and in some cases may even be enforced in another Member State. These began over 10 years ago with a convention on the mutual recognition of driving disqualifications.[51] After a substantial gap, this was followed by a rapid series of framework decisions dealing with other types of sentence. In 2005 a framework decision extended the principle of mutual recognition to 'financial penalties'—ie fines, so enabling a fine imposed by a court in one Member State to be enforced in another.[52] The following year a further framework decision did the same for confiscation orders.[53] In 2008 two further framework decisions were adopted, one to enable prison sentences to be enforced in other Member States[54] and another to enable the same to be done with probation orders and other 'alternative sanctions'.[55] To round it off, the same year produced a further framework decision requiring all Member States to give, within their own systems, the same official status to previous convictions imposed by the courts of other Member States as they give to previous criminal convictions imposed by their own courts.[56]

This 'mutual recognition' policy raises important issues which it is not possible to discuss fully here, but which nevertheless should be mentioned. One is whether mutual recognition, in its present form, is really workable. It was introduced, as everybody knows, as an expedient to avoid 'vertical solutions', but the view has been expressed that mutual recognition can only work when the laws of the countries concerned are broadly similar; thus to make it work properly some radical and centrally directed harmonisation will be required—which is one of the things that mutual recognition was intended to avoid. Another big issue is whether the mutual recognition programme, taken as a whole, is excessively authoritarian. Defence lawyers often say that it is unfairly favourable to prosecutors. If by this they really mean that prosecutors can now secure the conviction

[51] Convention under then Art K.3 of the Treaty of European Union on Driving Disqualifications. [1998] OJ C216. By Art 15, this comes into force 90 days after its ratification by the last of the states which were Members of the EU at the time of its adoption by the Council—an event which has still not occurred (though a number of Member States, including the UK and the Republic of Ireland, have made reciprocal arrangements).
[52] Council Framework Decision 2005/214/JHA of 24 February 2005 on the application of the principle of mutual recognition to financial penalties, [2005] OJ L76/16.
[53] Council Framework Decision 2006/783/JHA of 6 October 2006 on the application of the principle of mutual recognition to confiscation orders, [2004] OJ L335/8.
[54] Council Framework Decision 2008/909/JHA of 27 November 2008 on the application of the principle of mutual recognition to judgments in criminal matters involving deprivation of liberty (etc), [2008] OJ L327/27.
[55] Council Framework Decision 2008/947/JHA of 27 November 2008 on the application of the principle of mutual recognition to judgments and probation decisions (etc), [2008] OJ L337/102.
[56] Council Framework Decision 2008/675/JHA of 24 July 2008 on taking account of convictions in the Member States of the European Union in the course of new criminal proceedings, [2008] OJ L220/32.

of guilty clients who would otherwise go free, then this is a matter for rejoicing, not dismay; but if the criticism is that mutual recognition means that innocent people are more likely to be convicted wrongly, then—if this is really so—it is obviously worrying. A third big issue is whether the mutual recognition programme is actually effective. Apart from the Framework Decision on the European Arrest Warrant, the implementation of these instruments has been distinctly patchy and we are moving in the area of 'virtual law'. A fourth and final comment is how complicated this area of EU law has now become. In the previous paragraphs no fewer than nine different EU legal instruments have been examined. There is a strong case, surely, for pruning and simplification.[57]

C European Instruments Relating to Substantive Criminal Law

The last 15 years have seen an explosive growth of European instruments requiring Member States, if they have not already done so, to make various uniform adjustments to their substantive criminal law. In every case, the obligation so imposed is to make a given type of antisocial behaviour punishable; and, typically but not invariably, further duties are also imposed about the severity of punishment, the categories of person to whom the law applies and extra-territorial jurisdiction.

The range of matters covered by these instruments is wide and, broadly speaking, covers all the matters which, in the last few years, have agitated public opinion in the Member States to the point where the media are demanding action and the politicians are promising to provide it. They include commercial fraud,[58] corruption[59] and money-laundering;[60]

[57] On these and other issues, see G Vernimmen-Van Tiggelen, L Surano and A Weyembergh (eds), *The Future of Mutual Recognition in Criminal Matters in the European Union* (Bruxelles, Editions de l'Université Libre de Bruxelles, 2009).

[58] Council Framework Decision of 28 May 2001 combating fraud and counterfeiting of non-cash means of payment, [2001] OJ L149.

[59] Council Act 97/C 195/01 of 26 May 1997 drawing up, on the basis of Art K.3(2)(c) of the Treaty on European Union, the Convention on the fight against corruption involving officials of the European Communities or officials of Member States of the European Union, [1997] OJ C195. Council Framework Decision 2003/568/JHA of 22 July 2003 on combating corruption in the private sector, [2003]OJ L192.

[60] Dir 2005/60/EC of the European Parliament and the Council of 26 October 2005 on the prevention of the use of the financial system for the purpose of money laundering and terrorist financing, [2005] OJ L309.

terrorism;[61] organised crime;[62] drug-trafficking;[63] illegal immigration;[64] people-trafficking;[65] environmental pollution;[66] computer hacking;[67] child pornography and paedophilia;[68] and racism and xenophobia.[69] In all those cases, the interests affected by the behaviour in question are primarily those of the Member States, but instruments have also been adopted in order to strike at behaviour which primarily threatens the interests of Union itself—fraud against the Community budget[70] and counterfeiting the euro.[71] The type of instrument used has varied according to the date and to the subject matter. In the pre-Lisbon era, 'third pillar' instruments were mainly used—conventions—and then, after Amsterdam, framework decisions. In some cases, however, 'first pillar' instruments were used, and occasionally both types were used simultaneously, as a sort of legislative 'belt and braces'. Post-Lisbon, the instrument of choice is likely to be the directive.

In every case, these instruments begin by defining a type of behaviour and requiring Member States to make it criminally punishable. Very commonly, they continue by requiring a 'minimum maximum penalty'; the Framework Decision on organised crime, for example, requires Member States to take the necessary measures to ensure that involvement in a criminal organisation 'is punishable by a maximum term of imprisonment of between two and five years'.[72] These instruments usually require

---

[61] Council Framework Decision of 13 June 2002 on combating terrorism (2002/475/JHA), [2002] OJ L164/3.

[62] Council Framework Decision 2008/841/JHA of 24 October 2008 on the fight against organised crime, [2008] OJ L300/42.

[63] Council Framework Decision 2004/757/JHA of 24 October 2004 laying down minimum provisions on the constituent elements of criminal acts and penalties in the field of illicit drug trafficking, [2004] OJ L335.

[64] Council Framework Decision 2002/946/JHA of 28 November 2002 on illegal immigration etc, [2002] OJ L328; Dir 2002/90/EC of 28 November 2002 on the same topic, [2002] OJ L328.

[65] Council Framework Decision 2002/629/JHA of 19 July 2002 on combating trafficking in human beings, [2002] OJ L203.

[66] Dir 2005/35/EC of 7 September 2005 on ship-source pollution and on the introduction of penalties for infringements (and amendments), [2005] OJ L255.

[67] Council Framework Decision 2005/222/JHA of 24 February 2005 on attacks against information systems, [2005] OJ L69.

[68] Council Framework Decision 2004/68/JHA of 22 December 2003 on combating the sexual exploitation of children and child pornography, [2004] OJ L13.

[69] Council Framework Decision 2008/913/JHA of 28 November 2008 on combating certain forms and expressions of racism and xenophobia by means of criminal law, [2008] OJ L328/55.

[70] Convention drawn up on the basis of Art K.3 of the Treaty of European Union, on the protection of the European Communities' financial interests, 26 July 1995, [1995] OJ C316; second Protocol thereto, [1997] OJ C221/12.

[71] Council Framework Decision of 29 May 2000 on increasing protection by criminal penalties and other sanctions against counterfeiting in connection with the introduction of the euro, [2000] OJ L140/1.

[72] The Framework Decision also requires Member States to render punishable 'conduct by any person consisting of an agreement with one or more persons' to commit any of a

Member States to ensure that incitement and complicity are also punishable, and invariably require Member States to ensure that criminal liability extends to 'legal persons'. (Corporate criminal liability, though 'old hat' to common lawyers, to Continental lawyers is an exciting new development; and those responsible for drafting EU instruments clearly see it as a panacea.) Finally, they usually also require Member States to legislate so that the behaviour is punishable when committed on its national territory, by one of its nationals or for the benefit of a legal person that has its head office in the territory of that Member State. (If corporate criminal liability shows of the influence of the common law on Europe, these provisions about jurisdiction demonstrate the opposite trend. The common law has traditionally assumed that criminal jurisdiction should be based on territoriality alone, rejecting extensions such as 'active personality'.[73])

The most obvious point to make about this department of EU criminal law is that it is uniformly repressive. The tendency of every one of these instruments is to extend the scope of criminal liability or increase the severity of punishment; we have yet to see a European instrument that requires Member States to decriminalise behaviour or limit the penalties applicable. This has posed few problems at the political level for the UK, where 'criminal policy' in recent years has been to extend the number of criminal offences[74] and where already maximum penalties for offences are invariably far higher than those these EU instruments require.

D European Instruments Relating to Criminal Procedure

At present, there is just one EU instrument that potentially requires Member States to modify their criminal procedure, and this is the Framework Decision of 2001 on the standing of victims in criminal proceedings.[75] As previously mentioned, it was this instrument that gave rise to the *Pupino*[76] case. This instrument sets out a list of guarantees that Member States undertake to provide for the victims of criminal offences. Under Article 3, 'Each Member State shall take appropriate measures to ensure that its

range of criminal offences; and here, Member States must ensure a 'minimum maximum penalty' of between two and five years, or the penalty applicable to the completed offence, whichever is the greater.

[73] In deference to the UK and the Republic of Ireland, the provisions in these instruments about jurisdiction often permit Member States to decide that they will not apply the 'active personality' principle where the offence takes place outside their territory.

[74] It is widely said that, in the 19 years after the General Election in 1997, at least 3,000 new criminal offences were created. On this, see JR Spencer, 'The Drafting of Criminal Legislation: Need It Be So Impenetrable?' (2008) 67 *Cambridge Law Journal* 585, 587.

[75] [2001] OJ L82/1.

[76] Case C-105/3 *Criminal Proceedings Against Pupino*, Case C-105/03 [2005] ECR I-5285, [2006] QB 83 noted (2005) 64 *Cambridge Law Journal* 569.

authorities question victims only insofar as necessary for the purpose of criminal proceedings', and under Article 8(4),

> Each Member State shall ensure that, where there is a need to protect victims— particularly the most vulnerable—from the effects of giving evidence in open court, victims may, by decision taken in open court, be entitled to testify in a manner which will enable this objective to be achieved, by any appropriate means compatible with its basic rights.

Mrs Pupino, a teacher at an infant school, was accused of acts of cruelty to children in her care. As Italian criminal procedure then stood, for the children's evidence to be received it was necessary for them to attend the trial and give their evidence orally. This state of affairs was inconsistent with obligations imposed by the Framework Decision.[77]

Though this is the only instrument of this sort that currently exists, others are under serious discussion.

Of these, one is a proposal for an instrument requiring the criminal courts of all the Member States to treat as admissible evidence any material gathered in another Member State, provided that the laws of that Member State were respected when the evidence was collected. The background to this proposal is the previously mentioned difficulty that OLAF sometimes has in persuading the authorities of Member States to take action on its reports. One of the recurrent reasons Member States refuse to prosecute, it seems, is that the evidence OLAF provides was not gathered according to the procedures laid down for the collection of such evidence in their own criminal procedure codes—even though it was lawfully collected according to the rules of the Member State where it was gathered. To deal with this, a proposal for the 'free movement of evidence' was put forward at Tampere in 1999.[78] Three years later it surfaced again in a Commission Green Paper,[79] and again in another Commission Green Paper in 2009.[80]

What exactly is meant by this proposal is not clear. On a narrow interpretation, it merely means that where local formalities for evidence-gathering were complied with, the resulting evidence should not be rejected by the courts of another Member State merely because, had

---

[77] It is questionable whether the UK has complied with the Framework Decision, because at present English law would require a child witness to undergo a live cross-examination at the trial if the defendant pleaded not guilty.

[78] Tampere Presidency Conclusions, §36: 'evidence lawfully gathered by one Member State's authorities should be admissible before the courts of other Member States, taking account of the standards that apply there'.

[79] 'Green Paper on Criminal Law Protection of the Financial Interests of the Community and the Establishment of a European Public Prosecutor', COM(2001) 715 final, 11 December 2001. §6.3.4.1.

[80] 'Green Paper on Obtaining Evidence in Criminal Matters from One Member State to Another and Securing its Admissibility', COM(2009) 624 final. (Though part of the Commission's original proposal for a European Investigation Order, 'free movement of evidence' does not form part of the Draft Directive that is currently under discussion; see above n 51.)

the evidence been gathered there, different formalities would have been required. This 'locus regit actum' rule is a sensible one which already prevails in a number of Member States, including (it seems) the UK,[81] and to generalise it would not be revolutionary. On a wider reading, however, it could mean that any piece of evidence gathered lawfully in one Member State becomes automatically admissible in criminal proceedings in another Member State, irrespective of any rule of evidence that would otherwise exclude it, or whether that rule is concerned with formalities or based on some broader principle. On this interpretation, a written statement lawfully taken from a witness in state A, where written statements of absent witnesses are generally admissible in substitution for their oral testimony, would be automatically admissible in state B, under the law of which written statements from absent witnesses are generally excluded and oral evidence is normally required. The implications of this are worrying, to put it mildly.[82]

Another is a proposal—or, to be more exact, a series of proposals—to ensure that all Member States introduce measures to secure certain minimum safeguards for defendants.

Moves in this direction began in 2003,[83] shortly after the creation of the EAW. Their overt justification was the need to build the 'mutual trust' that is necessary for the proper functioning of 'mutual recognition'. The courts in Member States whose criminal procedure provides proper safeguards against the mistreatment of suspects and defendants, and against the risk of wrongfully convicting the innocent, will (so it is said) be unwilling to execute EAWs, and other 'mutual recognition' instruments, if they suspect that these safeguards are missing in the Member State whose order they are expected to enforce. But, as suggested earlier in this chapter, in the background also lay another and more fundamental reason: the notion that, in an 'area of freedom, justice and security', all citizens deserve a criminal justice system that is civilised, and in which certain basic safeguards are guaranteed.

In 2006, progress towards a new Framework Decision on defence rights was abruptly halted when, to its shame, the British government, initially in favour, used its political muscle to block it. No coherent reason was

---

[81] *R v McNab* [2001] EWCA Crim 1605, [2002] 1 Cr App R (S) 72, [2002] *Criminal Law Review* 129.

[82] On this, see JR Spencer, 'The Problems of Trans-border Evidence and European Initiatives to Resolve Them' (2006–2007) 9 *Cambridge Yearbook of European Legal Studies*, 465, 473ff.

[83] 'Green Paper from the Commission—Procedural Safeguards for Suspects and Defendants in Criminal Proceedings throughout the European Union', COM(2003)75 final, 19 February 2003; followed by 'A Proposal for a Council Framework Decision on Certain Procedural Rights in Criminal Proceedings throughout the European Union', COM(2004) 328, 28 April 2004; S Alegre 'EU Fair Trial Rights—Added Value or No Value?' [2004] *New Law Journal* 758.

ever given for this change of mind,[84] but the reason was probably that the government had just published a White Paper announcing its intention of 'Rebalancing the criminal justice system in favour of the law-abiding majority',[85] which it feared would lose its impact with the electorate if it appeared alongside headlines saying 'Brussels Forces UK to Give Criminals Yet More Human Rights'. By the autumn of 2009 the British government had changed its mind again, and it was actively backing new moves from the Commission towards EU instruments guaranteeing rights for criminal defendants.

These new moves consist of a 'roadmap' of intended future measures designed to safeguard the position of suspects and defendants during the police investigation and preliminary stages of a prosecution, which was approved by the Council in a resolution on 30 November 2009.[86] These proposed new measures concern (i) provision of adequate interpretation and translation; (ii) information to suspects about their legal rights; (iii) legal aid and advice; (iv) a right for persons detained to communicate with relatives, employers and consular authorities; (v) special safeguards for suspected or accused persons who are vulnerable; and—eventually—(vi) a Green Paper on pre-trial detention. At the time this chapter is written, the Commission is working on all of these, and an instrument designed to give effect to the first measure—interpretation and translation—was approved by the Council on 20 October 2010.[87]

III   EU CRIMINAL LAW—WHAT WILL IT BECOME?

As all readers will be well aware, the Lisbon Treaty has radically changed the previous constitutional arrangements for the making of what was earlier described as 'positive EU criminal law'.

First, gone is the 'third pillar', the special system under which legislation in the area of criminal justice was made by the Council using a special set of instruments (in particular, framework decisions), which could only be adopted by unanimity; instead, the EU now legislates in criminal justice matters by the same processes, and using the same instruments, as it does for everything else. The instruments are now regulations, directives, decisions, recommendations and opinions. The legislative process now involves the European Parliament, but no longer requires, as it used to, unanimity in the Council from all Member States. If push comes to

---

[84] See generally the House of Lords European Union Committee, 2nd Report of 2006–07, 'Breaking the Deadlock: What Future for EU Procedural Rights?', HL Paper 20.
[85] Home Office, July 2006.
[86] [2009] OJ C295/1.
[87] Directive 2010/64/EU of the European Parliament and of the Council of 20 October 2010 on the right to interpretation and translation in criminal proceedings, [2010] OJ L280/1.

shove, the legislation may proceed by a qualified majority vote; though to compensate for the loss of their veto, the UK and the Republic of Ireland managed to negotiate a set of 'opt outs' of labyrinthine complexity.[88] Furthermore, in future, EU criminal law measures, like all other EU measures, will be subject to full 'judicial control', including enforcement proceedings against recalcitrant Member States which fail to implement them.

Secondly, the powers of the EU to legislate in criminal justice matters have been restated by new provisions which are, fortunately, rather clearer than the arcane provisions of the TEU which they replace.

Article 82 TFEU deals (in effect) with criminal procedure. Having proclaimed the principle of 'mutual recognition', it provides that, to the furtherance of this end, the EU may (inter alia) 'lay down rules and procedures for ensuring recognition throughout the Union of all forms of judgments and judicial decisions', and further provides that, 'to the extent necessary to facilitate mutual recognition', it may also 'establish minimum rules' in relation to a number of criminal procedure matters: 'mutual admissibility of evidence between Member States', 'the rights of individuals in criminal procedure', 'the rights of victims of crime' and 'any other specific aspects of criminal procedure' which the Council has agreed upon by unanimity, with the consent of the European Parliament.

Article 83 TFEU deals (in effect) with substantive criminal law. It provides that the European Parliament and the Council may enact directives establishing

> minimum rules concerning the definition of criminal offences and sanctions in the areas of particularly serious crime with a cross-border dimension resulting from the nature or impact of such offences or from a special need to combat them on a common basis.

'Particularly serious crime' is defined as 'terrorism, trafficking in human beings and sexual exploitation of women and children, illicit drug trafficking, illicit arms trafficking, money laundering, corruption, counterfeiting of means of payment, computer crime and organised crime', plus other types of crime in future determined by the Council, acting unanimously and with the consent of the European Parliament. In addition the EU may also adopt directives defining crimes and prescribing punishments where 'the approximation of criminal laws and regulations of the Member States proves essential to ensure the effective implementation of a Union policy in an area which has been subject to harmonisation measures'.

As regards the impact of all this on the UK, public attention has mainly focused on wide powers the UK has secured to 'opt out' of those measures it does not like.[89] But no less important, I believe, is the fact that,

---

[88] On this see S Peers, 'In a World of Their Own? Justice and Home Affairs Opt-outs and the Treaty of Lisbon' (2007–08) 10 *Cambridge Yearbook of European Legal Studies* 383.
[89] In particular by Protocol 21; on this, see Peers, previous note.

where the UK has 'opted in' to a new measure, the government now has much wider powers than previously to implement it by using secondary legislation. Previously, where the implementation of a 'third pillar' measure required a change in the law, primary legislation would usually be necessary. But the European Union (Amendment) Act 2008 has extended the scope of section 2(2) of the European Communities Act 1972, which previously allowed the government to implement 'first pillar' measures by means of secondary legislation, so that in future all 'EU obligations' can be implemented by this method, including those in the area of criminal law. As before, this power cannot be used so as to create new criminal offences that are punishable with more than two years' imprisonment;[90] but, at least in theory, secondary legislation could now be used to implement EU measures requiring rearrangements of criminal procedure, however radical they might be.

So, against this background, what will be the 'big issues' in the future? There could be many, but here I propose to close this chapter by briefly mentioning only two.

The first is 'what will be the future shape of EU criminal law: vertical or horizontal?' As we have seen, this tension between these two rival models is already present. It is evident in the institutions: of the three EU organisations that exist to handle criminal law, one of them—OLAF—is 'vertical', carrying out is own investigations into EU fraud, and the other two—Europol and Eurojust—are 'horizontal', their essential tasks being to co-ordinate the crime-fighting efforts of the national authorities in the Member States. Thirteen years ago, the Corpus Juris project produced a blueprint for a 'vertical' future in the form of a European Public Prosecutor, albeit within the limited area of budgetary fraud, who would enforce a single, unified code of criminal offences by using a single, unified code of criminal procedure. As already mentioned, this solution did not please the Member States, which reacted by producing a rival 'horizontal' solution— mutual recognition and improved co-ordination through Eurojust—as a means to solve the problems of trans-border crime. The tension, though temporarily buried, is present in the criminal justice articles of the TFEU. Article 82, as we have seen, proclaims the principle of mutual recognition, but Article 86 provides a mechanism by which, in the future, a European Public Prosecutor could evolve from Eurojust; and there is pressure from within the Commission, and OLAF to see that it eventually does. In the next few years, we shall see whether, with a Union of 27 Member States and others keen to join, co-ordination between national police and pros-

[90] Schedule 2 of the European Communities Act 1972 still precludes the use of this method 'to create any new criminal offence punishable with imprisonment for more than two years or punishable on summary conviction with imprisonment for more than three months or with a fine of more than level 5 on the standard scale (if not calculated on a daily basis) or with a fine of more than £100 a day'.

ecuting authorities plus mutual recognition of decisions can really cope with the issues of budgetary fraud and trans-border crime.

The second big issue, I believe, is whether the EU can secure a decent deal for suspects and defendants in those Member States where it seems that present arrangements are seriously deficient. Every criminal justice system makes occasional mistakes, and our own (alas) is no exception. Regrettably, however, there are strong reasons to believe that the criminal justice systems of some Member States have problems that are systematic. In a press communication launching its 'Justice in Europe' campaign, Fair Trials International—a serious organisation—said this:

> Sadly, our own casework repeatedly demonstrates the human cost of existing co-operation measures. Under the European Arrest Warrant, for example, people from all across Europe are being sent to other EU Member States for the most minor offences, or to serve prison sentences imposed after unfair trials . . . we also have compelling evidence of the need to improve fair trial rights across the Union.

Some of the English case law relating to the EAW reinforces this disquieting impression.[91]

That the will exists to do this is shown by the adoption of the 'road-map' that was described earlier. Unfortunately, it is not entirely clear that the EU has the legislative powers to see that its good intentions are carried through. As we have seen, Article 82 of the TFEU subordinates the competence of EU to legislate in the area of criminal procedure to the need to promote 'mutual recognition'; the EU has no power, as such, to pass legislation requiring Member States to clean up their systems of criminal procedure, just because their current state of hygiene is questionable. There is an obvious difficulty about trying to gear an improvement in the position of suspects and defendants to the enhancement of mutual recognition, and this is the essential nature of mutual recognition, which is 'We'll enforce your courts orders without asking awkward questions, provided you will do the same for ours'.[92]

The 'vertical solution' of a single European Public Prosecutor, using a single set of European rules, has been widely attacked, at any rate in the

---

[91] A telling example is *R (Mann) v Westminster Magistrates Court and another*, [2010] EWHC 48 (Admin), where it seems clear that at the applicant's trial in Portugal he was denied adequate interpretation and the legal advice he received was grossly incompetent; alas, the blunders of his Portuguese defence lawyers were then matched by those of the lawyers who initially represented him in England.

[92] It is possible that, in future, the courts of the Member States may blunt the harsher effects of mutual recognition by invoking the provisions of the EU Charter of Fundamental Rights: for example, Art 49(3), which provides that '[t]he severity of penalties must not be disproportionate to the criminal offence'. However, the courts in the UK will be in a relatively weak position to do this, because the UK, together with Poland, extracted from the Lisbon negotiations a concession in the form of Protocol 30, which limits the effect of the Charter in those countries. On this, see J Vogel and JR Spencer, 'Proportionality and the European Arrest Warrant', 6 (2010) *Criminal Law Review* 474.

UK, as potentially authoritarian—often in language that is extraordinarily violent.[93] Paradoxically, it could provide better safeguards for defendants than the horizontal solution of mutual recognition, 'You scratch our national prosecutor's back, and we'll do the same for yours.'

[93] Typical is a letter published in the *Daily Telegraph* on 10 February 2010: 'The EPP would not be like our own Director of Public Prosecutions, but more like a chief of police with the powers of a judge. Uniformed police would execute his commands and have frightening powers such as ordering house searches (the dreaded knock on the door in the small hours). He could also order the arrest, interrogation and imprisonment of suspects (for months at a time, with no public hearing) . . . The establishment of an EPP will surely be the prelude to the imposition of Corpus Juris, a common criminal and judicial system for the EU, because, to enable him to function, the EPP will need such a set of rules. Corpus Juris adopts the Napoleonic (inquisitorial) method, and sweeps away our British system with all its inbuilt safeguards against coercion, such as *habeas corpus* and trial by jury. To ensure that the EU's writ runs throughout its vassal states, the European Gendarmerie Force (EGF) will doubtless be deployed. Once this trio of the EPP, Corpus Juris and the gendarmerie is in place, EU supremacy will be complete . . .'

19

Free Movement of Goods and Pre-emption of State Power

LAURENCE W GORMLEY

I PROLOGUE

I HAVE KNOWN Alan Dashwood for my entire professional career, and he has been a source of much inspiration and encouragement over the years. He is rightly renowned for his ability to spot, stimulate and nurture new talent in the law, without stifling it in any way. He challenges, discusses and is open to ideas; he is indeed a not uncritical observer of the European Union, demonstrating that it is possible to contribute fully to the development of the Union while pointing out what needs to be improved or changed. It is with very great pleasure that all his friends note that emeritus status merely gives him yet more time to engage in the practice of and research into the many fields of European law, and to encourage its constant improvement. May you long remain an inspiration to us all!

II INTRODUCTION

While the European Union is certainly as yet far from being a fully fledged federal order, it is undoubtedly, in Alan Dashwood's memorable characterisation, a constitutional order of states[1] with some clearly federalist aspects: the European Union is a political, legal, economic and financial order which has an arranged distribution of powers between its component members and itself,[2] opting for supremacy of central law over

---

[1] See, eg A Dashwood (1996) 31 *European Law Review* 113, 114.
[2] This is characteristic of federal systems; it is now made explicit in Arts 4(1), 5 TEU and 3–6 TFEU. For the consolidated text of the EU Treaty and the Treaty on the Functioning of the European Union, see [2010] OJ C83; for the consolidated version of the Euratom Treaty, see [2010] OJ C84, corr [2010] C181/1.

state law in the event of a conflict.[3] Despite the clear commitment in what is now Article 4(3) TEU to sincere co-operation and Union solidarity,[4] the Member States—at whatever level—still find it convenient to act first and be faced with the legal consequences later. Over the years this has been particularly true in relation to the free movement of goods, but has by no means been confined to that area of EU law. But to what extent do the Member States actually retain or have the power to act in law in a manner incompatible with EU law?[5] And can the free movement of goods case law shed any light on the powers of the Member States? The two most developed areas in this regard are free movement of goods in the presence of a common organisation of the market and free movement of goods in the presence of Union harmonisation, although the issue also arises more generally.

III   COMMON ORGANISATIONS OF THE MARKET

In many early judgments the interaction of the free movement of goods provisions of the Treaty and the provisions of the common organisations was somewhat fuzzy, not least due to the fact that older common organisations repeated integrally the text of what was then Articles

---

[3] This position is most firmly established in EU law, as is well known, but has always been a creature of case law. It did appear in Art I-6 of the Treaty establishing a Constitution for Europe ([2004] OJ C310/1), which never entered into force, but in the Treaty of Lisbon ([2007] OJ C306/1, corr [2009] OJ C290/1) reliance was again placed solely on the case law of the Court of Justice (see Declaration 17 attached to the Final Act, [2007] OJ C306/256). See, giving a discussion of approaches to primacy, D Chalmers et al, *European Union Law*, 2nd edn (Cambridge, Cambridge University Press, 2010) ch 5; PJG Kapteyn and P VerLoren van Themaat, *The Law of the European Union and the European Communities*, 4th edn (Alphen aan den Rijn, Kluwer Law International, 2008) 537–45. The Court had really little choice but to insist on the primacy of (then) Community law in Case 6/64 *Costa v ENEL* [1964] ECR 585, 593–94, as any other approach would have totally frustrated the concept of the same laws applying throughout the EU, with economic operators working under the same undistorted conditions of competition; it would have led to wholesale market fragmentation, as opposed to market integration. One advantage of the dismantling of the so-called pillar structure of the EU through the Lisbon changes is that it puts an end to discussion about whether primacy extended to measures outside the Community system.

[4] The literature on the predecessors to Art 4(3) TFEU is legion, but see in particular J Temple Lang, 'Art 10 EC: the Most Important "General Principle" of Community Law' in U Bernitz and J Nergelius et al (eds), *General Principles of EC Law in a Process of Development* (Alphen aan den Rhijn, Kluwer Law International, 2008) 75; 'The Development by the Court of Justice of the Duties of Cooperation of National Authorities and Community Institutions under Art 10 EC' (2008) 31 *Fordham International Law Journal* 1483.

[5] Literature specifically on pre-emption may well now enjoy a renaissance in no small part due to the most stimulating work by R Schütze, *From Dual to Cooperative Federalism The Changing Structure of European Law* (Oxford, Oxford University Press, 2009); see also R Schütze, 'Supremacy without Pre-emption? The Very Slowly Emergent Doctrine of Community Pre-emption' (2006) 43 *Common Market Law Review* 1023; ED Cross, 'Pre-emption of Member State Law in the European Economic Community: A Framework for Analysis' (1992) 29 *Common Market Law Review* 447 and earlier literature cited in these works.

30–36 EC in order to ensure that the free movement of goods could be relied upon in the agricultural field before the end of the transitional period.[6] Thus the European Court of Justice (the Court) was not always clear whether it was examining national measures against the scheme of common organisation or against the free movement of goods provisions of the Treaty, or against both sets of provisions.[7] Nevertheless, in relation to pre-emption, a number of points of interest are apparent, not least that the Court was clearly undecided how intensely and consistently a pre-emption doctrine should be expressed.

On the one hand, in the judgment in *Galli*,[8] it stated that 'the very existence of a common organization of the market in the sense of Article [40(1)(c) TFEU] has the effect of precluding Member States from adopting in the sector unilateral measures capable of impeding intra-Community trade'.[9] The logical conclusion followed that

> in sectors covered by a common organisation of the market—even more so where this organisation is based on a common price system—Member States can no longer interfere through national provisions taken unilaterally in the machinery of price formation as established under the common organisation.[10]

The only way in which the Member States could act was in accordance with the relevant regulations, by asking the competent authority at (then) Community level to initiate or authorise measures compatible with the single market which the common organisations established. Both the market organisations considered in *Galli* (cereals and oils and fats) involved price systems applicable at the production and wholesale stages. Thus, while at those stages the pre-emption doctrine applied, at the retail and consumption stages the Member States still enjoyed freedom of action, subject to compliance with other provisions of the (now TFEU) Treaty. Of these, in particular the free movement of goods set clear limits on their freedom of action. Michel Waelbroeck described this pre-emption approach as

> the clearest and most extreme expression of the conceptualist-federalist theory. [The judgment] considers that matters falling within the scope of a common organisation of the market are entirely withdrawn from possible interference

[6] The transitional period came to an end at midnight on 31 December 1969; see J-P Warner, AG in Case 5/79 *Procureur Général v Buys* et al [1979] ECR 3203, 3243, followed by the Court of Justice in Case 251/78 *Denkavit Futtermittel GmbH v Minister für Ernährung, Landwirtschaft und Forschung des Landes Nordrhein-Westfalen* [1979] ECR 3369, 3384.
[7] See, further, LW Gormley, *Prohibiting Restrictions on Trade within the EEC* (Amsterdam, North Holland, 1985) ch 4.
[8] Case 31/74 *Galli* [1975] ECR 47.
[9] Ibid, 64.
[10] Ibid.

by member States, even if the object of the interference is alien to the nature of the provisions constituting the Community regime.[11]

Yet this was not an attempt to exclude national action in every form of common organisation, as is apparent from a judgment handed down on the same day as that in *Galli*, in *Van der Hulst's Zonen*.[12] This time, the Court examined a much lighter scheme of common organisation of the market based essentially on quality standards, here in the context of exports rather than imports:[13] the judgment displayed much more of a willingness to examine the facts, aims and effects of measures. While the obligation not to undermine or create exceptions to the common organisation was clear,[14] its foundation in the duty of solidarity remained unstated. But of pre-emption there was no mention. Both VerLoren van Themaat and Waelbroeck[15] wondered whether the different character of the common organisations concerned might explain the difference in approach. While the judgment in *Van der Hulst's Zonen* is silent on this point, it seems most likely that their suggestion is correct. In *Galli*, though, the Court arrived at the same conclusion in respect of both the more and the less developed schemes of common organisation, as to national incapacity to regulate prices at the commonly organised stages.

Subsequent cases demonstrate a relatively speedy retreat from *Galli*.[16] Thus, already in *Tasca*[17] and *SADAM*,[18] in which the Court looked at the common organisation of the market in sugar, talk of pre-emption was abandoned: the possibility of national measures co-existing with common organisations even at the same stage (provided that they did not jeopardise the latter) was left open, although the Court felt that they would run a greater risk of jeopardising the common organisation than would national measures at other stages. The Court tested the national measures against the common organisation and against the free movement provi-

---

[11] M Waelbroeck, 'The Emergent Doctrine of Community Pre-emption—Consent and Re-delegation' in T Sandalow and E Stein (eds), *Courts and Free Markets* (Oxford, Clarendon Press, 1982) Vol II, 548, 559.

[12] Case 51/74 *PJ Van der Hulst's Zonen v Produktschap voor Siergewassen* [1975] ECR 79.

[13] The common organisation relating to live trees and other plants, bulbs, roots and the like, cut flowers and ornamental foliage.

[14] *Van der Hulst's Zonen*, above n 12, 94.

[15] In case notes in [1975] *Sociaal-Economische Wetgeving* 251 and (1977) 14 *Common Market Law Review* 94 respectively.

[16] This is true even though in *Tasca* & *SADAM* (discussed below) the Court quoted the pre-emption statements from *Galli*. The retreat is obvious because, having quoted that statement, the Court turned immediately to the result in *Galli*, phrased in terms of non-jeopardy. JA Usher, 'Effects of Common Organizations and Policies on the Powers of a Member State' [1977] 2 *European Law Review* 428, 434 rightly observed that the compatibility of national measures with a common organisation depends not on the general scope of the organisation as a whole, but on its specific provisions or, at the most, on its aims or objectives, which can, of course, be deduced from its provisions.

[17] *Tasca* [1976] ECR 291.

[18] *SADAM* [1976] ECR 323.

sions, although its behaviour later was far from consistent on this point.[19] However, vestiges of the language of pre-emption were not entirely lost. Thus, in *Van den Hazel* the Court proclaimed that, once a common organisation had been established in a given sector, Member States were under an obligation to refrain from taking any measure which might undermine or create exceptions to it;[20] on other occasions the Court has noted that, where exhaustive Union rules applied packaging requirements only to certain products, the Member States have no power to extend such requirements to other products.[21]

Where common rules are exhaustive, national competence is clearly displaced, although national rules pursuing other legitimate aims are uneffected (subject to compliance with the fundamental freedoms of the TFEU) unless and until such aims are covered by EU rules. This is in line with the vision of the Treaty and case law-based justifications for barriers to intra-Union trade being a temporary acceptance (subject to testing of the necessity and proportionality of the measures) pending EU measures (completely) occupying the field. In that line, it is hardly surprising that the Court rejected the argument that what is now Article 36 TFEU constituted a fund of reserved powers for the Member States.[22] Where the

---

[19] Sometimes testing takes place against the terms of both sets of provisions, sometimes against one set or the other, see eg Case 154/77 *Procureur du Roi v Dechmann* [1978] ECR 1573; Case 223/78 *Grosoli* [1979] ECR 2621; Case 5/79 *Procureur Général v Buys et al* [1979] ECR 3203; Cases 16–20/79 *Openbaar Ministerie v Danis* et al [1979] ECR 3327; Case 95/79 *Procureur du Roi v Kefger & Delmelle* [1980] ECR 103; Case 216/86 *Antonini v Prefetto di Milano* [1987] ECR 2919; Case 188/86 *Ministère public v Lefebre* [1987] ECR 2963.

[20] Case 111/76 *Officier van Justitie v Van den Hazel* [1977] ECR 901, 909. See also eg Case 83/78 *Pigs Marketing Board v Redmond* [1987] ECR 2347, 2371; Case 216/86 *Antonini v Prefetto di Milano* [1987] ECR 2919, 2932–33. See further (relating to a duty not to impede the proper functioning of the common organisation's machinery) Joined Cases 36 and 71/80 *Irish Creamery Milk Suppliers Association et al v Government of Ireland et al* [1981] ECR 735, 750–53; (relating to limits on national action) Case 222/82 *Apple & Pear Development Council v KJ Lewis Ltd et al* [1983] ECR 4083, 4121; (obligation to abstain from jeopardising measures, even where non-exhaustive regulation of a field is involved) Case 1/96 *R v Minister of Agriculture, Fisheries & Food, ex-parte Compassion in World Farming Ltd* [1998] ECR I-1251, 1295 (citing additional case law); Case C-428/99 *H van den Bor BV v Voedselvoorzieningsin—en verkoopbureau* [2002] ECR I-127, 161; Case C-507/99 *Denkavit Nederland BV v Minister van Landbouw, Natuurbeheer en Visserij et al* [2002] ECR I-169, 199.

[21] Case 255/86 *Commission v Belgium* [1988] ECR 693, 708. Another clear example of pre-emption through exhaustive occupation of the field is Case 218/85 *Association comité économique agricole regional fruits et legumes de Bretagne (CERAFEL) v Le Campion* [1986] ECR 3513, 3534 (the Member States had no power to extend to all producers the intervention rules laid down by producers' organisations; in that case the Court gave three possible reasons for preclusion of national action: exhaustive regulation of the matter by the common organisation, incompatibility with [Union] law or interference with the proper functioning of the common organisation.

[22] See, eg Case 35/76 *Simmenthal SpA v Italian Minister for Finance* [1976] ECR 1871, 1876, The same applies in relation to the case law-based justifications: see, eg Case 8/74 *Procureur du Roi v Dassonville* et al [1974] ECR 837, 852; Case 261/82 *Walter Rau Lebensmittelwerke v De Smedt PvbA* [1982] ECR 3961, 3972; Case C-39/90 *Denkavit Futtermittel*

common rules are non-exhaustive, national competence remains (subject to the above caveats) only in relation to the non-commonly regulated aspects. Although active expression of pre-emption is nowadays more lightly expressed than in *Galli*, its spirit and effect remain intact.

IV   HARMONISATION

In relation to harmonisation, the same ideas apply: the extent of pre-emption depends on the intensity of the harmonisation; the fact that the Member States are authorised to adopt within their own territory stricter measures than those laid down in a directive does not mean that the directive concerned has not exhaustively regulated the powers of the Member States in the area of protection concerned.[23] Reliance on the Treaty-based or case law-based justifications for barriers to intra-Union trade will no longer be possible if the Union measures are exhaustive.[24] Where Union legislation is adopted in stages or only covers certain aspects of a particular field, the Member States retain the right to apply their national rules, subject to compliance with the fundamental rules of the Treaties, in particular those on the free movement of goods, including the conditions under which justifications may be acceptable.[25] Thus reliance on Article 36 TFEU or on the case law-based justifications becomes

---

GmbH v Land Baden-Württemberg [1991] ECR I-3069, 3107; Case C-370/93 *Verein gegen Unwesen in Handel und Gewerbe Köln eV v Mars GmbH* [1995] ECR I-1923, 1940; Case C-448/98 *Guimont* [2000] ECR I-10663, 10689–90.

[23] Case C-169/89 *Gourmetterie Van den Burg* [1990] ECR I-2143, 2163; Case 1/96 *R v Minister of Agriculture, Fisheries & Food, ex-parte Compassion in World Farming Ltd* [1998] ECR I-1251, 1300.

[24] Eg Case 5/77 *Tedeschi v Denkavit Commerciale srl* [1977] ECR 2555, 1576–77; Case 148/78 *Pubblico Ministero v Ratti* [1979] ECR 1629, 1644; Case 251/78 *Firma Denkavit Futtermittel GmbH v Minister für Ernährung, Landwirtschaft und Forsten des Landes Nordrhein-Westfalen* [1979] ECR 3369, 3388; Case 190/87 *Oberkreisdirektor des Kreises Borken et al v Handelsonderneming Moormann BV* [1988] ECR 4689, 4720; Case 1/96 *R v Minister of Agriculture, Fisheries & Food, ex-parte Compassion in World Farming Ltd* [1998] ECR I-1251, 1296–97; Case C-241/01 *National Farmers' Union v Secrétariat général du gouvernement* [2002] ECR I-9079, 9126. Any appropriate checks must be carried out and protective measures adopted within the framework outlined by the harmonising directive, rather than unilaterally, eg Case C-323/93 *Société Civile Agricole du Centre d'Insémination de la Crespelle v Cooperative d'Elevage et d'Insémination du Département de la Mayenne* [1994] ECR I-5077, 5107, and the Member States must rely on mutual trust to carry out checks on their respective territories, eg Case C-5/94 *R v Ministry of Agriculture, Fisheries and Food, ex-parte Hedley Lomas (Ireland) Ltd* [1996] ECR I-2553, 2611; Case 1/96 *R v Minister of Agriculture, Fisheries & Food, ex-parte Compassion in World Farming Ltd* [1998] ECR I-1251, 1296–97.

[25] See, eg Case 53/80 *Officier van Justitie v Koninklijke Kaasfabriek Eyssen BV* [1981] ECR 409, 422; Case 40/82 *Commission v United Kingdom* [1982] ECR 2793, 2824; Case 227/82 *Van Bennekom* [1983] ECR 3883, 3904. The additional duty imposed now by Art 4(3) TFEU to ensure that national measures do not jeopardise the proper functioning of Union legislation (which has been noted above) applies here too.

increasingly otiose as complete harmonisation is achieved.[26] Harmonisation directives cannot expand the scope of Article 36 TFEU,[27] and both they and national measures adopted to implement them must be interpreted in accordance with the terms of Articles 34–36 TFEU.[28] While the Court has not eschewed the language of pre-emption, as in *British American Tobacco (Investments) and Imperial Tobacco*,[29] the tendency is to be sparing with references to lack of competence as an abstract concept, and to prefer to phrase the consequences of Union harmonisation in terms of concrete positive or negative obligations, sometimes with reference to what is now Article 4(3) TFEU.

V PRE-EMPTION MORE GENERALLY?

Pre-emption in the light of specific Union action is uncontroversial, even if the Court seems to prefer to use language which seems less inflammatory to eurosceptic politicians. The thought of pre-emption simply by virtue of a Treaty obligation seems a lot more controversial to say the least. Pre-emption by virtue, say, of Articles 34–36 TFEU is seen as going too far.[30] The obligation of the supremacy of EU law certainly requires national courts to disapply national legislation, rules or practices which are incompatible with the requirements of the free movement of goods, but could not an argument be made that the national authorities simply do not have the power to enact measures which are incompatible with (in this case) the free movement rules as elucidated by the Court of Justice in its case law?

The obvious difficulty is that the extent and scope of the free movement rules is in a constant state of evolution, and that it would be difficult to draw a clear dividing line as to the extent of pre-emption. A case can

---

[26] Case 227/82 *Van Bennekom* [1983] ECR 3883, 3904. In some cases the harmonising measure will expressly permit Member States to adopt supplementary measures, eg Case 4/75 *Rewe-Zentralfinanz eGmbH v Landwirtschaftskammer* [1975] ECR 843. Sometimes even complete schemes of harmonisation permit Member States to conduct spot checks to ensure that the harmonised rules have been complied with, but such spot checks must not take place so frequently that they amount to a disguised restriction on trade between Member States or a means of arbitrary discrimination, see Case 35/76 *Simmenthal SpA v Italian Minister for Finance* [1976] ECR 1871, 1887–88; Case 42/82 *Commisson v France* [1983] ECR 1013.

[27] Case 104/75 *De Peijper* [1976] ECR 613, 638.

[28] Case C-315/92 *Verband Sozialer Wettberb eV v Clinique Laboratories SNC et al* [1994] ECR I-317, 335.

[29] Case C-491/01 *R v Secretary of State for Health, ex-parte British American Tobacco (Investments) Ltd & Imperial Tobacco Ltd* [2002] ECR I-11453, 11578: 'The fact is that since the Community legislature made exhaustive provision in Directive 90/239 over the question of fixing the maximum tar yield of cigarettes, the Member States no longer had the power to enact individual rules in that area.' [1990] OJ L137/36–37.

[30] Eg ED Cross, above n 5, 453.

certainly be made that, once there is a clear line of authority that certain (types of) measures are unacceptable, the power of the Member States to act in a contrary manner should be a dead letter; indeed, even one judgment of the Court should suffice to make the point that certain actions are unlawful. However, this line of argument is ill-founded and has Lorelei characteristics. It fails to take account of the fact that judgments by the case law of the Court are viewed as means of negative integration, whereas pre-emption is better suited as a concept flowing from measures of positive integration. In other words, specific Union action (or exclusive Union competence by virtue of Article 3 TFEU) is necessary to generate the result of pre-emption. It might be convenient for litigants simply to say that national authorities do not have the power to act, but it is easier for national judiciaries simply to set aside any provision of national laws or other rules or any national practice which is incompatible with the obligations incumbent on the Member States by virtue of Union law.[31] Indeed, there is a strong case for the view that, even if a national legal system does not itself make provision for national courts to declare a law invalid, Union law itself requires the national courts to do so in cases of incompatibility of national law with directly applicable Union law,[32] although, as Schütze rightly recalls, the obligation is to disapply, and the Court has not been trying to say that the national rules were non-existent.[33] The obligation to disapply is (even though not always explicitly) the result of Article 4(3) TFEU. The conclusion must be that in relation to specific Treaty obligations there is no need for the Court of Justice to have to resort to the doctrine of pre-emption, and the decentralised Union judiciary is in a position—and has an obligation—to give a remedy in terms which are more palatable. In those areas where Union law is not directly applicable, and particularly when the measure concerned is not directly effective, the obligations on the national judiciary are markedly more nuanced, although the pressure to act in conformity with EU law is maintained.[34]

---

[31] This obligation does not restrict the power of the competent national courts to apply, from among the various procedures available under national law, those which are appropriate for protecting the individual rights conferred by Union law, see Case 34/67 *Firma Gebrüder Lück v Hauptzollamt Köln-Rheinau* [1968] ECR 245, 251; Joined Cases C-10/97–C-22/97 *Ministero delle Finanze v IN.CO.GE.'90 Srl et al* [1998] ECR I-6307, 6333.

[32] Case 106/77 *Amministrazione delle Finanze dello Stato v Simmenthal SpA* [1978] ECR 629, 644; Case C-213/89 *R v Secretary of State for Transport, ex-parte Factortame Ltd* et al [1990] ECR I-2433, 2474–75.

[33] R Schütze, 'Supremacy without Pre-emption? The Very Slowly Emergent Doctrine of Community Pre-emption' (2006) 43 *Common Market Law Review* 102, 1030.

[34] The competing interests involved are usefully summarised in Case C-98/09 *Sorge v Poste Italiane SpA* [2010] ECR I-not yet reported (24 June 2010), paras 50–55.

VI CONCLUDING OBSERVATIONS

Schütze,[35] following Zuleeg,[36] argues that, even in the presence of Union legislation, the underlying competence of the Member States remains undiminished: the pre-emptive effect of Union law takes place at the legislative level. Surely this can only be true of those areas in which Union law has not completely occupied the field. While Articles 3–6 TFEU state the division of competence between the Union and its Member States, they do not pretend to lay down an exhaustive allocation of areas of Union competence; they are merely a statement of existing areas in which there is exclusive Union competence, shared competence between the Union and the Member States or limited Union competence confined to supporting, co-ordinating or supplementing action by the Member States. The very fact that Union competence may become exclusive through Union action means that Union competence is still developing, and specific matters which may at one time be shared competence can (to the extent decided by the Union legislature) become the Union's exclusive competence. Once the Union is exclusively competent, any underlying national power to act must logically disappear. National parliaments are just as bound by the rules of Union law as any other organ of the Member States: to acknowledge that they still had underlying competence to act where the Union has become exclusively competent seems wrong in principle. It may be more politically acceptable to phrase matters in terms of pre-emption at the legislative level, but field pre-emption (the most far-reaching type of pre-emption) must apply to the legislator's power to legislate, not merely to the effects of legislation. The only sense in which the Lisbon settlement could be said to envisage an underlying competence to act remaining in the hands of the Member States is in the specific provision for Member States to again exercise their competence to the extent that the Union has decided to cease exercising its competence;[37] in other words, national competence becomes dormant in the presence of Union legislation and is reawakened by the abolition of Union legislation. A distinction between the (underlying) competence to legislate and the actual power to legislate — which moves in areas where exclusive competence is conferred on the Union by the Treaties[38] — would be envisaged by that approach.[39] Field

[35] Schütze, above n 33, 1030.
[36] M Zuleeg 'Vorbehaltene Kompetenzen der Mitgliedstaaten der Europäischen Gemeinschaft auf dem gebiete des Umweltschutzes' (1987) 6 *Neue Zeitschrift füre Verwaltungsrecht* 280, 281.
[37] See Art 2(2) TFEU.
[38] See Art 2(1) TFEU.
[39] This is reminiscent of the old analysis that the effect of the European Communities Act 1972 on parliamentary sovereignty was that Parliament was saying that in certain areas (in the fields and circumstances required by (now) Union law) it would refrain from exercising its competence to act, but it could reactivate such competence.

competence is not exclusively regulated by the Treaties, but can develop through Union action, as acknowledged by the case law of the Court: it is therefore inaccurate to argue that the Treaties alone provide an exhaustive list of areas in which pre-emption applies.

The free movement of goods forms a most stimulating set of examples of the various types of pre-emption which have been identified in the literature: field pre-emption, rule pre-emption and obstacle pre-emption.[40] In the first and third of these types, consideration of a common organisation or harmonised action is central; in the case of rule pre-emption, there seems to be some vagueness in the case law in the identification of the precise rule involved (largely because of the duplication of the provisions of the Treaty in the common organisations). It is submitted that, on policy grounds, it is inappropriate to apply pre-emption analysis in relation to the general Treaty rules relating to free movement, particularly as long as national courts conform to their obligations to uphold Union law. But the slightly naughty thought of upsetting small-minded local politicians by denying the very existence of parliamentary competence to legislate is perhaps a very hot, but certainly exquisite, potato to serve at a feast in a constitutional order of states.

---

[40] As to the theoretical basis of these three types of pre-emption, see Schütze, above n 33, 1038, and literature discussed there.

20

The Past, Present and Future of Competition Law in the European Union

PIET JAN SLOT

I INTRODUCTION

T HE EDITORS OF this *liber amicorum* for Alan Dashwood have suggested as my theme: 'the future of competition law in the European Union'. I have adjusted the subject somewhat in order to put the topic into perspective, hence the title: the development, the present status as well as the future of competition law. The editors have also asked all contributors to put the contributions in the context of Alan's favourite concept of EU law: 'a constitutional order of states'. This is a tall order for an essay about competition law since it is an area where the Community has exclusive competence. Nevertheless, as Amato[1] has argued, competition law addresses fundamental issues of a modern democracy. As will be discussed below in the final section, competition law has undergone a remarkable development as a result of which it is dealing with fundamental issues. In this sense, the development of competition law has led towards the creation of a constitutional order. Moreover, the changes effected by the Lisbon Treaty will further enhance the nature of this order.

Writing about the future of competition law, I was reminded of the following episode. On a journey returning from Nepal, we were transiting in Dacca, Bangladesh. Upon arrival, we were told that we would have a 24 hour delay. I went to the service desk of Biman Bangladesh Airlines and asked the agent whether that was tentative. The agent at the desk looked at me and declared solemnly: 'Sir, since it is future it will always be tentative'. In the end, we departed from Dacca with a delay of some 72 hours. I am therefore well aware of the risk I am taking in attempting to write about the future of competition law.

---

[1] G Amato, *Antitrust and the Bounds of Power. The Dilemma of Liberal Democracy in the History of the Market* (Oxford, Hart Publishing, 1997). Amato uses the term Antitrust Policy also referring to Competition Policy.

Competition law in the EU today has come a long way from what it was over 50 years ago, when the Rome Treaty entered into force on 1 January 1958. In the formative stages of the EEC, the European Court of Justice (ECJ) interpreted the main provisions of competition law with a view to market access and integration. While these themes still inspire many important competition law decisions, other objectives closer to the heart of the Member States' interest are being recognised. This is taking place in the area of the case law on free movement, but also in the case law on Article 106 TFEU and Articles 4(3) TEU and 101 TFEU.

I will give a brief overview of the developments over the past half century. I will start with a summary of the early and formative years, the period that ended in 1989 when the Merger Control Regulation entered into force. The second period lasted from 1989 until 1 May 2004, the entry into force of Regulation 1/2003.[2] The third period is characterised by the entry into force of the new procedural regime of Regulation 1/2003 and the accession of the new Member States, the former republics of Central and Eastern Europe. Finally, I will look into the crystal ball and offer some ideas about the development of competition law in the future.

This overview will allow me to address a more fundamental question about the role of competition law in the democracy of the EU or, to put it in terms of the theme of this *liber amicorum*, the constitutionality of EU competition law. I will turn to this theme first.

II   A CONSTITUTIONAL ORDER OF STATES

The term a 'constitutional order of states' was not coined by Alan to describe EU competition policy but, as I will demonstrate below, the development of competition policy in the EU can be seen as a peculiar species of this order. Competition policy in the EU has over time assumed traits of such a constitutional order both within the EU, in the relation with the Member States and internally in the Member States. The constitutional nature of competition policy has been very well analysed by Amato. He points out that antitrust law is the answer to a crucial problem of democracy. The dilemma for democracy is:

> How can private power be prevented from becoming a threat to the freedoms of others? But at the same time, how can power conferred on institutions for this purpose be prevented from itself enlarging to the point of destroying the very freedom it ought to protect?[3]

This essay will explore whether the development of competition policy in the EU has made a contribution to the dilemma to which Amato

---

[2] [2003] OJL1/1.
[3] Page 3.

pointed. As will be observed in the conclusions, EU competition law has evolved from a centralised administrative system to a multilayered system consisting of the EU and its Member Sates.

III THE EARLY AND FORMATIVE YEARS, 1958–89

A Introduction

Initially, the development of EEC competition policy followed very much a top-down approach with an administrative organ, the Commission, designing and enforcing it. Gradually, other actors entered the field, first the national courts and then, in their slipstream, arbitral panels. This happened because the ECJ ruled that Articles 85 and 86 EEC had direct effect.[4] The direct effect of Articles 85 and 86 also made it possible for national courts to ask the ECJ to give preliminary rulings.[5] This led to important judgments in cases such as *Delimitis* and *Pronuptia*.[6] The result was a new balance between the enforcer/legislator and the ECJ and the national courts. Subsequently, with a considerable time lag, the national competition authorities also assumed a role as enforcers and to some extent even as policy makers. This resulted in a rather complex system, of which it could no longer be said that the Commission was at the apex. This phenomenon was later reflected in the area of merger control, where Article 9 of Regulation 4064/89 provided for the possibility of referral from the Commission to the national competition authorities and Article 22(3) provided for the referral from the national competition authorities to the Commission. These mechanisms were expanded with the revision of the regulation in 2004. Article 4(5) of Regulation 139/2004 gives the undertakings concerned the right to request the Commission to examine the merger. The co-operative nature of the combined system of Union competition law and national competition law is also a distinct feature of Regulation 1/2003. Since the entry into force of this regulation the Commission has focused on the main elements of competition policy, such as the fight against major cartels and mergers, leaving the competition authorities of the Member States with the lesser infringements and local fine-tuning. This has accentuated the co-operative nature of the system. The creation of the network of competition authorities led to intensive

---

[4] See Commission Notice on the cooperation between the Commission and the courts of the EU Member States in the application of Arts 81 and 82 EC, [2004] OJ C101/54
[5] An overview of all references until 2004 can be found in B Rodger (ed), *Article 234 and Competition Law. An Analysis* (Kluwer, Wolters, 2008).
[6] For an analysis of the interaction between national courts, the ECJ and the legislator, see PJ Slot, *Le rôle du juge et du législateur dans le développement du droit communutaire et du droit dans les états membres* (Paris, Éditions A Pedone, 1998).

co-operation between the Commission and the national competition authorities.

In order to understand how this system evolved, it is necessary to give a brief sketch of its development since the entry into force of the Rome Treaty.

B   Regulation 17/62

In the first years after the entry into force of the Rome Treaty the general principles of Articles 85 and 86 EEC were implemented and subsequently applied. The Commission, pursuant to its mandate provided for in Article 87 EEC, drafted what became known as Regulation 17 to give effect to the principles of Articles 85 and 86 EEC. The Commission had gained some experience with enforcing the competition provisions of the ECSC Treaty, Article 65 on anticompetitive agreements and Article 66 requiring prior approval of mergers. After protracted negotiations, Regulation 17 was finally adopted by the Council on 6 February 1962.[7] This key regulation embodied a system of administrative a priori control of agreements having an anticompetitive effect. The regulation required the notification of both existing agreements and those that entered into force after 13 March 1962, the date of the entry into force of the regulation. Without notification, agreements that fell foul of Article 85(1) EEC could not be exempted under Article 85(3).[8] The system had the virtue of being simple, both for industry as well as for national courts. This system also allowed the Commission to develop a cartel policy, and that is precisely what the Commission did. During this period, the entire edifice of block exemptions and notices was built. These rules were rather detailed and tailored to fit specific sectors. The block exemption for the automobile industry was the clearest example. The notice on the effect on trade between the Member States and the *de minimis* notice were designed to manage the Commission's workload.

C   Developing the Policy

As was to be expected, the enactment of Regulation 17 led to a flood of notifications. The Commission had to devise a plan to deal with this enormous number of notifications. The first part of its strategy was to

---

[7] OJ 21 February 1962, 204–11. For a fuller account of this period see J Goyder and A Albors-Llorens, *Goyder's EC Competition Law*, 5th edn (Oxford, Oxford University Press, 2009) ch 4.

[8] Art 4 of Reg 17 exempted some agreements from the obligation to notify. They were not exempted from the prohibition of Art 81(1) EEC.

select from the notifications individual cases that represented the key elements of the provisions of the cartel prohibition in an effort to clarify and establish the main principles for a future policy. The major part of the notifications concerned vertical agreements, and in particular exclusive distribution and purchasing agreements. It was therefore no surprise that the Commission picked the *Consten-Grundig* case as a clear example of such agreements and territorial restrictions. It adopted a decision declaring such agreements to be contrary to Article 85(1) EEC. As the Commission hoped, the parties appealed to the ECJ, which clarified many key principles and, in so doing, confirmed the Commission's view.[9] The second prong of the Commission's approach to deal with the flood of notifications was the development of the system of notices and block exemptions.

From the point of view of substance, the emphasis in this period was on achieving market integration. The classical objectives of antitrust—the protection of the consumer and the small trader—were still largely absent. A first reference to the protection and promotion of small business appeared in the *Metro* judgment.[10]

Once the main challenges posed by the application of Article 85 EEC had been addressed, the Commission turned to the application of Article 86 EEC. Like its approach under Article 85 EEC, it started with some landmark cases defining the key concepts of the prohibition of abuse of a dominant position. In the absence of a notification mechanism, the Commission had to rely on complaints and its powers to bring infringement procedures. By its very nature, therefore, the Commission had fewer means to develop a policy on Article 86. It had to wait until suitable cases presented themselves. Consequently, it took quite some time before cases such as *United Brands*[11], *Hoffmann-LaRoche*[12], *Commercial Solvents*[13] and *Continental Can*[14] presented themselves. As was to be expected, these cases reached the ECJ, which did not fail to give them proper attention. The Court duly endorsed the Commission's interpretation of the key concepts.

During this period, the Commission did not address the politically sensitive subject matter of public undertakings and exclusive and special rights that was addressed in Article 90 EEC.[15]

---

[9] Cases 56 and 58/64 *Consten and Grundig v Commission* [1966] ECR 429.
[10] Case 26/76 *Metro v Commission* [1977] ECR 1875.
[11] Case 27/76 *United Brands v Commission* [1978] ECR 207.
[12] Case 85/76 *Hoffmann-La Roche v Commission* [1979] ECR 461.
[13] Joined Cases 6 and 7/73 *Istituto Chemioterapico Italiano and Commercial Solvents v Commission* [1974] ECR 22.
[14] Case 6/72 *Continental Can v Commission* [1973] ECR 215.
[15] The only judgment which briefly discusses Art 90(2) EEC is Case 10/71, *Muller v Porte de Mertet* [1971] ECR 738, which was a preliminary ruling.

D   Extraterritorial Jurisdiction

Conflicts of jurisdiction, resulting from the US extraterritorial application of its antitrust laws, were, as a result of the application of the Alcoa/effects doctrine,[16] quite common in those days.[17] These conflicts gave rise to the enactment of blocking statutes in several Member States preventing their companies from handing over documents to foreign authorities. The most far-reaching statutory provision was embodied in the UK Protection of Trading Interests Act of 1980, which provided for a claw-back provision should UK nationals suffer treble damage US antitrust awards. In the mid-seventies the Department of Justice (DOJ) Grand Jury conducted an investigation of the shipping sector which led to diplomatic protests from several EEC Member States. The problems were, for practical purposes, solved by the *Woodpulp I* 1988 judgment, in which the ECJ held that: 'The decisive factor is therefore the place where it is implemented'.[18] This was a cleverly designed formula which, on the face of it, is different from the US effects doctrine but in practice allows enforcement in the EU whenever its interests are at stake. This also opened the door for international agreements on mutual co-operation, the so-called negative and positive comity agreements. On the basis of these agreements, the antitrust authorities of the EU and the US nowadays co-operate actively and frequently.

D   Excluded Sectors

Towards the end of this period, the ECJ confirmed in the *Nouvelles Frontiéres* and *Ahmed Saeed* judgments[19] that the competition rules also applied in the air transport sectors. Earlier the ECJ had ruled that the competition rules apply to the banking sector.[20]

---

[16] 148 F.2d 416(2nd Circuit 1945).

[17] For a brief summary see Bellamy and Child, *European Community Law of Competition*, 6th edn (Oxford, Oxford University Press, 2008) 66–70; J Goyder and A Albors-Llorens, *Goyder's EC Competition Law*, 5th edn (Oxford, Oxford University Press, 2009) ch 22.

[18] Joined Cases 89, 104, 114, 116, 117 and 125–129/85 *Ahlstrom Osakeyhtio and Others v Commission* [1988] ECR 5193.

[19] Joined Cases 209–213/84 *Ministère Public v Lucas Asjes and Others (Nouvelle Frontieres)* [1986] ECR 1425; Case 66/86 *Ahmed Saeed Flugreisen and Silver Line Reisebüro GmbH v Zentrale zur Bekämpfung unlauteren Wettbewerbs* [1989] ECR 803.

[20] Case 172/80 *Zürchner v Bayerische Vereinsbank* [1981] ECR 2021.

IV THE APPLICATION OF RULES CONSOLIDATED, 1989–2004

A Merger Control

After a discussion of more than 20 years, the merger control system was finally enacted in 1989. It resulted in a large number of notifications. Although the great majority of the mergers were approved without much ado during the first phase, several mergers were only approved conditionally in the second phase.[21] The number of outright prohibitions was small. A landmark case was the prohibition of the *GE-Honeywell* merger. The Commission's decision was upheld by the Court of First Instance (CFI).[22] The merger had been approved by the US authorities. This led to a renewed debate about the necessity of closer co-operation between the authorities on both sides of the Atlantic as well as the need for similar substantive rules. In this period many other countries enacted their own merger control systems. This has led to networks of competition authorities—the European Competition Network (ECN) and the International Competition Network (ICN).

A side effect of the merger control system was that the numerous notifications, all of course providing extensive data about the relevant markets, gave the Commission a valuable insight into many markets. In this period several senior Commission officials joined the private sector, so major law firms became well informed as well.

For about 10 years the negative Commission decisions and the conditional decisions went unchallenged, mainly because the parties did not see the point of appealing a prohibition decision. Even if the decision was annulled, the merger could not be implemented subsequently.[23] This changed around the turn of the century with some spectacular judgments, such as *Airtours*[24] and *Schneider Electric*.[25] In both judgments the CFI annulled the Commission decision. The latter judgment led the wronged parties to bring a claim for damages. The CFI accepted the claim and ordered the Community to make good two-thirds of the loss represented by the reduction in the transfer price of Legrand. Moreover, the CFI ordered that the amount of that loss be assessed by an expert and that interest be awarded on the compensation relating to that loss.[26] Upon

---

[21] Under Reg 4064/89 conditions could only be imposed after the opening of the second phase this inflated the number of second phase decisions. The revised merger regulation, Reg 139/2004, allows conditional approvals.

[22] Case T-209/01 *Honeywell v Commission* [2005] ECR II-5527

[23] The CFI judgment could of course be appealed to the ECJ and the end result would be a fresh Commission decision approving the merger.

[24] Case T-342/99 *Airtours v Commission* [2002] ECR II-585.

[25] Case T-310/01 *Schneider Electric v Commission* [2002] ECR II-4071.

[26] Case T-351/03 *Schneider v Commission* [2007] ECR II-2237.

appeal, the ECJ set aside this part of the CFI judgment,[27] though the ECJ did accept the CFI's reasoning awarding damages for making good the loss represented by the expenses incurred by Schneider as a result of its participation in the resumed merger control procedure, which followed delivery of the *Schneider I* and *Schneider II* judgments.

B   Simplification of the Block Exemptions

An important development in this period was the gradual simplification of the block exemptions, in particular the block exemption regulation for vertical restraints, Regulation 2790/99.[28] By embodying the principle that what is not prohibited is allowed, this block exemption represented a major simplification. It should be remembered that the old system consisted of a blacklist of clauses that were prohibited outright. The regulation had a white list with clauses that were allowed and a third category of grey clauses which had to be assessed by the Commission, who would decide whether or not they were acceptable.

C   Liberalisation

This period is also characterised by the drive towards the completion of the internal market.[29] The internal market was to be completed by a major harmonisation programme. At the same time, the Commission started its action towards liberalisation of the closed sectors. It started to actively apply Article 90 EEC (subsequently 86 EC), notably in the telecom sector. In the important telecom judgment,[30] the ECJ confirmed the Commission's legislative power under Article 90(3) EEC. Other judgments defined the key concepts of the article. The definition of the concept of an undertaking delineated the scope of application of the competition rules in the public and private sector.[31] According to this case law, Member States are free to set up a public undertaking and to grant exclusive or special rights. However, Member States must not do so in such a way that a public undertaking must necessarily end up breaching the competition rules as soon as it starts its activities.[32]

Due to pressure from the Member States and the European Parliament, the Commission soon had to give up its use of Article 86(3) EC as the

---

[27] C-440/07 *Commission v Schneider* [2009] ECR II-2601, para 218.
[28] [1999] OJ L336/21.
[29] 'Completing the Internal Market', COM(85) 310 final (the White Paper).
[30] Case C-202/88 *France v Commission* [1991] ECR 1223.
[31] Case C-41/90 *Höfner v Macrotron* [1991] ECR I-1979.
[32] Case C-41/90 *Höfner v Macrotron* [1991] ECR I-1979; Case C-323/93 *Crespelle v Coopérative d'Elevage et d'Insémination Artificielle* [1994] ECR I-5077.

basis for legislation. Such legislation was henceforth based on Article 95 EC.[33] The results of this policy in the air transport and telecom sectors are now clearly visible for every citizen. In the first sector, Easy Jet, Ryan Air and Air Berlin have become household names for all but the business class traveller. The telecom sector has also developed beyond recognition, with the mobile phone sector the most obvious example. The liberalisation in the energy sector has been less spectacular, mainly as a result of a fierce opposition by the Member States and the incumbents. Directive 96/92 on the internal market for electricity and Directive 98/30 on the internal market for natural gas mark the first steps towards liberalisation. They embody the principles of third-party access, unbundling of production, transmission and distribution, as well as the (initially limited) freedom to choose the supplier.[34] Both directives were amended in 2003 and in 2009 to implement further liberalisation.[35]

It should be noted that the liberalisation policy was made possible because of the application of the free movement rules but also because gradually the Member States had all warmed up to the idea of the need for a national competition policy. During this period, most Member States adopted a national competition policy. The Euro agreements that were concluded with the former socialist countries all included copies of the EC competition rules.

V ACCESSION OF THE NEW MEMBER STATES AND THE ENACTMENT OF REGULATION 1/2003, 1 MAY 2004

A Accession

This period is first and foremost characterised by the accession of the new Member States. The significance of the accession for the development of Europe can hardly be exaggerated. The competition law regime in the EU was extended to the former planned economies of Central and Eastern Europe. The new Member States had gradually been prepared for the application and enforcement of the competition rules. The preparation had started in the early nineties with the Euro agreements, which all contained provisions modelled on Articles 81–90 EC. Many training

---

[33] For the air- and maritime transport sector this was Art 84(2) EEC.

[34] Dir 96/92 concerning common rules for the internal market in electricity, [1997] OJ L27/20 (also referred to as the Electricity Directive); and Dir 98/30, concerning common rules for the internal market in natural gas, [1998] OJ L 204/1 (also referred to as the Natural Gas Directive).

[35] Dir 2003/54 concerning common rules for the internal market in electricity, repealing Dir 96/92, [2003] OJ L176/37. Dir 2003/55 concerning common rules for the internal market in natural gas, repealing Dir 98/30 [2003] OJ L176/57; Dir 2009/72 concerning common rules for the internal market in electricity, [2009] OJ L211/55; Dir 2009/73 concerning common rules for the internal market in natural gas, [2009] OJ L211/94.

sessions and meetings were organised to create a competition law culture in the new Member States. Notwithstanding this extensive preparation, many disputes have arisen about the implementation and enforcement of the competition rules, some of them leading to spectacular claims often brought in arbitral proceedings.

B   Regulation 1/2003

A long and intensive negotiation process finally led to the enactment of Regulation 1/2003 at the same time as the new Member States' accession, thus avoiding what would have been a very complex transitional regime. A look at the transitional regime for the application of state aid (Articles 87 and 88 EC) shows how complex such a regime would have been.[36] The regulation represents a major shift in the enforcement of competition law to the level of the Member States. All Member States now have national competition authorities. It should be remembered that it was a requirement for accession of the new Member States to have the necessary authorities for the enforcement of competition rules. At the same time, the Commission issued a Notice on cooperation within the Network of Competition Authorities.[37] The judgments of the ECJ in *Courage*[38] and *Manfredi*[39] have stimulated the national courts to apply the competition rules. In 2004 the Commission also published a Notice on the co-operation between the Commission and the courts of the EU Member States in the application of Articles 81 and 82 EC.[40] In 2008 it published a White Paper on actions for damages.[41]

In the meantime, as arbitral tribunals were increasingly applying the competition rules, this has led to new questions. It should be noted that, according the *Nordsee* case law,[42] arbitral tribunals cannot make references for preliminary rulings. This has also led to Commission action whereby it submits comments in arbitral proceedings. The *Benetton* case[43] raised the issue of applying the competition rules *ex officio* at the final stage of the enforcement of the arbitral award.

---

[36] I note that this made it possible to avoid the complexities of the provisional validity regime of the *Bosch* case law, Case 13/61, *Kledingverkoopbedrijf de Geus en Uitdenboogerd v Robert Bosch*, [1962] ECR 45, in the sixties and seventies after the enactment of Reg 17.

[37] [2004] OJ C101, 43–53.

[38] Case C-453/99 *Courage v Crehan* [2001] ECR I-6297.

[39] Joined Cases C-295–298/04 *Manfredi v Lloyd Adriatico Assicurazion SpA* [2006] ECR I-6619.

[40] [2004] OJ C101, 54–64.

[41] 'White Paper on Damages Actions for Breach of the EC Antitrust Rules {SEC(2008) 404} {SEC(2008) 405} {SEC(2008) 406}', COM(2008) 0165 final.

[42] Case 102/81 *Nordsee v Reederei Mond* [1982] ECR 1095.

[43] Case C-126/97 *Eco Swiss China Time Ltd v Benetton International NV* [1999] ECR I-3055.

The entry into force of Regulation 1/2003 and especially the abolition of the possibility for the Commission to grant individual exemptions had far-reaching implications. Not only did this mean that the Commission had to redefine its enforcement tasks; the application of Article 81 was henceforth mainly dependent on the national courts and in their slipstream arbitral tribunals. This will not only have procedural consequences; in the course of time, it will inevitably lead to changes in the substance of the law. The Commission has, of course, retained its legislative powers, which it largely uses to adopt block exemptions and publish notices. It is no longer obliged to spend time on individual exemptions. A negative consequence is that the Commission no longer acquires valuable knowledge resulting from notifications. The notifications of mergers and the application of its power to investigate sectors of the economy have largely compensated for this.

The Commission has not made use of its power to issue decisions, finding that what are now Articles 101 and 102 TFEU are not applicable.

C   Pursuing High-profile Infringements

In this period we see the Commission pursuing a very active enforcement policy of imposing very high fines on hard-core cartels. In the calendar year 2007 the Commission imposed some €3.338 million in fines. In 2008 the fines amounted to €2.271 million.[44] In several of these cases applications for leniency have been the impetus for instituting the proceedings. In 2009 there were six cartel decisions, with €1.620 million fines. In the *Marine Hoses*, *Power Transformers* and *Heat Stabilizers* cases there was intensive co-operation with the US and Japanese authorities.[45] Note that these are all horizontal agreements of the hard-core type. In cases that are less hard core, the Commission is trying to take decisions on the basis of Article 9 of Regulation 1/2003 and to accept commitments.

The Commission's enforcement policy on abuse of dominant positions is equally characterised by the pursuit of high-profile cases. The *Microsoft* and *Intel* cases are prominent examples of this approach. The *Microsoft* case ended with a truce when Microsoft decided not to appeal against the judgment of the Grand Chamber of the CFI.[46] Yet both parties have been drawn into long and protracted discussions about the remedies. In the meantime, the effect of the decision can be seen from the features of the newly marketed Windows 7 operating system, which allows the

[44] The Commission adopted seven decisions: Nitrile Butadiene Rubber, International Removal Services, Sodium Chlorate Paper Bleach Producers, Aluminium Fluoride, Paraffin Wax, Bananas and Car Glass.
[45] Annual Report on Competition Policy 2009, para 66.
[46] Case T-201/04 *Microsoft v Commission* [2007] ECR II-3601.

client to install its own choice of internet browser. Intel has challenged the Commission decision.[47] In this case, the Commission and the perpetrators are also engaged in long and dogged fights about the interim remedies.

D   Sector Inquiries

Sector inquiries have become very popular with the Commission. They provide it with considerable insight, allowing it to take follow-up action. As such, they fill to some extent the gap that was created by the abolition of the notification. So far there have been three such inquiries, one into the retail banking sector, one into the energy sector and one into the pharmaceutical sector. The results of the banking inquiry have helped the Commission to face the avalanche of notifications of state aid measures in the financial sector. This was evident in the *Northern Rock* and *German Landesbanken* cases. The energy sector inquiry has so far resulted in five decisions, of which three are commitment decisions: the *Distrigas* commitment to open up the Belgian gas market; the *E.ON* and *RWE* commitments to opening of the German electricity and gas markets; and finally the *Gaz de France* commitment to open up the French gas market to allow competitors to import gas into France. One decision condemned the market-sharing agreement between *E.ON* and *GDF* on the German and French gas markets.[48] Follow-up action has also been taken in the pharmaceutical sector, where the Commission opened a case against *Laboratoires Servier* and some generic companies. The Commission may also want to consider revisiting the issue of parallel trade. I note in this context that the Union Courts have shown a willingness to have a good/ second look at the classical case law prohibiting bans on parallel trading (*GSK*,[49] among others). This may well oblige the Commission to reflect upon the conventional wisdom of treating parallel trading as being per se anti-competitive.

The Commission is envisaging further sector inquiries. When combined with commitment decisions, it may be an effective way of enforcing the competition rules, given the limits of its capacity.

---

[47] Case T-457/08 *Intel v Commission* [2008] OJ C301/60 (pending)

[48] See IP/09/1872 of 3 December 2009. See also the memo 09/536 of 3 December: frequently asked questions. See further the speeches by Commissioner Kroes on 3 December 2009 published on the DG Comp website http://ec.europa.eu/competition/index_en.html.

[49] Case T-168/01 *GlaxoSmithKline Services v Commission*, [2006] ECR II-2969.

E   Commitment Decisions

The use of commitment decisions is, of course, formally a new instrument created under Regulation 1/2003. It has some resemblance with the way the Commission previously used its power to grant individual exemptions. Under the old regime, the Commission often negotiated a limitation of restrictions of competition during the process of granting an individual exemption and subsequently granted the exemption conditionally. The instrument of commitment decisions allows the Commission to achieve results without having to go all the way by adopting a full infringement decision. It is therefore attractive for the Commission. It is also attractive for the undertakings concerned in that they may avoid ever increasing stiff fines. It is certainly less attractive from the perspective of legal protection. The first commitment decisions still have to be tested in the Union Courts. However, the very fact that the Commission can adopt the decision without having to prove that there was an actual infringement will necessarily have an effect on judicial protection. In the *GDF* case the Commission notes that *GDF 'might have'*[50] infringed Article 102 TFEU. Moreover, the commitments imposed can, of course, have a very considerable financial and commercial effect. The Commission observes that it can impose a fine of up to 10 per cent of the company's annual turnover if the firm were to break its commitments. If imposed, such fines will only underscore the shortcomings of this type of enforcement policy. This will be a very interesting area for future developments when the Commission's decisions are challenged before the Courts.

F   Merger Control

The amendment of the Merger Regulation resulted in a slight modification, lowering the thresholds. In the meantime, all Member States have enacted merger control rules which would seem to call for another lowering of the threshold. There has also been an enormous proliferation of merger control regimes all over the world, and we now have over 100 merger control systems. One of the latest was China, where on 1 August 2008 the Anti-Monopoly Law came into effect. The law applies to all state-owned or Chinese companies. The ministry, Mofcom, has in one year cleared 50 cases unconditionally and five conditionally (*InBev/Anheuser-Busch, Mitsubishi/Lucite, General Motors/Delphi, Pfizer/Wyeth* and *Panasonic/Sanyo*), and one merger was prohibited—*Coca-Cola/HuiYuan*. The latter decision has raised concerns about protectionism, although it should be

---

[50] Case COMP/39.316 *Gaz de France*. My italics.

remembered that in 2003 the Australian Competition Authority blocked Coca-Cola's acquisition of juice-maker Berri Limited on grounds that were very similar to those used in the Chinese case.

The policies of the Chinese authority, the Ministry of Commerce, will be closely followed by would-be investors in China. They will also be carefully watched by Chinese investors in other major economies, as they may have an effect on the way Chinese investors are treated abroad. One remembers, several years ago, the prohibition of the US authorities of the takeover of Conoco by China Petroleum. In the current economic and financial environment there seems to be a tendency to regulate and even restrict the nature and range of foreign investments in the US, the EU and other major jurisdictions.

Thus, co-operation will become an even more important topic for the future. We already see signs of such closer co-operation, eg the merger of Panasonic and Sanyo, where the Commission acted in close co-operation with the US and Japanese fair trade commissions in the context of the bilateral framework agreements.[51] Now co-operation with China is also enhanced on the legislation/personnel training aspect through the recently established EU–China competition dialogue. This may well lead in the future to a new bilateral agreement. The US Department of Justice has drawn up a list of current US antitrust investigations to help antitrust enforcement agencies of other jurisdictions review such deals or behaviour. On 25 November 2009 US senators John Kerry (D-Mass) and Orrin Hatch (R-Utah), along with 59 other senators, put pressure on the Commission to hurry up and complete its investigation of Oracle's proposed purchase of Sun Microsystems. The ECN and ICN provide forums for discussing these frictions in enforcement policy.

G   Article 102 TFEU

In February 2009 the Commission published a policy paper on Article 82 entitled 'Guidance on the Commission's Enforcement Priorities in Applying Article 82 of the EC Treaty to Abusive Exclusionary Conduct by Dominant Undertakings'.[52] As is indicated in the title, the paper is limited to exclusionary conduct, thus it does not deal with exploitative abuses. The paper is also limited in the sense that it only sets out the Commission's enforcement policies. At the moment of writing, it is still unclear what the Commission is going to do. In the paper the Commission refers regularly to consumer interest. This seems to reflect that during this period the substantive focus of EC competition law is now clearly also

---

[51] IP/09/1383.
[52] Communication from the Commission, [2009] OJ C45/7.

on consumer welfare. At the same time, it is not the only parameter, as the ECJ held in *T-Mobile and others*.[53]

H   Evaluation of Regulation 1/2003

The Commission has published a report on the functioning of Regulation 1/2003.[54] In this report it stresses that the enactment of Regulation 1/2003 has effected a system change that allows it to target its enforcement priorities to areas where it can make a significant contribution to the enforcement of Articles 81 and 82 EC.[55] The Commission concludes that Regulation 1/2003 has significantly improved the enforcement of Articles 81 and 82 EC, allowing it to become more proactive and address the competiveness of key sectors of the economy. It notes that co-operation in the ECN has contributed towards a coherent application and that the network is an innovative model of governance for the implementation of Community law by the Commission and Member State authorities. It also notes that there are areas that merit further attention.

VI   SINCE 1 DECEMBER 2009 WE HAVE ARTICLES 101 AND 102 TFEU

A   Changes in the Lisbon Treaty

Although the Lisbon Treaty has brought fundamental changes in EU law, the provisions on competition policy have changed numbers but not the substance. There are exceptions; one is Article 3 TEU that no longer makes a reference to 'a system of undistorted competition'. Instead, Protocol No 27 on the internal market and competition states that: 'considering that the internal market as set out in Article 3 of the Treaty on European Union

---

[53] Case C-8/08 *T-Mobile and others* [2009] ECR I-4529, para 38.

[54] [2003] OJ, L1/1.

[55] As the Commission puts it: '12. The change from a system of notification and administrative authorisation to one of direct application has been remarkably smooth in practice. Overall, neither the case practice of the Commission and the national enforcers, nor the experience reported by the business and legal community, indicate major difficulties with the direct application of Article 81(3) EC which has been widely welcomed by stakeholders. 13. The system change has supported a shift in priorities of the Commission, enabling it to focus its resources on areas where it can make a significant contribution to the enforcement of Articles 81 and 82 EC. This proactive approach is clearly illustrated by the launch of large scale inquiries in key sectors of the EU economy which directly impact consumers. The Commission has further implemented a more effects-based approach in all areas of antitrust case work and policy, outside the field of cartels. The more proactive stance of the Commission is further illustrated by an increase in the number of enforcement decisions adopted, compared with earlier periods.'

includes a system ensuring that competition is not distorted . . .'.[56] Will this make any difference? One could think in particular about the case law on Articles 3(1)(g), 10 and 81 EC. In this context, it is important to note that later case law no longer refers to Article 3(1)(g).[57] Furthermore, Article 10 EC is now found in Article 4(3) TEU. It therefore seems unlikely that the ECJ will no longer apply its case law. Moreover, since the jurisprudence of the ECJ leaves Member States a considerable margin of discretion,[58] it seems unlikely that this case law will be watered down.

Another amendment is found in Article 105 TFEU, where a new sentence is added: 'The Commission may adopt regulations relating to the categories of agreements in respect of which the Council has adopted a regulation or a directive pursuant to Article 83(2)(b).' This seems to codify the long-standing practice. Finally, Article 3(1)(b) TFEU lists competition as an area where the Union shall have exclusive competence: 'the establishing of the competition rules necessary for the functioning of the internal market'.

It may be questioned whether the fact that the competition rules are now explicitly designated as exclusive competence will have an impact on Article 3 of Regulation 1/2003, which requires national competition authorities to apply Articles 101 and 102 TFEU when applying national competition law to agreements or abuses of dominant positions that have an effect on trade between the Member States. I do not think it will; after all, these provisions have direct effect. Moreover, it is not uncommon for Member States or their emanations to implement Community law.

B   New Developments

Revision of the block exemption on vertical agreements started when the Commission published a draft of 28 July 2009 together with draft guidelines. The new regulation came into force in June 2010.[59]

Another development is that the Commission has been involved in arbitral proceedings writing submissions. There are also Commission state aid decisions that have taken into account that arbitral proceedings were going on. Similar developments may take place in the area of classical antitrust. In view of these developments, it may be time for the Commission to issue a communication on the application of the competition rules in arbitral proceedings.

---

[56] See R Barents, 'Constitutional Horse Trading: Some Comments on the Protocol' and R Lane, 'EC Competition Law Post Lisbon: A matter of Protocol' in *Liber Amicorum Piet Jan Slot* (Dordrecht, Kluwer, 2009) 123–32 and 167–79.

[57] See Case C-35/96, *Commission v Italy* [1998]ECR I-3886

[58] See N Reich, 'The "November Revolution" of the European Court of Justice: *Keck, Meng* and *Audi* Revisted' (1994) 31 *Common Market Law Review* 459.

[59] Reg 330/2010, [2010] OJ L102/1.

C Recasting Article 101 TFEU

The second paragraph of the preamble of Regulation 1/2003 states that there is need to rethink the arrangements for applying Article 81(3) EC. Now that it has been done, a further need to rethink may well be called for. In this context, it is relevant to note that a major part of the agreements are now covered by the block exemptions. In the literature, proposals are formulated to recast Article 101. The traditional bifurcation between Article 101(1) and 101(3) TFEU has, in my opinion, lost much of its appeal and usefulness, in particular now that national courts and national competition authorities can apply Article 101(3) as well. Of old, the division was between assessing whether there was a restriction of competition which had to be assessed in the legal and economic context[60] under Article 101(1) and the balancing of interest test under Article 101(3). The first provision had direct effect whereas the second did not. This often frustrated enforcement by national courts. Under Regulation 1/2003 national courts can apply both provisions. As a practical matter, it does not make a lot of sense for national courts to spend a considerable amount of time and effort on defining restrictions under Article 101(1) if subsequently such agreements will be exempted anyway. Therefore, national courts will start with the Article 101(3) test. However, it is very likely that in applying that test courts will undertake an overall assessment of the agreement. Although in theory a separate analysis of Article 101(1) is needed when agreements cannot be exempted, under Article 101(3) it is unlikely to happen. It is also not very likely that courts will apply the article conditionally, as the Commission often did in the past. Another reason to rethink that bifurcation is that the case law of the ECJ such as *Wouters*[61] has not convinced everybody. By contrast, the CFI judgment in *Métropole*[62] reflected the classical doctrine, clearly distinguishing between the Article 101(1) and 101(3) analysis.

Furthermore, the Commission and national competition authorities no longer spend time on issuing individual exemption decisions. One could ask whether the structure of Article 101 should be amended so as to merge the first and the third section. An amendment of the article itself may, taking the recent experience with Treaty amendments into account,

---

[60] Recently confirmed in Case C-8/08 *T-Mobile and Others*, judgment of 4 June 2009.
[61] Case C-309/99 *Wouters v NOVA* [2002] ECR I-1577
[62] Case T-112/99 *Métropole and Others v Commission* [2001] ECR II-2459. In paras 72ff the CFI rejects the applicants' thesis that there is a rule of reason in Community competition law, thereby, in para 77, also rejecting the argument that it is necessary to weigh the pro- and anti-competitive effects of an agreement when determining whether the prohibition laid down in Art 85(1) of the Treaty applies.

not be feasible for quite some time. But, as the US jurisprudence on the Sherman Act demonstrates, a lot can be done by the Courts.[63]

D   Human Rights

An area where we will certainly see discussions continuing is the area of protection of human rights in the context of competition law procedures, especially after the entry into force of the Lisbon Treaty.[64] The calls for a change of the system have become increasingly loud.[65] The central tenet of criticism is the fact that the Commission is both the prosecutor and the judge. At the time when Regulation 17 was enacted, the case law of the ECtHR on Article 6 was still in its infancy. In the EC, the only judicial protection provided for was laid down in Article 230 EC, which allows undertakings to whom decisions are addressed and those who are directly and individually concerned—ie those with standing—to challenge Commission decisions.[66] The Commission is of the opinion that the enforcement system of Regulation 1/2003 is in conformity with the case law of the ECtHR under Article 6 ECHR.[67] Nevertheless, at the end of 2009 it published three consultation documents,[68] two of which deal with procedures, and invited comments.

Another issue in this context is the application of the principle *ne bis in idem*. It is, in view of the fact that increasingly cartels are prosecuted on both sides of the Atlantic, less and less convincing to deny parties the protection of the time honoured principle.[69] This will require a change in the case law of the Union Courts.

As in many other areas of the law, the protection of fundamental rights

---

[63] See, for an extensive discussion, A Jones: 'An Analysis of Agreements under US and EC Antitrust Law—Convergence or Divergence' (2006) 51 *The Antitrust Bulletin* 691.

[64] Art 6(1) TEU recognises the rights, freedoms and principles set out in the Charter of Fundamental Rights. Art 6(2) provides that the Union shall accede to the ECHR. For a discussion on the impact of these changes see M Dougan, 'The Treaty of Lisbon 2007: Winning minds not hearts' (2008) 45 *Common Market Law Review* 661.

[65] See the leader in *The Economist*, 20–26 February 2010, and subsequently the article on p 57.

[66] For discussion of the intricacies of this provision in general, see, eg A Arnull, *The European Union and its Court of Justice*, 2nd edn (Oxford, Oxford University Press, 2006) ch 3 and PP Craig and G de Búrca, *EU Law: Text, Cases, and Materials*, 4th edn (Oxford, Oxford University Press, 2008) ch 11. For its application in the competition law field, see, eg R Whish, *Competition Law*, 6th edn (Oxford, Oxford University Press, 2009) 285–90 and C Kerse and N Khan, *EC Antitrust Procedure*, 5th edn (London, Sweet & Maxwell, 2005) ch 9.

[67] Commission Staff Working paper accompanying the Report on the Functioning of Regulation 1/2003, SEC(2009) 574 final.

[68] IP/10/2: Best practices for EU Antitrust/Competition proceedings; Best practices for the submission of economic evidence in antitrust/competition and merger cases; Guidance on the procedures of the European Commission's hearing officers.

[69] See WB van Bockel, *Ne bis in idem*, PhD thesis, Leiden (2009).

has been gaining increased attention, and judgments of the ECJ and, after 1989, also of the CFI have defined the scope of such rights in the area of competition law. In the *Kali & Salz* judgment of the ECJ,[70] the question was raised whether or not Article 2 of the EC Merger Control Regulation could also be applied to collective dominant positions. The applicants argued that such an interpretation could not be accepted as the regulation did not provide for legal protection of the companies that would thus be involved but were not party to the approval procedure. Another prominent case that should be noted under this heading is the *Roquette*[71] judgment, which was almost instantaneously incorporated into the text of Articles 20(8) and 21(3) of Regulation 1/2003.

The *TACA*[72] case and especially the position of, and appeals by, *DSR-Senator Lines*[73] illustrate the intricate relationship between EC procedural law and, in particular, the application of the general principles and fundamental rights as developed under Article 6 ECHR. The Commission adopted a decision against the Trans-Atlantic Conference Agreement imposing a fine on its members.[74] One of them, Senator Lines, was fined €13,750 million. As is standard practice, the Commission indicated that it would not take steps to recover the fine if Senator could provide a bank guarantee. Senator's dire financial situation made it impossible to get such a guarantee. Senator appealed against the Commission's decision and filed for interim measures. Its main argument was that, because it could not provide a bank guarantee, it would not be able to have full judicial recourse. After a failed attempt to reach a settlement, the President of the CFI rejected the request for interim measures.[75] An appeal to the President of the ECJ also failed.[76] Faced with the prospect of steps by the Commission to recover the fine, Senator brought an application to the ECtHR against all the Member States of the EC.[77] It alleged that, in denying the suspensory effect of the appeal, the Commission and the CFI, as well as the ECJ, had deprived the applicant of its fundamental right to have recourse to a judicial instance under Article 6 ECHR.

The Strasbourg Court scheduled a hearing for 22 October 2003. It so

---

[70] Joined Cases C-68/94 and C-30/95 *France v Commission* [1998] ECR I-1453, paras 172–75.

[71] Case C-94/00 *Roquette Frères SA v Directeur général de la concurrence, de la consommation et de la répression des fraudes, and Commission of the European Communities* [2002] ECR I-9011.

[72] Joined Cases T-191/98 and T-212–214/98 *Atlantic Container Line et al v Commission* [2003] ECR II-275.

[73] Ibid.

[74] [1999] OJ L95/1 in the so-called *TACA* Decision (Commission Decision 1999/13/EC of 16 September 1998).

[75] Case T-191/98 R *DSR-Senator Lines GmbH v Commission* [1999] ECR II-2531.

[76] Case C-364/99 P (R) *DSR-Senator Lines GmbH v Commission* [1999] ECR I-8733.

[77] *Senator Lines GmbH v 15 States of the European Union*, Series A No 256-A, (1993) 16 EHRR 297.

happened that the CFI annulled the Commission's decision in the *TACA* case on 30 September.[78] The ECtHR postponed the hearing and removed the case from the register after the judgment of the CFI was handed down. The Commission has refrained from taking steps to recover the fine during the procedure before the Strasbourg Court.

VII   CONCLUSIONS

Anno 2010 EU competition law has acquired a well-earned reputation worldwide and, as such, has served as an example for many other countries including China. Nevertheless, there are areas where some fine-tuning will be required. The debate about Article 102 TFEU will continue especially since the *Microsoft* case ended prematurely when Microsoft decided not to appeal against the CFI judgment. It is not expected that the Commission will seek major changes. Its paper only discusses enforcement priorities. Hence it will be for the Union Courts to try to balance the traditional views with the challenges of the new economy. This point was raised in the judgment of the US Court of Appeals in the US *Microsoft* case.[79] Another point raised in that case is the temporal dimension. In both the US and EC cases it took many years from complaint to a (final) court decision. The *Intel* case may also take many years. As was noted above, a fundamental revision of Article 101 TFEU should be considered.

The case law on Article 106 TFEU may well have reached its pinnacle, especially in view of the fact that quite a few Article 106 issues have been taken up in sector-specific Community rules, such as the directives on the internal market for electricity and natural gas as well as the regulations on conditions for access to the network for cross-border exchanges in electricity and natural gas transmission networks. In 2009 there was a third round strengthening these rules. The telecom sector regulation is another example. As sector-specific regulation reaches full maturity, it can be questioned whether competition law still has a role to play and, if so, what that role is.

There is a need to provide rules for imposing remedies and consequently legal protection. This was highlighted in the *Microsoft* case. It seems likely that we will see similar discussions in the *Intel* case. The legal framework for discussing remedies is largely absent and the process is not transparent.

In an increasingly global world economy there is a clear need for further developments in international co-operation. Merger control and the enforcement of hard-core cartels should be the prime focus of such co-ordinated action. In the area of merger control, procedural alignment

---

[78] *Atlantic Container Line*, above n 72.
[79] 253 F.3d 34, 10–13. Certiorari was denied.

is called for. Merging companies are increasingly faced with different deadlines in the respective jurisdictions. It goes without saying that this frustrates global mergers. It also creates considerable uncertainty for the people involved. A further step would be an alignment of the substantive rules.

The protection of human rights in competition law should be further increased. Such developments will be seen as a sign that competition law has evolved into a mature system of law reflecting the societal values of the twenty-first-century economy.

VIII A CONSTITUTIONAL ORDER?

Like other areas of EU law, competition law has undergone fundamental changes as a result of the ever-increasing embodiment of the rule of law and fundamental rights into the development and application of competition law. These developments were initiated by the ECJ and have finally been embodied in the Treaties, in Article 6 TEU. This is the answer of Union law to the second question raised by Amato. The power conferred on the institutions to apply competition law is reined in by the development and application of fundamental rights. The answer to the first question is that the development and application of the competition of the EU and the Member States is providing a check on private power. This is clearly reflected in the actions against Microsoft and Intel. In this respect, EU competition law increasingly assuming features similar to those of US antitrust law. These developments are the result of a worldwide recognition of the role competition law has to play in market economy. This started in the nineties in a context of an increasing role of the market with extensive deregulation and privatisation. In such an economic model, the introduction and increased enforcement of competition law is the logical consequence of the diminishing role of the state in the economy. In the EU this development was further stimulated by the large-scale accession of new Member States.

National courts could also play a role in addressing the problem of democracy; however, in the EU and its Member States the role of the national courts in enforcing competition law is still limited. This is largely due to the fact that the legal culture in the Member States does not stimulate private lawsuits.

Regulation 1/2003 can be seen as embodying a constitutional order of a special nature. First, the regulation embodies the principles of the rule of law referred to above. Secondly, the system of the regulation embodies an institutional framework in which the Commission is still the *primus inter pares* as far as enforcement is concerned, but the competition authorities of the Member States have increasingly assumed an important role in the functioning of the combined system of competition rules, comprising the Union rules as well as those of the Member States. Similar features are embodied in the merger control regulation.

21

The Future Shape of EU Energy Law and Policy

ANGUS JOHNSTON

BEFORE I HAD even arrived in Cambridge as a young lecturer in my first full-time academic post, Alan Dashwood had extended the hand of friendship. Soon after I arrived, we began our first co-authored project together, and I have been fortunate to enjoy his guidance, support and friendship ever since. He has always kindly indulged my perhaps more maverick legal interests, yet has also consistently insisted that energy law does not fall into that category. I am immensely grateful for all of this and hope that I may crave his indulgence one more time with this contribution on the future of EU energy law and policy. The twin themes of this chapter will be, first, the need for careful accommodation at the EU level of the diversity of Member State interests and concerns in the energy field (thus respecting the nature of the EU as a 'constitutional order of states')[1] and, second, the slow but real shift in EU (and some national) energy law and policy away from reliance upon market mechanisms and towards more complex regimes (involving market and other regulatory tools) to achieve a myriad of public interest goals.

I SHAPING THE DEBATE: 'ARE YOU A ROUNDY OR A SQUARY'?[2]

As a child, I vividly remember reading a short series of books by Roger Hargreaves, of 'Mr Men' fame, which started by posing the question: 'Are you a Roundy or a Squary?' As is clear from even its front cover, the implication is that one is rather happier as a 'Roundy' than as a 'Squary': when one reads further, one finds that Squaries' problem is that they are focused on material things like money and possessions, and on the work

---

[1] A Dashwood 'The Limits of European Community Powers' (1996) 21 *European Law Review* 113 and 'States in the European Union' (1998) 23 *European Law Review* 201.
[2] R Hargreaves *Are You a Roundy or a Squary?*; *I'm a Roundy, You're a Squary*; *Everybody's a Roundy or a Squary*; and *If You Aren't a Roundy, You're a Squary* (all Thurman Publishers, 1975).

needed to acquire them. Roundies, meanwhile, value things which the author portrays as 'really' important, like the natural world and principles such as freedom. While something of simplification, this provides a nice analogy to the development of European Union[3] law and policy in the energy sector: Squaries in the field may be taken as those who advocate the introduction of liberalisation and market processes, relying upon them to achieve the supply of energy of the type and to the extent that we need in an effective and efficient manner, while Roundies would prioritise other public interest goals, such as environmental and social protection, even if this would require the redesign (and even removal) of markets and regulation to achieve those objectives.

Alongside the first volume, there are also three other books by Hargreaves from the same period: *I'm a Roundy, You're a Squary*, and the more taxonomically inclined pair of *Everybody's a Roundy or a Squary* and *If You Aren't a Roundy, You're a Squary*. The implication of the series is clear: one has to be one or the other, and if you are not 'with' the Roundies, then you must be 'against' them. Naturally, in the real world of EU energy law and policy, such a straightforward division of loyalties cannot be identified. Indeed, the reality of the history of the European Union has been that different Member States have been more or less 'round' or 'square' in their approaches to law and policy in general, EU law and policy in particular, and EU energy law and policy most particularly for our purposes here.[4] The UK provides a case in point, having moved during its EU membership from a vertically integrated and publicly owned energy supply industry to the largely privatised, vertically separated companies which operate in the sector today.[5] By contrast, the German situation always involved a complex mixture of local and national, state and private ownership and operation of the sector,[6] while France consist-

---

[3] For ease of reference throughout, and now that the Treaty of Lisbon has entered into force, I will refer to the 'EU' to cover the current manifestation of the Treaties and their previous incarnations, except insofar as it is necessary to distinguish more precisely between the particular Treaties involved.

[4] For an early history, see N Lucas, *Energy and the European Communities* (London, Europa Publications, 1977). For an introduction to the background, see generally: F McGowan, *The Struggle for Power in Europe* (London, RIIA, 1994); and A Midttun (ed), *European Electricity Systems in Transition: A Comparative Analysis of Policy and Regulation in Western Europe* (Kidlington, Elsevier, 1996).

[5] See F McGowan, 'Ideology and Expediency in British Energy Policy' in F McGowan (ed), *European Energy Policies in a Changing Environment* (Heidelberg, Physica Verlag, 1996) ch 5; ED Cross, *Electric Utility Regulation in the European Union—a Country by Country Overview* (London, Chancery Law Publishing, 1996) ch 12; D Helm, *Energy, the State and the Market: British Energy Policy since 1979*, 2nd edn (Oxford, Oxford University Press, 2004); and S Dow, 'Energy Law in the United Kingdom' in M Roggenkamp, C Redgwell, I Del Guayo and A Rønne (eds), *Energy Law in Europe*, 2nd ed (Oxford, Oxford University Press, 2007) ch 15.

[6] See Cross, above n 5, above, ch 7; and J-C Pielow, H-M Koopmann and E Ehlers, 'Energy Law in Germany' in Roggenkamp et al (eds), above n 5, paras 9.11–9.16 and the references cited therein.

ently maintained both a strong degree of vertical integration and state involvement in the energy sphere.[7] Nevertheless, for the purposes of exposition, these basic shapes of policy sketched here are a useful device.

The different approaches to the energy sector were partly ideologically driven and partly due to differing natural resource bases and other factors (such as industrial relations and basic political practicalities and pragmatism); but they had to be accommodated at EU level in the formulation, development and application of EU-level energy law and policy.[8] The accommodation of this diversity in the legal and policy frameworks provides an excellent, if sometimes frustrating, illustration of the operation of a 'constitutional order of states' in action (or, indeed, inaction). Particular instances of these accommodations will be highlighted throughout this short contribution.

II 'HIP TO BE SQUARE'[9]

The history of EU-level energy legislation and policy is too long and involved to be treated in detail here, but a clear shift can be traced back to the Commission's White Paper on the Internal Market in 1985,[10] whose basic principles found detailed expression for the energy sector in the Commission's Working Document on an Internal Energy Market in 1988. That document, in line with the general philosophy of the Single Market Programme, identified the key precondition for progress in the energy industry as 'the greatest possible transparency with regard to potential obstacles'.[11] With specific reference to electricity, the Commission identified a number of potential obstacles to the creation of an internal electricity market, although the major focus was clearly on how the industry was organised in Europe. Aspects which were highlighted were those of unequal treatment of producer utilities as between Member States (such as fiscal and financial conditions, consent procedures for the authorisation of new construction, the cost of production depending on the cost of fuels where fuel choice policy varied significantly between Member States),

---

[7] See D Finon, 'French Electricity Policy: the Effectiveness and Limitations of Colbertism' in McGowan (ed), above n 5, ch 2; and Cross, above n 5, ch 2.

[8] For discussion of some of this process up to 1998, see A Johnston, 'Maintaining the Balance of Power: Liberalisation, Reciprocity and Electricity in the European Community' (1999) 17 *Journal of Energy and Natural Resources Law* 121, esp ss 1–3.

[9] Huey Lewis and The News (Capitol, 1986). NB: in concert, Huey Lewis now normally sings the song as '(Too) Hip to Be Square', as performed on their live album, *Live at 25* (available at http://en.wikipedia.org/wiki/Live at 25); a further sign of the changing times, perhaps?

[10] Commission, 'Completing the Internal Market', COM(1985) 310 final, available at http://europa.eu/documents/comm/white_papers/pdf/com1985_0310_f_en.pdf.

[11] Commission, 'Working Document on the Internal Energy Market', COM(1988) 232 final, available at http://aei.pitt.edu/4037/01/000179_1.pdf, para 34.

the compartmentalisation of national markets due to the largely internal character of the commercial usage of high-voltage interconnection systems (despite the fact that they had long been physically connected) and supplies to users at the distribution, large consumer and ordinary consumer levels. Also included on the list were taxation differences and the relative opacity of electricity costs and prices, without which any workable system of competition would be extremely difficult to achieve.

This all led, ultimately (and after much wrangling among the Member States and extensive industry lobbying from both energy companies and their customers), to three rounds of directives aimed at creating an internal energy market, as well as a number of other legislative and institutional developments designed to support and develop that market.[12] In conjunction with this, further EU-level steps were taken in this direction through the increasingly proactive and far-reaching enforcement of the free movement and competition rules by the Commission and private parties.[13] In short, the market-oriented process of liberalisation and 'regulation for competition' came into fashion during the 1980s, a trend with which the EU caught up during the 1990s and of which the Commission has proved a dedicated follower more or less ever since.

At national level,[14] this trend resulted in the liberalisation of the energy sector, often, but not always, coupled with privatisation: but the key focus was the introduction of competition wherever possible along the energy value chain, most particularly upstream in electricity generation and downstream in sales to customers and for the provision of so-called ancillary services (such as metering and maintenance). This trend chimed with 1980s US–UK capitalist and New Public Management consensus in this direction, infusing the state and its (management) activities with

[12] See PD Cameron, *Competition in Energy Markets: Law and Regulation in the European Union,* 2nd edn (Oxford, Oxford University Press, 2007) ch 1 and paras 2.01–2.63. Similar legislative developments can be tracked in other sectors such as rail and air transport, telecommunications, water and postal services.

[13] For a relatively early assessment, see PJ Slot, 'Energy and Competition' (1994) 31 *Common Market Law Review* 511. More recently, see C Jones (ed), *EU Energy Law, Volume II: EU Competition Law and Energy Markets,* 2nd revised edn (Leuven, Claeys & Casteels, 2007) and Cameron, *Competition in Energy Markets,* above n 12, esp chs 11–16. Most recently, see L Hancher and A Hauteclocque, 'Manufacturing the EU Energy Markets: the Current Dynamics of Regulatory Practice', EUI Working Paper, RSCAS 2010/01, who note that the Commission is pursuing often experimental regulatory goals via competition law, turning it from classic *ex post* correction of market failures into what they describe as 'quasi-ex ante regulatory' approach.

[14] For a general treatment of the economics, see D Newbery, *Privatization, Restructuring and Regulation of Network Utilities* (Cambridge, MA, MIT Press, 1999). It should, however, be noted that there has been strong French resistance to these developments throughout the E(E)C process in the 1980s and 1990s, continuing even today in the EU in certain areas and ways: a good introduction to the history of French energy policy in the twentieth century is provided by M Chick, *Electricity and Energy Policy in Britain, France and the United States since 1945* (Cheltenham, Edward Elgar, 2007), sections pertaining to France in chs 1, 2, 4, 5 and 6.

disciplines from the private/market sphere,[15] finding its ultimate expression in privatisation and liberalisation policies. These developments also responded to the criticism of the old regime that those in charge of running such public utilities bore none of the risks involved and were not in any meaningful sense held to account were such utilities to fail: the costs of any such failures were, ultimately, borne by customers and/or taxpayers (via state support and intervention).

III EVEN SQUARING THE CIRCLE . . .

Over the past few decades, there has been a growing reliance upon economically influenced, market-based mechanisms to secure and/or improve environmental protection. Their goal is to seek the least-cost, most efficient ways of achieving public interest goals.[16] Perhaps one of the first practical examples of this is to be found in the USA under the Clean Air Act Amendments 1990, introducing a 'cap-and-trade' scheme for sulphur oxide (SOx) emissions (a further scheme was later developed to cover nitrogen oxide emissions) in an attempt to tackle the problems of acid rain.[17] Probably the most famous, still highly topical and controversial, example remains the Kyoto Protocol,[18] leading to the UK[19] and now the

---

[15] Although note that US developments concerning market deregulation and liberalisation in the last 30 years have largely been confined to the state, rather than Federal, level (with the exception of natural gas transmission pipeline expansion and its concomitantly cross-state-border reach): see, eg Chick, *Electricity and Energy Policy*, above n 4, ch 6.

[16] For general discussion, see RN Stavins, 'Market-based Environmental Policies: What Can We Learn from US Experience (and Related Research)?' in J Freeman and CD Kolstad (eds), *Moving to Markets in Environmental Regulation: Lessons from Twenty Years of Experience* (New York, Oxford University Press, 2007) ch 2 (see also http://papers.ssrn.com/sol3/papers.cfm?abstract_idem=421720) and D Driesen, 'Alternatives to Regulation? Market Mechanisms and the Environment' in M Cave, R Baldwin and M Lodge (eds), *Oxford Handbook on Regulation* (Oxford, Oxford University Press, 2009) (see also: http://papers.ssrn.com/sol3/papers.cfm?abstract_idem=1268435) ch 10. The first suggestion to create an emissions trading programme as a rational approach to securing emissions reductions in an economically efficient manner was made by JH Dales, *Pollution, Property and Prices* (Toronto, University of Toronto Press, 1968). For more recent discussion of the history and practice of tradable emissions permits, see TH Tietenberg, *Emissions Trading: Principles and Practice*, 2nd edn (Washington, DC, Resources for the Future, 2006). Recent reports, however, suggest that the Obama administration in the USA may yet drop proposals for a US cap-and-trade carbon emissions regime, in the interests of securing enough votes to pass the Energy Bill, available at http://www.nytimes.com/cwire/2010/02/03/03climatewire-obama-says-senate-may-drop-cap-and-trade-pas-21189.html (accessed on 3 February 2010).

[17] For detailed discussion of the SO_x scheme, see A D Ellerman, P L Joskow, R Schmalensee, J-P Montero and E M Bailey, *Markets for Clean Air: the US Acid Rain Program* (Cambridge, Cambridge University Press, 2000).

[18] Kyoto Protocol to the Framework Convention on Climate Change (1998) 37 ILM 22.

[19] The Greenhouse Gas Emissions Trading Scheme Regulations 2003, SI 2003, No 3311: this was a complex, voluntary scheme with incentives for those who participated and which linked with the UK's Climate Change Levy and with Climate Change Agreements concluded between companies and government (where the former promised to make efficiency savings

EU Emissions Trading Scheme.[20] But there have been other manifestations of this trend in the energy sector, including various Member States' reliance upon Renewable Obligation Certificates[21] and other tradable certificates[22] to generate incentives for firms to behave in an environmentally sustainable manner, whether by trying to increase the share of electricity generated from renewable sources or to encourage measures to improve efficiency in, and reduce demand for, energy consumption.[23]

These devices all function by setting firm and legally binding targets to be achieved by those required to participate in the scheme which require an overall reduction (in emissions, or increase in renewable electricity generation) beyond that otherwise envisaged and then create tradable instruments which can be used to verify that those targets have been met across the relevant jurisdiction. If a certain participant can exceed the targets set, then they can sell their surplus to others: in this fashion, the least-cost abater (or improver) should be incentivised to do as much as is economic in exceeding the targets, allowing others to pay the market rate to benefit from each unit of the 'over-achievement' by others, leading to overall gains (whether reductions or increases, depending upon the scheme) in line with the targets set. Then, for the next reference period, new targets are set, usually more stringent than before, to ensure that the trajectory is maintained (and even improved). In this way, the goal is set by government in the public interest, but the choices are left to the market as to how best and most efficiently to ensure that they are achieved: hence the description of such devices as 'squaring the circle', since they aim to employ the disciplines of the market to achieve public interest goals in an efficient manner.[24]

---

in their emissions, which were not necessarily absolute cuts in total emissions). The Commission cleared the scheme, finding that its state aid elements were justifiable on environmental grounds: see Commission Press Release IP/01/1674, 28 November 2001.

[20] Originally Dir 2003/87/EC [2003] OJ L275/32; for allocations from 2012, see now the changes wrought by Dir 2009/29/EC [2009] OJ L140/63 (for a consolidated version, see http://eur-lex.europa.eu/LexUriServ/LexUriServ.do?uri=CONSLEG:2003L0087:20090625:EN:PDF).

[21] The most obvious example is the UK system (the current scheme is to be found in the regime of the Renewables Obligation Order 2009, SI 2009, No 785), but there are others who have adopted a so-called 'green certificate' scheme, including the Netherlands, Sweden and Italy.

[22] In the energy efficiency field, known as 'white certificates': both France (Law No 2005-781 of 13 July 2005) and Italy (Decree Law No 20/07 of 8 February 2007) have begun to use this instrument to encourage improved energy efficiency.

[23] For a helpful overview, see C Banet, 'The Use of Market-based Instruments in the Transition from a Carbon-based Economy' in DN Zillman, C Redgwell, Y Omorogbe and LK Barrera-Hernández (eds), *Beyond the Carbon Economy: Energy Law in Transition* (Oxford, Oxford University Press, 2008) ch 10; on energy efficiency, see B Barton, 'The Law of Energy Efficiency' in Zillman et al, n 43 above, ch 4.

[24] Cameron, *Competition in Energy Markets*, above n 12, para 1.59 and ch 17.

IV YET, INCREASINGLY, SQUARE PEGS IN ROUND HOLES?

Over the past few years, however, a shift in approach and aims can be charted, at both EU and some national levels. Recent legal and policy instruments have begun to prioritise the achievement of targets and goals. This development ties in closely with questions of accountability and political scrutiny of such areas of activity, even if it is often largely private actors who are involved in the delivery of services and, thus, the actual achievement of such targets on the ground. It is no exaggeration to suggest that these developments are an indication that the broader and deeper political implications of energy policy are becoming appreciated more widely outside government and industry circles, and are now exercising a direct influence within domestic and international political processes. In short, electorates are both more interested in, and (crucially) now increasingly holding governments responsible for, the achievement (or not, as the case may be) of energy and environmental goals. Yet the original market regimes constructed by those governments and legislators were not necessarily designed with the achievement of any specific goals in mind, other than the introduction of market mechanisms as a discipline for providing energy services in a more efficient manner.

A The Development and Operation of the European Emissions Trading Scheme[25]

The original development of the EU Emissions Trading Scheme (ETS), and the need to accommodate various interests in the negotiation and drafting process, led to some rather substantial difficulties in the operation of the scheme: for example, the decision taken to rely almost entirely upon the free allocation of allowances under the scheme (rather than an auctioning process),[26] leading to state aid questions about returns earned by energy companies.[27] The concern to achieve the goal of getting the system up and running was undoubtedly laudable, and one which provided an important opportunity for 'learning-by-doing' for the EU and its companies prior to

[25] See, generally, J Delbeke et al, *European Energy Law, Volume IV: EU Environmental Law—the EU Greenhouse Gas Emissions Trading Scheme* (Leuven, Claeys & Casteels, 2006); see also D Freestone and C Streck (eds), *Legal Aspects of Implementing the Kyoto Protocol Mechanisms: Making Kyoto Work* (Oxford, Oxford University Press, 2005), esp chs 16 and 17, and *Legal Aspects of Carbon Trading: Kyoto, Copenhagen and Beyond* (Oxford, Oxford University Press, 2009), esp chs 16 and 17.

[26] M Grubb and K Neuhoff, 'Allocation and Competitiveness in the EU Emissions Trading Scheme: Policy Overview' (2006) 6 *Climate Policy* 7.

[27] A Johnston, 'Free Allocation of Allowances under the EU Emissions Trading System—Legal Issues' (2006) 6 *Climate Policy* 115 (also available as Electricity Policy Research Group Working Paper 06/20 (2006) at http://www.electricitypolicy.org.uk/pubs/wp/eprg0620.pdf).

the expected operation of a global emissions trading scheme under the Kyoto Protocol (and beyond). Yet these compromises often had the effect of undermining the actual effectiveness of the EU ETS in achieving the goal of emissions reductions (at least in the EU ETS first and second reference periods): these difficulties undermined both the economic rationale behind the cap-and-trade system (excessive allocation, minimal incentive to reduce emissions, lack of sufficiently deterrent penalties for non-compliance, etc) and the achievement the environmental goal of emissions reductions (at least in the short term).[28] On the other hand, the very fact that these differing views and concerns were accommodated in the legislative process is indicative of the responsiveness of the EC legislative process to the concerns expressed by its Member States when pursuing innovative and far-reaching policies such as emissions trading. These same tensions have been apparent in the second phase of the scheme (for example in connection with the position of energy-intensive industries and so-called carbon leakage),[29] to which we will return shortly (see section IV.C(ii) below).

B   Other Emerging Issues

A myriad of issues has been raised by the combination of the EU's various goals (market, environment, security) and by their interaction with domestic and international political pressures.

(i)   'Fuel Poverty' Questions

In the early years of liberalisation, a commonly advanced argument was that increased competition across the system would lead to lower prices for customers;[30] indeed, to listen to some, it seemed that only if this were achieved could the process be judged a success. Of course, such a goal would always be difficult to achieve in absolute terms in the face of ever-scarcer primary energy resources and the environmental goals which were beginning to receive attention. The target of lower prices can only sensibly be analysed as a kind of counter-factual—ie lower than they would have been had we continued on the pre-existing course—and even this will be hard to show with any kind of analytical certainty or robustness. Nevertheless, it is clear that, as energy prices have risen and as they are

---

[28] For a balanced overview of these difficulties and the lessons to be learned from them, see AD Ellerman and P Joskow, *The European Union's Emissions Trading System in Perspective* (Pew Center on Global Climate Change, MIT, May 2008) (available at http://www.pewclimate.org/docUploads/EU-ETS-In-Perspective-Report.pdf).

[29] See K Neuhoff and F Matthes (eds), *The Role of Auctions for Emissions Trading* (Climate Strategies, October 2008).

[30] See W Patterson, *Transforming Electricity* (London, RIIA/Earthscan, 1999).

predicted to rise further in the future (if we are to achieve environmental goals such as the decarbonisation of the electricity supply network), the question of fuel poverty has risen rapidly up the political agenda. Specific measures to tackle this phenomenon are likely to remain at national level, since they typically mesh most closely with domestic taxation and/or social security regimes. Nevertheless, fuel poverty concerns have regularly been cited under the EU policy heading of secure supplies for all,[31] which interacts closely in the electricity field with the universal service obligation first recognised in EU law by Article 3(3) of the 2003 electricity internal market Directive[32] and the development of Public Service Obligations more generally (see section IV.D, below). And it is possible that future EU-level measures and actions will need to be fine-tuned to accommodate the possibility of restrictions upon competition to ensure that energy suppliers are in a financial position to be able to provide services to vulnerable customers (eg via cross-subsidy from those less unfortunate).

(ii) Binding Targets for Energy from Renewable Sources and the New EU Renewables Directive

One criticism of the first EU Renewables Directive was that the targets it set for Member States were only indicative in nature and not 'binding' in any real sense.[33] The European Parliament called for mandatory targets to be introduced, and these have now been adopted in Article 3 of the new Renewables Directive.[34] While various mechanisms are also introduced to keep Member States on track to achieve these targets (including the adoption of national renewable energy action plans (Article 4) and various associated reporting and information provision obligations), it seems that the only way to enforce these binding targets will be for the Commission to bring an enforcement action under Article 258 TFEU (ex-Article 226 EC), with the possible subsequent imposition of penalties under Article 260 TFEU (ex-Article 228 EC).[35] Whether this will prove to be either an

---

[31] See Commission Communication, 'An Energy Policy for Europe' COM(2007) 1 final (10 January 2007), para 3.17; and Recitals 36, 50 and 53, Arts 36(h) and 3(7) (8) of Dir 2009/72/EC [2009] OJ L211/55.

[32] Dir 2003/54/EC [2003] OJ L176/37; see now Art 3(3) of the latest electricity directive, Dir 2009/72/EC (above n 3).

[33] Dir 2001/77/EC [2001] OJ L283/33: see Art 3 in conjunction with the Annex's burden sharing of the overall EU target among the Member States.

[34] Dir 2009/28/EC [2009] OJ L140/16, in conjunction with Annex I thereto.

[35] On the use of Arts 226–88 EC, see A Bonnie, 'The Evolving Role of the European Commission in the Enforcement of Community Law: From Negotiating Compliance to Prosecuting Member States?' (2005) 1 *Journal of Contemporary European Research* 391 and P Wennerås, 'A New Dawn for Commission Enforcement under Arts 226 and 228 EC: General and Persistent (GAP) Infringements, Lump Sums and Penalty Payments' (2006) 43 *Common Market Law Review* 31. For discussion of the possible introduction of stronger enforcement mechanisms into the Directive (which suggestions were not taken up by the EU legislature), see A Johnston, K Neuhoff, D Fouquet, M Ragwitz and G Resch, 'The

effective deterrent or an effective enforcement mechanism in the event of default remains to be seen.[36]

However, the original Commission proposal[37] to allow a limited form of trading in Guarantees of Origin (GOs)[38] between private parties was removed from the final text, after objections from certain Member States (especially Germany) and the European Parliament.[39] Instead, the final form of the Directive contained a mechanism allowing only inter-government statistical transfers of specified amounts of renewable energy, allowing the recipient government to count that energy against its own renewables target: see Article 6 of the new Directive. Whatever the pros and cons of this retreat from a slightly more market-based, EU-mandated mechanism for renewables promotion, the fact thereof indicates genuine concern in both some Member States and the European Parliament that EU-level measures of this kind could undermine the viability and, in time, even preclude the use of alternative methods (such as feed-in tariffs) for encouraging renewable energy development. This provides a further illustration both of doubts as to the appropriateness of such market-oriented instruments and of the practical operation of the EU's constitutional order of states. In the absence of consensus on the need for, and shape of, EU-wide measures, the outcome of the legislative process reached a compromise which set ambitious and harder-edged EU targets to be achieved by each of the Member States and created a limited EU-level mechanism allowing some inter-Member State co-ordination (via the statistical transfer provision, joint projects (Article 7) and/or joint support schemes (Article 11) between Member States), while at the same time respecting a diversity of approaches across the Member States with regard to how best to achieve those targets.

Proposed New EU Renewables Directive: Interpretation, Problems and Prospects' [2008] *European Environmental Law Review* 126, 144–45.

[36] See the present author's presentation, 'How Binding Are the EU's "Binding" Renewables Targets?' at the CEEPR/EPRG European Electricity Workshop, Berlin, 15–16 July 2010, available at http://web.mit.edu/ceepr/www/about/Summer%202010/Johnston.pdf. Similar practical enforcement questions might be asked of the UK's much trumpeted adoption of binding national emissions reduction targets (80% by 2050) and binding carbon budgets under its recent Climate Change Act 2008.

[37] Commission, 'Proposal for a Directive on the Promotion of the Use of Energy from Renewable Sources', COM(2008) 19 final (23 January 2008), available at http://ec.europa.eu/energy/climate_actions/doc/2008_res_directive_en.pdf.

[38] In Art 2(g) of the Commission's Proposal (COM(2008) 19 final (23 January 2008)), a GO was defined as 'an electronic document which has the function of providing proof that a given quantity of energy was produced from renewable sources'

[39] See Johnston et al, 'The Proposed New EU Renewables Directive', above n 35, for detailed analysis of the proposal concerning inter-private party trade in such Guarantees of Origin. The new definition concerning GOs is found in Art 2(j) of Dir 2009/28/EC (above n 34), which emphasises that a GO is 'an electronic document which has the *sole* function of providing proof to a final customer that a given share or quantity of energy was produced from renewable sources' (emphasis added), thus excluding the use of GOs as a tradable certificate.

(iii) Security of Supply: Measures and Investments

In the face of blackouts,[40] questions concerning Russian gas supplies
(transit through the Ukraine, alternative pipeline routes)[41] and fears
concerning possible terrorist attacks on critical infrastructure,[42] it seems
likely that 'security of supply' will become one of the key features of
EU energy law and policy in the near future. Unpacking exactly what
the 'security of supply' concept contains is no easy task, and this is not
the place to attempt it. Briefly, it encompasses both short- and long-term
security, and technical, practical and geopolitical aspects: key elements
include regular/continuous supply, affordable cost and access to supplies,
as well as the physical integrity and safety of the relevant infrastructure. It
is thus something of a catch-all concept, rendering its precise presentation
and analysis difficult at the best of times.[43]

From relatively humble beginnings in the wake of the oil shocks of the
1970s,[44] the EU has become increasingly concerned, both as a whole and
as individual Member States, with securing energy supplies and reducing
dependence upon imports from outside the EU.[45] While the Commis-

[40] For analysis of European instances and responses, see UCTE, 'Security of Electricity
Supply: Roles, Responsibilities and Experiences within the EU' (January 2006); ERGEG,
'Final Report: The Lessons to be Learned from the Large Disturbance in the European Power
System on the 4th of November 2006' (E06-BAG-01–06, 6 February 2007), available at http://
www.energy-regulators.eu/portal/page/portal/EER_HOME/EER_PUBLICATIONS/CEER_
ERGEG_PAPERS/Electricity/2007/E06-BAG-01–06_Blackout-FinalReport_2007–02–06.pdf);
and E Van der Vleuten and V Lagendijk, 'Interpreting Transnational Infrastructure Vul-
nerability: European Blackout and the Historical Dynamics of Transnational Electricity
Governance' (2009) 38 *Energy Policy* 2053.

[41] On the first Russo-Ukrainian gas crisis, see K Westphal, 'Energy Policy between Mul-
tilateral Governance and Geopolitics: Whither Europe?' (2006) 4 *Internationale Politik und
Gesellschaft* 44. On the 2009 repeat performance, see S Pirani, J Stern and K Yafimava,
'The Russo-Ukrainian Gas Dispute of January 2009: a Comprehensive Assessment' (Oxford,
OIES, February 2009), available at http://www.oxfordenergy.org/pdfs/NG27.pdf.

[42] See AEA, 'Study on Risk Governance of European Critical Infrastructures in the ICT
and Energy Sector: Final Report to the European Commission' (4 September 2009), available
at http://ec.europa.eu/energy/infrastructure/studies/doc/2009_10_risk_governance_report.pdf.

[43] For analysis, see S Haghighi, *Energy Security: The External Legal Relations of the
European Union with Major Oil and Gas Supplying Countries* (Oxford, Hart Publishing,
2007) ch 1; and B Barton, C Redgwell, A Rønne and D Zillman (eds), *Energy Security:
Managing Risk in a Dynamic Legal and Regulatory Environment* (Oxford, Oxford University Press, 2004).

[44] Although the first EEC legislation concerning oil stocks in fact dates from 1968—Dir
68/414/EEC [1968] OJ L308/14 (with its various amendments, now codified in Dir 2006/67/
EC [2006] OJ L217/8)—specific measures aimed at mitigating crude oil and petroleum supply
difficulties were adopted in 1973 and 1977 (Dir 73/238/EEC [1973] OJ L228/1 and Dir
77/706/EEC [1977] OJ L292/9, respectively).

[45] See the Commission's Green Papers: 'Towards a European Strategy for the Security of
Energy Supply', COM(2000) 769 final (29 November 2000) (and its subsequent Communication reporting thereon: COM(2002) 321 final (26 June 2002)) and 'A European Strategy
for Sustainable, Competitive and Secure Energy', COM(2006) 105 final (8 March 2006);
and see COM(2007) 1 final, above n 31. See, generally, Cameron, *Competition in Energy
Markets*, above n 12, ch 18.

sion has consistently argued that liberalisation and competition strengthen
security of supply by ensuring that market actors receive the right signals
about investment and demand, the internal market directives for both electricity and gas contain a number of provisions allowing Member States to
take measures to ensure and promote supply security. Some of those provisions specifically authorise derogations from market liberalisation and
competition provisions,[46] albeit in what are in practice a relatively limited
range of circumstances due to their wording and the enduring applicability of the trade and competition provisions of what is now the TFEU (see
its Articles 101–108). Further, recent proposals and measures have shown
an increasing willingness on the Commission's part at least to propose the
pursuit of more interventionist policies in the name of security of supply.
To date, the EU has adopted specific directives concerning security of
supply in both the electricity[47] and natural gas[48] sectors, and more recently
passed a regulation on Union financing for key energy projects[49] as part
of a package to stimulate economic recovery in the wake of the financial
crisis. At the time of writing, heated debate continued in the Council over
a proposed regulation in the field of gas supply security,[50] which turns
on the extent to which EU-level minimum standards for supply security
should be imposed. This has created much controversy among Member
States, given that a 'one-size-fits-all' policy fails to take into account significant variations across Member States with regard to their exposure to
supply security difficulties.[51] This, again, illustrates clearly the two themes

---

[46] Arts 42 and 3(2) (14) of the electricity directive, Dir 2009/72/EC, above n 31; see also
Art 7 of the electricity regulation, Reg 1228/2003/EC [2003] OJ L176/37, and Arts 3, 36
and 46 of the gas directive, Dir 2009/73/EC [2009] OJ L211/94. One should note that the
market can operate positively in the security of supply field, responding to supply shortages
by providing a clear price signal to that effect, leading to interactions between providers
across the value chain to cover that shortage; of course, the 'cost' of reliance upon such a
mechanism is price volatility, which can cause difficulties (eg re fuel poverty, on which see
Section B(i), above).

[47] Dir 2005/89/EC [2006] OJ L33/22.

[48] Dir 2004/67/EC [2004] OJ L127/92.

[49] Reg 663/2009/EC [2009] OJ L200/31, which includes a detailed annex listing the eligible projects and the envisaged Community contribution to each. It should be noted that
the Regulation pursues environmental sustainability and economic recovery goals alongside
supply security, while endeavouring to distribute these investments 'taking into account an
adequate geographical balance' (Recital 4), again illustrating the complex policy combinations and compromises at work in the sector when seeking to act on the EU level.

[50] 'Proposal for a Regulation Concerning Measures to Safeguard Security of Gas Supply',
COM(2009) 363 final (16 July 2009), available at http://eur-lex.europa.eu/LexUriServ/LexU-
riServ.do?uri=COM:2009:0363:FIN:EN:PDF; for discussion and critique, see P Noël and S
Findlater, 'A Comment on the Draft EU Regulation on Security of Gas Supply' (EPRG, University of Cambridge, 3 July 2009), available at http://www.eprg.group.cam.ac.uk/wpcontent/
uploads/PN_SF_Comment%20on%20the%20draft%20Regulation(2).pdf.

[51] For suggestions on how to resolve these difficulties, see P Noël, 'Ensuring Success for
the EU Regulation on Gas Supply Security' (EPRG, ECFR, 9 February 2010), who favours
a 'bottom-up' approach focusing on Member States' adoption of regular national energy
security assessments and action plans, which are published across the EU so as to incentivise information- and experience-sharing among Member States.

emerging from this contribution: negotiating difficulties at the EU level due to diversity in Member States' positions concerning how supply security issues might affect them alongside recognition that reliance upon the market alone is unlikely to be sufficient to ensure the achievement of a public interest goal (here, security of gas supplies).

C   Greater (Political) Commitment to Achieving Goals, and Less Faith in the Market Process to Reach Those Goals:[52] the Challenges of Environmental Policy

From these brief examples, it starts to become clear that the orientation of EU law and policy in the energy sphere is in the process of shifting away from a clear and overriding goal of 'regulation for competition',[53] towards a more complex balance between market and other public interest objectives. While this complexity has always been more or less present in most Member States' domestic energy law and policy, this shift at the EU level has only recently become pronounced. Some of the pressures 'from below' on EU law and policy are discussed below and they suggest that the trend on the EU level discussed in the preceding subsection is likely to continue in the years to come.

(i)   Promoting the Generation of Electricity from Renewable Sources

An examination of the UK's Renewables Obligation (RO) regime and its tradable Renewables Obligation Certificates (ROCs)[54] when compared with the German system of feed-in tariffs and supported prices for electricity generated from renewable sources has shown that, while both systems have led to increased renewables deployment, the German system has been far more successful in getting significant amounts of renewable generation built.[55] It also shows that ROCs which cover all

[52] Eg F Matthes, 'Do We Need the Return of State Planning to Overcome the Climate Change Challenge?' in A Giddens, S Latham and R Liddle (eds), *Building a Low-carbon Future: the Politics of Climate Change* (London, Policy Network, 2009) ch 4.

[53] See the discussion in Cameron, *Competition in Energy Markets*, above n 12, ch 1 and the references cited therein.

[54] Which system functions by imposing an obligation upon electricity suppliers to source an increasing proportion of their electricity from renewable sources, evidenced by submitting ROCs to prove that they have met that obligation or else paying a buy-out price to the extent that they have failed to do so. The proportion was 9.1% in 2008–09 and is currently 9.7% for 2009–10.

[55] A Johnston, A Kavali and K Neuhoff, 'Take-or-Pay Contracts for Renewables Deployment' (2008) 36 *Energy Policy* 2481 (also available as Electricity Policy Research Group Working Paper 07/07 (2007) at http://www.electricitypolicy.org.uk/pubs/wp/eprg0707.pdf). In early 2010, the UK renewables share of generation was around 5.5%, which is well short of the 30% projected to be required to meet the UK's 2020 energy targets. In Germany, renewables penetration is already well in excess of 25%.

different kinds of renewable generation sources do not provide incentives to develop diversity and innovation across the range of such sources: for example, the renewable technology currently closest to unsubsidised viability in the electricity market is wind power, and thus ROC prices on the market tend, roughly, to stabilise around the levels required to support wind generation. Yet that price level will not provide sufficient support to encourage the development of renewable generation using other technologies, such as solar power and tidal power. The UK has acknowledged this latter problem in the latest incarnation of the RO scheme by creating a 'banding' regime for ROCs,[56] under which some technologies will have to generate more electricity, and others less, to qualify for each ROC granted.[57]

This empirical evidence suggests that a market response[58] which provides significant development of renewable electricity generation capacity requires medium- to long-term guarantees about returns on up-front investment and about stability of government policy in the area.[59] Such guarantees themselves would seem to imply at least some insurance against the uncertainties of the free market, particularly when competing against other generation sources whose costs are subject to very different cycles and constraints (such as natural gas or coal). Of course, this picture would be incomplete without mentioning the constraints imposed by planning legislation: many developers in the renewables field complain[60] that the time, expense and uncertainty of the planning[61] process in the UK are a

[56] Renewables Obligation Order 2009, SI 2009, No 785, on which see Ofgem, 'Renewables Obligation: Guidance for Generators over 50kW' (27 March 2009), available at http://www.ofgem.gov.uk/Sustainability/Environment/RenewablObl/Documents1/Large%20Gen%20Guidance%202009%20-%20for%20publication.pdf.

[57] Thus, eg landfill gas earns only 0.25 ROC per MWh generated, sewage gas or biomass 0.5 ROC, onshore wind 1.0 ROC and offshore wind 1.5 ROCs, while wave, tidal stream, solar photovoltaic, geothermal and microgeneration receive 2.0 ROCs per MWh: for the full list and definitions, see Ofgem, ibid, 33. (Note that pre-existing microgeneration will be transferred to, and new microgeneration will fall under, the new feed-in tariff regime from 1 April 2010.)

[58] Indeed, ss 41–43 of the UK's Energy Act 2008 also empowered the creation of a feed-in tariff scheme to support small-scale (<5 MW) renewable generation, and the government has now announced that such a scheme will be introduced (available at http://www.decc.gov.uk/en/content/cms/news/pn10_010/pn10_010.aspx and http://www.decc.gov.uk/en/content/cms/consultations/elec_financial/elec_financial.aspx). The scheme will be called 'Clean Energy Cashback' and will enter into force in England and Wales on 1 April 2010: see http://www.energysavingtrust.org.uk/Generate-your-own-energy/Sell-your-own-energy/Clean-Energy-Cashback-Feed-in-Tariffs for details.

[59] For an interesting and original contribution on securing stability over time in government policy for respecting international agreements, see R Ismer and K Neuhoff, 'Commitments Through Financial Options: an Alternative for Delivering Climate Change Obligations' (2009) 9 *Climate Policy* 9.

[60] See, eg Centrica's forceful views of 5 November 2007, reported at http://uk.reuters.com/article/idUKL0228070200711o5 (although in many respects directed towards constructing gas storage capacity, the issues are much the same).

[61] Such concerns are being highlighted by commentators across the world: on the USA see, eg JR Nolon, 'Climate Change and Sustainable Development: the Quest for Green

major explanation for the UK's relatively slow development of renewable electricity generation. Much of this is clearly due to the domestic system and its operation,[62] but that has itself been shaped by EU environmental legislation over the years, including the Directives on Environmental Impact Assessment,[63] Strategic Environmental Assessment[64] and Public Access to Environmental Information.[65]

(ii) Legal Challenges by Member States to the Commission's Role in the Operation of the EU ETS

In the autumn of 2009, successful challenges were brought by Poland and Estonia to the Commission's decisions on their National Allocation Plans (NAPs) under the EU ETS,[66] which plans had sought to grant more allowances domestically than the Commission was willing to approve. It seems that these plans to allocate more allowances were due to fears of high domestic costs imposed on business by tighter allowance caps (and the resulting risk of 'carbon leakage'—whereby emitting industries leave the EU for countries without emissions caps and then import their production back into the EU, while another intra-EU emitter emerges to use the new space under the EU emissions cap, thus increasing overall global emissions). For the Commission, these proposals were excessive when compared with the projected emissions which would actually occur in those (and other) countries during the reference period: to allow such high allocation levels would have been to move away from the economic rationale for the cap-and-trade system and back to political deal-making with domestic industry interests. It should be noted that the Commission refused to concede that the judgments would lead to any extra allowances

Communities—Parts I and II' (2009) 64(10) *Planning & Environmental Law* 3 and 64(11) *Planning & Environmental Law* 3, respectively.

[62] And has led to recent changes in UK legislation, endeavouring to simplify and speed up the approval process for large infrastructure projects: see the Planning Act 2008, whose Part 3 covers 'nationally significant infrastructure projects' including energy in ss 15–21. It is perhaps a measure of how complicated the previous system had become that the 2008 Act itself contains 242 sections and 13 schedules.

[63] Dir 85/337/EEC [1985] OJ L175/40 (as amended by Directives 97/11/EC [1997] OJ L73/5 and 2003/35/EC [2003] OJ L156/17), on which see COM(2009) 378 final (23 July 2009).

[64] Dir 2001/42/EC [2001] OJ L197/30, on which see COM(2009) 469 final (14 September 2009).

[65] Dir 2003/4/EC [2003] OJ L41/26, implementing some of the obligations imposed by the Århus Convention (on Access to Information, Public Participation in Decision Making and Access to Justice in Environmental Matters (1999) 38 ILM 517) and building upon the earlier Dir 90/313/EEC [1990] OJ L158/56 (which was repealed by Dir 2003/4/EC).

[66] Cases T-183/07 *Poland v Commission* and T-263/07 *Estonia v Commission*, judgments of 23 September 2009.

making it on to the market.[67] In essence, the result of the judgments was that the Commission had to reach new formal decisions on the matter, which it did on 11 December 2009, again rejecting the NAPs of Poland and Estonia on various grounds of incompatibility with the guiding criteria for such NAPs laid down in the EU ETS Directive.[68]

The key consequence was that the Court of First Instance found that the Commission lacked the power under the Directive to fix the maximum level for the total quantity of allowances to be allocated by any given Member State. This is, so the Court said, because the Directive lays down a division of powers between Member States and the Commission which specifically envisages that the Member State shall develop a NAP which states the total quantity of allowances it intends to allocate (see Articles 9(1) and 11(2) of the Directive). The Commission's role is to check compatibility of the NAP with the Directive's Annex III and Article 10 criteria, which role does not include constraining the Member State's discretion in taking the final decision on the total quantity of allowances to be allocated.

These are very fine distinctions, and this is borne out by the Commission's recent Decisions again rejecting the proposed NAPs of both Poland and Estonia. In them, the Commission pointed out the grounds of inconsistency with the allocation criteria but specifically refrained from making suggestions of what allocations would be 'acceptable' to the Commission, lest this be construed as attempting to fix the allocations itself and thus intruding upon the Member State's powers under the Directive.

Given that the new EU ETS Directive[69] (which was adopted prior to these judgments) will remove Member States' powers to determine their own NAPs from 2012, it may prove difficult to argue against the Court's interpretation of the legislation as it stands, since otherwise one would have to ask why the change in the Commission and Member States' respective roles would have been needed in the new Directive. Neverthe-

---

[67] First, the Commission made plain that it had to take new decisions on the two National Allocation Plans in question, making clear that in the interim no new allowances could be issued and pointing out that the actual emissions observed were in line with those envisaged by the Commission in its original decisions: see Press Release IP/09/1355, 24 September 2009 and 'Commission Says Poland, Estonia cannot issue more carbon allowances' (25 September 2009), available at http://euobserver.com/9/28720/?rk=1. Subsequently, on 3 December 2009 the Commission announced that it had decided to appeal against the CFI's judgments in these cases (pending Cases C-504 and 505/09, respectively), available at http://www.eubusiness.com/news-eu/climate-warming.1s4.

[68] P/09/1907, and http://ec.europa.eu/environment/climat/emission/pdf/pl_decision_en.pdf and http://ec.europa.eu/environment/climat/emission/pdf/et_decision_en.pdf for the text of the two decisions (on, respectively, the Polish and Estonian NAPs), all of 11 December 2009.

[69] Dir 2009/29/EC [2009] OJ L140/63: see esp Art 9 (which replaces NAPs with an EU-wide quantity of allowances published by the Commission, which quantity is to reduce in a linear manner year on year, by 1.74%) and Arts 10, 10a, 10b and 10c (which harmonise the criteria by which Member States are to auction and, in a limited range of cases, allocate allowances).

less, given the fact that observed emissions have actually been lower than some of the Member States had suggested (and in fact more in line with the estimates made by the Commission in its decisions on the NAPs), it seems likely that some diplomatic solution will be reached without significantly increasing the overall amount of allowances in circulation. However, the whole episode illustrates Member States' tendencies to resort to political manipulation of the allocation criteria and quantities when such decisions are left in their hands: this undermines the use of such market-based mechanisms to achieve environmental goals and threatens the new EU approach to designing markets more effectively to deliver environmental objectives.

The market, meanwhile, reacted to these judgments with a significant drop in the carbon price (by as much as 3.9 per cent according to one report), reflecting uncertainty[70] as to the overall supply volume of allowances in the system and the predictability of that supply in the future. This uncertainty is underlined by the fact that six other Member States[71] have applications pending before the CFI on similar grounds to those relied upon in the Polish and Estonian cases. Others have hurried to reassure campaigners and markets alike that the extent of such uncertainty is likely to be small at worst.[72]

(iii) National Concerns about Achieving Emissions Reductions Targets under the EU ETS: Securing a Minimum Carbon Price?

There have been suggestions in the policy community that the achievement of genuine CO_2 reductions under the current meshed European and national systems within the EU will require a much higher carbon price, with a minimum price to safeguard and encourage investment decisions by business and financiers, and to incentivise innovation, research and development. This has become particularly pressing in the face of reductions in emissions due to the recent recession across the EU, which has led to significant falls in the carbon price. Yet no moves have been made at EU level to secure such a minimum price under the EU ETS. This has led to discussions in some Member States (such as the UK)[73]

---

[70] See Norton Rose's short report (in late September 2009) on the CFI's judgments, the first sub-heading of which is 'Where to Now for Market Certainty?', available at http://www.nortonrose.com/knowledge/publications/2009/pub23247.aspx?page=all&lang=en-gb.

[71] The cases concern: Bulgaria (T-499/07); the Czech Republic (T-194/07); Hungary (T-221/07); Latvia (T-369/07); Lithuania (T-368/07); and Romania (T-483 and 484/07).

[72] See C Egenhofer, 'Court Ruling Need Not Cause Carbon Market to Unravel' (CEPS, 1 October 2009), available at http://www.ceps.be/book/court-ruling-need-not-cause-carbon market-unravel.

[73] Most recently (8 February 2010), the UK Parliament's Environmental Audit Committee has considered this issue and called for the government seriously to consider measures, including a carbon tax, to set a floor for carbon prices: to set a floor for carbon prices to set a floor for carbon prices (see the press release at http://www.parliament.uk/parliamentary_

about introducing some form of domestic carbon tax to ensure a minimum carbon price.[74]

The aim of such a tax would be to design the market so as to incentivise and facilitate the 'right' kinds and amounts of (environmentally sustainable, etc) investment. Essentially, a tax-based system would seek to establish a carbon tax (z) on top of the cost of an emissions allowance (x), at a level to ensure that the overall 'cost of carbon' always reached at least a certain minimum amount (y), ie $x + z \geq y$. In practice, the easiest way to achieve this would be a uniform carbon tax, charged at the level of y. Then a rebate could be given to anyone holding an emissions allowance to the market value of that allowance, subject to the limit that no rebate payment would be any greater than the original level of the tax charged (ie y). Thus, if the market price of emissions allowances were to exceed the tax (ie $x > y$), then effectively the tax would not impose an extra cost[75] beyond the need to purchase emissions allowances (whether at the original auctions or subsequently on the market). Meanwhile, so long as that market price was below the up-front level of the tax (ie $x < y$), the tax would add the necessary increment to ensure the desired minimum carbon price. The result would be the creation of a minimum price for carbon set at the level of the carbon tax; that carbon price could rise higher where the market price of allowances exceeded the minimum level set by the tax, but it could not fall below the floor set by that tax. This tax mechanism would also be open to amendment over time,[76] should

committees/environmental_audit_committee/eacpno80210.cfm; and the report, 'The Role of Carbon Markets in Preventing Dangerous Climate Change', available at http://www.pub-lications.parliament.uk/pa/cm200910/cmselect/cmenvaud/290/29002.htm, esp s 4). Carbon taxes are already levied in Finland, the Netherlands, Sweden, Denmark, the UK and France (in order of the date of their introduction): for an overview, see J Sumner, L Bird and H Smith, 'Carbon Taxes: A Review of Experience and Policy Design Considerations', National Renewable Energy Laboratory (USA) Technical Report NREL/TP-6A2-47312 (December 2009), available at http://www.nrel.gov/docs/fy10osti/47312.pdf.

[74] See, on the general question, P Wood and F Jotzo, 'Price Floors for Emissions Trading', FEEM Working Paper 118.2009 (7 January 2010), available at http://papers.ssrn.com/sol3/papers.cfm?abstract_idem=1532701, suggesting that firms should pay some form of extra fee or tax to implement such a 'price floor' policy.

[75] This excludes the enforcement costs associated with such a tax regime, which includes both compliance costs for the companies concerned and the cost to the state of running the system of taxation and rebates: no doubt the state's costs in running that system would swallow much of the extra net revenue generated by the tax. Thus, the overall welfare costs and benefits of such a tax system would need to be examined very carefully and compared to alternative possible schemes when conducting a regulatory impact assessment, and might yet amount to a further argument against such an approach (see the subsequent paragraph in the text).

[76] Of course, care would have to be taken to ensure that these tax levels were not too readily manipulated by the rough and tumble of domestic politics, whether in raising such taxes to an excessively high level or (perhaps more likely) allowing them to fall in the face of pressure from business or other lobbyists. Lack of certainty in this regard would undermine the whole purpose of introducing such a tax regime in the first place, and would perhaps suggest that the level of any such tax should be determined by an independent

it become clear that a lower or higher minimum carbon price would be more appropriate to achieve the goal of emissions reductions.

It may also be argued that an alternative way to achieve this goal would be to introduce reserve prices under the mechanism for auctioning allowances under the EU ETS. Under the latest incarnation of the EU ETS Directive,[77] an auctioning process will be used for allocations of allowances from 2013 onwards: to date, the vast majority of allowances has been allocated for free, with only very small proportions (up to 5 per cent in the first phase and up to 10 per cent in the second) being auctioned. Under a system mainly based on auctioning, a provision adopted at EU level allowing for the setting of reserve prices in such auctions would provide (depending upon its precise formulation) a harmonised solution to this problem across the EU, unlike the suggestions in the preceding paragraph (which would proceed on the basis of national taxation measures in any Member State which wished to introduce them). This might well be a preferable approach,[78] so far as general EU law considerations are concerned, since one could envisage a range of difficult questions being raised with regard to the domestic taxation proposal. For example, the rules on internal taxation under Article 110 TFEU (ex-90 EC) may prove challenging, particularly if the national system were to respond to potential protests by large domestic electricity consumers by imposing some form of border tax adjustments against imported products which would not be subject to the higher effective UK carbon price. Alternatively, EU state aids law might prove a challenge if the response to such imports were instead to exempt certain domestic emitters from the tax, and of course such exemptions would themselves call into question whether the very goals of the tax-based approach to securing a minimum carbon price would actually be achieved.

While neither of these approaches would signal an abandonment of the market process altogether, they would amount to an acknowledgment that

---

regulator or government agency. These possibilities suggest that industry might not ascribe sufficient credibility to a tax-based system as a long-term, reliable instrument, which in turn might dampen enthusiasm for the necessary investment to develop technology and deploy it effectively and in good time.

[77] See Art 10, Dir 2009/29/EC [2009] OJ L140/63.

[78] Although it must be conceded that there may be little appetite among the Commission, Council and European Parliament to return to the amendment of the EU ETS so soon after the adoption of the 2009 Directive. Thus, much may turn on whether a reserve auction price might be introduced into the EU ETS through the Commission's envisaged Regulation on auctioning, to be adopted under Art 10(4) of the new Directive by 30 June 2010 conducted according to the 'regulatory committee with scrutiny' variant of the comitology process, under Art 23(3) of Dir 2009/29/EC. Nevertheless it also seems inconsistent to pursue unilateral measures at a time when the interdependence between EU Member States' energy systems and needs is increasingly accepted: see, eg PD Cameron, 'From Producer to Consumer: the UK's Changing Energy Strategy in the EU' in P Andrews-Speed (ed), *International Competition for Resources: The Role of Law, the State and of Markets* (University of Dundee Press, Dundee 2008) 45.

there is a need for greater regulatory intervention in that market process (or, at least, a more involved and nuanced approach to designing that market) to ensure that the goals for which it was created are actually achieved in practice.

D   Ownership Unbundling and the General Quid Pro Quo of EU Legislative Bargaining

The ownership unbundling (OU)[79] of vertically integrated energy companies was a key feature in the intense debates over the third energy package: it aimed to secure greater competition and cross-border trade, and to reduce the ability and/or incentives for vertically integrated (VI) incumbents to exploit their market power to keep markets less open and accessible to new entry by competitors. Yet one might also question whether such OU will secure the number and scale of investments needed to meet the EU's multifarious energy goals (of competition, environment and energy security). Ultimately, reluctance in some Member States to accept a simple OU rule for transmission networks led to a compromise which adopted full OU as the default position but allowed Member States to derogate from this (Article 9(8) of Directive 2009/72/EC). This could be done either by designating an 'Independent System Operator' (Articles 13 and 14: essentially, this allows the maintenance of a pre-existing legally unbundled transmission system operator as part of a VI operation, with additional regulatory oversight), subject to the Commission's approval, or by using the provisions in Chapter V of the Directive to create an Independent Transmission Operator (Articles 17ff: this creates a complex and detailed regime subjecting a legally unbundled transmission operator to far more extensive institutional requirements (Trustee, Supervisory Board, Compliance Programme) and regulatory oversight to ensure the independence of the transmission element of the business).

One can clearly speak of a quid pro quo process in the enhancement of the EC energy liberalisation directives over their three iterations to date.[80] For example, from minimal early beginnings, public service obligations (PSOs)[81] and consumer protection[82] questions have become much more

---

[79] For an outline, see A Johnston, 'Ownership Unbundling: Prolegomenon to a Legal Analysis' in M Bulterman, L Hancher, A McDonnell and H Sevenster (eds), *Views of European Law from the Mountain*—Liber Amicorum *Piet Jan Slot* (Kluwer Law International, Alphen aan den Rijn, 2009) ch 23.

[80] I have discussed elsewhere the difficult, multi-faceted genesis and problematic implications of the 'reciprocity' clauses in the first set of energy liberalisation Directives: see Johnston, above n 8.

[81] In the electricity sector, see DG TREN's Interpretation Note, 'Public Service Obligations' (16 January 2004), and now Art 3(2)(6) (Arts 14 and 15 of Dir 2009/72/EC, above n 31).

[82] Compare the relevant provisions in the first, second and third liberalisation packages: eg Annex I to the electricity internal market directive on consumer protection measures has

prominent and detailed in EC-level rules. These developments can be seen as the price paid in return for securing the almost universal application of Regulated Third Party Access rules,[83] the requirement to establish a national energy regulator(y function),[84] agreement by Member States to speeding up the market opening timetable[85] and the push towards ownership unbundling and away from vertical integration. This also tracks the introduction of Article 16 EC[86] by the Treaty of Amsterdam (now Article 14 TFEU), as well as the development of case law concerning PSOs and services of general economic interest under what is now Article 106 TFEU (ex-Article 86 EC)[87] and cognate provisions (eg the grant of concessions in cases like *Altmark-Trans*[88] and the conditions for avoiding the application of Article 107 TFEU (ex-Article 87 EC)).

V   SQUARING OFF . . . AND CUTTING CORNERS?

> *And this circle doesn't fit its little square,*
> *It bulges with opportunity . . . bulges.*[89]

Writing in early 2010, one important but as yet unanswered question about the future of EU energy law and policy must be the impact of the Treaty of Lisbon in the energy field. In particular, the TFEU contains new provisions which for the first time provide a separate legal basis upon which the Union may adopt measures in the energy field.[90] At the same time, the TFEU explicitly reserves autonomy to Member States over

grown with every amendment, while also becoming more detailed (it now spans two pages in the Official Journal: see Dir 2009/72/EC at [2009] OJ L211, 90–91). On such consumer protection issues in the EU utilities sector generally, see P Nihoul, 'The Status of Consumers in EC Liberalisation Directives' (2009) 3 *Yearbook of Consumer Law* 67.

[83] See Arts 32 and 34 of the electricity directive, Dir 2009/72/EC (above n 31), and the slightly more nuanced position in Arts 32–36 and 38 of the gas directive, Dir 2009/73/EC (above n 46).

[84] Arts 35–41 of the electricity directive, ibid, and Arts 39–44 of the gas directive, ibid.

[85] Art 33 of the electricity directive, ibid, and Art 37 of the gas directive, ibid.

[86] See M Ross, 'Article 16 EC and Services of General Interest: from Derogation to Obligation' (2000) 25 *European Law Review* 22 and 'Promoting Solidarity: from Public Services to a European Model of Competition' (2007) 44 *Common Market Law Review* 1057.

[87] Eg the *Energy Import–Export* cases of 1997, concerning various national import and export monopolies in electricity and natural gas: Cases C-157/94 *Commission v Netherlands* [1997] ECR I-5699,; C-158/94 *Commission v Italy* [1997] ECR I-5789, C-159/94 *Commission v France* [1997] ECR I-5815 and C-160/94 *Commission v Spain* [1997] ECR I-5851, on which see PJ Slot, 'Annotation' (1998) 35 *Common Market Law Review* 1183

[88] Case C-280/00 *Altmark Trans GmbH and Regierungspräsidium Magdeburg v Nahverkehrsgesellschaft Altmark GmbH and Oberbundesanwalt beim Bundesverwaltungsgericht* [2003] ECR I-7747.

[89] The Wonderstuff, 'Circlesquare' (Polydor, 1994).

[90] See Title XXI, Art 194 TFEU.

their own natural resources.[91] This may, perhaps, be seen as another quid pro quo development, this time in the process of negotiating the Lisbon Treaty: the price to be paid for a new Union competence in the energy field, independent of competition and internal market grounds, was the need to provide safeguards for Member States in highly sensitive areas, such as a given Member State's decisions about its future energy mix, exploitation of its natural resources and the structure of industries of particular national significance.

A similar trend might be seen in the relegation of 'competition' from the 'activities' of the Union (the old Article 3(1)(g) EC)[92] to 'Protocol No 27 on the Internal Market and Competition': is this likely to be significant in practice? Most[93] have argued that it will not lead to substantive changes in, for example, the Court of Justice's case law.[94] Yet, presentationally, it illustrates a change in attitude towards the prima facie centrality of competition to the internal market. Perhaps it is best understood as a marker in the Treaty which shows the difficulties that will be faced in the years to come when trying to reach a balance concerning the often competing economic and other goals now embodied in the EU Treaties. In many ways, these different goals have long been contained within the founding Treaties, but it is the current (and likely future) political and economic climate which is now bringing such conflicts more clearly to the fore.[95]

Of course, alongside these points, the general reforms made to the Union's decision-making processes will have an impact upon EU-level law-

---

[91] Under Title XX on the environment, see Art 192(2)(c) TFEU (prescribing the consultation procedure vis-à-vis the European Parliament and preserving unanimity in Council voting on 'measures significantly affecting a Member State's choice between different energy sources and the general structure of its energy supply'); and see Art 194(2), second sentence, which provides that energy measures adopted under Art 194 TFEU: '. . . shall not affect a Member State's right to determine the conditions for exploiting its energy resources, its choice between different energy sources and the general structure of its energy supply, without prejudice to Art 192(2)(c)'.

[92] See now Art 3(3) TEU and, concerning competence, Arts 3(1)(b) and 4(2)(a) TFEU.

[93] Albeit with some caution, R Barents, 'Constitutional Horse-trading: Some Comments on the Protocol on the Internal Market and Competition' in Bulterman et al (eds), *Views of European Law from the Mountain* (above n 79) ch 9. Logically, this should be correct, given that protocols have the same legal status as the text of the Treaties themselves: see the old Art 311 EC and, after the Treaty of Lisbon, Art 51 TEU.

[94] Particularly in those cases concerning Member State obligations under the norm of Arts 10 and 81/82 EC, such as Case 267/86 *Van Eycke v ASPA NV* [1988] ECR 4769, and Cases C-245/91 *Criminal proceedings against OHRA Schadeverzekeringen NV*, C-185/91 *Bundesanstalt für die Güterfernverkehr v Gebruder Reiff GmbH & Co KG* and C-2/91 *Criminal proceedings against Wolf W Meng* [1993] ECR I-5872, 5841 and 5791 respectively.

[95] For a similarly difficult issue of competition between market and other (here, labour and social protection) goals, see the Court of Justice's judgments in Cases C-341/05 *Laval un partneri* [2007] ECR I-11767, C-438/05 *ITWF v Viking Line* [2007] ECR I-10779, C-319/06 *Commission v Luxembourg* [2008] ECR I-4323 and C-346/06 *Rüffert* [2008] ECR I-1989, discussed by C Barnard, '*Viking and Laval*: An Introduction' (2008) 10 *Cambridge Yearbook of European Legal Studies* 463 and AC Davies, 'One Step Forward, Two Steps Back? The *Viking* and *Laval* Cases in the ECJ' (2008) 38 *Industrial Law Journal* 126.

and policy-making in most fields, including energy. New developments[96] concerning the input of national parliaments, a wider range of Council legislative meetings being held in public and the expansion of the range of areas subject to ordinary legislative procedure will all make subtle but distinct changes to the functioning of the EU's institutions and, concomitantly, to their law and policy output.

Perhaps the key question for future EU energy law and policy will be how best to combine the Commission's push (through DG Competition) to secure well-functioning energy markets across Europe with the pursuit of other priorities, such as environmental goals and security of supply considerations (in all of its many, many facets: fuel poverty and price questions; geopolitics; system stability and reliability). Increasingly, it seems that more direct approaches are being taken, opting for public procurement of desired energy generation and transmission capacity and types (which seek to accommodate competition concerns via competitive tendering processes),[97] allied with other techniques which try to increase available information for energy customers in the hope that they will take, for example, environmentally sustainable purchasing decisions for themselves (eg labelling initiatives to encourage green purchasing decisions and greater efficiency in energy usage).[98] Wherever these new policies may lead, the energy sector seems certain to present fascinating future challenges for EU and national law and policy, and for the interaction between these two levels, all of which will continue to test and refine the notion of the EU as a 'constitutional order of states'.

---

[96] Discussed (with reference to the proposals for a Treaty Establishing a Constitution for Europe, but covering the identical substance contained in the Treaty of Lisbon) in A Dashwood and A Johnston, 'The Institutions of the Enlarged EU under the Regime of the Constitutional Treaty' (2004) 41 *Common Market Law Review* 1481.

[97] See Recital 43 and Art 8 of Dir 2009/72/EC (above n 31), requiring Member States to provide for a tendering process for new generation capacity in the interests of security of supply. From a wide and growing literature on EU public procurement law, see S Arrowsmith and P Kunzlik (eds), *Social and Environmental Policies in EC Procurement Law: New Directives and New Directions* (Cambridge, Cambridge University Press, 2009), esp ch 9 (Kunzlik); C Bovis, *EC Public Procurement: Case Law and Regulation* (Oxford, Oxford University Press, 2006); C de Koninck, *European Public Procurement: The European Public Procurement Directives and 25 Years of Jurisprudence by the Court of Justice of the European Communities* (Kluwer, Law International, Alphen aan den Rijn, 2008); and P-A Trepte, *Public Procurement in the EU: A Practitioner's Guide* (Oxford, Oxford University Press, Oxford 2007).

[98] At EU level, see Art 3(9) of Dir 2009/72/EC, above n 31.

22

The Role of National Judges in Implementing Uniform Rules of Jurisdiction and Choice of Law in the European Union

RICHARD PLENDER*

I INTRODUCTION

THE FOCUS ON the internal market as the basis for EU legislation in the field of private international law (in particular, the Brussels I[1] and Rome I and II[2] Regulations) has produced some unexpected consequences and challenges for national judges. The determination of the jurisdiction of the national court is by no means unusual in the work of national judiciaries; and the recognition and enforcement of foreign judgments is a frequent occurrence at the national level. So it is that national courts, particularly those with commercial competence, have cause to interpret and apply the Brussels I Regulation more frequently than the European Court of Justice. It might have been thought that, given the principle of national procedural autonomy, national procedural law would remain unaffected by developments in EU law. However, the need for uniformity in the internal market has now been said to extend to private international law. As a consequence, EU law has had a significant impact on the procedural role of national judges.

The true basis on which the Brussels and Rome Regulations can be considered 'necessary for the proper functioning of the internal market'

---

* I am grateful to Louise Merrett for her advice and assistance with this chapter.

[1] Reg 44/2001 on jurisdiction and the recognition and enforcement of judgments in civil and commercial matters, [2001] OJ L12/23. This instrument is commonly called the Brussels Regulation to distinguish it from Reg 1347/2000 of 29 May 2000 on jurisdiction and the recognition and enforcement of judgments in matrimonial matters and in matters of parental responsibility for children of both spouses, [2000] OJ L160/19, 'the Brussels II bis Regulation'.

[2] Reg 593/2008 [2008] OJ L177/6.

continues to be questioned, notwithstanding the European Court's Opinion 1/03[3] ('the Lugano Opinion'), in which Professor Dashwood appeared as counsel for the UK. The matter cannot even now be considered as settled: the Commission's Green Paper on the effective enforcement of judgments in the European Union[4] raised questions about a review of Article 4 of the Brussels I Regulation; and the effects of the Court of Justice's Opinion in *Lugano*, together with the effects of the Lisbon Treaty on the EU's external competence, has excited interest, not least in the Legal Affairs Committee of the European Parliament. So Professor Dashwood's submissions in the Lugano Convention case (in particular, that Brussels I does not entail a complete harmonisation of the rules of Member States on conflicts of jurisdiction) may yet come to be revisited.

But the importance and practical consequences of the internal market justification can be seen very clearly in two areas, which I will examine in turn. First, I will argue that the internal market justification restricts the ability of national judges to make use of traditional tools of commercial litigation in England, namely the *forum non conveniens* stay and the anti-suit injunction. According to *Owusu v Jackson*[5] and *Turner v Grovit*,[6] such national tools can no longer be used in EU cases as not all Member States judges have such devices available to them and thus the uniform application of the jurisdictional rules in Brussels I is impaired.

The second area I will consider raises a different issue. An unexpected consequence of EU legislation in certain areas, here the Fourth Motor Insurance Directive, which extends the right to bring an action directly against an insurer throughout the EU, has been to require national judges to solve novel questions of characterisation in the context of jurisdiction and choice of law.

II NATIONAL COURTS' JUDGES USE OF STAYS AND ANTI-SUIT INJUNCTIONS

The role of *forum non conveniens* in the exercise of the court's adjudicatory discretion is a key feature of the traditional English rules of jurisdiction. Prior to *Turner v Grovit* it was common for English courts, particularly in the commercial division of the High Court, to issue anti-suit injunctions prohibiting a litigant from commencing or continuing legal proceedings before a court of another state. The Court of Justice declared in *Turner v Grovit* that the issuance of such an injunction to restrain proceedings in the court of another Member State is incompatible with the Brussels I

---

[3] Opinion 1/03 pursuant to Art 300(6) of the EC Treaty, [2006] ECR I-1417
[4] COM(2008) 128.
[5] [2005] *Owusu v Jackson* QB 801.
[6] Case C-159/02 *Turner v Grovit* [2004] ECR 3565.

Regulation, even when the court granting the injunction is satisfied that the party invoking the jurisdiction of another court has acted in bad faith.

Conversely, in a case where England is not the most appropriate forum to hear a case, English courts have traditionally made extensive use of stays on the grounds of *forum non conveniens*. The European Court of Justice has restricted the use of this remedy in the case of *Owusu v Jackson*.

The importance in English law of the principle of *forum non conveniens* is to be explained by reference to the special position of the English commercial court in international litigation. Parties to commercial contracts having no connection with England commonly agree to submit disputes to the English courts, upon the principle that English courts are neutral, predictable and swift. The English courts, for their part, proceed on the premise that, where parties to a contract have agreed to submit to their jurisdiction, it cannot have been their intention that parallel proceedings should be brought elsewhere, unless there is some exceptional reason for doing so. In short, an English court will restrain a party from doing what it has undertaken not to do. In cases involving contests of jurisdiction between English and non-EU courts, anti-suit injunctions remain a powerful tool, and for such cases the speech of Lord Hobhouse in *Turner v Grovit*[7] remains the highest authority in outlining the grounds on which such injunctions will be granted. Conversely, in cases where England has not been chosen and is not the most appropriate forum to hear the case, courts will choose not to exercise jurisdiction but instead will grant a stay of proceedings in favour of the appropriate forum.

Standard Bank Plc & Anor v Agrinvest International Inc & Ors[8] affords a recent example of a decision in the Commercial Court, on an application for an anti-suit injunction and a non-liability declaration. It is a good example of the sort of case where traditionally the anti-suit injunction has been utilised. The bank had granted to Agrinvest an option to purchase promissory notes on payment of an option fee. Simultaneously, the bank entered into a master sale agreement with Agrinvest, which expressly provided for English law and jurisdiction. Under the master sale agreement, Agrinvest sold shares of a particular Egyptian company to the bank, agreeing to later repurchase them. But later, when share prices of the Egyptian company crashed, it opted out of the option contract and failed to repurchase the shares. The bank then initiated monetary claims against the company in England. Meanwhile the bank served a notice to Agrinvest for sale of its land in Mississippi. However, Agrinvest initiated proceedings in Mississippi against the bank, alleging that it was not liable to the bank for any monetary claim and that the bank was liable for

---

[7] *Turner v Grovit* [2001] 1 WLR 107.
[8] *Standard Bank Plc & Anor v Agrinvest International Inc & Orrs* [2007] EWHC 2595 (Comm).

breach of contract in relation to the sale of the shares. Further, Agrinvest initiated claim against the bank in Egypt alleging that the company was unable to exercise the option to purchase the promissory notes because the bank had wrongfully caused the price of the Egyptian company's shares to fall. Consequently the bank applied for a permanent injunction restraining the Mississippi and Egyptian proceedings on the ground that the agreement had an exclusive jurisdiction clause. The bank also sought a non-liability declaration.

These were the (somewhat convoluted) circumstances in which the court was required to determine whether the bank was entitled to the anti-suit injunction and the declaration sought. The interpretation of the master sale agreement clearly suggested that the parties were bound by the express jurisdictional clause in the agreement. Agrinvest had not shown any good reason why it should not be held to its master sale agreement. Therefore the court, exercising its discretion, granted an injunction restraining the company from prosecuting its claims against the bank relating to the agreement either in Mississippi or in Egypt. Both those proceedings were unconscionable, vexatious and oppressive, and were calculated to frustrate the English proceedings. Further, in circumstances where the company had not exercised its option to purchase the promissory notes, the bank could not be liable for refusing to implement the agreement. Therefore, a declaration of non-liability was made in favour of the bank. Moreover, the company's allegation that the bank had breached the contract in respect of sale of shares was time-barred.

Since *Turner v Grovit*, such an order can no longer be made if proceedings are taking place in the courts of another Member State. However, even in cases clearly falling within the scope of the Brussels I Regulation, there may be cases where the courts can effectively by-pass the decision in *Turner v Grovit* by making a declaration of non-liability, which would tend to preclude a successful suit in the courts of another Member State. In other words, although an anti-suit injunction is no longer available, use can be made of the *lis alibi pendens* provisions in Brussels I in order to make sure litigation can take place only in England. A good example of the use of a declaration of non-liability is *Polskie Ratownictwo Okretowe v Rallo Vito & C SNC and Another.*[9] Hamblen J was presented with a claim arising from the refloating of a fishing vessel off Lampedusa (Italy). Various tug companies, including the claimant, an Italian domiciliary, had been contacted with a view to refloating the vessel, but a contract was entered into between the claimant and the defendants. The defendants complained that the claimant had damaged the vessel and also caused loss to cargo. The claimant issued a claim form, seeking a declaration

---

[9] *Polskie Ratownictwo Okretowe v Rallo Vito & C. SNC and Another* [2009] EWHC 2249 (Comm).

that it was not liable for breach of contract or duty to the defendants. The defendant argued that under the Brussels I Regulation it could be sued only in Italy. The claimant subsequently served the claim form on the defendant out of jurisdiction.

The judge held that English courts had jurisdiction in accordance with Article 23 of the Regulation (which regulates jurisdiction agreements in favour of Member States) because there was evidence on record to show that the claimant and the defendants had, by way of an oral and implied contract, agreed to be subjected to the jurisdiction of the English courts. He held that the towage contract had been finally agreed and concluded orally over the telephone. Further, a failure to raise an objection within a reasonable time was detrimental to the defendants' cause since they had failed to vigilantly react to a situation of urgency whereby express instructions to mobilise the tug had to be given almost immediately. Because England was then the court first seized under the jurisdiction agreement, this prevented further proceedings in Italy.

Although the principles explained by Lord Hobhouse in *Turner v Grovit* remain intact in cases involving a contest between English courts and the courts of a non-contracting state, it is possible that even in such cases there is now less enthusiasm than previously for defending an English jurisdiction clause by an anti-suit injunction. In *Deutsche Bank v Highland Crusader Offshore Partners*[10] a Court of Appeal comprising Carnwath, Toulson and Goldring LJJ held that an agreement to submit disputes to English courts in an international finance agreement in standard form was not inconsistent with the prosecution of parallel proceedings elsewhere. An appeal against an anti-suit injunction restraining the institution of proceedings in Texas was therefore allowed. It seems that in a case falling outside the Brussels I Regulation the English courts will not apply to a choice of forum clause the presumption established by Article 23 of the Brussels I Regulation, whereby a court chosen by the parties as having jurisdiction to resolve disputes arising under a contract is to have exclusive jurisdiction unless the parties have agreed otherwise. Here the court ruled that a non-exclusive jurisdiction agreement could not provide the basis for an anti-suit injunction if it was not inconsistent with the agreement to sue elsewhere.

The availability of *forum non conveniens* stays in cases where the jurisdiction of the national court is based on EU rules of jurisdiction was considered in *Lubbe & Others v Cape plc*.[11] The House of Lords determined whether England was the *forum conveniens* for determination of the asbestos-related claims of South African miners who were alleged to have suffered damage in South Africa in the course of their employment

---

[10] *Deutsche Bank v Highland Crusader Offshore Partners* [2009] EWCA 725.
[11] *Lubbe & Others v Cappe Plc* [2000] UKHL 41.

by a company registered in England. It was contended that the claimants were entitled to bring their action in England, by reason of Article 2 of the Brussels I Convention and that such jurisdiction could not be precluded by conditions of *forum conveniens*. Declining to deal with that issue at all, Lord Bingham said:

> I am unwilling to stay the plaintiffs' proceedings in this country. It is accordingly unnecessary to decide whether the effect of Article 2 is to deprive the English court of jurisdiction to grant a stay in a case such as this. Had it been necessary to resolve that question, I would have thought it necessary to seek a ruling on the applicability on Article 2 from the European Court of Justice, since I do not consider the answer to that question to be clear.

Thus, the House of Lords in *Lubbe v Cape* thought that the issue was not clear. When the issue did eventually arrive in the European Court of Justice, that Court ruled that jurisdiction based on Article 2 of Brussels I could not be declined on grounds of *forum non conveniens* and therefore a stay was not permitted in such circumstances.

The issue of *Owusu v Jackson* has been raised again in the recent decision of the Court of Appeal in *Choudhary v Bhatter*.[12] In that case Mr Bhatter challenged the jurisdiction of the English court to determine a claim made against him restraining him from acting in relation to the business of a jute company registered in England but trading in Calcutta. David Donaldson QC, sitting as a High Court judge, held that, in the light of *Owusu v Jackson*, he was bound to accept jurisdiction in relation to the company and that the order sought was an order in relation to the company. On an appeal by Mr Bhatter, the Court of Appeal (Ward, and Stanley Burnton LJJ and Sir John Chadwick) held that proceedings brought against Mr Bhatter were not proceedings relating to winding up or analogous proceedings. Ward LJ, in a judgment with which the others agreed, stated that the judgment in *Owusu v Jackson* provided no direct authority on the question whether a court of a Member State was precluded from declining the jurisdiction, if any, conferred on it by Article 22 of the Regulation (which gives exclusive jurisdiction in proceedings concerning the dissolution of companies to the courts of the place of the seat of the company) in respect of a person not domiciled in a Member State on the ground that a court of a non-contracting state would be a more appropriate forum for the trial of the action.

In a comment on that judgment, Andrew Dickinson noted that

> in what might be termed a 'surprising decision' the English Court of Appeal has apparently ruled that Art 22 of the Brussels I Regulation (exclusive jurisdiction) does not apply to proceedings against persons not domiciled in a Member State, and left open the possibility that (even if Art 22 did apply to such cases) the English court would (notwithstanding the ECJ's decision in *Owusu v Jackson*)

---

[12] *Choudhary v Bhatter* [2009] EWCA Civ 1176.

be entitled to decline jurisdiction on *forum conveniens* grounds. On this view, in proceedings concerning a company with its seat in England, the English court would not be mandated to accept jurisdiction by Art 22(2) in a case to which that Article applies (the Court also held that the dispute in question did not fall within Art 22(2), thereby providing an alternative ground for its decision to decline jurisdiction where the dispute had a close connection to India). This despite the fact that Article 4(1) is expressed to be 'subject to Articles 22 and 23' and Art 22 is expressed to apply 'regardless of domicile'.[13]

I beg to differ with Andrew Dickinson's analysis of the judgment of the Court of Appeal. Ward LJ did not decide that Article 22 of the Brussels I Regulation is inapplicable to proceedings against persons not domiciled in a Member State, nor did he leave open the possibility that, if Article 22 did apply, the English court would be entitled to decline jurisdiction on *forum conveniens* grounds (that would be plainly inconsistent with *Owusu v Jackson*). Had Ward LJ reached that conclusion, it would indeed have been surprising (in Mr Dickinson's word). The judgment of Ward LJ is to be explained on the ground that the proceedings against Mr Bhatter were not 'proceedings relating to winding up or analogous proceedings' and thus did not engage Article 22 at all. They were not, in effect, proceedings against the company but were truly proceedings against Mr Bhatter *in personam*. The matter may be tested in this way: if the action against Mr Bhatter had been for damages, would Article 22 of the Brussels I Regulation have mandated the English court to assume jurisdiction? The answer, I suggest, is plainly in the negative.

III NATIONAL COURTS' JUDGES INTERPRETATION OF UNION RIGHTS

So far we have examined how national tools such as anti-suit injunctions can no longer be used in EU cases as not all Member State judges have such devices available to them and so the uniform application of the jurisdictional rules in Brussels I would be impaired. A different example of the problem raised by uniformity concerns the creation of new causes of action, for example, under the Motor Insurance Directive. The need for national judges to implement and apply such causes of action has led to difficult issues of characterisation not faced by common law lawyers before. The issue arises when an insurer is sued in England on the basis of a statutory provision commonly found in continental countries whereby a claimant may bring an action directly against the insurer of an alleged tortfeasor. Article 11(2) of the Brussels I Regulation provides that Articles

---

[13] A Dickinson 'Non-domiciled Parties and the Brussels I Regulation: A Phantom Menace'; conflictoflaws.net.

8, 9 and 10 thereof shall apply to actions brought by the injured party directly against the insurer, where such direct actions are permitted. Such direct actions are now permitted in all Member States pursuant to Council Directive 2000/26.[14] Where such a direct action is brought in an English court, it may have to determine whether the claim sounds in contract or in tort, for on that point depends the measure of damages available.

The Commission's opinion on a draft regulation of 2003[15] affords some support for the argument that the insurer's obligation is of a contractual character, for it states that the right of persons who have suffered damage to take direct action against the insurer of the person claimed to be liable shall be governed by 'the law applicable to the non-contractual liability', unless the person who has suffered damage prefers to base his/her claims on the law applicable to the insurance contract. The accompanying explanatory memorandum appears to reinforce the impression that the insurer's obligation is contractual, in providing that 'the scope of the insurer's obligations is determined by the law relating to the insurance contract'. In the UK, the legislation designed to implement the Fourth Motor Insurance Directive are the European Communities (Rights against Insurers) Regulations. These also appear to proceed on the premise that the obligation of the insurer is contractual. Regulation 3(2) provides that the insurer shall be liable to the claimant 'to the extent that he is liable to the insured person'.

Further support for the proposition that the insurer's obligations are of a contractual nature may perhaps be derived from the judgment of Clarke LJ (as he then was) in *Through Transport Mutual Assurance Association (Eurasia) Ltd v New India Assurance Co Ltd*.[16] This case, which had to be determined on the basis of the Brussels I Regulation, arose from a dispute between an Indian insurance company (New India) and a P & I Club (Through Transport). New India had insured a cargo of textiles which were lost in the course of carriage from Calcutta to Moscow via Finland. One of the members of Through Transport had issued the bills of lading and the CMR waybill for the goods but had gone into liquidation. New India therefore instituted proceedings against Through Transport in Finland, relying on section 67 of the Finnish Insurance Contracts Act 1994. This authorised the making of claims directly against the insurer of the person liable. Through Transport then applied for an anti-suit injunction in London, relying on a term of its agreement with its members provid-

---

[14] Dir 2000/26 on the approximation of the laws of the Member States relating to insurance against civil liability in respect of the use of motor vehicles [2000] OJ L181/65.

[15] No significant change was made in the wording of the (then) Art 14 in the Commission's Communication to the Parliament on the draft Rome II Regulation, Eur-Lex 52006PC0566, 27 September 2006. Nor did a significant change appear in its Opinion on the Council's Common Position, Eur-Lex 52007PC0126, 14 March 2007.

[16] [2005] 1 Lloyd's Rep 67.

ing for arbitration of disputes in London. Moore-Bick J (as he then was) granted the injunction. The Court of Appeal set the injunction aside. Giving reasons, Clarke LJ made the following comments on the nature of the obligation imposed on the insurer by the Finnish enactment:

> The judge held that the claim is in substance to enforce against the Club as insurer the contract made by the Insured . . . The claim under the Act is not therefore in any sense independent of the contract of insurance but under or in accordance with it . . . In all the circumstances we agree with the judge that, although the Act gives the claimant a right of action directly against the insurer without the need for the formalities of an assignment, what he obtains is essentially a right to enforce the contract in accordance with its terms.

This decision is also relevant to the first point I have addressed, that is, the availability of anti-suit injunctions in European cases. The effect of *Through Transport* on this point has now been reversed by the European Court in *Allianz SpA v West Tankers Inc*[17] upon a reference from the House of Lords.[18] The European Court extended the 'mutual trust' set out in *Turner v Grovit* to proceedings brought in aid of arbitration, notwithstanding the exclusion of arbitration from the material scope of the Brussels I Regulation. The Court's reasoning was that the *effet utile* of the Brussels I Regulation precluded an anti-suit injunction against proceedings in another EU Member State even where it was alleged that the matter should be subject to arbitration.

As to the issue of characterisation, Article 18 of Rome II deals with direct actions against the insurer of the person liable and provides that

> The person having suffered damage may bring his or her claim directly against the insurer of the person liable to provide compensation if the law applicable to the non-contractual obligation or the law applicable to the insurance contract so provides.

Thus, Article 18 also seems to envisage a role for the law of the contract. Conversely, it may be argued that to characterise the obligation owed by an insurer to a claimant pursuant to Article 18 of the Rome II Regulation as an obligation arising under its contract with the insured would be to lose sight of the fact that the Rome II Regulation is concerned with non-contractual obligations. Moreover, it might be said that to characterise the obligation as one of a contractual character would be to court serious difficulties in any case in which the policy of insurance contains a choice of law or even a choice of forum clause. The person having suffered damage could not successfully invoke the law applicable to the non-contractual obligation in the courts of the Member State whose law is applicable to the non-contractual obligation if she/he were to be confronted with the

[17] Case C-185/07 *Allianz SpA v West Tankers Inc* [2009] ECR I-663.
[18] *West Tankers*: [2007] UKHL 4, [2007] 1 Lloyd's Rep 391.

defence that the insurer's obligation is derived from a contract which specifies some other applicable law.[19]

The point arose more recently in *Maher v Groupama Grand Est.*[20] In that case, Mrs Maher brought an action on her own behalf and as testatrix of the estate of her late husband in the Mayor's and City of London Court against the insurer of a driver of a motor vehicle which collided in France with the Mahers' Land Rover, causing injury to Mrs Maher and the death of her husband. The insurer accepted jurisdiction and liability but contended that the extent of damages and any question of interest were to be assessed by reference to French law, since the liability assumed by the insurer was tortious (and the proper law of the tort was French law, where the accident took place). Moore-Bick LJ, following the judgment of Sharp J in *Knight v AXA*,[21] held that, although the insurer's liability was indeed tortuous, damages were to be assessed by reference to English law as the *lex fori*, since matters of remedy were regarded as procedural in nature and governed by the *lex fori*. It should be noted that this aspect of the decision would now be regulated by Article 15(c) of the Rome II Regulation,[22] which provides that the law applicable to the tort governs 'the existence, the nature and the assessment of damage or the remedy claimed'.

In relation to the claim for interest, while the existence of a right to recover interest as a head of damage was properly to be classified as a substantive matter to be determined by reference to the *lex causae*, the question for determination was whether section 35A created a substantive right or a remedy. As regards the question of interest, Hobhouse J had been right in *Midland International Trade Services v Al Sudairy*[23] when he said that section 35A of the Supreme Court Act created a remedy rather than a substantive right to interest. Although the existence of a right to recover interest as a head of damage was a matter of French law, being the law applicable to the tort, the court had available to it the remedy created by section 35A of the 1981 Act. So, in the exercise of its discretion, the court might well include any relevant provisions of French law relating to the recovery of interest, but the decision whether to grant an award of interest or not was one for the *lex fori*. Mummery LJ and Etherton J agreed with Moore-Bick LJ.

I venture the opinion that the judgment of Moore-Bick LJ was not only correct but consistent with elementary principles of private international law. What it demonstrates is that, even if the Brussels I Regulation is

---

[19] A Dickinson, *The Rome II Regulation: The Law Applicable to Non Contractual Obligations* (Oxford, Oxford University Press, 2008) para 14.99.

[20] *Maher v Groupama Grand Est.* [2009] EWCA Civ 1191.

[21] *Knight v AXA* [2009] EWHC 1900.

[22] Reg 864/2007, [2008] OJ L169/40.

[23] Judgment of 11 April 1990.

conducive to the proper functioning of the internal market, it does not eliminate the risk of forum-shopping.

IV   CONCLUSIONS

The extent to which the proper functioning of the internal market requires uniformity in national procedural rules and rules of private international law remains controversial. The decisions of the Court of Justice in *Turner v Grovit* and *Owusu v Jackson* have made considerable inroads into the traditional role of national judges in managing commercial litigation, justified, in part at least, on just such internal market considerations. I stated in opening that national courts frequently have cause to interpret and apply the Brussels I Regulation. Those who seek guidance on the meaning and effect of the Brussels I Regulation and the practical consequences of the internal market justifications will find a rich source of authority in recent decisions of the English courts. Useful guidance can also be found as to how national judges will be called on to characterise new EU wide rights. In this contribution I have had to be extremely selective and have referred to only a sample of the decisions of English courts on the subject. I do not doubt that if Alan Dashwood finds the time to distil and analyse them, in future years, he will enlarge substantially on the contribution to the subject that he made in the book that he wrote with Richard Hacon and Robin White, *A Guide to the Civil Jurisdiction and Judgments Convention*.[24]

---

[24] A Dashwood, R Halcon and R White, *A Guide to the Civil Jurisdiction and Judgments Convention* (Deventer/Antwerpen, Kluwer, 1987).

Part IV

Europe in the Wider World

23

Member States as Trustees of the Union Interest: Participating in International Agreements on Behalf of the European Union

MARISE CREMONA

I INTRODUCTION[1]

THIS CHAPTER DISCUSSES the legal effects of a seemingly paradoxical situation: an international agreement falls within the exclusive competence of the European Union, yet the Member States are parties to the agreement and the Union is not. This situation emphasises the importance of the role the Member States continue to play within the framework of EU foreign policy, even in fields where the EU has apparently displaced the Member States completely. It serves as a reminder that the EU, as an international actor, operates as a complex organisation—a constitutional order—which continues to include the Member States. The members of this constitutional order of states operate both in their own right as international actors and as EU Member States, with the obligations which flow from that status. While not common, the participation of the Member States in international agreements falling within exclusive Union competence is not as unusual as we might imagine and it gives rise to a number of interesting legal questions as to the status of the agreement, if any, in Union law and the Member States'

---

[1] In this chapter the following citation practice will be followed: the abbreviation 'TEU' used after a Treaty article refers to the Treaty on European Union in the version in force after 1 December 2009; 'TFEU' refers to the Treaty on the Functioning of the European Union; 'EC' after a Treaty article refers to a provision of the European Community Treaty in the version in force until 30 November 2009; similarly, 'EU' refers to an article of the Treaty on European Union in the version in force until that date. Where events prior to 1 December 2009 are mentioned, reference is made where appropriate to the European Community (EC) rather than European Union (EU).

obligations under Union law arising as a consequence. It may occur for several reasons.

1. It is decided that it is in the Union interest, for political or other reasons, that the Member States rather than the Union should participate in an agreement.

The classic example of this is the European Road Transport Agreement (ERTA or AETR). It will be recalled that the Court of Justice, having found that the conclusion of the AETR fell within exclusive Community competence, accepted the political judgment of the Council that it would have been disruptive of the ongoing negotiations to substitute the Community for its Member States at such a late stage.[2] In such a case the Court took the view that the Member States party to the agreement are acting on behalf of the Community, and in its interests:

> In carrying on the negotiations and concluding the agreement simultaneously in the manner decided on by the Council, the Member States acted, and continue to act, in the interest and on behalf of the Community in accordance with their obligations under article 5 of the Treaty.[3]

The Regulation that gave effect to the AETR within the Community (and now Union) recognises this explicitly in its preamble:

> Whereas, since the subject matter of the AETR Agreement falls within the scope of Regulation (EEC) No 543/69, from the date of entry into force of that Regulation the power to negotiate and conclude the Agreement has lain with the Community; whereas, however, the particular circumstances in which the AETR negotiations took place warrant, by way of exception, a procedure whereby the Member States of the Community individually deposit the instruments of ratification or accession in a concerted action but nonetheless act in the interest and on behalf of the Community.[4]

The Regulation then provides that 'In ratifying or acceding to the AETR the Member States, having regard to the Council recommendation of 23 September 1974, shall act on behalf of the Community'.[5] Regulation 561/2006, which currently gives effect to the AETR within the Union, also refers to the AETR in its preamble and to the need for the Member States to act together in the Community interest, especially where developments to Community law may require an amendment to AETR.[6]

In the case of the AETR, the regulation from which the Community's (exclusive) competence was derived came into force during the course of

[2] Case 22/70 *Commission v Council* (AETR) [1971] ECR 263, paras 82–90.
[3] Case 22/70 *Commission v Council* (AETR) [1971] ECR 263, para 90. Art 5 became Art 10 EC and is now Art 4(3) TEU.
[4] Reg (EEC) 2829/77 [1977] OJ L334/11.
[5] Ibid, Art 2(1).
[6] Reg (EC) 561/2006 [2006] OJ L102/1, preamble paras 10 and 11.

the negotiations and the Community thus came late to the table. In this case the choice, accepted by the Court, was to continue with Member State-only participation. An alternative (and more common) solution to this situation would be to conclude the agreement, and the legal questions that arise then derive from the phenomenon of mixity; here the focus will instead be on agreements to which the Union is not a party.

2. It may be the case that only states, and not regional economic integration organisations (REIOs) such as the EC or EU, are entitled to participate in the agreement.

This is the case for agreements concluded under the aegis of many UN agencies, such as the ILO and the IMO.[7] In Opinion 2/91 the Court was asked to determine Community competence in relation to ILO Convention No 170, which the Community as such would not be able to conclude. Procedures had been devised by agreement between Council and Commission to accommodate the negotiation of ILO Conventions falling within Community competence. The Court said, in the context of ruling on the scope of its own jurisdiction, that 'In any event, although, under the ILO Constitution, the Community cannot itself conclude Convention No 170, its external competence may, if necessary, be exercised through the medium of the Member States acting jointly in the Community's interest'.[8]

Later in the judgment the Court, having held that aspects of ILO Convention No 170 fell within exclusive Community competence and aspects within shared competence, goes on to stress the importance of the duty of co-operation in this context. This duty, based on Article 4(3) TEU (ex-Article 10 EC, also referred to in the *AETR* judgment) could then be regarded as the basis for the Member States' duty to the Community— and now Union—in relation to the agreement.

3. It may be that when the agreement was originally concluded the Member States were competent; since then, however, EC exclusivity has 'supervened'.

A classic example would be the GATT. Thus, our third initial example is the *International Fruit Company* case.[9] This differs from the others in that it is not a question of the Member States concluding the agreement on

---

[7] As far as the ILO is concerned, see Opinion 2/91 (ILO Convention No 170) [1993] ECR I-1061; as far as the IMO is concerned, see Case C-45/07 *Commission v Greece* [2009] ECR I-00701; both cases are discussed further below.

[8] Opinion 2/91 [1993] ECR I-1061, para 5.

[9] In Cases 22–24/72 *International Fruit Company* [1972] ECR 1219, the Court held that, although the Community was not then a formal party to the GATT, it was nevertheless bound by it as a result of the transfer by the Member State GATT parties to the Community of competence in the fields covered by the GATT. The focus of this case was on the binding nature of the GATT as far as Community secondary legislation is concerned, rather than the obligations on the Member States.

behalf of the Community; rather, the Court holds that, since the Member States have conferred exclusive competence in the matters covered by the GATT to the Community, the Community should be held bound by the GATT, in what is termed functional succession to the Member States.

> It therefore appears that, insofar as under the EEC Treaty the Community has assumed the powers previously exercised by Member States in the area governed by the General Agreement, the provisions of that agreement have the effect of binding the Community.[10]

The Court does not say here anything directly about the obligations that might flow for Member States within Community law from this development; but the implication, borne out by later cases, is that compliance with the GATT by the Member States has become a matter for Community—and now Union—law.[11]

As we have seen, the obligation on the Member States in these cases flows ultimately from Article 4(3) TEU, which requires Member States to 'take any appropriate measure, general or particular, to ensure fulfilment of the obligations arising out of the Treaties' and to 'facilitate the achievement of the Union's tasks'. In matters of exclusive competence, the Member States may act only by way of Union authorisation.[12] In a case involving internal measures in the field of fisheries conservation (a matter of exclusive competence) the Court referred to the Member States as acting as 'trustees of the common interest' and the consequent need to act collaboratively within the institutional framework. The Member States, acting in a field of exclusive Union competence and as trustees of the common, or Union, interest, are subject to the supervision of the Commission:

> As this is a field reserved to the powers of the Community, within which Member States may henceforth act only as trustees of the common interest, a Member State cannot therefore, in the absence of appropriate action on the part of the Council, bring into force any interim conservation measures which may be required by the situation except as part of a process of collaboration with the Commission and with due regard to the general task of supervision which Article 155 [see now Article 17 TEU] . . . gives to the Commission.[13]

The legal questions I will explore below arise out of the fact that the

[10] *International Fruit Company*, ibid, para 18.
[11] See Cases 267–269/81 *Amministrazione delle Finanze v SPI SpA* [1983] ECR 801, para 15.
[12] See, eg Case 41/76 *Suzanne Criel, née Donckerwolcke and Henri Schou v Procureur de la République* [1976] ECR 1921, para 32; Case 174/84 *Bulk Oil* [1986] ECR 559; Case C-70/94 *Werner* [1995] ECR I-3189; Case C-83/94 *Leifer and Others* [1995] ECR I-3231. Art 2(1) TFEU provides that 'Where the Treaties confer on the Union exclusive competence in a specific area, only the Union may legislate and adopt legally binding acts, the Member States being able to do so themselves only if so empowered by the Union or for the implementation of acts of the Union'.
[13] Case 804/79 *Commission v United Kingdom* [1981] ECR 1045, para 30.

international agreements in the above examples are not formally a 'Union agreement' within the scope of Articles 216 and 218 TFEU, and thus the matters regulated by those provisions, including the binding nature of the agreement as far as the Union is concerned and its place in the Union legal order, are not expressly resolved. To what extent can the provisions of Articles 216 and 218 TFEU apply by analogy? Do the three factual/legal scenarios given above lead to different answers to any of these questions? In what follows, we will look at the negotiation and then conclusion of the agreement, the status of the agreement in Union law and the jurisdiction of the Court of Justice, and the obligations that Union law imposes on the Member States in these circumstances.

II NEGOTIATING AND CONCLUDING AGREEMENTS 'ON BEHALF OF' THE EU

A The Formation of a Common Negotiating Position by the Member States

Where an agreement is to be negotiated by the Member States instead of the Union (although it falls within exclusive Union competence), the Member States are obliged to establish a joint negotiating position within the framework of the common institutions and this will be binding on them. Thus, in *AETR* the Court held:

> [The Council decided that] throughout the negotiations and at the conclusion of the agreement, the States would act in common and would constantly co-ordinate their positions according to the usual procedure in close association with the Community institutions, the delegation of the Member State currently occupying the presidency of the Council acting as spokesman . . .
>
> [T]he Council's proceedings dealt with a matter falling within the power of the Community, and . . . the Member States could not therefore act outside the framework of the common institutions. It thus seems that insofar as they concerned the objective of the negotiations as defined by the Council, the proceedings of 20 March 1970 could not have been simply the expression or the recognition of a voluntary co-ordination, but were designed to lay down a course of action binding on both the institutions and the Member States, and destined ultimately to be reflected in the tenor of the Regulation.[14]

The role of negotiator given by Article 218 TFEU to the Commission is here taken by the Member States co-ordinated through the Council and Presidency. In *AETR* the Commission had complained that the decision to act through the Member States in this way thereby deprived it of its role; in accepting that the Member States should negotiate and conclude

---

[14] Case 22/70 AETR, n 2 above, paras 49, 52 and 53.

the agreement on behalf of the Community, the Court accepted this result. However, it does refer to the need for the Council and Commission 'to reach agreement . . . on the appropriate methods of cooperation with a view to ensuring most effectively the defence of the interests of the Community'.[15]

It may be desirable and possible in other cases for the Commission to negotiate the agreement. In the case of the ILO, a working agreement was reached and contained in a Council decision of 22 December 1986 which applies to cases where an ILO Convention covers matters within exclusive Community competence and which provides that the Council will authorise the Commission to negotiate and to speak on behalf of the Community in the Conference.[16] In Opinion 2/91 the Court stressed the application of the duty of co-operation in this regard:

> In this case, cooperation between the Community and the Member States is all the more necessary in view of the fact that the former cannot, as international law stands at present, itself conclude an ILO convention and must do so through the medium of the Member States. It is therefore for the Community institutions and the Member States to take all the measures necessary so as best to ensure such cooperation both in the procedure of submission to the competent authority and ratification of Convention No 170 and in the implementation of commitments resulting from that Convention.[17]

We may ask to what extent the obligation on the Member States in such cases—based as it is on exclusive Union competence—goes beyond the duty of co-operation operative in the case of mixed agreements. The quotation from Opinion 2/91 just cited implies that it is of the same nature, though perhaps more urgently required ('cooperation . . . is all the more necessary'). If the duty of co-operation in the case of mixed agreements in cases of shared competence is ultimately a best efforts obligation,[18] it could be argued by contrast that in the case we are considering here, where the Member States are acting on behalf of the Union, the obligation is to negotiate through a common position or not to conclude the agreement at all.[19] The common position may be given expression through the adoption 'within the Council' either of a negotiating mandate for the Commission or, in cases where the Commission is not given the power to negotiate, through an agreed negotiating position such as was adopted for the AETR. In the case of the AETR, the Court held that it had the power to review the legality of the 'proceedings' of the Council as a binding measure,

---

[15] Ibid, para 87.

[16] See further Opinion 2/91, n 7 above, part IV.

[17] Opinion 2/91, n 7 above, paras 37–38.

[18] M Cremona, 'Defending the Community Interest: the Duties of Cooperation and Compliance' in M Cremona and B de Witte (eds), *EU Foreign Relations Law—Constitutional Fundamentals* (Oxford, Hart Publishing, 2008) 168.

[19] Cf *Commission v Greece*, n 7 above, considered further below.

although not adopted as a formal decision, under what is now Article 263 TFEU (at the time Article 173 EEC). Were the Member States to act not through the Council but by 'common accord', this may not be reviewable, but the exclusive nature of the Union's competence will colour the Court's characterisation of the act as a Member State or a Council act.[20]

B The Decision to Authorise the Member States to Conclude the Agreement

In fields within exclusive Union competence, the Member States may act only with Union authorisation.[21] This implies that under Union law (not, of course, as a matter of international law) they should not conclude such an agreement without Union authorisation. This may be given ad hoc (as with AETR) or by way of a more general authorisation. Since the Council is the institution that normally concludes Union agreements (Article 218(2) TFEU, ex-Article 300 EC) the authorisation should be given by the Council, although the Commission may act in specific cases under implementing powers. Although in the *AETR* case the Court accepted an informal, though binding, decision in the Council without an explicit legal base, there is an argument for saying that the decision should be adopted on the same legal basis as would form the basis for a decision to conclude the agreement (were it to be concluded by the Union), and this might well imply a role for the European Parliament, depending on the substantive legal base. This would be a way of preserving the institutional balance, although it would not necessarily mirror exactly the procedure for concluding a Union agreement. This would be particularly important where the decision not only authorised but also required the Member states to conclude the agreement.[22]

As we have seen, Member States may be authorised to conclude agree-

---

[20] In Joined Cases C-181/91 and C-248/91 *European Parliament v Council and Commission* [1993] ECR I-3685, paras 12 and 14, the Court held: 'acts adopted by representatives of the Member States acting, not in their capacity as members of the Council, but as representatives of their governments, and thus collectively exercising the powers of the Member States, are not subject to judicial review by the Court... [However] it is not enough that an act should be described as a "decision of the Member States" for it to be excluded from review under Art 173 of the Treaty. In order for such an act to be excluded from review, it must still be determined whether, having regard to its content and all the circumstances in which it was adopted, the act in question is not in reality a decision of the Council.' It should be noted that in this case the Court stressed the right of the Member States to act collectively outside the Council given the shared nature of competence in the field; in *AETR* the Court held that competence being exclusive the Member States 'could not act' outside the common institutions: see text at n 14 above.

[21] See the cases at n 12 above and Art 2(1) TFEU.

[22] See the discussion below on Case C-370/07 *Commission v Council* [2009] ECR I-08917, in the context of a Council decision establishing a common position for the Member States to adopt within the framework of the CITES Convention.

ments on behalf of the Union where the Union itself is not entitled to become a party. Thus, in 2002 the Council adopted a decision authorising the Member States to ratify the 'Bunkers Convention' on civil liability for oil pollution damage. The preamble explains the rationale clearly:

> The Community . . . has sole competence in relation to Articles 9 and 10 of the Bunkers Convention inasmuch as those Articles affect the rules laid down in Regulation (EC) No 44/2001. The Member States retain their competence for matters covered by that Convention which do not affect Community law. Pursuant to the Bunkers Convention, only sovereign States may be party to it; there are no plans, in the short term, to reopen negotiations for the purpose of taking into account Community competence for the matter. It is not therefore possible for the Community to sign, ratify or accede to the Bunkers Convention at present, nor is there any prospect that it will be able do so in the near future . . . The substantive rules of the system established by the Bunkers Convention fall under the national competence of Member States and only the provisions of jurisdiction and the recognition and enforcement of the judgments are matters covered by exclusive Community competence . . . The Council should therefore authorise the Member States to sign, ratify or accede to the Bunkers Convention in the interest of the Community, under the conditions set out in this Decision.[23]

In this example, Member States are to make a declaration at the time of ratification or accession that as between the EU Member States, recognition and enforcement of judgments are covered by Community rules.[24] The decision also requires the Member States to use their best endeavours to ensure the amendment of the Bunkers Convention to allow the Community to become a contracting party.[25] Similar examples have been the 2004 Council Decision authorising the Member States to ratify the 2003 Protocol to the 1992 International Convention on the Establishment of an International Fund for Compensation for Oil Pollution Damage,[26] and the 2002 Council Decision authorising the Member States, in the interest of the Community, to sign the 1996 Hague Convention

[23] Council Decision (EC) 2002/762 of 19 September 2002 authorising the Member States, in the interest of the Community, to sign, ratify or accede to the International Convention on Civil Liability for Bunker Oil Pollution Damage, 2001 (the Bunkers Convention), [2002] OJ L256/7, preamble paras 3–7. Note that Denmark is not covered by the Decision, by virtue of its opt-out from Title IV EC Treaty, nor is it affected by the Community's exclusive competence arising from Reg 44/2001/EC.
[24] This Declaration, although not binding, is similar in effect to a disconnection clause; on such clauses see further M Cremona, 'Disconnection Clauses in EU Law and Practice' in C Hillion and P Koutrakos (eds), *Mixed Agreements Revisited* (Oxford, Hart Publishing, 2010).
[25] Council Decision (EC) 2002/762, n 23 above, Art 5.
[26] Council Decision (EC) 2004/246 of 2 March 2004 authorising the Member States to sign, ratify or accede to, in the interest of the European Community, the Protocol of 2003 to the International Convention on the Establishment of an International Fund for Compensation for Oil Pollution Damage, 1992, and authorising Austria and Luxembourg, in the interest of the European Community, to accede to the underlying instruments, [2004] OJ L78/22.

on Parental Responsibility, which was concluded within the framework of the Hague Conference on Private International Law.[27]

The imposition of conditions on the conclusion of international agreements by Member States is not new. A relatively early example is the regulation which sets out the conditions under which the Member States should ratify and implement the Convention on a Code of Conduct for Liner Conferences, drawn up under the auspices of the United Nations Conference on Trade and Development.[28]

Where authorisation is given to a Member State on an individual basis, a distinction needs to be made between those cases where the Member State acts on its own account, albeit under Union authorisation, and those where it acts on behalf of the Union. In the first case, the authorisation is given on the ground that it is not contrary to the Union interest for the Member State to conclude the agreement, but since the Member State is not acting in the Union interest we will not discuss these cases further here.[29]

In the second case, the Member State acts on behalf of the Union and in its interest. Examples include those cases where individual Member States are authorised by Council decision, adopted under Article 219 TFEU (ex-Article 111(3) EC), to conclude agreements with third countries respecting the use of the Euro. These are cases where the special relationship between one Member State and the third country concerned provides a political rationale for the procedure. Thus Italy has been authorised to

[27] Council Decision (EC) 2003/93 of 19 December 2002 authorising the Member States, in the interest of the Community, to sign the 1996 Hague Convention on jurisdiction, applicable law, recognition, enforcement and cooperation in respect of parental responsibility and measures for the protection of children, [2003] OJ L48/1; see also Council Decision (EC) 2008/431 authorising those Member States who have not already done so to ratify or accede to the Convention [2008] OJ L151/36. The Member States are again required to make a declaration as to the application of Community rules to the recognition and enforcement of judgments between Member States, in particular here Reg (EC) 1347/2000 on jurisdiction and the recognition and enforcement of judgments in matrimonial matters and in matters of parental responsibility for children, [2000] OJ L160/19.

[28] Council Reg (EEC) 954/79 of 15 May 1979 concerning the ratification by Member States of, or their accession to, the United Nations Convention on a Code of Conduct for Liner Conference,s [1979] OJ L121/1. This Regulation was repealed with effect from 18 October 2008 following the application of EC competition rules to maritime transport and the consequent incompatitibility of shipping conferences with Community competition law: Reg (EC) 1490/2007 of 11 December 2007, [2007] OJ L332/1.

[29] For examples see Council Reg (EC) No 664/2009 of 7 July 2009 establishing a procedure for the negotiation and conclusion of agreements between Member States and third countries concerning jurisdiction, recognition and enforcement of judgments and decisions in matrimonial matters, matters of parental responsibility and matters relating to maintenance obligations, and the law applicable to matters relating to maintenance obligation,s [2009] OJ L200/46; Reg (EC) 662/2009 of 13 July 2009 establishing a procedure for the negotiation and conclusion of agreements between Member States and third countries on particular matters concerning the law applicable to contractual and non-contractual obligations [2009] OJ L200/25.

conclude agreements with San Marino[30] and with Vatican City;[31] France with Monaco.[32] Portugal was authorised to continue its monetary agreement with Cape Verde,[33] and France its agreements with the UEMOA (Union économique et monétaire ouest-africaine), the CEMAC (Communauté économique et monétaire de l'Afrique Centrale) and the Comores.[34] In the case of the agreements with San Marino, Vatican and Monaco, the Council decision set out the negotiating position of the Community and provided for its conclusion by the Member State subject to the possibility of referral to the Council. The agreements themselves are published in the Official Journal.

C   Are There Circumstances In Which the Member States Could Be Required to Conclude an Agreement?

If we envisage an agreement which falls within exclusive Union competence but which the Union cannot conclude, should the Member States be under an obligation to conclude the agreement? Given the problems for the integrity of the legal order that might arise if some but not all Member States were to become parties, it could be argued that such an obligation would flow from Article 4(3) TEU, based on the need to represent the interests of the Union, and on the rationale for the presence of exclusivity— the need to protect the unity of the Common Market and the uniform application of Union law.

Mixed agreements provide an analogy here: in the case of 'bilateral' mixed agreements, such as Association Agreements, the Union act of conclusion will wait until all Member States have ratified. Accession treaties generally contain a specific clause obliging the new Member State to accede to certain mixed agreements;[35] there is no such clause for agree-

---

[30] Council Decision (EC) 1999/97, [1999] OJ L30/33; Monetary Agreement between the Italian Republic, on behalf of the European Community, and the Republic of San Marino [2001] OJ C209/1.

[31] Council Decision (EC) 1999/98, [1999] OJ L30/35; Monetary Agreement between the Italian Republic, on behalf of the European Community, and the Vatican City State and, on its behalf, the Holy See, [2001] OJ C299/1.

[32] Council Decision (EC) 1999/96, [1999] OJ L30/31; Monetary Agreement between the Government of the French Republic, on behalf of the European Community, and the Government of His Serene Highness the Prince of Monaco [2002] OJ L142/59.

[33] Council Decision (EC) 1998/744, [1998] OJ L358/111.

[34] Council Decision (EC) 1998/683, [1998] OJ L320/58.

[35] See, eg Act concerning the conditions of accession of the Czech Republic, the Republic of Estonia, the Republic of Cyprus, the Republic of Latvia, the Republic of Lithuania, the Republic of Hungary, the Republic of Malta, the Republic of Poland, the Republic of Slovenia and the Slovak Republic and the adjustments to the Treaties on which the European Union is founded, [2003] OJ L236/33, Art 6.

ments of the type considered here (such as some ILO Conventions), but arguably there should be.[36]

D   Can the Court Give an Opinion Under Article 218(11) TFEU?

Under Article 218(11) TFEU (ex-Article 300(6) EC), the Council, Commission, European Parliament or a Member State may request an opinion from the Court of Justice as to the compatibility of an 'envisaged agreement' with the Treaties. In Opinion 2/91 the Court held that this provision could be applied to the envisaged ILO Convention although the Community itself was not to be a party. The Court held that

> the request for an opinion does not concern the Community's capacity, on the international plane, to enter into a convention drawn up under the auspices of the ILO but relates to the scope, judged solely by reference to the rules of Community law, of the competence of the Community and the Member States within the area covered by Convention No 170.[37]

Article 218(11) TFEU also provides that if the opinion as to compatibility is negative, the agreement may not enter into force 'unless it is amended or the Treaties are revised'. The principle behind this provision will apply in the situation we are considering here, but it cannot have exactly the same effect: this provision has the effect of removing the Council's power to adopt a decision concluding an incompatible agreement.[38] The Member State acts concluding an incompatible agreement (even one within exclusive Union competence) cannot be declared invalid by the Court of Justice. However, it is certainly the case that, were the Member States to conclude such an agreement, they would be acting contrary to their Union law obligations.

---

[36] In the case of ILO Convention No 170, part of which the Court held was a matter of exclusive Community competence, only a few Member States had in fact ratified it at the time of writing: Germany, Italy, Luxembourg, Poland and Sweden.

[37] Opinion 2/91, n 7 above, para 4.

[38] Thus the decision concluding it may be declared invalid. This would not, however, invalidate the agreement in terms of international law; see C-327/91 *France v Commission* [1994] ECR I-3641; C-13/07 *Commission v Council* (removed from register on the 10 June 2010), Opinion of AG Kokott, para 173: 'The annulment of a prior decision establishing the Community position would not alter the fact that Vietnam's accession to the WTO is binding under international law on the Community and its Member States because infringements of provisions of internal law cannot in principle, according to the general rules of international law, have any bearing on the competence to conclude treaties and agreements.'

E   Subsequent Developments in Union Law

This last point raises the issue of subsequently arising incompatibilities between a Member State agreement and Union law. We will discuss below the status of the agreement and its relationship with Union law, including secondary law. Here we may note that the Member States may be under an obligation to seek to bring an agreement to which they are party into line with developments in Union law. Regulation 561/2006, which currently gives effect to the AETR within the Union, also refers to the AETR in its preamble and to the need for the Member States to act together in the Community interest:

> Since the subject matter of the AETR falls within the scope of this Regulation, the power to negotiate and conclude the Agreement lies with the Community. If an amendment to the internal Community rules in the field in question necessitates a corresponding amendment to the AETR, Member States should act together to bring about such an amendment to the AETR as soon as possible, in accordance with the procedure laid down therein.[39]

The parallel between the second sentence here cited and Article 351(2) TFEU (ex-Article 307(2) EC) is striking. While Article 351 TFEU only applies to agreements concluded by Member States prior to their accession to the EU and expressly recognises (in paragraph 1) the obligations of Member States towards the third countries involved, in both cases Member States have a Union law obligation to resolve incompatibilities between their international law obligations and Union law, and in both cases the Member States should act together.[40]

III   THE LEGAL STATUS OF AGREEMENTS CONCLUDED BY MEMBER STATES 'ON BEHALF OF' THE EU

We will here discuss essentially the extent to which Article 216(2) TFEU (ex-Article 300(7) EC) might apply by analogy or extension to agreements concluded by Member States on behalf of the Union. The issues arising include whether the agreement is binding on the Union as well as on the Member States, who is responsible for its implementation, does the Court have jurisdiction to interpret it and does it take precedence over secondary Union law?

---

[39] Reg (EC) 561/2006, [2006] OJ L102/1, preamble paras 10–11.
[40] See, eg Case C-205/06 *Commission v Austria* (BITS) [2009] ECR I-01301, paras 43–44.

A Is the Agreement Binding on the Union?

Under Article 216(2) TFEU, agreements concluded by the Union are binding on the Union and its institutions (as well as the Member States). In the cases where a single Member State concludes an agreement on behalf of the Union, which would include, for example, the delegation to Italy already mentioned of the power to conclude agreements on the use of the euro with San Marino and Vatican City, we can take the view that the agreement will be binding on the Union. The decision authorising Italy to conclude those agreements was in fact based on Article 111(3) EC, which provided that agreements concluded under that provision are binding on the Community (now Union), the European Central Bank and the Member States.

These are rather special cases, and it is only in the case of GATT and the Customs Nomenclature Convention that the Court has explicitly declared an agreement to which only the Member States are parties to be binding on the Community.[41] It is possible that the same principle might be applied to other agreements but caution should be exercised: it is not merely that all Member States are party to the agreement; it must be shown that there has been a transfer of power to the Union in the field covered by the agreement. In *Intertanko*, for example, the Court held in connection with the MARPOL Convention:

> it does not appear that the Community has assumed, under the EC Treaty, the powers previously exercised by the Member States in the field to which Marpol 73/78 applies, nor that, consequently, its provisions have the effect of binding the Community . . . In this regard, Marpol 73/78 can therefore be distinguished from GATT 1947 within the framework of which the Community progressively assumed powers previously exercised by the Member States, with the consequence that it became bound by the obligations flowing from that agreement (see to this effect, in particular, *International Fruit Company and Others*, paragraphs 10 to 18). Accordingly, this case law relating to GATT 1947 cannot be applied to MARPOL 73/78. It is true that all the Member States of the Community are parties to Marpol 73/78. Nevertheless, in the absence of a full transfer of the powers previously exercised by the Member States to the Community, the latter cannot, simply because all those States are

---

[41] On GATT see n 9 above; on the Nomenclature Convention, see Case 38/75 *Douaneagent der NV Nederlandse Spoorwegen v Inspecteur der invoerrechten en accijnzen* [1975] ECR 1439, para 21. We may argue that Art 6(3) TEU (ex-Art 6(2) EU) does the same for the ECHR but as this Convention does not concern a field of exclusive competence, and as the Member States are not parties on behalf of the Union, the logic is a different one and it falls outside the scope of this chapter; the same could be said of the argument of the CFI that the United Nations Charter binds the Community as a matter of Community law: Case T-315/01 *Kadi v Council and Commission* [2005] ECR II-3649.

parties to Marpol 73/78, be bound by the rules set out therein, which it has not itself approved.[42]

A similar conclusion was reached in a case which raised the issue of the status in Union law of the International Convention on Civil Liability for Oil Pollution Damage and the International Convention on the Establishment of an International Fund for Compensation for Oil Pollution Damage. The Court held, citing *Intertanko*, that the Community is not bound by either the Liability Convention or the Fund Convention:

> In the first place, the Community has not acceded to those international instruments and, in the second place, it cannot be regarded as having taken the place of its Member States, if only because not all of them are parties to those conventions . . .[43]

Although, as we have seen, the Council had expressly authorised the Member States, in the interests of the Community, to ratify or accede to the 2003 Protocol to the Fund Convention, the Court took the view that this made no difference since the Protocol did not apply to the facts at issue in the case.[44] The result is somewhat unsatisfactory since the Court was thereby unable to give a clear ruling on the relationship between two different liability regimes (that based on the international conventions and that based on the EC's waste directive[45]), even though by its authorising decision of 2004 the Council had indicated support for the international regime. It is not clear how the Court would have reasoned if the Protocol itself had been directly relevant to the case, but it seems that, in the absence of a concluding act, it is only in exceptional cases that an international agreement may bind the Union.

In the absence of such a concluding act which would render the agreement itself an integral part of Union law,[46] the contents of an agreement may be transformed into binding Union law by a legislative act which incorporates the agreement itself into the legislation designed to implement its provisions. Thus, Regulation 2829/77 was titled 'on the bringing into force' of the AETR and provided that the AETR would apply to

---

[42] Case C-308/06 *The Queen, on the application of International Association of Independent Tanker Owners (Intertanko) and Others v Secretary of State for Transport* [2008] ECR I-04057, paras 48–49.

[43] Case C-188/07 *Commune de Mesquer v Total France SA and Total International Ltd* [2008] ECR I-4501, para 85.

[44] Ibid, para 86; see n 26 above.

[45] Dir 75/442/EEC of 15 July 1975 on waste, [1975] OJ L194/39; unlike Dir 2004/35/EC on environmental liability ([2004] OJ L143/56), Dir 75/442 makes no mention of the Liability and Fund Conventions. The Court merely finds that the Member States in enacting national liability rules may follow the scheme established by the Conventions but must at the same time ensure full compliance with Dir 75/442. On *Intertanko* and *Commune de Mesquer* see further M Mendez, 'The Legal Effect of Community Agreements: Lessons from the Court', PhD thesis (defended at the EUI, 2009) 267–76.

[46] Case181/73 *Haegeman* [1974] ECR 449.

the relevant types of international road transport operations.[47] We find another example in the regulation originally implementing the Convention on International Trade in Endangered Species of Wild Fauna and Flora (CITES), which attached the Convention as an annex and provided in Article 1, 'The Convention, as set out in Annex A, shall apply throughout the Community under the conditions laid down in the following articles. The objectives and principles of the Convention shall be respected in the application of this regulation.'[48]

In considering the implications of whether and how the Union may be 'bound' by an agreement to which it is not a party, and of these forms of incorporation, we need to consider two issues in particular: the first is responsibility—as a matter of Union law—for implementation of the agreement, and the second is the place of the agreement in the Union legal order and more particularly the extent to which it can take precedence over secondary law.

B Implementing the Agreement as a Matter of Union Law

Member States who are party to an agreement 'on behalf of' the Union and in the Union interest are under not only an international law obligation to comply with the agreement but also a Union law obligation. If the provisions of an agreement are expressly incorporated into a Union instrument, then the obligation of the Member States will flow from that instrument, but even in the absence of such incorporation a Union law-based obligation may be derived from Article 4(3) TFEU. The Member States participate in the agreement not only as sovereign states but also as Member States of (and under the authorisation of) the Union. Here I think we can again draw an analogy with mixed agreements, where the Member States participate in their own right but also with commitments as Union Member States:

> [I]n ensuring compliance with commitments arising from an agreement concluded by the Community institutions, the Member States fulfil, within the Community system, an obligation in relation to the Community, which has assumed responsibility for the due performance of the agreement . . . Since the Convention and the Protocol thus create rights and obligations in a field covered in large measure by Community legislation, there is a Community

---

[47] See n 4 above; the same is true of the Regulation currently in force, Reg (EC) 561/2006 of 15 March 2006 on the harmonisation of certain social legislation relating to road transport, [2006] OJ L102/1.

[48] Council Reg (EEC) 3626/82 of 3 December 1982 on the implementation in the Community of the Convention on international trade in endangered species of wild fauna and flora, [1982] OJ L384/1. This Regulation has now been replaced by Council Reg (EC) 338/97, [1997] OJ L61/1, which provides in Art 1, 'This Regulation shall apply in compliance with the objectives, principles and provisions of the [CITES] Convention.'

interest in compliance by both the Community and its Member States with the commitments entered into under those instruments.[49]

In the situations we are considering here, of course, the agreement has not been 'concluded by the Community institutions' and the Union has not directly 'assumed responsibility' for its implementation, but the principle and the Union interest in compliance by the Member States seem to be the same. This argument is supported by *SPI & SAMI*, where the Court held that it had jurisdiction to interpret the GATT whether the point at issue was national or Community law:

> In that regard it does not matter whether the national court is required to assess the validity of Community measures or the compatibility of national legislative provisions with the commitments binding the Community [ie GATT].[50]

Thus, for the Member States, as trustees of the Union interest, compliance with the agreement is a Union law obligation which may be enforceable by the Court.[51]

Is there a corresponding obligation on the Union, albeit not bound directly via Article 216 TFEU? The Member States, as parties to the agreement, may be in the uncomfortable position of being bound in international law by an agreement which they have no power to implement (since the subject matter is within exclusive Union competence). Indeed, in the case of the ILO, the ILO itself, when accepting that an agreement—although it must be concluded by the EU Member States—may be negotiated by the Commission, declared that 'Member States alone can be held liable for failure to comply with those undertakings, even if the breach of the provisions of such a convention is attributable to a Community measure adopted by majority decision'.[52] It can be argued that the possession of exclusive competence and the fact that the Member States act under Union authorisation in concluding the agreement give rise to a responsibility for its implementation. As a matter of Union law, therefore, and as a corollary to the Union's exclusive competence and the Article 4(3) TFEU obligation on the Member States, there must be an obligation on the institutions flowing from the duty of co-operation to ensure that the agreement is implemented. If the agreement is found to be binding on the Union institutions either directly through the GATT case law or indirectly through incorporation, this will of itself entail an obligation to implement it and to enact any necessary legislation. In fact, in *Commission*

---

[49] Case C-239/03 *Commission v France (Étang de Berre)* [2004] ECR I-9325, paras 26 and 29.

[50] Cases 267–269/81 *Amministrazione delle Finanze v SPI SpA* [1983] ECR 801, para 15.

[51] As far as GATT is concerned, see Case C-61/94 *Commission v Germany* [1996] ECR I-3989.

[52] Document, drawn up by the Governing Body of the International Labour Office on 12 February 1981, supplemented by another document dated 31 May 1989, as cited in Opinion 2/91, n 7 above, Part IV.

v Greece, the Court asserted the exclusive competence of the Community to take initiatives designed to ensure compliance with international rules incorporated into a Community regulation.[53]

C   The Agreement as Part of the Union Legal Order

Union agreements are an integral part of the Union legal order and as such are subject to the interpretive jurisdiction of the Court of Justice. It seems clear that agreements concluded by a single Member State on behalf of the Union (such as the monetary agreements already referred to) are also 'Union agreements' in this sense. What of agreements such as the AETR, concluded by all Member States in a field of exclusive Union competence? In *SPI & SAMI*, as we have seen, the Court held that it had jurisdiction to interpret the GATT.[54] In *Libor Cipra* the Court held, with respect to the AETR:

> [I]n ratifying or acceding to [the AETR], the Member States acted in the interest and on behalf of the Community . . . According to Article 2(2) of Regulation No 3820/85, the AETR Agreement is to apply, instead of the provisions of that regulation, to international road transport operations to and/or from non-member countries which are Contracting Parties to the agreement . . . In the light of the foregoing, it must be held that the AETR Agreement forms part of Community law and that the Court has jurisdiction to interpret it.[55]

This phrasing is reminiscent of the Court's statement in *Haegeman*, referring to agreements concluded by the Community.[56] But is the position of agreements such as the AETR to be completely assimilated to Union agreements? The case law since *Haegeman* has made it clear that the binding nature of agreements concluded by the Community (and now the Union) entails that they have primacy over acts of secondary Union law.[57] In the specific, and not often applied, *Nakajima* case law, the Court has been prepared to assess the legality of secondary legislation in the light of the GATT on the basis that it was both binding on the Community and

---

[53] Case C-45/07 *Commission v Greece*, n 7 above; this case is discussed further below. Reg (EC) 725/2004 of 31 March 2004 on enhancing ship and port facility security, [2004] OJ L129/6 is intended to provide a basis for the harmonised implementation and monitoring of Chapter XI-2 of the International Convention for the Safety of Life at Sea (the SOLAS Convention) and the International Ship and Port Facility Security Code (the ISPS Code).

[54] See n 50 above.

[55] Case C-439/01 *Libor Cipra and Vlastimil Kvasnicka v Bezirkshauptmannschaft Mistelbach* [2003] ECR I-00745, paras 23–24.

[56] *Haegeman*, n 46 above.

[57] *Commission v Germany*, n 51 above, para 52; *Intertanko*, n 42 above, paras 42–45; Joined Cases C-402/05P and C-415/05P *Yassin Abdullah Kadi and Al Barakaat International Foundation v Council and Commission* [2008] ECR I-6351, paras 306–07.

expressly implemented by the relevant secondary law.[58] In a case such as the AETR, however, where the agreement becomes 'part of Union law' by virtue of incorporation via an act of secondary law, it might be difficult to argue that its provisions have primacy over secondary law. Incorporation by these means is a different legal process from the act of conclusion which, although by way of secondary act (normally a Council decision), has a legal effect determined by Article 216(2) TFEU.

Indeed, the Court in *Intertanko* casts doubt on the applicability of the provisions of an international agreement as a basis for reviewing the legality of secondary legislation even where the purpose of that legislation (in the words of Directive 2005/35 on ship-source pollution) 'is to incorporate international standards for ship-source pollution into Community law'.[59] The Court held that:

> Since the Community is not bound by Marpol 73/78, the mere fact that Directive 2005/35 has the objective of incorporating certain rules set out in that Convention [Marpol] into Community law is likewise not sufficient for it to be incumbent upon the Court to review the directive's legality in the light of the Convention.[60]

Although both Directive 2005/35 and the Court refer to 'incorporating' the Marpol standards, the directive at issue here does not in fact reproduce those standards; it is designed to harmonise and ensure effective Member State implementation of the standards by establishing rules regarding infringements, penalties and enforcement. It can therefore be distinguished from the incorporation of the AETR (at issue in *Libor Cipra*[61]) and also the incorporation of the SOLAS Convention and the International Ship and Port Facility Security Code (ISPS Code) in Regulation 725/2004/EC, at issue in *Commission v Greece*.[62] Nevertheless, as an agreement to which all Member States are parties, Marpol is not without legal effect:

---

[58] Case C-69/89 *Nakajima All Precision Co Ltd v Council* [1991] ECR I-2069; in paras 30–32 the Court held, 'the new basic regulation . . . was adopted in order to comply with the international obligations of the Community, which, as the Court has consistently held, is therefore under an obligation to ensure compliance with the General Agreement and its implementing measures . . . In those circumstances, it is necessary to examine whether the Council went beyond the legal framework thus laid down . . . and whether, by adopting the disputed provision, it acted in breach of Art 2(4) and (6) of the Anti-Dumping Code.' The principle has mainly been applied in anti-dumping cases; for an example of an application of *Nakajima* outside the dumping context see Case C-352/96 *Italy v Council* [1998] ECR I-6937; for an example of a refusal to apply *Nakajima* reasoning to legislation designed to implement a Dispute Settlement Body ruling, see Case T-19/01 *Chiquita v Commission* [2005] ECR II-315; Case C-377/02 *Van Parys* [2005] ECR I-1465.

[59] [2005] OJ L255/11.

[60] *Intertanko*, n 42 above, para 50.

[61] *Libor Cipra*, n 55 above.

[62] *Commission v Greece*, n 7 above; Reg (EC) 725/2004 on enhancing ship and port facility security, [2004] OJ L129/6: the Regulation explicitly requires Member States to apply the international rules, and the relevant provisions of the SOLAS Convention and the ISPS Code are annexed to the Regulation.

> In view of the customary principle of good faith, which forms part of general international law, and of Article 10 EC, it is incumbent upon the Court to interpret those provisions [of secondary law which fall within the field of application of Marpol 73/78] taking account of Marpol 73/78.[63]

The fact that there is no single rule, equivalent to Article 216(2) TFEU, determining the effect of these agreements in the Union legal order means that their effect will vary according to the precise way in which the legislation incorporates them either expressly or by reference, or implements them. Thus it seems that in exceptional cases, where there has been a full transfer of powers to the Union in the field covered by an agreement, the Union may be bound by the agreement itself, and in such cases the *Nakajima* doctrine suggests that, where secondary legislation is expressly designed to give effect to the agreement, it may take priority over the secondary Union law in question. It might also be argued that, in cases where the Council does not simply authorise the Member States to conclude an agreement but actually requires them to do so, its decision should carry the same legal effects as a decision actually concluding the agreement. On the other hand, in cases where the effect of the agreement in Union law is dependent on its incorporation in secondary legislation, it is difficult to argue that it should prevail over that legislation. Nevertheless, where Union legislation is designed to implement an international agreement in an area of exclusive Union competence, the Court may interpret that agreement in order to give effect to the principle of consistent interpretation (that is, to avoid conflict between the agreement and Union law). And in *Libor Cipra* the AETR was interpreted with a view to its being applied by a national court in the same way as a regulation, as a result of its having been incorporated into Community law by that regulation.

D   The Formation of Positions in Institutions Set Up by the Agreement

Certain agreements may set up institutional structures and mechanisms for the negotiation of updated or new rules. If the Union is not a party to the underlying agreement, or a member of the relevant institutions, we need to establish the ongoing Union-based obligations on the Member States within such organs and the mechanisms whereby a common Union position may be established and defended.

The Union is not a member of the IMO, nor is it a party to the International Convention for the Safety of Life at Sea (SOLAS Convention)

---

[63] *Intertanko*, n 42 above, para 52. This principle of consistent interpretation has of course also been applied to the GATT and WTO in cases where *Nakajima* does not apply: see *Commission v Germany*, n 51 above, para 52; Case C-89/99 *Groeneveld* [2001] ECR I-5851.

and the International Ship and Port Facility Security Code (ISPS Code).
In *Commission v Greece*,[64] the Court was asked to determine whether
a Member State was entitled to put forward national proposals within
the IMO connected with the monitoring of compliance with the SOLAS
Convention and ISPS Code, given that implementation of these international rules was governed within the Community by a regulation.[65] The
parties do not seem to have disputed that—given the regulation—the
measure fell within the scope of exclusive Community competence. Greece
argued, however, that the *AETR* ruling, which would prevent a Member
State from entering into an international agreement on the subject on its
own account, did not extend to submitting a proposal in the context of
its participation in the IMO. The Court disagreed, holding that Greece
had initiated a procedure which could lead to the adoption by the IMO
of new rules, that the adoption of such new rules would have an effect
on the regulation, and that as a consequence the Member State was in
breach of its obligations under Articles 10, 71 and 80(2) EC.[66] Although,
then, Greece was not directly entering into an obligation which would
affect the regulation, it was setting in motion a procedure that might lead
to such an effect in a context where the regulation sought to harmonise
implementation of the international rules. To the argument that, since the
Community was not a member of the IMO, the Community interest had
to be defended by Member States (and that Greece was acting in this
interest), the Court was clear:

> The mere fact that the Community is not a member of an international
> organisation in no way authorises a Member State, acting individually in
> the context of its participation in an international organisation, to assume
> obligations likely to affect Community rules promulgated for the attainment
> of the objectives of the Treaty. Moreover, the fact that the Community is
> not a member of an international organisation does not prevent its external
> competence from being in fact exercised, in particular through the Member
> States acting jointly in the Community's interest.[67]

A non-binding arrangement agreed within the Council relating to
participation in the IMO did not, in the view of the Court, envisage
such unilateral action in the absence of an agreed common position and,
even if it had, it could not have the effect of permitting a Member State
to act in contravention of the Union's exclusive powers.[68]

This case illustrates the importance—indeed, the necessity—of forming

[64] *Commission v Greece*, n 7 above.
[65] Reg 725/2004/EC of 31 March 2004 on enhancing ship and port facility security,
[2004] OJ L129/6.
[66] For further discussion see M Cremona, 'Extending the Reach of the AETR principle:
Comment on *Commission v Greece* (C-45/07)' (2009) 34 *European Law Rev* 754.
[67] *Commission v Greece*, n 7 above, paras 30 and 31.
[68] Compare the role of a binding inter-institutional agreement in a case of shared competence in Case C-25/94 *Commission v Council* (FAO agreement) [1996] ECR I-1469.

a common position with respect to proposals of this kind. The duty of co-operation operates here on the Commission, as well as on the Member States. In the IMO case, Greece argued that the Commission was in breach of this duty, since it had not tabled the Greek proposal for discussion before the relevant Community committee prior to its submission by Greece. Whereas Advocate General Bot felt that the Commission had done enough to 'promote co-ordination at Community level',[69] the Court seems to have taken the view that the Commission could have done more. However, both agreed that, even if the Commission had failed in its performance of the duty of co-operation, this did not entitle the Member State to 'unilaterally adopt, on its own authority, corrective or protective measures designed to obviate any breach by an institution of rules of Community law'.[70]

Assuming such a common position is adopted by the Council, what is its legal status? This question was under consideration in a case involving CITES (the Convention on International Trade in Endangered Species).[71] Again, we have a convention to which the Union is not a party, and a framework—the Conference of the Parties (COP)—for the amendment of convention annexes listing protected species. The Union has observer status in the COP and, as we have already seen, the CITES Convention has been implemented in the EU by means of a regulation.[72] The case concerned the need for a statement of reasons, including a legal base, for a Council decision establishing a common position for the Member States in a meeting of the COP.[73]

For Union agreements, Article 218(9) TFEU (ex-Article 300(2) EC) establishes a procedure for establishing the Union position in a body set up by an agreement, where that body is to adopt decisions having legal effects.[74] In the case of CITES, as the Advocate General points out in her opinion, the Council decision does not establish a position of the Union, since the Union does not participate as a party in the COP, but rather a position to be adopted by the Member States. In addition, since the decision in this case is addressed to the Member States, it differs from

---

[69] *Commission v Greece*, n 7 above, Opinion of AG Bot, paras 41–43.

[70] *Commission v Greece*, ibid, para 26, citing by analogy Case C-5/94 *Hedley Lomas* [1996] ECR I-2553. For a critique of this position see Cremona, n 66 above.

[71] Case C-370/07 *Commission v Council*, judgment 1 October 2009 [2009] OJ C282/4.

[72] See n 48 above.

[73] For the obligation to state the reasons on which a legal act is based, see Art 296 TFEU (ex-Art 253 EC). In this case the Commission had proposed a dual trade and environment legal base; the Council adopted the decision with no stated legal base. The Council argued that the 'decision' envisaged in Art 300(2) EC (now Art 218(9) TFEU) is a different type of legal act from the 'decision' referred to in Art 253 EC.

[74] The Council acts on a proposal from the Commission or the High Representative of the Union for Foreign Affairs and Security Policy, normally by qualified majority but unanimously where the agreement covers a field for which unanimity is required for the adoption of a Union act, for association agreements and agreements with candidate states.

a decision adopted under Article 218(9) which does not have a direct addressee but rather determines the conduct of another institution (the Commission). Nevertheless, it is clear from its wording that the act in question is a Council measure addressed to the Member States—and not only a decision of the representatives of the Member States meeting in Council—and is thus amenable to judicial review under Article 263 TFEU (ex-Article 230 EC).[75] The Court took the view that any act designed to have binding legal effects, which may therefore be the subject of an action for annulment, is subject to the obligation to state reasons, and in particular its legal basis.[76] This act was legally binding; it followed that 'the contested decision must be reasoned and must therefore indicate the legal basis on which it is founded in order, in particular, that the Court may be able to exercise its powers of review'.[77] The need for a legal base was also derived from the principle of conferred powers ('having only conferred powers, the Community must tie the contested decision to a Treaty provision which empowers it to approve such a measure'[78]) and the implications of different legal bases for both institutional balance and the division of competence between the Union and the Member States.[79] Neither the Advocate General nor the Court took a view on whether Article 218(9) TFEU should be the appropriate procedural legal basis in such cases, where a Member State rather than a Union agreement was at issue, merely saying that both a procedural and a substantive legal basis should be referred to in the decision.

IV   CONCLUSION

This chapter has taken as its starting point the fact that there are circumstances in which the Member States alone may become, or remain, parties to international agreements falling within exclusive Union competence. This may occur because the Union is excluded from participation by the international legal framework within which the agreement is negotiated, because it is regarded as being in the Union interest for the Member States to participate or because exclusive competence has arisen after the conclusion of an agreement by the Member

---

[75] Cf the *AETR* case, n 2 above; both the AG and the Court, however, distinguish the decision in this case from that taken in the case of the AETR as regards the obligation to state reasons.

[76] *Commission v Council*, n 71 above, para 42.

[77] Ibid, para 45.

[78] Ibid, para 47.

[79] Responding to a UK argument that a duty to state reasons would be incompatible with the flexibility needed in international negotiations, the Court held that the degree of detail required may vary, the minimum being the need to cite an explicit legal basis: *Commission v Council*, n 71 above, para 52.

States. The paper has explored the Union law obligations that arise for the Member States in these circumstances, as well as the status of such agreements within the Union legal order. In such cases, the Member States are said to act on behalf, and in the interests, of the Union, although the implications of this lie within Union law rather than at the international level. The Union's exclusive competence requires that the Member States act under Union authorisation, and that Union negotiating positions are formulated and adhered to. Duties of compliance and implementation are a matter of Union obligation as well as international law, and competence to implement the agreement will lie primarily with the Union rather than the Member States.

Although there is no formal legal link between the Union and the agreement in terms of either international or Union law, there are different ways in which the agreement may become part of Union law. Where there has been a complete transfer of competence to the Union, the agreement may directly bind the Union itself, including the institutions, by analogy with Article 216(2) TFEU. However, it is more usual for the agreement to be incorporated into Union law by way of secondary legislation, either by way of referral or by including (parts of) the agreement in the legislation itself. The Court of Justice will have jurisdiction to interpret the agreement and will apply the principle of consistent interpretation. Whether the agreement will take priority over secondary legislation—so that incompatibility may lead to the invalidity of that legislation—will depend on whether, and the mechanism whereby, the agreement becomes part of Union law, as well as the nature of the agreement itself.

The cases discussed here show that the phenomenon is not all that unusual. Although these agreements are in some senses anomalous, and their position in the Union legal order may be ambiguous, we find that what might appear to be a clear-cut distinction between exclusive and shared competence in fact reveals a more complex interaction between Member States and the Union in their international relations: for a variety of reasons, even where the Union is exclusively competent the Member States may not be completely eclipsed. These agreements also illustrate the constraints under which the Member States—although fully sovereign states—operate at an international level as a result of their Union obligations; the way in which the international identity of the Union may be represented by the Member States alongside the Union; and the accommodations possible between the demands of the Union's constitutional order and the practical exigencies of international treaty-making.

24

The 'Succession Doctrine' and the European Union

ROBERT SCHÜTZE*

I INTRODUCTION: TREATY SUCCESSION AND THE EUROPEAN UNION

THE LAW OF succession represents one of the unruliest parts of international law.[1] Should a new subject of international law be bound by the old obligations of its 'predecessor'? Two theories exist in classic international law to provide answers to this problem. The 'continuity theory' is inspired by the Roman law of inheritance.[2] Based on the idea of (universal) succession, it insists on the continuity of sovereignty that passes—with all rights and obligations—from the old to the new subject of international law. The theory thus protects the validity of obligations assumed under international treaties. The 'clean slate' theory, by contrast, emerges out of the 'subjectivist' philosophy of the nineteenth century. The view denies succession: sovereignty cannot be transferred from a 'predecessor' to a 'successor'. The new international subject exercises its jurisdiction 'solely because it has acquired the possibility of expanding its own sovereignty in the manner dictated by its will'.[3] This second view has—with one (or two) exception(s)[4]—become the dominant philosophy

---

* Special thanks go Jan Klabbers and the editors for their comments and advice.

[1] A Verdross and B Simma, *Universelles Völkerrecht: Theorie und Praxis* (Berlin, Duncker & Humblot, 1984) 608: 'Die Lehre von der Staatennachfolge bildet den umstrittsten Teil des Volkerrechts'; B Stern, 'La Succession d'Etats' (1996) 262 *Recueil des Cours* 27: 'La succession d'Etats apparaît comme l'un des problèmes les plus complexes du droit international'.

[2] DP O'Connel, *State Succession in Municipal Law and International Law—Volume I* (Cambridge, Cambridge University Press, 1967) 9.

[3] Ibid, 14.

[4] The traditional exception to the 'clean slate' theory is 'territorial treaties'. The exception is codified in Arts 11 and 12 of the 1978 Vienna Convention, and in Gabcikovo-Nagymaros Project (Hungary/Slovakia) (1997) ICJ Reports 7, the International Court of Justice considered these provisions to reflect customary international law (ibid, para 123). In the 1990s, a second exception to the clean-slate theory was seriously considered: human rights treaties. As territorial treaties 'binds successor States by virtue of attaching to the territory itself' (M Shaw, 'State Succession Revisited' (1994) 5 *Finnish Yearbook of International Law* 34, 79), human rights treaties were said to 'attach' to the inhabitants of the State (R Mullerson, 'The Continuity and Succession of States, by Reference to the former USSR and Yugoslavia' (1993) 42 *International and Comparative Law Quarterly* 473, 490;

in the twentieth century: a new member of the international community starts 'with a clean slate in respect of treaty obligations'.[5]

Would international law apply this solution to treaty successions within unions of states? When states unite they may create a new subject of international law. Should we view this phenomenon in terms of succession? And, if so, should the union start with a 'clean slate'; or, should it be bound by the international agreements of its Member States? This chapter looks for answers to these questions in the context of the European Union. I will start with the 'external perspective' of international law and investigate its normative responses to treaty continuity and succession within unions of states (Section II). A third section will adopt the 'internal perspective' of the European Union and analyse the doctrine of functional succession as established in the European legal order. In addition to a constitutional regime protecting the continuity of international treaties concluded by the Member States prior to accession, the Union has indeed considered itself to have functionally succeeded to some of its Member States' international treaties. What are the constitutional conditions for a functional succession in the European Union's 'constitutional order of states'?[6] And has this European view matched the perspective of international law?

II   EXTERNAL PERSPECTIVE: FUNCTIONAL SUCCESSION IN INTERNATIONAL LAW

Classic international law struggles with 'composite' subjects.[7] Its—partial—blindness towards 'unions of states' is embodied in the traditional

---

MT Kamminga, 'State Succession in Respect of Human Rights Treaties' (1996) 7 *European Journal of International Law* 469, 482). However, the view has been criticised as not reflecting international practice (*cf* A Rasulov, 'Revisiting State Succession to Humanitarian Treaties: Is there a Case for Automaticity?' (2003) 14 *European Journal of International Law*, 141).

  [5] C Jenks, 'State Succession in Respect of Law-Making Treaties' (1952) 29 *British Yearbook of International Law* 105, 107. However, the 1978 Vienna Convention on the Succession of States in respect of Treaties would not codify this completely. Drafted against the backdrop of 'the profound transformation of the international community brought about by the decolonization process' (preamble 1), the Convention sharply distinguishes between a succession leading to 'newly independent States' and a succession through the 'uniting and separation of [old] States'. The former cases are governed by the 'clean slate' theory (*cf* Art 16), while the latter situation follows the 'continuity' theory. The codification has been considered a failure and has been criticised for not fully reflecting international custom (*cf* Resolution 3/2008 on 'Aspects of the Law of State Succession' adopted by the International Law Association (73rd Conference, Brazil, 2008)).

  [6] For the characterisation of the European Union as a 'constitutional order of states', see A Dashwood, 'The Limits of European Community Powers' (1996) 21 *European Law Review* 113, 114.

  [7] *Cf* R Schütze, 'Federalism and Foreign Affairs: Mixity as an (Inter)national Phenomenon'

conception of succession in 'statist' and 'territorial' terms.[8] Succession in the restrictive sense is thus 'limited to cases arising from *territorial changes*' between states.[9] However, in a wider sense of the term,[10] succession will equally occur 'whenever a party to a treaty joins with another State in a relationship by which its capacity to contract international obligations is either annulled or restricted, though it retains some constitutional identity'.[11] Should the Member States be absolved from their previous international obligations—due to the 'functional changes' brought about by a transfer of powers to the union? And should the union 'succeed' to the treaty obligations of its Member States? The idea of functional succession has received eminent support,[12] but it nonetheless remains a sensitive issue:

> The question is delicate because it is one where the rules of international law and of the constitution of the union intersect; and the international rule

in C Hillion & P Koutrakos (eds), *Mixed Agreements Revisited* (Oxford, Hart Publishing, 2010) 57.

[8] Art 2(b) of 1978 Vienna Convention defines 'succession of States' as 'the replacement of one *State* by another in the responsibility for the international relations of *territory*' (emphasis added).

[9] EJS Castrén, 'On State Succession in Practice and Theory,' (1954) 24 *Nordisk Tidsskrift International Ret* 55 (emphasis in original).

[10] EJS Castrén, 'Aspects Récents de La Succession d'Etats' (1951) 78 *Recueil des Cours* 379, 386: 'Par succession juridique internationale, au sens large, on entend, selon la conception indiquée, le transfer de toute sorte de droits et d'obligations internationaux entre sujets du droit international intervenant sur la base du droit international, soit en vertu de traits, sout autrement.'

[11] DP O'Connell, 'State Succession and the Effect Upon Treaties of Entry into a Composite Relationship' (1963) 39 *British Yearbook of International Law* 54.

[12] For an affirmation of the doctrine of functional succession in federal states, see U Scheuner, 'Die Funktionsnachfolge und das Problem der staatsrechtlichen Kontinuität' in T Maunz (ed), *Vom Bonner Grundgesetz zur Gesamtdeutschen Verfassung—Festschrift von Nawiasky* (Isar, München, 1956) 9, 34: 'Funktionennachfolge bedeutet Verknüpfung von Rechten und Pflichten zu denjenigen Aufgaben (Hoheitsrechten), mit denen sie verbunden waren in der Weise, daß sie beim Wechsel der Zuständigkeiten auf den neuen Träger dieser Funktionen übergehen. Sie ist kein gebietlicher, sondern ein funktioneller Tatbestand der Rechtskontinuität. Daher beschränkt sich in der Hauptsache der Anwendungsbereich der Funktionennachfolge auf dasjenige Feld staatlicher Gestaltung, wo solche Veränderungen funktioneller Art in der Regel allein vorkommen, den Bundesstaat . . .' For the idea of 'functional' succession in the context of international organisations, see GG Fitzmaurice (1952) 29 *British Yearbook of International Law* 1, 9: 'If, for the concept of territorial area, there is substituted that of functional field, then the position might be stated as follows: that just as a territorial area passing from one state to another carries with it all rights and obligations specifically appertaining to that area in a territorial manner, so a functional field 'passing' from one international organisation to another (in the sense that the former is distinguished but the latter is created expressly to fulfil the same general purposes, and the extinction of the former is carried out largely on that basis) carries with it the rights, obligations, and functions connected with that field, and appertaining to the capacity to act in it.' On the issue of functional succession within International Organisations, see generally: H J Hahn, 'Continuity in the Law of International Organization' (1994) 13 *Zeitschrift für öffentliches Recht* 167. According to Art 1 TEU (Lisbon), the (new) European Union 'shall replace and succeed the European Community'.

is itself concerned with the effects on treaties of the constitutional change resulting from the formation of the union. The argument for treating unions of States as a special case is that, as sovereign States, they created a complex of treaty relations with other States and ought not to be able completely at will to terminate all those treaties by joining a federal or other union. In other words, the argument is that the principle of continuity should displace the 'clean slate' principle in the case of the formation of a union and the moving treaty frontier principle in the case of the addition of a state to a union. Today, this argument may, perhaps, be thought to have added force in view of the growing tendency of States to group themselves in new forms of associations where the line between international organisations and unions of States becomes somewhat blurred.[13]

Let me analyse the diverse responses to the question of treaty succession in federal unions in this second section. I start by looking at the 'general' answers offered by international law, before focusing on the 'special' answer offered by the European Convention of Human Rights vis-à-vis the status of the European Union and its Member States.

A   Treaty Succession and Unions of States

How has international law, history and theory, responded to the normative phenomenon of treaty succession within 'unions of states'? Historically, international praxis has been mixed. When Texas joined the United States in 1845, the United States insisted on discontinuity. It refused to honour the treaty obligations of its new Member State and claimed that Texas's pre-accession treaties had lapsed.[14] In *Terlinden v Ames*,[15] a different conclusion was reached. The case concerned the 1852 Extradition Treaty between the United States and Prussia. Having been arrested in the United States and about to be extradited to Prussia, Terlinden petitioned for the writ of habeas corpus on the grounds that the treaty between the United States and the Kingdom of Prussia 'was terminated by the creation of the German Empire and the adoption of the Constitution of the said Empire in AD 1871'.[16] The Supreme Court rejected this view:

> Undoubtedly treaties may be terminated by the absorption of powers into other nationalities and the loss of separate existence . . . Cessation of independent

---

[13] Fifth Report 'On Succession in Respect of Treaties' (Special Rapporteur: Sir Humhrey Waldock) [1972] *Yearbook of the International Law Commission—Volume II* (herinafter Waldock Report) 1, 29.

[14] This view might have been inspired by the Supreme Court's judgment in *Holmes v Jennison*, 39 US 540 (1840), according to which the states of the Union lose all their treaty-making power. The fact that Texas had 'constitutionally' survived as a 'state' endowed with autonomous internal powers was treated as irrelevant (*cf* DP O'Connell, above n 11, 79).

[15] *Terlinden v Ames*, 184 US 270 (1902).

[16] Ibid, 273.

existence render[s] the execution of treaties impossible. But where sovereignty in that respect is not extinguished, and the power to execute remains unimpaired, outstanding treaties cannot be regarded as avoided because of impossibility of performance. This treaty was entered into by His Majesty the King of Prussia . . . [before] the adoption of the Constitution of the German Empire . . . [T]he Constitution created a composite state instead of a system of confederated states, and even that it was called a confederated Empire rather to save the *amour propre* of some of its component parts than otherwise, it does not necessarily follow that the Kingdom of Prussia lost its identity as such, or that treaties theretofore entered into by it could not be performed either in the name of its King or that of the Emperor. We do not find in this Constitution any provision which in itself operated to abrogate existing treaties or to affect the status of the Kingdom of Prussia in that regard.[17]

The Supreme Court's judgment reflected the solution favoured by (then) contemporary German constitutional theory.[18] Because the German Member States remained international persons with (limited) treaty powers, their accession to the federal Empire would not automatically discontinue their international obligations. Member States' international treaties survived as long as they did not violate federal law.[19] However, where the Member States had transferred powers to the Union and the latter had exercised them in a way that conflicted with pre-accession treaties, the Federation would not consider itself internationally bound to succeed to the treaties of its Member States.[20] Functional succession was *not* regarded as an international reflex to a constitutional shift of power.

What 'theoretical' solutions have been proposed by modern international law? The doctrine of functional succession within unions of states was addressed by the 1968 Resolution of the International Law Association. It offered the following solutions:

[17] Ibid, 283–85. The Court ultimately appeared to find that the question whether the treaty had been terminated was controlled by 'state practice': 'extradition from this country to Germany, and from Germany to this country, has been frequently granted under the treaty, which has thus been repeatedly recognised by both governments as in force'. The German government had therefore continued officially to recognise the 1852 Prussian Treaty 'as well as similar treaties with other members of the Empire, so far as the latter has not taken specific action to the contrary or in lieu thereof', ibid, 285–86 (with reference to P Laband, *Das Staatsrecht des Deutschen Reiches—Volume 2* (Scientia, 1964), 167ff).
[18] A Haenel, *Deutsches Staatsrecht* (Berlin, Duncker & Humblot, 1892) 547ff, esp 557; Laband, ibid.
[19] Laband (ibid, 169): 'besteht die Kompetenz der Einzelstaaten zum Abschluß von Staatsverträgen fort, so lange das Reich von seiner Kompetenz noch keinen Gebrauch gemacht hat'.
[20] This was clarified in a decision of the Weimar Reichsfinanzhof of 18 June 1930 on the double-taxation treaty between Prussia and Luxembourg (cf (1933) 3 *Zeitschrift für ausländisches öffentliches Recht und Völkerrecht* 155, 156): 'Es gibt keinen Rechtsatz des Völkerrechts, aus dem zu folgern wäre, daß das Reich, nachdem es die Einkommensteuer in Anspruch genommen und durch Reichsgesetz geregelt hat, in die völkerrechtlichen Verpflichtungen eingetreten ist, die die Länder in den von ihnen mit auswärtigen Staaten abgeschlossenen Doppelbesteuerungsverträgen übernommen hatten'). For the subsequent constitutional practice within the Federal Republic of Germany, see Scheuner, above n 12.

In cases of unions or federations of States, treaties, unless they otherwise provide, remain in force within the regional limits prescribed at the time of their conclusion *to the extent to which their implementation is consistent with the constitutional position established by the instrument of union or federation.* In such a case where the treaty remains in force, the question whether the union or federation becomes responsible for performance of the treaty is *dependent on the extent to which the constituent governments remain competent to negotiate directly with foreign States* and to become parties to arbitration proceedings therewith.[21]

Treaty continuity is consequently seen as analytically distinct from the problem of treaty succession. Treaty continuity depends solely on the (in)compatibility of the treaty with the union constitution. Succession, by contrast, depends on the distribution of treaty-making powers within the union. Where the Member States retain treaty-making powers for the subject matter of the treaty, no succession has occurred. By contrast, where the external powers on the matter have been transferred to the union, the latter automatically succeeds its Member States.[22] This view represented a compromise between the clean slate and the continuity theory. Treaties that violated the union's constitution would lapse. But in the absence of a constitutional conflict, treaty obligations would continue to tie the Member States, or—where the union had assumed the treaty-making powers—the union by means of a doctrine of functional succession.[23]

The International Law Commission favoured an even stronger succession doctrine for unions of states.[24] The Waldock Report, having narrowed the topic to that of 'federal states',[25] proposed the following principles.

---

[21] Parts of the Resolution are reproduced in Waldock Report, above n 13, 26 (emphasis added).

[22] This solution was justified by the following considerations: 'Respecting responsibility for treaty-performance, the Committee acknowledges that it is controversial whether the central or local government is responsible. However, it believes that considering the machinery of international negotiation, the central government remains responsible unless the local government remains competent to negotiate internationally within the treaty field. Any other solution is likely, in the Committee's opinion, to be administratively abortive and to frustrate the implications of treaty continuity through the process of administrative change.' *cf* Note 2, Interim Report of the Committee on the Succession of New States to the Treaties and Certain other Obligations of their Predecessors (International Law Association, Report of the Fifty-third Conference, 1968), reproduced in Waldock Report, above n 13, 26.

[23] The view went against E Castrén, above n 10, 443: 'Les traités conclus avec des Etats tiers par les Etats members avant la constitution de l'Etat fédéral s'éteignent pour autant que les Etats members sont privés du droit de traiter dans le demaine en question. Ces traités ne sont pas transférés *ipso jure* au nom de l'Etat fédéral, celui-ci, ainsi qu'il a ete indique, constituant un nouveau sujet du droit international.'

[24] *Cf* Waldock Report, above n 13.

[25] The Report distinguished 'between unions of States which create a new political entity only on the plane of international law and organizations, and unions which also create a new political entity on the plane of internal constitutional law'. The former—like the United Nations—would 'fall completely outside the concept of union of States for the purposes of succession of States'. The latter category comprised 'federations of States'—like the United States of America—and only these 'constitutional unions' would be covered by the report

First, it claimed to have identified 'a rule prescribing the continuance in force *ipso jure* of the pre-federation treaties of the individual States within their respective regional limits'.[26] This rule discarded normative conflicts between the (new) union constitution and prior international treaties of the Member States. The continuity of pre-union treaties should, in particular, not depend on the distribution of power to perform the treaty. 'Such an approach to the question is thought to go too far in introducing internal constitutional provisions into a rule of international law[.]'[27] Even more radical was the second principle: 'a treaty which continues in force binds the *Union of States*',[28] which suggested an automatic succession of the union to all international treaties of the Member States. This conclusion inspired the 1978 Vienna Convention on Succession of States in respect of Treaties. Article 31 of the Convention deals with a succession in unions of states and reads:

> 1. When two or more States unite and so form one successor State, any treaty in force at the date of the succession of States in respect of any of them continues in force in respect of the successor State unless:
> (a) the successor State and the other State party or States parties otherwise agree; or
> (b) it appears from the treaty or is otherwise established that the application of the treaty in respect of the successor State would be incompatible with the object and purpose of the treaty or would radically change the conditions for its operation.
> 2. Any treaty continuing in force in conformity with paragraph 1 shall apply [principally] only in respect of the part of the territory of the successor State in respect of which the treaty was in force at the date of the succession of States[.] [29]

(ibid, 18). The European Union, admitted to represent a 'hybrid' union, was expressly excluded (ibid): 'For the present purposes, it must suffice to say that, while [the] E[U] is not commonly viewed as a union of States, it is at the same time not generally regarded as being simply a regional international organisation. The direct effects in the national law of the member States of regulatory and judicial powers vested in [Union] organs gives to [the] E[U], it is said, a semblance of a quasi-federal association of States. Be that as it may, from the point of view of succession, [the] E[U] appears without any doubt to remain on the plane of intergovernmental organisation. Thus, [Art 351 TFEU] unmistakably approaches the question of the pre-Union treaties of member States with third countries from the angle, not of succession or of the moving treaty frontier rule, but of the rules governing the application of successive treaties relating to the same subject matter (Art 30 of the 1969 Convention on the Law of Treaties).'

[26] Ibid, 29.
[27] Ibid, 30.
[28] Ibid, 32.
[29] Art 31 of the Convention is subject to a 'Resolution relating to incompatible treaty obligations and rights arising from a uniting of States'. It recognised 'the desirability of resolving such questions through a process of consultation and negotiation, [and] recommends that if a uniting of States gives rise to incompatible obligations or rights under treaties, the successor State and the other states parties to the treaties in question make every effort to resolve the matter by mutual agreement'.

The provision is said to reflect international custom but poorly.[30] It may be criticised for a number of reasons. First, the international norm disregarded the distinction between a unification of two states into a new state and the incorporation of one state into another.[31] Secondly, the solution adopted by Article 31 favours a succession of the union for all Member State treaties—unless this conflicts with the object or application of the treaty. This principle rejects a rule of non-succession in situations where the treaty violates the union constitution. The absence of a compromise between (international) continuity and (national) discontinuity marginalises the idea that the union constitutes—theoretically—a new subject of international law.[32] The universal succession principle ignores thus situations where the Members States survive as (limited) subjects of international law.[33] Finally, confining itself to situations in which states unite to form a 'successor state', the provision excludes its application to unions of states. This state-centred focus of Article 31 precluded from the very beginning direct answers to the normative problems of treaty continuity and succession in the European Union.[34] And in the absence of a clear doctrine of functional

---

[30] A Aust, *Modern Treaty Law and Practice* (Cambridge, Cambridge University Press, 2000), 306: 'the Convention is largely an example of the progressive development of international law, rather than a codification of customary law'. For a severe critique of the Convention, see DP O'Connell, 'Reflections on the State Succession Convention' (1979) 39 *Zeitschrift für ausländisches öffentliches Recht und Völkerrecht 725*.

[31] S Oeter, 'German Unification and State Succession' (1991) 51 *Zeitschrift für ausländisches öffentliches Recht und Völkerrecht* 349, 355. In the situation where a state is absorbed by another state, the continuity rule for both states is 'utterly meaningless' (ibid): 'A general rule like that—if existing at all—would enormously hinder states created by a process of unification of previously different states to advance the further process of unification, since the separation of the different territories of the former states in different legal orders would be cemented by the (territorially limited) application of the old treaties.'

[32] It is a rule of customary international law that 'new' international persons are not bound by the 'political treaties' of its predecessors, cf R Jennings and A Watts, *Oppenheim's International Law—Volume I: Peace* (Oxford, Oxford University Press, 2008) 211: 'no succession takes place with regard to rights and duties of the extinct state arising from its purely political treaties'; cf also Aust, above n 30, 307.

[33] On German federalism and foreign affairs, see Schütze, above n 7, 65ff.

[34] The Commentary to the Convention ([1974] *Yearbook of the International Law Commission—Volume II* 162, 253) explained: 'Being concerned only with the uniting of two or more States into one State, association of States having the character of intergovernmental organizations such as, for example, the United Nations . . . fall completely outside the scope of the articles; as do some hybrid unions which may appear to have some analogy with a uniting of States but which do not result in a new State and do not therefore constitute a succession of States. One example of such a hybrid is [the] E[U], as to the precise legal character of which opinions differ. For the present purpose, it suffices to say that, from the point of view of succession in respect of treaties, [the] E[U] appears to keep on the plane of intergovernmental organizations. Thus, [Art 351 TFEU] unmistakably approaches the question of the pre-Union treaties of member States with third countries from the angle of the rules governing the application of successive treaties relating to the same subject matter (article 30 of the Vienna Convention).' HG Schermers, 'Succession of States and International Organizations' (1975) 6 *Netherlands Yearbook of International Law* 103, 111 subsequently criticised the ILC Draft for being 'certainly too black and white a construction'), and found: 'The concept of the fully sovereign State is outdated. States are no longer the only entities which can perform acts in the international community'.

succession for unions of states, international law had to develop alternative legal mechanisms.

B Bridging the Gap: the (limited) Direct Responsibility of Member States

How has international law dealt with the absence of a doctrine of succession for (hybrid) unions of states? How has it bridged the gap between its state-centred ideal and the reality of unions of states? We find an illustration of this problem—as well as a solution—in the relationship between the European Convention of Human Rights and the European Union.[35] The Union is not (yet) a party to the international Convention.[36] The latter, then, cannot formally bind the Union. Nor has the European Convention system found the European Union to have (partly) 'succeeded' its Member States.[37] Could the Member States thus escape their international obligations under the Convention by transferring decision-making powers to the European Union? In order to avoid a normative vacuum, the European Convention system created an alternative mechanism to functional succession. To bridge the normative gap created by the presence of the Union as a new subject of international law, it developed the doctrine of the (limited) direct responsibility of the states for acts of the Union.

[35] For an analysis of the relationship between 1947 GATT and the EC, see R Uerpmann-Wittzack, 'The Constitutional Role of International Law' in A von Bogdandy and J Bast (eds), *Principles of European Constitutional Law* (Oxford, Hart Publishing, 2009) 131, 149: 'Public international law contains rules on the succession of states. Such succession has not taken place, however, with regard to the EC. The rules of state succession are applicable when territorial [!] sovereignty over an area is passed from one state to another. In the case of the EC, this is not what has happened. The EC is not a state. In particular it has not replaced its member States as territorial sovereignties but has just taken over some of their functions. One could ask if such a functional succession leads to the transfer of obligations of international law; however, such a functional succession has thus far been recognised neither by international treaties nor by customary international law as a reason for a legal succession.' The author argues, however, that the EC had been integrated into 1947 GATT by means of an 'implied accession'. For the same conclusion, see A Zimmermann, *Staatennachfolge in völkerrechtlichen Verträge* (Heidelberg, Springer, 2000), 716. See also T Kunuhi, 'State Succession in the Framework of GATT' (1965) 59 *American Journal of International Law* 268.

[36] For a long time, accession to the European Convention was confined to States (*cf* Art 4 of the Statute of the Council of Europe). This has recently changed with the amendment to Art 59 of the Conventions, para 2 of which now states: 'The European Union may accede to this Convention.' From the 'internal' perspective of European law, the new Art 6(2) TEU (after Lisbon) imposes a constitutional obligation to accede: 'The Union shall accede to the European Convention for the Protection of Human Rights and Fundamental Freedoms.'

[37] *Confédération Française Démocratique Du Travail v European Communities* (alternatively, their Member States) (1978) 13 DR 231, 240: 'In so far as the application is directed against the European Communities as such the Commission points out that the European Communities are not a Contracting Party to the European Convention on Human Rights (Art 66 of the Convention). To this extent the consideration of the applicant's complaint lies outside the Commission's jurisdiction ratione personae.'

The birth and evolution of this alternative to a doctrine of functional succession is instructive. Having originally found that the Union constituted an autonomous subject of international law whose actions could not be attributed to its Member States,[38] the European Commission of Human Rights and its Court subsequently changed views. In *M & Co v Germany*,[39] the Commission found that, whereas 'the Convention does not prohibit a Member State from transferring powers to international organisations', 'a transfer of powers does not necessarily exclude a *State's responsibility under the Convention with regard to the exercise of the transferred powers*'.[40] This would not, however, mean that the state was to be held responsible for all actions of the federal Union: 'it would be contrary to the very idea of transferring powers to an international organisation to hold the Member States responsible for examining [possible violations] in each individual case'.[41] What, then, were the conditions for this *limited* state responsibility? Consistent with its chosen emphasis on state responsibility, the Commission would not concentrate on the concrete decision of the Union, but on the state's decision to transfer powers to the Union. This transfer of powers was deemed 'not incompatible with the Convention provided that within that organisation fundamental rights will receive an *equivalent protection*'.[42] Member States would consequently not be responsible for every—compulsory—European Union act that violated the European Convention.[43] In *Bosphorus*,[44] the European Court of Human Rights justified this 'middle ground' position as follows:

---

[38] Ibid. The Commission held that the complaint was 'outside its jurisdiction ratione personae since the [Member] States by taking part in the decision of the Council of the European Communities had not in the circumstances of the instant case exercised their "jurisdiction" within the meaning of Art 1 of the Convention'.

[39] *M & Co v Federal Republic of Germany* (1990) 64 DR 138.

[40] Ibid, 145 (emphasis added).

[41] Ibid, 146.

[42] Ibid, 145 (emphasis added).

[43] The decision thus introduced a distinction between the state execution of compulsory Union acts—for which there would only be limited review—and voluntary or discretionary state acts that would be subject to a full review. In *Matthews v the United Kingdom* (1999) 28 EHRR 361 the European Court of Human Rights rejected to view Council Decision 76/787, [1976] OJ L278 and the 1976 Act concerning elections to the European Parliament as acts of the European Union. In the (correct) view of the Court they 'constituted international agreements which were freely entered into by the United Kingdom'. The Court consequently found that the UK, together with all the other Member States, was fully responsible under Art 1 of the Convention (ibid, para 33). The Court here dealt with European primary law that was 'authored' by the Member States—not the European Union. (On the European law principles governing the authorship of an act, see R Schütze, 'The Morphology of Legislative Powers in the European Community: Legal Instruments and the Federal Division of Powers' (2006) 25 *Yearbook of European law* 91, 98ff.) The same reasoning applies, *mutatis mutandis*, to discretionary national acts. Discretionary national acts are national acts—not Union acts—and therefore subject to a full review; cf *Bosphorus Hava Yollari Turizm ve Ticaret Anonim Sirketi v Ireland* (2006) 42 EHRR 1, paras 148 and 157.

[44] *Bosphorus*, ibid.

The Convention does not, on the one hand, prohibit Contracting Parties from transferring sovereign power to an international (including a supranational) organisation in order to pursue co-operation in certain fields of activity. Moreover, even as the holder of such transferred sovereign power, that organisation is not itself held responsible under the Convention for proceedings before, or decisions of, its organs as long as it is not a Contracting Party. On the other hand, it has also been accepted that a Contracting Party is responsible under Article 1 of the Convention for all acts and omissions of its organs regardless of whether the act or omission in question was a consequence of domestic law or of the necessity to comply with international legal obligations. Article 1 makes no distinction as to the type of rule or measure concerned and does not exclude any part of a Contracting Party's 'jurisdiction' from scrutiny under the Convention.

In reconciling both these positions and thereby establishing the extent to which a State's action can be justified by its compliance with obligations flowing from its membership of an international organisation to which it has transferred part of its sovereignty, the Court has recognised that absolving Contracting States completely from their Convention responsibility in the areas covered by such a transfer would be incompatible with the purpose and object of the Convention... In the Court's view, State action taken in compliance with such legal obligations is justified as long as the relevant organisation is considered to protect fundamental rights, as regards both the substantive guarantees offered and the mechanisms controlling their observance, in a manner which can be considered at least equivalent to that for which the Convention provides. By 'equivalent' the Court means 'comparable'; any requirement that the organisation's protection be 'identical' could run counter to the interest of international co-operation pursued.[45]

For acts of a 'supranational' Union, the Court would thus not conduct a 'normal' review.[46] Where the Union protected human rights in an 'equivalent' manner to that of the Convention, the European Court of Human Rights would operate a 'presumption' that the states had not violated the Convention by transferring powers to the European Union. This presumption translates into a lower review standard for acts adopted

---

[45] Ibid, paras 152–55 (emphasis added).

[46] For a criticism of this point, see Joint Concurring Opinion of Judges Rozakis et al (ibid, paras 3–4): 'The right of individual application is one of the basic obligations assumed by the States on ratifying the Convention. It is therefore difficult to accept that they should have been able to reduce the effectiveness of this right for persons within their jurisdiction on the ground that they have transferred certain powers to the European [Union]. For the Court to leave to the [Union's] judicial system the task of ensuring "equivalent protection, without retaining a means of verifying on a case-by-case basis that that protection is indeed "equivalent", would be tantamount to consenting tacitly to substitution, in the field of [European] law, of Convention standards by a [Union] standard which might be inspired by Convention standards but whose equivalence with the latter would no longer be subject to authorised scrutiny . . . In spite of its relatively undefined nature, the criterion "manifestly deficient" appears to establish a relatively low threshold, which is in marked contrast to the supervision generally carried out under the European Convention on Human Rights.'

by the European Union,[47] since the presumption of equivalent protection could only be rebutted where the actual treatment of human rights within the Union was 'manifestly deficient'.[48] The lower review standard was designed to allow for European integration and represented a compromise between two extremes: no control through the application of the clean slate doctrine and full control through a doctrine of international succession. This compromise was 'the price for Strasbourg achieving a level of control over the EU, while respecting its autonomy as a separate legal order'.[49]

III   INTERNAL PERSPECTIVE: FUNCTIONAL
SUCCESSION IN EUROPEAN LAW

When the European Union came into existence in 1958, it had not been born into a normative vacuum. The six Member States of the Union were extensively linked with each other and with third states in a complex network of bilateral and multilateral treaties. In what ways would the emergence of the European Union affect these contractual connections? From the beginning, the European legal order provided a mechanism that would ensure the continuity of prior Member States' agreements. These international agreements could be enforced against European Union law, but the Member States would be under a European Union legal obligation to seek amendment or denunciation (A). The constitutional guarantee of (limited) treaty continuity would—subsequently—be complemented by a European doctrine of functional succession under which the Union considers itself bound by international treaties of its Member States (B).

(A)   Survival without Succession: Article 351 and prior Member State Agreements

(i)   The 'Supremacy' of International Treaties: Internal and External Limits

The European legal order confirmed from the very beginning the continuity of prior contractual engagements of its Member States with third countries:

---

[47] J Callewaert, 'The European Convention on Human Rights and European Union Law: A Long Way to Harmony' (2009) *European Human Rights Law Review* 768, 773: 'through the *Bosphorus*-presumption and its tolerance as regards "non manifest" deficiencies, the protection of fundamental rights under [European] law is policed with less strictness than under the Convention'.

[48] *Bosphorus*, above n 43, paras 156–57.

[49] S Douglas-Scott, 'A Tale of Two Courts: Luxembourg, Strasbourg and the Growing European Human Rights Acquis' (2006) 43 *Common Market Law Review* 629, 639.

The rights and obligations arising from agreements concluded before the entry into force of this Treaty between one or more Member States on the one hand, and one or more third countries on the other, shall not be affected by the provisions of this Treaty.[50]

The provision went beyond the ordinary international law principle of *res inter alios acta*. It not only acknowledged the continued normative force of Member States' prior international treaty obligations in the European legal order, but also codified their 'precedence' over (subsequently) conflicting European law.[51] The Union legal order would 'suspend' its own law—even primary law—to allow for the implementation of these international agreements.

Would this constitutionally guaranteed continuity apply to all international treaties concluded by the Member States prior to the Union; or was there a category of agreements beyond the solution suggested by Article 351 TFEU? The Court has answered this question in the past: the provision 'is of general scope and applies to any international agreement, irrespective of subject matter'.[52] But would there be internal or external limits to the 'precedence' of prior international treaties? The Court clarified that there existed internal limits to the protective provision:

[T]he terms 'rights and obligations' in [Article 351] refer, as regards the 'rights', to the rights of third countries and, as regards the 'obligations', to the obligations of Member States and that, by virtue of the principles of international law, by assuming a new obligation which is incompatible with rights held under a prior treaty, a State *ipso facto* gives up the exercise of these rights to the extent necessary for the performance of its new obligation . . . In fact, in matters governed by the [European] Treat[ies], th[ese] Treat[ies] take precedence over agreements concluded between Member States before its entry into force[.][53]

Teleologically, Article 351(1) would thus only allow Member States to implement their obligations towards third states.[54] Member States could

---

[50] Art 234 EEC. The Amsterdam Treaty amended the provision textually to include 'accessions' to the Union (*cf* Art 307 EC). The Lisbon Treaty has adjusted the wording to refer to the TEU and the TFEU. The new vessel for the old Art 234 EEC is now Art 351 TFEU. For an analysis of this provision in Europe's 'constitutional order of states', see also J Heliskoski, Chapter 28 below.

[51] K Lenaerts and P van Nuffel, *Constitutional Law of the European Union* (London, Sweet & Maxwell, 2003) 751. The concept of 'precedence' or 'supremacy' is perhaps not the best concept to capture the relationship, for international agreements of the Member States do not form part of the European legal order.

[52] Case C-466/98, *Commission v United Kingdom* [2002] ECR I-9427, para 23.

[53] Case 10/61, *Commission v Italy* [1962] ECR 1, 10–11.

[54] What happens when a former 'third' state becomes a member of the European Union? This occurred in Case C 3/91, *Exportur SA v LOR SA and Confiserie du Tech SA* [1992] ECR I-5529, where the ECJ had to deal with a bilateral convention between France and Spain. The Court emphasised, as a preliminary point, that the accession of Spain to the EU had changed its perspective: 'it should be observed that the national court rightly considered that the provisions of a convention concluded after 1 January 1958 by a Member

not rely on the norm to enforce their rights; nor could they rely on the provision to fulfil their international obligations *inter se*. However, the Union would generally acknowledge the 'supremacy' of prior international obligations of the Member States over conflicting European law. Article 351 TFEU 'would not achieve its purpose if it did not imply a duty on the part of the institutions of the [Union] *not to impede the performance of the obligations of Member States which stem from a prior agreement*'.[55] This was a severe incursion into the integrity and autonomy of the European legal order, which had to be interpreted restrictively. The Court has thus insisted that 'when an international agreement allows, but does not require, a Member State to adopt a measure which appears to be contrary to European law, the Member State must refrain from adopting such a measure'.[56]

These internal limitations are complemented by external limitations. The Court recently clarified their existence in *Kadi*.[57] While admitting that Article 351 would principally justify derogations from primary Union law, the Court insisted that the provision 'cannot, however, be understood to authorize any derogation from the principles of liberty, democracy and respect for human rights and fundamental freedoms enshrined in [ex] Article 6(1) EU as a foundation of the Union'.[58] In the opinion of the Court, 'Article [351 TFEU] may in no circumstances permit any challenge to the principles that form part of the very foundations of the [Union] legal order'.[59] The Union's constitutional core constitutes a limit to the supremacy of prior international treaties concluded by the Member States.

State with another State could not, from the accession of the latter State to the [Union], apply in the relations between those States if they were found to be contrary to the rules of the Treaty. It is therefore necessary to determine whether the provisions of the Franco-Spanish Convention are compatible with the rules of the Treaty on the free movement of goods': ibid, para 8 (emphasis added). The bilateral convention had become an *inter se* agreement and was, consequently, fully assimilated to the regime applicable to national unilateral measures: ibid, para 39.

[55] Case 812/79, *Attorney General v Juan C. Burgoa* [1980] ECR 2787, para 9 (emphasis added). This was confirmed in Case C-158/91, *Criminal Proceedings against Jean-Claude Levy* [1993] ECR I-4287, para 22 (emphasis added): 'In view of the foregoing considerations, the answer to the question submitted for a preliminary ruling must be that the national court is under an obligation to ensure [that the relevant European legislation] . . . is fully complied with by refraining from applying any conflicting provision of national legislation, unless the application of such a provision is necessary in order to ensure the performance by the Member State concerned of obligations arising under an agreement concluded with non-member countries prior to the entry into force of the EEC Treaty.'

[56] Case C-324/93, *The Queen v Secretary of State for Home Department, ex-parte Evans Medical Ltd and Macfarlan Smith Ltd* [1995] ECR I-563, para 32.

[57] Case 402/05P *Kadi and Al Barakaat International Foundation/Council and Commission* [2008] ECR I-6351. The facts of the case will be discussed below (below n 85).

[58] Ibid, para 303. Art 6(1) EU (before Lisbon) stated: 'The Union is founded on the principles of liberty, democracy, respect for human rights and fundamental freedoms, and the rule of law, principles which are common to the Member States.'

[59] Ibid, para 304.

This external limit to the provision protects the constitutional identity of the European Union from an—unjustified—loyalty to the international obligations of its Member States. Where the very foundations of the Union would be compromised, the latter is not obliged to bow in self-denial towards a—still illiberal—international legal order. The Union is constitutionally entitled to sets its foundational values above the Member States' international obligations.

(ii) Temporal Limits to Treaty Continuity: Article 351 (2) TFEU

Within the substantive limits of Article 351(1), Member States' prior international obligations may be enforced against European Union law. Yet this European right to enforce international law is balanced by a European duty imposed by paragraph 2. The Member States of the Union must try to eliminate normative incompatibilities between their international agreements and European law: 'To the extent that such agreements are not compatible with the Treaties, the Member States or States concerned shall take all appropriate steps to eliminate the incompatibilities established.'[60] Is Article 351(2) stronger than a 'best effort' obligation?[61] Could the procedural obligation solidify into an obligation of result? Was there, in other words, a temporal deadline that Member States could not miss? And from what moment would the duty to remove the normative incompatibilities begin?

The closest the European Court has come to requiring a solid result is *Commission v Portugal*.[62] Portugal had claimed that Article 351(2) would '*not* impose the obligation to achieve a specific result, in the sense of requiring them, regardless of the legal consequences and political price, to eliminate the incompatibility'.[63] The constitutional duty to denounce an agreement should arise only 'exceptionally and in extreme situations', 'since denunciation is a measure which in principle gives rise to international liability'.[64] The Court disagreed. No restrictive interpretation of the procedural duty imposed by Article 351(2) TFEU was in order, since 'the balance between the foreign-policy interests of a Member State and the [Union] interest is already incorporated in [Article 351]'.[65] True, the Member States had a choice as to which steps to take, but they were 'nevertheless under an obligation to eliminate any incompatibilities existing between a pre-[Union] convention and the [European] Treat[ies]'. When

---

[60] Art 351(2) TFEU.
[61] M Cremona, 'Defending the Community Interest: the Duties of Cooperation and Compliance' in M Cremona and B de Witte (eds), *EU Foreign Relations Law—Constitutional Fundamentals* (Oxford, Hart Publishing, 2008) 133.
[62] Case C-84/98, *Commission v Portugal* [2000] ECR I-5215.
[63] Ibid, para 30 (emphasis added).
[64] Ibid, para 33.
[65] Ibid, para 59.

'a Member State encounters difficulties which make adjustment of an agreement impossible, an obligation to denounce that agreement cannot therefore be excluded'.[66] This Union-friendly construction of Article 351 gave some teeth to the procedural obligation in paragraph 2.[67]

But when would the European obligation to renegotiate or renounce start? The Court gave a—strong and surprising—answer in a series of cases dealing with bilateral investment treaties of the Member States.[68] The Commission had claimed that the international investment treaties had to be denounced or renegotiated—even if these treaties were not yet incompatible with existing EU legislation. The Member State(s) responded that there were no actual incompatibilities,[69] to which the Commission replied that due to Article 351 the effectiveness of Union legislation was impaired, because:

> the period of time required for the denunciation or renegotiation of the agreements at issue would have the consequence that the [Member States] would be obliged, in the intervening period, under international law, to continue to apply the agreements in question.[70]

This was a radical argument that turned Article 351 against itself: the Member States would be under an immediate obligation to renegotiate or renounce their prior international agreements, because the (temporary) 'supremacy' granted to them under the provision may compromise the uniform application of European Union law.

The Court shared this new vision. The obligation to denounce or renegotiate would not require an actual conflict between the international treaty and European Union legislation. International agreements that did 'not contain a provision allowing the Member State concerned to exercise

---

[66] Ibid, para 58. For an elaborate discussion of when denunciation may be necessary see P Koutrakos, *EU International Relations Law* (Oxford, Hart Publishing, 2006) 313–16.

[67] J Klabbers, 'Moribund on the Fourth of July? The Court of Justice on Prior Agreements of the Member States' (2001) 26 *European Law Review* 187, 197.

[68] Cf Cases C-205/06 *Commission v Austria* [2009] ECR I-1301, C-249/06, *Commission v Sweden* [2009] ECR 1335 and C-118/07 *Commission v Finland,* [2009] ECR I-000. For two recent analyses of these judgments, see P Koutrakos, 'Annotation on Case C-205/06, *Commission v Austria* and Case C-249/06, *Commission v Sweden*' (2009) 46 *Common Market Law Review* 2059, as well as E Denza, 'Bilateral Investment Treaties and EU Rules on Free Transfer: Comments on *Commission v Austria, Commission v Sweden and Commission v Finland*' [2010] *European Law Review* 263. The subsequent analysis concentrates on the Court's judgment in *Commission v Sweden*.

[69] Ibid, para 18: 'The situation envisaged in the second paragraph of [Art 351 TFEU] will therefore arise only following the actual adoption of the measures authorised by the relevant provisions and in circumstances where mechanisms derived from international law, and designed to remedy an incompatibility in a given case, do not exist or are inadequate. Only then may the Commission commence an action based on infringement of the second paragraph of [Art 351 TFEU], by relying on an actual restrictive measure, the genuine conflict between that measure and the agreement at issue, and the measures which may or may not have been adopted in order to bring an end to that conflict.'

[70] Ibid, para 16.

its rights and to fulfil its obligations as a member of the [Union]' would, as such, constitute an obstacle to the effectiveness of European law.[71] In the absence of a 'disconnection clause' giving preference to EU law, the Court found that 'the possibility of relying on other mechanisms offered by international law' was 'too uncertain in its effects' to guarantee the full effectiveness of European law.[72] If the reasoning were exported into other areas of European law, this—radically novel—interpretation of Article 351(2) would henceforth require the Member States to denounce or renegotiate all their prior international agreements that fall within the scope of European law. For it is no longer actual conflict with existing European legislation that triggers the obligations under paragraph 2; any international agreement falling within the competence of the Union would be incompatible with the effectiveness of (subsequently adopted) European legislation.

(B) Survival with Succession: The Theory and Practice of Functional Succession

In the absence of a doctrine of succession in international law, only treaties to which it is a formal party will internationally bind the Union. But has the Union considered itself materially bound by the international treaties of its Member States? The wording of Article 351 TFEU did not—unlike Article 106 Euratom[73]— envisage the (consented) succession of the Union to (prior) international agreements of its Member States.[74] And in *Burgoa*, the Court expressly rejected the argument that the provision could be the

---

[71] Ibid, para 38.

[72] Ibid, para 41. The Court's 'cursory approach' to the international law principle *clausula rebus sic stantibus* has been criticised (Koutrakos, above n 68, 2070). However, from the Court's point of view the European legal order constitutes a 'constitutional' or 'domestic' legal order and the application of the rebus sic stantibus principle may indeed be doubtful (*cf* Arts 27 and 46 of the 1969 Vienna Convention of the Law of Treaties). On this point, see also J Klabbers, *An Introduction to International Institutional Law* (Cambridge, Cambridge University Press, 2009) 103.

[73] Art 106 Euratom reads: 'Member States which, before the entry into force of this Treaty, have concluded agreements with third States providing for cooperation in the field of nuclear energy shall be required to undertake jointly with the Commission the necessary negotiations with these third States in order to ensure that the rights and obligations arising out of such agreements shall as far as possible be assumed by the [Union]. Any new agreement ensuing from such negotiations shall require the consent of the Member State or States signatory to the agreements referred to above and the approval of the Council, which shall act by a qualified majority.'

[74] KM Meessen, 'The Application of Rules of Public International Law within Community Law' (1976) 13 *Common Market Law Review* 485: 'The provision that treaty commitments of the Member States vis-à-vis third states "shall not be affected" excluded any attempt on the part of the [Union] to have the rules of state succession concerning unions of states applied to its own formation. The non-application of these rules must be regarded as operating in two directions: the treaty commitments of the Member States are neither cancelled nor are they automatically transferred to the [Union].'

direct source for a constitutional duty to assume these obligations: Article 351 'is directed *only* to permitting the Member State concerned to perform its obligations under the prior agreement and does not bind the [Union] as regards the non-member country in question'.[75]

The self-binding of the Union would therefore have to find a different rationale. The rationale was borrowed from the idea of 'state succession'. Since the Union is not a 'state', the concept had to be applied analogously. The doctrine of Union succession was a doctrine of functional succession: 'we are dealing with a succession that is neither territorial nor general, but a succession of a functional and limited kind'.[76] Union succession would not be based on a transfer of territory, but on a transfer of functions.[77] The 'transfer of powers' from the Member States to the Union would trigger 'a substitution or succession in the meaning of international law'. '[B]y taking over, by virtue of the Treaties, certain competences and certain powers previously exercised by the Member States, the [Union] equally had to assume the international obligations that controlled the exercise of these competences and powers[.]'[78] But would the Union automatically assume all international obligations of its Member States within the scope of the powers transferred to it? What were—from the European legal order's perspective—the conditions for a functional succession of the Union to Member States' international treaties? And what would happen if this European perspective did not match the perspective of international law?

---

[75] Case 812/79 *Attorney General v Juan C Burgoa* [1980] ECR 2787, para 9 (emphasis added).

[76] P Pescatore, 'La Cour de Justice des Communautés Européennes et la Convention Européenne des Droits de l'Homme' in F Matscher and H Petzold (eds), *Protecting Human Rights: The European Dimension* (Cologne, Heymann, 1988) 441, 450 (my translation).

[77] On the application of the idea of 'succession' see Petersmann, EU 'Artikel 234 EEC' in H von der Groeben, H von Boeckh, J Thiesing (eds), *Kommentar zum EWG-Vertrag* (Baden-Baden, Nomos, 1974) 736, 745–46 (rn 8): 'In Übereinstimmung mit dem Rechtsgutachten des IGH betr. "Reparations for Injuries Suffered in the Services of the UN" (ICJ Rep 1949, ss 174ff) kann die (analoge) Anwendbarkeit allgemeinen Völkerrechts auf eine mit eigener Völkerrechtspersönlichkeit ausgestattete Internationale Organisation wie die EWG (vgl Art 210 EWGV) nur funktionell vom Gründungsvertrag der Organisation sowie von den Erfordernissen der völkerrechtlichen Grundsätze des Vertrauensschutzes und der Rechtssicherheit her ermittelt werden . . . [Es] liegt eine analoge Anwendung der erwähnten Staatensukzessionsregeln dahingehend nahe, da gemeinschaftsrechtlich bewirkte Kompetenzverschiebungen innerhalb präföderaler Wirtschaftsgemeinschaften ähnlich wie bundesstaatliche Zuständigkeitsverschiebungen vom internationalen Vertragspartner hinzunehmen sind und den völkerrechtlichen Erfüllungsanspruch des internationalen Vertragspartners ändern können.'

[78] P Pescatore, *L'ordre juridique des Communautés Européennes* (Liège, Presse universitaire de Liège, 1975) 147–48: 'un effet de substitution ou de succession au sens du droit international: en assumant, en vertu des traités, certaines compétences et certains pouvoirs précédemment exercés par les Etats membres, la Communauté a dû reprendre, également, les obligations internationales qui réglaient l'exercice de ces compétences et pouvoir' (my translation).

(i) The European Court and the Practice of Union Succession

When and where would the Union consider itself the legal successor to its
Member States' international treaties? The European Court announced the
European doctrine of succession in relation to the General Agreement on
Tariffs and Trade (1947) in *International Fruit*.[79] Formally, the Union was
not a party to the international treaty, but Dutch traders had nonetheless
challenged the legality of various European measures restricting the
importation of apples from third countries as contrary to Article XI of
GATT. Confirming that the legality of a Union measure may only be
reviewed against an international treaty binding the Union,[80] the Court
moved to the famous passage that would create the doctrine of Union
succession:

> The [Union] has assumed the functions inherent in the tariff and trade policy,
> progressively during the transitional period and in their entirety on the expiry
> of that period, by virtue of [Articles 206 and 207 TFEU]. *By conferring those
> powers on the [Union], the Member States showed their wish to bind it by
> the obligations entered into under the General Agreement.* Since the entry
> into force of the EEC Treaty and, more particularly, since the setting up of
> the common external tariff, the transfer of powers which has occurred in the
> relations between Member States and the [Union] has been put into concrete
> form in different ways within the framework of the General Agreement and
> has been recognized by the other contracting parties . . . *It therefore appears
> that, insofar as under the [European] Treat[ies] the [Union] has assumed the
> powers previously exercised by Member States in the area covered by the
> General Agreement, the provisions of that agreement have the effect of binding
> the [Union].*[81]

Functional succession seemed to emanate from the exclusive nature of
the Union's powers under the Common Commercial Policy (CCP).[82] This
ingenious solution cut the Gordian knot in the entangled relationship
between the GATT, the Union and the Member States: for if the Union
had succeeded the Member States in relation to GATT, it could centrally
determine the extent to which GATT obligations affected European Union
law. The succession doctrine seemed to have become a dead letter, when

---

[79] Joined Cases 21–24/72, *International Fruit Company NV v Produktschap voor
Groenten en Fruit* [1972] ECR 1219.

[80] Ibid, para 7.

[81] Ibid, paras 14–16 and 18 (emphasis added). In Joined Cases 267, 268 and 269/81,
*Amministrazione delle Finanze dello Stato v Societa Petrolifera Italiana SpA (SPI) and SpA
Michelin Italiana (SAMI)* [1983] ECR 801, para 17, the ECJ clarified that, following the
introduction of the common customs tariff on 1 July 1968, the Union had 'assumed its full
powers in relation to the sphere covered by GATT'.

[82] The Court of Justice had not yet 'officially' declared the CCP to be an exclusive competence of the Union. However, the doctrine of succession was a precursor to that development:
see R Schütze, 'Dual Federalism Constitutionalised: the Emergence of Exclusive Competences
in the EC Legal Order' (2007) 32 *European Law Review* 3, 6–10.

the Union became a formal member of the World Trade Organization. For more than three decades, the succession doctrine remained quiet. (Emblematically, the Court passed silently over the succession theory in the context of the European Convention of Human Rights.[83])

In the last decade the succession doctrine has experienced a constitutional revival in the context of the United Nations Charter. Formally, the European Union is not a member of the United Nations and has traditionally considered itself not materially bound by its resolutions.[84] The relationship was 'unsettled' by the General Court in *Kadi*.[85] The applicants had challenged the legality of European Union regulations, inter alia, on the grounds that their fundamental Union rights had been violated. The contested European regulations had reproduced the relevant UN Security Council Resolutions.[86] The Union institutions, having intervened in the proceedings, argued that 'the Charter of the United Nations prevail[s] over every other obligation of international, [European] or domestic law' to the effect that Union human rights standards should be inoperative.[87] How did the General Court position the European Union legal order vis-à-vis the United Nations? While admitting that under public international law the Union was not formally bound by UN law, the Court still found that 'the [Union] *must be considered to be bound* by the obligations under the Charter of the United Nations in the same way as its Member States, *by virtue of the Treaty establishing it*'.[88] How did the Court come to this novel interpretation? The Court's reasoning ran as follows:

> By concluding a treaty between them [the Member States] could not transfer to the [Union] more powers than they possessed or withdraw from their obligations to third countries under that Charter. On the contrary, their desire to fulfil their obligations under that Charter follows from the very provisions

[83] For an analysis of the European legal order's past perspective on its (ambivalent) relationship with the European Convention of Human Rights, see R Schütze, 'EC Law and International Agreements of the Member States—An Ambivalent Relationship?' (2006–07) 9 *Cambridge Yearbook of European Legal Studies* 387, 399ff. This relationship between the European Union and the European Convention will change once the former accedes to the latter.

[84] According to Art 4 UN Charter, only states can become full members. For the 'traditional' approach of the European legal order to the UN legal order, see Case C-84/95 *Bosphorus Hava Yollari Turizm ve Ticaret Anonim Sirketi v Minister for Transport et al* [1996] ECR 3953 as discussed in R Schütze, 'On Middle Ground: The European Community and Public International Law', EUI Working Paper 2007/13, 16ff.

[85] Case T-315/01 *Kadi v Council and Commission* [2005] ECR II-3649.

[86] The challenge principally concerned Council Reg (EC) 881/2002 imposing certain specific restrictive measures directed against certain persons and entities associated with Osama bin Laden, the Al-Qaeda network and the Taliban, and repealing Reg 467/2001, [2002] OJ L139/9. The Regulation aimed to implement UN Security Council Resolution 1390 (2002) laying down the measures to be directed against Usama bin Laden, members of the Al-Qaeda network and the Taliban and other associated individuals, groups, undertakings and entities.

[87] *Kadi*, n 85, para 177.

[88] Ibid, para 193 (emphasis added).

of the Treaty [on the Functioning of the European Union] and is made clear in particular by [Article 347] and the first paragraph of [Article 351] . . .

By conferring those powers on the [Union], the Member States demonstrated their will to bind it by the obligations entered into by them under the Charter of the United Nations. Since the entry into force of the Treaty establishing the European Economic Community, the transfer of powers which has occurred in the relations between Member States and the [Union] has been put into concrete form in different ways within the framework of the performance of their obligations under the Charter of the United Nations . . . *It therefore appears that, insofar as under the [European] Treat[ies] the [Union] has assumed powers previously exercised by Member States in the area governed by the Charter of the United Nations, the provisions of that Charter have the effect of binding the [Union][.][89]*

This view proposed a radical change in the relationship between the United Nations and the European Union legal order. The Court acknowledged a positive obligation on the Union to implement UN Security Council Resolutions by invoking the functional succession doctrine. The doctrine was thus revived and extended 'by analogy' to the United Nations Charter.[90] This extension was highly debatable.[91] The point was not clarified by the (appeal) judgment delivered by the European Court of Justice.[92] The Court passed silently over the succession analogy—a silence that was a result of judicial economy. For the Court found, as we saw in Section III.A(i), that even if functional succession had taken place 'the obligations imposed by an international agreement cannot have the effect of prejudicing the constitutional principles of the [European] Treat[ies], which include the principle that all [Union] acts must respect fundamental rights'.[93] The recognition of this external limit made an analysis of the doctrine of functional succession unnecessary.

Thankfully, the Court came back to the succession doctrine and clarified its contours in subsequent jurisprudence. Three principles seem to govern functional succession. First, for the succession doctrine to come into operation all the Member States must be parties to an international treaty.[94] Second, the fact that the international treaty is concluded after

---

[89] Ibid, paras 195–203 (references omitted, emphasis added).

[90] The 'analogy' is emphatically underlined in paras 195, 196, 200, 201 and 203.

[91] For a critical analysis of the functional succession idea in the context of economic sanctions, see M Nettesheim, 'UN Sanctions against Individuals—A Challenge to the Architecture of European Union Governance' (2007) 44 *Common Market Law Review* 567, 585. For the opposite view, see P Eeckhout, *External Relations of the European Union* (Oxford, Oxford University Press, 2004) 438.

[92] *Kadi and Al Barakaat International Foundation*, above n 57.

[93] Ibid, para 181. The author had made this point prior to the Court's judgment in Schütze, above n 84, 26–27.

[94] Case C-188/07 *Commune de Mesquer v Total* [2008] ECR I-4501, para 85, 'In the first place, the [Union] has not acceded to those international instruments and, in the second place, it cannot be regarded as having taken place of its Member States, if only because not all of them are parties to those conventions'. By insisting that all Member States be

1958 seems not to be relevant.[95] Third, the Union would not succeed to all international treaties concluded by all Member States that fell within the sphere of its transferred powers. This was clarified in *Intertanko*.[96] The case concerned the question whether the Union was bound by the 'International Convention for the Prevention of Pollution from Ships' (Marpol 73/78)—an international treaty to which all Member States are parties. Was this a sufficient condition for a functional succession? The Advocate General rejected this view by placing *International Fruit* into its constitutional context:

> GATT is an agreement of the Member States which was already in existence when the [Union] was established, but at the time of the judgment in *International Fruit Company* the relevant trade-policy powers had been *transferred in their entirety to the [Union]*. Therefore, the [Union] alone was able to act within the areas covered by GATT. Accordingly, and with the agreement of both the Member States and the other parties to GATT, the [Union] acted on behalf of the Member States within the framework of GATT. Unlike in the case of trade policy, *in the present case the [Union] has no exclusive competence under the Treaty* to lay down rules on the discharge by ships of pollutants into the sea. This competence—either under [Article 100 (2) TFEU] concerning transport policy or [Article 192 TFEU] concerning policy on the environment—is instead competitive in nature, that is to say, it remains with the Member States so long and insofar as it is not exercised by the [Union].[97]

The Court followed this view. '[I]n the absence of a *full transfer of the powers* previously exercised by the Member States to the [Union], the latter cannot, simply because all those States are parties to Marpol 73/78, be bound by the rules set out therein, which it has not itself approved.'[98] Succession thus required the 'full transfer of the powers' to the Union. But what did this mean? Would the European succession doctrine be confined to the sphere of the Union's *constitutionally* exclusive powers? Or did the doctrine extend to situations of *legislative* exclusivity, that is, situations whereby the subsequent exercise of an internal competence led to the creation of an exclusive implied external power? The Court has shown a preference for the wider version of the succession doctrine in *Bogiatzi*—a case involving the Warsaw Convention for the Unification of

---

parties to an international agreement before functional succession occurs, the European legal order avoids the—strange—rule within Art 31 of the 1978 Convention on State Succession according to which the Union is bound but only in relation to the territory of the pervious contracting parties.

[95] Case 308/06 *Intertanko and others v Secretary of State for Transport* [2008] ECR I-4057.
[96] Ibid.
[97] Opinion of Advocate General Kokott in *Intertanko*, paras 41–42 (emphasis added).
[98] *Intertanko*, above n 95, para 49 (emphasis added). See also the earlier Case C-379/92, *Criminal proceedings against Peralta* [1994] ECR I-3453, para 16.

Certain Rules Relating to International Carriage by Air.[99] The Convention fell within the Union's transport policy—a shared competence. Yet this was not a sufficient reason for the Court to reject the idea of a functional succession by the Union to the Convention. Indeed, it considered whether the Union—through the adoption of three regulations based on Article 100 (2) TFEU—had 'assumed the powers previously exercised by the Member States in the field to which the Warsaw Convention applies'.[100] Legislative exclusivity was thus seen as capable of triggering functional succession. However, for a 'full transfer' to take place, European legislation would need to pre-empt the Member States from the substantive scope of the international treaty completely.

In conclusion, the European doctrine of functional succession considers the European Union bound by international treaties to which it is not formally a party if all the Member States are contracting parties and the treaty falls within an area in which the Union has assumed 'exclusive' responsibility.[101] The Court has been willing to adopt a wide version of functional succession by extending the succession doctrine to legislative exclusivity. (This broadens the scope of international obligations to which the Union may succeed—even if legislative exclusivity is, generally, in decline in the European legal order.[102]) This extension of the succession doctrine to legislative pre-emption has constitutionally curious consequences. If the adoption of European legislation leads to functional succession, the international agreement materially binding the Union will have a higher hierarchical status than ordinary legislation.[103] The European legislator might thus be bound and limited by an international agreement to which it had never given its consent, and whose elevated rank would—theoretically—prevent it overruling its content subsequently. This undemocratic consequence should entice the Court to reconsider its jurisprudence in the future.

---

[99] Case C-301/08, *Bogiatzi v Deutscher Luftpool and others* [2009] ECR I-10185.
[100] Ibid, paras 27–33.
[101] In *Intertanko*, above n 95, Advocate General Kokott argued that the exclusivity of the Union competence is not a sufficient condition (paras 43–44), 'Irrespective of whether or not the [Union's] competence is now exclusive, there must also be doubts as to whether such an assumption of powers resulting from the exercise of competence is sufficient as a basis on which to conclude that the Member States' obligations under international law are binding on the [Union]. In any event, the assumption of trade-policy powers, to which GATT related, was laid down expressly in the Treaty . . . Furthermore, it has not been submitted that the [Union] acted as the successor to the Member States in connection with Marpol 73/78 or that such action was agreed to by the other parties, as in the case of GATT.' The Advocate General confirmed her views in Case 533/08 *TNT Express Nederland BV v AXA Versicherung AG* [2010] ECR I-000.
[102] For an analysis of this decline, see R Schütze, *From Dual to Cooperative Federalism: The Changing Structure of European Law* (Oxford, Oxford University Press, 2009) ch 4.
[103] Cf Case 61/94 *Commission v Germany (IDA)* [1996] ECR 3989, para 52: 'primacy of international agreements concluded by the [Union] over provisions of secondary legislation'.

(ii)   Bridging the Gap: The Member States as 'Trustees' of the Union

In the absence of an international doctrine of functional succession, international law continues to view the Member States as sovereign subjects bound by the treaties concluded with third states.[104] By contrast, European Union law suggests that whenever the Union assumes exclusive responsibility for an area the Union will be bound by the international agreement—if all the Member States are parties—by means of the European doctrine of functional succession. The perspectives of international and European law thus diverge. This divergence creates a normative incommensurability: while international law insists on the Member States as—exclusive—parties to an international treaty, European law insists that solely the European Union is entitled to (re)negotiate and (re)conclude the agreement. We saw above how international law may 'bridge' this normative gap: it disregards the internal distribution of power between the Union and the Member States by insisting that the Member States have remained—within the limits of the 'equivalence doctrine'—directly responsible subjects of international law.

How has European law bridged the gap between the Union's internal power and its international inability to conclude an agreement? The European constitutional answer is the mechanism of the Member States acting as 'trustees' of the Union.[105] In parallel to situations where the Union could not exercise its exclusive competences, because the European legislator was internally unable to act,[106] the trustees doctrine has been applied to situations where the Union cannot act externally because it is not allow to conclude an international treaty. The application of the trustees doctrine to this situation is a result of the state-centred structure of international law.[107] Where the Union is—internationally—prevented from exercising its exclusive competences, it will thus have to authorise its Member States to conclude or amend an international treaty on its behalf. An illustration of this international 'inability' can be found in the structure of the ILO. Because membership of the ILO is limited to states,[108] the European Union will be unable to conclude any of the ILO's international conventions—even if they fall within its (subsequently) exclusive external competence. To bridge this legal handicap, the European

---

[104] See above, Section II.B.

[105] For an extensive discussion of the doctrine to the context of the external relations of the European Union, see M Cremona, below Chapter 23.

[106] Case 804/79 *Commission v United Kingdom* [1981] ECR 1045. For a discussion of this case, see R Schütze, *From Dual to Cooperative Federalism: The Changing Structure of European Law* (Oxford, Oxford University Press, 2009) 179ff.

[107] Ibid, para 37: 'In this case, cooperation between the [Union] and the Member States is all the more necessary in view of the fact that the former cannot, as international law stands at present, itself conclude an ILO Convention and must do so through the medium of the Member States.'

[108] Art 1 (2) of the ILO Constitution.

legal order insists that the external competence of the Union 'be exercised through the medium of the Member States acting jointly in the [Union's] interest'.[109] The Court thereby protects the Union interest through a variety of constitutional duties.[110]

IV CONCLUSION: FUNCTIONAL SUCCESSION AND THE EUROPEAN UNION

The problem of succession is particularly crucial in transformation periods of international society.[111] It was thus hotly debated during decolonisation in the 1960s[112] and the dissolution of the Eastern bloc in the 1990s. Sadly, the international law of succession has not (yet) paid much attention to a great transformation of international law: the rise of international co-operation and (inter)national unions. One such union is the European Union, and this chapter has tried to investigate the solutions offered by international and European law with regard to treaty continuity and succession. The following conclusions have been reached.

First, international law is still struggling with 'compound' subjects like unions of states. This is reflected in the unclear principles governing treaty continuity and succession within federal unions. International practice is mixed, and the 1978 Vienna Convention on Succession of States in respect of Treaties is not very helpful. Being confined to the uniting of states into a successor state, the Convention not only falls victim to the state-centricity of classic international law; the codification has widely been regarded as imperfect. Worst of all, the rule adopted in Article 31 of the Convention ignores—even for federal states—that the Member States may survive as (independent) subjects of international law with (limited) treaty powers.

Secondly, in the absence of general guidelines on functional succession within unions of states, alternative mechanisms were developed in specific contexts. Thus, when the European Convention system had to determine its relationship to the European Union it rejected the doctrine of functional succession and developed its own solution. The European Court of Human Rights favours a compromise between the 'continuity theory' and the 'clean slate theory': the limited direct responsibility of the Member States for acts of the European Union. The continuity of the Member States obligations under the Convention is here affirmed, yet it is limited so as to take account of the 'real existing' European Union as

---

[109] Opinion 2/91 (Convention No 170 of the International Labour Organization concerning safety in the use of chemicals at work) [1993] ECR I-1061, para 5

[110] For a discussion of these duties, see Cremona, below ch 23.

[111] Stern, above n 1, 27.

[112] For an excellent account of the succession doctrine during the decolonisation period, see M Craven, *The Decolonization of International Law: State Succession and the Law of Treaties* (Oxford, Oxford University Press, 2007).

an independent subject of international law. This 'bridging mechanism' will become superfluous once the European Union accedes to the Convention—a process that is under way.

Thirdly, the European legal order has developed its own perspective on the continuity of, and succession to, Member State treaties. As regards the former, the European legal order was originally clear and generous. Article 351 TFEU allowed Member States to fulfil their international obligations against any conflicting European law, yet it imposed a procedural European obligation to renegotiate or denounce the treaty in the future. In the last decade, the European Court has significantly lessened this tolerant stance in order to protect the autonomy and integrity of the European legal order. Not only has it set external limits to the supremacy of prior international treaties over European law to judicially safeguard the Union's 'constitutional identity'; it appears to have come to require an immediate application of Article 351(2) for all Member State treaties falling within the scope of the European legal order.

Fourthly, the European Union has developed its own theory and practice of functional succession. The Union considers itself materially bound by those international agreements that were concluded by all its Member States and fall within its exclusive competence. The scope of the doctrine of functional succession is thus relatively limited (even if the Court were to include subsequent or legislative exclusivity). Nonetheless, there arrive moments when—viewed from its internal perspective—only the Union can conclude or (re)negotiate an international agreement; yet under international law, the Member States continue to be seen as eligible contracting partners. To bridge this normative gap, the European legal order has developed the 'trustees doctrine'. The Member States are authorised to conclude the international treaty on behalf of the Union. This internal constitutional arrangement will need to stay in place as a second best solution as long as international law retains its (partial) blindness toward compound international subjects.

25

Enlarging the Constitutional Order of States

CHRISTOPHE HILLION*

I INTRODUCTION

ONE OF ALAN Dashwood's numerous legacies to EU law scholarship is his characterisation of the European Union as a 'constitutional order of states'—the title of this collection. In an article published in the *Cambridge Yearbook of European Legal Studies* (another of his legacies), he explained the notion in the following way:

> The European Union is a new kind of polity. On the one hand, the Member States have pooled their sovereignty in many important matters, and have accepted the discipline of acting together through common institutions. On the other hand, they retain the legal and political quality of states . . . recognised by other international actors as full subjects of public international law. And for their own peoples, they represent the main focus of collective loyalty and the main forum of democratic political activity. I call that remarkable construction 'a constitutional order of states'.[1]

The purpose of this chapter is to establish to what extent the EU enlargement policy relates to that notion. More specifically, have 'Member States pooled their sovereignty [and] accepted the discipline of acting together through common institutions' with respect to the accession of additional Member States?

Enlargement is a unique policy of the Union in that it entails the production of primary law, viz an accession treaty, in principle immune from judicial review by the European Court of Justice.[2] Indeed, enlargement has often been located outside the scope of application of EU norms. This chapter intends to demonstrate that, in spite of its special characteristics, that policy is not totally exempt from the 'discipline' which, in Alan's definition, is inherent in the Union as a constitutional order of states.

* Many thanks to Catherine Barnard, Francis Jacobs, Alan Mayhew and Anne Myrjord for all their insightful comments and suggestions. The usual disclaimer applies.
[1] A Dashwood, 'The Elements of a Constitutional Settlement for the European Union' (2001) 4 *Cambridge Yearbook of European Legal Studies* 1.
[2] Joined Cases 31/86 and 35/86 *LAISA and CPC España v Council* [1998] ECR 2285; Case C-445/00 *Austria v Council* [2003] ECR I-8549.

The increasing participation of EU institutions in the shaping and conduct of the enlargement procedure is a sign of Member States' growing acceptance of such a discipline. At the same time, the latter is, perhaps more than in other EU policies, highly dependent on their good will. Indeed, in recent years some of the Member States have unilaterally introduced new elements into the procedure and the policy, thus showing disregard for the commonality intrinsic to the constitutional order. Finding the right balance between the 'state' and the 'constitutional' elements is essential to the effectiveness of any EU policy, including enlargement. The current trend amongst Member States towards ignoring the discipline carries the risk of depriving the enlargement provisions of their *effet utile*. The question is whether the constitutional order of states itself can limit the creeping nationalisation of the enlargement process. In particular, could the Court of Justice, hitherto almost absent from the procedure, have any role to play in this respect?

A   Common Discipline and Institutions in the EU Enlargement Process

Enlargement is exclusively governed by provisions laid down in EU primary law. The Union cannot be enlarged without having recourse to the specific procedure established by the Treaty. According to Article 49 TEU (Lisbon):

> Any European State which respects the values referred to in Article 2 and is committed to promoting them may apply to become a member of the Union. The European Parliament and national parliaments shall be notified of this application. The applicant State shall address its application to the Council, which shall act unanimously after consulting the Commission and after receiving the consent of the European Parliament, which shall act by a majority of its component members. The conditions of eligibility agreed upon by the European Council shall be taken into account.
>   The conditions of admission and the adjustments to the Treaties on which the Union is founded which such admission entails shall be the subject of an agreement between the Member States and the applicant State. This agreement shall be submitted for ratification by all the contracting States in accordance with their respective constitutional requirements.

Furthermore, the procedure involves the 'Member States' as such, rather than as 'High Contracting Parties' as per Article 1 TEU. In other words, they do not only act (using Alan Dashwood's words) qua 'states . . . recognised by other international actors as full subjects of public international law', they also act as Members of the Constitutional Order.

Thus, the enlargement procedure is more than simply an inter-state negotiation for the purpose of increasing the number of contracting parties to the Treaties founding the Union. While Article 49 TEU makes it plain that the Union's enlargement entails common action by the Member

States, its first paragraph also foresees an essential role for the institutions: the Council, the European Council, the Commission and the Parliament. Indeed, a comparison between the different versions of the enlargement provisions in the successive Treaties shows that the involvement of the common institutions has increased, thus counter-balancing the apparent primary role of the Member States.[3] Hence, Article 8 of the 1986 Single European Act introduced the requirement that the European Parliament (EP) should consent to any Community expansion, by an absolute majority of its members.[4] The Lisbon version of the procedure also includes a new obligation to inform the European Parliament of any new application for membership.

In practice too, the positions of the EU institutions in the enlargement procedure have consistently been bolstered, particularly those of the Commission and of the European Council, working in tandem with the Council. Such involvement has developed in an incremental fashion, through ad hoc arrangements carved out in consideration of the particular needs of each expansion process, and to a great extent outside Treaty provisions. Unorthodox interactions between the institutions have been apparent in (i) the elaboration of the accession conditions, (ii) the establishment and management of the 'pre-accession strategy' and (iii) the accession negotiations.

(i)   Accession Conditions

As regards the definition of accession criteria, the development of novel institutional arrangements was particularly noticeable following the Copenhagen European Council in 1993, which set out the so-called 'Copenhagen criteria', following earlier proposals from the European Commission.[5] These criteria were subsequently elaborated notably at the European Council meetings in Madrid in 1995, and in Helsinki in 1999.[6]

---

[3] Note that the enlargement procedure of the European Coal and Steel Community Treaty did not envisage any role for the Member States as such. Art 98 ECSC stipulated that: 'Any European State may apply to accede to this Treaty. It shall address its application to the Council, which shall act unanimously after obtaining the opinion of the High Authority; the Council shall also determine the terms of accession, likewise acting unanimously. Accession shall take effect on the day when the instrument of accession is received by the Government acting as depository of this Treaty.'

[4] Only the stillborn Treaty establishing the European Political Community had foreseen such a parliamentary involvement. See Art 116(3) EPC. See further C Hillion, 'EU Enlargement' in G de Búrca and P Craig (eds), *The Evolution of EU Law* (Oxford, Oxford University Press, 2011).

[5] See Report by the Commission to the European Council, Edinburgh, 11–12 December 1992, 'Towards a Closer Association with the Countries of Central and Eastern Europe', SEC(92) 2301 final; Communication by the Commission to the Council, in view of the meeting of the European Council in Copenhagen, 21–22 June 1993, 'Towards a Closer Association with the Countries of Central and Eastern Europe', SEC(93) 648 final.

[6] Presidency Conclusions, Madrid European Council, 15–16 December 1995; Presidency Conclusions, Helsinki European Council, 10–11 December 1999. M Cremona, 'Accession to the European Union: Membership Conditionality and Accession Criteria' (2001) 25 *Polish*

Through these seminal summits, the European Council, with the help of the Commission, thus refined the substantive rules of accession to the EU, supplementing the general provisions of Article 49 TEU. Both thereby became key actors in defining the overall normative framework for conducting the enlargement policy.

(ii)   Pre-accession Strategy

At its Essen meeting in 1994,[7] the European Council established the 'pre-accession strategy', previously envisaged in various Commission proposals.[8] It entailed growing co-operation between the Commission, the Council and European Council, for the purpose of preparing applicants' accession.

A case in point is the management of the so-called Accession Partnership (AP), the key instrument of the strategy.[9] On the basis of a framework regulation adopted by the Council, the Commission drafted APs for each candidate, containing lists of principles, priorities, intermediate objectives and conditions on which the applicant's adaptation should focus to for it to meet the Copenhagen criteria. Each AP was then presented to the Council for adoption by qualified majority voting, and then to the candidate.[10] In addition, and at the behest of the European Council,[11] the Commission started producing detailed evaluations of each applicant's performance in implementing the APs, in annual 'progress reports', on the basis of which the Council could determine the pace of the accession process. Indeed, the AP Regulation established a system of sanctions

---

Yearbook of International Law 219; F Hoffmeister, 'Earlier Enlargements' in A Ott and K Inglis (eds), *Handbook on European Enlargement* (TMC Asser Press, 2002) 90; C Hillion, 'The Copenhagen Criteria and Their Progeny' in C Hillion (ed), *EU Enlargement: a Legal Approach* (Oxford, Hart Publishing, 2004) 17.

[7] Presidency Conclusions, Essen European Council, 9–10 December 1994.

[8] Communication from the Commission to the Council, 'The Europe Agreements and Beyond: A Strategy to Prepare the Countries of Central and Eastern Europe For Accession', COM(94) 320 final; Communication from the Commission to the Council, 'Follow Up to Commission Communication on "The Europe Agreements and Beyond: A Strategy to Prepare the Countries of Central and Eastern Europe for Accession"', COM(94) 361 final.

[9] Council Reg 622/98 on assistance to the applicant States in the framework of the pre-accession strategy, and in particular on the establishment of Accession Partnerships, [1998] OJ L85/1.

[10] Art 2 of Council Reg 622/98, above n 9.

[11] The 1997 Luxembourg European Council decided that '[f]rom the end of 1998, the Commission will make regular reports to the Council, together with any necessary recommendations for opening bilateral intergovernmental conferences, reviewing the progress of each Central and Eastern European applicant State towards accession in the light of the Copenhagen criteria, in particular the rate at which it is adopting the Union *acquis* . . . The Commission's reports will serve as the basis for taking, in the Council context, the necessary decisions on the conduct of the accession negotiations or their extension to other applicants. In that context, the Commission will continue to follow the method adopted by Agenda 2000 in evaluating applicant States' ability to meet the economic criteria and fulfil the obligations deriving from accession' (Presidency Conclusions, Luxembourg European Council, 12–13 December 1997, pt 29).

whereby the Council, on a proposal from the Commission, could review the pre-accession financial assistance if progress in meeting the Copenhagen criteria was found insufficient.

The regular reporting on candidates' progress contrasts with previous accession procedures in which only two opinions were given by the Commission on each membership application. It is also noticeable that the Commission provided an assessment of the progress of the candidates in meeting all the Copenhagen accession criteria, including the political conditions, such as the protection of minorities.[12] By articulating and promoting the wider Union's acquis in relation to potential Member States, and in controlling their compliance with accession requirements, the Commission acted well beyond its traditional function of 'guardian of the [EC] Treaty' vis-à-vis Member States. In effect, it became closely involved in defining the prototype of an EU Member State, in political, economic, legislative, administrative and judicial terms.[13]

(iii)   Accession Negotiations

The involvement of the EU institutional framework in the enlargement policy has also materialised at the level of accession negotiations. While Treaty provisions suggest that the latter essentially involve the Member States on the one hand and the applicant state on the other, in practice institutions have been directly associated with the conduct of these negotiations.[14] For example, the common position presented by the Council Presidency in accession conferences is first unanimously agreed within the General Affairs Council, on the basis of drafts prepared by the Commission on each of the chapters, for each of the candidates.[15]

---

[12] G Toggenburg (ed), *Minority Protection and the Enlarged European Union: The Way Forward* (Budapest, LGI Books, 2004); P Van Elsuwege, 'Minority Protection in the EU—Challenges Ahead' in K Inglis and A Ott (eds), *The Constitution for Europe and an Enlarging Union: Unity in Diversity?* (Groningen, Europa Law Publishers, 2005) 259; G Sasse, 'The Politics of Conditionality: The Norm of Minority Protection Before and After EU Accession' (2008) 15 *Journal of European Public Policy* 842; O De Schutter, 'The Framework Convention on the Protection of National Minorities and the Law of the European Union', CRIDHO Working Paper 2006/01; C Hillion, 'The Framework Convention for the Protection of National Minorities and the European Union', Council of Europe Report (2008).

[13] For a critical view on this development, in terms of the EU institutions interfering in (newly acquired) Member State's sovereignty, see eg A Albi, 'Europe Agreements in the Light of Sovereignty and Legitimacy: The Case of Estonia' in A Kellermann, J de Zwaan and J Czuczai (eds), *EU Enlargement—The Constitutional Impact at EU and National Level* (The Hague, Asser Press, 2001) 195.

[14] The role of the institutions had already been noted by Puissochet in the context of the first enlargement, see J-P Puissochet, *L'Elargissement des Communautés Européennes* (Paris, Editions Techniques et Economiques, 1974).

[15] Indeed, the decision to open accession negotiations is taken by the European Council, while the Negotiating Framework, which determines the principles, the substance and the procedures of the negotiations, is adopted by the General Affairs Council; see eg the Negotiating Framework for Iceland, doc 12228/10, available at http://ec.europa.eu/enlargement/pdf/iceland/st1222810_en.pdf [Last visited on 10 September 2010].

The foregoing review of key elements of the enlargement process illustrates that it largely involves the Union's institutions, not only because the Treaty so requires, but also as a result of generous ad hoc arrangements, including phases of the procedure where Member States are in principle in charge. Having recognised the eastern enlargement as 'political necessity and historic opportunity',[16] the latter have readily admitted that enlargement can be prepared and organised through the common institutions. They have even allowed practices which are at odds with the Treaty provisions, most notably the principle enshrined in Article 13(2) TEU that 'each institution shall act within the limits of the powers conferred on it in the Treaties, and in conformity with the procedures, conditions and objectives set out in them'. The increased role of the institutions, particularly since the enlargement to Central and Eastern Europe, has been codified by the Treaty of Lisbon. Not only does it formally consolidate the paramount role of the European Council in establishing the normative framework of accession, it also, albeit implicitly, acknowledges the monitoring tasks of the institutions vis-à-vis the candidate. Indeed, Article 49 TEU requires that, to be eligible, the applicant state must respect the values referred to in Article 2, and show commitment to promoting them.

B   Reassertion of Member States' Control over EU Enlargement

When preparing for the Union's enlargement to Central and Eastern Europe (the fifth expansion), Member States showed an acceptance of the discipline of acting together through common institutions. However, the end of the fifth enlargement process (ie the accession of Bulgaria and Romania) marked a progressive rebalancing of the procedure in favour of Member States' control and, almost as a corollary, a loosening of such discipline.[17] This tendency is expressed both (i) at the EU level in the way the procedure is implemented and (ii) at national level.

(i)   Evolving Reading of Article 49(1) TEU

The Treaty provisions on enlargement have long been brief and vague, offering ample room for interpretation. For its part, the Court of Justice has played only a minimum role in ensuring 'that in the interpretation and application of [these provisions] the law is observed', and this despite the full jurisdiction it has been granted since the original EEC Treaty.

---

[16] Presidency Conclusions, Madrid European Council, 15–16 December 2006.
[17] The reasons are multifarious, an analysis of which would go beyond the scope of this contribution. See further House of Lords, 'The Further Enlargement of the EU: Threat or Opportunity?', European Union Committee 53rd Report of Session 2005–06.

Asked once about Article 237 EEC,[18] the Court considered in *Mattheus v Doego* that it establishes:

> a precise procedure encompassed within well-defined limits for the admission of new Member States, during which the conditions of accession are to be drawn up by the authorities indicated in the article itself. Thus the legal conditions for such accession remain to be defined in the context of that procedure without it being possible to determine the content judicially in advance.[19]

In view of such limited judicial intervention, the interpretation of the Union's enlargement rules has essentially fallen on the Member States and the EU political institutions. In this exegetic exercise, the quest for objectiveness, consistency, and *effet utile* has been less instrumental than political considerations and expediency. The reading of the accession procedure has thus varied. This is particularly conspicuous in the aftermath of the fifth enlargement, and notably as regards the role of EU institutions in the context of Article 49(1) TEU.

In principle, the candidate's application is to be sent to the Council, which then decides by unanimity after the Commission has provided its opinion and the EP has given its consent. While the procedure suggests that the Council only decides once the other institutions have been consulted, in practice, the Council takes decisions at an earlier stage. In particular, the Commission does not provide or even prepare its opinion without having been requested to do so by the Council. Indeed, while the practice had hitherto been to decide to invite the Commission to start to prepare its opinion by simple majority, now it appears that single Member States feel entitled to block, or at least hold up, the Council's request to the Commission.

Thus, the Commission's invitation to prepare an Opinion on Albania's application was withheld as a result of the German government's intention first to consult its parliament on the matter, allegedly in application of the revised Lisbon ratification law, adopted following the *Lisbon* judgment of the German Constitutional Court.[20] The procedure of Article 49 TEU was resumed after the German approval, six months later, when the Council eventually '*decided* to implement the procedure laid down in Article 49 of the Treaty on the European Union. Accordingly, the Commission [was] *invited* to submit its opinion'.[21]

---

[18] According to the old Art 237 EEC, any European State may apply to become a member of the Community. It shall address its application to the Council, which, after obtaining the opinion of the Commission, shall act by means of a unanimous vote. The conditions of admission and the amendments to this Treaty necessitated thereby shall be the subject of an agreement between the Member States and the applicant state. Such agreement shall be submitted to all the contracting states for ratification in accordance with their respective constitutional rules.

[19] Case 93/78 *Mattheus v Doego* [1978] ECR 2203.

[20] *Lissabon-Urteil*, judgment of 30 June 2009 (BVerfGE 123, 267).

[21] 16 November 2009; 15913/09 (Presse 328) (emphasis added).

This incident shows that the Council does not automatically transmit the candidate's application to the Commission. Rather, it first has to '[decide] to implement the procedure' of Article 49 TEU. It (and thus each of the Member States) thereby acquires the ability to assess the admissibility of the application, before the Commission and indeed the Parliament have had a chance to voice their views. It may be wondered whether this evolution sits comfortably with the procedural requirements of Article 49(1) TEU, which stipulate that the Council's formal decision on the application is to be taken after the Commission has formally presented its opinion and the Parliament has given its consent.[22] The duplication of the Council decision weakens the role of the other EU political institutions and de facto changes the nature of the procedure of Article 49(1) TEU: in principle inter-institutional, in practice intergovernmental.

(ii)   *Increased National Interference with the Enlargement Procedure*

While the enlargement procedure is set out by EU primary law and involves EU institutions (Article 49(1) TEU), it also has a national dimension (Article 49(2) TEU). The Member States and the candidate country not only negotiate the agreement containing the 'conditions of admission and necessary adjustments to the Union's founding Treaties', they also ratify that agreement 'in accordance with their respective constitutional requirements'.

Recent practice suggests that the national facet of the EU enlargement policy has been reinforced, particularly in the aftermath of the 2004 enlargement and the negative referenda on the Constitutional Treaty, notably through the strengthening of the 'constitutional requirements' within the Member States. An essential procedural element in the enlargement process, the definition of procedural requirements has evolved, notably in consideration of internal (or bilateral) issues, with significant effect on the overall procedure.

A particularly glaring example of such a trend is the French constitutional requirement introduced in 2008 that future accession treaties be ratified by referendum. According to the first paragraph of new Article 88-5 of the French Constitution:[23]

> Any Government Bill authorizing the ratification of a treaty pertaining to the accession of a state to the European Union shall be submitted to referendum by the President of the Republic.

---

[22] Practice shows that a Commission's positive opinion may be ignored by the Council, as exemplified by the second British application.

[23] This version of Art 88(5) has come into effect upon the coming into force of the Treaty of Lisbon, in accordance with Art 2 of Constitutional Act No 2008-103 of 4 February 2008 and Art 47 of Constitutional Act No 2008-724 of 23 July 2008.

Notwithstanding the foregoing, by passing a motion adopted in identical terms in each House by a three-fifths majority, Parliament may authorize the passing of the Bill according to the procedure provided for in paragraph three of article 89.[24]

Disclosing the political expediency of the French constitutional amendment,[25] the requirement of Article 88-5 is, however, not applicable to accessions that 'result from an Intergovernmental Conference whose meeting was decided by the European Council before July 1, 2004'.[26] The purpose of this time limitation to the referendum requirement was to ensure that the latter would not concern the Accession Treaty with Croatia, but would in any event apply to Turkey and subsequent admissions.

Admittedly, the second paragraph of Article 88-5 foresees a possible exception to the referendum requirement if Parliament so decides, 'by passing a motion adopted in identical terms in each House by a three-fifths majority'. In this case, Parliament may authorise the passing of the bill by the two chambers, convened in Congress. And to be approved, the bill must be passed by a three-fifths majority of the votes cast.[27] The French Constitution thus exceptionally allows for parliamentary ratification of future accession treaties, but on the demanding condition that it is supported by a double qualified majority. In any event therefore, future accessions to the Union are being made more difficult as a result of the revamped French constitutional requirement.[28]

Member States have also strengthened their grip on other stages of the procedure. Following the *BvfG* judgment on the Lisbon Treaty, the amended German ratification law foresees an increased involvement of the Bundestag in EU affairs.[29] In particular, the law explicitly requires

[24] Art 89(3) of the Constitution foresees that 'a Government Bill to amend the Constitution shall not be submitted to referendum where the President of the Republic decides to submit it to Parliament convened in Congress; the Government Bill to amend the Constitution shall then be approved only if it is passed by a three-fifths majority of the votes cast. The Bureau of the Congress shall be that of the National Assembly.'

[25] France had autonomously vetoed the accession of the UK on two occasions, while organising a referendum in April 1972 to ratify its Treaty of Accession.

[26] Art 47 of Constitutional Act No 2008-724 of 23 July 2008.

[27] According to Art 89(3), a government bill is not submitted to referendum where the President of the Republic decides to submit it to Parliament convened in Congress, ie the meeting of the two chambers. To be approved, the bill must be passed by a three-fifths majority of the votes cast.

[28] Other Member States are considering introducing specific constitutional requirements for ratifying accession treaties in the form of, for example, a two-thirds qualified majority in Parliament (eg The Netherlands; see Kamerstukken TK 30874, Nos 1–3). Some Member States are also inspired by the French arrangement (eg Austria; see Government Programme 2007–2020, available at http://www.austria.gv.at/DocView.axd?CobId=19512, 8)

[29] 'Gezets zur Änderung des Gesetzes über die Zusammenarbeit von Bundesregierung und Deutschem Bundestag in Angelegenheiten der Europäischen Union' (EuZBBG; available at http://www.bundesrat.de/nn_8396/SharedDocs/Beratungsvorgaenge/2009/0701-800/715-09.html). Prior to the judgment, the Bundestag had already proposed that the German gov-

that the German government seeks the opinion of the parliament on the opening of accession negotiations.[30] Since then, the consultation requirement has been invoked at various stages of the enlargement procedure, and not only for the specific decision to open accession talks. This is illustrated by the 'Albanian application' episode, referred to above, in which the law was brought into play prior to the decision to request the Commission's opinion.[31] While the government is not bound by the opinion of the Bundestag, in the specific field of enlargement, they are explicitly asked to seek a common position.[32] Were the German Parliament to give a negative opinion on the matter, EU enlargement could be stalled.

The creeping nationalisation of enlargement, exemplified by these two legal developments, is also typified by the increasing impact of bilateral issues on the accession process. For instance, Croatia's membership prospect has been undermined as a result of the border dispute with Slovenia. Another case in point is the name issue between Greece and (the former Yugoslav Republic of) Macedonia, which has prevented the opening of accession negotiations with the latter, despite the favourable recommendation from the Commission. Enlargement of the Union is thus being hijacked by some Member States using their relative power vis-à-vis applicants to settle bilateral issues to their advantage.[33]

Perhaps more worryingly, the nationalisation of the EU enlargement procedure has led to Member States tempering the fundamentals of integration with domestic concerns. An illustration of this phenomenon can be found in the EU negotiating framework for Turkey.[34] The document envisages that the Accession Treaty could include 'permanent safeguard clauses' with respect notably to movement of persons, agricultural and structural policies. As it has been suggested elsewhere, such clauses would put at risk the functioning of the internal market. More generally, they

---

ernment seek its approval before the start of new accession negotiations, as recalled in the House of Lords report, above n 14, 20.

[30] §3(1)2 EuZBBG.

[31] The slowing down effect of the German law has been all the more significant because the consultation of the Bundestag requires prior translation of relevant background documents, notably the Commission reports, mostly written in English. It should, however, be noted that §9(1) EuZBBG stipulates that the involvement of the Bundestag should not hold up the EU decision-making process.

[32] This is foreseen in §10(2) EUZBBG, which also stipulates that the Bundesregierung has the right to take a decision that contradicts the position of the Bundestag for 'important reasons of foreign or integration policy'. Both institutions can turn to the Bundesverfassungsgericht if they consider that their rights are violated by the other institution ('Organstreitverfahren', laid down in detail in the Bundesverfassungsgerichtsgesetz). I am grateful to Thomas Ackermann and Jens-Uwe Franck for their helpful explanations of these points.

[33] In its 2009 strategy paper, the Commission specifically referred to the tendency of bilateral issues hampering the enlargement process (see COM(2009) 533, 6).

[34] Negotiating Framework, 3 October 2005.

could strike at the heart of the EU legal order,[35] and in particular at the principle of equality of EU citizens and states.[36]

From having been driven through common institutions, EU enlargement is increasingly held hostage by Member States' domestic considerations, and unilateral actions. This tendency challenges the discipline which is fundamental to the constitutional order, thus raising the question of preserving the latter's effectiveness against too much encroachment by the Member States.

C Getting the Balance Right between 'Constitutional' and 'State' Elements?

As shown above, Member States increasingly assert their specific interests in the context of enlargement, thus defying the discipline envisaged by the Treaty-based procedure. In particular, the notion of 'constitutional requirements' has been instrumentalised to the extent that it risks making a 'mockery of the [EU enlargement] process'.[37] Is this national *dérive* inevitable and unstoppable? Are there ways to restore some sense of EU discipline?

The strongest incentive to discipline within the Constitutional Order emanates from the Court of Justice. In principle, the greater its power, the less dependency on the 'good will' of Member States to promote common action. Jurisdiction is the basis of the Court's power. Already acknowledged in the founding Communities treaties, the Court's jurisdiction over the accession procedure entails that enlargement is not immune from judicial control. The establishment of the multi-pillar EU by the Maastricht Treaty did nothing to change this. Article L TEU made it clear that the Court had unrestricted jurisdiction over the Final Provisions of the Treaty, which included the enlargement procedure enshrined in Article O TEU. Under the Lisbon dispensation, Article 49 TEU is equally subject to the Court's jurisdiction as articulated in Article 19 TEU and Article 275 TFEU. In principle, therefore, the Court of Justice is expected to ensure that in the interpretation and application of the provisions of Article 49 TEU, the law is observed.[38]

---

[35] C Hillion, 'Negotiating Turkey's Membership to the European Union—Can Member States Do as They Please?' (2007) 3 *European Constitutional Law Review* 269.

[36] Case 231/78 *Commission v UK* [1979] ECR 1447, para 9. This principle of equality is enshrined in Art 4(2) TEU.

[37] House of Lords, above n 14.

[38] Whether and how that jurisdiction would be exercised in practice remains to be seen. On this point, it may be noted that in *Coyle v Smith* the US Supreme Court was asked to adjudicate on the terms of admission of a state (Oklahoma) to the Union. The jurisdiction of the Court was questioned on the ground that the power of Congress to admit new states is a political power uncontrollable by the courts. The Supreme Court was not moved by the argument, and looked into the merits of the case (*Coyle v Smith* (1911) 221 US 559).

However, the existence of jurisdiction is a necessary, but not sufficient, condition for the Court's power to encourage discipline. It is the exercise of such jurisdiction that creates a genuine pressure to act together. As indicated by the *Mattheus* judgment referred to earlier, the Court's jurisdiction as regards the enlargement procedure is exercised with caution. Nonetheless, in its pronouncement, the Court of Justice stated that the enlargement provisions establish 'a precise procedure *encompassed within well-defined limits* for the admission of new Member States'.[39] While the Court did not specify what these limits are, the phraseology of the ruling suggests that they are located in the enlargement procedure itself, but may also derive from other parts of EU primary law more generally.[40]

If the enlargement procedure is not immune from the application of rules and principles underpinning the EU legal order, and from the judicial control by the Court of Justice, it may be worth speculating briefly on the possible forms such a control would take. In particular, are there judicial means to address the nationalisation of the EU enlargement policy, and to preserve the integrity of the Treaty procedure? Two avenues could be envisioned: one based on non-compliance with procedural and substantive requirements and the other founded on a breach of the obligation of loyal co-operation.

(i)   Non-compliance with Procedural and Substantive Requirements

In case of a violation of the 'well-defined limits' referred to by the Court in *Mattheus*, the annulment of one of the many Council decisions adopted in relation to enlargement could be sought on the basis of Article 263 TEU. A Council decision could thus be disputed on the ground that one of the essential procedural requirements of Article 49 TEU has not been complied with. For instance, the European Parliament could be tempted to challenge the Council's refusal to consider an application from a European state,

---

[39] Emphasis added.

[40] Hence, limits applying to the procedure could stem from the 'very foundations of the Community', which the Court of Justice emphasised in its *Kadi* judgment (Joined Cases C-402/05 P and C-415/05 P *Kadi and Al Barakaat International Foundation v Council and Commission* [2008] ECR I-6351, paras 282 and 304) and in its first *EEA* Opinion (Opinion 1/91 [1991] ECR I-6079, paras 35 and 71), as well as from the general principles of Union law, eg equality, proportionality, protection of legitimate expectations; for more on these see T Tridimas, *The General Principles of the EU Law* (Oxford, Oxford University Press, 2006); P Craig, *EU Administrative Law* (Oxford, Oxford University Press, 2006). Limits may also derive from the rules of regional organisations such as the European Convention for the Protection of Human Rights and Fundamental Freedoms, notably once the Union has acceded to the Convention (as envisaged by Art 6(2) TEU), and from international law (eg the Vienna Convention on the Law of Treaties), particularly in view of the insistence, in the Treaty of Lisbon, on the Union's respect for the principles of the UN Charter and of international law (Art 21 TEU). See also JL da Cruz Vilaça and N Piçarra, 'Y a-t-il des limites matérielles à la révision des traités instituant les Communautés européennes?'(1993) 29 *Cahiers de Droit Européen* 3.

on the ground that the Treaty gives it the right to give its consent before the Council so decides. Indeed, delaying tactics in Council to postpone indefinitely the invitation to start the procedure, as in the Albanian episode referred to above, could be addressed through an action to establish a failure to act, on the basis of Article 265 TFEU.

The action for annulment could equally be triggered in case of violation of the substantive limits of Article 49 TEU, or other substantive requirements derived from the Treaty. For instance, if an agreement negotiated and concluded under Article 49 TEU were to contain permanent limitations to the application of fundamental freedoms, thus not offering full membership to the acceding state, it could be argued that the agreement is not an accession treaty but an external agreement of an advanced form. The legal basis of the negotiation and conclusion of such an agreement would thus have to be altered, and so would the procedure. Alternatively, the agreement would have to be renegotiated so as to ensure its compatibility with the substantive requirement of membership deriving from Article 49 TEU, which the Court is empowered to interpret.[41]

For example, if the Treaty of Accession with Turkey were to include permanent safeguard clauses in the field of movement of persons, regional and agricultural policies, the Treaty in question would arguably fall short of offering full membership to Turkey, amounting instead to the 'privileged partnership' sought by several Member States.[42] The choice of legal basis for the conclusion of the agreement could therefore not be Article 49 TEU, but eg Article 216 and/or Article 8 TEU (substantive legal basis), together with Article 218 TFEU (procedural legal basis). Thus, the suggestion, sometimes made by some politicians, that the current negotiations with Turkey could lead to such a privileged partnership is based on the erroneous assumption that the procedure of Article 49 TEU can be used for this purpose.

(ii) Infringement of Loyal Co-operation

Another ground for a more active involvement by the Court in preserving the integrity of the Treaty enlargement procedure could be that Member States have violated their obligation of loyal co-operation enshrined in Article 4(3) TEU: 'The Member States shall facilitate the achievement of the Union's tasks and refrain from any measure which could jeopardise the attainment of the Union's objectives.'

---

[41] The Court could, for instance, be asked to shed light on the notion of 'conditions of admission and the adjustments to the Treaties on which the Union is founded which such admission entails'; see in this respect Case C-413/04 *European Parliament v Council* [2006] ECR I-11221 and Case C-414/04 *European Parliament v Council* [2006] ECR I-11279.

[42] See the coalition agreement of the current CDU–CSU–FDP German government, available at www.cdu.de/doc/pdfc/091215-koalitionsvertrag-2009-2013-englisch.pdf, 166–67.

More precisely, the Court might be asked, notably by the Commission, to sanction actions or omissions on the part of Member States or institutions (eg the Council)[43] that would jeopardise the attainment of the Union's objective[44] of enlarging to include a state whose membership prospect has been acknowledged by the European Council and with whom accession negotiations have begun.

The rationale would be that the effectiveness of the procedure to achieve that objective, ie Article 49 TEU, ought to be guaranteed. Measures at EU or national levels that would make it impossible for those provisions to operate in practice would arguably endanger the attainment of the Union's objectives, in infringement of Article 4(3) TEU. A scenario which appears legally feasible, though politically distant, would be that the Commission on this basis starts enforcement proceedings against a state which has introduced constitutional requirements that would make it virtually impossible for it to ratify the accession Treaty.

II CONCLUDING REMARKS

Enlargement, both as a policy and a procedure, may well be analysed through Alan's prism of the EU as a constitutional order of states. The accession treaty, the essential legal instrument underpinning the accession process, is aimed at modifying the constitutional order by increasing the number of states that compose it, and by expanding the discipline it entails to new territories.

Indeed, the enlargement procedure includes both strong 'constitutional' and 'state' components whose relative significance varies depending on the context, and in particular as a function of Member States' political will to enlarge the constitutional order. Clearly, either of the two constitutive elements of the constitutional order (constitutional/state) can be inflated, depending on Member States' choice. The more political will displayed on the part of the Member States, the more the constitutional elements of the enlargement policy appear to prevail in the way enlargement is conducted. Conversely, the more scepticism towards enlargement, the less discipline of acting together may be detected in the reading and practice of the procedure. This suggests that the constitutional *acquis* is fragile.

Nonetheless, the constitutional order of states does have some tools for self-preservation. In particular, the Court of Justice's jurisdiction on

---

[43] Art 13 (1) and (2) TEU.

[44] Enlargement more generally appears to remain one of the Union's aims. The preamble of the TFEU still refers to the Member States' call to other peoples of Europe, while the specific procedure for enlargement has not been totally disposed of. It could indeed be argued, using the Court's jurisprudence exposed at para 226 of its *Kadi* judgment (above n 35), that Art 49 TEU is the expression of an EU 'implicit underlying objective' of enlargement.

enlargement rules and its jurisprudence on loyal co-operation could help circumscribe the abuse of the 'state' elements of the procedure. The question is how far the reassertion of Member States' control over enlargement can go before these hitherto-unused tools of the constitutional order are set in motion.

26

Very Small States and the European Union: the Case of Liechtenstein

MARC MARESCEAU*

I INTRODUCTION

THE AUTHOR OF this chapter had the great pleasure to work closely with Alan in the framework of a Jean Monnet Centre of Excellence project on recent law and practice in the field of EU external relations and to edit with him a book under this title.[1] One of the chapters in that volume attempted a comparative study of the EU's relations with Andorra, San Marino and Monaco,[2] but Liechtenstein was not included in that analysis. The reason for that had to do with the great complexity of Liechtenstein's relations with the EU as a result of its membership of the European Economic Area, differentiating it considerably from the other very small states. This *liber amicorum* offers a unique opportunity not only to fill this gap but also to pay tribute to a great lawyer, a very distinguished colleague and, last but not least, a good friend. In a volume like this, exploring the constitutional order of states, the specific position of very small states also deserves attention all the more since literature on this topic is scarce, but writing on the relations between the EU and these states is always a difficult challenge. These relations are particularly difficult as a result of the specific history of these countries, which explains why they were not absorbed by their bigger neighbour or neighbours. The integration of most of these neighbours into the expanding EU while the very small states remain on the sideline gives rise to multiple questions about the type of political and

---

* The author had the opportunity to discuss with HSH Prince Nikolaus von Liechtenstein, Ambassador of Liechtenstein to the EU, various aspects covered in this contribution and would like to express his gratitude for the useful comments. All views and opinions expressed are the responsibility of the author.

[1] A Dashwood and M Maresceau (eds), *Law and Practice of EU External Relations—Salient Features of a Changing Landscape* (Cambridge, Cambridge University Press, 2008) 484.

[2] Ibid, 270–308.

legal frameworks organising their relations with the EU. [3] However, today, neither the EU nor the very small states themselves have a clear vision of the future form and content of this relationship. The overall picture of the very small states' relationships with the EU depicts certain common characteristics but also illustrates how diversified their respective relationships are and how each has developed their own bilateral frameworks with the EU, sometimes on the initiative of the EU, sometimes on their own initiative. Among the very small states concerned, in many respects Liechtenstein occupies a unique position.

A short background on Liechtenstein's place in Europe is useful for a better understanding of the country's complex relations to the EU. Liechtenstein was part of the 'Confederation of the Rhine' established by Napoleon, and has been a sovereign state since 1806. It is a very small country, with a surface area of only 160 km² and approximately 36,000 inhabitants, 35 per cent of whom are foreigners. Liechtenstein has a written constitution, the current version of which dates back to 1921. This constitution, amended on numerous occasions, reflects a compromise between the ruling monarch (the Prince) and the Parliament. Liechtenstein is a constitutional and hereditary monarchy, with the Princes von und zu Liechtenstein as sovereigns. [4] Specific characteristics of the Liechtenstein constitutional system are, among other things, the dual basis of the exercise of power by the Prince and the Parliament. This 'constitutional dualism' establishes, broadly speaking, a balance of power, but the Prince's powers are real. A very specific feature of Liechtenstein's constitutional system is the prominent role of direct democracy via popular initiatives or referenda. Another unique feature, which has no equivalent in existing monarchies in the world, is that the Liechtenstein Constitution explicitly allows for citizens to introduce an initiative to abolish the monarchy. Seen from this perspective, one can say that the ruling Prince has a passive democratic legitimation.

Liechtenstein's international legal personality is well established. In 1990 it became a member of the UN before the other small European states Andorra, San Marino and Monaco. It has also been a member of the Council of Europe since 1978 and was again the first very small state to become a member of that organisation. Moreover, unlike the other very small states, Liechtenstein has acceded to the WTO (in 1995).

Another important aspect of Liechtenstein's specificity is its close relationship with Switzerland. In 1923, Liechtenstein established a customs

---

[3] For more details, see 'The Relations between the EU and Andorra, San Marino and Monaco', ibid.

[4] The House von Liechtenstein acquired the estates of Schellenberg and Vaduz in the seventeenth century and the County of Vaduz in the eighteenth century. It also gave its name to what became 'Fürstentum Liechtenstein' (the 'Principality of Liechtenstein'). The Liechtenstein dynasty is one of the oldest noble families of the European continent.

union with its neighbour.[5] As a result of this, trade and customs agreements concluded by Switzerland with third countries are also applied by Liechtenstein. Logically, the 1972 Free Trade Agreement between the EEC and Switzerland, signed before the EU's first enlargement, was made valid for Liechtenstein, and to this end an additional agreement was formally concluded between the latter and the EEC.[6] The special relationship with Switzerland was further accentuated through various other bilateral agreements between the two countries, such as the 1980 *Währungsvertrag* (Currency Treaty), which included Liechtenstein in the currency area of Switzerland. Consequently, the Swiss franc is the currency used in Liechtenstein and Swiss rules on monetary, credit and currency policy are also applied in Liechtenstein. Moreover, in 1978 the *Patentschutzvertrag* (Patent Protection Treaty) created a common area for the protection of patents. It is evident that, as a result of such a close relationship with Switzerland, the relations between the latter and the EU inevitably also directly affect Liechtenstein. In other words, EU–Switzerland relations cannot be disconnected from the Switzerland–Liechtenstein bilateral relations. This triangular relationship can be addressed only summarily within the framework of this contribution.

When EFTA was created in 1960, Liechtenstein became an associate member and, in 1991, it joined the organisation as a full member. In 1992, Liechtenstein, in a truly visionary and daring move as a very small state, became a party to the European Economic Area Agreement (EEA)[7] and, consequently, after the entry into force of this agreement, became associated with the EC.[8] Contrary to what happened in Switzerland, the Agreement was approved by the Liechtenstein population through a popular referendum. Certainly, Liechtenstein's participation in such a far-reaching integration agreement as the EEA constituted a formidable challenge for the principality and meant a considerable limitation of its sovereignty in a number of vital areas,[9] next to the ones already undertaken as a result of the customs union with Switzerland and the other bilateral agreements with its neighbour.

For the purpose of this contribution, Liechtenstein's complex relationship with the EU will be examined in the context of the following aspects. First, the European dimension of the controversy on Liechtenstein's con-

---

[5] Liechtenstein had been in a customs union with the Austro-Hungarian Empire since 1852, but this agreement was terminated in 1919. It was the collapse of the Austro-Hungarian Empire which was at the origin of Liechtenstein's external reorientation towards its other neighbour, Switzerland.

[6] See [1972] OJ L 300/189.

[7] For text of the EEA Agreement, see [1994] OJ L 1/3.

[8] The EEA is '[an] Agreement of association' (Art 1 EEA).

[9] On the effect of the EEA Agreement on the concept of sovereignty for a very small state such as Liechtenstein, see N von Liechtenstein, 'Die europaïsche Integration als Testfall liechtensteinischer Souveränität' (2006) 105 *Jahrbuch des historischen Vereins für das Fürstentum Liechtenstein* 155–67, in particular 158–63.

stitutional dualism is briefly addressed. The second part concentrates on Liechtenstein's EEA membership, including the issue of confiscated Liechtenstein property in the aftermath of World War II. Notwithstanding the extensive substantive scope of the EEA, Liechtenstein's relations towards the EU have been broadened considerably and go significantly beyond the EEA framework. In particular, tax co-operation and banking secrecy issues have recently occupied a prominent position in the global EU–Liechtenstein bilateral agenda and this contribution pays attention to these themes. Unfortunately, restrictions of space do not allow us to go into other aspects of EU–Liechtenstein relations, such as Liechtenstein's position in relation to the Schengen and Dublin Conventions. Suffice it to say that the association of Liechtenstein to these Conventions is foreseen for 2010. This contribution concludes with some brief comments on Liechtenstein's possible future European orientation.

II   LIECHTENSTEIN'S CONSTITUTIONAL DUALISM: A EUROPEAN ISSUE?

Besides participation in the activities of the Council of Europe, one of the main goals of Liechtenstein's application for membership of the Council was to assert its international legal personality.[10] Because of its status as a very small state, Liechtenstein initially met certain difficulties but, as mentioned above, was eventually able to join the Council in 1978. Liechtenstein's membership of the Council may subsequently have facilitated the membership of Andorra, San Marino and Monaco. However, the relations between Liechtenstein and the Council have at times been strained because of the place and role of the Prince in the Liechtenstein constitutional structure. Since the ensuing controversy touches upon the very basis on which European democracy is founded, it also indirectly affected Liechtenstein's relations with the European Union.

In the last decade of the twentieth century a political and legal controversy erupted on the position and role of the monarch in Liechtenstein's constitutional system. The Prince did not see his function as confined to a merely representative role. In the past, the Prince's rights had to some extent been eroded in favour of the government. It was the organisation, and particularly the timing, of the EEA referendum which became the catalyst for a constitutional crisis. The Prince wanted a referendum prior to the Swiss referendum—in itself a sensible decision in light of the fact that afterwards the Swiss population rejected EEA member-

---

[10] See M Seiler, 'Kleinstaaten im Europarat' in E Busek and W Hummer (eds), *Der Kleinstaat als Akteur in den internationalen Beziehungen*, Liechtenstein Politische Schriften (Schaan, Verlag der Liechtensteinischen Akademischen Gesellschaft, 2004) vol 39, 292–317, in particular 297–98 and 301–02.

ship—while the government considered the choice of a date to be its own prerogative. The government was of the opinion that Liechtenstein's first priority was its relations with Switzerland and that organising the EEA referendum in Liechtenstein before the referendum in Switzerland could jeopardise these relations. The controversy quickly shifted to a more general debate on the place of the monarch in Liechtenstein's constitutional framework and, in particular, the Prince's constitutional rights to dismiss members of the government and the government itself, as well as to dissolve Parliament.[11] In the course of the controversy, other prerogatives came under discussion, such as nomination of judges.[12] The Prince had expressed his intention to propose amendments to the Constitution, clarifying and reinforcing his constitutional powers. In addition, he also threatened to leave Liechtenstein if voters failed to back those constitutional amendments.

In the broad constitutional debate that followed, the controversy was brought before the Parliamentary Assembly of the Council of Europe by a group of citizens of the principality, arguing that the amendments proposed by the Prince were not in conformity with the fundamental principles of the Council of Europe. Following this move, the Bureau of the Parliamentary Assembly asked the Venice Commission, an advisory body set up by the Council of Europe in 1990 to advise the emerging democracies after the fall of communism, to make an assessment of the constitutional reforms as proposed by the Prince. In its opinion, the Venice Commission, elaborating on the possible fundamental tensions between the monarchic principle and the democratic principle, observed 'that the monarchies in the member States of the Council of Europe have all been reformed in a way making them compatible with democratic principles'. It had to be regarded as a part of the European constitutional heritage that, where monarchies exist, the power of the monarch was regulated in such a way as to avoid conflict with the democratic principle. In the words of the Venice Commission, 'European monarchs do not have wide political powers and the tendency, after the establishment of the Council of Europe, has been to further reduce their powers'. Consequently, the Venice Commission stated in rather outspoken terms that if the Prince's proposals were approved, they would present a decisive shift with respect to the present Constitution of Liechtenstein. The princely initiative, if accepted, would moreover constitute 'a serious step backwards', isolating Liechtenstein in Europe and damaging its position in the Council of Europe, even

---

[11] For a comprehensive account of Liechtenstein's recent constitutional history, see D Beattie, *Liechtenstein. A Modern History* (Triesen, van Eck Publishers, 2004) 193–215.

[12] This became particularly acute as a result of the Herbert Wille 'affair', which led to a ruling by the European Court of Human Rights stating that there had been a violation of the European Convention by Liechtenstein (Arts 10 and 13) and awarding damages; see ECtHR, *Wille v Liechtenstein*, App No 28396/95, judgment 28 October 1999.

making 'its membership of the Council of Europe problematic'.[13] The Venice Commission concluded that 'even if there is no generally accepted standard of democracy, not even in Europe, both the Council of Europe *and the European Union*[14] do not allow the *acquis européen* to be diminished'. Certainly, the reference in the opinion to the European Union was somewhat unexpected and even surprising. It probably intended to imply that the EU should also have reacted against what was going on domestically in Liechtenstein.

Notwithstanding the Venice Commission's criticism, on 14–16 March 2003 the popular referendum was held and a large majority of the Liechtenstein population agreed with the Prince's initiatives.[15] Logically, the results of the constitutional referendum made it difficult for the instances of the Council of Europe to pursue the matter further. The Parliamentary Assembly of the Council of Europe wisely decided not to initiate the monitoring procedure but instead to open instead a 'constructive dialogue' with Liechtenstein. This resulted in the establishment of an *ad hoc* Committee of the Bureau of the Assembly with a mandate to study, together with the Parliament of Liechtenstein, the constitutional and political practices in the country. In 2006 the Committee concluded that, as a result of the constitutional amendments, there had indeed been a change of balance of power in favour of the Prince, while the general trend of constitutional monarchies had been to reduce the political powers of the constitutional monarch. However, it was too early to make a definitive judgment and, moreover, the Committee had itself been unable to make a unanimous proposal to the Bureau.[16] This finally led the Bureau to decide that the dialogue with Liechtenstein could be concluded.[17]

As far as the EU is concerned, in its bilateral relations with Liechtenstein, it does not seem that the issue of the constitutional controversy has ever been raised formally or even informally, and the very strong focus on this particular point by various instances of the Council of Europe seems not to have affected the EU–Liechtenstein bilateral relations. At first sight, and in the light of the intensity of the issue at the level of the Council of Europe, this might be surprising. It might be thought, especially after the large popular approval of the constitutional amendments, that the Council of Europe's direct intervention in Liechtenstein's constitutional debate while the EU remained silent was something of a storm in a teacup. The frameworks in place, Liechtenstein's membership of the

---

[13] Venice Commission, Strasbourg, 16 December 2002, Opinion No 227/2002. For a (very) critical assessment of this opinion, see G Winkler, *The Council of Europe. Monitoring Procedures and the Constitutional Autonomy of the Member States* (Wien–New York, Springer, 2006) 60–181.

[14] Emphasis added.

[15] The results were: 64.32% of the votes in favour, 35.68% against.

[16] See Doc 10940 Addendum, 31 May 2006.

[17] See Doc 10940, 26 June 2006.

Council of Europe, its acceptance of the jurisdiction of the European Court of Human Rights and its close relationship with the EU, mainly but not exclusively through the EEA, and, last but not least, the ultimate and decisive say of the population itself through direct democracy, even with the possibility of a vote of no confidence towards the monarch and also the possibility of abolishing the monarchy, would appear more than sufficient safeguards against any non-democratic orientation of the principality. In the extremely unlikely hypothesis that the Prince were to use his prerogatives in a clearly unacceptable way from the point of view of the application of the fundamental principles of the Council of Europe, this would undoubtedly affect Liechtenstein's relations with the EU.

III   LIECHTENSTEIN'S EEA MEMBERSHIP

The rejection of the EEA by Switzerland created multiple political and legal problems in the bilateral relations between Liechtenstein and Switzerland, which could be solved only through direct contacts between these two countries. The main difficulty was to combine the simultaneous existence of the EEA Agreement with the customs union with Switzerland, which was not part of the EEA. On 2 November 1994, a bilateral agreement between Liechtenstein and Switzerland was signed amending the 1923 Custom Union Agreement to allow Liechtenstein's participation in the EEA.[18] Article 3(1) of the Agreement establishes that both the law of the customs union and the EEA Agreement are applicable in the Liechtenstein legal order but, should ever a conflict arise, the EEA Agreement will prevail over the 1923 Agreement.[19] After the conclusion of the 1994 Agreement, the EEA Council acknowledged, by Decision No 1/95 of 10 March 1995, that the condition laid down in Article 121(b) of the EEA Agreement, namely that the good functioning of the Agreement was not impaired by the regional union between Switzerland and Liechtenstein, was fulfilled.[20] Consequently, the EEA Agreement in relation to Liechtenstein could enter into force on 1 May 1995. It

---

[18] For text, see *Liechtensteinisches Landesgesetzblatt* No 77 (1995).

[19] In 2001, the EFTA States signed the Vaduz Convention, adapting the 1960 EFTA Convention to the new situation created by on the one hand the EEA Agreement and on the other hand the signature of the *Bilaterals I*, covering a series of seven agreements between the EC and Switzerland. A specific protocol regarding free movement of persons between Switzerland and Liechtenstein was also agreed upon, laying down the principle that Liechtenstein applies to Swiss nationals treatment equal to that of EEA citizens 'under the special solution granted to Liechtenstein in the EEA', while Switzerland, for its part, applies to Liechtenstein nationals the rules laid down in the EC–Switzerland Agreement on free movement of persons, which was part of the agreements of the 'package' of the Agreements of *Bilaterals I* between the EC and Switzerland.

[20] See Decision EEA Council No 1/95 of 10 March 1995 on the entry into force of the EEA Agreement for the Principality of Liechtenstein, [1995] OJ L86/54.

should be recalled that Liechtenstein follows a monist approach towards the relationship between national and international law. Questions of primacy and direct effect of EEA law are very much approached in the same way in Liechtenstein as in the EU.

In order to address Liechtenstein's position in the EEA, first some general comments are made on Liechtenstein's EEA compliance record and then attention is paid to two key pillars of the EEA: movement of goods and movement of persons. In addition, when reviewing Liechtenstein's place in the EEA, it is impossible not to say a word about the EEA enlargement controversy in which Liechtenstein played a pivotal role.

A   Compliance with the EEA *Acquis*

The EEA Agreement obviously covers a large part of the relations between the EU and Liechtenstein. The EEA *acquis* includes the EU's Internal Market with its four freedoms: free movement of goods, persons, services and capital. It also covers so-called 'horizontal policies', incorporating co-operation in the field of social policy, consumer protection, environment, statistics and company law. While these areas, strictly speaking, fall outside the free movement *acquis*, they are nevertheless considered indispensable for the smooth achievement of the EEA objectives and constitute Part V of the EEA Agreement. The relevant *acquis communautaire* in these areas is further explicitly identified in annexes and is binding upon those EFTA countries that are members of the EEA. In addition, EFTA countries in the EEA also co-operate in certain so-called 'flanking policies', such as R&D, education, tourism and culture. Needless to say, all this constitutes a huge package of substantive EU *acquis*. Since Liechtenstein is the only very small state to be part of the EEA, its situation is obviously different from the other very small European states. Seen from this angle, of all the very small European states, Liechtenstein is the most integrated with the EU.

It is interesting to note that Liechtenstein's status as a very small EEA member does not seem to have adversely affected its global commitments towards and implementation record for the EEA *acquis*. Certainly, in a few cases, the EFTA Court found that Liechtenstein had not properly implemented its EEA obligations by, for example, not taking the necessary legislative measures for the implementation of directives within the time limit[21] and, perhaps more seriously, that it had infringed certain basic

---

[21] See Case E-5–9/05 *EFTA Surveillance Authority v Liechtenstein* [2006] EFTA Court Report 144 on non-implementation of a series of Community Directives on electronic communication networks and services; Case E-5/01 *EFTA Surveillance Authority v Liechtenstein* [2001] EFTA Court Report 287 on non-implementation of the Council Directive relating to legal expenses insurance; Case E-6/06 *EFTA Surveillance Authority v Liechtenstein* [2007] EFTA Court Report 298 on non-implementation of the Council Directive relating to the

rules relating to free movement.[22] But there is no indication that these infringements of EEA law, which on the whole remain very limited, have anything to do with structural problems related to Liechtenstein's status as a very small state. On the contrary, various *Scoreboards* published by the EFTA Surveillance Authority indicate that Liechtenstein is simply the best EFTA pupil of the EEA class.[23]

In this context it is worth recalling that one of the important tasks of the EFTA Surveillance Authority (ESA) is to monitor the implementation and application of the EEA *acquis* by the EFTA members of the EEA. Due incorporation of regulations and due implementation of directives are a priority for the ESA. While in the EU regulations are directly applicable in each EU Member State, they are made part of the internal legal order of the EFTA States, according to Article 7 EEA.[24] In Iceland and Norway this means that legal measures have to be taken to integrate regulations in the national legal order. In Liechtenstein, however, regulations are automatically part of the domestic legal order, which facilitates their smooth application. A considerable number of infringement procedures have been initiated by the ESA against Norway and Iceland for non- or wrong incorporation of regulations. Logically, for Liechtenstein this is not an issue, and it is only in very rare cases that Liechtenstein has failed to comply with a regulation.[25] In this respect, it should be mentioned that the EEA Agreement does not require individuals and economic operators to rely directly on EEA rules and that the EEA Agreement does not provide that non-implemented EEA rules take precedence over conflicting national rules. When conflict occurs between national law and non-implemented EEA law, 'the Contracting Parties may decide whether, under their

assessment and management of environmental noise; Case E-3/09 *EFTA Surveillance Authority Liechtenstein* on non-implementation of the Council Directive relating to reinsurance

[22] Eg the Liechtenstein national provisions limiting means of security for costs in court proceedings to various forms of security of domestic origin constituted restrictions of the principle of free movement of capital, Case E-10/04 *Paolo Piazza v Paul Schutze* AG [2005] EFTA Court Report 76. For the judgments of the EFTA Court on right of establishment, see nn 34 and 35.
[23] See, eg *Scoreboard* (2009), 6–7, which observes, in the context of implementation of Internal Market directives, that 'Liechtenstein achieved, once again, its best results so far', while *Scoreboard* (2010) notes that '[b]y reducing its transposition deficit from 0.5% to 0.4%, Liechtenstein achieved its best result ever'. A negative note is the transposition delay, which has recently increased in Liechtenstein, but, with only four infringement proceedings for EEA obligations, Liechtenstein has the lowest number of such proceedings out of 30 EEA States.
[24] On the legal significance of Art 7 EEA in general and for the EFTA Court in particular, see the illuminating comments by C Baudenbacher, 'The EFTA Court Ten Years On' in C Baudenbacher, P Tresselt and T Örlygsson (eds) *The EFTA Court Ten Years On* (Oxford, Hart Publishing, 2005) 24–30.
[25] In Case E-5/06 *EFTA Surveillance Authority v Liechtenstein* [2007] Court Report 298, the EFTA Court concluded that Liechtenstein, by applying a requirement of residence for entitlement to the helplessness allowance, had failed to comply with Council Reg 1408/71 on the application of social security schemes as part of the EEA *acquis*.

national legal order, national administrative and judicial organs can apply the relevant EEA rule directly, and thereby avoid violation of EEA law in a particular case'.[26] Consequently, the EEA Agreement 'does not require that a provision of a directive that has been made part of the EEA Agreement is directly applicable and takes precedence over a national rule that fails to transpose the relevant EEA rule correctly into national law'.[27] The EFTA Court also reminded the contracting parties 'which have introduced principles of direct effect and primacy of EEA law in their internal legal order'—something not irrelevant for Liechtenstein—that they 'remain under an obligation to correctly transpose directives into national law'.[28]

(i)   Movement of Goods

With regard to movement of goods, Liechtenstein applies the EEA *acquis*. There are no judgments of the EFTA Court on the question of free movement of goods involving Liechtenstein. The ESA also seems to have dealt with few or no cases concerning Liechtenstein.

The leading legal instrument regarding the necessary adjustments to the EEA Agreement in the field of free movement of goods, as a result of Liechtenstein's participation in the EEA, remains Decision No 1/95 of the EEA Council, mentioned above. However, the specific relationship between Liechtenstein and Switzerland has led to a declaration by the EEA Council on the application of Protocol 4 on the rules of origin in Liechtenstein–Switzerland trade relations, indicating the conditions under which Swiss customs authorities may issue movement certificates (EUR1) and under what conditions the term 'exporter' used in Protocol 4 also covers exporters in Switzerland in respect of goods originating in the EEA. Another particularity, laid down in Annex I to Decision No 1/95 of the EEA Council, is that, for products covered by Chapters II (Feeding stuffs) and III (Phytosanitary measures) of the EEA Agreement, 'Liechtenstein may apply Swiss legislation deriving from its regional union with Switzerland on the Liechtenstein market in parallel with the legislation implementing the acts referred to in the Chapters'. Annex II further provides that, for products covered by the acts to which it refers, as a result of its regional union with Switzerland, Liechtenstein may also apply Swiss technical regulations, standards, testing and certifications in addition to EEA legislation. Clearly, this amounts to accepting the principle of parallel marketability for the goods covered by the acts. The application of this principle is the result of Liechtenstein's involvement in two distinct

---

[26] See EFTA Court in judgment of 10 October 2007, Case E-1/07 [2007] Report 248, following a request for an advisory opinion by the Fürstliches Landesgericht on the interpretation of Council Dir 77/249/EEC to facilitate the effective exercise by lawyers of freedom to provide services, para 40.

[27] See EFTA Court judgment, ibid, para 43.

[28] Para 41.

economic areas, which are governed by different and seemingly irreconcilable rules. As Advocate General Colomer rightly observed:

> two legal systems meet in one place: one governs relations between Switzerland and Liechtenstein, the other regulates the latter's membership of the EEA. If there is no conflict between the systems, they are permeable; as a general rule, nothing prevents a product from Switzerland moving from the territory of its partner to that of another EEA member, and *vice versa*. If, on the other hand, there is conflict, the barriers are raised and the markets are sealed, so that goods authorised in Liechtenstein can be exported to the other Contracting Parties to the Agreement only if they comply with EEA rules. In conclusion, goods which enjoy unimpeded freedom of movement within the customs union do not, merely because of that, enjoy the same freedom within the EEA.[29]

No serious problems seem to have arisen regarding the application of this important principle. However, in the *Novartis* case[30] the European Court of Justice was asked to assess whether the grant of a marketing authorisation for a medicinal product in Switzerland, which is automatically recognised in Liechtenstein, was to be considered as the 'first authorisation' to place the product on the market when later, for the same product, marketing authorisations within the Community had also been granted under the authorisation procedure as laid down in Directive 65/65/EEC. The issue was that the determination of the date of the authorisation necessarily also affected the duration of the protection, granted as a result of Council Regulation 1768/92 of 18 June 1992 concerning the creation of a supplementary protection certificate for medicinal products.[31] In the same judgment, the Court acknowledged that the EEA Agreement recognises

> that two types of marketing authorisation may co-exist in the principality of Liechtenstein, namely marketing authorisations issued by the Swiss authorities, which because of the regional union between Switzerland and that State are automatically recognised in the latter, and marketing authorisations issued in Liechtenstein in accordance with Directive 65/65.[32]

Since a marketing authorisation for a medicinal product issued by the competent Swiss authorities is automatically recognised by Liechtenstein in the context of its regional union with Switzerland, it had to be considered as a first authorisation within the meaning of Regulation 1768/92. Moreover, such an interpretation was fully consistent with the purpose of the Regulation.[33]

[29] Opinion Advocate General Colomer, in Cases C-207/03 and C-252/03 *Novartis* [2005] ECR I-3209, para 39. On Liechtenstein's parallel participation in two different economic areas, see GS Baur, 'Die *parallele Verkehrsfähigkeit* und analoge Verfahren als Prinzipien des Europarechts' in *Aktuelle Rechtsfragen 1996. Liber Amicorum zum sechzigsten Geburtstag von Theodor Bühler* (Zürich, Schulthess, 1996) 83–104.
[30] *Novartis*, ibid.
[31] For the text of this regulation, see [1992] OJ L182/1.
[32] Para 29.
[33] Para 31.

(ii)   Movement of Persons and Right of Establishment

On the whole, the fundamental principle of free movement of persons, one of the four fundamental freedoms of the Internal Market, has been applied without specific or serious problems. Certainly, a number of questions have arisen, particularly in the field of establishment and a few rulings of the EFTA Court do concern discriminatory aspects of Liechtenstein's legislation imposing residence requirements for at least one managing director of a Liechtenstein company (*Gewerbegesetz*/Business Act), or at least one member of the board of directors of a Liechtenstein company (*Personen- und Gesellschaftsrecht*/Persons and Companies Act). In both cases the EFTA Court found that such residence requirements constituted unjustified restrictions on the right of establishment.[34] In another ruling, the EFTA Court examined the compatibility of the *Gesetz vom 21 Oktober 1992 über die Banken und Finanzgesellschaften* (Banking Act), stipulating that at least one member of the management board and one member of the executive management of a bank established in its territory had to reside in Liechtenstein. According to Liechtenstein, such a residence requirement was necessary in order to protect the good functioning and reputation of the banking sector. Moreover, a resident requirement contributed to ensuring familiarity with local circumstances, promoted compliance with national legislation, and facilitated supervision and enforcement of national law. However, the EFTA Court found that the residence requirement had the effect of placing nationals of other EEA States at a disadvantage compared to Liechtenstein nationals. The residence requirement, according to the Court, constituted covert discrimination and was therefore a restriction in the sense of Article 31 EEA providing for the abolition of all restrictions on establishment between EEA states.[35] After this judgment, Liechtenstein adopted new legislation, but this has led to further action by the ESA against Liechtenstein. In the view of the ESA, Liechtenstein, by requiring the members of the management board and of the executive management of banks established in Liechtenstein to be in a position to actually and flawlessly perform their functions and duties, has failed to fulfil its obligations under the EEA Agreement.

In the same case, a second action was also brought, this time for residence requirements for lawyers, patent lawyers, auditors and trustees,

---

[34] Case E-3/98 *Herbert Rainford-Towning* [1998] EFTA Court Report 205 and Case E-2/01 *Dr Franz Martin Pucher* [2002] EFTA Court Report 44.

[35] Case E-8/04 *EFTA Surveillance Authority v Liechtenstein* [2005] EFTA Court Report 46. In another judgment the EFTA Court found that the 'single practice rule' applied for certain medical professions forbidding the operation of more than one practice, regardless of location, infringed Art 31 EEA on the freedom of establishment, Cases E-4/00 *Johann Brändle* [2000–2001] EFTA Court Report 125; Case E-5/00 *Dr Jozef Mangold* [2000–01] EFTA Court Report 165 and Case E-6/00 *Tschannet* [2000–01] EFTA Court Report 205.

imposing proof of a residence from where an applicant is able to perform his duties effectively and on a regular basis. On 6 January 2010 the EFTA Court, as could have been expected, found the Liechtenstein legislation to constitute a restriction on free movement. These restrictions, based on economic motives or in respect of ethical standards or the need to react quickly in the event of a crisis (in the case of management of a bank), were considered not to be justified and constituted infringements of Article 31 EEA.[36]

While these cases do not relate directly to Liechtenstein's situation as a very small state, the same cannot be said of the specific rules defined in Protocol 15 to the EEA Agreement on the transitional periods on movement of persons (Switzerland and Liechtenstein). When becoming an EEA member, Liechtenstein was allowed to keep in force national provisions submitting entry, residence and employment to prior authorisation until 1 January 1998, in the context of relations between Liechtenstein and the EC Member States and other EFTA states (Article 5(1)). And, more importantly, with regard to EC nationals (and nationals of other EFTA states), Liechtenstein was also allowed to keep in force until the same date 'quantitative limitations for new residents, seasonal workers and frontier workers'. These quantitative limitations were to be gradually reduced (Article 5(2)). However, in this context it is important to mention the EEA Council Declaration made in relation to Decision No 1/95, where the Council 'recognises that Liechtenstein has a very small inhabitable area of rural character with an unusually high percentage of non-national residents and employees'. Moreover, the Council also 'acknowledges the vital interest of Liechtenstein to maintain its own national identity'. Consequently, the EEA Council agreed:

> that in the context of the review of the transitional measures provided for in the Agreement, account should be taken of the elements which, according to the Declaration by the Government of Liechtenstein on the specific situation of the country, might justify the taking of safeguard measures by Liechtenstein as provided for in Article 112 of the EEA Agreement, ie an extraordinary increase in the number of nationals from the EC Member States or the other EFTA States, or in the total number of jobs in the economy, both in comparison with the number of the resident population . . . Furthermore, the Contracting Parties shall in case of difficulties endeavour to find a solution which allows Liechtenstein to avoid having recourse to safeguard measures. It is understood that an equal treatment must be ensured for the nationals of the States, Contracting Parties to the EEA Agreement, and that only the increase in the number of nationals of the above States should be taken into account in the review.

---

[36] Case E-1/09 EFTA *Surveillance Authority v Liechtenstein*, nyr.

By the Decision of 17 December 1999, and in accordance with Article 9(2) Protocol 15, the EEA Joint Committee extended the 'transitional period' to 31 December 2006.[37] Liechtenstein's specific geographical situation 'still [justified] the maintenance of certain conditions on the right of taking up residence in that country', and the Decision also defined how to calculate the quota for residence permits available annually for nationals of EEA states exercising an economic activity in Liechtenstein. Before 31 December 2006, the Joint Committee was asked to carry out a review 'on the basis of which it may, *duly taking into account the specific geographic situation of Liechtenstein and to the extent necessary*, decide to maintain such measures that may be deemed appropriate'.[38] However, it appeared that in 2006 such a decision was not deemed necessary since, with the entry into force of the EEA Enlargement Agreement (see below), an arrangement was accepted 'on the specific geographic situation of Liechtenstein' allowing for a review every five years.[39] Consequently, such a review could have occurred in 2009 but, at the time of writing, no new decision seems to have been taken in this respect. However, in light of what has already been mentioned regarding Liechtenstein's very small inhabitable area and its vital interest, it is difficult to imagine that on this point any future review could lead to dramatic changes for the principality.

B   The EEA Enlargement Controversy

It is certainly not the purpose of this chapter to enter into the details of the impact of EU enlargement on the EEA as a whole. However, the fact that Liechtenstein is a party to the EEA has given rise to a number of specific questions with regard to the effect of EU enlargement on the EU's relations with the principality. In this respect, Article 128 EEA should be recalled. This provision stipulates that any European state becoming a member of the Union 'shall apply to become a Party to the EEA Agreement' and the terms and conditions for such participation shall be subject to an agreement between the contracting parties and the applicant state. This means that any candidate for EU membership has to enter into negotiations not only with the EU but also with the EFTA members of the EEA, something which has been largely ignored in existing literature on EU enlargement. From a legal point of view, and notwithstanding the fact that this is not explicitly mentioned in Article 128 EEA, an agreement with the latter has to be reached before accession to the EU takes place. In other words, the candidate state must formally adhere to the EEA in

---

[37] Decision No 191/1999 amending Annexes VIII (Right of establishment) and V (Free movement of workers) to the EEA Agreement, [2007] OJ L124/20.
[38] Emphasis added.
[39] See [2004] OJ L130/59.

order to become a EU member. This, in itself, is not surprising since the EEA is already part of the EU *acquis*. The EEA Enlargement Agreement with the 10 applicant states for the fifth EU enlargement was signed on 11 November 2003[40] and introduced, among other things, the necessary adjustments to the main text of the EEA Agreement. Besides the fact that, geographically speaking, the Internal Market is considerably extended, an important element of the EEA Enlargement Agreement was the insertion of a new Protocol 38a on the EEA Financial Mechanism, laying down the financial contribution of the EFTA states and members of the EEA 'to the reduction of economic and social disparities in the European Economic Area through the grants to investment and development projects in the priority sectors listed in Article 3 [of the Protocol]'. The total amount foreseen was 600 million euro, covering the period from 2004 to 2009 in annual tranches of 120 million euro. Norway contributed 567 million euro, which is around 95 per cent of the total contribution. The contribution by Liechtenstein amounted to 4.5 million euro for the 2004 EEA enlargement.[41] The EFTA contribution to the EEA enlargement with Romania and Bulgaria, including Norway's financial contribution to bilateral co-operation, was 150 million and Liechtenstein's share for the enlargement with Romania and Bulgaria was respectively 0.51 and 0.22 million euro. At the time of writing, the EFTA/EEA countries were negotiating the new financial envelope of the 2010–2014 contribution.[42]

While all this can easily be understood, one point needs to be explained further. A complex political but also legal issue has arisen with Liechtenstein in the context of the EEA enlargement. To properly understand this, it is necessary to go back into history, specifically to the aftermath of World War II. The Principality of Liechtenstein, squeezed between a Nazi neighbour and neutral Switzerland, also remained neutral throughout the war and was never occupied by Nazi Germany.[43] After the war, Czechoslovakia adopted the Beneš Decrees. Among them was Decree No 12 of 21

---

[40] For text, see [2004] OJ L130/1 (on the provisional application). For the conclusion and entry into force, see [2006] OJ L149/28.

[41] The cost-sharing principle for the EEA Financial Mechanism regarding the EFTA countries in the EEA was established by Decision 5/2004/SC of 23 September 2004 of the EFTA Standing Committee (see No 1040576). It laid down a formula based on gross domestic product for the three most recent years.

[42] On 19 August 2010, after the completion of this text, Norway, Iceland and Liechtenstein signed the Agreement to Finance the New Financial Mechanism 2009–2014 for 988.5 million euro. Liechtenstein's share is around 1% and represents roughly 10 million euro (or 2 million euro per year).

[43] A small part of the Liechtenstein population was in favour of a German 'Anschluss', and in 1939 German Nazi groups were on the point of invading Liechtenstein at Feldkirch. This, however, was probably against Hitler's will and the attempt by the Nazis to incorporate Liechtenstein in the Reich was discontinued. On this particularly salient episode of Liechtenstein history, see the impressive study of P Geiger, *Krisenzeit. Liechtenstein in den Dreissigerjahren 1928–1939* (Vaduz-Zürich, Historischer Verein für das Fürstentum Liechtenstein–Chronos Verlag, 2000) vol 2, 365–68.

June 1945 on the 'Confiscation and expedited distribution of agricultural properties of Germans, Hungarians, traitors and collaborators and certain organisations and institutes'. In 1946 the Beneš Decrees were approved by a Czechoslovak constitutional act.[44] Somewhat strangely, Beneš Decree No 12 applied to property owned by 'German people' regardless of their citizenship, and also to property owned by Liechtenstein nationals, including the properties of Prince Franz Jozef II of Liechtenstein, notwithstanding Liechtenstein's neutrality throughout the war.[45] As one might expect, after the war the application of these measures was challenged by the Prince before the Administrative Court in Bratislava, a challenge which was rejected in 1951 in what was a largely politically motivated judgment, at a time when Czechoslovakia was already a communist country. Later the Federal Republic of Germany signed the (provisional) Convention on the Settlement of Matters Arising out of the War and the Occupation, which entered into force in 1955. In this convention, Germany renounced its right to raise objections to measures carried out with regard to confiscated German property. In 1990, this was reconfirmed by the Treaty on the Final Settlement signed between Germany and its former enemies.

The issue of the confiscation of Liechtenstein property, as a result of the application of the Beneš Decrees, has never been properly settled. The least that can be said is that it is remarkable that in the Decrees property owned by Liechtenstein nationals was assimilated to 'enemy property'. One of the direct consequences of this assimilation was that after the war no diplomatic relations between Liechtenstein and Czechoslovakia were re-established. This situation endured even after the political transformation of Czechoslovakia and the subsequent split of Czechoslovakia into the two separate countries, the Czech and Slovak Republics, in 1993.[46] Only very recently has there been a change in situation (see below), while various attempts at a judicial solution of the dispute have failed. In this respect, the *Pieter van Laer Painting* case should be mentioned.

In 1991 a painting by the seventeenth-century Dutch master, which had belonged to the von Liechtenstein family for centuries but had been confiscated as a result of Beneš Decree No 12, was lent by a Czechoslovak museum to a museum in Cologne. Prince Hans-Adam II of Liechtenstein instituted proceedings before a German court in order to obtain restitution of the painting. However, on the basis of the Settlement Convention between Germany and the allied powers mentioned above, the German court declined jurisdiction. The Prince's claim was rejected again

---

[44] Act No 57/1946 of 28 March 1946.

[45] Swiss property was also expropriated, but in 1949 a bilateral agreement on compensation for confiscated Swiss assets had been concluded between Switzerland and Czechoslovakia.

[46] For a detailed analysis, see R Marxer, 'Liechtensteins Beziehungen zur Tschechoslowakei und zu deren Nachfolgestaaten seit 1945' (2006) 105 *Jahrbuch des historischen Vereins für das Fürstentum Liechtenstein* 131.

on appeal. He then lodged an application with the European Commission of Human Rights and the case was brought before the European Court of Human Rights in 1998. On 12 July 2001 the European Court, without looking at the merits of the dispute itself (that is to say, into the question of whether the assimilation of Liechtenstein nationals, and in particular the applicant's father, to 'persons of German nationality' was against the general rules of public international law or German *ordre public*), held that there had been no violation of Article 6, paragraph 1 of the European Convention, which guarantees everyone the right to have any claim relating to civil rights and obligations brought before a court. Within the limited power of judicial review exercised by the European Court,

> it cannot be said that the German court's interpretation of Chapter 6, Article 3, of the Settlement Convention was inconsistent with previous German case law or that its application was manifestly erroneous or was such as to lead to arbitrary conclusions.[47]

However, the Court's reference to 'previous German case law' is enigmatic because prior to this case no dispute in the context of the application of the Beneš Decrees had ever arisen in Germany concerning the assimilation of Liechtenstein property to German property.[48]

A month before the European Court's ruling, the Principality of Liechtenstein had also instituted proceedings before the International Court of Justice (ICJ) against Germany for treating property of Liechtenstein nationals as German assets without ensuring any compensation for the loss of that property to its owners and to the detriment of Liechtenstein itself. The ICJ, while recognising that there was a dispute between Liechtenstein and Germany, something Germany had denied, accepted Germany's preliminary objection that the Court lacked jurisdiction *ratione temporis* to decide the dispute. Liechtenstein had based the Court's jurisdiction on Article 1 of the European Convention for the Peaceful Settlement of Disputes, but Article 27 of the same Convention stipulated that provisions of the Convention did not apply to disputes relating to facts or situations prior to the entry into force of the Convention as between the parties to the dispute. Basically, the ICJ follows a line of thought comparable to that of the European Court of Human Rights in that it held that the dispute relates to facts or situations prior to the entry into force of the European Convention for the Peaceful Settlement of Disputes. The ICJ recognised that the *Pieter van Laer Painting* case triggered the dispute. However, according to the Court, the critical issue was not the date on

[47] ECtHR, *Prince Hans-Adam II of Liechtenstein v Germany*, App No 42527/98, judgment of 12 July 2001, para 65.

[48] It is also surprising that the Municipality of Cologne could apparently accept on loan from a Czechoslovak museum a painting which was part of the Prince's confiscated property. In doing so, consciously or unconsciously, it indirectly contributed to support the Czechoslovak position on the confiscation of Liechtenstein property.

which this dispute arose but the date of the facts or situations in relation to which the dispute arose. In other words 'the source or real cause of the dispute is to be found in the Settlement Convention and the Beneš Decrees'. Consequently, the Court found that it lacked temporal jurisdiction to hear the case. Again, it must be observed that, because it was the first time that German courts had been faced with a claim from a Liechtenstein national after the entry into force of the European Convention on Dispute Settlement, the ICJ's reference to 'German courts [which] have consistently held that the Settlement Convention deprived them of jurisdiction to address the legality of any confiscation of property treated as German property by the confiscating State'[49] does not address this point convincingly.[50] This was also the view of Judge Kooijmans, who expressed a dissenting opinion and who rightly observed '[that] the pivotal issue is not that the German courts in the *Pieter van Laer Painting* case confirmed the previous case law, but they applied it—for the first time—to neutral assets, and thus introduced a new element'.[51] Furthermore, it is intriguing that the question to what extent a treaty may create obligations for a third party is not properly addressed, the more since in World War II Liechtenstein was a neutral state.[52]

In the light of what has already been discussed, it is clear that EEA enlargement has caused particular problems for Liechtenstein, since Liechtenstein did not have 'normal bilateral relations' with the Czech Republic and Slovakia. Liechtenstein—and this is understandable since it was clearly a victim of an improper extension of the scope of the Beneš Decrees—insisted that the assimilation of Liechtenstein property to German assets was paramount to denying the sovereign character of Liechtenstein. In 2003, a critical year for the EEA enlargement, two *aides-mémoire* on this issue were sent by Liechtenstein to all the parties involved in the preparation of the enlargement. In the *aide-mémoire* of 4 April 2003,[53] Liechtenstein stated that the EEA goal aimed at 'establishing a dynamic and homogeneous European Economic Area' on the basis of equality and reciprocity of rights and duties could not be met with the Czech Republic and the Slovak Republic as EEA Members. In the second *aide-mémoire*, of 23 September 2003,[54] Liechtenstein submitted a draft for a joint decla-

---

[49] ICJ, *Case Concerning certain property* (*Liechtenstein v Germany*), judgment of 10 February 2005, para 50.

[50] For a view supporting the Court's interpretation, see B Delmartino, 'The End of the Road for the Prince? Sixty Years after the Czechoslovak Confiscation of Liechtenstein Property' (2006) 19 *Leiden Journal of International Law* 441, in particular 455–56.

[51] Para 13. For other dissenting voices, see Opinions by judges Elaraby, Owada and Berman.

[52] See also the dissenting opinion of Judge Berman, in particular para 29.

[53] For text, see Regierung des Fürstentums Liechtenstein, aide-mémoire, Vaduz, 4 April 2003.

[54] For text, see Regierung des Fürstentums Liechtenstein, aide-mémoire, Vaduz, 23 September 2003.

ration with the Czech and Slovak delegations. For the Czech Republic,[55] this draft read as follows:

> The Czech Republic hereby expressly declares that it respects the Principality of Liechtenstein without reservation as a sovereign and recognised state since 1806. The Principality of Liechtenstein expresses likewise the recognition of the Czech Republic as a sovereign state since 1 January 1993.

However, in response to this request, the Czech Republic was only willing to make a declaration recognising the Principality of Liechtenstein under international law with immediate effect, but such a declaration did not, contrary to the wish of Liechtenstein, refer to Liechtenstein being a sovereign state since 1806. Consequently, Liechtenstein, in its second *aide-mémoire*, insisted again that both the Czech Republic and Slovak Republic 'unconditionally declare that they respect the Principality of Liechtenstein as a sovereign state of long standing'. The expression 'long standing' obviously meant that there would not have been an interruption of sovereignty of Liechtenstein before, during and after World War II. With regard to the unsolved question of the confiscated Liechtenstein property, Liechtenstein proposed 'to resolve these issues in the future on a bilateral level, provided only that the Czech and Slovak side declare their readiness to enter into such negotiations with the objective of seriously reaching a final solution'.

The train of thought in Liechtenstein's reasoning needs little explanation. Accepting Liechtenstein's sovereignty before and during World War II necessarily implied that the application of Beneš Decree No 12 to Liechtenstein property had no legal basis. While no adequate diplomatic solution for the issue was found, Liechtenstein, under heavy pressure from all sides, nevertheless initialled the EEA Enlargement Agreement on 3 July 2003, but when it came to the actual signing of the Agreement, as scheduled on 14 October 2003, Liechtenstein aired its discontent and simply refused to sign. Moreover, in a gesture of EFTA solidarity, Norway and Iceland also preferred not to go ahead with the signing procedure.[56] Although legally Liechtenstein could have blocked or at least have further delayed the EEA enlargement, the extent of the political and legal ramifications of such an eventuality was such that this would necessarily also have seriously complicated the EU's enlargement with the Czech Republic and Slovakia. This was a bridge too far and involved a dimension of political responsibility that the principality simply could not bear. In the end, Liechtenstein gave in without having obtained anything from the two candidate states.

The EEA Enlargement Agreement entered into force simultaneously with the EU Accession Treaty on 1 May 2004, but it was clear that the ques-

---

[55] For the Slovak Republic the same formulation for a joint declaration was suggested.
[56] See Marxer, above n 45, 143–44.

tion of the confiscation of Liechtenstein property was far from solved. Therefore, in subsequent bilateral agreements with the EC, Liechtenstein continued to draw attention to this issue. Thus, at the signing on 7 December 2004 of the Agreement with the EC on taxation of savings income, Liechtenstein reiterated the same position,[57] but the unilateral declaration was not formally added to the Agreement itself. It is therefore obvious that this matter can only be fully solved through diplomatic negotiations, failing which by judicial settlement. A particular difficulty in connection with the Liechtenstein claim resides in the fact that the effect of any review of the confiscation measures regarding Liechtenstein property and/ or compensation for this confiscation might also affect the confiscation measures regarding German and Hungarian properties. Legally speaking, however, the two situations are distinct, so a Pandora's box effect need not necessarily be feared. It was also clear that the EU was not interested in taking up this question in the pre-accession phase of the EU enlargement process with the two candidate states, notwithstanding the fact that it was an unresolved dispute with a neighbouring country that threatened this process as a result of the obvious interconnection of the EEA and EU *acquis*. It is also noteworthy that the refusal by the two (then candidate) states to accept any judicial settlement of the dispute did not seem to pose a particular problem for the EU.

There is now perhaps some hope for evolution on the diplomatic front. On 13 July 2009 Liechtenstein and the Czech Republic decided to establish diplomatic relations.[58] This could signal a possible new approach and it certainly implies a considerable concession by Liechtenstein. However, it does not yet mean that the dispute regarding the confiscated Liechtenstein property, as such, is solved. Both parties have only agreed to set up a 'Historical Commission' to examine the joint history of Bohemia, Moravia, Silesia and the House of Liechtenstein, as well as the relationship between the two countries throughout the twentieth century. It is not specified what power will be given to the work of this Commission. Diplomatic relations with Slovakia were re-established on 21 December 2009, but the property dispute with that country also remains so far unsolved.

IV   TAX CO-OPERATION AND BANKING SECRECY

This chapter is certainly not the place to examine the various difficulties in establishing an EU fiscal policy, but certain initiatives in that area have considerably affected relations with the EU's neighbours. In recent years,

---

[57] This was again repeated at the moment of ratification. For text, see *Bericht und Antrag der Regierung*, No 3/2004, 18.
[58] See press communiqué of the Government of Liechtenstein, 'Liechtenstein and the Czech Republic Establish Diplomatic Relations', 13 July 2009.

the EU has been able to make progress domestically in the area of taxation through Council Directive 2003/48 EC on taxation of savings income in the form of interest payments[59] and, externally, in 2004, through the bilateral agreements that have been signed with Switzerland as well as with Andorra, Liechtenstein, San Marino and Monaco. The conclusion of these agreements was a *conditio sine qua non* for the entry into force of the Community Directive itself. In other words, synchronisation of application of the Directive on the one hand and of the bilateral agreements in question on the other hand was indispensable.[60] The five bilateral agreements provide for the application of a tax on interest payments similar to the one which, according to the Directive, three EU Member States (Austria, Belgium, Luxembourg) were also allowed to apply at intra-EU level. While the Directive laid down the principal of automatic exchange of information, the three Member States were, as a transitional measure, allowed to apply 'equivalent measures' in the form of a retention tax.

With the five neighbouring countries of the EU, including Liechtenstein, there is, on the basis of the 2004 Agreements, no automatic exchange of information, and the principle of banking secrecy has been left largely intact. Granting of information on bank details is only foreseen on conduct constituting tax fraud 'under the laws of the requested state or the like'. Consequently, it is the laws of the requested state which determine whether information exchange is going to take place. It is precisely this limitation of the scope of application of the 2004 Agreements that has come under severe pressure in recent years, aggravated all the more as a result of the worldwide financial crisis. Generally speaking, this challenge has taken different forms. Initiatives have, or had, already been developed at multilateral level through the Financial Action Task Force, the IMF, the Council of Europe, the G20 and the OECD.[61] In particular, the pressure from the G20 through its London April 2009 meeting[62] and the efforts made by the OECD have contributed substantially to creating a political momentum for improving good governance in tax matters. The work of the OECD deserves special mention. The OECD has set up a Global Forum on Taxation, aimed at achieving what it calls 'a global playing field' in which all significant financial centres meet high standards of transparency and effective exchange of information in taxation matters.

---

[59] [2003] OJ L157/38.

[60] See Art 17, para 2 of the Directive.

[61] For an interesting overview of the various initiatives, see GS Baur, 'Will New Developments in Global Economic and Financial Policy Erode International Law and the Sovereignty of States? — The Example of Liechtenstein' in MG Kohen (ed), *Promoting Justice. Human Rights and Conflict Resolution through International Law. Liber Amicorum Lucius Caflisch* (Leiden, Brill Nijhoff, 2007) 1018–36.

[62] See, eg G20 communiqués 'The Global Plan for Recovery and Reform' and 'Strengthening the Financial System', declaring that 'the era of banking secrecy' was over.

A list of so-called 'unco-operative tax havens' had been established, but gradually jurisdictions identified in that list have made commitments to implement OECD standards. In 2007 only three countries still remained on the OECD blacklist: Andorra, Liechtenstein and Monaco.[63] Liechtenstein's initial response to the OECD tax policy initiatives was perhaps the most outspokenly negative. For example, in March 2006, the Crown Prince of Liechtenstein, expressing widespread feeling in Liechtenstein, declared that there was simply insufficient political support in the principality for such co-operation.[64] Liechtenstein had introduced an adequate legislative framework to tackle crime-related money laundering and the principle of banking secrecy did not protect criminal or terrorist activity. This was thought to be sufficient and 'tax evasion', as opposed to 'tax fraud', was not considered to be a criminal offence. Banking secrecy was something 'very firmly anchored in the population'. On this point, the Liechtenstein approach was very similar to that of Switzerland. Liechtenstein wished to continue to function as an important offshore financial centre and was afraid that a further weakening of banking secrecy could jeopardise this objective.

However, apart from the actions at multilateral level, the issue of Liechtenstein as a tax haven was brought into sharp focus when in February 2008 a highly publicised tax scandal erupted in Germany following an investigation for tax evasion by German taxpayers. It appeared that substantial tax evasion *inter* alia through private-purpose funds (*Stiftungen*) had been taking place in Liechtenstein. Apart from the size of the investigation and the very high profile of some suspected individuals, what added extra colour to the investigation was the direct involvement of the German intelligence service, which appeared to have bought data stolen from a Liechtenstein bank. In a rather surreal atmosphere, the Liechtenstein Prime Minister was due in Berlin for a long-planned official visit a few days after the scandal had broken out. The day before the visit, the Crown Prince had used particularly strong words to express his disgust at what was going on in Germany. Germany was accused of mounting an attack on Liechtenstein and of using investigative methods, including spying on citizens, which were totally unacceptable from the point of view of respect of the rule of law.[65] Moreover, all this happened at a moment in time when negotiations for an agreement on combating fraud, including tax information exchange with the EU and its Member States, were

---

[63] San Marino was never included since it had already accepted the OECD Code of Conduct for international tax cooperation in 2000.

[64] See 'Sound of Silence from Liechtenstein. Principality Rejects OECD's Calls to Scrap Banking Secrecy', *International Herald Tribune*, 21 March 2006.

[65] Fürstentum Liechtenstein. Press release, statements by HSM Hereditary Prince Alois von und zu Liechtenstein and Deputy Prime Minister Dr Klaus Tschütscher on the recent events, 19 February 2008; see also 'Prince Hits Out against "Attack" on Tax Haven', *Financial Times*, 20 February 2008; and 'Lilliput's Giantslayer', *Financial Times*, 23–24 February 2008.

at an advanced stage. Chancellor Merkel, for her part, accused Liechtenstein of encouraging lawbreaking in Germany by offering financial services promoting tax evasion. For Germany, the controversy clearly had an EU dimension as well, and the consequent problems therefore had to be tackled at European level. The Chancellor explicitly referred to the possibility of blocking Liechtenstein's entry into the Schengen zone and warned Liechtenstein, without providing further details, of the danger of isolation in the European continent.[66] It is worthwhile noting that, apparently, Germany did not seem willing to use diplomatic channels to air its discontent. Rather, it preferred a direct and frontal action through the media.

The German clampdown on Liechtenstein banking secrecy was not without effect within the EU. Awareness had been growing in an increasing number of EU Member States that banking secrecy rules needed substantive review, but obtaining unanimity among the Member States remained a difficult matter since at least two of them (Austria and Luxembourg) continued to be opposed to rapid and thorough changes. Against this background, it proved particularly difficult for the EU to move forward firmly. Nevertheless, the impact of the German tax evasion incident on Liechtenstein's approach regarding international tax co-operation has been profound. Combined with the growing feeling that the principle of banking secrecy should be relaxed in the light of the banking crisis, Liechtenstein (and some other countries) was forced into providing more transparency in tax matters, as demonstrated through various initiatives taken in 2008 and 2009. On the one hand, substantive concessions have been made by Liechtenstein in the negotiations on the mixed anti-fraud agreement with the EU, while, on the other hand, bilateral negotiations on tax co-operation between Liechtenstein and individual third countries have been successfully completed. As far as the negotiations with the EU are concerned, Liechtenstein's position has changed substantially.

Signs of a change in the Liechtenstein approach could already be discerned from 2007 onwards, but the clearest indication of a major political shift on this issue was the 'Liechtenstein Declaration' of 12 March 2009, committing Liechtenstein to OECD standards on transparency and information exchange in tax matters, and expressing a willingness to conclude bilateral tax agreements with individual states that could go even beyond OECD standards. A direct effect of this commitment was Liechtenstein's removal in May 2009 from the OECD blacklist of unco-operative tax havens.[67] Even before this move, after the eruption of the German tax inquiry, Liechtenstein had indicated, in 2008, that it wanted to move away from the image of being an unco-operative tax haven and that it wished

---

[66] See 'Merkel Ultimatum over Tax Haven Rules', *Financial Times*, 21 February 2008.
[67] Andorra and Monaco have also been removed from that list.

to put an end to the tax row. On the basis of this new approach, bilateral negotiations on the anti-fraud agreement with the EU were concluded in June 2008, and on 10 December 2008 the European Commission adopted a proposal for a Council Decision on the signature of the agreement.[68] The draft agreement covered various forms and modalities of assistance regarding illegal activities in connection with trade in goods and services, including evasion of value-added taxes.[69] The most sensitive part of the agreement concerned Liechtenstein's assistance on fraud affecting direct taxes, which went considerably beyond what was foreseen in the 2004 Savings Tax Agreement. Specifically with regard to 'Stiftungen' and other forms of investment controlled by a fiduciary where the founder and owner are not publicly registered, the draft agreement stipulated that a party

> shall not reject a request for administrative assistance in the form of exchange of information solely because the information is held by a bank, other financial institutions, nominee or person acting in agency or a fiduciary capacity or because it relates to ownership interests in a person, nor when the information is already available to its competent administrative authorities.

Certainly, seen from a Liechtenstein perspective, these were large concessions. Notwithstanding strong calls from the European Parliament to the Council of Ministers in favour of signature and conclusion of the agreement,[70] the ECOFIN Council of 10 February 2009, at the instigation of the German Minister of Finance, refused to accept the draft and urged the Commission to continue the negotiations with Liechtenstein 'in order to obtain such changes in the text of the draft agreements to ensure effective administrative assistance and access to information with regard to all forms of investment, in particular foundations and trusts'. The Council expected Liechtenstein 'to encompass in the agreement with the European Community and its Member States at least a similar scope of obligations as Liechtenstein recently agreed with third countries'. As a matter of fact, this last sentence could only be understood in the light of the Tax Information Exchange Agreement that Liechtenstein had signed with the US on 8 December 2008.[71] This agreement provides for information exchange upon request where, under US law, there is any suspicion concerning tax offences by US taxpayers with assets in Liechtenstein. In other words, the agreement with the US is an agreement on tax co-operation, while the anti-fraud agreement with the EU aimed at countering fraud and other irregular activities detrimental to public financial interests. Suspicion of

---

[68] COM(2008) 839 final.

[69] For text, see ibid.

[70] See Draft Report by Rapporteur Ingeborg Grässle, Committee on Budgetary Control, 2008/0234 (CNS).

[71] For text, see http://www.ustreas.gov/press/releases/reports/us%20liechtenstein%20tiea.pdf.

fraud needed therefore to be sufficiently well founded before a request for co-operation could be initiated. A new draft agreement with the EU was renegotiated in 2009 in which additional concessions by Liechtenstein were made in order to ensure the effective exchange of information on tax matters. The OECD practice and the bilateral agreement Liechtenstein had signed with the US are the main sources of inspiration for these amendments. The result of this exercise is a hybrid and particularly complicated draft which is supposed to be a 'model agreement' for Switzerland and the other very small European states as well. However, at the time of writing, the agreement has not yet been signed as a result of political reservations by Austria and Luxembourg. These two Member States oppose the signature of the text because they consider that such an agreement with Liechtenstein would trigger the end of the regime as established under the Savings Tax Directive and would require them to exchange information automatically. For the moment, the position of Austria and Luxembourg is that a global package of 'good governance measures' in taxation matters is needed, and this implies a fundamental revision of the Savings Tax Directive itself and the conclusion of a series of anti-fraud agreements with the five European countries concerned, not just with Liechtenstein alone. As already mentioned, this blockage has not prevented Liechtenstein from going ahead with the signature of a series of bilateral tax co-operation agreements with third states (EU members and non-members) based on the OECD model, providing for an exchange of information upon request. As a result of these agreements, Liechtenstein was removed from the OECD tax haven 'grey list'[72] on 11 November 2009. This recent and rapid evolution towards bilateral tax co-operation agreements between Liechtenstein and a large number of individual EU Member States is probably not without impact on the contents of the agreement the EU intends to sign with Liechtenstein, and questions may perhaps be raised on the co-existence of the two types of agreements alongside each other.

V CONCLUSION

It is no exaggeration to qualify Liechtenstein's relationship to the EU as being unique. Clearly, its status as a very small state in the heart of the European Union, its very close relationship with another non-EU

---

[72] The OECD 'grey list' had been approved by the G20 and had been published on 2 April 2009. This list identified 38 countries or territories, including EU Member States such as Austria, Belgium and Luxembourg but also Switzerland, which had committed themselves to OECD standards but had not yet fully implemented them in practice. Countries could be removed from the list after signature of 12 bilateral agreements for exchange of information based on the OECD model.

member, Switzerland, also encircled by the EU, its EEA membership and exemplary integration in this very demanding structure, and its additional commitments far beyond the strict EEA *acquis* make Liechtenstein a very special neighbouring partner of the EU. While all these characteristics can be seen as illustrations of strength, Liechtenstein's relations with the EU nevertheless have their fragile side. This has much to do with what is going on in the EU's direct proximity as a whole. For Liechtenstein, the EEA and Switzerland are crucial points of reference, enhancing the specificity of its European identification. But the EEA, with only three EFTA members left—Norway, Iceland and Liechtenstein—and also in the light of Iceland's application for EU membership, whatever the outcome of that may be—is itself under further strain. It is difficult to predict how the EEA, without structural readjustments, will continue to function in the hypothesis of an EU accession by Iceland. Perhaps a possible future option is an advanced framework for further integration in the Internal Market of other very small states,[73] but the value added by this line of thought for Liechtenstein particularly may be rather limited. Another orientation for Liechtenstein could lie in an even closer relationship with Switzerland, but Switzerland's relationship with the EU might also evolve in the future. Certainly, Switzerland is not Liechtenstein, but the particularly pointed attacks against banking secrecy in Liechtenstein were, or are, an indirect warning for Switzerland and it is difficult to ignore the possible spillover effects of these initiatives in Switzerland.

One of the side effects—probably most unwanted for the EU—of all this pressure on Liechtenstein is that it might lead that country to contemplate the option of applying for EU membership. Ultimately, Liechtenstein must consider the advantages of not being part of the EU while being forced to approximate most of its legislation to that of the EU, whether within or outside the EEA framework. Seen from this perspective, a possible request for the accession of Liechtenstein to the EU is therefore, perhaps, becoming less surreal than may previously have appeared. Certainly, in this hypothesis, it will be necessary to reflect in depth on the different modes possible for the future relations. A *sui generis* EU Member State status for the very small states, taking due account of their specificity but integrating them in the wider European framework, is perhaps one of the options that deserves to be explored further. But instead of EU accession, an advanced association status or an agreement based on the new Article 8 TEU resulting from the Treaty of Lisbon also remains a possibility. It must be recalled that Article 8 provides a legal basis for an agreement developing 'a special relationship' with neighbouring countries and a declaration on Article 8 stipulates that the EU is willing to take into account 'the

---

[73] For an example of a reflection in that direction regarding Andorra, see J-C Berthélemy, J Llimona and M Maresceau, *Andorre-Union Européenne. Vers le Marché Intérieur* (Andorra, Ministeri d'Afers Exteriors, 2009).

particular situation of the small-sized countries which maintain specific relations of proximity with it'. The question for Liechtenstein is, however, whether and to what extent the association or Article 8 TEU option can go beyond the present status quo, which is already one of very advanced integration. One possible drawback to these options is that progress in the relations with the EU could well result in a further one-way-street approach, based on unilateral EU requests, if not EU diktats, and this for Liechtenstein is not necessarily the most attractive perspective for an optimal future relationship with the Union.

27

The Internal Legal Effects of the EU's International Agreements and the Protection of Individual Rights

FRANCIS G JACOBS

I INTRODUCTION

AN ESSAY WRITTEN by way of tribute to Alan Dashwood can happily start from the first enlargement of the European Community nearly 40 years ago: the accession of the UK, Denmark and Ireland (but regrettably not Norway) on 1 January 1973, and its legacy. Throughout that period, Alan has studied, and helped to shape, the legal order of what is now the European Union.

Alan has taken a keen interest in the external relations of the European Union, so it is particularly appropriate to reflect on the internal legal effects of the EU's international agreements. Under the title assigned to me, this essay will seek to look back over the development of the rich case law of the ECJ; to sketch where we stand today; and to take a glimpse into the future, looking briefly at some issues raised by the prospect of EU accession to the European Convention on Human Rights.

That first enlargement marked the merger of two separate legal traditions, the 'civil law' tradition shared in many respects by the six founding Member States and the 'common law' systems of the UK and Ireland, with Denmark having aspects of both traditions as well as a strong Nordic element.

One respect in which the traditions differed was in their approach to international law. The UK, Denmark and Ireland were firmly in the so-called 'dualist' camp, in which treaties are said to have legal effect internally not upon ratification but only if they have been incorporated by legislation into internal law. The position in the original six Member States was more nuanced, with variations between dualism and 'monism', a conception of international and municipal law as part of a single system.[1]

---

[1] See the contributions in FG Jacobs and S Roberts (eds), *The Effects of Treaties in Domestic Law* (London, Sweet & Maxwell, 1987).

A closer study shows, however, that the distinction between dualism and monism is not altogether helpful. A dualist system, for example, can sometimes be more receptive in practice to treaties than monist systems, especially where its courts are alert to interpret national legislation consistently with treaties. It may therefore be more helpful not to look at the label but rather to see how a legal system, and in particular its courts, deal with treaties, whether incorporated or not.

II THE APPROACH OF THE COURT OF JUSTICE

Given the varieties of approach under the national laws of the Member States, it was of crucial importance to decide what approach to take to treaties binding on the Community; and at around the same period, in the early 1970s, the ECJ had to make some fateful decisions on that issue.[2]

Ten years earlier, in 1963, the ECJ was confronted, in *van Gend en Loos*,[3] with the national approaches to the EEC Treaty itself. Several Member States argued before the Court, consistently or not with their national law, that the Treaty could not be enforceable in the national courts. The ECJ famously ruled to the contrary. In the early 1970s the Court faced similar questions, and similar arguments, concerning treaties binding on the Community: in 1972 the ECJ ruled on the direct effect of the General Agreement on Tariffs and Trade (GATT), to which, in its view, the Community must be regarded as a party by way of succession to the rights and obligations of the Member States. In considering the issue of direct effect, in *International Fruit Company*,[4] the Court had regard, following its approach to the EEC Treaty in *van Gend en Loos*,[5] to 'the spirit, the general scheme and the terms of the General Agreement'. It reached a negative conclusion on the very principle of direct effect of the GATT, just as, many years later, it reached a negative conclusion on the successor to the GATT, the World Trade Organization (WTO) Agreement.

But the Court took a more positive view of the effect of treaties in the EC legal order in the *Haegeman* case in 1974,[6] which concerned the Association Agreement with Greece. Here the Court was so bold as to rule that the provisions of the Agreement 'form an integral part of Community

---

[2] Reference may be made in passing to the broad view taken by the Court of the treaty-making power of the European Community, starting with the *ERTA* case; highly controversial at times, that case law is now only of historical interest as a result of the broad provisions introduced by the Lisbon Treaty with effect from 1 December 2009: see in particular Art 37 of the Treaty on European Union (TEU) and Art 216 of the Treaty on the Functioning of the European Union (TFEU).

[3] Case 26/62 *van Gend en Loos* [1963] ECR 1.

[4] [1972] ECR 1219.

[5] Case 26/62 *van Gend en Loos* [1963] ECR 1.

[6] Case 181/73 *Haegeman* [1974] ECR 449.

law'—which might be seen as a direct assertion of the monist position, and certainly one intended to give full effect to treaties.

The Court also held that it had jurisdiction to give preliminary rulings on the interpretation of the Agreement, on the ground that the Agreement, being concluded by the Council, was an act of the institutions of the Community under Article 177 EEC—now Article 267 TFEU.

That was a crucial development, since it had the consequence that the Court could impose a single interpretation on the treaties concluded by the Community, rather than leave their interpretation to the Member States or their national courts, which would hardly have been conducive to a consistent and uniform interpretation, or to the Council and Commission of the EC, which might have resulted in politically inspired interpretation.

The adoption of a single interpretation by the Court was of course of particular importance when it came to questions of direct effect. The issue arose in *Bresciani*, decided in 1976;[7] if the issue had been decided by the national courts, it would no doubt have been decided differently in different systems. The ECJ, by a similar process of reasoning to *van Gend en Loos*, held that the provision in question did have direct effect. And it appeared that, in this context at least, for a provision of such an agreement to have direct effect, it was a necessary and sufficient condition that the provision conferred rights on individuals which national courts must protect. For that purpose, the provision had to be sufficiently clear, precise and unconditional.

Thus there is a close connexion between the two aspects of the title of this chapter: the internal legal effects of the EU's international agreements (which has essentially come to be seen as the question of direct effect) and the protection of individual rights.

Moreover, it seems that it is not always helpful to draw a dividing line between questions of direct effect and questions of interpretation, as is sometimes done in this field. The question of direct effect is, of course, also a question of interpretation. Moreover, the answer to the question requires an interpretation of the treaty as a whole and/or of the substantive provisions which are invoked in the instant case. For that reason, no objection can properly be taken where the Court, empowered under the EU Treaty to rule on 'interpretation', rules, as in *van Gend en Loos*, *International Fruit* and *Bresciani*, on the 'effect' of a treaty.

Ever since the 1970s, the Court has been ready to ascribe direct effect to the EC's bilateral agreements—including mixed agreements—but has sometimes had reservations about some multilateral agreements. But it is not the character of the agreement as bilateral or multilateral that is decisive; rather, it is other features of the agreement in question.

Similarly with the interpretation of the substantive provisions of the

---

[7] Case 87/75 *Bresciani* [1976] ECR 129,

agreements: here there is a progressive development in the approach of the Court to bilateral agreements, with an increasing willingness to give the provisions the same meaning as in the 'progressive' internal Community context, whereas in the context of multilateral agreements there is sometimes a tendency to apply the traditional principles of treaty interpretation as reflected in the Vienna Convention on the Law of Treaties.

It is unnecessary here to recount in detail the development of the jurisprudence, as the story has been frequently told.[8] But the conclusions that can be drawn are still perhaps in some respects novel.

Whereas in earlier periods the Court seemed hesitant about according direct effect, in recent case law the Court has rather consistently—and often rather rapidly—rejected objections to direct effect, with the limited but important exceptions particularly of the GATT/WTO Agreement and, more recently, of the United Nations Convention on the Law of the Sea.

This tendency towards recognition of direct effect can be illustrated both where the Court examines the issue of the direct effect of the agreement as a whole and where it examines the direct effect of a particular provision.

The Court's approach might be criticised, however, for not always distinguishing the two issues; moreover, when it does so, it regularly addresses them in what may seem the wrong sequence. The Court generally considers first the specific provision of the agreement, applying the classic tests of whether the provision is clear, precise and unconditional; it then considers the agreement as a whole. It might have seemed more logical to take the reverse order: it seems that it would make little sense to analyse the provision and conclude that it is apt to have direct effect but then to negate that conclusion on the ground that the agreement as a whole is not apt to have such effect. In practice, however, in the exceptional case where the Court considers that the agreement is not apt to have direct effect, it does start with the analysis of the agreement as a whole, as it did with the GATT in the *International Fruit Company* case.[9] Once the Court had reached the conclusion that that Agreement, taken as a whole, did not lend itself to direct effect, it was able to refrain from examining the specific provisions in issue.

Let us first illustrate the positive approach of the Court by reference to some more recent cases, and then examine some qualifications which may be needed.

The Court's increasingly positive approach to treaties in its recent case law can be conveniently illustrated by the trio of cases *Pokrzeptowicz-*

---

[8] See, eg the very full study by M Maresceau, 'Bilateral Agreements Concluded by the European Community' (2006) 309 *Collcted Courses of the Hague Academy of International Law* 125; see also M Mendez, 'The Legal Effect of Community Agreements: Maximalist Treaty Enforcement and Judicial Avoidance Techniques' (2010) 21 *European Journal of International Law* 83.

[9] See Maresceau, above n 8, 293–94.

Meyer,[10] *Kolpak*[11] and *Simutenkov*.[12] In the first two cases the Court was concerned with provisions of an Association Agreement, a 'Europe Agreement' intended to lead to accession to the European Union. In the the third case the Agreement was with Russia and had no such aim. In contrast to its earlier case law, where the aim and object of the agreement was a decisive factor, the Court here reached a similar 'progressive' result in all three cases on very different treaties.

In the *Pokrzeptowicz-Meyer* case the question was raised whether the non-discrimination principle in Article 37(1) of the Agreement had direct effect.[13] Ms Pokrzeptowicz-Meyer, a Polish national, had claimed the incompatibility with that principle of a provision of national (German) law according to which posts for foreign-language assistants might be the subject of employment contracts of limited duration whereas, for other teaching staff performing special duties, recourse to such contracts must be individually justified by an objective reason.

According to the Land Nordrhein-Westfalen, Article 37(1) of the Agreement was incapable of having direct effect because the provision opened with the phrase 'Subject to the conditions and modalities applicable in each Member State'. In its submission, that phrase qualified the prohibition of discrimination on grounds of nationality and Article 37(1) could not, therefore, be considered to be unconditional within the meaning of the Court's case law on direct effect. That submission did indeed find some support in the Court's earlier case law.

The Court, however, appeared to have little difficulty in concluding that the provision in issue had direct effect, despite the presence of terms which under its earlier case law might have been regarded as precluding such effect. The Court referred instead to its case law on discrimination on grounds of nationality in the context of the free movement of workers for nationals of EU Member States, notably its judgment in *Spotti*[14] concerning precisely the right of a worker employed under a contract for a limited period to remain in employment on the expiry of that period. The Court thus interpreted the pertinent provision of the Association Agreement with Poland in the same way as Article 39(2) (now Article 45(2) TFEU). According to the Court, although the 'similar wording' as such was not in itself sufficient to adopt the same interpretation, 'the aim and context' of the provision did not justify any different interpretation from the one given in *Spotti*. As a consequence, the Polish applicant could rely

[10] Case C-162/00 *Land Nordrhein-Westfalen v Beata Pokrzeptowicz-Meyer* [2002] ECR I-1049.
[11] Case C-438/00 *Kolpak* [2003] ECR I-4135.
[12] Case C-265/03 *Simutenkov* [2005] ECR I-2579.
[13] Case C-162/00 *Land Nordrhein-Westfalen v Beata Pokrzeptowicz-Meyer* [2002] ECR I-1049.
[14] Case C-272/92 *Spotti* [1993] ECR I-5185.

on the non-discrimination principle against Germany to the same extent as applicants relying on the former Article 39 EC.

The Court took a similar approach in *Kolpak*, where it extended its intra-EU ruling in *Bosman*[15] to the interpretation of the non-discrimination principle of the Association Agreement with Slovakia.[16] The Court thus transposed to the Association Agreement with Slovakia the famous *Bosman* ruling, given on the EC Treaty itself but in the then novel context of professional football, to the effect that the principle of non-discrimination on grounds of nationality, a cornerstone of the EC Treaty, applies to rules laid down by sporting associations which determine the conditions under which professional sportsmen can engage in gainful employment; that principle therefore precludes a limitation, based on nationality, on the number of players who may be fielded in a football team at the same time. Maros Kolpak was a Slovak national, lawfully resident in Germany and goalkeeper for a German handball team. He applied for an unrestricted handball licence, ie one that was not marked with the letter 'A' (*Ausländer*, foreigner) since only a maximum of two players with an 'A' licence were entitled to be fielded at the same time. Kolpak claimed that the Slovak Republic was a state whose nationals were entitled to participate without restriction in competitions under the same conditions as German and Community players by reason of the prohibition of discrimination resulting from the combined provisions of the EC Treaty and the Association Agreement with Slovakia.

The Court accepted that the provision of the Agreement did have direct effect, and indeed, although this was not spelt out, that it had a form of 'horizontal' direct effect, since it could be relied upon by Kolpak against the sports federation. The Court concluded that the non-discrimination principle laid down in this provision

> must be construed as precluding the application to a professional sportsman of Slovak nationality, who is lawfully employed by a club established in a Member State, of a rule drawn up by a sports federation in that State under which clubs are authorised to field, during league or cup matches, only a limited number of players from non-member countries that are not parties to the Agreement on the European Economic Area.[17]

The Court followed a similar line of argument in *Simutenkov*, where a provision of the Partnership and Cooperation Agreement with Russia was in question.[18] The applicant, a Russian national lawfully employed as a professional footballer in Spain, had been granted by the football federation a licence issued to nationals of third states (states other than

---

[15] Case C-413/93 *Bosman* [1995] ECR I-4921.
[16] Case C-438/00 *Kolpak* [2003] ECR I-4135.
[17] Para 58 of the judgment.
[18] Case C-265/03 *Simutenkov* [2005] ECR I-2579.

Member States of the EU and of the European Economic Area). His application for the type of licence issued to nationals of Member States had been refused on the basis of national rules which provided that such a licence could be issued only to nationals of Member States and which restricted the fielding of third-state nationals in national games. He challenged that refusal before the Spanish courts on the basis that the distinction made by the rules between nationals of Member States of the EU and the EEA, on the one hand, and Russian nationals, on the other, was contrary to the non-discrimination principle laid down in Article 23(1) of the Partnership and Cooperation Agreement with Russia.[19]

Although the Agreement did not establish a special relationship of the traditional kind between the Community and Russia, and still less was a preparatory step towards accession, but provided merely for co-operation between the parties, the Court of Justice took the view that those considerations did not preclude direct effect.

Moreover, the Court interpreted the provision 'progressively', in the same way as it had interpreted it in an intra-EU context. The facts were similar to those in *Kolpak*, with the sport changed from football to handball and the scene changed from Germany to Spain. But the Agreement with Russia was of a different character. However, although the Agreement was not concluded in order to establish an association with the Community, but merely with a view to co-operation, the Court concluded that the difference in context and purpose of the two agreements could not result in a difference in meaning of the principle of non-discrimination in the two agreements. It is interesting to observe that the Court did not compare the nature and purpose of the partnership agreement with those of the EC Treaty. Article 23(1) of the Partnership Agreement therefore produced a right to equal treatment similar to that established in *Kolpak* and in *Bosman*. It followed from those rulings that a limitation on participation in matches between clubs based on the nationality of the players could not be justified on sporting grounds. No other justifications for such limitation had been advanced.

The Court's approach to direct effect in *Simutenkov* seems particularly far-reaching and represents a departure from the earlier case law.

Indeed, it seems as if the nature of the Agreement is now no longer an obstacle to direct effect, so long as the Agreement contains provisions which, as the Court put it in *Simutenkov*, directly govern the position of

---

[19] Art 23(1) of the Partnership and Cooperation Agreement with Russia provided that, subject to the laws, conditions and procedures applicable in each Member State, the Community and its Member States had to ensure that the treatment accorded to Russian nationals legally employed in the territory of a Member State was free from any discrimination based on nationality, as regards working conditions, remuneration or dismissal, as compared to its own nationals. The contracting parties were not prevented from applying their own national rules concerning, amongst other things, working conditions to the extent that in so doing they did not nullify or impair the benefits accruing to any party under the Agreement.

individuals; the only real requirement is now that the substantive provisions themselves satisfy the requirements of direct effect, ie that they are clear, precise and unconditional: and even the requirement of unconditionality, as we have seen, has been diluted.

Could it even be suggested that the reference in judgments to the nature of the agreement has in recent cases become little more than a ritual refrain in which an agreement of almost any nature could be said nevertheless to be capable of having direct effect? Is the reference to the nature of the agreement, or its object and purpose, any longer meaningful on the issue of direct effect?

Such a reference is perhaps a relic of an earlier period in which the Court was more cautious, and placed more emphasis on the category of agreement in question. Thus an association agreement designed essentially to confer benefits on the other party at the Community's expense should be held, for that very reason, to have direct effect, and so to be enforceable within the Community, even though there was no reciprocity; the Court accordingly rejected arguments by Member States that such an agreement should not be enforceable in the absence of reciprocity. Similarly, agreements designed to facilitate the other party's accession to the Community should be accorded direct effect in view of the intended close relationship with that party. On the other hand, an ordinary arm's-length trade agreement with a commercial partner might not be accorded direct effect.

The recent cases before the Court suggest that the Court may be going down a different route, in which different types of agreement are treated in the same way. But it would be wrong to assume too much, if only because recent cases may not be wholly representative. The recent cases have predominantly been cases in which the Agreements 'directly govern the position of individuals', and in which the fundamental principle of equal treatment, within a Member State of the European Union, is at issue. It is perhaps that material context which has led the Court to adopt a more positive approach to direct effect. The position might be different if the Court were to be confronted by a very different type of scenario, for example under a traditional trade agreement, where the issue was one of, say, the exhaustion of intellectual property rights, or some other provision of an essentially commercial character. However, it may be that in such a case the Court would nonetheless accept the direct effect of the agreement but rule, if that proved appropriate, that in view of the nature of the agreement its terms could not be interpreted in accordance with the interpretation of the terms of the EC Treaty.

Something similar is also true of interpretation of the substantive provisions of the Agreement. In recent cases, the Court's new approach to direct effect is mirrored, as we have seen, by its approach to interpretation: the Court is increasingly ready to apply the same interpretation as it has developed for the EC Treaty. But again the same qualification may be necessary: how far are the recent cases truly representative?

In fact, examples can be found in very recent case law of a more cautious approach. In *Katsivardas*[20] the Court refused to recognise the direct effect of the most-favoured-nation clause of the Cooperation Agreement with the Cartagena Agreement and the Member States thereof. In *Fokus Invest*,[21] following its recent decision in *Grimme*,[22] the Court held that the freedom of establishment guaranteed by the Agreement with Switzerland extended only to natural, not to legal, persons. The Court explicitly based that view on the fact that the Swiss Confederation had chosen not to join the internal market of the European Union and that, consequently, the interpretation given to the provisions of Union law concerning that market cannot be automatically applied by analogy to the Agreement.

In the politically charged recent case of *Brita*, which concerned the interpretation of the EC–Israel Association Agreement and the EC–PLO Association Agreement, the Court relied heavily and explicitly on the classic rules of treaty interpretation contained in the Vienna Convention on the Law of Treaties in ruling on the importation into the EU of goods originating in the West Bank.[23]

It remains to be seen, therefore, how far the new approach of the Court of Justice to agreements with third countries will extend; but we have certainly witnessed, in recent years, a positive evolution in that approach. Before summarising the conclusions to be drawn, it is necessary to consider how far multilateral agreements should be considered separately.

III MULTILATERAL TREATIES

As observed above, it is sometimes suggested that there is a broad distinction reflected in the ECJ case law between bilateral and multilateral agreements, the Court being more progressive on the former than the latter. As often, the picture is more complex. There is certainly a distinction between the GATT/WTO family of treaties and the 'personal' provisions of bilateral treaties. However, there is no doubt that many multilateral treaties are 'an integral part of the European Union legal order' which the ECJ therefore has jurisdiction to interpret by way of a preliminary ruling: this is true, for example, of the Montreal Convention (on international carriage by air).[24]

Multilateral treaties may also have direct effect: indeed, the very first

[20] Case C-160/09 *Katsivardas*, judgment of 20 May 2010.
[21] Case C-541/08 *Fokus Invest*, judgment of 11 February 2010.
[22] Case C-351/08 *Grimme*, judgment of 12 November 2009.
[23] Case C-386/08 *Brita*, judgment of 25 February 2010.
[24] Case C-63/09 *Walz v Clickair*, judgment of 6 May 2010.

case in which the ECJ held a treaty concluded by the Community to have direct effect concerned a multilateral treaty.[25]

Moreover, at least where a challenge is made by a Member State, direct effect in the customary sense is not necessary for the Court to entertain the challenge: the Court made this clear in the biotechnology case, where the Court was prepared to consider a challenge by the Netherlands to the Biotechnology Directive, a challenge based in part on a multilateral convention on biodiversity, without raising any issue of direct effect.[26] So an EU measure can be challenged on the basis of (even) a multilateral treaty, even though that treaty does not have direct effect in the sense of conferring rights on individuals

The recent *Intertanko* case is particularly interesting in this respect.[27] There, an EU directive was challenged as contrary both to a multilateral convention on maritime pollution (MARPOL) and to the UN Convention on the Law of the Sea (UNCLOS). The challenge based on MARPOL foundered inter alia because the Member States' powers had not been fully transferred to the European Union. As for UNCLOS, although a multilateral, indeed global, treaty of immense scope, it binds the European Union and forms an integral part of the EU legal order, but it 'does not establish rules intended to apply directly and immediately to individuals and to confer upon them rights and freedoms capable of being relied upon against States'.[28] Thus a treaty can be invoked by individuals—in contrast to Member States—in order to challenge an EU measure only where the treaty has direct effect.

A further consideration regarding multilateral treaties concluded by the EU follows from the rule, now stated in Article 216(2) TFEU, that all such treaties are binding on the Member States. Thus, even if they do not have direct effect, they may be justiciable before the ECJ, if only because the Commission may bring infringement proceedings against Member States. That would have been unlikely in the earlier years of the Community, but is now not infrequent. Examples are proceedings against Germany for non-compliance with a GATT agreement;[29] proceedings against France for infringement of the Barcelona Convention and the Mediterranean Sea Protocol;[30] and proceedings against the Netherlands for infringing provisions of the Association Agreement with Turkey (provisions which would, it seems, have direct effect).[31]

The Court has also held, in relation to UNCLOS—although, as we have seen, it has declined to review compliance with UNCLOS at the

---

[25] *Bresciani*, above n 7.
[26] Case C-377/98 *Netherlands v European Parliament and Council* [2001] ECR I-7079.
[27] Case C-308/06 *Intertanko* [2008] ECR I-4057.
[28] Para 64 of the judgment.
[29] Case C-61/94 *Commission v Germany* [1996] ECR I-3989.
[30] Case C-239/03 *Commission v France* [2004] ECR I-9325.
[31] Case C-92/07 *Commission v Netherlands*, judgment of 29 April 2010.

suit of individuals—that it does have jurisdiction to assess Member State compliance with that Convention in infringement proceedings, where the Convention provisions at issue come within the scope of the European Union's competence.[32]

IV CONCLUSIONS ON THE CASE-LAW

Overall, the Court of Justice has been remarkably positive in its approach to agreements concluded by the Community.

This is true in the first place of asserting jurisdiction to interpret the provisions of agreements, and also of related instruments such as decisions of Association Councils: although here the Court's exercise of jurisdiction can be traced back to the earliest cases.

Secondly, it is true of the Court's conception of the Community's treaty-making power.

Thirdly, it is apparent in the Court's consistent assertion that treaties concluded by the Community form an integral part of Community law.

Fourthly, it is apparent in the Court's willingness to ascribe direct effect to a treaty.

Fifthly, it is generally true of the Court's approach to the interpretation of the substantive provisions of the treaty.

A Treaty Which Raises Some New Questions: the European Convention on Human Rights

Article 6(2) of the Treaty on European Union, as amended by the Lisbon Treaty, imposes an obligation on the European Union to accede to the European Convention on Human Rights. That obligation raises many questions, but should be considered here mainly in the context of the EU's external relations, the effects of accession within the EU legal order and the impact of accession on the constitutional order of states.

As is well known, initially the Court refused to accept challenges to EC measures on grounds of fundamental rights, apparently fearing the impact on the primacy of EC law. Gradually, and perhaps partly in response to the concerns expressed by national constitutional courts, it shifted to a diametrically opposite position. Ultimately the Court even seemed excessively concerned, sometimes bringing in human rights principles when they appeared superfluous. In that change of heart, the Court increasingly relied on the ECHR, and its jurisprudential formulation was taken over in the Maastricht and Amsterdam Treaties.

---

[32] Case C-459/03 *Commission v Ireland* [2006] ECR I-4635, para 121.

In terms of the external relations and the effects of accession, the following points seem noteworthy:

(i)   The Obligation to Accede

However commendable the idea of accession may be, it is odd to impose an obligation on the European Union to accede to the ECHR when the fulfilment of that obligation is not solely within the powers of the European Union and its Member States. With the belated entry into force in 2010 of the 14th Protocol to the Convention, the Convention has been amended so as to permit accession by the European Union, as the Convention was drawn up for states and hitherto allowed only states to be parties, so that that particular obstacle has been overcome—and there seems political agreement on all sides in favour of EU accession. As is often the case with such grand designs, however, the devil is in the detail. The Convention is still designed for states, and substantial amendments may be needed to fit the European Union into its scheme. Accession therefore requires negotiation with the other 20 state parties to the Convention on a number of difficult issues; agreement has to be reached on all of those issues; and the resulting treaty has to be ratified by all 47 state parties to the Convention. It might have been more appropriate for the obligation on the EU to be framed not as an obligation to accede, but as an obligation to use its best endeavours to accede. The EU Member States are also in the strange position of being in a sense on both sides of the negotiation, as being Member States of the Council of Europe and also, of course, parties to the Convention.

A further difficulty in complying with the obligation to accede might arise from the possibility that the European Court of Justice, which is of course closely affected by accession, might be asked for an opinion on the compatibility with the EU Treaties of the proposed agreement on the terms of accession. In the past, some members of the Court, in their private capacity, expressed views favourable to accession—and there should no longer be debate on the principle of accession, since it appears to be mandated by the Treaty. However, the possibility cannot be excluded that the Court might give an unfavourable opinion on certain of the proposed terms of accession, or lay down certain conditions. In that event, the agreement could not enter into force without such terms being renegotiated; and it cannot be certain that all the non-EU Member States, at least, would be willing to accept the views of the ECJ. Indeed, the Court has already expressed certain views on what it deems desirable in the way in which accession should be effected.[33]

---

[33] See the discussion document of the Court of Justice, 5 May 2010.

(ii)   The Scope of Accession

It seems to be broadly agreed within the European Union and the Council of Europe that accession should be subject to the principle of equality: the position of the European Union should reflect as closely as possible the position of the states. Of course, the principle of equality cannot be interpreted blindly: it must take account of relevant differences. In some respects, the European Union cannot be treated as a state. Difficult questions may arise from the need to respect the specific features of EU law, and in particular for the EU institutions and the ECJ in particular to have unfettered control of the division of competences internally between the European Union and its Member States. But the principle of equality, taking due account of such differences, must be applied rather strictly. It would thus certainly seem to preclude some ideas which have been floated by some EU Member States: for example, that EU 'primary legislation' should not be subject to the jurisdiction of the Strasbourg Court. In principle, the European Union should be fully subject to the control of the Strasbourg Court, such control being the principal object of EU accession.

Whether the European Union should also accede to all the protocols adding additional rights to the Convention is considered briefly below.

(iii)   The Internal Legal Effects of Accession

Let us look briefly nowat the internal legal effects of accession. As we have seen, treaties concluded by the European Union are, in accordance with Article 216(2) TFEU, binding both on the European Union and on its Member States. However, that may raise difficulties in the case of the ECHR. Which of the obligations are obligations of the European Union and which are of the Member States? In relation to other so-called 'mixed' agreements, the European Union and its Member States have sometimes sought to draw up a list of their respective competences, but that would be inappropriate in the case of the ECHR. As regards judgments of the Strasbourg Court, it may be only in the light of the Court's final judgment that it is possible to see the dividing line between the responsibility of the European Union and the responsibility of its Member States. Yet the European Union will seek to insist that it is the European Union, not the Strasbourg Court, which decides, as between the Union and its Member States, on issues of competence, and thus on responsibility.

A further question arises in relation to the protocols to the Convention which have from time to time been adopted to 'update' the Convention by providing for additional rights: these are Protocols 1, 4, 6, 7, 12 and 13. What would the position be if the European Union were to ratify protocols which had not been ratified by all the Member States? Those are Protocols 4, 7, 12 and 13. Would such protocols be binding on the

European Union Member States which had not ratified them by virtue of the principle that treaties concluded by the European Union are binding on its Member States? The answer would seem to be no: only the European Union itself and those Member States which had ratified the protocol in question would be answerable for an alleged breach. Ratification of a protocol by the European Union could only be in relation to the exercise of its own competence and certainly could not confer jurisdiction on the Strasbourg Court over a state which had not ratified the protocol. Even if other EU Member States were indirectly affected by an adverse judgment of the Strasbourg Court, for example because compensation was payable out of the EU budget, that could not mean that those states were themselves in breach of the protocol rights.

What does seem clear beyond doubt, as regards the internal legal effects of accession to the Convention and protocols, is that the provisions of the Convention and protocols laying down individual rights and freedoms would be accepted as having direct effect. Such provisions could indeed be regarded as the archetype of provisions having direct effect. That would be so notwithstanding the flexibility of some of the provisions, for example the element of discretion conferred on states by the notion of a 'margin of appreciation' used by the Strasbourg Court.

(iv)   Participation in the European Court of Human Rights and the Committee of Ministers of the Council of Europe

It will no doubt be urged on the European Union side that the Union should participate fully in the organs applying the Convention: so there should be a judge appointed in respect of the EU, and full participation in the Committee of Ministers. Questions of principle and of detail are likely to arise: among them, will the EU judge be eligible to sit in all cases? Will it be possible for two judges from the same state to sit in the same case? Similarly, will the EU appointee to the Committee of Ministers be a permanent appointment? Will he serve in proceedings before the Committee of Ministers in all cases?

Execution of judgments of the Court

Execution of judgments of the Strasbourg Court is entrusted to the Committee of Ministers of the Council of Europe: the Foreign Ministers of the 47 Member States of the Council of Europe, or their deputies stationed in Strasbourg. In recent years, the Committee of Ministers has taken its responsibility for execution of the judgments of the Court increasingly seriously. An obvious difficulty which may result from EU accession is that an EU act found by the Court to breach the Convention might be treated more favourably than a state act, given that a majority of the Committee of Ministers would represent EU Member States: currently 27 out of 47, but the proportion would rise in the event of further enlargements of the EU. (The same question might even arise in relation to judges hearing a case against the EU, since there might in such a case be a majority of judges from the EU and its Member States; but the judges should of course be presumed to be wholly independent.)

(v)   Concluding Remark

At a time when some of the major issues on the effect of treaties concluded by the European Union appear to have been resolved—although many interesting questions remain—it is perhaps apposite that important new issues of a wholly new kind are raised by the prospect of EU accession to the ECHR. Those questions mentioned above are only a selection of issues which have been raised; and, as so often with the law, others will no doubt arise which have not yet been imagined.

The Lisbon Treaty resolves some long-standing problems with its provisions on the treaty-making power of the European Union, but the Lisbon Treaty's commitment to accession to the European Convention on Human Rights will raise many new problems, which will doubtless exercise legal minds for many years to come.

28

The Obligation of Member States to Foresee, in the Conclusion and Application of their International Agreements, Eventual Future Measures of the European Union

JONI HELISKOSKI*

I BACKGROUND, SCOPE AND PURPOSES

THIS CHAPTER ADDRESSES the question of obligations of the Member States, under European Union law[1], to foresee, in the context of the conclusion and application of their international agreements with third countries, acts or measures that the Union may take in its own right in future. To put it in another way, the question is whether the exercise of Member States' competence to conclude or apply international agreements may be circumscribed by Union law specifically by a prospect of the Union exercising its competence—it being understood that actions of Member States could, under certain circumstances, compromise the effectiveness of the measures that may eventually be taken by the Union.

In more concrete terms, the nature of the questions to be addressed in what follows may be illustrated by means of the issues that have arisen in the recent case law of the Court of Justice, that is: the obligations incumbent on Member States when they negotiate and ratify bilateral

---

* While the author has acted as agent for the Finnish government in Case C-205/06 *Commission v Austria*, Case C-249/06 *Commission v Sweden*, Case C-118/07 *Commission v Finland* and Case C-246/07 *Commission v Sweden*, the views expressed are personal.
[1] While terminology resulting from the entry into force of the Treaty of Lisbon is taken account of throughout the paper, it may, however, still be more appropriate to refer to 'Community' or 'Community law' in certain contexts (eg when judgments delivered under the EC Treaty are discussed).

international agreements on a subject matter in respect of which a Union agreement is being negotiated;[2] the obligation of Member States to eliminate incompatibilities between their existing international agreements and measures that may in future be adopted by the Union;[3] and the obligations of Member States when they exercise their rights as contracting parties to an international agreement in an area where action by the Union is envisaged.[4] As these examples serve to demonstrate, the issue to be addressed does not concern the scope or nature of the Union's external competence but rather the obligations under Union law that the Member States are required to respect when they exercise their competence.[5] In this sense, this chapter not only draws upon the distinction—consistently emphasised in the work of *Alan Dashwood*—between, on the other hand, the conferment upon the Union of certain competence and, on the other hand, the obligations of Union law incumbent upon the Member States that may not involve any correlative powers of the Union;[6] by focusing on the obligations incumbent on the Member States in the conduct of their external relations, the chapter also serves to illustrate the fact that the Member States retain their character as states at the international level— a circumstance referred to as justifying the designation of the European Union as 'a constitutional order of states'.[7]

The analysis in this chapter will focus on the relevant case law of the Court of Justice. While the general principles of Union law laid down by Article 4(3) TEU (ex-Article 10 EC)[8] are certainly relevant in the present context, the fact remains that there are no provisions in either the TEU or the TFEU that specifically govern the present matter. Of course, account will have to be taken of the fact that in areas where the Union has competence to 'carry out actions to support, co-ordinate or supplement the actions of the Member States' (Article 6 TFEU), the exercise of that competence does not 'supersede' the competence of the Member States in those areas (Article 2(5) TFEU). Likewise, in the areas of research, technological development and space, as well as those of development co-operation and

---

[2] See Case C-266/03 *Commission v Luxembourg* [2005] ECR I-4805 and Case C-433/03 *Commission v Germany* [2005] ECR I-6985.

[3] See Case C-205/06 *Commission v Austria*, judgment of 3 March 2009; Case C-249/06 *Commission v Sweden*, judgment of 3 March 2009; and Case C-118/07 *Commission v Finland*; judgment of 19 November 2009.

[4] See Case C-246/07 *Commission v Sweden*, judgment of 20 April 2010.

[5] For a recent and particularly helpful general analysis of the obligations constraining the exercise of the external competence of the Member States under EU law, see M Cremona, 'Defending the Community Interest: the Duties of Cooperation and Compliance' in M Cremona and B de Witte (eds), *EU Foreign Relations Law. Constitutional Fundamentals* (Oxford, Hart Publishing, 2008) 125.

[6] See, eg his inaugural lecture, 'The Limits of European Community Powers' (1996) 21 *European Law Review* 113, 114.

[7] See A Dashwood, 'The Relationship between the Member States and the European Union/European Community' (2004) 41 *Common Market Law Review* 355.

[8] See also Art 24(3) TEU.

humanitarian aid, the exercise of the Union's competence 'shall not result in Member States being prevented from exercising theirs' (Article 4(3)–(4) TFEU).[9] However, these are all provisions dealing with the nature of the Union's competence and not specifically with the question of Union law obligations of the Member State to foresee future Union measures in the conclusion of new international agreements and in the application of existing ones.[10] Secondary law, too, is by definition of little avail for the present purposes: the hypothesis is precisely to look at situations where the Union has not yet taken any action by way of the adoption of rules of secondary law.

The chapter is structured as follows. I shall first deal with the question of the application of 'pre-accession'[11] agreements covered by Article 351 TFEU (ex-Article 307 EC) (Section II). The obligation of the Member States, as parties to such agreements, to foresee measures that may eventually be adopted by the Union has recently arisen before the Court of Justice in the so-called Bilateral Investment Treaties (BITs) cases.[12] Secondly, I shall address 'post-accession' agreements (Section III) and deal with both the conclusion of new agreements (Section III.A) and the application of existing agreements (Section III.B).

Finally, two aspects are excluded from the scope the analysis: the areas of a priori exclusive Union competence (as any Member State competence is by definition ruled out)[13] and the question of the exercise of Member State competence in the specific context of the conclusion of mixed agreements (ie the question of whether and when the Member States may

---

[9] There are also a number of provisions expressly indicating that the Union's competence in a particular subject matter or area does not affect the right of the Member States to maintain or conclude agreements in the subject matter or area concerned. See, eg the provisions stating that the Union's external competence in the fields of the environment (Art 191(4), second subpara, TFEU, ex-Art 174(4), second subpara, EC)), development cooperation (Art 209(2), second subpara, TFEU, ex-Art 181, second para, EC) as well as economic, financial and technical cooperation with third countries (Art 212(3), second subpara, TFEU, ex-Art 181a(3), second subpara, EC)—respectively—is without prejudice to Member States' competence to negotiate in international bodies and to conclude international agreements. See also Protocol (No 23) on External Relations of the Member States with Regard to the Crossing of External Borders, annexed to the TEU and the TFEU and Declaration (No 36) on Art 218 of the TFEU concerning the negotiation and conclusion of international agreements by Member States relating to the area of freedom, security and justice, annexed to the Final Act of the Intergovernmental Conference which adopted the Treaty of Lisbon.

[10] It may, however, be noted that under Art 22 TEU the European Council now has the power to identify the strategic interests and objectives of the Union not only in the area of the Common Foreign and Security Policy but in all areas of the Union's external action.

[11] Ie agreements concluded before 1 January 1958 or, for acceding states, before the date of their accession, between one or more Member States on the one hand, and one or more third countries on the other hand.

[12] See above n 3.

[13] By the concept of a priori exclusive Union competence, reference is made to the category of Union competence now covered by Art 3(1) TFEU, as opposed to the situations of exclusive Union competence envisaged in para 2 of the provision concerned.

become parties to a mixed agreement when the Union's competence is non-exclusive Union).

II   PRE-ACCESSION AGREEMENTS
COVERED BY ARTICLE 351 TFEU

A   Preliminary Observations

The first and second paragraphs of Article 351 TFEU read as follows:

> The rights and obligations arising from agreements concluded before 1 January 1958 or, for acceding States, before the date of their accession, between one or more Member States on the one hand, and one or more third countries on the other, shall not be affected by the provisions of the Treaties.
>
> To the extent that such agreements are not compatible with the Treaties, the Member State or States concerned shall take all appropriate steps to eliminate the incompatibilities established. Member States shall, where necessary, assist each other to this end and shall, where appropriate, adopt a common attitude.

For the present purposes, the question is whether Article 351 TFEU, as interpreted by the Court of Justice, requires the Member States to prevent conflicts from arising between, on the one hand, their existing pre-accession international agreements with third countries and, on the other hand, measures that may in future be taken by the Union's institutions (or the powers of the institutions that have not yet been exercised).

In order to address this question, it is necessary to look at the concept of 'incompatibility' within the meaning of the second paragraph of Article 351 TFEU in the Court's case law.

B   The Case Law

A case that has sometimes been invoked in favour of a broad understanding of the concept of 'incompatibility' under Article 351 TFEU is *Burgoa*.[14] In the judgment concerned, the Court of Justice explained that: 'Article 234 [now Article 351 TFEU] is of general scope and it applies to any international agreement, irrespective of subject matter, which is *capable of affecting the application* of the Treaty'.[15]

It could be argued that the phrase 'capable of affecting the application of the Treaty' also covers the incompatibilities that may arise between, on the one hand, measures that are adopted by the Union institutions and, on the other hand, an international agreement concluded by a Member State.

---

[14] Case 812/79 *Burgoa* [1980] ECR 2787.
[15] Ibid, para 6 of the judgment (emphasis added).

In the submission of the present author, the judgment in *Burgoa* provides no authority for defining the concept of incompatibility under Article 351 TFEU.

First, the case did not concern the question of an incompatibility between an international agreement of a Member State and a power-conferring provision of the EC Treaty. Secondly, in the circumstances of the case, no conflict between a Member States' international obligations and the Treaty was found to exist. The case raised the issue of whether fishing vessels registered in a third country could validly be made subject to a regime requiring them to obtain an authorisation for a fishery zone lying between 12 and 200 nautical miles from the baselines (as had in fact been provided in the relevant Community regulations) in a situation where the London Fisheries Convention[16] (to which both the Member State and the third country concerned were parties) only referred to the zone extending up to 12 miles. However, an agreement had been reached between the Community and the third country concerned providing, inter alia, that each of the parties could require vessels of the other party fishing in its waters to hold a licence. Consequently, the Court held that the interim regime the Community had set up through its own internal rules fell within the framework of the relations established between the Community and the third country concerned, and those relations were superimposed on the regime that had previously applied in those zones by virtue of the London Convention.[17] Hence, no substantive conflict between the Community rules and the provisions of the Convention was found to exist.

It is thus necessary to look at those cases where an incompatibility under Article 351 TFEU has actually been found to exist. It is well established that, in principle, a conflict, or an incompatibility, under Article 351 TFEU, may arise between, on the one hand, obligations resulting from an agreement concluded by a Member State and, on the other hand, obligations incumbent upon that Member State by virtue of provisions of the Treaties directly giving rise to obligations incumbent upon the Member States.[18] It is equally well settled case law that an incompatibility may arise between, on the one hand, obligations resulting from an agreement concluded by a Member State and, on the other hand, secondary Union law.[19] For the present purposes, however, the question is whether an incompatibility under Article 351 TFEU may arise between, on the one hand, an agreement concluded by a Member State and, on the other hand, Treaty provisions from which no obligations flow directly for the

---

[16] Fisheries Convention (London, 9 March 1964), 581 UNTS 8432.
[17] Ibid, para 24 of the judgment.
[18] See, eg Case C-216/01 *Budějovický Budvar* [2003] ECR I-13617.
[19] See, eg Joined Cases C-62/98 and C-84/98 *Commission v Portugal* [2000] ECR I-5171.

Member States (or with measures that may in future be adopted by the Union institutions).

In the first place, reference could be made to the opinion of Advocate General Tizzano in the *Open Skies* cases,[20] which clearly illustrates the problem. These cases concerned the compatibility with the EC Treaty of bilateral air transport agreements concluded between eight Member States of the Community and the US. In his opinion, the Advocate General addressed the question of whether an incompatibility could arise between, on the one hand, the Community's external competence and, on the other hand, an agreement covered by the first paragraph of Article 307 of the EC Treaty (now Article 351 TFEU). In his view, bilateral agreements concluded by Member States before the entry into force of the EC Treaty (or, the accession by a given Member State to the Union):

> may well give rise, in substantive terms, to an issue of compatibility with specific provisions of the Treaty (for example, Article [43 EC, now Article 49 TFEU]) or with provisions of secondary law (for example, the regulations on air transport), and in that case, as we will see, the question of the application of Article [307 EC, now Article 351 TFEU] will certainly arise.[21]

In the opinion of the Advocate General, however, the same did not apply to the provisions of the EC Treaty the function of which was to confer upon the Community a certain competence. The mere existence of a Community competence could not give rise to an incompatibility in the sense of Article 307 EC:

> [I]n terms of competence, by contrast, the issue of compatibility with Community law cannot arise, for the obvious reason that supervening external competence of the Community in matters previously regulated by agreements of the Member States does not suffice in itself to render those agreements incompatible with the rules and principles governing the division of powers. Nor, clearly, can the AETR judgment be of relevance in this respect, since it concerns only agreements concluded following the exercise of an internal power. It seems to me, therefore, that there is no basis for bringing the first paragraph of Article [307] into play in this connection.[22]

In the judgments in the *Open Skies* cases, the Court did not pronounce on the question of application of Article 307 EC, as none of the disputed agreements were considered to fall within the scope application of the first subparagraph thereof.

There is, however, case law indicating that, in order for the obligation

---

[20] See the Opinion of AG Tizzano in Case C-466/98 *Commission v United Kingdom*; Case C-467/98 *Commission v Denmark*; Case C-468/98 *Commission v Sweden*; Case C-469/98 *Commission v Finland*; Case C-471/98 *Commission v Belgium*; Case C-472/98 *Commission v Luxemburg*; Case C-475/98 *Commission v Austria*; and Case C-476/98 *Commission v Germany*, [2002] ECR I-9427.

[21] Para 113 of the Opinion.

[22] Ibid (emphasis added).

of a Member State to 'take all appropriate steps to eliminate the incompatibilities established' pursuant to the second paragraph of Article 351 TFEU to be triggered, those incompatibilities should have a certain degree of clarity, that is, they should have been established sufficiently clearly for the Member State concerned. Hence, in *Commission v Austria*[23] the Court of Justice addressed the question of compatibility of the ILO Convention No 45 concerning the employment of women on underground work in mines[24] with Council Directive 76/207/EEC of 9 February 1976 on the implementation of the principle of equal treatment for men and women as regards access to employment, vocational training and promotion, and working conditions.[25] After first having concluded that the obligations flowing from the Convention were indeed incompatible with Articles 2 and 3 of the Directive, the Court noted that the only occasion (following the accession of Austria to the Union) on which that Member State could have denounced the Convention under the rules laid down in Article 7(2) thereof was during the year following 30 May 1997. Given that the Commission's first letter to Austria on the subject had dated from 29 September 1998, 'the incompatibility of the prohibition laid down by that convention with the provisions of Directive 76/207 had *not been sufficiently clearly established* for that Member State to be bound to denounce the convention'.[26]

In those cases where the question of the interpretation of Article 351 TFEU has arisen in the context of references for a preliminary ruling, the Court's approach appears to have been equally cautious. The standard practice of the Court has been to leave the task of determining the existence of an incompatibility to the national court,[27] and to require the national court to ascertain whether a possible incompatibility between the Treaty and the bilateral convention can be avoided by interpreting that convention, to the extent possible and in compliance with international law, in such a way that it is consistent with Union law.[28]

More recently, the Court has been directly confronted with a question of the existence of an incompatibility under Article 351 TFEU in the *BITs* cases.[29] In those proceedings, the Commission claimed that the defendant Member States—Austria, Finland and Sweden—had failed to fulfil their obligations under the second paragraph of Article 351 of the TFEU by not having taken appropriate steps to eliminate incompatibilities between, on the one hand, Articles 57(2) EC (now Article 64 (2)–(3) TFEU), 59

---

[23] Case C-203/03 *Commission v Austria* [2005] I-935.
[24] Geneva, 30 May 1937, 40 UNTS 627.
[25] [1976] OJ L39/40.
[26] Para 62 of the judgment (emphasis added).
[27] Case C-158/91 *Levy* [1993] ECR I-4287, para 21; Case C-124/95 *Centro-Com* [1997] ECR I-81, para 58.
[28] Case C-216/01 *Budějovický Budvar* [2003] ECR I-13617, para 169.
[29] See above n 3.

EC (now Article 66 TFEU) and 60(1) EC (now Article 75/215 TFEU)[30] and, on the other hand, the provisions on transfer of capital contained in investment agreements the Member States had concluded with certain third countries. Articles 64, 66 and 75/215 TFEU provide the Council with the power to adopt measures restricting the movement of capital to or from third countries in certain circumstances, whereas the provisions of the relevant investment treaties seek to guarantee the free transfer of capital between the Member State and third country concerned. Irrespective of the fact that no measures had actually been taken on the basis of above Treaty provisions, the Court agreed with the Commission and held that:

> [the] *powers of the Council*, which consist in the unilateral adoption of restrictive measures with regard to third countries on a matter which is identical to or connected with that covered by an earlier agreement concluded between a Member State and a third country, *reveal an incompatibility with that agreement where*, first, *the agreement does not contain a provision allowing the Member State concerned to exercise its rights and to fulfil its obligations as a member of the Community* and, second, there is also no international-law mechanism which makes that possible.[31]

This means that, in principle, an incompatibility can arise between an international agreement of a Member State and a power-conferring provision of the TFEU, irrespective of whether the powers concerned have actually been exercised by institutions of the Union. In order to prevent such an incompatibility from arising, Member States may therefore be required to foresee the eventual exercise by the Union of its powers, by ensuring that the Member State concerned is allowed, in the words of the Court of Justice, 'to exercise its rights and to fulfil its obligations as a member of the Union'.

C   Analysis

So far, the *BITs* case law remains the sole occasion when the Court has clearly recognised that an 'incompatibility' within the meaning of Article 351 TFEU may arise between an international agreement of a Member State and a power-conferring provision of the Treaties. In all other cases, the incompatibilities detected by the Court have concerned either provisions of the EC Treaty directly giving rise to obligations incumbent

---

[30] Art 215 TFEU 'combines' ex-Arts 60 and 301 EC, and its scope of application *ratione materiae* covers 'economic and financial relations' with third countries (as well as restrictive measures against natural or legal persons and groups or non-state entities). Art 75 TFEU covers restrictive measures necessary for the pursuance of the objectives related to the area of freedom, security and justice.

[31] Case C-205/06 *Commission v Austria*, para 37 (emphasis added). See also Case C-249/06 *Commission v Sweden* para 38, and Case C-118/07 *Commission v Finland*, para 31.

upon the Member States (as opposed to power-conferring provisions) or rules of secondary law. Even in these cases, the approach of the Court in establishing an incompatibility has been a cautious one.

The general picture emerging of the Court's case law suggests that the scope of application of the principles laid down by the Court of Justice in the *BITs* judgments should be a narrow one and confined to the specific nature of the provisions of Articles 64, 66 and 75/215 TFEU. The rationale of the *BITs* judgments clearly relates to the requirement of effectiveness of measures that the Council may take in the specific circumstances provided for in Articles 64, 66 and 75/215 TFEU.[32] As the Court explained, those provisions confer upon the Council a power to restrict movements of capital and payments between Member States and third countries 'in certain specific circumstances'[33] and, in order to ensure their effectiveness, the measures in question 'must be capable . . . of being applied immediately'.[34] It is in the light of these specific characteristics of the powers concerned that the Court reached the conclusion that the renegotiation *ex post facto* of the agreements or the reliance on other mechanisms offered by international law as means of removing eventual actual incompatibilities should not be considered as sufficient to guarantee the practical effectiveness of the measures concerned.[35]

III POST-ACCESSION AGREEMENTS OF THE MEMBER STATES

Unlike the case of pre-accession agreements, the situation of post-accession agreements calls for a twofold analysis in the present context. It seems appropriate to distinguish between, on the one hand, the obligations incumbent upon a Member State in a situation where the conclusion of a new agreement is envisaged and, on the other hand, the obligations

---

[32] In a similar vein is P Koutrakos, 'Annotation on Case C-205/06, *Commission v Austria* and Case C-249/06, *Commission v Sweden*' (2009) 46 *Common Market Law Review* 2059, 2076. In Case C-118/07 *Commission v Finland*, the Court stated (in response to the argument that the consequence of granting the Commission's application would be to confer on the second para of Art 307 EC a scope which is unduly wide) that '. . . this judgment in no way prejudices the obligations of the Member States in other circumstances and merely holds, as stated earlier, that the exercise of the powers conferred on the Council in relation to the movement of capital might be hindered by the very existence of the bilateral agreements at issue and by the terms in which they are drafted' (para 49). For a critical review of the BITs judgments, see E Denza, 'Bilateral Investment Treaties and EU Rules on Free Transfer: Comment on *Commission v Austria*, *Commission v Sweden* and *Commission v Finland*' (2010) 35 *European Law Review* 263. See also N Lavranos, 'Protecting European Law from International Law' (2010) 15 *European Foreign Affairs Review* 265.

[33] Case C-205/06 *Commission v Austria*, para 35.

[34] Ibid, para 36.

[35] See also paras 49–54 of the Opinion of AG Poiares Maduro in Case C-205/06 *Commission v Austria* and Case C-249/06 *Commission v Sweden*.

a Member State is required to respect in the application of its existing agreements.

A   Conclusion of New Agreements by Member States

(i)   *Preliminary Observations*

Leaving aside the areas of an a priori exclusive Union competence, as well as the exclusive competence that may arise out of 'necessity' within the meaning of Opinion 1/76,[36] it has been a basic principle of the Union's external relations law since the *AETR* judgment[37] that the Member States retain their external competence until common rules are adopted by the Union. In other words, 'the Member States, whether acting individually or collectively, only lose their right to assume obligations with non-member countries as and when common rules which could be affected by those obligations come into being'.[38]

It is an equally well-established principle of Union law that, even when no such common rules have been adopted and, consequently, a matter continues to fall within the competence of the Member States, the latter must exercise that power in a manner that is in conformity with their obligations under the Treaties.[39]

The question arises, however, as to whether the requirement of the Member States to exercise their competence in conformity with EU law involves obligations specifically based on the existence of a prospect of the Union exercising its own competence—obligations that are deemed to constrain the exercise of Member States' competence to conclude international agreements.

---

[36] Opinion 1/76, Draft Agreement establishing a European laying-up fund for inland waterway vessels, [1977] ECR 741. See Opinion 1/94, Competence of the Community to conclude international agreements concerning services and the protection of intellectual property, [1994] ECR I-5267, para 85, and Art 3(2) TFEU.

[37] Case 22/70 *Commission v Council* [1971] ECR 263.

[38] Opinion 1/94 [1994] ECR I-5267, para 77. *Cf*, however, Opinion 1/03, Competence of the Community to conclude the new Lugano Convention on jurisdiction and the recognition and enforcement of judgments in civil and commercial matters, [2006] ECR I-1145, where the Court held that '. . . it is not necessary for the areas covered by the international agreement and the Community legislation to coincide fully. Where the test of "an area which is already covered to a large extent by Community rules" (Opinion 2/91, paragraphs 25 and 26) is to be applied, the assessment must be based not only on the scope of the rules in question but also on their nature and content. *It is also necessary to take into account not only the current state of Community law in the area in question but also its future development, insofar as that is foreseeable at the time of that analysis* (see, to that effect, Opinion 2/91, paragraph 25)' (para 126, emphasis added).

[39] See, eg Case C-466/09 *Commission v United Kingdom* [2002] ECR I-9427, para 41.

(ii) The Case Law

The well-known *Kramer* case[40] is usually regarded as an authority on how external competence is transferred from the Member States to the Community. In the judgment, however, the Court also addressed the question of the obligations circumscribing the exercise of the Member States' competence within a transitional period before the Community's competence was deemed to have become exclusive. From this perspective, the *Kramer* case may also be relevant insofar as it concerns the obligation of the Member States to foresee, in the context of the conclusion and application of their international agreements, measures that may eventually be adopted by the Union.

In *Kramer*, the question was whether the Member States were, at the time, still competent to assume the international commitments resulting from recommendations of the North-East Atlantic Fisheries Commission—an organ set up under the North-Atlantic Fisheries Convention, to which a number of other Member States were parties along with certain third states—or whether that competence had been transferred to the Community by virtue of Article 102 of the 1973 Act of Accession. Under the provision concerned, the Council was required to determine, from the sixth year after the accession at the latest, conditions for fishing with a view to ensuring protection of the fishing grounds and conservation of the biological resources of the sea. The Court held that, while the Community certainly had acquired the requisite external competence, the Member States had nonetheless retained a transitional competence to assume the commitments concerned in view of the fact that the Community had not at the time fully exercised its competence in the matter. However, pending the adoption of the relevant measures by the Community, the Member States were 'bound by Community obligations in their negotiations within the framework of the Convention and of other comparable agreements'.[41] More specifically, it followed from all of the relevant factors, including Article 5 EEC (now Article 4(3) TEU), Article 116 EEC[42] and Article 102 of the Act of Accession, that:

> Member States participating in the Convention and in other similar agreements [were] now not only under a duty not to enter into any commitment within the framework of those conventions which could *hinder the Community in carrying out the tasks entrusted to it by Article 102 of the Act of Accession*, but also under a duty to proceed by common action within the Fisheries Commission. It further [followed] therefrom that *as soon as the Community institutions had initiated the procedure for implementing the provisions of the said Article 102, and at the latest within the period laid down by that Article*, those institutions

---

[40] Joined Cases 3, 4 and 6/76 *Kramer* [1976] ECR 1279.
[41] Ibid, para 40 of the judgment.
[42] Art 116 EEC was repealed by the Treaty of Maastricht.

and the Member States will be under a duty to use all the political and legal means at their disposal in order *to ensure the participation of the Community in the Convention* and in other similar agreements.[43]

Thus, the exercise of Member States competence was circumscribed by the prospect of Community measures being adopted by the end of the period provided for in Article 102 of the Act of Accession. It is evident that the rationale of the obligations concerned related specifically to the timetable set out in Article 102 of the Act of Accession for the exercise of the relevant Community competence. In the judgment, the Court also made it plain that the transitional competence of the Member States would cease to exist at the end of the period concerned at the latest, the result being that the conservation of the biological resources of the sea was to be conceived of as an area falling within the Community's exclusive competence.[44] In this sense, the obligations of the Member States were construed within the specific context of an 'emerging exclusive Community competence'.

More recently, the question of the significance of the prospect of Union measures being adopted for the Union law obligations incumbent on the Member States has arisen in *Commission v Luxembourg*[45] and *Commission v Germany*,[46] both cases concerning the negotiation, ratification and bringing into force of, as well as the refusal to terminate, by Member States, bilateral agreements with third countries on inland waterway transport. In those cases, the Commission accused the Member States concerned not only of infringing the Community's exclusive competence but also of breaching their obligations under Article 10 EC (now Article 4(3) TEU) by negotiating, concluding, ratifying and bringing into force the contested bilateral agreements after the Council had authorised the Commission to negotiate a multilateral agreement on behalf of the Community on the same subject. By so doing, the Commission claimed, the Member States concerned had 'compromised' or 'jeopardised' the implementation of the Council's decision in the sense that the negotiation by the Commission of a Community agreement, as well as the subsequent conclusion thereof by the Council, had been made more difficult by the interference from the Member States.

The Court accepted the Commission's arguments.[47] It first observed that the duty of genuine co-operation provided for in Article 10 EC is of general application and does not depend either on whether the Com-

---

[43] Joined Cases 3, 4 and 6/76 *Kramer* [1976] ECR 1279, para 40 of the judgment (emphasis added).

[44] See Case 804/79 *Commission v United Kingdom* [1981] 1045.

[45] Case C-266/03 *Commission v Luxembourg* [2005] ECR I-4805.

[46] Case C-433/03 *Commission v Germany* [2005] ECR I-6985.

[47] Case C-266/03 *Commission v Luxembourg*, paras 57ff, and Case C-433/03 *Commission v Germany*, paras 60ff.

munity competence is exclusive or on any right of the Member States to enter into obligations towards non-member countries. Referring to its own previous case law,[48] the Court then recalled that the Member States are subject to 'special duties of action and abstention' in a situation in which the Commission has submitted to the Council proposals which, although they have not been adopted by the Council, represent the point of departure for concerted Community action. The adoption by the Council of a decision authorising the Commission to negotiate a multilateral agreement on behalf of the Community marks 'the start of a concerted Community action at international level' and requires, for that purpose, 'if not a duty of abstention on the part of the Member States, at the very least a duty of close cooperation between the latter and the Community institutions'.[49] It followed that, by proceeding to ratify and implement those agreements without co-operating or consulting with the Commission, the Member States concerned had compromised the achievement of the Community's tasks and the attainment of the objectives of the EC Treaty.[50]

(iii) Analysis

Both the *Kramer* case and the more recent case law of *Commission v Luxembourg* and *Commission v Germany* show that Union law may circumscribe the freedom of the Member States to conclude new international agreements (or, in general, assume new international commitments), should the Member States' action be capable of undermining the measures which the Union institutions are envisaging to take. Whilst the *AETR* effect only becomes operative as and when common rules adopted by the Union institutions come into being, the cases concerned are illustrative of what Rass Holdgaard has called the 'extension of the temporal scope of the duty of loyal co-operation'[51] in the case law of the Court. For the present

---

[48] Case 804/79 *Commission v United Kingdom* [1981] 1045. The Court does not mention that in *Commission v United Kingdom* the Community was recognised to possess an exclusive competence and, due to disagreement in the Council, the Commission proposals concerned had not been adopted.

[49] Case C-266/03 *Commission v Luxembourg*, para 60 and Case C-433/03 *Commission v Germany*, para 66.

[50] As AG Tizzano explained in Case C-433/03 *Commission v Germany*, '[the ratification of bilateral agreements by a Member States in a field in which the Community is preparing to negotiate and conclude its own agreements] is likely to limit, if not undermine, the common action which the institutions are preparing to take and, in any event, prevents them from presenting themselves as the architects of a common position on the part of all the Member States, unless it is at the same time guaranteed that the agreement concluded by the Member State in question is in accordance with the common interest and follows the line desired and decided by the Community bodies. Still less then can it be guaranteed that the rules laid down in the Member State's agreement will exactly reflect the terms that the Community intends to lay down in the common agreement' (para 83 of the Opinion).

[51] R Holdgaard, *External Relations Law of the European Community. Legal Reasoning and Legal Discourses* (Alphen aan den Rijn, Kluwer Law International, 2008) 128–31.

purposes, the following conclusions may be drawn from the cases.

First, it needs to be stressed that in *Kramer* the obligations incumbent on the Member States were probably based on the specific circumstances of an 'emerging exclusive competence of the Community' in the area of the conservation of the biological resources of the sea. Article 102 of the 1973 Act of Accession established a specific time limit within which the Community was required to adopt the relevant measures of conservation in the area concerned. Therefore, the conclusions of the Court may not be applicable in areas where competence is shared between the Union and the Member States. However, the judgments in *Commission v Luxembourg* and in *Commission v Germany* show that the exercise of Member States competence may also be circumscribed by a prospect of the exercise of the Union competence that is less specific, should the action to be taken by the Union be sufficiently foreseeable. In the cases concerned, the 'special duties' of the Member States were deemed to have been created by a decision of the Council authorising the Commission to negotiate a multilateral agreement. However, the mere submission of a Commission proposal would not seem to be sufficient for such duties to be created; the adoption of a Council decision authorising the Commission to negotiate on behalf of the Union would also be required.[52]

Secondly, insofar as the nature of the obligations incumbent upon the Member States are concerned, it would be appropriate to employ the distinction drawn by Marise Cremona between obligations of substantive compliance, on the one hand, and obligations of a procedural nature, on the other hand; the former are based on the principle of primacy of Union law and, in particular, the need to comply with the provisions of the Treaty, the general principles of Union law and Union law based on the exercise of (internal or external) competence. The latter are based on the duty of co-operation and—in contrast to the obligations of substantive compliance—embody more flexible obligations to inform and consult.[53] In the light of these concepts, the *Kramer* judgment would seem to involve both a substantive and a procedural aspect: on the one hand, an obligation not to hinder the Union in carrying out the tasks and, on the other hand, a duty to proceed by common action within the organs set up by the agreement concerned. In *Commission v Luxembourg* and *Commission v Germany*, however, the obligations to foresee the conclusion of a future Union agreement are to be seen purely as procedural obligations without a requirement of substantive compliance.[54]

---

[52] See Case C-433/03 *Commission v Germany*, para 67. See also Holdgaard, above n 51, 130.

[53] See Cremona, above n 5, 129, 164–65 and 168–69.

[54] See also C Hillion, 'Tous pour un, un pour tous! Coherence in the External Relations of the Union' in M Cremona (ed), *Developments in EU External Relations Law* (Oxford, Oxford University Press, 2008) 10, 28.

B Application of Existing Post-accession Agreements by Member States

(i) Preliminary Observations

In the application of their existing post-accession agreements, the Member States are required, on the one hand, to refrain from taking measures that either might affect common rules in the sense of the *AETR* case law[55] or be in conflict with provisions of the Treaties directly giving rise to obligations incumbent upon the Member States[56] and, on the other hand, to take measures to bring their existing international commitments into conformity with subsequent secondary legislation.[57] For the present purposes, however, the question is whether Member States are under an obligation to refrain from taking measures under an existing international agreement as a result of a prospect of the Union acting in its own right in future, either as a party to the agreement concerned or otherwise, in the area covered by measures envisaged by a Member State (or Member States). New light has recently been shed on this question by the judgment in *Commission v Sweden*[58]—the so-called *PFOs* case concerning the application of the Stockholm Convention on Persistent Organic Pollutants.[59]

(ii) The Case Law

In brief, the *PFOs* case raises the question of whether Sweden was entitled to submit a proposal to add a particular group of substances— perfluoroctane sulphonates (PFOs)—to the Stockholm Convention in a situation where the substances concerned were not, at the time, covered by any instrument of Community legislation. In March 2005—that is, before the submission of Sweden's proposal—the Council had adopted conclusions containing a common position on the substances to be proposed for listing in the annexes to the Convention. In the conclusions, the Council had recommended that the Community and the Member States

> consider the further proposal of up to three additional substances [and that], as a first priority, their experts explore the list of substances under the United Nations Economic Commission for Europe (UNECE) Long Range Transboundary Air Pollution (LRTAP) Protocol on Persistent Organic Pollutants

---

[55] See Case C-45/07 *Commission v Greece* judgment of 12 February 2009, not yet reported.

[56] See Case C-307/97 *Saint-Gobain ZN* [1999] ECR I-6161, paras 57–59 and Case C-55/00 *Gottardo* [2002] ECR I-413, paras 31–35.

[57] See Case C-170/98 *Commission v Belgium* [1999] ECR I-5493.

[58] *Commission v Sweden*, above n 4.

[59] [2006] OJ L209/3. The Community and the Member States, with the exception of Italy and Malta, are parties to the Convention (21 December 2010).

(POPs Protocol) [60] as the source for these substances since these are already controlled as POPs[61] in the EU.[62]

On 6 July 2005—still before the submission of the proposal—the Council's Working Party on the international environment had concluded that a common proposal to add PFOs to the Protocol would be made once the Commission had submitted a proposal on control measures at the Community level. A few days later, and without waiting for the Commission's proposal, Sweden unilaterally proposed the addition of PFOs to the Convention. The Commission considered that, by submitting this proposal even though it was aware that the Community was engaged in drafting legislation on that substance, Sweden had breached Article 10 EC (now Article 4(3) TEU) and Article 300(1) EC (now Article 218(1)–(4) TFEU). The case therefore raises the question of whether a Member State is required, in the context of the application of an international agreement to which it is a party (in this case, alongside with the Union), to take account of the prospect of the Union exercising its competence in a matter related to the action envisaged by that Member State.

In his Opinion Advocate General Poiares Maduro agreed with the Commission and concluded that Sweden had failed to fulfil its obligations under Article 10 EC on the ground that the Community's decision-making process had been undermined by the submission of the contested proposal.[63] In the view of the Advocate General, a Member State should 'engage fully and in good faith' in a Community decision-making process in a field covered by a mixed agreement. More precisely, Member States should, first, co-operate with the Community decision-making process; and, secondly, 'refrain from taking individual action, *at least for a reasonable period of time, until a conclusion to that process has been reached*'.[64] In respect of Sweden's actions, the Advocate General concluded that Sweden had failed to discharge the second part of the above duty; given that no conclusion had been reached with the Community decision-making procedure on the question of whether PFOs ought to be added to the Stockholm Convention, Sweden should have refrained from acting at least until that procedure had been (or was deemed to have been) brought to an end.

The Court also concluded that Sweden had breached Article 10 EC.

---

[60] [2004] OJ L81/37. The Community and the Member States, with the exception of Greece, Ireland, Malta, Poland, Portugal and Spain, are parties to the Protocol (21 December 2010).

[61] Pursuant to Reg (EC) No 850/2004 of the European Parliament and of the Council of 29 April 2004 on persistent organic pollutants and amending Dir (79/117/EEC), [2004] OJ L158/7.

[62] Council doc No 6770/05 (3 March 2005) (footnotes added).

[63] See paras 47ff of the Opinion.

[64] Emphasis added. The AG referred to Case C-266/03 *Commission v Luxembourg*, para 60, and Case C-433/03, *Commission v Germany*, para 66.

According to the Court, failure by Sweden to fulfil its obligations was constituted essentially by two sets of circumstances. First, by acting unilaterally, Sweden had unlawfully 'dissociated itself' from a 'common strategy' (deemed to have been established by the above mentioned Council conclusions and the minutes of the Working Party) not to propose, at the time, listing PFOs in the Annex to the Stockholm Convention;[65] unlike the Advocate General, however, the Court seems to leave it open as to whether the obligation of Member States to refrain from acting is provisional (that is, applicable only insofar as the common strategy is deemed to exist) or permanent. Given that such a strategy was in any case considered to exist at the time of Sweden's action, there was no need to rule on that issue. Secondly, the breach by Sweden of Article 10 was also constituted by the fact that the unilateral proposal '[had] consequences for the Union' since 'the Union [*sic!*] is a party to that convention [and] could be bound by the resulting amendment'.[66] This second set of circumstances—that is, the fact of the Union in its own right being a party to the agreement—suggests that the principles on the obligations of Member States relied on by the Court apply only in the case of mixed agreements.

(iii)   Analysis

Until the judgment in the *PFOs* case, there had been no case law of the Court of Justice specifically addressing the question of the obligation of Member States to foresee future measures of the Union in the context of the application of their existing agreements. In the *PFOs* case, the Court laid down a relatively strict obligation for Member States not to 'dissociate themselves' from a 'common strategy' of the Union in the application of an international agreement. At the same time, the requirements for such a strategy to exist are not very high: conclusions of the Council (which are political to their nature), minutes of a Council working party (ie a preparatory body with no decision-making powers) and events subsequent to the action of a Member State the legality of which is to be reviewed,[67] taken together, may be conducive to the existence of a 'common strategy'. Defined in this way, it is arguable that the obligation of Member States to abstain from action goes further than the procedural obligation to 'inform and consult' laid down in *Commission v Luxembourg* and *Commission v Germany*. In *PFOs*, the obligation incumbent on a Member State could probably be described as either a provisional (binding as long as a 'common strategy' is regarded to exist) or permanent obligation of abstention.[68] Such a heavy circumscription of the exercise of Member State

---

[65] Case C-246/07 *Commission v Sweden*, paras 89–91.
[66] Ibid, paras 100–01.
[67] Case C-246/07 *Commission v Sweden*, paras 88–89.
[68] In Cremona's typology (see the text accompanying n 53 above), the obligation con-

competence one may involve the risk of blurring the essential distinction between exclusive and shared Union competence. However, the conclusion in *PFOs* appears to be linked with the nature of the Stockholm Convention as a mixed agreement. Therefore, equally far-reaching constraints may not be imposed on Member States when they apply agreements (either bilateral or multilateral) to which the Union in its own right is not a contracting party.

IV   GENERAL CONCLUSIONS

Specific conclusions have already been drawn in respect of each of the situations addressed above, and there is no need to repeat those observations at this stage. What remains to be made is a more general summary of the main observations.

It emerges from the analysis of the relevant case law that there are various situations in which Union law may require the Member States, in the context of the conclusion or application of their international agreements with third countries, to take account of the prospect of the Union exercising its competence in future in a subject matter or an area that may have incidence upon a given agreement of a Member State (or Member States). In the light of the case law, at least the following three situations, or rationales, emerge:

1.   **The institutions are deemed to have initiated a Union decision-making procedure or agreed upon a common strategy.**

It follows from the Court's judgments in *Commission v Luxembourg* and *Commission v Germany* that, once the Commission has submitted to the Council proposals on Union action, the Member States become subject to 'special duties of action and abstention'. Moreover, the Court has held that the adoption by the Council of a decision authorising the Commission to negotiate a Union agreement results, if not in a duty of abstention on the part of the Member States, at least in a duty of close co-operation between the latter and the Union's institutions. The fact that the involvement of least two of the institutions is required for the duties concerned to be created implies that there is a requirement for the Union decision-making procedure to have made certain progress. In other words, there should be a sufficiently foreseeable prospect of action by the Union that needs to be protected from being undermined by individual initiatives or actions of Member States. The more recent judgment in the *PFOs* case is based on similar principles, but the Court appears to go further in circumscribing the Member States' freedom of action; the threshold

cerned might probably still fall within the category of procedural obligations (as opposed to substantive obligations of compliance).

for the existence of a 'common strategy'—from which a Member State
is not entitled to dissociate itself—is not very high, and is certainly more
open-ended than in *Commission v Luxembourg* and *Commission v Germany*. However, the Court's emphasis on the consequences that actions
of a Member States are bound to have for the Union strongly suggests
that the *PFOs* case law is intended to apply in the specific context of
mixed agreements.

2. **There is a primary law obligation requiring the Union institutions
to adopt rules of secondary law by a certain moment in time.**

This principle, familiar from the *Kramer* case, shares the same rationale
as the previous one, the main difference being the role played by a specific
Treaty-based obligation for the institutions to exercise their powers by a
certain time limit. The significance of this aspect of the *Kramer* case law
is, however, likely to be rather limited for the following reasons. First, the
reasoning of the Court appears to have been based on the conception of
the conservation of the biological resources of the sea as an area of an
'emerging' exclusive Community competence; therefore, similar logic may
not apply in other areas where competence is usually shared between the
Union and the Member States. Secondly, the TEU and the TFEU (unlike
the Treaty of Amsterdam, for example)[69] do not appear to contain primary
law obligations falling within this category, which, of course, decreases
the practical relevance of this element of the *Kramer* case law.

3. **A specific need to safeguard the practical effectiveness of the measures to be taken by the Union follows from the very nature of the powers
of the institutions.**

The third and final instance where Union law clearly requires Member
States to foresee measures that may be taken by the Union in future brings
us back to where the present analysis started from—the judgments of the
Court of Justice in the *BITs* cases. It follows from the judgments that the
Member States are under an obligation to foresee the exercise of Union
competence based on Articles 64, 66 and 75/215 TFEU by eliminating
incompatibilities between, on the one hand, those provisions and, on the
other hand, the provisions on transfer of capital contained in their bilateral investment agreements with third countries. Unlike the two other
situations covered above, the obligations concerned are not based on a
foreseeable (or even remote) prospect of the Union competence being
exercised but rather on the requirement to guarantee the practical effectiveness of the measures concerned. This requirement is specific to the
Treaty provisions in question and, accordingly, the principles put forward
by the Court in the *BITs* judgments may hardly be regarded as being of
a more general application.

---

[69] See, eg Art 30 TEU and Arts 61, 62, 63 and 67 EC, all amended by the Treaty of
Lisbon.

By way of a more general conclusion, it is submitted that the Court's case law reveals a certain tendency towards imposing, on the basis of Article 4(3) TEU, more far-reaching constraints on the exercise of the Member States' competence to conclude and apply international agreements. The recent judgments in the *BITs* cases and in the *PFOs* case serve as an unequivocal confirmation of this trend. In the case of the application of mixed agreements, in particular, the *PFOs* judgment shows that, even in matters falling within shared competence, the Court of Justice is determined to prevent 'solo performances' by individual Member States from compromising the prospects for action by the Union in its own right.

29

Third Time Lucky:
The Pre-history of the
Common Security and
Defence Policy

DAVID SCANNELL*

I INTRODUCTION

E UROPE'S PRESENT ATTEMPT to co-ordinate its activity in
the security and defence domain is not new. In the early 1950s,
an ambitious attempt was made to pleach the security and defence
capacities of European nations into a single framework. This was the
abortive attempt to create a purely supranational European Defence Community (EDC). Again in the early 1960s, an attempt was made to achieve a
measure of security and defence policy integration among European states.
This was the so-called Plan Fouchet, which lay at the opposite end of the
spectrum of integration models, being purely intergovernmental in character. It too failed. It therefore comes as no surprise that Europe's latest
attempt to achieve a measure of security and defence integration—the
Common Security and Defence Policy (CSDP)[1]—is neither purely supranational (the assets deployed in pursuit of CSDP objectives being Member
State, not EU, assets) nor purely intergovernmental in character (CSDP
objectives being EU, not Member State, objectives).

* Being historical in character, this chapter is heavily dependent on the accounts of others.
I have relied in particular upon Edward Fursdon's masterful account of the history of
the EDC (E Fursdon, *The European Defence Community: A History* (London, Macmillan,
1980)) to provide a framework for the historical context of the European Defence Community Treaty. I am grateful to James Flynn QC (of Brick Court Chambers) for his comments
on an earlier draft.
    [1] The CSDP has undergone a series of name changes over the past decade. Before the
Treaty of Lisbon amendments, the CSDP was most commonly referred to as the European
Security and Defence Policy (ESDP).

II   THE POST-WAR SECURITY ENVIRONMENT

Battle-scarred and bankrupt, post-war Europe had two security issues to address. First was the need to provide a credible counterbalance to the massive Soviet army, which had remained deployed on the territory of Eastern Europe after the conclusion of hostilities.[2] Second was the issue of how to allow Germany to rearm, if at all. The two issues were linked, since it was apparent that a contribution from Germany would be necessary to crenellate Europe's position between East and West.

A   The Dunkirk and Brussels Treaties

An aggressive German military renaissance in the aftermath of World War II was never really probable,[3] yet it was the fear of such a hegemony that gave rise to the Franco-British Treaty of Dunkirk of 4 March 1947.[4] This was largely due to the agency of the French, for whom the remilitarisation of Germany was especially anathema.[5] The preamble of the Dunkirk Treaty openly proclaimed it to be 'a Treaty . . . with the object of preventing Germany from becoming again a menace to peace'.[6] At its heart was a mutual assistance clause,[7] providing that the contracting parties would provide 'all the military and other support and assistance in [their] power' in the event of the other becoming engaged in hostilities.

To a lesser extent,[8] the same concern about German aggression gave rise to the Dunkirk Treaty's multilateral equivalent, the Brussels Treaty (BT) of 17 March 1948.[9] The BT extended the mutual assistance clause

---

[2] R Jenkins, *Churchill* (London, Macmillan, 2001) 787; TC Achilles, 'US Role in Negotiations that Led to Atlantic Alliance: Part I' NATO Review (August 1979) 5; G Aybet *The Dynamics of European Security Cooperation, 1945–1991* (Macmillan Press, 1997) ch 3, 60.

[3] S Dockrill, *Britain's Policy for West German Rearmament, 1950–1955* (Cambridge, Cambridge University Press, 1991) 6.

[4] Treaty of Alliance and Mutual Assistance, Dunkirk, 1947, Cmnd 7217, was ratified on 8 September 1947.

[5] ES Furniss, *France: Troubled Ally, De Gaulle's heritage and prospects* (New York, Harper & Row, 1960) 8–10.

[6] Dunkirk Treaty (1947), above n 4, preamble.

[7] Art II.

[8] There is evidence to suggest that the Brussels Treaty may also have been motivated by Ernest Bevin's desire to provide a 'third force' between the US and the USSR or, alternatively, to secure Marshall Plan aid, which was linked to European efforts to provide a meaningful defence against Soviet aggression: Aybet, above n 2, 61–62; Report of 25 November 1997 submitted on behalf of the Committee for Parliamentary and Public Relations of the Western European Union pursuant to Order 66 of the WEU Assembly, WEU Assembly doc. No 1583, Explanatory Memorandum, Introduction.

[9] Treaty of Economic, Social and Cultural Collaboration and Collective Self-Defence, Brussels, 1948, Cmnd 7599, Treaty Series No 1. Proposed initially by Ernest Bevin, it was signed by the Benelux countries, France and the UK and entered into force on 25 August 1948.

to the Benelux countries[10] and provided that the Consultative Council of the Brussels Treaty Organisation (BTO), established by the Treaty, would convene immediately to decide on 'the attitude to be adopted and the steps to be taken in case of a renewal by Germany of an aggressive policy'.[11] The 6th recital to the Treaty spoke of the Contracting Parties' resolve '[t]o take such steps as may be held to be necessary in the event of a renewal by Germany of a policy of aggression'.

The long-term relevance of the Dunkirk and Brussels treaties was doubtful from the outset. Both were directed at an illusory target.

B   The North Atlantic Treaty

Unlike the German threat, events in Czechoslovakia, Norway and Berlin[12] had clearly shown that the Soviet threat was real. In the immediate postwar years, the US patiently allowed the UK and France to fret about Germany—how could it, or they, do otherwise?—but kept its own eyes on the Soviet Union.

The United Nations Charter of 26 June 1945 had provided a legal framework within which regional security arrangements might be accommodated with a view to ensuring 'individual or collective self-defence if an armed attack occurs against a Member of the United Nations'.[13] It was within this framework that negotiations opened in Washington on 6 July 1948 on a trans-Atlantic security arrangement involving the five BTO states, Canada and the US.[14] The North Atlantic Treaty,[15] including a mutual assistance clause,[16] was signed in Washington on 4 April 1949,[17] creating the North Atlantic Treaty Organisation (NATO).

In addition to establishing a formal transatlantic security partnership, NATO's infrastructure provided a forum within which the US could voice

---

[10] Art IV BT. Art IV became Art V of the Modified Brussels Treaty in 1954. See below n 106.

[11] Art VIII, 2nd para BT.

[12] N Henderson, *The Birth of NATO* (London, Weidenfeld and Nicolson, 1982) 11–12; W Park, *Defending the West: A History of NATO* (Brighton, Wheatsheaf, 1986) 6.

[13] UN Charter, San Francisco, 26 June 1945, Treaty Series No 67 (1946), Cmnd 7015, Art 51.

[14] The Vandenberg Resolution of 11 June 1948 (Resolution 239) had paved the way for long-term US involvement in European security matters within the framework of Art 51 of the UN Charter. More immediate catalysts for the conclusion of the Washington Treaty were Stalin's orchestration of the Berlin Blockade and Ernest Bevin's importunate message to General Marshall, transmitted on 10 March 1948, concerning Norwegian security: Henderson, above n 12, 11–12.

[15] UKTS 56 (1949), Cmnd 7789; 34 UNTS 243; (1949) AJIL, Supp 159.

[16] Art 5.

[17] By the US, Canada, the UK, France, Italy, the Benelux countries, Denmark, Iceland, Norway and Portugal.

its strongly held opinion[18] that Europe should take a hand in its own security by formalising inter-state co-operation in the field of defence.[19] There was little doubt in the minds of the Americans that this could only be achieved by including West Germany as a security partner[20] and slowly, with passing years, the UK and France came to share that view. West Germany could not be allowed to languish in penury, undefended and making no contribution to a Western effort to resist the Soviet Union.[21]

C   The Supranational Approach; 'le Plan Pleven'

The invasion of South Korea by North Korea on 25 June 1950 is widely credited as having revitalised the European effort, under increasing US pressure,[22] to establish within Europe a defence structure capable of matching the military might of the Soviet Union[23] and, more particularly, to accommodate West Germany into that structure.[24]

At a debate in the Consultative Assembly of the Council of Europe on 11 August 1950, Winston Churchill went so far as to table a motion for

[18] The US's military strength was not the only reason why its voice within the NATO framework was stentorian. Following the detonation by the Soviet Union of a nuclear device on 22 September 1949, which Grosser says that this device was detonated on 14 July (A Grosser, *The Western Alliance: European-American Relations since 1945* (New York, Continuum, 1980)), Dockrill in August (Dockrill, above n 3, 9), President Truman had hurriedly signed the Mutual Defence Assistance Act into law and the US sought to link the financial aid to NATO states for which the Act provided to the integration of defence plans for the North Atlantic area.

[19] Park, above n 12, 18–19.

[20] E Fursdon, *The European Defence Community: A History* (London, Macmillan, 1980) 22 and 69; Aybet, above n 2, 71; F Gauzy, 'Le réarmement de la République fédérale d'Allemagne et la CED (1951–1954)' in M Dumoulin (ed), *La communauté européenne de défense, leçons pour demain?/The European Defence Community, Lessons for the Future?*, Euroclio, Etudes et documents, No 15 (Bruxelles, Bern, Berlin, Frankfurt/M, New York, Wien, PIE–Peter Lang, 2000) 31–50. The US clearly wanted Europe to do more than create bodies like the intergovernmental Council of Europe (established in London on 5 May 1949), described by Grosser, above n 18, 120–21, as an 'ineffectual shell'. See also, Dockrill, above n 3, 85.

[21] Grosser, above n 18, 123.

[22] President Truman's response is set out in US Department of State, *Bulletin*, 3 July 1950.

[23] J Pinder, *The Building of the European Union*, 3rd edn (Oxford, Oxford University Press, 1998) 8; A Forster and W Wallace, 'Common Foreign and Security Policy, From Shadow to Substance?' in H Wallace and W Wallace (eds), *Policy-Making in the European Union*, 4th edn (Oxford, Oxford University Press, 2000) ch 17, 463; Fursdon, above n 20, 67; Park, above n 12, 16; Aybet, above n 2, 71; RA Wessel, 'The State of Affairs in EU Security and Defence Policy: The Breakthrough in the Treaty of Nice' (2003) 8 *Journal of Conflict and Security Law* 265, 267; T Sinai, 'The Common European Security and Defence Capability: The Creation of a 'Holistic' Security Actor', Working Paper (Centre for Applied Policy Research, Munich, 2001) 24.

[24] Andrew and Gordievsky explain convincingly why the attribution of the invasion to Soviet policy is, in fact, misguided (C Andrew and O Gordievsky, *KGB* (London, Hodder and Stoughton, 1990) 401, citing D Dimbleby and D Reynolds, *An Ocean Apart* (London, BBC/Hodder and Stoughton, 1988) 190).

the creation of a European army. The Assembly, no doubt believing that the motion was reflective of British policy, went so far as to adopt it (with riders). However, Churchill never actually expected Britain to participate in his proposed European army[25] and, once that was more widely appreciated, the motion slipped over the political horizon.

The US resumed the initiative at the end of August 1950, proposing the remilitarisation of West Germany within NATO. NATO, of course, is not a supranational organisation. The national armies of its member countries remain intact and subject to national command and control. For the French, the notion of an operationally autonomous German army including a general staff remained execrable, and it was with a view to preventing this that, in advance of the scheduled NATO Defence Committee meeting at which it was expected that the NATO solution would be endorsed,[26] France sought to devise an alternative, supranational, solution to the problem of German rearmament.[27] The result of France's lucubration was 'le Plan Pleven',[28] proposing the establishment of a *Communauté Européenne de Défense*, a supranational EDC.

The dispatch with which the detail of the EDC proposal was devised is explained by the fact that the proposal relied heavily on the blueprint for a supranational system of governance contained within the Schuman Plan,[29] which was later to become the European Coal and Steel Community Treaty (ECSC).[30] That Treaty had broached the dilemma of West German economic reliance on coal and steel[31]—then the stuff of war—by supranationalising the means of production of these strategic commodities in France and Germany, creating a continuum of stability and prosperity

[25] Churchill himself was later to remark, on the proposal to establish a European Army, 'I meant it for them, not for us': D Weigall, 'British Perceptions of the European Defence Community' in PMR Stirk and D Willis (eds), *Shaping Post-War Europe: European Unity and Disunity 1945–1957* (London, Pinter, 1991) 94.

[26] The meeting was scheduled to take place on 28 October 1950.

[27] J Monnet, *Mémoires* (London, Collins, 1978) 345; Aybet, above n 2, 70–72.

[28] René Pleven was Prime Minister of France at the time of the plan's adoption, in the form of a Declaration, by the French cabinet, on 23 October 1950. The name of the Plan, like the Schuman Plan, is rather misleading, belying the fact that its chief architect was Jean Monnet.

[29] Robert Schuman was French Minister for Foreign Affairs when, in September 1949, he was asked by the NATO Council (NAC) to examine the reintegration of West Germany into Western Europe (as to which, see Fursdon, above n 20, 55). Jean Monnet, French Commissaire-Général of the Plan for the Modernisation and Equipment of France, was largely responsible for drafting the ECSC. Indeed, the 'Monnet Plan' only became the 'Schuman Plan' upon its approval by the French Cabinet and by Dr Konrad Adenauer on 9 December 1950.

[30] The Treaty of Paris, establishing the European Coal and Steel Community, was signed 18 April 1951 by France, Germany, Italy and the Benelux countries and entered into force on 23 July 1952. It expired on 23 July 2002 (Art 97 ECSC). The subject matter of the Treaty was then subsumed into the domain of the EC.

[31] German coal and steel production was concentrated in the Ruhr and Saar valleys. As to UK/US insistence that production in these valleys should resume after the war, see, for example, Pinder, above n 23, 5.

through mutual dependence[32] and ultimately playing an important security role in its own right.[33]

The Pleven Plan was presented at the 28 October meeting and met with an initially guarded response.[34] However, later West German objections to the NATO solution, coupled with French inveteracy on the issue of equal treatment for Germany within NATO's military structure, left the US with little option but to commit itself to the Plan as the only feasible solution to European security and defence.[35]

III   THE TREATY OF THE EUROPEAN DEFENCE COMMUNITY

The Treaty of Paris[36] (TEDC), the constituent instrument of the EDC, comprised 132 articles, 12 associated protocols, a common declaration by Foreign Ministers on the Treaty's duration and six further agreements.

The preamble began with a reference to the Charter of the United Nations before alluding to the purposes to be pursued by the EDC, chief among them the maintenance of peace and the defence of Western Europe through 'the fullest possible integration . . . of the human and material elements of [Member State] Defence Forces assembled within a supra-national European organisation'.[37] The core objective of the Treaty therefore adumbrated the derelict Council of Europe resolution of 11 August 1950: the establishment of a European army. Ancillary to this objective was that of ensuring the most rational and economical use of Member State resources by means of a common budget and a common armaments programme.[38] In the longer term, the preamble recognised that

[32] Address by Dr Javier Solana, 'Europe: Security in the Twenty-First Century', Olof Palme Memorial Lecture, Stockholm, 20 June 2001.

[33] For an historical perspective, see J Gillingham, *Coal, Steel, and the Rebirth of Europe, 1945–1955: The Germans and French from Ruhr Conflict to Economic Community* (Cambridge, Cambridge University Press, 1991); AS Milward, *The Reconstruction of Western Europe 1945–1951* (1984); AH Robertson, *European Institutions*, 3rd edn (London, Stevens/ New York, Matthew Bender, 1973); and DW Urwin, *The Community of Europe: A History of European Integration since 1945*, 2nd edn (London, Longman, 1995). On the key US and French players in the ECSC/TEDC process, see D Spierenburg and R Poidevin, *The History of the High Authority of the European Coal and Steel Community: Supranationality in Operation* (London, Weidenfeld & Nicolson, 1994); R Dwan, 'The European Defence Community and the Role of French-American Elite Relations (1950–1954)' in Dumoulin, above n 20, 63–89; W Isaacson and E Thomas, *The Wise Men: Six Friends and the World They Made* (New York, Simon & Schuster, 1986).

[34] Dockrill, above n 3, 42.

[35] Grosser, above n 18, 123; Aybet, above n 2, 75.

[36] European Defence Community Treaty, Paris, 27 May 1952, Cmnd 9127, Miscellaneous No 11 (1954).

[37] Preamble, 2nd Recital.

[38] Also provided for in Art 1, Part I Chapter II (European Defence Forces), Part IV (Financial Provisions) and Part V (Economic Provisions).

the Treaty might constitute 'a new and essential step towards the creation of a united Europe'.[39]

The TEDC contained an automatic support clause which provided that '[a]ny armed attack against any of the Member States in Europe or against the European Defence Forces shall be considered an armed attack on all Member States'.

The Member States and the European Defence Forces shall afford to the State or forces so attacked all the military and other aid in their power.[40]

As between the Benelux countries and France, therefore, Article 2(3) TEDC did not entail any additional accretion of international responsibilities, since it duplicated the mutual assistance clauses of the Dunkirk and Brussels Treaties. As with the Dunkirk and Brussels Treaties, it was to apply automatically in the case of an armed attack and was to have been geographically restricted to Europe. It is to be contrasted, however, with the weaker security guarantee of the North Atlantic Treaty's automatic support clause, which provided that an armed attack against one or more Member States would be considered an armed attack against all Member States and that each Member State would in such event assist the attacked party by taking '*such action as it deems necessary*, including the use of armed force, to restore and maintain the security of the North Atlantic area'.[41]

It was expressly envisaged that the structure of the Community and the internal organisation of its institutions would in time evolve into a deeper federal or confederal structure, as provided for in Article 38 TEDC.[42] This article had been proposed by the Italian Prime Minister Alcide de Gasperi at the Paris Conference of Foreign, Defence and Finance Ministers of the six ECSC states in December 1951.[43] It was intended to be the omphalos of the Treaty, within which a political superstructure would be developed which would ultimately supersede and accommodate the security and defence framework from which it had emerged, as well as the ECSC.

The EDC was therefore always intended to be a provisional arrangement. Although a Defence Community with a political core was to be established, it was contemplated that, within a year or so, the entire structure would 'turn itself inside out', resulting in a political community with a defensive core.[44]

---

[39] Preamble, 6th Recital.

[40] Art 2(3) TEDC.

[41] North Atlantic Treaty (1949), Art 5. Emphasis added.

[42] Art 8 (2) TEDC.

[43] AS Milward, *The European Rescue of the Nation-State*, 2nd edn (Oxon, Routledge, 2000) 333.

[44] On the premature, and unsuccessful, activation of Art 38 TEDC by the Foreign Ministers of the six ECSC states, see Spierenburg and Poidevin, above n 33, 45. The assumption that the EDC would burgeon to become a European federation or confederation is again apparent from Art 128, 2nd para TEDC.

Part I, Chapter II, containing Articles 9–18 of the Treaty, dealt with the newly established 'European Defence Forces', describing in detail the manner in which units were to be made available to the EDC by its Member States. Subject to very limited exceptions (such as the protection of Heads of State), Member State armed forces were to be almost entirely 'Europeanised'. The assets of the EDC were to be EDC assets, not Member State assets deployed in pursuit of EDC objectives. The competent NATO Supreme Commander was to be responsible for organising, equipping, training, preparing and commanding the European Defence Forces,[45] while day-to-day training, etc was to be undertaken by the Board of Commissioners, under Article 74(1). The EDC would therefore have rendered impossible the notion of state armies marching under a national flag by pooling Member State assets into a single European Defence Force, under NATO command.

The EDC was to occupy a lower position than NATO in the hierarchy of Western security and defence, and the TEDC was interlarded with provisions designed to ensure the smooth simultaneous operation of NATO and the EDC. In particular, Article 2(2) provided that the EDC would 'ensure the security of Member States against any aggression by taking part in Western defence *within the framework of the North Atlantic Treaty*'.[46]

The roles, functions and competences of the EDC's institutions were provided for in Part II of the Treaty (Articles 19–67). In many respects, The Board of Commissioners, Common Assembly, Council of Ministers and Court of Justice were to have been similar to the European Union's Commission, Parliament, Council and Court.

One of the features of the TEDC which distinguished it from the ECSC was its overt references to supranationalism. The ECSC, though it dealt with the substantially less controversial matter of the regulation of coal and steel markets, had obviated such references and had been ratified without substantial difficulty,[47] giving rise to a perception that references to supranationalism were best avoided in such treaties.[48]

However, references to the supranationality of the EDC Board of Commissioners were more than mere descriptive flourishes. The proposed institutions of the EDC were indeed conceived to be more supranational

[45] Art 18 TEDC.
[46] Emphasis added. Also relevant here are Arts 5, 47 and 128 TEDC.
[47] On the ratification process generally, see Spierenburg and Poidevin, above n 33, 32–34.
[48] Schaad has argued that it was primarily due to the sense of caution instilled by the EDC experience that the participants at the Messina Conference of 1955 sought to avoid references to supranationalism in the adoption of the Messina Resolution of 2 June 1955 (MPC Schaad, *Bullying Bonn: Anglo-German Diplomacy on European Integration, 1955–61* (Basingstoke, Macmillan in association with St. Antony's College, Oxford, 2000) 16). See also, DA Gowland and A Turner, *Reluctant Europeans: Britain and European Integration 1945–1998* (Harlow, Longman, 2000) 112.

than the institutions of the present European Union. The Board of Commissioners, for instance, was to take decisions by a majority vote of its members present,[49] while the European Commission under the European Economic Community Treaty acted by a majority of the number of members provided for in Article 157 of the EEC Treaty.[50] The Board was to have enjoyed substantial powers, which were to include powers of appointment of high-ranking military personnel.[51]

The EDC Assembly, too, was to have been far more supranational than the Assembly originally constituted under the later EEC Treaty. In addition to the de Gasperi provision, considered above, the Assembly was to have enjoyed a *locus standi* commensurate with the Council and the Member States to bring appeals before the EDC Court of Justice against decisions or recommendations of the Board of Commissioners[52] and a *locus standi* commensurate with the Member States and the Board of Commissioners to bring appeals against proceedings of the Council.[53] It will be recalled that the EEC Assembly enjoyed no such standing under Article 173 EEC, as originally framed.[54]

The jurisdiction of the Court of Justice of the EDC was also to have been extensive (even extending to a penal jurisdiction), consistent with the supranational character of the proposed Community. The Court was to have enjoyed powers under conditions set forth in a Jurisdictional Protocol and Statute[55] to give rulings with regard to punishable offences.[56] In particular, the Community was to ensure that the European Defence Forces and their members conformed in their conduct to the rules of the law of nations. Violation of such rules by the Forces or by its members was to have been punished.[57] It was envisaged that a common military penal code would be adopted in due course[58] so that the Court could act as a military tribunal, though that code, of course, never materialised.

The Financial Provisions of the Treaty, contained in Part IV, provided[59] that the revenue of the Community was to include contributions paid

---

[49] Art 24(1) TEDC.

[50] Art 163, 2nd para EEC. This voting requirement continues to apply under the TEC: Art 219, 2nd para TEC.

[51] See, in particular, Art 31 TEDC.

[52] Art 54(1) TEDC.

[53] Art 57, para 1 TEDC.

[54] Arts 173 and 175 EEC. See now, Arts 230 and 232 TEC. The amendment of Arts 173 and 175 EEC was preceded by a series of activist ECJ decisions gradually extending the *locus standi* of the European Parliament: Cases 138 and 139/79 *Roquette Frères v Council* and *Maizena v Council* [1980] ECR 3333 and 3393; Case 294/83 *Partie Ecologiste 'Les Verts' v Parliament* [1986] ECR 1339; Case C-70/88 *Parliament v Council* (Chernobyl) [1990] ECR I-2041.

[55] As to which, see Art 67 TEDC.

[56] Art 61 TEDC.

[57] Art 81(1) TEDC.

[58] Art 61 *bis* TEDC.

[59] In Art 93 TEDC.

by Member States, the Community's own revenue and revenue generated by dealing with property[60] and received by way of external aid.[61]
Among the noteworthy provisions of the Treaty coming under the heading of 'Economic Provisions' (Part V) was Article 107, pursuant to which
the production, import and export of war materials from or to third
countries, measures directly concerning establishments intended for the
production of war materials and the manufacture of prototypes and technical research concerning war materials was to have been prohibited,
subject to the granting of a permit to do so by the Board of Commissioners.[62] Extensive powers were to have been conferred on the Board of
Commissioners to demand information from firms which may have been
involved in infringements of the prohibition and to request the Court to
impose fines, including daily fines, on firms evading their obligations or
knowingly communicating false information.[63]

Finally, the General Provisions of Part VI of the TEDC dramatically
exemplify to what extent the EDC, had it come into existence, would
have surpassed any subsequent attempt at European supranational governance. A 'fidelity clause', instantly evocative of the later Article 5 EEC
(later Article 10 TEC and now, in substance, Article 4, paragraph 3 TEU),
was included, providing that

> Member States shall undertake to take all general or special measures necessary
> to ensure the implementation of the obligations resulting from the decisions
> and recommendations of the institutions of the Community, and to help the
> latter in the accomplishment of its task.
>
>   Member States shall undertake to refrain from any measure incompatible
> with the provisions of the present Treaty.

Though a rare example of a provision of the TEDC which was not
quite as directive as its later EEC descendant, given the fertility of
Article 5 EEC as a progenitor of Community obligations devolving upon
Member States, it is not fanciful to suppose that EDC law might, in the
fullness of time, have developed to the advanced state later attained by
EC law, encompassing such concepts as direct effect and supremacy, as
well as ancillary notions such as implied competence and obligations of
interpretation and reparations.

---

[60] Under Art 7 TEDC.

[61] Under Art 99, para 4 TEDC.

[62] Two very detailed annexes were appended to Art 107 TEDC, one listing the categories
of materials forbidden under Art 107 (including machine guns, ammunition and explosives),
the other listing items in respect of which the Board of Commissioners would not grant
permits except by unanimous decision of the Council (including nuclear, chemical, biological and long-range weaponry).

[63] Art 108 TEDC. The maximum imposable fine was to have been 1% of the annual
turnover of the violating firm (the word undertaking does not appear in the TEDC), while
the maximum daily fine was to have been 5% of the average daily turnover for each day
of delay: Art 108(2) TEDC.

Articles 123 and 124 TEDC are equally interesting. The former reads:

> 1. In case of grave and urgent necessity, the Council, provisionally, shall assume or confer on the organs of the Community or on any other appropriate body, the powers necessary to meet the position, within the limits of the general mission of the Community and in order to ensure the realisation of its objectives. Such a decision shall be taken unanimously . . .,

the latter, that:

> [i]n any case not provided for in the present Treaty in which a decision or a recommendation of the Board of Commissioners shall appear necessary to ensure the proper functioning of the Community and the realisation of its objectives within the limits of its general mission, such decision or recommendation may be taken, on approval of the Council acting unanimously.[64]

The combined effect of these Articles went far beyond that of the modern Articles 352–53 TFEU. The reference, for example, in Article 123(1) to 'the general mission of the Community' is arguably wider than a reference to the 'objectives' thereof, which were expressly enumerated in Article 1 of the Treaty, so that there is an element of *Kompetenz-Kompetenz* here, the Council enjoying the power to effect *des petites révisions* in order to optimise the effectiveness of the Community at times of crisis.[65]

The elasticity of the Treaty is equally apparent from Article 125, which expressly conferred power on the Council to modify the Treaty, by unanimous decision, 'if unforeseen difficulties revealed by experience arise in connection with [its] application', provided that such modifications did not prejudice the provisions of Article 2 of the Treaty or the balance of inter-institutional power.

IV THE FAILURE OF THE EDC

The EDC Treaty was signed in Paris on 27 May 1952 by the ECSC Member States: Germany, France, Italy and the Benelux countries. Progress in the period 1952–54 was at best desultory, however. Though formulated by the French, it had become ever more apparent that without the stated endorsement of the US, NATO and the UK the Treaty would fail, so that even by the time the Treaty was initialled in Paris on 9 May 1952 it had accumulated a miscellany of parallel Conventions (such as the

---

[64] Art 124, 1st para TEDC.

[65] Cases of 'grave and urgent necessity' were deemed to result from the position provided for in Art 2(3) TEDC (any armed attack against any of the Member States in Europe or against the European Defence Forces, as noted above) or in the Treaty between the EDC Member States and the UK (also of 27 May 1952: Miscellaneous No 9 (1952), Cmnd 8562, Annex A) or in the additional protocol relating to the guarantees of assistance between the Member States of the EDC and NATO, or from a declaration to this effect by the Council, acting unanimously: Art 123 (1), 2nd sub-para TEDC.

Bonn Convention, designed to provide for German equality outwith the EDC Treaty provisions), communiqués, security guarantees,[66] protocols and declarations of support, all designed to boost French confidence in the Treaty.

On 27 August 1954, the much-anticipated debate on the EDC Treaty opened in the Assemblée Nationale. Prime Minister Mendès-France's speech on the following day was at best uninspiring, at worst treacherous,[67] serving to empty the forthcoming vote of any prospect of success. On 30 August, a 'guillotine'[68] motion was introduced by deputy Herriot under the terms of which the Treaty should be rejected without detailed consideration (or a vote) on the ground that it was not suitable for discussion. The motion was passed (in large part as a result of cross-party voting), signalling the demise of the EDC.

A   Reasons for the Failure of the EDC

A variety of reasons for the EDC's failure has been advanced over the years, ranging from the thesis that it was 'foredoomed to failure'[69] to a conspiracy theory suggesting a Franco-Soviet pact to sabotage the Treaty in return for Soviet assistance in securing a settlement of the Indo-China war at the Geneva Conference.[70] There may very well be a little truth in each of the theories. Nevertheless, there were four principal reasons for the EDC's failure:

1. the refusal of successive British governments to participate in the Community;
2. the supranational character of the Community, as devised under the TEDC;
3. the death of Stalin; and

[66] In addition to a series of British declarations of support and association, NATO gave a security guarantee at its 1952 North Atlantic Council conference in Lisbon in terms that an attack on the EDC would constitute an attack on NATO for the purposes of its automatic support clause. Deighton mentions a $100m loan given to the ECSC by the US in an attempt to secure the safe passage of the EDC (A Deighton, 'Britain and the Creation of the WEU' in A Deighton (ed), *Western European Union 1954–1997: Defence, Security, Integration* (Oxford, European Interdependence Research Unit, St Antony's College, 1997) 15, fn 14, citing P Winand, *Eisenhower, Kennedy and the United States of Europe* (Basingstoke, Macmillan, 1993) 62.

[67] See, eg J Aimaq, 'Rethinking the EDC: Failed Attempt at Integration or Strategic Leverage?' in Dumoulin, above n 20, 91, 134; Dwan, above n 33, 88, fn 90, citing a letter from David Bruce, US Ambassador to France 1949–52 and Under Secretary of State 1952–53, to John Foster Dulles, 14 September 1954, General Correspondence and Memoranda, Confidential, Box 2, Dulles Papers, Princeton.

[68] A *motion préalable*.

[69] Milward, above n 43, 119.

[70] Fursdon, above n 20, 273, who rejects the theory.

4. the obsoleteness of one of the main objectives of the TEDC.[71]

(i) The Refusal of Successive British Governments to Participate in the Community

British resistance to the EDC is in large part attributable to its parlous financial position in 1945,[72] which served to focus British policy on the consolidation of financial, political and industrial strength rather than on the assumption of further commitments on mainland Europe.[73] The post-war Attlee government was anxious to ensure that Britain remained a world power into the future, but this could only be achieved with US support.[74] Inevitably, therefore, the UK favoured the US policy of advocating German rearmament through NATO.

Ideally, of course, the US would have liked to have reduced her own defence costs and exposure to Europe by inducing Britain to participate in continental affairs. Without British participation, the US was unwilling to give unqualified support to autonomous continental European defence and security initiatives.[75] Nevertheless, in the period between 1950 and 1954, Britain retained her policy of resistance to membership of any form of federal European structure coupled with peripheral participation as an interested observer of the EDC process.[76]

Churchill's post-war return to power, in October 1951, rekindled European hopes that the traditional British posture of scepticism towards European integration would be forsworn. However, it soon became apparent that Britain would continue under the new administration its policy of observing the EDC debate while making limited commitments to ensure

---

[71] Other suggested reasons for failure have included the hostility with which the Plan was received by the French media, by iron and steel interests in France and by the French army: DF Navarrete and RMF Egea, 'The Common Foreign and Security Policy of the European Union: A Historical Perspective' 7 *Columbia Journal of European Law* 41, 47–8, citing B Bruneteau, *Histoire de l Unification Européenne* (Paris, Armand Colin, 1996) 95; P Pitman, 'Interested Circles: French Industry and the Rise and Fall of the European Defence Community (1950–1954)' in Dumoulin, above n 20, 51, 51. On the internal French dynamics which operated against ratification, see R Aron and D Lerner, *France Defeats EDC* (New York, Praeger, 1957). These include Mendès-France's failure to support the TEDC in the French Assembly: Dwan, above n 33, 88, citing Bruce, above n 67.
[72] Grosser, above n 18, 43 and 60; Gowland and Turner, above n 48, 16ff; Park, above n 12. There were, of course, other psychological, structural and historical reasons for the UK's refusal to participate, as to which see, in particular, Schaad, above n 48, 2–5. Milward describes the Britain inherited by its post-war politicians as 'an almost empty simulacrum of world power': Milward, above n 43, 347. See also, Gowland and Turner, above n 48, 16.
[73] Gowland and Turner, above n 48, 9–11.
[74] Dockrill, above n 3, 8–9. On the 'special relationship', see R Hague, 'The Anglo-American Special Relationship in Retrospect' in M Clarke and R Hague (eds), *European Defence Co-operation, America, Britain and NATO* (London, Manchester University Press in association with the Fulbright Commission, 1990); and Gillingham, above n 33, 121–37.
[75] Dockrill, above n 3, 19.
[76] See, in particular, Gowland and Turner, above n 48, 55–61.

its success.[77] For Churchill in 1951, the clear priority was the reversal of Britain's economic and political decline and, as his health declined with advancing age, he was reasonably content to leave the question of Europe to his non-integrationist Foreign Secretary and protegé, Anthony Eden.[78] At the heart of Churchill's resistance to the idea were concerns as to its possible effectiveness on account of its supranational features.[79]

Certainly, the extent to which the UK ultimately supported the EDC[80] was such as to negate a suggestion that it was not committed to Europe.[81] On the other hand, there is no doubt that the fact that the UK's support fell short of seeking accession to the EDC played no small part in the demise of the TEDC.[82] Indeed, it has even been suggested that Gaullist opposition to the TEDC in France was partly based on disenchantment with Britain and a feeling that, without British participation, the Community could never work.[83]

(ii)   The Supranational Character of the EDC

Whatever chance there may have been for the TEDC to succeed as a purely intergovernmental organisation, there was no realistic prospect of success when the Community proposed the eviction of military and security matters from its traditional home at the heart of national sovereignty.[84]

Churchill never wavered from his belief that supranationalism and military sovereignty were fundamentally incompatible[85] and in this matter he

---

[77] Grosser, above n 18, 121; Jenkins, above n 2, 854–55.

[78] Jenkins, above n 2, 857; Dockrill, above n 3, 80–81.

[79] Gowland and Turner, above n 48, 59, and, amusingly, Jenkins, above n 2, 855. Most military men, it seems, despised the EDC proposal (Gillingham, above n 33, 263)—even in France (P Vial, 'Le militaire et le politique: le maréchal Juin et le général Ely face à la CED (1948–1954)' in Dumoulin, above n 20, 135–58) and Belgium (P Deloge, 'L'armée belge et la CED' in Dumoulin (ibid), 161–68).

[80] British support for the EDC was approved in Cabinet on 4 September 1951. A technical association followed, which later became a security guarantee and, on 14 March 1952, a treaty relationship: Cmnd 8512, April 1952. Further British undertakings of support followed: Memorandum Regarding UK Association with the EDC (1954). On 14 April 1954, Eden announced to the House of Commons that Britain would be prepared to second an armoured division to the EDC (Hansard(54), Vol 526, cols 1141–47) and, on the eve of the anticipated French debate on the EDC, the UK endorsed the US undertaking to regard the North Atlantic Treaty (1949) as a treaty of unlimited duration, removing a further impediment to the TEDC's ratification by its contracting parties. See generally, Dockrill, above n 3, 95, 103.

[81] A Deighton, 'Britain and the Creation of the WEU, 1954' in Dumoulin, above n 20, 283, 305.

[82] Fursdon, above n 20, 17, 20; Schlaim, Jones and Sainsbury, 'British Perceptions of the European Defence Community' in Stirk and Willis (above n 25), 100; Dockrill, above n 3, quoting Eisenhower.

[83] F Seydoux, *Mémoires* (Paris, Bernard Grasset, 1975) 172ff.

[84] M Trybus, 'On the Application of the EC Treaty to Armaments' (2000) 25 *European Law Review* 663, 664.

[85] Jenkins, above n 2; Dockrill, above n 3, 81.

was *ad idem* both with his own foreign secretary, Anthony Eden[86], and with Eden's predecessor, Ernest Bevin.[87] Significantly, the French Prime Minister, Pierre Mendès-France, also doubted the practicality of a supra-national structure for military co-operation and when, in July 1954, it became apparent that British and US guarantees of support would not be sufficient to ensure a positive vote on the TEDC in the Assemblée, he proposed, unsuccessfully, a series of amendments to the negotiated Treaty, notwithstanding its ratification in four of the six participating states,[88] which were designed to strip the Community of its supranational char-acter.[89] France and the UK were not alone, moreover, in their dislike of the TEDC's supranational character; initial reservations in Scandinavia,[90] Holland,[91] Belgium[92] and Spain[93] were also attributable in part to this feature.

(iii) The Death of Stalin

It has been suggested that one of the chief reasons underpinning the Plan Pleven was the need to provide a credible European defence against the threat of Soviet attack from the East. The death of Stalin on 5 March 1953[94] did not diminish that threat, but it did serve to remove from the EDC process much of the urgency which had characterised it theretofore. French opponents of the Treaty were now in the position of being able to argue with some conviction that it was unnecessarily and indeed dangerously isolationist to advocate a defence treaty to which the USSR would not be invited to accede.[95]

---

[86] Dockrill, above n 3, 84. Dockrill also explains that the Pentagon, from the very earliest days of the Plan Pleven, entertained serious reservations as to the military effectiveness of a defence organisation based upon a limitation of national sovereignties: ibid, 30.

[87] Gowland and Turner, above n 48, 55–56.

[88] The Netherlands had ratified the TEDC on 20 January, Belgium on 11 March, West Germany on 29 March and Luxembourg on 7 April 1954.

[89] Mendès-France was not alone in holding this view. French popular opinion had turned against the Treaty by 1954, being opposed to the relinquishment of military sovereignty for the sake of European unity: B Buzan, M Kelstrup, P Lemaître, E Tromer and O Wæver, *The European Security Order Recast, Scenarios for the Post-Cold War Era* (London, Pinter Publishers, 1990) 146; Dockrill, above n 3, 114; H Wyatt-Walter, *The European Community and the Security Dilemma, 1979–92* (London, Macmillan Press, 1997) 25.

[90] A G Harryvan and J van der Harst, 'From Antagonist to Adherent: The Netherlands and the European Defence Community' in Dumoulin, above n 20, 169, 172.

[91] Ibid.

[92] Deloge, above n 79, 164ff.

[93] V Gavin and I Munte, 'Spain's Position on the EDC: A Look at the Spanish Press' in Dumoulin, above n 20, 207, 211.

[94] Closely followed by the Korean armistice, in 1954.

[95] Forster and Wallace, above n 23, 463; Fursdon, above n 20, 217; Jenkins, above n 2, 860.

(iv)   The Obsoleteness of One of the Main Objectives of the TEDC

Although less immediately obvious than the explanations for the failure of
the TEDC advanced above, the proposition can be put, if only tentatively,
that the foundations upon which the TEDC was constructed were so
unsteadfast as to cast doubt on the architectural integrity of the project
from the very beginning. Milward has argued that although the political
line of negotiation, leading ultimately to the ECSC and beyond, and the
military line of negotiation were confluent for a brief period between
1950 and 1954, the latter was never going to succeed.[96] The reason
for this was simply that the military security of the post-war state did
not require integration; 'indeed a sovereign German army in a politically
unified western Europe was seen almost as much as a threat to security as
its future guarantee'.[97] At most, the traditional solution of military alliance
was indicated and ultimately, of course, it was precisely within such a
framework that West German military sovereignty was rehabilitated.

Milward's view invites the criticism that it was precisely in order to
prevent the emergence of a militarily sovereign Germany with full command over its own army which had led to the Plan Pleven, but the view
disguises a more significant point concerning the viability of the Plan
from the time of its inception. If it is accepted that France's first priority
in advocating the Treaty was to prevent German accession to the Washington Treaty and, beyond that, to prescind an outcome involving full
German sovereignty, then it was indeed, in Milward's words, 'foredoomed
to failure'.[98] Whatever the credibility of the Soviet military threat in the
1950s, it was to this problem that American and British minds had turned
after the war and it was manifest even at this time that the design of
an effective counter-threat could only be hindered by luxuriating in the
attempt to deny equality of treatment to a West Germany which would
inevitably become economically stronger over time. The EDC served to
deflect attention away from a substantial security problem towards an
insubstantial one.

Two conclusions can be drawn from this line of reasoning. First, the
attempt to deny equality of treatment to all participating states in the
EDC project hampered its development since, at the very least, US and
UK endorsement of the project hinged on its potential military effectiveness.[99] Secondly, so long as the *raison d'être* of the TEDC was the
containment of Germany, it remained of doubtful value. Without a clear
and legitimate justification, and unable to prove its potential effectiveness,

[96] Milward, above n 43, 119.
[97] Ibid.
[98] Ibid.
[99] Dockrill, above n 3, 76.

the EDC project was always going to amount to a mere diversion from the NATO solution advocated by the US in early 1950.

V THE LEGACY OF FAILURE; THE WESTERN EUROPEAN UNION AND BEYOND

The EDC having foundered, the remilitarisation of Germany again became imperative. Two possibilities lay open to the West. First, the redrafting within the NATO framework of the TEDC in such a manner as might permit UK participation. However, this approach was not favoured by Dr Adenauer since it would have institutionalised the marginalisation of West Germany, which was not a NATO Member State. The other possibility was German accession to NATO, French fears of German military renaissance being placated by appropriate safeguards.

There was, however, a third way; the enfolding of West Germany into the Western defence and security structure provided by the Brussels Treaty of 17 March 1948. Although Anthony Eden (by then the UK Prime Minister) claimed that this approach had come to him in an epiphanic moment while taking Sunday morning ablutions at his Wiltshire cottage in early September 1954,[100] the identity of the true originator of the proposal remains a mystery.[101] Whatever the provenance of the Brussels Treaty solution, at its heart was German (and Italian) accession to the Treaty, appropriately modified, with a view to its eventual entry into NATO. In return, Germany would pledge to accept self-imposed military restrictions with a view to attenuating the fears which continued to linger in Europe as the legacy of the Second World War.

At a conference held in London on 28 September 1954 involving the US, Canada, the UK and the ECSC Member States, it was agreed that the Brussels Treaty approach would be taken[102] and, on 3 October 1954, the Final Act, containing six parts and five annexes, was signed. According to its terms, Italy and Germany would accede to the Brussels Treaty, thereafter known as the 'Modified' Brussels Treaty, from which references

[100] A Eden, *Full Circle—The Memoirs of the Rt Hon Sir Anthony Eden* (London, Cassell, 1960) 149–151; J Wheeler-Bennett and A J Nicholls, *The Semblance of Peace: the Political Settlement after the Second World War* (London, 1972) 593.
[101] Certainly, the idea had been mooted well before September 1954. Other candidates include Harold Macmillan (on 27 August 1954): H Macmillan, *Tides of Fortune* (London, Macmillan, 1969) 481 and Wheeler-Bennett and Nicholls, above n 100, 596; Pierre Mendès-France: Fursdon, above n 20, 311, citing P Mendès-France, *Choisir* (Stock, Paris, 1974) 77; Dutch Foreign Minister Dirk Stikker (in 1952): Fursdon, above n 20, 311; Italian Foreign Minister Ducci and Britons, Frank Roberts and Christopher Steel: ibid, 312. Paul Van Zeeland, the Belgian Foreign Minister, is also said to have had this idea in 1952: Dockrill, above n 3, 146.
[102] On the London Conference, see Dockrill, above n 3, 143.

to German aggression were deleted. Other changes to the Treaty included the provision of an Assembly and of an armaments agency for Western Europe.[103] Germany would be admitted to NATO.[104] The changes were refined at meetings held in Paris on 20–22 October, for submission to the North Atlantic Council at its scheduled meeting on 23 October 1954. In the papers drafted in preparation for the Paris series of meetings, the nomenclature 'Western European Union' appeared for the first time.[105]

The ratification process was completed on 5 May 1955, paving the way for German membership of NATO.[106] The Soviet Union, its policy of obstructionism finally having been overcome by the West, gathered its seven satellite nations to itself and formed the Warsaw Pact by way of countermeasure against the perceived threat from NATO.[107]

VI EUROPEAN SECURITY AND DEFENCE DURING AND AFTER THE COLD WAR

So it was that the contours of post-war European security and defence were defined and so they remained throughout the cold war, until the twilight of the twentieth century. The intervening period was in fact one of relative stability in Europe,[108] creating an ideal climate for the wreathing of the strands of Western European statehood into an ever more elaborate garment of solidarity in the economic and political spheres. The demise of the EDC and the successful creation of the WEU had sundered the relationship between supranationalism and the high politics of defence.[109] Once the EDC had failed, the process of supranationalisation and functional integration begun by the European unity movement of the 1940s and continued by the ECSC was carried forward through ever-

[103] Part II, Final Act.
[104] Part IV, Final Act.
[105] Fursdon, above n 20, 328. The Modified Brussels Treaty (MBT) created the Western European Union, comprising a Council of Ministers (established pursuant to Protocol No 1), a Parliamentary Assembly (also so established) and an Agency for the Control of Armaments ('ACA'), under the authority of the Council (established under Art VIII MBT).
[106] The MBT entered into force on 6 May 1955 and, on 11 May 1955, an agreement was signed giving the WEU the status of a legal entity under international law.
[107] These nations were Albania, Bulgaria, Czechoslovakia, East Germany, Hungary, Poland and Romania. The Warsaw Pact was established on 14 May, almost two weeks to the day from Germany's admission to NATO.
[108] JJ Mearsheimer, 'Back to the Future: Instability in Europe after the Cold War' [1990] *International Security* 15, 15. On the question of whether Europe was more or less secure after the Cold War, see JC Garnett 'European Security after the Cold War' in J Davis (ed), *Security Issues in the Post-Cold War World* (Cheltenham, Edward Elgar, 1996); T Marauhn, *Building a European Security and Defence Identity: The Evolving Relationship between the Western European Union and the European Union* (Bochum, UVB-Universitätsverlag Dr N Brockmeyer, 1996).
[109] Aybet, above n 2, 95.

wider and deeper economic integration (initially without overt reference to political union).[110]

A The Intergovernmental Approach; 'le Plan Fouchet' and Beyond

Security and defence issues were not entirely forgotten, however. Before the Single European Act's institutionalisation of European Political Cooperation, President de Gaulle had proposed a form of purely intergovernmental political union,[111] embracing a common foreign and defence policy, 'To help to build Western Europe into a political, economic, cultural and human grouping, organized for action and for defence . . .'[112]

This proposal had resulted in due course in the 'Fouchet Plan',[113] which urged the establishment of a union of states with a common foreign and defence policy which would 'contribute to the strengthening of the Atlantic Alliance'.[114] A second Fouchet Plan followed, proposing an even greater erosion of the supranational elements of the then EEC and greater independence from NATO. Both failed, not only because of an insistence among the other five Member States that the economic competences of the Community should remain unaffected by any attempt to institution-alise political union, but, more generally, because they perceived the Plan to be excessively intergovernmental.

It would seem, then, that the French, in the fifties and again in the sixties, unwittingly posited the parameters within which any attempt at security and defence co-operation in Europe might be viable. At one end of the spectrum was the EDC, which failed largely because it was too supranational. At the other was the Fouchet Plan, which failed largely because it was too intergovernmental and not supranational enough.

The Single European Act (SEA) had referred to security, though only in respect of political and economic matters[115] and without prejudice to co-operation within the Western European Union (WEU) and NATO frameworks.[116] For the duration of the cold war, indeed, the extent of

[110] The final communiqué of the Messina Conference of the six ECSC Member States in June 1955 had insisted that the next attempts to unify Europe had to be undertaken in the economic field: U Kitzinger, *The Politics and Economics of European Integration* (Greenwood Press, Westport, CT, 1963) 14.

[111] 5 May 1960.

[112] Quoted in H Mayer, 'Germany's Role in the Fouchet Negotiations' [1996] *Journal of European Integration History* No 2, 39, 43.

[113] On the Fouchet Plans generally, see CWA Timmermans, 'The Uneasy Relationship between the Communities and the Second Union Pillar: Back to the "Plan Fouchet"?' [1996] *Legal Issues of Economic Integration* 61–70; Mayer, above n 112, and documents available online from the Centre Virtuel de la Connaissance sur l'Europe at http://www.ena.lu/.

[114] First Fouchet Plan, 10 November 1961.

[115] Art 30(6)(a) SEA.

[116] Art 30(6)(c) SEA.

the Soviet nuclear threat was such that only the United States could cred-
ibly counter it[117] and European security co-operation was largely confined
to the attempt to define a European security identity within the Atlantic
Alliance.[118] However, the thawing of the cold war in the early 1990s,[119]
which created an altogether different security environment in Europe,[120]
coupled with Europe's failure to speak with a single voice during the first
Gulf War and the opening salvoes of the Balkan conflict, precipitated
calls for increased European foreign policy co-ordination at the time of
the Maastricht IGC which opened in Rome on 15 December 1990. The
Common Foreign and Security Policy ('CFSP') introduced by the TEU
and later refined by the Treaty of Amsterdam ('TA')[121] and the Treaty of
Nice ('TN'),[122] was expressly stated to apply to 'all areas of foreign and
security policy',[123] 'including the eventual framing of a common defence
policy, which might in time lead to a common defence.'[124] The relevant
provisions were, however, contained within a separate Title of the TEU[125]
to which what became known before the Lisbon Treaty as the 'Community method' of governance did not apply. Further, the relevant provisions
clearly indicated that the WEU was to be the primary organisation responsible for security and defence issues.[126]

[117] H Bull, 'Civilian Power Europe: A Contradiction in Terms?' (1982) *Journal of
Common Market Studies* 149.
[118] Aybet, above n 2, ch 4.
[119] The events of 1989–91 are described by Laurent as 'earth-shattering' (P-H Laurent,
'European–American Security Co-operation and Conflict, 1955–1995' in Dumoulin, above
n 20, 345, 345).
[120] The speeches of the Secretary General/High Representative are useful in this regard:
examples include: (i) address by Dr Javier Solana, 'Where Does the EU Stand on Common
Foreign and Security Policy?', Forschungsinstitut der Deutschen Gesellschaft für Auswärtige
Politik (Berlin), 14 November 2000; (ii) Solana, above n 32; (iii) address by Dr Javier Solana,
'European Security and Defence Policy (ESDP) and its Social Basis', Berlin, 29 June 2001; (iv)
address by Dr Javier Solana to the Economist Conference, 6 Government Roundtable, 'Leadership Strategy in the Security Arena: Changing Parameters for Global Recovery', Athens, 19
April 2002; (v) address by Dr Javier Solana to the Swedish EU 2004 Committee, 'Europe's
Place in the World: The Role of the High Representative', Stockholm, 25 April 2002; (vi)
address by Dr Javier Solana to the Danish Institute of International Affairs, 'Europe's Place
in the World', Copenhagen, 23 May 2002; (vii) address by Dr Javier Solana, 'CFSP: the State
of the Union', Institute for Security Studies, Paris, 1 July 2002; (viii) address by Dr Javier
Solana to the Permanent Council of the OSCE, 'The European Union and the Organisation for Security and Cooperation in Europe: the shape of future cooperation', Vienna, 25
September 2002; and (ix) address by Dr Javier Solana at the conference 'NATO: The Next
50 Years—Cooperation for Security and Stability in Southeastern Europe', Athens, 18 April
2002. See also European Parliament Resolution 2000/2005 (INI) on the establishment of a
CESDP after Cologne and Helsinki, A5-0339/2000, preamble, Recital B.
[121] Signed on 2 October 1997. Entered into force on 1 May 1999.
[122] Signed on 26 February 2001. Entered into force on 1 February 2003.
[123] Art J.1(1) TEU (TM).
[124] Art J.4(1) TEU (TM).
[125] Title V.
[126] A Missiroli, 'Background of ESDP (1954–1999)', Institute for Security Studies, Paris
(2004); Wessel, above n 23.

B Kosovo

Perhaps more than any other factor, the Balkan crisis of the 1990's demonstrated to the European Union the nature of the post-cold war security environment. More immediately, however, it demonstrated the inadequacy of the European Union's foreign policy tools.[127] It has been said, quite bluntly, by the SG/HR that '[i]f European Security and Defence Policy had a shape it would be the shape of the Western Balkans.'[128] When diplomacy broke down in Kosovo between 25 March and 10 June 1999, only military intervention remained as a strategic option with which to stabilise the situation and prevent a humanitarian catastrophe. The capacity to implement that strategic option was shown to be piteously beyond the EU's reach, however. Most of the vital missions in Kosovo were flown by US B-2's and F-117's since these were the only planes capable of flying at night, in any weather, evading defences and delivering pinpoint strikes. For similar reasons, US planes flew two thirds of the transport, refuelling and intelligence missions. It took months for most Allies to pre-position their KFOR contingents in Macedonia and to deploy them into Kosovo.[129]

---

[127] S Lucarelli, 'Europe's Response to the Yugoslav Imbroglio' in KE Jørgensen (ed), *European Approaches to Crisis Management* (The Hague, Kluwer Law International, 1997) ch 3, 35. The EU's inability to participate on equal terms with the US in Kosovo is the most commonly cited cause of the revival of the European security and defence debate. See, eg J Howorth, 'European Defence and the Changing Politics of the European Union: Hanging Together or Hanging Separately?' 39 *Journal of Common Market Studies* (2001), 765, 767; R Rummel, 'From Weakness to Power with the ESDP?' (2002) 7 *European Foreign Affairs Review*, 453, 469 (mentioning the post-Cold War security environment); J Roper (Lord), 'Keynote Art: Two Cheers for Mr. Blair? The Political Realities of European Defence Co-operation' (2000) 38 *Journal of Common Market Studies* (Supp. (The European Union)), 8; B Crowe (Sir) 'A Common European Foreign Policy—Is It Achievable?', Royal Institute of International Affairs, Chatham House, London, 18 June 2002 (seminar); S Peers 'Common Foreign and Security Policy 1999–2000' (2001) 20 *Yearbook of European Law*, 531, 531; E Pond, 'Kosovo: Catalyst for Europe' (1999) 22 *The Washington Quarterly* 77; A Bailes, 'Under a European Flag' (2000) Foreign Policy Draft Publication; A Hyde-Price, 'Decision-making: The Second Pillar' in A Arnull and D Wincott (eds), *Accountability and Legitimacy in the European Union* (Oxford, Oxford University Press, 2002) ch 3, 41, 49; G Müller-Brandeck-Bocquet, 'The New CFSP and ESDP Decision-Making System of the European Union' (2002) 7 *European Foreign Affairs Review*, 257, 258; M Vaïsse, 'L'Europe sans défense: du blocus de Berlin à Sarajevo' in Dumoulin, above n 20, 359, 371–72; Sinai, above n 23, 26; Missiroli, above n 126; A Treacher, 'From Civilian Power to Military Actor: The EU's Resistable Transformation' (2004) 9 *European Foreign Affairs Review*, 49, 57; successive European Council Presidency Conclusions; European Parliament Resolution, above n 120, preamble, Recitals F. and G.

[128] Summary of the intervention of Dr Javier Solana, SG/HR, at the Regional EU Conference on Conflict Prevention, Helsingborg, 30 August 2002.

[129] S Talbot, 'America's Stake in a Strong Europe', Royal Institute of International Affairs conference on the Future of NATO, 7 October 1999; J Dempsey, 'NATO Enlargement', *Financial Times*, 20 November 2002, 19.

C   St Malo

The British Government was keenly aware of the lessons to be drawn from Kosovo,[130] including the fact that the re-unification of Germany and the end of the cold war might presage a US disengagement from European security matters,[131] resulting in a diminished NATO role.[132] Europe simply had to be in a position to act in circumstances where the US, via NATO, did not wish to become involved.[133] It was the assimilation of this lesson, coupled with the British government's wish to prove to its electorate and to the rest of the Union that it was willing and able to take a lead in Europe, despite its refusal to participate fully in European Monetary Union,[134] that provided the context for the Franco-British St Malo Declaration of December 1998.[135] By the Declaration, Britain and France sought to provide the impetus necessary for the full implementation of the European Union's CFSP provisions relating to security and defence, mentioned above: '[t]he Union must have the capacity for autonomous action, backed up by credible military forces, the means to decide to use them and a readiness to do so, in order to respond to international crises'.

It was this historic Joint Declaration that set in train the remarkable series of European Council meetings elaborating the CSDP within the CFSP framework.[136]

[130] T Blair, press conference after the informal Pörtschach EU summit (Austria), 24–25 October 1998; G Robertson, UK Secretary of State for Defence, Informal Conference of Defence Ministers of the EU, Vienna, 3–4 November 1998, speaking notes, reproduced with the permission of the British Ministry of Defence in (1999) 4 *European Foreign Affairs Review* 121.

[131] Laurent, above n 119, 350ff.

[132] CG Cogan, *Oldest Allies, Guarded Trends: The US and France since 1940* (Westport, CT, Praeger, 1994) 194.

[133] Howorth, above n 127, 782–83; G Robertson,) 'European Defence: Challenges and Prospects' (2001) 39 *Journal of Common Market Studies* 791, 794–95. US support for CSDP has been schizophrenic, ranging from guarded support (M Albright, 'The Right Balance Will Secure NATO's Future', *Financial Times*, 7 December 1998) to scepticism (Laurent, above n 119, 356).

[134] Sinai, above n 23, 28 and 30; Wessel, above n 23, 273; P Koutrakos, 'Constitutional Idiosyncracies and Political Realities: The Emerging Security and Defense Policy of the European Union' (2003) 10 *Columbia Journal of European Law*, 69, 81; Roper, above n 127, 9–10; B Donnelly and U Rüb, 'In Europe's Defence?', European Policy Brief, Issue 2, December 2003.

[135] Franco-British Joint Declaration on European Defence, adopted at the Franco-British summit, St Malo, 3–4 December 1998.

[136] For a preliminary analysis of the early development of the CSDP after St Malo, see S Hoffmann, 'Towards a Common European Foreign and Security Policy?' (2000) 38 *Journal of Common Market Studies* 189; and 'European Defence Autonomy?' (2000) 42 *Survival* (special issue) 5–112.

VII   CONCLUSIONS – A HEURISTIC APPROACH TO EUROPEAN SECURITY AND DEFENCE?

A number of conclusions can be drawn from the failure of the EDC project and its legacy. Each can be seen to have been learnt by the Member States of the European Union, reflected as they are in the approach now being taken to the implementation of the CSDP.

First, it is apparent that security and defence matters reside within the core of national sovereignty and are seen by European states as matters to be sedulously protected from the agency of supranationalism. Certainly, a purely intergovernmental approach, such as that proposed by the Plan Fouchet, is unrealistic since it ignores the subtle interplay between defence and commercial policy, but a purely supranational approach involving the relinquishment of national sovereign control over the assets to be deployed in pursuit of defence policy objectives appears to be unfeasible in the European context. Among the guiding principles of the CSDP is the principle of 'voluntariness', meaning that the Member States contribute these assets on the basis of national, sovereign, decisions, both as to quantity and quality, in order to implement decisions taken within the Council of the European Union on the basis of unanimity. The voluntariness principle is also reflected in the arrangements relating to the financing of CSDP military operations.

Secondly, the natural corollary of the fact that the assets of the CSDP are Member State assets is that certain Member States, which control the lion's share of Europe's military hardware, will exert greater influence on the shaping of policy than other Member States. It is plain, both on first principles and on the basis of the EDC experience, that the UK, France and, for that matter, Germany, simply must agree in order for progress to be made in CSDP matters.[137] One of the idiosyncrasies of the CSDP is that the European Council has played an unexpected role, of the kind normally expected of the Council, in fleshing out the detail of the policy. The more expected European Council role – the provision of the necessary impetus for the development of the Union and the definition of the general political guidelines thereof[138] – has in large part been played by the UK and France, each of the key European Council meetings being preceded by 'guiding' Franco-British Declarations, of which the St Malo Declaration is simply the most celebrated.[139]

---

[137] Donnelly and Rüb, above n 134.

[138] Art 4, para 1 TEU.

[139] Franco-British summit, London, 25 November 1999 (Pre-Helsinki); Franco-British summit, London, 29 November 2001 (Pre-Laeken); Franco British summit, Le Touquet, 4 February 2003, Declaration on strengthening European cooperation in security and defence (Pre-Brussels, deciding on more rapid reaction times); Franco-British summit, London, 24 November 2003 (issue of autonomous EU planning).

Third, not least because of the importance of UK participation in the CSDP, NATO and, by extension, the US, must be involved. Significant efforts have been made by Member States to ensure co-operation between the EU and NATO as the former develops its military presence on the international scene. The second sub-paragraph of Article 42(7) TEU now expressly provides that:

> commitments and cooperation in this area [ie security and defence including mutual assistance] shall be consistent with commitments under the North Atlantic Treaty Organisation, which, for those States which are members of it, remains the foundation of their collective defence and the forum for its implementation.

Fourth, the EDC experience has taught European states the lesson that equality must be ensured between all participating nations. The concept of *Gleichberechtigung*, which formed the basis of Dr Adenauer's rejection of the August 1950 US proposal to rearm West Germany within the NATO framework, has itself become an identifiable principle of the CSDP.[140]

Finally, full recognition of the 'voluntariness' of the CSDP and of the equality of participating nations must extend to the recognition of difference, where it exists. Each of the contracting parties to the TEDC harboured its own security and defence interests, and was defined by idiosyncratic security and defence postures.[141] This is no less true today of the Member States of the European Union. The second sub-paragraph of Article 42(2) TEU now provides that the Union's CSDP 'shall not prejudice the specific character of the security and defence policy of certain Member States' and, again, this admonition has had a formative influence on the CSDP.

The CSDP is being driven forward for practical political reasons. The pre-history of the CSDP helps to explain the manner in which the policy is moving.

---

[140] Cologne European Council, 3–4 June 1999, Presidency Conclusions.

[141] On the reactions of certain European states to the EDC proposal, see Deloge, above n 79 (Belgium); Harryvan and van der Harst, above n 90 (Netherlands); M af Malmborg, 'How Can Defence Issues be Avoided in European Integration? Sweden, the EDC and the Eden Plan' in Dumoulin, above n 20, 247–63 (Sweden); GI Munte, above n 93 (Spain); G Skogmar, 'The Attitudes of Denmark and Norway towards West German Rearmament and the EDC (1950–1954)' in Dumoulin, above n 20, 235–45 (Denmark and Norway); and A Varsori, 'Italian Diplomacy and the *"querelle de la CED"*' in Dumoulin, above n 20, 181–206 (Italy).

30

The Nexus Between the European Union's Common Security and Defence Policy and Development

PANOS KOUTRAKOS

I INTRODUCTION

THE FUNCTIONING OF the Union as a constitutional order of states entails a balancing exercise between the Member States and the Union, between what the former may do, either individually or collectively, and what the Union is endowed with the competence to do. This exercise is constant, intense and continuously redefined by a number of factors, not least the assertiveness of the Union institutions, the approach of the Court of Justice and the political will of the Member States.

The relationship between the Common Security and Defence Policy (CSDP), on the one hand, and development, on the other, provides a useful and topical microcosm of the coexistence between the Union and the Member States, and the management of the two policies illustrates clearly the various issues to which the ensuing balancing exercise gives rise. The CSDP is about civilian and military assets used 'on missions outside the Union for peace-keeping, conflict prevention and strengthening international security in accordance with the principles of the United Nations Charter'.[1] Organised on the basis of purely intergovernmental principles, the CSDP has been at the centre of both legal and political developments in the recent years. The developments which have shaped the Union's current constitutional structure, from the drafting, ratification process and death of the Treaty Establishing a Constitution for Europe to the inception and tumultuous ratification process of the Lisbon Treaty, have centred on the international role of the Union in general and its security and defence policy in particular. Furthermore, the Union has carried

---

[1] Art 42(1) TEU.

out a significant number of missions in Europe, Asia and Africa, and has been steadily trying to raise its profile as a security actor.

On the other hand, development co-operation is about the reduction and, in the long term, the eradication of poverty.[2] Organised on the basis of the so-called Community method, involving very substantial funds and endowing the Commission with considerable powers, its prominence in the Union's external relations armoury renders it at the centre of any debate about the Union's external action. Furthermore, the parallel nature of the competence with which the Union is endowed in the area[3] ensures the continuous co-existence of Union action with national measures.

In recent years, there has been an increasing link between CSDP and development: the objectives of the latter constitute a precondition for security, and missions carried out by the former have a distinct development dimension. However, this linkage may raise important legal and policy questions: on the one hand, it may blur the boundaries between the distinct sets of rules which govern CSDP and development; on the other hand, it has repercussions for the subject matter and direction of these policies, hence raising questions about the securitisation of development and the 'developmentalisation' of security.

This chapter examines the implications of this relationship and the impact which its management may have for both policies, as well as for the Union actors and the Member States. It is structured as follows. First, it sets out the approach of the Union institutions and the Member States to the relationship between security and defence and development policies. Secondly, it outlines the development dimension in certain CSDP missions and examines the issues which these missions raise about their conduct. Thirdly, it examines the approach of the Court of Justice to the definition of the demarcation line between the two policies.

II   THE NEXUS BETWEEN CSDP AND DEVELOPMENT

Primary law defines the scope of security and defence policy in broad terms. The Common Foreign and Security Policy encompasses 'all areas of foreign policy and all questions relating to the Union's security'.[4] As for the CSDP, which is 'an integral part of the common foreign and security policy',[5] it provides the Union 'with the operational capacity to act on

---

[2] Art 208(1) TFEU. Art 21(2)(d) TFEU, which sets out the objectives of the Union's overall external action, refers to fostering the sustainable economic, social and environmental development of developing countries, with the primary aim of eradicating poverty.

[3] Art 4(4) TFEU. See also Joined Cases C-181/91 and C-248/91 *European Parliament v Council and Commission* [1993] ECR I-3685, and Case C-316/91 *European Parliament v Council* [1994] ECR I-625.

[4] Art 24(1) TEU.

[5] Art 42(1) TEU.

missions outside its territory for peace-keeping, conflict prevention, and strengthening international security in accordance with the principles of the United Nations Charter'.[6]

Furthermore, the reorganisation of external relations by the Lisbon Treaty highlights what has been recognised as a matter of policy, namely that the CSDP and development are both significant components of the Union's external relations. Article 21 TEU sets out the principles and objectives which guide the entire spectrum of the Union's external action, including both the CSDP and development. Article 21(1) TEU refers to democracy, the rule of law, human rights and fundamental freedoms, human dignity, equality and solidarity, and the principles of the United Nations Charter and international law. Article 21(2) TEU sets out the objectives of the Union's external action, which include, amongst others, the safeguarding of the Union's fundamental interests and security, the preservation of peace, the prevention of conflicts and the strengthening of international security, as well as the fostering of sustainable development. These principles and objectives are to be respected and pursued by the Union 'in the development and implementation of the different areas of the Union's external action . . . and of the external aspects of its other policies'.[7]

Therefore, the Lisbon Treaty defines a distinct link which binds, amongst others, security, defence and development policies, and renders them an organic part of the indissoluble whole which the Union's external action is designed to be. In doing so, primary law expresses a position which has been acknowledged by the Union actors for some time. On the one hand, the European Security Strategy, endorsed by the European Council in December 2003, clearly states that security 'is a precondition of development'[8] and defines the instruments for crisis management and conflict prevention at the Union's disposal as including political, diplomatic, military and civilian, trade and development activities.[9]

On the other hand, The European Consensus on Development, a policy document drawn up by the Council, the Commission and the European Parliament, as well as the representatives of the governments of the Member States meeting within the Council,[10] sets out the main parameters of the development policy and places it within the broader context of the Union's other policies. It acknowledges that security and development 'are important and complementary aspects of EU relations with third countries' and points out that '[w]ithin their respective actions, they con-

---

[6] Ibid.

[7] Art 21(3) TEU.

[8] 'A Secure Europe in a Better World—European Security Strategy' (Brussels, 12 December 2003), 2. This is reinforced further below, where it is stated that security 'is the first condition for development' (13).

[9] Ibid, 11.

[10] [2006] OJ C46/1.

tribute to creating a secure environment and breaking the vicious cycle of poverty, war, environmental degradation and failing economic, social and political structures'.[11] It refers specifically to non-proliferation, and highlights, amongst others, the multidimensional aspects of poverty eradication, viewing conflict prevention and state fragility as central aspects of development policy.[12] Therefore, the EU institutions and Member States construe both security and defence and development policies broadly and set out a relationship which works both ways: security is a precondition for development, and development is essential for security.

This link has become more prominent in recent years. The Report on the Implementation of the European Security Strategy, adopted in 2008, includes a distinct section entitled 'Security and development nexus' in which it is pointed out that 'there cannot be sustainable development without peace and security, and without development and poverty eradication there will be no sustainable peace'.[13] It then goes on to refer to the various dimensions of development which have an impact on the Union's security and defence policy, including public health, human rights and sexual violence, state fragility, and natural resources.

The increasing prominence of the nexus between security and defence and development policies must be viewed in the light of two considerations. First, security has been defined in increasingly broad terms, a phenomenon by no means confined to the European Union.[14] The terrorists attacks of 11 September 2001 and the renewed focus of international politics on anti-terrorism, the ensuing emphasis on failed states and the ways in which they breed terrorism and instability, and the various technological advances provide some explanation of the broad construction of security which prevails in international relations.[15] Secondly, rather than originating in the core of the policies which defined the genesis of European integration, the CSDP emerged gradually over the years and as a consequence of both internal factors (such as the success of economic integration and its inevitable spill-over effects,[16] and the steady enlargement

[11] Ibid, para 37.

[12] See also 'EU Strategy for Africa: Towards a Euro-African Pact to Accelerate Africa's Development', COM(2005) 489 fin, (Brussels, 12 October 2005).

[13] 'Providing Security in a Changing World' (Brussels, 11 December 2008) 8.

[14] It is interesting that US President Obama has appointed a Cyber Security Coordinator who reports to the National Security Council (*New York Times*, 21 December 2009). See also WK Clark and PL Levin, 'Securing the Information Highway' (2009) 88(6) *Foreign Affairs* 2.

[15] In the last few years, issues such as food security and environmental change have been brought gradually to the centre of our understanding about security. On the former, the US Secretary of State Hillary Clinton wrote that food security is not only about food, but 'it is all about security' (*The Guardian*, 16 October 2009). On the latter, see S Dalby, *Security and Environmental Change* (Cambridge, Polity Press, 2009).

[16] The Laeken Declaration (European Council, 14–15 December, 2001) 2 asks: 'Does Europe not, now that is finally unified, have a leading role to play in a new world order, that of a power able both to play a stabilising role worldwide and to point the way ahead for many countries and peoples?'

process), and external developments (such as the growing expectations of third countries and the wars in the Balkans in the 1990s).[17] Therefore, it was inevitable that it should have drawn on the existing policies of the Union legal order from the development of which it emerged, and to which it was linked organically, albeit in a legally distinct manner.

III DEVELOPMENT DIMENSIONS IN CSDP MISSIONS

In relation to state fragility, both the European Consensus on Development and the Report on the European Security Strategy refer specifically to, amongst others, governance reforms, rule of law, anti-corruption measures and the building of viable state institutions.[18] In relation to the CSDP, the Union has carried out over 20 missions in Europe, Asia and Africa. Whilst the nature of these missions has varied considerably,[19] a number of them pursue these objectives. This section will focus on two types of missions, namely rule of law and security sector reform. As the former is a civilian mission and the latter military, they provide a snapshot of the ways in which CSDP practice reflects the nexus between security and development.

A central theme of development policy,[20] rule of law reform has been pursued by the Union on the basis of a number of CSDP operations. EUJUST THEMIS was launched in Georgia in July 2004 and lasted for a year.[21] It was the smallest CSDP mission and expired on 14 July 2005. Its objective was to assist the Georgian authorities to develop a strategy for reforming the criminal justice system. In effect, it dispatched a number of senior legal experts who, along with Georgian legal assistants, were located within a number of Georgian authorities.

Furthermore, EUJUST LEX (Iraq) was launched on July 2005[22] and

---

[17] For the development of the EU security and defence policy, see M Trybus, *European Union Law and Defence Integration* (Oxford, Hart Publishing 2005) 9ff.

[18] See above n 8, 4; above n 13, para 37.

[19] For an analysis of the missions, see G Grevi, D Helly, and D Keohane (eds), *ESDP: The First Ten Years* (Paris, ISS, 2009); S Blockmans (ed), *The European Union and Crisis Management-Policy and Legal Aspects* (The Hague, TMC Asser Press 2008); idem (ed), *The European Union and Peace Building: Policy and Legal Aspects* (The Hague, TMC Asser Press 2010).

[20] See MJ Trebilcock and RJ Daniels, *Rule of Law Reform and Development-Charting the Fragile Path of Progress* (Cheltenham, Edward Elgar, 2008).

[21] Joint Action 2004/523/CFSP [2003] OJ L228/21, amended by Joint Action 2004/638/CFSP [2004] OJ L291/7.

[22] See Joint Action 2005/190/CFSP [2005] OJ L62/37, which has been amended a number of times (by Joint Action 2006/413/CFSP [2006] OJ L163/17, Joint Action 2006/708/CFSP [2006] OJ L291/43, Joint Action 2007/760/CFSP [2007] OJ L305/58, Joint Action 2008/304/CFSP [2008] OJ L105/10, Joint Action 2008/480/CFSP [2008] OJ L163/50, Joint Action 2009/475/CFSP [2009] OJ L156/57 and Joint Action 2010/330/CFSP [2010] OJ L140/12, the latter extending its duration until 30 June 2012).

focuses on the Iraqi criminal justice system by providing training for the Iraqi police, judiciary and prison authorities. It aims 'to improve the capacity, co-ordination and collaboration of the different components of the Iraqi criminal justice system'[23] 'in full respect for the rule of law and human rights'.[24] In practical terms, it achieves this by drawing up courses for judges, investigating magistrates, senior police and prison officers, and by organising work secondments for such officials.

Finally, and more recently, EULEX KOSOVO, the biggest civilian mission undertaken so far, was established in February 2008 in order to

> assist the Kosovo institutions, judicial authorities and law enforcement agencies in their progress towards sustainability and accountability and in further developing and strengthening an independent multi-ethnic justice system and multi-ethnic police and customs service, ensuring that these institutions are free from political interference and adhering to internationally recognised standards and European best practices.[25]

In practical terms, the mission monitors, mentors and advises the police, judiciary and customs authorities, and is entrusted with executive responsibilities, in effect enjoying the power to investigate and prosecute serious and sensitive crimes.[26]

Security sector reform is prominent in the European Security Strategy in the context of support for fragile states.[27] So far, the Union has undertaken missions in the Democratic Republic of Congo (EUSEC RD Congo) and Guinea-Bissau (EU SSR Guinea-Bissau). The former was launched in 2005 and aimed to provide practical support for the integration of the Congolese army and good governance in the field of security,[28] and, later on, to support the restructuring and rebuilding of the Congolese.[29] The mission in Guinea-Bissau was launched in June 2008 and aims to support the local authorities in implementing a national security sector reform

---

[23] Art 2(1) Joint Action 2005/190/CFSP (n 22 above).

[24] Art 2(2) Joint Action 2005/190/CFSP (ibid).

[25] Art 2 of Joint Action 2008/124/CFSP [2008] OJ L42/92. This measure was amended by Joint Action 2009/445/CFSP [2009] OJ L148/33 and Council Dec 2010/322/CFSP [2010] OJ L145/13, which extended the duration of the mission until 14 June 2012.

[26] For an assessment of the mission so far, see S Keukeleire, A Kalaja and A Çollaku, 'The European Union's Policy on Kosovo' in P Koutrakos (ed), *European Foreign Policy— Legal and Political Aspects* (Cheltenham, Edward Elgar, 2011) (forthcoming); see also M Spernbauer, 'EULEX Kosovo-Mandate, Structure and Implementation: Essential Clarifications for an Unprecedented EU Mission', CLEER Working Paper 2010/5.

[27] See also 'EU Concept for ESDP support to Security Sector Reform (SSR)' Council Doc 12566/4/05 (Brussels, 13 October 2005), para 17.

[28] Council Joint Action 2005/355/CFSP [2005] OJ L112/20, amended by Council Joint Action 2005/868/CFSP [2005] OJ L318/29; Council Joint Action 2006/303/CFSP [2006] OJ L112/18; Council Joint Action 2007/192/CFSP [2007] OJ L87/22, replaced by Joint Action 2007/406/CFSP [2007] OJ L151/52, which was then amended by Joint Action 2008/491/CFSP [2008] OJ L168/42; Joint Action 2009/509/CFSP [2009] OJ L172/36, replaced by Joint Action 2009/709/CFSP [2009] OJ L246/33.

[29] Art 1 of Joint Action 2007/406/CFSP (n 28 above).

strategy.[30] This is a small mission which entails officials from Member States being placed with the local military, police and prosecution authorities to assist them in the development of detailed implementation plans for downsizing/restructuring the armed forces and security forces, as well as advising them on the definition of their capacity-building needs (such as training and equipment, facilitating subsequent mobilisation of, and engagement by, donors).

The development dimension of these missions is readily apparent. Joint Action 2008/112/CFSP, for instance, on the security sector reform in Guinea-Bissau, states in its second recital that 'security sector reform in Guinea-Bissau is essential for the stability and sustainable development of that country'.[31] A clear indication of how it straddles CSDP and development policy is that both the Council Secretariat and the Commission have put forward their own understanding of what security sector reform entails for these respective spheres of activity.[32] Both documents stress the multifarious dimensions of security sector reform (SSR), and articulate principles for its conduct which are quite similar (such as respect for local ownership, democratic norms, internationally accepted human rights, the rule of law and coherence within the overall framework of EU policy). Drawing on them, the Council then went on to articulate a policy framework for security sector reform in a brief document, the starting point of which is the dual character of SSR:[33] 'Together the two concepts [that is about EC and ESDP support] constitute a policy framework for engagement in Security Sector Reform, stressing the importance for the EU to take a comprehensive and cross-pillar approach to SSR recognising the fact that SSR is a holistic, multi-sector and long-term process encompassing the overall functioning of the security system as part of governance reforms'.

The bifurcated nature of SSR is not confined to policy statements. In parallel to the CSDP missions, there have been considerable initiatives in the context of the Union's external financial instruments.[34] For instance, the Financing Instrument for Development Cooperation focuses, amongst others, on co-operation in the area of governance, democracy, human rights and support for institutional reforms, and refers specifically to fostering co-operation and policy reform in the fields of security and justice, especially as regards asylum and migration, the fight against drugs and

---

[30] Council Joint Action 2008/112/CFSP [2008] OJ L40/11, amended by Council Joint Action 2009/405/CFSP [2009] OJ L128/60; Council Joint Action 2009/841/CFSP [2009] OJ L303/70; Joint Action 2009/841/CFSP [2009] OJ L303/70.

[31] Ibid.

[32] Above n 27; 'A Concept for European Community Support for Security Sector Reform', COM(2006) 253 fin (Brussels, 24 May 2006).

[33] Council Conclusions of 12 June 2006.

[34] See P Doelle and A Gouzée de Harven, 'Security Sector Reform: a Challenging Concept at the Nexus between Security and Development' in D Spence and P Fluri (eds), *The European Union and Security Sector Reform* (London, John Harper Publishing, 2008) 38.

other trafficking, including trafficking in human beings, corruption and money laundering.[35] More specifically, the Commission has funded programmes in Congo involving the organisation of seminars and studies on reconciliation and security sector reform, the improvement of living conditions and security for the families of the newly integrated brigades and their host communities, and the establishment of an integrated system for human resources management within the Congolese National Police. Similarly, it launched a programme in Guinea-Bissau nine months prior to the CSDP mission, providing technical assistance for the security sector reform through a team of three experts tasked to advise the national Defence Ministry and the Committee for Technical Cooperation on the institutional framework of SSR, on legal reforms needed, on definition of the instruments for compensation and reintegration and on pension schemes for former security personnel, as well as the preparation of censuses and the effective co-ordination between donors and the government. The Commission noted that its initiative helped introduce the SSR CSDP mission to local authorities.[36]

Therefore, the CSDP–development nexus has given rise to sets of initiatives which are carried out in parallel and are viewed as mutually reinforcing.[37] This raises certain substantive, structural and constitutional issues. In addition to giving rise to a rapprochement of objectives, the management of the nexus is underpinned by similar substantive principles. The principle of local ownership is a case in point. It has become one of the main guiding principles of the EU's development policy. According to the European Consensus on Development,

> [t]he EU is committed to the principle of ownership of development strategies and programmes by partner countries. Developing countries have the primary responsibility for creating an enabling domestic environment for mobilising their own resources, including conducting coherent and effective policies. These principles will allow an adapted assistance, responding to the specific needs of the beneficiary country.[38]

This has also been a central tenet of the CSDP rule of law and security sector reform missions.[39] And yet, the osmosis between distinct policies does not necessarily justify the application of the same principles. On the one hand, the application of the principle of local ownership has given rise to considerable problems in the conduct of CSDP missions.

---

[35] Council Reg 1905/2006 [2006] OJ L378/41.

[36] See SEC(2009) 932, 'Commission Staff Working Paper Accompanying Annual Report from the European Commission on the Instrument for Stability in 2008', COM(2009) 341, 18.

[37] It is interesting that the EU Concept for ESDP support to Security Sector Reform was written by the Council Secretariat 'in close consultation with the Commission'.

[38] Above n 10, para14.

[39] See above n 27, para 27, and the Council Conclusions, above n 33, para 3.

For instance, the EUJUST THEMIS staff found it difficult to co-operate with the Georgian authorities tasked with policy reform, so much so that they found it necessary to get the Georgian Justice Minister invited by the Political Security Committee in Brussels in order to make some progress.[40] And in Guinea-Bissau, the small mission staff was met with such internal upheaval and disagreements that they found it difficult to even identify their interlocutors.[41] On the other hand, the conditions which a CSDP mission faces on the ground may be such as to raise the intensity of its intervention to levels which the principle of local ownership can hardly envisage, the mission in Kosovo being a case in point.[42]

Furthermore, the management of the nexus between CSDP and development needs to meet the challenges of coherence and consistency. In accordance with Article 21(3) TEU, the Union 'shall ensure consistency between the different areas of its external action and between these and its other policies'. This task is assigned to the Council and the Commission, assisted by the High Representative of the Union for Foreign Affairs and Security Policy. And the broader the concepts of security and development have been construed and the higher the intensity of their interactions, the greater the emphasis on the coherence of the Union's external action. This is stressed in both the European Security Strategy and the European Consensus on Development. In fact, eight years prior to the adoption of the latter, the Council had adopted a Resolution on Coherence between the Community development co-operation and its other policies.[43]

Quite apart from this institutional preoccupation with it, the challenge which coherence presents for the management of the nexus of CSDP and development is indicative of the greater challenge which coherence presents for the EU external action as whole. This has been at the centre of the group therapy process which the Union has undergone since the adoption of the Laeken Declaration on the Future of the European Union,[44] which

---

[40] See X Kurowska, 'EUJUST THEMIS (Georgia)' in Grevi et al (eds), above n 19, 201, 206.

[41] See D Helly, 'EU SSR Guinea-Bissay' in ibid, 369, 373.

[42] See Keukeleire et al, above n 26. However, this leap between the choices made by the EU in the context of its CSDP operations and the local wishes is not confined to the missions referred to in this chapter: see, eg A Juncos, 'Of Cops and Robbers: the EU and the Problem of Organized Crime in Bosnia' in B Balamir-Coskun and B Demirtas-Coskun (eds), *Neighborhood Challenge: The European Union and its Neighbours* (Boca Raton, FL, Universal Publishers, 2009) 47.

[43] It was adopted by the Development Council on 5 June 1997. This was followed by the European Parliament's B5-0117/2000 Resolution on the coherence of the various policies with development policy [2000] OJ C339/208, and the Commission's 'Policy Coherence for Development', COM(2005) 134 fin. Furthermore, and following a request by the Council, on 19 November 2002 the Commission refers specifically to progress in terms of coherence in its annual report on development policy.

[44] European Council, 14–15 December 2001. The focus on the international role of the Union was apparent in it: 'Does Europe not, now that is finally unified, have a leading role to play in a new world order, that of a power able both to play a stabilising role worldwide and to point the way ahead for many countries and peoples?' (2).

initiated the process of reform of the Union's Treaties in December 2001 and has led to the entry into force of the Lisbon Treaty. This is clearly illustrated by the mandate of the 2007 Intergovernmental Conference, which mentions coherence in its very first paragraph. An assessment of whether the grand objectives about the coherence of the Union's international role have been met is beyond the scope of this chapter.[45] However, it is interesting to note the recent complications which the nexus between development and security policy has caused in relation to the introduction of one of the most widely acclaimed innovations introduced by the Lisbon Treaty, namely the European External Action Service (EEAS).

It is recalled that the Service shall assist the High Representative in fulfilling her mandate, and shall comprise officials from relevant departments of the Council General Secretariat and the Commission, as well as diplomats seconded from the Member States (Article 27(3) TEU). The High Representative is responsible for representing the Union for matters relating to the common foreign and security policy (Article 27(2) TEU), and for assisting the Council and the Commission to ensure the consistency between the different areas of the Union's external action and between these and its other policies (Article 21(3) TEU). Where does this leave development co-operation? Should it be integrated in the task entrusted to the EEAS or should it become a distinct and autonomous policy within the Union's external action? The Commission was hostile to the former, as it felt that it would undermine its powers as set out in Article 17(1) TEU; these include the Union's external representation, with the exception of the common foreign and security policy, the execution of the budget and the management of programmes and the exercise of co-ordinating, executive and management functions as laid down in primary law.

These are sensitive matters insofar as their resolution touches upon issues of efficiency and effectiveness, as well as institutional powers deeply entrenched through successive rounds of Treaty amendments. Indeed, the proposal made by the High Representative in March 2010 which relied upon the requirement of consistency and suggested the integration of development policy in the functions of the EEAS, referring specifically to the EU external co-operation programmes such as the Development Cooperation Instrument and the European Development Fund, turned out to be controversial. Most non-governmental organisations viewed it as a Trojan horse which would undermine both the integrity of development policy and the powers of the Commission.[46] The Parliament, on the

---

[45] See S Duke, 'Consistency, Coherence and EU External Action: The Path to Lisbon and Beyond' in Koutrakos (ed), above n 26; P Koutrakos, 'Primary Law and Policy in EU External Relations—Moving Away from the Big Picture?' (2008) 33 *European Law Review* 666.

[46] See, eg the press statement of 26 April 2010 issued by CIDSE, Oxfam International, APRODEV, CONCORD, EUROSTEP and One International (http://www.concordeurope. org/Files/media/0_internetdocumentsENG/5_Press/1_Press_releases/5_Press_releases_2010/ MEDIA-STATEMENT-on-EEAS-26-04-2010—EN.pdf) (last accessed on 1 August 2010).

other hand, was keen not only to avoid the contamination of the Community (now Union) method which governs development co-operation by the intergovernmental features of the EEAS, but also to increase its leverage on the conduct of the EU's external action by intervening directly on the funding of the Service, and the appointment of Heads of Delegation.

Following intense inter-institutional haggling, the final outcome, set out in Decision 2010/427/EU establishing the organisation and functioning of EEAS,[47] follows the logic of integrating development in the EEAS functions. However, it does so by seeking to square the circle and engaging in a very delicate balancing exercise. The High Representative is responsible for the co-ordination between all the EU financial instruments, but the management of these programmes remain under the responsibility of the Commission,[48] and the EEAS shall 'contribute to the programming and management cycle' of these instruments, and shall be responsible for 'preparing Commission decisions on the strategic, multi-annual steps within the programming cycle'.[49] All proposals are to be prepared following Commission procedures, and the role of the Commissioner responsible for development is pronounced; for instance, in relation to the European Development Fund and the Development Cooperation Instrument in particular, that is, the programmes involving the majority of the development policy budget, both the EEAS and the Commission are to make any proposals under the supervision of the Development Commissioner.[50]

Whether the compromise outlined above is workable remains to be seen.[51] For the purposes of this analysis, suffice it to point out that it shares the vague language and the keen commitment to square the circle which is apparent in other strands of the security–development nexus.[52] For instance, the Council Conclusions on a policy framework for security sector reform are striking in their generality:

> The EU has a broad range of civilian and military instruments which are able to support SSR activities. A case-by-case analysis is based on a situation specific approach is always needed to assess whether any proposed activities are most appropriately carried out through ESDP or Community action or a

[47] [2010] OJ L201/30. This Decision is accompanied by a Declaration by the High Representative on political accountability ([2010] OJ C210/1, and [2010] OJ C217/12), which sets out the practicalities of the interactions between the High Representative and the European Parliament.

[48] Ibid, Art 9(1) and (2).

[49] Ibid, Art 9(3).

[50] Ibid, Art (4).

[51] See the scepticism expressed in Editorial, 'Habemus European External Action Service' (2010) 35 *European Law Review* 607.

[52] See European Parliament legislative resolution of 8 July 2010 on the proposal for a Council decision establishing the organisation and functioning of the European External Action Service (A7-02278/2010).

combination of both with the objectives of ensuring effective and coherent EU external action in this area.[53]

Whilst understood for practical reasons and political expediency, the lofty language and complex arrangements which govern the management of the security–development nexus cannot hide two problems. First, to turn the policy statements about the intrinsic link between security, defence and development policies into tangible action requires a leap of faith which the pre-occupations of the Union institutions with their own powers renders exceedingly difficult for them to take. Secondly, once this leap has been taken, the compromises which it entails and the vague language in which these are couched render the effectiveness of the agreed system of rules and procedures subject to the personality of the relevant post holders, and the willingness of the institutions to co-operate. Not only is such an arrangement hardly conducive to the certainty and stability required for any effective administration, but also the energy and time wasted in turf wars about the legal basis of external measures in other areas (such as trade and environment) bode ill for its success.[54] The following section will elaborate on this in relation to two cases brought before the Court of Justice which highlight the problem of delineating between, and managing, the relationship of security, defence and development policies.

IV   THE CSDP-DEVELOPMENT NEXUS
BEFORE THE COURT OF JUSTICE

The Court of Justice has had the opportunity to rule on the relationship between security and development in two judgments. In the first one, the *Philippines Borders* case,[55] it does so indirectly. This concerned a Commission decision financing a project relating to the security of the borders of the Philippines. That decision was adopted in implementation of Council Regulation 443/93 on financial and technical assistance to, and economic co-operation with, the developing countries in Asia and Latin America.[56] Its aim was to contribute to the fight against terrorism and international crime and enhance the internal security and stability of the Philippines. However, the European Parliament argued that these objectives were beyond the scope of the economic co-operation provided for by the Council Regulation and, in pursuing them, the Commission did not have the authority to approve the financing of that project.

---

[53] Above n 33, para 4.
[54] See P Koutrakos, 'Legal Basis and Delimitation of Competence in EU External Relations' in M Cremona and B De Witte (eds), *EU Foreign Relations Law—Constitutional Fundamentals* (Oxford, Hart Publishing, 2008) 171.
[55] Case C-403/05 *European Parliament v Commission* [2007] ECR I-9045.
[56] [1992] OJ L52/1.

The Court accepted that conclusion and annulled the Commission decision. Although it acknowledged the broad objectives of development policy as laid down in ex-Articles 177–81 EC (Articles 208-211-TFEU), it ruled that the Council Regulation, which set out the framework within which assistance to developing countries would be provided, makes no reference either to the fight against terrorism and international crime or to the internal stability and security of the Philippines. It also pointed out that there is nothing in the contested decision to indicate how the objective pursued by the project could contribute effectively to making the environment more conducive to investment and economic development, which were the proper objectives of the Regulation.

The judgment appears to require a specific link between the external relations activity and the development objectives in order to justify the conduct of the former within the framework set out by the latter. However, the temptation to consider it as suggesting a restrictive interpretation of development policy altogether should be resisted. Instead, it should be recalled that the ruling was rendered in a very specific context which was defined by a secondary measure and the acceptable scope of the Commission's implementing powers.[57]

It is in the second case where the Court's understanding of the delineation between security and development emerges more clearly. This is Case C-91/05 *Commission v Council (re: ECOWAS)*,[58] about non-proliferation of small arms and light weapons in Africa. The European Union has been an active player in the field of non-proliferation of weapons in general, as well as the small arms and light weapons in particular.[59] In Joint Action 2002/589/CFSP,[60] it sets out a number of principles and measures in order to prevent the further destabilising accumulation of small arms. In particular, it provides for financial and technical assistance by the Union to various programmes and projects which make a direct contribution to this objective.

In this context, the Council adopted Decision 2004/833/CFSP,[61] and in doing so implemented the above Joint Action by contributing to the Economic Organisation of West African States (ECOWAS). This contribution consisted of providing financial and technical assistance to ECOWAS in order to set up the Light Weapons Unit within its structure and converting the Moratorium on Small Arms and Light Weapons into a binding Convention between the ECOWAS states.

---

[57] See M Cremona, 'Annotation on Case C-403/05 *European Parliament v Commission*' (2008) 45 *Common Market Law Review* 1727, 1739–40.

[58] [2008] ECR I-3651.

[59] See P Koutrakos, 'The Non-Proliferation Policy of the European Union' in M Evans and P Koutrakos (eds), *Beyond the Established Legal Orders—Policy Interconnections Between the European Union and the Rest of the World* (Oxford, Hart Publishing, forthcoming).

[60] [2002] OJ L191/1.

[61] [2004] OJ L359/65.

The Commission challenged both the Joint Action and the Decision as violating the Community's competence: it argued that they pursued development objectives and therefore ought to have been adopted under ex-Article 177 EC (now Article 208 TFEU). It put forward three main arguments. First, the Union should not do what the Community could do, even if the competence of the latter was shared and had not been exercised. This was based on ex-Article 47 TEU, which provided that 'nothing in [the TEU] shall affect the Treaties establishing the European Communities' and which the Commission viewed as defining a fixed boundary between CFSPP and EC competence. Secondly, development policy necessarily encompasses the combating of the proliferation of small arms and light weapons, as co-operation in this area presupposes a minimum degree of stability. Therefore, the decommissioning of small arms and light weapons is essential to achieving the objectives of development co-operation.[62] Thirdly, the Commission argued that both the objective and the substantive content of Decision 2004/833/CFSP suggested that they could have been adopted in the context of development policy: one of its objectives was the improvement of the prospects for sustainable development in West Africa, while the provision of financial and technical assistance constituted a typical form of assistance in the context of development co-operation.

On the other hand, the Council argued that ex-Article 47 TEU could not be interpreted in a way which would be detrimental to the competences enjoyed by the Union in the area of foreign and security policy. Secondly, it argued that both non-proliferation of small arms and light weapons and the more general objective of preserving peace and strengthening international security were CFSP objectives which might only incidentally affect the prospects for sustainable development; otherwise, a broader interpretation of development co-operation would render the Community's competence unlimited, and deprive the CFSP of any practical effect. Finally, the Council suggested that the objective of the contested Decision was part of the fundamental objective of the CFSP, namely the preservation of peace and the strengthening of international security, and argued that the scope of CFSP activities might not be limited by precluding the Union from using the same instruments as those employed in the area of development co-operation.

In its ruling, the Court made three main points. First, it accepted that ex-Article 47 TEU should be interpreted strictly, and held that

> a measure having legal effects adopted under Title V of the EU Treaty affects the provisions of the EC Treaty within the meaning of [ex] Article 47 EU whenever it could have been adopted on the basis of the EC Treaty, it being

---

[62] To that effect, the Commission relies upon the Cotonou Agreement, Art 11(3) of which refers specifically to activities addressing an excessive and uncontrolled spread, illegal trafficking and accumulation of small arms and light weapons.

unnecessary to examine whether the measure prevents or limits the exercise by the Community of its competences.[63]

In other words, it suggests a very strict reading of the autonomy of development policy under the previous constitutional arrangements.

Secondly, it suggested a broad interpretation of development policy as, in addition to the sustainable economic and social development, the smooth and gradual integration into the world economy and the campaign against poverty, it encompasses the development and consolidation of democracy and the rule of law, respect for human rights and fundamental freedoms, and compliance with UN and other international commitments. However, it pointed out that it is necessary that any measure adopted under development co-operation contributes to the pursuit of this policy's economic and social development objectives.

Thirdly, the Court suggested that, whilst measures aimed at combatingthe proliferation of small arms and light weapons can contribute to the elimination or reduction of obstacles to the economic and social development of developing countries, they fall within the scope of development policy only if, in the light of their aim and content, their main purpose is the implementation of that policy. Relying on its earlier case law on legal basis, the Court then pointed out that, if a measure pursues both CFSP and development co-operation objectives, it should be ascertained which is the main objective and which is incidental, as the former would dictate the appropriate legal basis.[64] If, however, the measure pursues both development and CFSP objectives simultaneously without either being incidental to the other, a joint legal basis is precluded under ex-Article 47 TEU. It is for this reason that 'the Union cannot have recourse to a legal basis falling within the CFSP in order to adopt provisions which also fall within a competence conferred by the EC Treaty on the Community'.[65]

Focusing on the contested decision, the Court concluded that it pursued both the CFSP objective of tackling a threat to peace and security and the development objective of eliminating or reducing obstacles to the sustainable development of co-operating developing countries. It then ruled that neither objective is incidental to the other: the preamble mentions sustainable development in its first paragraph, and the provision of technical and financial assistance is a typical development co-operation measure.[66]

---

[63] Above n 61, para 60.

[64] Ibid, para 73

[65] Ibid, para 77.

[66] It is pointed out that, '[w]hile there may be some measures, such as the grant of political support for a moratorium or even the collection and destruction of weapons, which fall rather within action to preserve peace and strengthen international security or to promote international cooperation, being CFSP objectives stated in Art 11(1) EU, the decision to make funds available and to give technical assistance to a group of developing countries in order to draft a convention is capable of falling both under development cooperation policy and the CFSP' (para 105).

The judgment in *ECOWAS* must be examined in the light of the Lisbon Treaty, which has redefined the constitutional balance of powers between CFSP, and therefore CSDP, and development. Whilst ex-Article 47 TEU gave precedence to preserving the integrity of the Community legal order, the new provision of Article 40 TEU adds another dimension:

> Similarly, the implementation of the policies listed in [Articles 3–6 TFEU] shall not affect the implication of the procedures and the extent of the powers of the institutions laid down by the Treaties for the exercise of the Union competences under [Chapter 2 TEU which deals with CFSP and CSDP].

In addition to being given this elevated constitutional status, the specificity of CFSP rules is expressly acknowledged.[67]

The *ECOWAS* judgment has been analysed in detail and well.[68] This section will focus on the light it sheds on our understanding of the ways in which security and development objectives may be served by Union measures, as well as the principles governing the choice of the appropriate legal basis.

A main tenet of the judgment is the broad construction of both security and defence, and development co-operation policies. This is suggested by the ample reference to policy documents adopted by the Union institutions and the Member States. For instance, as suggested above in this chapter, the European Consensus on Development[69] is a document firmly based on an understanding of development co-operation as a policy with economic, political, social and security dimensions, all of which are intrinsically linked. The Court referred to it at length, twice: to acknowledge that measures aiming to prevent fragility in developing countries, including the non-proliferation of small arms and light weapons, can contribute to tackling the economic and social development problems of those countries; and secondly, to argue that the objective of a security and defence policy instrument to tackle the non-proliferation of small arms and light weapons may be served by development co-operation, as well as security and defence policy measures.[70] In effect, the above propositions are two sides of the same coin: in the context of EU external relations, the economic and social and the security and defence are intertwined because each is achieved by a wider range of policy responses than might have originally

---

[67] See Art 2(4) TFEU.

[68] See A Dashwood, 'Article 47 TEU and the Relationship between First and Second Pillar Competences' in A Dashwood and M Maresceau (eds), *Law and Practice of EU External Relations* (Cambridge, Cambridge University Press, 2008) 70; J Heliskoski, 'Small Arms and Light Weapons within the Union's Pillar Structure: An Analysis of Art 47 TEU' (2008) 33 *European Law Review* 898; C Hillion and R Wessel, 'Competence Distribution in EU External Relations after ECOWAS: Clarification or Continued Fuzziness?' (2009) 46 *Common Market Law Review* 551.

[69] See above n 10.

[70] Reference is also made to the Development Council Resolution on small arms, adopted on 21 May 1999, paras 69 and 89 of the judgment (above n 61).

been envisaged. In this part of the judgment, the Court gives voice to one of the main tenets of the Union's international role as defined after the terrorist attacks of 11 September 2001.

However, to construe development and security and defence policy in broad terms is one thing; to allow this understanding to obscure the dividing line between these policies is quite another. The Court's conclusion that neither the security nor the development objectives of the provision of financial and technical assistance for the non-proliferation of small arms and light weapons is incidental to the other is problematic. The analysis of the content of the contested decision is confined to presenting the provision of technical and financial assistance as a typical development co-operation measure. However, this overly instrumental logic confines security and defence policy to a core of the most fundamental security actions, easily recognisable and categorised as such. The Court refers expressly to the grant of political support for a moratorium and the collection and destruction of weapons as measures which would aim, primarily, to preserve peace and strengthen international security.[71] However, this type of categorisation is too tidy and schematic, and fails to engage with the intricacies of the multifarious dimensions of security and defence policy. What makes it even more problematic is the extent to which the Court substantiates its decision on the basis of policy documents adopted by the Union institutions and the Member States. These are policy documents drafted in vague language and aimed at articulating political objectives as to how best to position the Union on the world stage. In doing so, they also seek to strike the balance between competing claims to power made by the Union's actors. One wonders what their appropriate role in judicial reasoning is, as the latter seeks to define the demarcation line between different sets of rules which entail different constellations of power between the Union and the Member States, as well as between the Union institutions.[72]

The above approach is all the more serious as it bears on the choice of legal basis. Far from being an exact science, the identification of the weight which a Union measure attaches to the various objectives it pursues is bound to be fraught with ambiguities. This is so even in areas which are not as constitutionally charged as the demarcation line between security and defence and development policies. In the light of the broad construction of these areas, to ascertain whether a given objective is the main component of a measure, whether it is incidental or whether it is indissolubly linked to other objectives is more often than not far from clear. The case law on the legal basis of the measures with trade and environmental objectives illustrate this clearly: the Court's conclusions

---

[71] Ibid, para 105.
[72] It is interesting, though, that neither the European Security Strategy (above n 8) nor its 2008 Implementation Report (above n 13) are mentioned in the judgment.

that the Cartagena Protocol is mainly an environmental measure with incidental trade implications,[73] that the Energy Star Agreement is a trade measure with incidental environmental implications[74] and that the Rotterdam Convention serves trade and environmental objectives equally[75] have created a body of case law difficult to follow, and applied principles in a way which is even more difficult to predict.[76] In the area of security and defence and development policies, rather than clarifying it, the Court's approach in *ECOWAS* makes the choice of legal basis even more complex and less predictable.

Furthermore, the difficulties inherent in the strict monitoring of the choice of legal basis suggested by the Court are bound to whet the already healthy appetite of the Union institutions for legal disputes. This slows down the decision-making process and takes away energy and time which the EU institutions would put to much better use if focused on the effectiveness of the Union's international action and the monitoring of the consistency of its activities. This author has made this point in relation to the legal basis disputes involving trade and environmental policies.[77] This is even more apt in relation to the areas discussed in this chapter, not only because of the profound constitutional implications for the functioning of the Union as a constitutional order of states, but also given the vital role which inter-institutional co-operation plays in order to enhance the coherence of the Union's external action. After all, for all the institutional innovations and procedural amendments introduced by the Lisbon Treaty, coherence will become a rhetorical imperative unless the Union's institutions develop functional synergies in order to give effect to it.

There is another message which the judgment in *ECOWAS* conveys, and it has to do with the Court of Justice. The difficult tests which govern the choice of legal basis, the ambiguous ways in which they are applied by the Court of Justice, the reliance upon policy documents couched in language difficult to guide judicial reasoning and the increasing number of inter-institutional disputes all suggest that the role of the Court of Justice in this area is bound to become more pronounced. This in itself may not appear controversial, or surprising. After all, the case law of the Court of Justice has been pivotal in the genesis and development of the law of EU external relations, and the proliferation of judgments in the area

---

[73] *Opinion 2/00 (re: Cartagena Protocol)* [2001] ECR I-9713.

[74] Case C-281/01 *Commission v Council (re: Energy Star Agreement)* [2002] ECR I-12049.

[75] Case C-94/03 *Commission v Council (re: Rotterdam Convention on the Prior Informed Consent Procedure for certain hazardous chemicals and pesticides in international trade)* [2006] ECR I-1.

[76] M Cremona, 'External Relations of the EU and the Member States: Competence, Mixed Agreements, International Responsibility, and Effects of International Law', EUI Working Paper LAW No 206/22, n 50; P Koutrakos, 'Annotation on Case C-94/03 *Commission v Council* and Case C-178/03 *Commission v Parliament and Council*' (2007) 44 *Common Market Law Review* 171.

[77] See Koutrakos, above n 60.

of external relations in recent years leaves no doubt about it. However, the implications of the increasing recourse to Europe's judges in order to address legal basis choices of the kind appearing in *ECOWAS* should not be underestimated: on the one hand, it politicises further a matter with inherent political repercussions, and renders the Court of Justice directly at the centre of a most controversial arena; on the other hand, and given the emphasis on the synergy between the wide range of policies and instruments available for the Union's international role, it introduces an element of uncertainty in an area which, due to its centrality and political sensitivity, least requires it.

V CONCLUSION

The CSDP–development nexus has emerged strongly at various initiatives pursuant to which the Union seeks to define its international role. From the security policy point of view, it follows from the increasingly broad definition which security has been given in the last 10 years, both within the Union and beyond. This chapter has outlined the impact which the management of this nexus has on the functioning of the Union as a constitutional order of states.

This has raised a question about the nature of the main principles governing the conduct of CSDP. As far as development policy is concerned, its increasing interactions with security policy have given rise to a lively debate about its securitisation.[78] The broad understanding of security which prevails in international relations, the timid steps of the Member States in the area of Union's defence policy and the emphasis of the missions on the soft end of the security and defence spectrum all raise the question whether CSDP has been 'developmentalised' to a certain extent. It is interesting that both the European Security Strategy and the 2008 Implementation Report should refer to the unique range of instruments at its disposal as the main assets of the Union's international role. Given its experience on development co-operation and the prominent role of the latter in the Union's international relations, the 'developmentalisation' of CSDP would be hardly surprising. Whether this would enhance its effectiveness and visibility, though, and, if so, under what conditions, is another matter altogether.

Another important issue is the role of the Union's institutions. The

---

[78] See, eg A Hadfield, 'Janus Advances? An Analysis of EC Development Policy and the 2005 Amended Cotonou Partnership Agreement' (2007) 12 *European Foreign Affairs Review* 39; R Picciotto, 'Aid and Conflict: The Policy Coherence Challenge' (2004) 4 *Conflict, Security and Development* 543; N Woods et al, 'Reconciling Effective Aid and Global Security: Implications for the Emerging International Development Architecture' Global Economic Governance Working Paper 19 (2005).

intrinsic links between CSDP and development which emerge as a matter of practice require the Union's institutions to dedicate less time and energy on legal basis squabbles and approach the conduct of the policies with imagination and in a spirit of co-operation. Unfortunately, their record so far provides little ground for optimism, and raises the prospect of the management of the CSDP–development nexus becoming more dependent on the intervention of the Court of Justice. This would be consistent with the latter's increasingly prominent role in the area of the Union's external relations. However, the greater the intensity of the interactions between the two policies and more prominent their position in the Union's international action, the more politicised the management of the CSDP–development nexus would become. In this context, the institutions should think hard as to how best to tackle the ensuing challenges. Should they decide to test the limits of their powers by increasing recourse to Europe's judges, they would do so at their peril.

31

The Role of the European Commission in Tackling Terrorism: the Example of Passenger Name Records

JONATHAN FAULL*

I INTRODUCTION

AS AN ACADEMIC and founding editor of the *European Law Review*, Alan Dashwood played an important role in my early interest in European law and policy. It is therefore a particular honour to contribute to this book of essays. Far beyond my personal gratitude for his friendship, influence and guidance, European law, very much in its infancy in this country when Alan started his academic career, owes a great deal to his meticulous and inspiring work as a teacher, writer, editor, legal adviser and barrister. A generation of students, the EU institutions, the British government, several universities and all those who welcome the development and the integrity of the EU's legal system can rejoice in his work.

Alan wrote in the first editorial in the *European Law Review* in November 1975 that 'the *Review* will have proved its worth if it is able to contribute to establishing (and maintaining) the law of the European Communities as a familiar part of the stock-in-trade of judges, legal practitioners and administrators'.[1] Well, that mission was certainly accomplished.

I have been asked to consider a sombre subject: the role of the European Commission in tackling terrorism. This would have surprised me as a topic of discussion back in Sussex in the early 1970s. Not because terrorism was not yet born—alas, it was all too present in our minds—but because what became known as justice and home affairs (hereinafter

---

* The views expressed herein are personal. The author thanks Despina Vassiladou and James Ogilvie for their invaluable help in preparing this article.
[1] A Dashwood (1975–76) 1 *European Law Review* 1.

JHA) was a development in EU law and policy many would have judged inconceivable at the time.[2]

As for the Commission, it was busy with the Common Market and dreaming of economic and monetary union, not of JHA. I do not set out to trace the development of JHA through successive treaty changes. In retrospect, and without succumbing to the facile view that what happened was somehow inevitable, as if responding to deep historical currents and legal logic, one can see how free movement led to Schengen, which begat information sharing, law enforcement co-operation and mutual recognition. The tragic events of 11 September 2001 made this all the more necessary and added an international dimension to the whole endeavour. Fundamental rights law became even more important as the Union began to legislate and enter into international agreements on matters relating directly to the individual's liberty and security. Now we have a well-developed set of JHA policies, under its third five-year programme.[3] Meanwhile, for followers of bureaucracy, the little task force nestled in the Commission's Secretariat General became a Directorate-General in 1999 with Antonio Vitorino as Commissioner and my late predecessor, Sir Adrian Fortescue, as its first director general. It came under the responsibility of Commission Vice-Presidents Franco Frattini (2005–08) and Jacques Barrot (2008–09). Now in the Barroso II Commission, the portfolio the Directorate-General have been split into two, with one Commissioner for fundamental rights, justice and citizenship and another for immigration, borders and security. Make of those developments what you will; I like to think that they signify a certain maturity and recognition of the importance of the whole policy area in the EU.

What, then, is the Commission's role in tackling terrorism in Alan Dashwood's constitutional order of states? It is, of course, to propose and enforce legislation, and to lend a co-ordinating hand to Member States. The Lisbon Treaty has, it is often said, abolished the Union's pillars, but it leaves many vestiges in place which legal archaeologists will dig around in for many years to come. The distinctions of such historical importance to JHA law between the first and third pillars (and between Schengen and not) will remain very much alive. The constitutional order of states is not a neat one, as states have taken different views about the extent and the modalities of sharing sovereignty. JHA is a good example of the complex legal geometry of the EU. It should not be surprising that it gave rise to the first formal instance of enhanced co-operation, in the controversial matter of divorce law.[4] In this chapter, I will concentrate on another of

---

[2] It was not until the Rome European Council in December 1975 that the TREVI network was created.

[3] Tampere 1999, The Hague 2004, Stockholm 2009.

[4] Council Decision of 12 July 2010 authorising enhanced cooperation in the area of law applicable to divorce and legal separation, [2010] OJ L189/12.

the Commission's tasks: to negotiate international agreements, or, in the case of the old third pillars, to assist the Council Presidency in doing so.

The European Union faces a continuing threat from people and organisations who commit acts of terrorism in EU countries or against its citizens and interests abroad. These terrorists may be foreigners or 'home-grown' EU citizens.

The European Security Strategy[5] states:

> Terrorism puts lives at risk; it imposes large costs; it seeks to undermine the openness and tolerance of our societies and it poses a growing strategic threat to the whole of Europe. Increasingly, terrorist movements are well-resourced, connected by electronic networks, and are willing to use unlimited violence to cause massive casualties. The most recent wave of terrorism is global in its scope and is linked to violent religious extremism . . .

II PASSENGER NAME RECORDS AS A SECURITY TOOL

I will illustrate some of the recent legal issues arising from the fight against terrorism by reference to the saga, far from over, of passenger name records (PNR), the data provided by passengers and collected by carriers[6] for the purpose of making reservations and carrying out the check-in process. They record each passenger's details and travel requirements and are held in air carriers' reservation and departure control systems.[7] The airline collects the information in order to provide and charge for the service of air transport. Under orthodox data protection principles, one would expect that, once the flight has taken place and been paid for, the data would be destroyed, except perhaps for post-sale service and marketing purposes. But lo and behold, the PNR contain nuggets of information in which public authorities, especially those responsible for law enforcement, may well be interested. Attached to a name and address are an itinerary, choice of seat, mode of payment, perhaps a credit card number, a travel agent or an internet address, a telephone number, baggage information, a choice of meal or medical assistance.

PNR data are different from advance passenger information (API). API is the biographical information taken from the machine-readable part of a passport and contains a person's name, passport number, date and place of birth and nationality. API data are mostly used for combating illegal

[5] The European Security Strategy, 'A Secure Europe in a Better World', available at www.consilium.europa.eu/uedocs/cmsUpload/78367.pdf, 4, identifies terrorism as a 'key threat' for the EU.

[6] I will limit my remarks to air travel, but other means of transport also generate PNR which may be of interest to public authorities.

[7] Statewatch maintains a comprehensive, critical data base on PNR: http://www.statewatch.org/pnrobservatory.htm.

immigration, border management and carrying out identity checks as part of border controls, although in some cases the data are also used by law enforcement authorities in order to identify persons fleeing arrest warrants or otherwise wanted or sought. API data are thus primarily used as an identity verification tool. The use of API is becoming increasingly common around the world, with more than 30 countries using it systematically,[8] while more than 40 are in the process of setting up such systems.[9]

Although PNR and API are both passenger data, PNR are mainly used as a criminal intelligence tool rather than to check identity. The value of PNR data for law enforcement purposes lies mainly in the following: (i) PNR make it possible to carry out a risk assessment of all passengers on the basis of fact-based rules in advance of the passengers' arrival or departure. They allow law enforcement authorities to focus on those passengers who fit into the fact-based rules and who were previously unsuspected, rather than subjecting all passengers to on-the spot assessment by border guards; (ii) PNR can be made available well in advance of a flight's arrival or departure and hence give law enforcement authorities more time for processing, analysis and any follow-up action; (iii) with PNR it is possible to match specific addresses, telephone numbers and credit cards connected to criminal offences to an actual person; and (iv) through matching PNR against other PNR, it is possible to identify associates of suspects, for example people travelling together, or sharing a travel agent or credit card.

The use of PNR data by law enforcement authorities is not a new phenomenon. They have been used for almost 60 years, mainly by customs. Modern technology now makes it possible to receive, analyse and store such data electronically and in advance of travel.

As a result, it is now possible to use PNR data in the following ways:

- reactively: in investigations, prosecutions, unravelling of criminal networks;
- in real time, to prevent crime, place people under surveillance or arrest before a crime is committed or because a crime has been or is being committed, by running PNR data against predetermined fact-based risk indicators and databases of persons and objects sought;
- proactively: for trend analysis and development of fact-based travel and general travel behaviour patterns, creating risk indicators, which can then be used in real time as above.

---

[8] Some examples include Australia, Brazil, Canada China, Cuba, India, Japan, Mexico and the US—information sourced from IATA.

[9] Some examples include Indonesia, Kuwait, Peru, Russia, Saud Arabia, Singapore and Thailand—information sourced from IATA.

Although there are various EU laws regulating the collection and processing of personal data for law enforcement purposes,[10] PNR data provide unique opportunities for law enforcement. Traditionally law enforcement authorities collected certain types of data, like fingerprints, DNA and criminal records. In these cases, the EU may regulate their exchange between Member States for the purpose of enhancing police and judicial co-operation and protecting data privacy. Law enforcement authorities may also obtain access in certain circumstances to other types of data collected by Member States for different purposes, for example immigration, asylum, vehicle registration and citizenship registration. Law enforcement authorities may also seek access to databases constituted by private parties, for example telecommunications companies, internet service providers (ISP) and travel companies (PNR). Access is regulated in different ways. depending on the type of data and their functionalities. For example, within the EU, telecommunications and ISP data are retained by the undertakings which collect them and access by law enforcement authorities is authorised and conducted on a case-by-case basis, while PNR are received, retained and processed in their entirety by the law enforcement authorities.

So, for the first time, data are collected and processed for large numbers of presumptively innocent people, proactively and to create fact-based risk indicators.

III   PNR AGREEMENTS

Following the 11 September 2001 terrorist attacks, the US was the first country in the world to regulate the electronic retention and processing of PNR data in the ways described above. It enacted legislation in November 2001 requiring each air carrier operating passenger flights to and from the US to transfer to US Customs and Border Protection (which became part of the newly created Department of Homeland Security) the PNR data of passengers in advance of a flight's departure.[11] Under EU data protection rules, carriers processing data in the EU could not transfer data to a country outside of the EU in the absence of a specific legal basis and unless the country which received the data is found to provide an

---

[10] 'Communication on the Overview of Information Management in the Area of Freedom, Security and Justice', COM(2010) 385 final, 20.7.2010.

[11] Uniting and Strengthening America by Providing Appropriate Tools Required to Intercept and Obstruct Terrorism (USA PATRIOT) Act of 2001.

'adequate'[12] level of protection of personal data.[13]

This led to an untenable situation for airlines. On the one hand, they risked being fined or even having their landing rights withdrawn if they failed to transfer PNR data to the US, while on the other hand they would violate EU law in the absence of a proper legal basis and an adequacy decision. In June 2002 the Commission, while acknowledging the security interests at stake, informed the US authorities that their PNR requirements could conflict with EU and Member States' legislation on data protection, which imposes conditions on the transfer of personal data to third countries. It also informed the US authorities that it could not accept the extraterritorial application of US PNR legislation in the absence of an agreement between the two parties to that effect.

As a result, the EU and the US entered into negotiations for an agreement on transfer of air passenger data with an adequate level of data protection. These negotiations led to the conclusion of an agreement in 2004 between the EC (as it then was) and the US on the processing and transfer of PNR data by air carriers to the US Department of Homeland Security (DHS),[14] which was based on and accompanied by a Commission adequacy decision.[15] The adequacy decision itself was based on a series of undertakings given by the US to the EU on the way it would treat EU-origin PNR data. The undertakings raised the standard of data protection as regards PNR data as to make it acceptable for the EU. On the basis of these specific undertakings, the Commission was able to find that the US afforded an adequate level of data protection to PNR data, and on this basis agreed to the transfer of the data to the US.

The conclusion of the agreement was based on Article 95 of the EC Treaty, a general provision on measures approximating laws for the establishment and functioning of the internal market. The agreement provided the legal basis upon which the carriers could transfer PNR data to the US.

The European Parliament was officially consulted prior to the conclusion of the agreement by the EU, but did not issue an opinion within the specified time limit. The Council therefore proceeded to conclude the agreement in accordance with Article 300(3) of the EC Treaty. The European Parliament, which was dissatisfied both with the contents of the agreement and the adequacy decision, and the procedure leading to its conclusion, challenged the validity of agreement and the adequacy decision

---

[12] 'Adequate' is a false friend of nearly identical words in other languages—*adéquat* in French, for example—which could have been better rendered as 'equivalent' or 'satisfactory'. An American negotiator once said, with some justification, that it is hard not to hear the adverb 'barely' before it.

[13] Art 25 of the Data Protection Directive, Dir 95/46/EC on the protection of individuals with regard to the processing of personal data and the free movement of such data, [1995] OJ L281/31.

[14] [2004] OJ L183/83.

[15] [2004] OJ L235/11.

before the European Court of Justice, arguing that the adequacy decision did not comply with Directive 95/46/EC on the protection of individuals with regard to the processing of personal data.[16]

Before the Court delivered its judgment, Canada enacted legislation requiring air carriers operating flights to and from Canada to transfer passengers' API and PNR to the Canadian Border Services Agency. As a result, and for the same reasons, the EU and Canada entered into negotiations for an agreement on transferring API and PNR data to the Canadian authorities while ensuring an adequate level of data protection for the transferred data. These negotiations led to the conclusion of an agreement in 2006 between the EC and Canada. The agreement consisted of three instruments: (i) commitments by the Canadian Border Service Agency to the EU on the handling of API/PNR data;[17] (ii) a Commission adequacy decision based on the Commitments;[18] and (iii) an international agreement.[19] The agreement was concluded by the Council on the basis of Article 95 of the Treaty establishing the European Community. This time Parliament did not bring an action for annulment.

On 30 May 2006 the European Court of Justice delivered its judgment[20] as regards the validity of the US PNR Agreement. The Court ruled that neither the Commission's decision finding that PNR data are adequately protected by the US nor the Council decision approving the conclusion of an agreement on their transfer to that country was founded on an appropriate legal basis. In other words, the agreement was based on the wrong pillar. The Court held that 'the transfer of PNR data . . . constitutes processing operations concerning public security and the activities of the State in areas of criminal law'. The fact that the PNR data were collected by private operators for commercial purposes and that it is they who arrange for transfer of the data to the USA did not prevent that transfer from being regarded 'as necessary for safeguarding public security and for law enforcement purposes' and thus as data processing excluded from the first pillar Data Protection Directive's scope.[21] The transfer fell within a framework established by public authorities relating to public security. The adequacy decision of the Commission and the Council decision concluding the agreement were thus annulled. The Court suspended the application of its judgment for five months, to enable a new agreement to be negotiated with the US.

The Court made two clear findings: (1) the agreement fell outside the scope of Directive 95/46/EC as defined in its Article 3(2); and (ii) Article

---

[16] [1995] OJ L281/31.
[17] [2006] OJ L91/53.
[18] [2006] OJ L91/49.
[19] [2006] OJ L82/14.
[20] Joined Cases C-317/04 and C-318/04 *Parliament v Council* [2006] ECR I-4635.
[21] Dir 95/46/EC on the protection of individuals with regard to the processing of personal data and the free movement of such data, [1995] OJ L281, 31, Art 3(2).

95 TEC was the wrong legal basis. The Court did not go as far as to state expressly what would have been the correct legal basis. This provoked discussions between the EU institutions and other bodies on whether the correct legal basis should have been police and judicial co-operation under what was then Title VI TEU or common foreign and security policy under what was then Title V TEU. In other words, it was not a matter for the first pillar, but it was not clear whether the second or third pillar applied.

The opinion of Advocate General Bot on the validity of the Data Retention Directive 2006/24/EC seemed to put an end to speculation regarding the interpretation of the PNR judgment.[22] In distinguishing between the two cases, the AG considered the judgment of the Court in the US PNR case and stated that 'the international dimension of the co-operation put in place and the methods of collaboration established between air carriers and the CBP, methods which bring it, in my view, within the area covered by Title VI of the EU Treaty, thus constitute two fundamental differences vis-à-vis the situation at issue in the present case.'[23] The Court's judgment in the data retention case held in relation to the US PNR judgment that 'the subject matter of that decision was data-processing which was not necessary for a supply of services by the air carriers, but which was regarded as necessary for safeguarding public security and for law-enforcement purposes'.[24] Following these clarifications, it became clearer that PNR agreements were a matter of police and judicial co-operation, not common foreign and security policy.

The judgment confirmed the correctness of the decision of the Council to negotiate a new agreement with the US pursuant to Articles 24 and 38 of the EU Treaty, ie under the provisions on police and judicial co-operation. This led to an interim agreement for the intermediate period of one year between the annulment of the first agreement by the Court and the conclusion of a long-term agreement with the US.[25] The interim agreement was accompanied by the same set of US undertakings as the 2004 Agreement.[26]

A long-term agreement between the EU and the US was signed in July 2007, accompanied by a letter from the US to the EU containing commitments on the way that the US will treat EU-originating PNR data.[27] These instruments set out a series of conditions on the processing of PNR data by DHS, aimed at ensuring an adequate level of data protection by the US authorities. Together, they form the legal framework for the transfer

[22] Case C-301/06 *Ireland v Parliament and Council* [2009] ECR I-593.
[23] Para 119.
[24] Para 88.
[25] [2006] OJ L289/27.
[26] [2006] OJ C259/1.
[27] [2007] OJ L204/16.

and processing of such passenger data by the US authorities, which was again adopted pursuant to Articles 24 and 38 of the EU Treaty.

This format was a creative solution developed in order to ensure the 'adequacy' of data protection for EU-originating PNR data by the US. Following the judgment of the European Court of Justice, which decided that the purposes of the PNR agreements were outside the scope of the Data Protection Directive 95/46/EC, there was no applicable EU procedure for making 'adequacy findings'. However, data protection remained a fundamental right in the EU, and the EU had to comply with the requirements of the Council of Europe's Convention 108 for the Protection of Individuals with Regards to Automatic Processing of Personal Data.[28] Since the US was not a contracting party to this Convention, the EU had to find a way to continue authorising the transfers of data to the US without breaching the Convention. Through the solution found by the EU, the US would commit itself to ensuring an 'adequate' standard of data protection by a series of commitments contained in a letter accompanying the agreement.

As regards the legal basis, the correctness of this choice was reinforced by a commitment by the US that:

> in order to foster police and judicial co-operation, DHS will encourage the transfer of analytical information flowing from PNR data by competent US authorities to police and judicial authorities of the Member States concerned and, where appropriate, to Europol and Eurojust. DHS also expects that the EU and its Member States will likewise encourage their competent authorities to provide analytical information flowing from PNR data to DHS and other DHS authorities concerned.

The European Parliament[29] and the data protection authorities[30] were critical of the agreement, which, in their view, did not ensure an adequate level of data protection. Their main criticisms were directed against provisions of the agreement and the commitments relating to the use of sensitive data, the excessive and disproportionate length of the period during which the data would be retained, the wide purpose limitation, the failure to guarantee the right to judicial redress to non-US citizens and the loose regulation of onward transfers.

In 2008, following repeated requests, the EU concluded an agreement with Australia for the transfer of PNR data for the fight against terrorism and serious transnational crime.[31] The agreement was accompanied by an annex, which contained several commitments on the way Australia will treat EU originating PNR data, following a similar format to the US Agreement. The agreement and the annex set out a series of conditions

[28] CETS No 108.
[29] Resolution No P6_TA(2007)0347 of 12 July 2007.
[30] Opinion 5/2007 of the Article 29 Data Protection Working Party, available at http://ec.europa.eu/justice/policies/privacy/docs/wpdocs/2007/wp138_en.pdf.
[31] [2008] OJ L213/49.

on the processing of PNR data by Australian authorities, aimed at ensuring an adequate level of protection of the data. This agreement was again signed pursuant to (then) Articles 24 and 38 of the EU Treaty.

The European Parliament[32] and Member States' data protection authorities criticised this agreement, albeit to a much lesser degree than the one with the US. The main criticism was the alleged lack of clear purpose limitation, which was said to give rise to uncertainty. Even though the main purpose of the agreement was the fight against terrorism and serious transnational crime, other secondary purposes were seen by the Parliament as creating uncertainty.

Both the 2007 Agreement with the US and the 2008 Agreement with Australia entered into provisional application immediately upon their signature. However, according to Article 24(5) TEU:

> No agreement shall be binding on a Member State whose representative in the Council states that it has to comply with the requirements of its own constitutional procedure; the other members of the Council may agree that the agreement shall nevertheless apply provisionally.

Before all Member States completed their constitutional procedures, on 1 December 2009 the Treaty of Lisbon entered into force. As a result, the conclusion of the two PNR agreements could no longer be based on the procedure provided for in Articles 24 and 38 TEU as those articles ceased to exist. Although the conclusion procedure had started under those two articles, it would have to continue under the new rules of Article 218 of the Treaty on the Functioning of the European Union. Under Article 218(6), the Council now needed the European Parliament's consent before concluding the agreements:

The Council, on a proposal by the negotiator, shall adopt a decision concluding the agreement:

> Except where agreements relate exclusively to the common foreign and security policy, the Council shall adopt the decision concluding the agreement:
> (a) after obtaining the consent of the European Parliament in the following cases:
> . . .
> (v) agreements covering fields to which either the ordinary legislative procedure applies, or the special legislative procedure where the consent of the European Parliament is required.
> . . .

The European Parliament was therefore asked officially by the Council to consent to the conclusion of the US and Australia PNR agreements. It became clear that a positive vote on consent was unlikely, bearing in mind the Parliament's critical resolutions. If consent was refused, the

---

[32] Resolution No P6_TA(2008)0512 of 22 October 2008.

agreements would have to be terminated. Such an abrupt termination of the two PNR agreements would have serious adverse effects on air carriers and passengers. Flights to the US and Australia would leave the carriers exposed to penalties by the two countries for failure to transfer the PNR data or by the Data Protection Authorities of the Member States for sending the data in the absence of an agreement.

The European Parliament's official response to the request for consent came in the form of a resolution in May 2010[33] calling upon the Commission to renegotiate the two agreements on terms acceptable to Parliament. In the resolution, Parliament provided a series of minimum requirements with which the two agreements and any future PNR agreements should comply. However, Parliament decided to postpone a vote on consent for the time being.

Parliament did not postpone its vote until such time as new agreements are concluded. It would reassess the postponement on the basis of progress achieved in the renegotiations. This is indicative of Parliament's understanding of its new institutional role, further illustrated in February 2010 when Parliament withheld its consent[34] for the conclusion of the agreement between the EU and the US on the processing and transfer of financial messaging data for the purposes of the US 'Terrorist Finance Tracking Program'.[35]

At the same time, the fact that Parliament chose to postpone its vote rather than risking the difficult consequences that the withholding of its consent would have had showed that it wished to play a constructive role in the formulation of the EU's external PNR policies. More countries, namely New Zealand and South Korea, are already using PNR data for law enforcement purposes, and the latter has made a formal request to the EU for the conclusion of a PNR agreement.[36] Other countries have either enacted PNR legislation and/or are currently considering doing so: Japan, Saudi Arabia, South Africa and Singapore. Within the EU, the UK already has a PNR system, while France, Denmark, Belgium, Sweden and the Netherlands have either enacted relevant legislation and/or are currently testing using PNR data. Several other Member States are considering setting up PNR systems.

Against this background, the Commission announced that it intends to issue a communication on PNR external strategy and to seek negotiating mandates from the Council to renegotiate the US and Australia PNR agreements, on the basis of the minimum requirements listed in the European Parliament resolution of May 2010. These requirements include,

---

[33] P7_TA-(2010)0144, 5 May 2010.
[34] P7_TA(2010)0029, 11 February 2010.
[35] [2010] OJ L8/11.
[36] New Zealand has no direct or transfer flights with the EU and does not requirement any PNR data from the EU.

for example, a clearer purpose limitation, restrictions on onward transfers to third countries and possibilities for all passengers to enforce their data protection rights. The same requirements will form the basis for any future PNR agreements with other countries.

In the meantime, the EU had been considering whether it should develop a PNR system of its own. After conducting an impact assessment[37] on the issue, in November 2007 the Commission adopted a proposal for a Council Framework Decision for the use of PNR data for law enforcement purposes.[38] Its legal basis was Title VI of the Treaty of European Union, which was the former third pillar. The proposal was still being negotiated when the Treaty of Lisbon entered into force on 1 December 2009. As a result of the fundamental Treaty changes which modified the decision-making procedure, the proposal of the Commission became void and no longer exists.

The Stockholm programme[39] called upon the Commission to present an EU PNR proposal to prevent, detect and investigate terrorism and serious crime. The Commission is currently assessing the situation and considering a new proposal for an EU PNR system under the new Treaty rules. Firm support for this policy by the majority of Member States, coupled with the constructive attitude of Parliament, suggest that the European Union will soon have its own PNR system.

IV   CONCLUSION

PNR has raised many interesting legal and institutional issues and the PNR saga is far from over. All the PNR agreements will have to be renegotiated following the European Parliament's 2010 resolution, the EU PNR proposal is still to be adopted by the Commission, while a series of other countries are waiting in line to reach agreements with the EU. Given that we are now operating under the new decision-making procedures of the Treaty of Lisbon and that the data protection rules of the EU are under revision, it seems inevitable that complex legal challenges lie ahead.[40]

---

[37] SEC(2007)1453, 6 November 2007.
[38] COM(2007)654, 6 November 2007.
[39] Council Document No 17024/09 of 2 December 2009.
[40] For a critical US insider's account of EU–US relations on PNR and other related issues, see SA Baker, *Skating on Stilts: Why We Aren't Stopping Tomorrow's Terrorism* (Stanford, Hoover Institution Press, 2010).

Index